McDougal Littell

# Algebra Readiness

McDougal Littell
A DIVISION OF HOUGHTON MIFFLIN COMPANY
Evanston, Illinois • Boston • Dallas

ISBN-13: 978-0-618-90084-8
ISBN-10: 0-618-90084-5      456789—DSV—11 10 09 08

Internet Web Site: http://www.mcdougallittell.com

# California Reviewers

## McDougal Littell's
## California Algebra Readiness

**Rick Austin**

Mathematics Teacher
Daniel Lewis Middle School
Paso Robles, CA

**Karen Cliffe**

Mathematics Curriculum Specialist
Sweetwater Union High School District
Chula Vista, CA

**Ed Kohn**

Professional Development Facilitator
Los Angeles Unified School District
Los Angeles, CA

**Gregory T. Miyata**

ETT/ImaST II Lead Coach/Advisor
Robert Louis Stevenson Middle School
Los Angeles, CA

**Rudy Sass**

Mathematics Teacher
Orangeview Junior High School
Anaheim, CA

# Chapter 1

# Expressions, Unit Analysis, and Problem Solving

## STARTING THE CHAPTER

California Standards

| | | |
|---|---|---|
| | Preview Vocabulary | 2 |
| | Review Prerequisite Skills | 3 |
| Gr. 7 NS 1.2, Gr. 7 AF 2.1 | **1.1 Write and Evaluate Powers** | 6 |
| | Activity 1.1: Investigating Powers | 4 |
| Gr. 7 NS 1.2, Gr. 7 AF 2.1 | **1.2 Use Order of Operations** | 12 |
| | Activity 1.2: Investigating Order of Operations | 10 |
| Gr. 7 NS 1.2, Gr. 7 AF 4.2 | **1.3 Use Formulas** | 18 |
| | Activity 1.3: Investigating Perimeter and Area | 16 |
| Gr. 7 MG 1.3 | **1.4 Use Unit Analysis** | 26 |
| | Activity 1.4: Investigating Unit Conversions | 24 |
| Gr. 7 AF 1.1 | **1.5 Write and Evaluate Algebraic Expressions** | 32 |
| | Activity 1.5: Evaluating Expressions | 30 |
| Gr. 7 AF 4.2, Gr. 7 MR 2.5 | **1.6 Use a Problem Solving Plan** | 38 |
| | Activity 1.6: Using Problem Solving Strategies | 36 |
| **Problem Solving** | **Problem Solving and Reasoning** | 42 |

## ASSESSMENT

Mid-Chapter Review, 22

Mid-Chapter Test, 23

Chapter Review Game, 44

Chapter Summary and Review, 45

Chapter Test, 48

Multiple Choice Chapter Test, 49

# Chapter 2

# Fractions

**STARTING THE CHAPTER**

| | | |
|---|---|---|
| **California Standards** | Preview Vocabulary | **50** |
| | Review Prerequisite Skills | **51** |
| Preparing for Gr. 7 NS 1.2 | **2.1 Simplify Fractions** | **54** |
| | Activity 2.1: Modeling Equivalent Fractions | **52** |
| Preparing for Gr. 7 NS 1.2 | **2.2 Write Mixed Numbers and Improper Fractions** | **60** |
| | Activity 2.2: Modeling Mixed Numbers and Improper Fractions | **58** |
| Gr. 7 NS 1.2 | **2.3 Add and Subtract Fractions with the Same Denominator** | **66** |
| | Activity 2.3: Fractions with the Same Denominator | **64** |
| Gr. 7 NS 1.2 | **2.4 Add and Subtract Fractions with Different Denominators** | **74** |
| | Activity 2.4: Fractions with Different Denominators | **72** |
| Gr. 7 NS 1.2 | **2.5 Multiply Fractions** | **80** |
| | Activity 2.5: Modeling Fraction Multiplication | **78** |
| Alg. 2.0 | **2.6 Find Reciprocals** | **86** |
| | Activity 2.6: Modeling Reciprocals | **84** |
| Gr. 7 NS 1.2 | **2.7 Divide Fractions** | **92** |
| | Activity 2.7: Modeling Fraction Division | **90** |
| **Problem Solving** | **Problem Solving and Reasoning** | **96** |

**ASSESSMENT**

Mid-Chapter Review, 70

Mid-Chapter Test, 71

Chapter Review Game, 98

Chapter Summary and Review, 99

Chapter Test, 102

Multiple Choice Chapter Test, 103

## Chapter 3 — Decimals and Percents

**STARTING THE CHAPTER**

| California Standards | | |
|---|---|---|
| | Preview Vocabulary | 104 |
| | Review Prerequisite Skills | 105 |
| Gr. 7 NS 1.2 | **3.1 Add and Subtract Decimals** | 108 |
| | **Activity 3.1:** Modeling Decimal Addition and Subtraction | 106 |
| Gr. 7 NS 1.2 | **3.2 Multiply Decimals** | 114 |
| | **Activity 3.2:** Modeling Decimal Multiplication | 112 |
| Gr. 7 NS 1.2 | **3.3 Divide Decimals** | 120 |
| | **Activity 3.3:** Modeling Decimal Division | 118 |
| Gr. 7 NS 1.3, Gr. 7 NS 1.5 | **3.4 Convert Between Fractions and Decimals** | 128 |
| | **Activity 3.4:** Converting Between Fractions and Decimals | 126 |
| Gr. 7 NS 1.3 | **3.5 Write Percents as Fractions and Decimals** | 134 |
| | **Activity 3.5:** Percents, Decimals, and Fractions | 132 |
| Gr. 7 NS 1.3 | **3.6 Write Decimals and Fractions as Percents** | 140 |
| | **Activity 3.6:** Writing Decimals and Fractions as Percents | 138 |
| Gr. 7 NS 1.3 | **3.7 Find a Percent of a Number** | 146 |
| | **Activity 3.7:** Finding a Percent of a Number | 144 |
| | **Problem Solving** Problem Solving and Reasoning | 150 |

**ASSESSMENT**

Mid-Chapter Review, 124

Mid-Chapter Test, 125

Chapter Review Game, 152

Chapter Summary and Review, 153

Chapter Test, 156

Multiple Choice Chapter Test, 157

# Chapter 4

# Integers

**California Standards**

**STARTING THE CHAPTER**

| | | |
|---|---|---|
| | Preview Vocabulary | 158 |
| | Review Prerequisite Skills | 159 |
| Alg. 2.0 | **4.1 Compare and Order Integers** | **162** |
| | Activity 4.1: Comparing Numbers Using a Number Line | 160 |
| Gr. 7 NS 1.2 | **4.2 Add Integers** | **168** |
| | Activity 4.2: Investigating Integer Addition | 166 |
| Gr. 7 NS 1.2 | **4.3 Subtract Integers** | **174** |
| | Activity 4.3: Investigating Integer Subtraction | 172 |
| Gr. 7 NS 1.2 | **4.4 Multiply Integers** | **182** |
| | Activity 4.4: Investigating Integer Multiplication | 180 |
| Gr. 7 NS 1.2 | **4.5 Divide Integers** | **188** |
| | Activity 4.5: Investigating Integer Division | 186 |
| **Problem Solving** | **Problem Solving and Reasoning** | **192** |

**ASSESSMENT**

Mid-Chapter Review, 178

Mid-Chapter Test, 179

Chapter Review Game, 194

Chapter Summary and Review, 195

Chapter Test, 198

Multiple Choice Chapter Test, 199

# Chapter 5

# Rational Numbers and Their Properties

## STARTING THE CHAPTER

**California Standards**

| | Preview Vocabulary | 200 |
| | Review Prerequisite Skills | 201 |
| Gr. 7 NS 1.5 | **5.1 Compare and Order Rational Numbers** | 204 |
| | Activity 5.1: Identifying Numbers on a Number Line | 202 |
| Gr. 7 NS 1.2 | **5.2 Add and Subtract Rational Numbers** | 210 |
| | Activity 5.2: Adding Rational Numbers Using a Ruler | 208 |
| Gr. 7 AF 1.3 | **5.3 Use the Properties of Addition** | 216 |
| | Activity 5.3: Investigating Addition Properties | 214 |
| Gr. 7 NS 1.2 | **5.4 Multiply and Divide Rational Numbers** | 224 |
| | Activity 5.4: A Rational Number Game | 222 |
| Gr. 7 AF 1.3 | **5.5 Use the Properties of Multiplication** | 230 |
| | Activity 5.5: Investigating Multiplication Properties | 228 |
| Gr. 7 AF 1.3 | **5.6 Use the Distributive Property** | 236 |
| | Activity 5.6: Modeling the Distributive Property | 234 |
| | **Problem Solving**    **Problem Solving and Reasoning** | 240 |

### ASSESSMENT

Mid-Chapter Review, 220

Mid-Chapter Test, 221

Chapter Review Game, 242

Chapter Summary and Review, 243

Chapter Test, 246

Multiple Choice Chapter Test, 247

# Chapter 6

# Exponents

**STARTING THE CHAPTER**

**California Standards**

Gr. 7 NS 2.1, Alg. 2.0

Gr. 7 NS 2.1, Alg. 2.0

Gr. 7 NS 2.1

Gr. 7 NS 2.1

| | | |
|---|---|---|
| | Preview Vocabulary | 248 |
| | Review Prerequisite Skills | 249 |
| **6.1** | Multiply Powers with the Same Base | 252 |
| | Activity 6.1: Investigating Products of Powers | 250 |
| **6.2** | Divide Powers with the Same Base | 258 |
| | Activity 6.2: Investigating Quotients of Powers | 256 |
| **6.3** | Use Zero and Negative Exponents | 266 |
| | Activity 6.3: Zero and Negative Exponents | 264 |
| **6.4** | Simplify Expressions Involving Exponents | 272 |
| | Activity 6.4: Investigating Expressions Involving Exponents | 270 |
| Problem Solving | Problem Solving and Reasoning | 276 |

**ASSESSMENT**

Mid-Chapter Review, 262

Mid-Chapter Test, 263

Chapter Review Game, 278

Chapter Summary and Review, 279

Chapter Test, 282

Multiple Choice Chapter Test, 283

# Square Roots and the Pythagorean Theorem

**STARTING THE CHAPTER**

California
Standards

| | | |
|---|---|---|
| | Preview Vocabulary | 284 |
| | Review Prerequisite Skills | 285 |
| Alg. 2.0 | **7.1 Find Square Roots of Perfect Squares** | 288 |
| | Activity 7.1: Finding Side Lengths of Squares | 286 |
| Alg. 2.0 | **7.2 Approximate Square Roots** | 294 |
| | Activity 7.2: Using Squares to Approximate Square Roots | 292 |
| Gr. 7 MG 3.3 | **7.3 Use the Pythagorean Theorem** | 302 |
| | Activity 7.3: Investigating Right Triangles | 300 |
| Gr. 7 MG 3.3 | **7.4 Use the Converse of the Pythagorean Theorem** | 308 |
| | Activity 7.4: Investigating Sides and Angles of Triangles | 306 |
| | **Problem Solving** Problem Solving and Reasoning | 312 |

**ASSESSMENT**  Mid-Chapter Review, 298

Mid-Chapter Test, 299

Chapter Review Game, 314

Chapter Summary and Review, 315

Chapter Test, 318

Multiple Choice Chapter Test, 319

# Chapter 8

# Equations in One Variable

**California Standards**

**STARTING THE CHAPTER**

| | |
|---|---|
| Preview Vocabulary | 320 |
| Review Prerequisite Skills | 321 |

Preparing for
Gr. 7 AF 4.1,
Gr. 7 AF 1.1

**8.1 Solve Equations Involving Addition or Subtraction** — 324
Activity 8.1: Equations Involving Addition or Subtraction — 322

Preparing for
Gr. 7 AF 4.1,
Gr. 7 AF 1.1

**8.2 Solve Equations Involving Multiplication or Division** — 330
Activity 8.2: Equations Involving Multiplication — 328

Gr. 7 AF 1.1,
Gr. 7 AF 4.1

**8.3 Solve Two-Step Equations** — 336
Activity 8.3: Modeling Two-Step Equations — 334

Gr. 7 AF 1.1,
Gr. 7 AF 4.1

**8.4 Solve Equations with Fractions and Decimals** — 344
Activity 8.4: Solving Equations with Fractions and Decimals — 342

Alg. 4.0,
Alg. 5.0

**8.5 Solve Equations Using the Distributive Property** — 350
Activity 8.5: Modeling Multi-Step Equations — 348

Gr. 7 AF 4.2

**8.6 Solve Rate Problems** — 356
Activity 8.6: Modeling Rate Problems — 354

**Problem Solving**   **Problem Solving and Reasoning** — 360

**ASSESSMENT**

Mid-Chapter Review, 340

Mid-Chapter Test, 341

Chapter Review Game, 362

Chapter Summary and Review, 363

Chapter Test, 366

Multiple Choice Chapter Test, 367

# Chapter 9

# Inequalities in One Variable

**STARTING THE CHAPTER**

**California Standards**

| | | |
|---|---|---|
| Preview Vocabulary | | 368 |
| Review Prerequisite Skills | | 369 |

Gr. 7 AF 1.1

**9.1** Write and Graph Simple Inequalities — 372
Activity 4.1: Investigating Solutions of Simple Inequalities — 370

Gr. 7 AF 1.1, Preparing for Gr. 7 AF 4.1

**9.2** Solve Inequalities Involving Addition or Subtraction — 378
Activity 9.2: Inequalities Involving Addition or Subtraction — 376

Gr. 7 AF 1.1, Preparing for Gr. 7 AF 4.1

**9.3** Solve Inequalities Involving Multiplication or Division — 386
Activity 9.3: Inequalities Involving Multiplication or Division — 384

Gr. 7 AF 1.1, Gr. 7 AF 4.1

**9.4** Solve Two-Step Inequalities — 392
Activity 9.4: Using Tables to Solve Two-Step Inequalities — 390

**Problem Solving**    Problem Solving and Reasoning — 396

**ASSESSMENT**    Mid-Chapter Review, 382

Mid-Chapter Test, 383

Chapter Review Game, 398

Chapter Summary and Review, 399

Chapter Test, 402

Multiple Choice Chapter Test, 403

# Chapter 10

# Linear Equations in Two Variables

**STARTING THE CHAPTER**

**California Standards**

| | | |
|---|---|---|
| | Preview Vocabulary | 404 |
| | Review Prerequisite Skills | 405 |

Preparing for Gr. 7 AF 3.3 — **10.1** Graph in the Coordinate Plane — 408
Activity 10.1: Using a Map — 406

Gr. 7 AF 3.3 — **10.2** Graph Linear Equations in Standard Form — 414
Activity 10.2: Modeling Graphs of Equations in Two Variables — 412

Gr. 7 AF 3.3 — **10.3** Graph Horizontal and Vertical Lines — 420
Activity 10.3: Modeling Graphs of Horizontal and Vertical Lines — 418

Gr. 7 AF 3.3 — **10.4** Graph Linear Equations Using Intercepts — 428
Activity 10.4: Using Intercepts — 426

Gr. 7 AF 3.3 — **10.5** Find Slopes of Lines — 434
Activity 10.5: Modeling Slopes of Lines — 432

Gr. 7 AF 3.3 — **10.6** Graph Equations in Slope-Intercept Form — 440
Activity 10.6: Investigating Slope and y-Intercept — 438

Gr. 7 AF 3.4, Gr. 7 AF 4.2 — **10.7** Solve Direct Variation Problems by Graphing — 446
Activity 10.7: Investigating Direct Variation — 444

Gr. 7 AF 3.4, Gr. 7 AF 4.2 — **10.8** Solve Direct Variation Problems Using Algebra — 452
Activity 10.8: Writing Direct Variation Equations — 450

**Problem Solving** Problem Solving and Reasoning — 456

**ASSESSMENT**

Mid-Chapter Review, 424

Mid-Chapter Test, 425

Chapter Review Game, 458

Chapter Summary and Review, 459

Chapter Test, 462

Multiple Choice Chapter Test, 463

Contents **xiii**

# Contents of Student Resources

## Looking Ahead
pages 465–475

**Topic 1** Write and Graph Equations in Two Variables ... 466

**Topic 2** Write and Graph Inequalities in Two Variables ... 468

**Topic 3** Write and Graph Systems of Equations ... 472

**Topic 4** Write and Graph Systems of Inequalities ... 474

## Skills Review Handbook
pages 476–497

### Number Sense
Place Value ... 476

Comparing and Ordering Whole Numbers ... 477

Comparing and Ordering Decimals ... 478

Rounding ... 479

Adding and Subtracting Whole Numbers ... 480

Multiplying Whole Numbers ... 481

Dividing Whole Numbers ... 482

Ratios ... 483

Factors and Multiples ... 484

### Algebra and Functions
Converting Units of Measurement ... 486

Converting Between Metric Units and Customary Units ... 487

### Measurement and Geometry
Perimeter and Area ... 488

Circumference and Area of a Circle ... 490

Surface Area and Volume ... 492

### Statistics, Data Analysis, and Probability
Reading Bar Graphs ... 494

Reading Circle Graphs ... 495

### Mathematical Reasoning
Problem Solving Strategies ... 496

## Extra Practice for Chapters 1–10
pages 498–507

## Tables
pages 508–513

Symbols and Formulas ... 508

Geometric Formulas ... 509

Properties ... 510

Measures ... 512

Squares and Square Roots ... 513

## English-Spanish Glossary
pages 514–532

## Index
pages 533–543

## Credits
page 544

## Selected Answers
pages SA1–SA17

# Why Get Ready for Algebra?

You may be asking yourself why algebra is so important that you need Algebra Readiness just to get ready for it. Is algebra so different from the mathematics you have already learned that you need some help getting ready? Read on!

## Why is algebra important?

Algebra is the first step on a path that leads to all higher mathematics courses. That path may take you to a career in mathematics, science, engineering, or information technology. Or it may take you to a career that does not directly involve mathematics but that still requires you to think logically and solve problems. No matter where the path takes you in terms of a career, you will still find algebra to be a useful tool when making decisions in everyday life. Algebra Readiness will prepare you to step onto the path to your future and move ahead.

## Why is algebra different?

Algebra provides a new opportunity to use the power of mathematics. In algebra, you will learn to recognize mathematical relationships and to generalize patterns. You will use variables and mathematical symbols to represent and solve real-world problems. You will learn not only to perform mathematical procedures such as equation solving but also to justify those procedures and extend their usefulness. Algebra Readiness will give you the tools you need to begin.

# California Mathematics Content Standards for Algebra Readiness

California has selected a number of standards from Grade 7 and Algebra 1 to be the basis of an Algebra Readiness course. The standards fall into the following groups:

- **4 Number Sense (NS) standards from Grade 7**
- **7 Algebra and Functions (AF) standards from Grade 7**
- **2 Measurement and Geometry (MG) standards from Grade 7**
- **All of the Mathematical Reasoning (MR) standards from Grade 7**
- **3 standards from Algebra 1**

The following tables list these standards and describe why they are important for algebra and where they appear in this book.

| Number Sense (NS) Standards from Grade 7 | |
|---|---|
| **Standards** | **Why and Where** |
| **Gr. 7 NS 1.2** Add, subtract, multiply, and divide rational numbers (integers, fractions, and terminating decimals) and take positive rational numbers to whole-number powers. | In algebra, you will need to perform operations on all types of numbers when you simplify expressions, solve equations, and evaluate functions. In this book, you will work with the following types of numbers: |
| **Gr. 7 NS 1.3** Convert fractions to decimals and percents and use these representations in estimations, computations, and applications. | • whole numbers in Chapter 1, <br> • fractions in Chapter 2, <br> • decimals and percents in Chapter 3, <br> • integers in Chapter 4, |
| **Gr. 7 NS 1.5** Know that every rational number is either a terminating or a repeating decimal and be able to convert terminating decimals into reduced fractions. | • rational numbers, including negative fractions and decimals, in Chapter 5, <br> • and irrational numbers in Chapter 7. |
| **Gr. 7 NS 2.1** Understand negative whole-number exponents. Multiply and divide expressions involving exponents with a common base. | In algebra, when you work with polynomials and other expressions that involve exponents, you need to understand exponents. In this book, exponents: <br> • are explained in the very first lesson of the book, <br> • appear in every lesson on multiplication in Chapters 2–5, <br> • and are given exclusive treatment in Chapter 6. |

# Algebra and Functions (AF) Standards from Grade 7

| Standards | Why and Where |
|---|---|
| **Gr. 7 AF 1.1** Use variables and appropriate operations to write an expression, an equation, an inequality, or a system of equations or inequalities that represents a verbal description (e.g., three less than a number, half as large as area A). | In algebra, you will need to translate English phrases and sentences into mathematical expressions, equations, and inequalities. You can then apply properties and rules to simplify expressions, solve equations and inequalities in one variable, and graph equations and inequalities in two variables. |
| **Gr. 7 AF 1.3** Simplify numerical expressions by applying properties of rational numbers (e.g., identity, inverse, distributive, associative, commutative) and justify the process used. | In this book, translating words into symbols and applying properties and rules include: |
| **Gr. 7 AF 2.1** Interpret positive whole-number powers as repeated multiplication and negative whole-number powers as repeated division or multiplication by the multiplicative inverse. Simplify and evaluate expressions that include exponents. | • writing and evaluating expressions in Chapter 1, <br> • using the properties of rational numbers in Chapter 5, <br> • using the rules of exponents in Chapter 6, <br> • solving linear equations in one variable in Chapter 8, |
| **Gr. 7 AF 3.3** Graph linear functions, noting that the vertical change (change in $y$-value) per unit of horizontal change (change in $x$-value) is always the same and know that the ratio ("rise over run") is called the slope of a graph. | • solving linear inequalities in one variable in Chapter 9, <br> • graphing linear equations in two variables (and, in particular, direct variation equations) in Chapter 10, <br> • and writing and graphing linear equations and inequalities in two variables in Looking Ahead. |
| **Gr. 7 AF 3.4** Plot the values of quantities whose ratios are always the same (e.g., cost to the number of an item, feet to inches, circumference to diameter of a circle). Fit a line to the plot and understand that the slope of the line equals the ratio of the quantities. | |
| **Gr. 7 AF 4.1** Solve two-step linear equations and inequalities in one variable over the rational numbers, interpret the solution or solutions in the context from which they arose, and verify the reasonableness of the results. | |
| **Gr. 7 AF 4.2** Solve multistep problems involving rate, average speed, distance, and time or a direct variation. | |

## Measurement and Geometry (MG) Standards from Grade 7

| Standards | Why and Where |
|---|---|
| **Gr. 7 MG 1.3** Use measures expressed as rates (e.g., speed, density) and measures expressed as products (e.g., person-days) to solve problems; check the units of the solutions; and use dimensional analysis to check the reasonableness of the answer. | In algebra, analyzing the units of the measurements given in a problem helps you set up a mathematical model and check the results obtained from the model. In this book, unit analysis is first discussed in Lesson 1.4 and then used throughout. |
| **Gr. 7 MG 3.3** Know and understand the Pythagorean theorem and its converse and use it to find the length of the missing side of a right triangle and the lengths of other line segments and, in some situations, empirically verify the Pythagorean theorem by direct measurement. | In algebra, the appearance of square roots when using the Pythagorean theorem gives you exposure to numbers that are not rational. In this book, work with square roots and the Pythagorean theorem occurs in Chapter 7. |

## Mathematical Reasoning (MR) Standards from Grade 7

| Standards | Why and Where |
|---|---|
| **Gr. 7 MR 1.0** Students make decisions about how to approach problems: | In algebra, you will need to engage in mathematical reasoning, such as making generalizations, providing justifications, and recognizing relationships. Mathematical reasoning takes time to develop, and its development occurs while learning the concepts and skills of algebra. |
| **Gr. 7 MR 1.1** Analyze problems by identifying relationships, distinguishing relevant from irrelevant information, identifying missing information, sequencing and prioritizing information, and observing patterns. | |
| **Gr. 7 MR 1.2** Formulate and justify mathematical conjectures based on a general description of the mathematical question or problem posed. | In this book, opportunities for reasoning occur: |
| **Gr. 7 MR 1.3** Determine when and how to break a problem into simpler parts. | • in the Draw Conclusions exercises that are part of pre-lesson activities throughout the book, |
| **Gr. 7 MR 2.0** Students use strategies, skills, and concepts in finding solutions: | • in exercises labeled "Reasoning" in the practice for every lesson, |
| **Gr. 7 MR 2.1** Use estimation to verify the reasonableness of calculated results. | • and in the Problem Solving and Reasoning feature at the end of every chapter. |
| **Gr. 7 MR 2.2** Apply strategies and results from simpler problems to more complex problems. | |
| *MR standards continue on the next page.* | |

| Standards | Why and Where |
|---|---|
| **Gr. 7 MR 2.3** Estimate unknown quantities graphically and solve for them by using logical reasoning and arithmetic and algebraic techniques.<br><br>**Gr. 7 MR 2.4** Make and test conjectures by using both inductive and deductive reasoning.<br><br>**Gr. 7 MR 2.5** Use a variety of methods, such as words, numbers, symbols, charts, graphs, tables, diagrams, and models, to explain mathematical reasoning.<br><br>**Gr. 7 MR 2.6** Express the solution clearly and logically by using the appropriate mathematical notation and terms and clear language; support solutions with evidence in both verbal and symbolic work.<br><br>**Gr. 7 MR 2.7** Indicate the relative advantages of exact and approximate solutions to problems and give answers to a specified degree of accuracy.<br><br>**Gr. 7 MR 2.8** Make precise calculations and check the validity of the results from the context of the problem.<br><br>**Gr. 7 MR 3.0** Students determine a solution is complete and move beyond a particular problem by generalizing to other situations:<br><br>**Gr. 7 MR 3.1** Evaluate the reasonableness of the solution in the context of the original situation.<br><br>**Gr. 7 MR 3.2** Note the method of deriving the solution and demonstrate a conceptual understanding of the derivation by solving similar problems.<br><br>**Gr. 7 MR 3.3** Develop generalizations of the results obtained and the strategies used and apply them to new problem situations. | Mathematical reasoning plays an important role in solving problems, whether the problems are purely mathematical or come from the real world. In this book, opportunities for problem solving occur:<br><br>• in every lesson, because every lesson has problem solving examples and exercises,<br><br>• particularly in Lesson 1.7, which presents a general problem solving plan and the use of verbal models to transition from words to symbols,<br><br>• and in the Problem Solving and Reasoning feature at the end of every chapter. |

## Standards from Algebra 1

| Standards | Why and Where |
|---|---|
| **Alg. 2.0** Students understand and use such operations as taking the opposite, finding the reciprocal, taking a root, and raising to a fractional power. They understand and use the rules of exponents [excluding fractional powers]. | In algebra, the use of variables is fundamental. Knowing how to write, interpret, and manipulate mathematical statements involving variables allows you to solve complex problems. In this book, variables are: |
| **Alg. 4.0** Students simplify expressions before solving linear equations and inequalities in one variable, such as $3(2x - 5) + 4(x - 2) = 12$ [excluding inequalities]. | • introduced in Lesson 1.5 and used in Chapters 2–6 in the form of algebraic expressions to be simplified or evaluated, <br><br> • used in Chapter 7 to define square roots and to state the Pythagorean theorem, |
| **Alg. 5.0** Students solve multistep problems, including word problems, involving linear equations and linear inequalities in one variable and provide justification for each step [excluding inequalities]. | • and used in Chapters 8–10 in the form of linear equations and inequalities to be solved or graphed. |

# Pre-Course Test

## Number Sense

### Place Value (Skills Review p. 476)

**Write the number in expanded form.**

**1.** 23.6378      **2.** 1,267,869.2      **3.** 102.367      **4.** 31,267.671

### Comparing and Ordering Whole Numbers (Skills Review p. 477)

**Copy and complete the statement using <, >, or =.**

**5.** 23 _?_ 49      **6.** 128 _?_ 671      **7.** 2972 _?_ 2927      **8.** 1003 _?_ 1256

### Comparing and Ordering Decimals (Skills Review p. 478)

**Order the numbers from least to greatest.**

**9.** 3.27, 3.2, 3.3, 3.1      **10.** 1.05, 1.5, 1.25, 1.1      **11.** 14.2, 14.36, 14.8, 14.1

### Rounding (Skills Review p. 479)

**Round the number to the place value of the digit in red.**

**12.** 52.36      **13.** 2,368,248.1      **14.** 379.1574      **15.** 213.871

### Operations (Skills Review pp. 480–482)

**Find the sum or difference.**

**16.** 268 + 137      **17.** 4125 − 1275      **18.** 23 + 1284      **19.** 682 − 627

**Find the product.**

**20.** 38 × 27      **21.** 1287 · 237      **22.** 635 × 4267      **23.** 1597 · 34,586

**Find the quotient.**

**24.** 652 ÷ 2      **25.** 3275 ÷ 5      **26.** 128 ÷ 12      **27.** 25,367 ÷ 245

### Ratios (Skills Review p. 483)

**Find the specified ratio.**

**28.** Students with dogs to students with cats

**29.** Students with no pet to students with cats

**30.** Students with dogs to total number of students in the class

| Pet | Number of students with pet |
|---|---|
| Dog | 12 |
| Cat | 10 |
| No pet | 5 |

## Factors and Multiples *(Skills Review p. 484)*

**Find the greatest common factor of the pair of numbers.**

**31.** 8, 14
**32.** 36, 24
**33.** 125, 75
**34.** 232, 120

**Find the least common multiple of the pair of numbers.**

**35.** 5, 9
**36.** 12, 32
**37.** 56, 112
**38.** 220, 100

# Algebra and Functions

## Converting Units of Measurement
*(Skills Review pp. 486–487)*

**Copy and complete. If necessary, round to the nearest whole number.**

**39.** 320 sec = _?_ min
**40.** 240 in. = _?_ ft
**41.** 42 m = _?_ cm

**42.** 5200 mL = _?_ L
**43.** 46 lb = _?_ ton
**44.** 6 gal = _?_ c

**45.** 4 kL ≈ _?_ gal
**46.** 3 m ≈ _?_ ft
**47.** 6 g ≈ _?_ oz

# Measurement and Geometry

## Perimeter and Area *(Skills Review p. 488)*

**Find the perimeter of the figure.**

**48.** Square

6 cm

**49.** Rectangle

4 in.

8 in.

**50.** Triangle

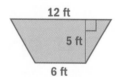

5 ft   3 ft
7 ft

**Find the area of the figure.**

**51.** Rectangle

4 yd

5 yd

**52.** Trapezoid

12 ft

5 ft

6 ft

**53.** Parallelogram

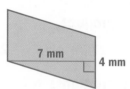

7 mm   4 mm

## Circumference and Area of a Circle *(Skills Review p. 490)*

**Find the circumference and area of the circle. Give your answers in terms of π and as decimals rounded to the nearest tenth.**

**54.**

3 ft

**55.**

5 cm

**56.**

12 yd

## Surface Area and Volume (Skills Review p. 492)

**Find the surface area and volume of the solid. For a cylinder, give your answers in terms of $\pi$ and as decimals rounded to the nearest tenth.**

**57.** Cube

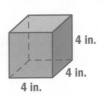

4 in.
4 in.
4 in.

**58.** Rectangular prism

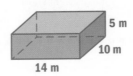

5 m
10 m
14 m

**59.** Cylinder

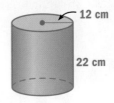

12 cm
22 cm

# Statistics, Data Analysis, and Probability

## Reading Bar Graphs (Skills Review p. 494)

**In Exercises 60–62, use the bar graph, which shows the results of a survey on favorite type of juice.**

**60.** Which type of juice was chosen by the greatest number of people?

**61.** How many more people chose apple juice than chose grape juice?

**62.** Which juices were chosen by fewer than 10 people?

*Favorite Type of Juice*

Students: 0 2 4 6 8 10 12 14

Grape, Apple, Orange, Fruit Punch

## Reading Circle Graphs (Skills Review p. 495)

**In Exercises 63–65, use the circle graph, which shows the results of a survey about the type of movie people most recently saw.**

**63.** How many people last saw a comedy?

**64.** How many people last saw a drama or an action movie?

**65.** How many people saw a movie other than a drama or a documentary?

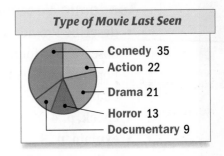

*Type of Movie Last Seen*

Comedy 35
Action 22
Drama 21
Horror 13
Documentary 9

# Mathematical Reasoning

## Problem Solving Strategies (Skills Review p. 496)

**66.** Jill is 13 years old. In 5 years she will be twice the age of her cousin. How old is her cousin?

**67.** In how many different ways can you make $.60 in change using quarters, dimes, and nickels?

**68.** Jack builds a rectangular animal pen using 20 fence posts placed every 4 feet along the perimeter of the pen. What is the greatest possible area of the animal pen?

# Expressions, Unit Analysis, and Problem Solving

## Vocabulary for Chapter 1

### Key Mathematical Vocabulary

- **power, p. 6**
- **expression, pp. 12, 32**
- **order of operations, p. 12**
- **unit analysis, p. 26**

### Academic Vocabulary

- **describe** Provide a statement of your observations for a given situation. For example, see Exercises 20 and 21 on page 15.
- **check, p. 4**
- **explain, p. 8**
- **estimate, p. 15**
- **compare, p. 28**

**Finding soccer statistics by evaluating an algebraic expression, page 35**

# Review Prerequisite Skills

## REVIEW VOCABULARY

- sum, p. 480
- difference, p. 480
- product, p. 481
- quotient, p. 482
- area, p. 488
- perimeter, p. 488

**VOCABULARY CHECK**

**Copy and complete the statement.**

1. The _?_ of a figure is the distance around it.

2. The _?_ of a figure is the number of square units enclosed by the figure.

**SKILLS CHECK**

**Find the sum or difference.** (Review p. 480 for 1.2–1.3, 1.5–1.6.)

3. $14 + 465$

4. $640 + 559$

5. $7837 + 2593$

6. $594 - 339$

7. $9018 - 65$

8. $23{,}227 - 19{,}193$

**Find the product.** (Review p. 481 for 1.1–1.6.)

9. $112 \times 9$

10. $62 \times 99$

11. $801 \times 30$

**Find the quotient.** (Review p. 482 for 1.1–1.6.)

12. $240 \div 15$

13. $315 \div 21$

14. $1152 \div 18$

**Find the perimeter of the triangle.** (Review p. 488 for 1.3.)

15.
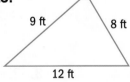
9 ft   8 ft
12 ft

16.
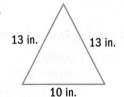
13 in.   13 in.
10 in.

17.
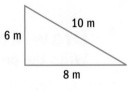
6 m   10 m
8 m

**Copy and complete.** (Review p. 486 for 1.4.)

18. $50 \text{ min} = \underline{\ ?\ } \text{ sec}$

19. $96 \text{ in.} = \underline{\ ?\ } \text{ ft}$

20. $3 \text{ yd} = \underline{\ ?\ } \text{ in.}$

## Let's Explore
### Investigating Powers

| Goal | Materials |
|---|---|
| Write repeated multiplication as a power. | • pencil and paper |

**QUESTION** **How can you write repeated multiplication as a power?**

A *power* is a way of writing repeated multiplication. The *base* of a power is the factor, and the *exponent* of a power is the number of times the factor is used. In the power below, the base 3 is used as a factor 2 times.

**2 is the exponent.**

**3 is the base.** ⟶ $3^2 = 3 \cdot 3$

**EXPLORE 1** *Evaluate powers* ••••••••••••••••••••••••••

**1** **Copy** and complete the table. The table helps you evaluate some powers.

| Power | Base | Number of factors | Expanded form | Evaluate |
|---|---|---|---|---|
| $3^2$ | 3 | 2 | $3 \cdot 3$ | 9 |
| $2^4$ | 2 | 4 | $2 \cdot 2 \cdot 2 \cdot 2$ | ? |
| $6^3$ | 6 | 3 | ? | ? |
| $4^4$ | 4 | ? | ? | ? |
| $7^4$ | ? | ? | ? | ? |

**2** **Check** your results by comparing your completed table with a partner's completed table. If your answers are different, explain your thinking and try to determine the correct answer together.

## Draw Conclusions
**Write the product as a power.**

**1.** $10 \cdot 10$        **2.** $8 \cdot 8 \cdot 8 \cdot 8$        **3.** $7 \cdot 7 \cdot 7 \cdot 7 \cdot 7$

**Evaluate the power.**

**4.** $4^3$        **5.** $9^2$        **6.** $2^5$

**Gr. 7 NS 1.2** Add, subtract, multiply, and divide rational numbers (integers, fractions, and terminating decimals) and **take positive rational numbers to whole-number powers.**
**Gr. 7 AF 2.1** Interpret positive whole-number powers as repeated multiplication and negative whole-number powers as repeated division or multiplication by the multiplicative inverse. **Simplify and evaluate expressions that include exponents.**

**EXPLORE 2** *Use powers for repeated multiplication* .......

**1** **Find** the number of sections formed by folding a piece of paper in half. Open the paper and count the number of sections formed.

**2** **Copy** the table and record the number of sections you counted from Step 1.

| Folds | 1 | 2 | 3 | 4 | 5 |
|---|---|---|---|---|---|
| Sections | 2 | ? | ? | ? | ? |

**3** **Refold** the paper from Step 1. Then fold the paper in half again. Count the number of sections formed and record this in your table. Keep folding, counting, and recording until you have completed 5 folds.

**4** **Write** the number of sections you recorded in your table as a product of 2s and as a power of 2. For example, 4 can be rewritten as $2 \cdot 2$ and as $2^2$. Add *Products of 2s* and *Power of 2* rows to your table and write each number of sections as a product of 2s and as a power of 2.

| Folds | 1 | 2 | 3 | 4 | 5 |
|---|---|---|---|---|---|
| Sections | 2 | 4 | ? | ? | ? |
| Product of 2s | 2 | $2 \cdot 2$ | ? | ? | ? |
| Power of 2s | $2^1$ | $2^2$ | ? | ? | ? |

# Draw Conclusions

**7.** What can you conclude about the relationship between the number of folds and the exponent in the corresponding power of 2?

**8.** How many sections would be formed if you folded a piece of paper 6 times? Extend and complete your table for 6, 7, and 8 folds.

# Write and Evaluate Powers

## VOCABULARY and CONCEPTS

A **power** is a way of writing repeated multiplication. The **base** of a power is the factor, and the **exponent** of a power is the number of times the factor is used. A number raised to the first power, such as $7^1$, is usually written without the exponent. A number raised to the second power, such as $7^2$, can be described as the number *squared*. A number raised to the third power, such as $7^3$, can be described as the number *cubed*.

$$\underset{\text{power}}{\underbrace{7^{\overset{\text{exponent}}{3}}}} = 7 \cdot 7 \cdot 7 \qquad \text{7 is a factor 3 times.}$$

base     exponent

**EXAMPLE 1**  *Writing Powers*

**Write the product as a power.**

**a.** $3 \cdot 3 \cdot 3 \cdot 3 \cdot 3 \cdot 3$        **b.** $5 \cdot 5 \cdot 5 \cdot 5$

**Solution**

**a.** $3 \cdot 3 \cdot 3 \cdot 3 \cdot 3 \cdot 3 = 3^6$     **3 is a factor 6 times.**

**b.** $5 \cdot 5 \cdot 5 \cdot 5 = 5^4$     **5 is a factor 4 times.**

### Practice for Example 1

**Write the product as a power.**

**1.** $10 \cdot 10 \cdot 10$        **2.** $9 \cdot 9 \cdot 9 \cdot 9 \cdot 9 \cdot 9 \cdot 9$

**3.** $8 \cdot 8 \cdot 8 \cdot 8 \cdot 8$        **4.** $6 \cdot 6$

**EXAMPLE 2**  *Evaluating Powers*

**Evaluate the power.**

**a.** $3^3$        **b.** $9^2$        **c.** $2^4$

**Solution**

**a.** $3^3 = 3 \cdot 3 \cdot 3$     **Write 3 as a factor 3 times.**
      $= 27$     **Multiply.**

**b.** $9^2 = 9 \cdot 9$     **Write 9 as a factor 2 times.**
      $= 81$     **Multiply.**

**c.** $2^4 = 2 \cdot 2 \cdot 2 \cdot 2$     **Write 2 as a factor 4 times.**
      $= 16$     **Multiply.**

**Gr. 7 NS 1.2** Add, subtract, multiply, and divide rational numbers (integers, fractions, and terminating decimals) and **take positive rational numbers to whole-number powers.**
**Gr. 7 AF 2.1** Interpret positive whole-number powers as repeated multiplication and negative whole-number powers as repeated division or multiplication by the multiplicative inverse. **Simplify and evaluate expressions that include exponents.**

## Practice for Example 2

**Evaluate the power.**

**5.** $4^5$        **6.** $8^3$        **7.** $5^1$

**EXAMPLE 3** *Writing and Evaluating Powers* · · · · · · · · · · ·

**Write the verbal phrase as a power. Then evaluate.**

**a.** 4 to the third power        **b.** 3 to the fourth power

**Solution**

**a.** Write as a power: $4^3$
Evaluate: $4^3 = 4 \cdot 4 \cdot 4$
$= 64$

**b.** Write as a power: $3^4$
Evaluate: $3^4 = 3 \cdot 3 \cdot 3 \cdot 3$
$= 81$

## Practice for Example 3

**Write the verbal phrase as a power. Then evaluate.**

**8.** 9 to the third power        **9.** 4 to the fourth power

**EXAMPLE 4** *Using a Power in a Real-World Problem* · · · · · · ·

A chessboard has 8 columns and 8 rows of small squares. How many small squares does the chessboard contain? Write your answer as a power. Then evaluate.

**Solution**

$$8 \quad \times \quad 8 = 8^2 = 64$$

columns     rows

▶ **Answer** The chessboard contains 64 small squares.

## Practice for Example 4

**10.** You need to contact members of your marching band. You call 5 members after school. Those 5 members each call 5 more members by dinnertime. That evening, those additional members each call 5 others. How many band members are called that evening? Write your answer as a power. Then evaluate.

**Copy and complete the statement.**

1. In the power $2^3$, 2 is called the ? .

2. A(n) ? is a way of writing repeated multiplication.

**Write the product as a power.**

3. $8 \cdot 8 \cdot 8$
    4. $3 \cdot 3 \cdot 3 \cdot 3$
    5. $6 \cdot 6 \cdot 6 \cdot 6 \cdot 6$

6. $9 \cdot 9 \cdot 9$
    7. $2 \cdot 2 \cdot 2 \cdot 2 \cdot 2 \cdot 2$
    8. $10 \cdot 10$

**Match the verbal phrase with the power.**

9. five to the fourth power
    **A.** $4^5$

10. seven to the ninth power
    **B.** $2^8$

11. eight squared
    **C.** $5^4$

12. nine to the seventh power
    **D.** $7^9$

13. four to the fifth power
    **E.** $9^7$

14. two to the eighth power
    **F.** $8^2$

**Evaluate the power.**

15. $2^3$
    16. $9^2$
    17. $5^3$

18. $3^5$
    19. $4^3$
    20. $10^4$

**Write the verbal phrase as a power. Then evaluate.**

21. 6 to the second power
    22. 10 to the third power

23. 3 to the fourth power
    24. 2 to the fifth power

25. 8 to the third power
    26. 5 to the second power

27. **REASONING** What is the value of $3^8$ if $3^7 = 2187$? *Explain* how you found your answer.

28. An area rug is shown at the right. Write the number of small squares in the rug as a power. How many squares is this?

29. In the metric system of measurement, 1 meter is the same as $10^2$ centimeters. Evaluate the power to find the number of centimeters in 1 meter.

30. Computers store information in units called bits and bytes. There are 8 bits in 1 byte of data. Write the number of bits in 1 byte as a power of 2.

# Practice

**Write the power in words.**

**1.** $3^8$ **2.** $9^4$ **3.** $4^5$

**4.** $8^3$ **5.** $4^9$ **6.** $5^4$

**Write the product as a power.**

**7.** $2 \cdot 2 \cdot 2 \cdot 2 \cdot 2 \cdot 2$ **8.** $13 \cdot 13 \cdot 13$

**9.** $6 \cdot 6 \cdot 6 \cdot 6$ **10.** $12 \cdot 12 \cdot 12 \cdot 12 \cdot 12$

**11.** $5 \cdot 5 \cdot 5 \cdot 5 \cdot 5 \cdot 5 \cdot 5$ **12.** $4 \cdot 4 \cdot 4 \cdot 4$

**Evaluate the power.**

**13.** $2^5$ **14.** $7^4$ **15.** $10^3$

**16.** $3^5$ **17.** $6^3$ **18.** $1^4$

**Write the verbal phrase as a power. Then evaluate.**

**19.** 7 squared **20.** 5 to the fourth power

**21.** 6 to the fourth power **22.** 13 to the first power

**23.** 12 cubed **24.** 1 to the twelfth power

**Write the number as a power.**

**25.** 25 **26** 121 **27.** 64

**28.** 81 **29.** 1000 **30.** 256

**31.** Write each number in the pattern as a power: 1, 4, 9, 16, 25, . . .

**32. REASONING** What is the value of $4^6$ if $4^7 = 16{,}384$? *Explain* how you found your answer.

**33.** Computers store information in units called bytes. A kilobyte is $2^{10}$ bytes. Evaluate the power to find the number of bytes in 1 kilobyte.

**34.** In the metric system of measurement, there are 1000 milligrams in 1 gram. Write the number of milligrams in 1 gram as a power.

**35.** In the metric system of measurement, there are 1000 grams in 1 kilogram. Write the number of grams in 40 kilograms as a power.

**36.** The solid figure at the right is a cube and is made of cubical blocks that are all the same size. How many blocks make up the cube? Write the number of blocks that make up the cube as a power.

# Activity 1.2

## Let's Explore
## Investigating Order of Operations

**Goal**
Determine the order of operations.

**Materials**
• six index cards

**QUESTION**  **In what order should you perform operations?**

To make sure everyone gets the same result when evaluating an expression such as 2 + 3 • 4, mathematicians have agreed on a set of rules called the *order of operations*.

**EXPLORE**  *Evaluate expressions using order of operations*

**1** **Make** operation cards.

Make six operation cards by writing each of the phrases below on a separate slip of paper.

| Multiply | Divide | Add |
|---|---|---|

| Subtract | Evaluate inside parentheses | Evaluate powers |
|---|---|---|

**2** **Determine** the order of operations.

For each expression in the table below, describe the order of operations you would follow to get the value of the expression. Use the operation cards you created in Step 1 to complete each row. Note that some expressions require two operations and some require three.

| Expression | Value | 1st operation | 2nd operation | 3rd operation |
|---|---|---|---|---|
| $5 + 5 \div 5$ | 6 | ? | ? | ? |
| $4 \cdot 3^2$ | 36 | ? | ? | ? |
| $50 - 5 \cdot 2^3$ | 10 | ? | ? | ? |
| $(12 - 5)^2$ | 49 | ? | ? | ? |
| $2 \cdot (8 - 3)^2$ | 50 | ? | ? | ? |

**Gr. 7 NS 1.2** Add, subtract, multiply, and divide rational numbers (integers, fractions, and terminating decimals) **and take positive rational numbers to whole-number powers.**
**Gr. 7 AF 2.1** Interpret positive whole-number powers as repeated multiplication and negative whole-number powers as repeated division or multiplication by the multiplicative inverse. **Simplify and evaluate expressions that include exponents.**
**Also addresses Gr. 4 AF 1.2**

**③** **Arrange** your operation cards.

Based on your results from Step 2, arrange your operation cards to show the order of operations you should use when you evaluate an expression.

**④** **Test** your order.

Use the order you created in Step 3 to complete the table. If your order does not result in the value shown, revise the order of your operation cards until it does.

| Expression | Value | 1st operation | 2nd operation | 3rd operation |
|---|---|---|---|---|
| $10 - 3 \times 2$ | 4 | ? | ? | ? |
| $4 \times 3^2$ | 36 | ? | ? | ? |
| $(8 - 5) \cdot 2^3$ | 24 | ? | ? | ? |

# Draw Conclusions

**1.** Based on the order of your operation cards, what order of operations should you use to evaluate an expression?

**Evaluate the expression.**

**2.** $12 - (8 + 3)$

**3.** $5 + 3 \times 2$

**4.** $25 + 4 \div 2$

**5.** $4 + (14 - 6)$

**Tell whether the statement is *true* or *false*. If it is false, give the correct value for the expression.**

**6.** $10 + 3 \times 7 = 91$     **7.** $6 \times 9 - 2^3 = 46$     **8.** $6 + (12 \div 2) \times 3 = 36$

**In Exercises 9 and 10, use the tables below.**

| Expression | Value |
|---|---|
| $8 - 4 + 2$ | 6 |
| $15 - 3 + 2$ | 14 |
| $9 + 5 - 6$ | 8 |

| Expression | Value |
|---|---|
| $24 \div 6 \times 2$ | 8 |
| $18 \div 3 \times 2$ | 12 |
| $4 \times 5 \div 2$ | 10 |

**9.** How do you evaluate an expression when addition and subtraction are the only operations in the expression?

**10.** How do you evaluate an expression when multiplication and division are the only operations in the expression?

# Use Order of Operations

## VOCABULARY and CONCEPTS

A **numerical expression** consists of numbers, operations, and sometimes *grouping symbols*.

**Grouping symbols** indicate operations that should be performed first. The most common grouping symbols are parentheses ( ) and brackets [ ]. A fraction bar, which is used to indicate division, is also a grouping symbol.

To **evaluate an expression** means to find the value of the expression.

To make sure everyone gets the same result when evaluating an expression, mathematicians use a set of rules called the **order of operations**:

1. Evaluate expressions inside grouping symbols.
2. Evaluate powers.
3. Multiply and divide from left to right.
4. Add and subtract from left to right.

---

**EXAMPLE 1**  *Using the Order of Operations* • • • • • • • • • • • • • • • • •

**Skills Review**

Performing operations with whole numbers, pp. 480–482

**a.** $24 - 3 + 7 = 21 + 7$     First subtract 3 from 24.
$= 28$     Then add 21 and 7.

**b.** $3 \times 8 \div 2 = 24 \div 2$     First multiply 3 and 8.
$= 12$     Then divide 24 by 2.

**c.** $9 - 2 \times 4 + 3 = 9 - 8 + 3$     First multiply 2 and 4.
$= 1 + 3$     Next subtract 8 from 9.
$= 4$     Then add 1 and 3.

### Practice for Example 1

**Evaluate the expression.**

**1.** $6 + 2 - 5$      **2.** $8 - 4 + 7$      **3.** $3 \times 12 \div 2$

**4.** $3 \times 8 \div 2$      **5.** $10 \div 5 + 5$      **6.** $15 - 3 \times 4$

---

**EXAMPLE 2**  *Using Order of Operations with Powers* • • • • • • • •

**a.** $10 - 3^2 = 10 - 9$     First evaluate the power.
$= 1$     Then subtract.

**b.** $5 \cdot 2^3 = 5 \cdot 8$     First evaluate the power.
$= 40$     Then multiply.

Gr. 7 NS 1.2 Add, subtract, multiply, and divide rational numbers (integers, fractions, and terminating decimals) and take positive rational numbers to whole-number powers.
Gr. 7 AF 2.1 Interpret positive whole-number powers as repeated multiplication and negative whole-number powers as repeated division or multiplication by the multiplicative inverse. Simplify and evaluate expressions that include exponents.
Also addresses Gr. 4 AF 1.2

## Practice for Example 2

**Evaluate the expression.**

**7.** $3 \times 4^2$          **8.** $2^4 - 6$          **9.** $2 \times 3^3 - 14$

**EXAMPLE 3** *Using Grouping Symbols*

**a.** $15 \div (4 - 1) = 15 \div 3$     **First evaluate inside grouping symbols.**

                $= 5$            **Then divide.**

**b.**    $\dfrac{14 - 2}{3 + 1} = \dfrac{12}{4}$     **Evaluate the numerator and the denominator.**

                $= 3$            **Then divide.**

## Practice for Example 3

**Evaluate the expression.**

**10.** $16 \div (2 + 6)$      **11.** $\dfrac{18}{17 - 11}$      **12.** $\dfrac{1 + 8}{2 + 1}$

**EXAMPLE 4** *Using Order of Operations*

Student musicians are having a benefit concert. Admission is $4 per adult and $2 per student. Suppose 50 adults and 35 students are admitted. Evaluate $4 \cdot 50 + 2 \cdot 35$ to find the total amount paid for admissions.

**Solution**

You need to evaluate the expression $4 \cdot 50 + 2 \cdot 35$.

$4 \cdot 50 + 2 \cdot 35 = 200 + 70$     **First multiply 4 and 50 and multiply 2 and 35.**

               $= 270$         **Then add 200 and 70.**

▶ **Answer** The total amount paid for admissions is $270.

## Practice for Example 4

**13.** You buy 4 notebooks for $2 each, 5 mechanical pencils for $3 each, and 2 binders for $5 each. Evaluate $4 \cdot 2 + 5 \cdot 3 + 2 \cdot 5$ to find the total cost.

**14.** A ski resort charges $40 per adult and $30 per student for a one-day pass. Evaluate $2 \cdot 40 + 4 \cdot 30$ to find the cost for 2 adult and 4 student one-day passes.

**Identify the operation that is performed first when the expression is evaluated.**

**1.** $4 + 3 \cdot 5$

**2.** $\dfrac{9 + 7}{2}$

**3.** $(12 + 6) \div 6$

**4.** $\dfrac{10}{7 - 2}$

**5.** $3 \times 6 \div 2$

**6.** $5 + 2 \times 3^4$

**Identify the operation that is performed last when the expression is evaluated.**

**7.** $8(11 - 6)$

**8.** $3 + 4^2$

**9.** $\dfrac{10}{5 - 3}$

**10.** $5 + 3 \times 6 \div 2$

**11.** $\dfrac{5 \times 3}{7 - 2}$

**12.** $9^2 - 2 \times 4^2$

**Evaluate the expression.**

**13.** $4 + 6 \times 3$

**14.** $9^2 - 15$

**15.** $5 \times 9 - 3$

**16.** $(37 - 12) \times 2$

**17.** $(6 - 2) \times 7$

**18.** $14 \times 2 - 64 \div 4$

**19.** $15 \div 3 + 4$

**20.** $18 + 3 \div 3$

**21.** $\dfrac{3 + 3}{6 - 3}$

**22.** $(31 - 3 \times 7) \div 2$

**23.** $\dfrac{5^2 + 2}{7 - 4}$

**24.** $(8^2 - 48) \div 4^2$

**Tell whether the statement is *true* or *false*. If it is false, give the correct value for the expression.**

**25.** $16 - 4 \times 3 = 36$

**26.** $19 + 8 \div 2 = 23$

**27.** $(9 - 6) \div 3 = 1$

**28.** $4^2 - 6 \times 2 = 20$

**29.** $30 - 5 + 4 \times 3 = 3$

**30.** $6 - (27 - 9) \div 3 = 0$

**31.** $125 - 20 \times 4 \div 2 = 210$

**32.** $179 - 63 \times 2 = 232$

**33.** $15 + 6^3 - 28 = 203$

**34.** **REASONING** Copy and complete $16 + 33 - 11 \times 2 = 27$ by inserting parentheses to make the statement true.

**35.** Your local cable television company charges a one-time $50 hookup fee and then charges $45 per month for extended basic cable service. Evaluate the expression $50 + 45 \times 12$ to find the cost of getting cable for the first year.

**36.** Entrance to a popular amusement park costs $40 for a person who is 4 feet tall or taller and $20 for a person who is shorter than 4 feet. To determine the total cost for 5 people who are over 4 feet tall and 3 people who are under 4 feet tall to enter the park, evaluate the expression $5 \times 40 + 3 \times 20$.

**37.** Rosario mows the front lawn and the back lawn. Both lawns are rectangular. The dimensions of the front lawn are 20 feet by 16 feet, and the dimensions of the back lawn are 32 feet by 10 feet. Evaluate the expression $20 \times 16 + 32 \times 10$ to find the total area she mows.

# Practice

**Evaluate the expression.**

**1.** $19 + 7 \times 3$

**2.** $(12 - 8) \times 2$

**3.** $21 \times 2 - 54 \div 9$

**4.** $3 \times 12 \div 4 + 11$

**5.** $46 - 3^3$

**6.** $12 \times (5 - 2)$

**7.** $99 \div 11 + 7$

**8.** $26 - 18 + 3 \times 5$

**9.** $(104 - 87) \times (56 + 8)$

**10.** $7 \times 2^4 - 32$

**11.** $\dfrac{6 + 6}{6 - 2}$

**12.** $\dfrac{6 - 2}{2}$

**13.** $(4^2 + 1) - 15$

**14.** $\dfrac{5^2 + 2}{3^2}$

**15.** $8 \times (3 + 1) \div 2^2$

**Match the expression with the best estimate of its value.**

**16.** $22 + 19 \times 3$     **A.** 60

**17.** $11 \times 9 - 59$     **B.** 80

**18.** $119 + 41 \div 4$     **C.** 40

**19.** $18 + 121 \div 3$     **D.** 130

**FIND THE ERROR** *Describe* and correct the error in evaluating the expression.

**20.**
$$14 + 3 \times 8 = 17 \times 8$$
$$= 136$$

**21.**
$$5^2 \times 2 - 15 = 10^2 - 15$$
$$= 100 - 15$$
$$= 85$$

**22. REASONING** Copy and complete $40 - 3 \times 4 + 6 = 10$ by inserting parentheses to make the statement true.

**23.** Samantha makes $7 per hour mowing lawns and $6 per hour cleaning a house. If she mows lawns for 5 hours and cleans for 9 hours, how much money does she earn? Use the expression $7 \times 5 + 6 \times 9$.

**24.** A speeding ticket costs $100 plus $20 for each mile per hour over the speed limit that the violator was traveling. Use the expression $100 + 8 \times 20$ to find the amount of a ticket for someone going 8 miles per hour faster than the speed limit.

**25.** During a basketball game, you made 6 two-point baskets and 3 three-point baskets. To find out how many points you scored for your team, evaluate the expression $2 \times 6 + 3 \times 3$.

**26.** Maria is making a dress that requires 3 yards of red ribbon and 2 yards of blue ribbon. She wants to make identical dresses for herself and four of her friends. How much ribbon does she need for all of the dresses? Use the expression $3 \times 5 + 2 \times 5$.

# Let's Explore

## Investigating Perimeter and Area

**Goal**
Find the perimeter and area of a rectangle.

**Materials**
• graph paper

**QUESTION** **How can you find the perimeter and area of a rectangle?**

Recall that a rectangle is a four-sided figure with four right angles and opposite sides equal in length.

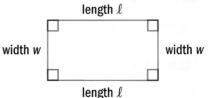

**EXPLORE 1** *Find the perimeter of a rectangle* ...............

**1** **Draw** a rectangle with a length of 10 units and a width of 6 units on graph paper.

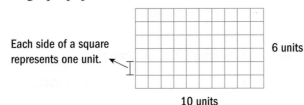

Each side of a square represents one unit.

6 units

10 units

**2** **Count** the number of units around the outside of the rectangle to find its perimeter.

▶**Answer** There are 32 units around the outside of the rectangle. So, the perimeter of the rectangle is 32 units.

## Draw Conclusions
**Find the perimeter of the rectangle.**

**1.**

**2.**

**3.**

**Use graph paper to draw and label a rectangle with the given length $\ell$ and width $w$. Then find the perimeter.**

**4.** $\ell = 5$ units
$w = 3$ units

**5.** $\ell = 11$ units
$w = 7$ units

**6.** $\ell = 10$ units
$w = 3$ units

**7.** Copy and complete the statement: The perimeter of a rectangle is equal to the sum of $\underline{\ ?\ }$ times the length and $\underline{\ ?\ }$ times the width.

**Gr. 7 NS 1.2 Add,** subtract, **multiply,** and divide **rational numbers** (integers, fractions, and terminating decimals) and take positive rational numbers to whole-number powers.

**EXPLORE 2**  *Find the area of a rectangle*

**1** **Draw** a rectangle with a length of 10 units and a width of 4 units on graph paper.

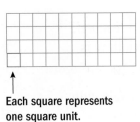

↑ Each square represents one square unit.

**2** **Count** the number of square units that cover the rectangle to find its area.

▶ **Answer**  There are 40 square units that cover the rectangle. So, the area of the rectangle is 40 square units.

## Draw Conclusions

**In Exercises 8–10, find the area of the rectangle.**

**8.**

**9.**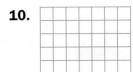

**10.**

**In Exercises 11–13, use graph paper to draw a rectangle with the given length *l* and width *w*. Then find the area.**

**11.** $l$ = 8 units
  $w$ = 7 units

**12.** $l$ = 6 units
  $w$ = 3 units

**13.** $l$ = 9 units
  $w$ = 5 units

**14.** Copy and complete the statement: The area of a rectangle is equal to the  ?  of the length and the width.

**15.** Recall that a square is a rectangle with all four sides having the same length. Copy and complete each statement.

  **a.** The perimeter of a square is equal to  ?  times the side length.

  **b.** The area of a square is equal to the side length raised to the  ?  power.

# Use Formulas

## VOCABULARY and CONCEPTS

A **variable** is a letter used to represent one or more numbers. A **formula** gives a relationship between two or more variables. Some common formulas are shown below.

### Perimeter and Area of a Rectangle

The perimeter $P$ of a rectangle with length $\ell$ and width $w$ is

$$P = 2\ell + 2w.$$

The area $A$ of a rectangle with length $\ell$ and width $w$ is

$$A = \ell w.$$

### Perimeter and Area of a Square

The perimeter $P$ of a square with side length $s$ is

$$P = 4s.$$

The area $A$ of a square with side length $s$ is

$$A = s^2.$$

### Distance, Rate, and Time

Distance traveled $d$ is equal to the speed (rate of travel) $r$ times the travel time $t$.

$$d = rt$$

### Total Cost

The total cost $T$ of $n$ items is the cost $c$ of one item (the *unit cost*) times the number of items.

$$T = cn$$

---

**EXAMPLE 1** *Finding Perimeter and Area* • • • • • • • • • • • • • • • • •

International soccer is played on a rectangular field that has a length of 100 meters and a width of 64 meters. What are the perimeter and the area of the soccer field?

### Solution

**Skills Review**
Perimeter and area, p. 488

| | |
|---|---|
| $P = 2\ell + 2w$ | **Write perimeter formula.** |
| $= 2(100) + 2(64)$ | **Substitute 100 for $\ell$ and 64 for $w$.** |
| $= 200 + 128$ | **Multiply.** |
| $= 328$ | **Add.** |
| $A = \ell w$ | **Write area formula.** |
| $= 100(64)$ | **Substitute 100 for $\ell$ and 64 for $w$.** |
| $= 6400$ | **Multiply.** |

▶ **Answer** The perimeter of the soccer field is 328 meters, and the area is 6400 square meters.

## Practice for Example 1

**1.** A picture frame holds a picture that has a length of 6 inches and a width of 4 inches. What are the perimeter and the area of the picture?

**EXAMPLE 2** *Finding Distance Traveled*

A sea turtle travels at an average rate of about 20 kilometers per day. How far can a sea turtle travel in 4 days?

**Solution**

$$d = rt$$ Write the formula for distance traveled.

$$= 20 \cdot 4$$ Substitute 20 for $r$ and 4 for $t$.

$$= 80$$ Multlply.

▶ **Answer** A sea turtle can travel 80 kilometers in 4 days.

## Practice for Example 2

**2.** A runner ran a race at a steady speed of 0.15 mile per minute in 40 minutes. How far did the runner run?

**EXAMPLE 3** *Finding Total Cost*

A school is purchasing 35 microscopes that cost $119 each for the science department. What is the total cost?

**Solution**

$$T = cn$$ Write the formula for total cost.

$$= 119 \cdot 35$$ Substitute 119 for $c$ and 35 for $n$.

$$= 4165$$ Multiply.

▶ **Answer** The total cost for 35 microscopes that cost $119 each is $4165.

## Practice for Example 3

**3.** Kayla bought 26 jars of poster paint. She paid $3 for each jar. What was the total cost of her purchase?

**Find the perimeter and area of the rectangle.**

**1.**
12 in., 8 in.

**2.**
8 yd, 4 yd

**3.**
3 cm, 5 cm

**Find the perimeter and area of the square.**

**4.**
5 ft, 5 ft

**5.**
3 m, 3 m

**6.** 2 in., 2 in.

**Find the distance traveled for the given rate *r* and time *t*.**

**7.** $r = 4$ feet per second, $t = 20$ seconds

**8.** $r = 2$ miles per hour, $t = 7$ hours

**9.** $r = 3$ inches per minute, $t = 25$ minutes

**10.** $r = 9$ kilometers per hour, $t = 12$ hours

**Find the total cost of *n* items having unit cost *c*.**

**11.** $c = \$8$ per ticket, $n = 6$ movie tickets

**12.** $c = \$12$ per CD, $n = 4$ CDs

**13.** $c = \$15$ per shirt, $n = 3$ shirts

**14.** $c = \$21$ per book, $n = 5$ books

**15. REASONING** *Describe* how to find the side length of a square if you know the perimeter of the square.

**16. REASONING** *Describe* how to find the average rate at which you traveled if you know the distance you traveled and the amount of time you traveled.

**17.** A computer screen is 13 inches long and 10 inches wide. Find the perimeter and the area of the computer screen.

**18.** A photograph is 5 inches wide and 7 inches long. What are the perimeter and the area of the photograph?

**19.** A bird flew at an average speed of 5 miles per hour for 3 hours. How far did the bird fly?

**20.** A dolphin swam at an average speed of 8 kilometers per hour for 5 hours. How far did the dolphin swim?

**In Exercises 21–23, use the table at the right, which shows the cost of merchandise at a concert.**

**21.** Find the cost of 8 patches.

**22.** Find the cost of 6 stickers and 2 hats.

**23.** Find the cost of 3 patches, 1 hat, and 4 shirts.

| Item | Cost |
|------|------|
| Sticker | $7 |
| Patch | $3 |
| Hat | $10 |
| Shirt | $20 |

# B Practice

**Find the perimeter and area of the rectangle.**

**1.** 4 in. / 5 in.

**2.** 1 ft / 7 ft

**3.** 6 yd / 3 yd

**Find the perimeter and area of the square.**

**4.** 9 cm / 9 cm

**5.** 8 in. / 8 in.

**6.** 1 m / 1 m

**Find the distance traveled for the given rate _r_ and time _t_.**

**7.** $r = 52$ miles per hour, $t = 6$ hours

**8.** $r = 4$ meters per minute, $t = 13$ minutes

**9.** $r = 8$ feet per second, $t = 21$ seconds

**10.** $r = 12$ centimeters per hour, $t = 14$ hours

**Find the total cost of _n_ items having unit cost _c_.**

**11.** $c = \$3$ per watermelon, $n = 6$ watermelons

**12.** $c = \$38$ per skateboard, $n = 4$ skateboards

**13.** $c = \$69$ per bookcase, $n = 2$ bookcases

**14.** $c = \$99$ per phone, $n = 3$ phones

**15. REASONING** *Describe* how to find the length of a rectangle if you know the area and the width of the rectangle.

**16. REASONING** *Describe* how to find the cost of one notebook if you know the number of notebooks purchased and the total cost of the notebooks.

**17.** You plant a square flower bed that has a side length of 6 feet. What are the perimeter and the area of the flower bed?

**18.** The rectangular tablet that the Statue of Liberty holds is about 24 feet long and 14 feet wide. What are the perimeter and the area of the Statue of Liberty's tablet?

**19.** Sound travels through iron at a speed of 6 kilometers per second. In 4 seconds how far does sound travel through iron?

**In Exercises 20–22, use the table at the right, which shows the cost of art supplies.**

**20.** Find the cost of 6 tubes of acrylic paint.

**21.** Find the cost of 4 tubes of oil paint and 2 canvases.

**22.** Megan has \$20 to spend on art supplies. Does she have enough money to buy 3 tubes of acrylic paint and a set of brushes? *Explain.*

| Item | Cost |
|---|---|
| Tube of acrylic paint | \$2 |
| Tube of oil paint | \$3 |
| Set of brushes | \$15 |
| Small canvas | \$9 |

**VOCABULARY**
- power, p. 6
- base, p. 6
- exponent, p. 6
- numerical expression, p. 12
- grouping symbols, p. 12
- evaluate an expression, p. 12
- order of operations, p. 12
- variable, p. 18
- formula, p. 18

**Vocabulary Exercises**

1. Copy and complete: A _?_ consists of numbers, operations, and sometimes grouping symbols.

2. What are the variables in the formula $P = 4s$?

## 1.1 Write and Evaluate Powers .................... pp. 6–9

**EXAMPLE** **Write as a power: 6 to the fifth power. Then evaluate.**

Write as a power: $6^5$

Evaluate: $6^5 = 6 \cdot 6 \cdot 6 \cdot 6 \cdot 6 = 7776$

**Write the verbal phrase as a power. Then evaluate.**

3. 3 to the fourth power

4. 8 to the third power

## 1.2 Use Order of Operations .................... pp. 12–15

**EXAMPLE** $18 \div (13 - 4) = 18 \div 9$ **First evaluate inside the grouping symbols.**

$= 2$ **Then divide.**

**Evaluate the expression.**

5. $7 + 6 \times 5$

6. $7^2 + 12$

7. $\dfrac{4^3 - 4}{10}$

## 1.3 Use Formulas .................... pp. 18–21

**EXAMPLE** A science department is buying 3 laboratory ovens that cost $355 each. What is the total cost?

$T = cn$ **Write the formula for total cost.**

$= 355 \cdot 3 = \$1065$ **Substitute 355 for $c$ and 3 for $n$, then multiply.**

8. An athletic department is buying 12 volleyballs that cost $19 each. What is the total cost?

**Write the product as a power.**

**1.** $2 \cdot 2 \cdot 2$  **2.** $3 \cdot 3$  **3.** $10 \cdot 10 \cdot 10 \cdot 10$  **4.** $16 \cdot 16 \cdot 16 \cdot 16$

**Evaluate the power.**

**5.** $4^2$  **6.** $5^3$  **7.** $1^8$  **8.** $3^5$

**Write the verbal phrase as a power. Then evaluate.**

**9.** 11 to the second power  **10.** 6 to the third power

**11.** 5 to the fourth power  **12.** 2 to the fifth power

**Evaluate the expression.**

**13.** $2 + 4 \times 7$  **14.** $17 - 3 \times 2$  **15.** $(13 - 8) \times 4$  **16.** $(9 + 20) \times 3$

**17.** $5^2 - 1$  **18.** $6^2 + 5$  **19.** $\dfrac{36}{4 - 1}$  **20.** $\dfrac{24 + 8}{24 - 8}$

**Find the perimeter and area of the rectangle or square.**

**21.**

2 ft
5 ft

**22.**
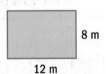
8 m
12 m

**23.**
3 cm
3 cm

**24.**
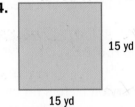
15 yd
15 yd

**Find the distance traveled for the given rate *r* and the time *t*.**

**25.** $r = 55$ miles per hour, $t = 4$ hours  **26.** $r = 2$ millimeters per minute, $t = 8$ minutes

**27.** $r = 40$ miles per day, $t = 7$ days  **28.** $r = 10$ kilometers per second, $t = 3600$ seconds

**Find the total cost of *n* items having unit cost *c*.**

**29.** $c = \$2$ per decoration, $n = 75$ decorations  **30.** $c = \$20$ per dinner, $n = 10$ dinners

**31.** $c = \$48$ per uniform, $n = 2$ uniforms  **32.** $c = \$40$ per book, $n = 16$ books

**In Exercises 33 and 34, use the information on the menu to answer the question.**

**33.** What is the total cost of 4 tacos and 2 orders of nachos?

**34.** What is the toal cost of 2 hamburgers and 2 boxes of popcorn?

| Item | Cost |
| --- | --- |
| Taco | $3 |
| Popcorn | $3 |
| Nachos | $4 |
| Hamburger | $5 |

## Let's Explore
## Investigating Unit Conversions

**Goal**
Convert among customary units of length.

**Materials**
• number cube

**QUESTION** **How do you convert among customary units of length?**

You can use equivalent measures to write *conversion factors* to convert from one unit of measurement to another. Some equivalent measures of length are shown below.

> **Equivalent Measures of Length**
> 12 in. = 1 ft          3 ft = 1 yd          1760 yd = 1 mi
> 36 in. = 1 yd          5280 ft = 1 mi

Dividing one side of an equivalence by the other side gives an expression equal to 1. This fraction is known as a conversion factor.

For example, use the equivalence 3 ft = 1 yd to get $\frac{3 \text{ ft}}{1 \text{ yd}} = 1$. The fraction $\frac{3 \text{ ft}}{1 \text{ yd}}$ is a conversion factor that can be used to convert a measurement in yards to a measurement in feet.

**EXPLORE 1** *Use conversion factors* • • • • • • • • • • • • • • • • • • • • •

**1** **Write** conversion factors for customary units of length. Copy the expressions below and fill in the missing units of length so that each expression is equal to 1.

$$\frac{12 \boxed{?}}{1 \boxed{?}} = 1 \qquad \frac{1 \boxed{?}}{36 \boxed{?}} = 1 \qquad \frac{1 \boxed{?}}{1760 \boxed{?}} = 1 \qquad \frac{5280 \boxed{?}}{1 \boxed{?}} = 1$$

**2** **Find** how many feet are equivalent to 24 yards. *Explain* how to use one of the conversion factors to find the answer.

## Draw Conclusions

1. How many inches are equivalent to 20 yards? *Explain* how to use one of the conversion factors to find the answer.

2. How many miles are equivalent to 10,560 feet? *Explain* how to use one of the conversion factors to find the answer.

**EXPLORE 2**  *Play a game involving conversions* · · · · · · · · · · · · ·

1. **Make** a recording sheet. Each person in your group will need a recording sheet like the one below.

| Round | Yards | Feet | Inches |
|-------|-------|------|--------|
| 1 | ? | ? | ? |
| 2 | ? | ? | ? |
| 3 | ? | ? | ? |
| 4 | ? | ? | ? |
| 5 | ? | ? | ? |
| 6 | ? | ? | ? |
| 7 | ? | ? | ? |

2. **Start** rolling. Determine who will go first. The first person will roll a number cube. The value he or she rolls will be put in the *Feet* column of the table. Then convert the number of feet to inches. Switch rollers.

3. **Aim** for the target. Once everyone in your group has had one turn, the first person should roll again. This time the value of his or her roll can be put in either the *Yards* or the *Feet* column. Your goal by the end of 7 rounds is for the value of your rolls to total 1000 inches without going over.

4. **Continue** rolling. Repeat Step 3 until each member of your group has rolled 7 times. At the end of 7 rounds, find the total number of inches and determine who is the closest to 1000 inches without going over. Make sure to show your other group members how you found your total.

## Draw Conclusions

3. What conversion factor did you use to convert yards to inches?

4. What conversion factor did you use to convert feet to inches?

5. Is it possible for a player's total to be less than 100 inches? *Explain.*

6. What is the maximum number of inches a player could get without going over 1000?

# Use Unit Analysis

## VOCABULARY and CONCEPTS

### Measures Involving Quotients

Some measures involve quotients of quantities measured in different units and are commonly called **rates**. A **unit rate** has a denominator of 1 unit when the rate is written as a fraction. When a unit rate is expressed verbally, it often contains the word *per*, which means "for every."

For example, "12 miles per hour" is a unit rate for speed expressed as a verbal phrase. As a fraction, it is expressed as $\frac{12 \text{ mi}}{1 \text{ h}}$.

### Measures Involving Products

Some measures involve products. For example, a person-day is a unit of measure that represents one person working for one day. To find the number of person-days needed to complete a project, multiply the number of people working on a project by the number of days they work on the project.

### Unit Analysis

When solving problems involving units, use **unit analysis**, or *dimensional analysis*, to make sure that the units used in your answers are correct.

---

**EXAMPLE 1** *Speed and Unit Analysis* . . . . . . . . . .

**Skills Review**
Converting units of measurement, p. 486

An airplane flies 590 miles per hour for 120 minutes. How many miles does it travel?

**Solution**

Use unit analysis to solve the problem. First make sure that the units for the rate and the time are compatible. In this case, convert minutes to hours.

$$120 \text{ minutes} \cdot \frac{1 \text{ hour}}{60 \text{ minutes}} = 2 \text{ hours} \qquad \textbf{Use the conversion factor } \frac{1 \text{ h}}{60 \text{ min}}.$$

Then calculate the distance traveled.

$$d = rt \qquad \textbf{Write the formula for distance traveled.}$$

$$= \frac{590 \text{ miles}}{1 \text{ hour}} \cdot 2 \text{ hours} \qquad \textbf{Substitute. Cross out the common unit.}$$

$$= 1180 \text{ miles} \qquad \textbf{Multiply.}$$

▶ **Answer** The plane travels 1180 miles in 120 minutes.

## Practice for Example 1

**1.** A hiker walked for 480 minutes at an average rate of 5 kilometers per hour. How many kilometers did the hiker walk?

**EXAMPLE 2**  *Density and Unit Analysis*

You can calculate the mass $m$ of an object using the formula $m = DV$ where $D$ is the density of the object and $V$ is the volume of the object.

Use the table to find the mass of the sample of copper.

| Sample | Density (grams per cubic centimeter) | Volume (cubic centimeters) |
|---|---|---|
| Copper | 9 | 21 |
| Palladium | 12 | 16 |

**Solution**

$$m = DV \qquad \text{Write the formula for mass.}$$

$$= \frac{9 \text{ g}}{1 \text{ cm}^3} \cdot 21 \text{ cm}^3 \qquad \text{Substitute. Cross out the common unit.}$$

$$= 189 \text{ g} \qquad \text{Multiply.}$$

▶ **Answer** The mass of the copper sample is 189 grams.

### Practice for Example 2

**2.** What is the mass of the sample of palladium in the table? Is this mass greater than or less than the mass of the copper sample?

**EXAMPLE 3**  *Person-Days and Unit Analysis*

It usually takes 4 persons working 6 days to paint the walls in a particular school. How many days would it take for 3 persons to paint the walls? Use unit analysis to find the answer.

**Solution**

First find the number of person-days needed to paint the walls.

4 persons • 6 days = 24 person-days    **Multiply persons by days to get person-days.**

Then find the number of days it would take 3 persons to paint the walls.

$$\frac{24 \text{ person-days}}{3 \text{ persons}} = 8 \text{ days} \qquad \textbf{Divide person-days by persons to get days.}$$

▶ **Answer** It would take 3 persons 8 days to paint the classroom walls.

### Practice for Example 3

**3.** It takes 12 persons working 3 days to plant an acre of young trees. How many days would it take 4 persons to plant an acre of young trees?

**Write the unit rate as a fraction.**

**1.** 25 feet per second

**2.** 13 grams per cubic centimeter

**3.** $3 per gallon

**4.** 70 kilometers per hour

**5.** 19 ounces per cubic foot

**6.** $2 per pound

**Copy and complete the statement by finding the missing number or unit.**

**7.** $30 \underline{\ ?\ } \cdot \dfrac{2 \text{ mi}}{1 \text{ h}} = 60 \text{ mi}$

**8.** $9 \underline{\ ?\ } \cdot 5 \text{ hours} = 45 \text{ person-hours}$

**9.** $\dfrac{? \text{ lb}}{1 \text{ ft}^3} \cdot 8 \text{ ft}^3 = 32 \text{ lb}$

**10.** $20 \text{ sec} \cdot 4 \underline{\ ?\ } = 80 \text{ ft}$

**11.** $6 \text{ persons} \cdot \underline{\ ?\ } \text{ days} = 30 \text{ person-days}$

**12.** $\dfrac{3 \text{ g}}{1 \text{ cm}^3} \cdot 2 \underline{\ ?\ } = 6 \text{ g}$

**REASONING Tell whether each answer seems reasonable. *Explain.***

**13.** You estimate that it will take 3 hours to drive 600 miles.

**14.** A given number of people are working on a job in which 12 person-days are needed to complete the job. You calculate that it will take 24 days to complete the job.

**In Exercises 15 and 16, use the table, which shows the density and volume of three mineral samples. Use the formula *m = DV* and unit analysis to answer the question.**

**15.** What is the mass of the anhydrite sample?

**16.** Compare the masses of the halite and hematite samples.

| Sample | Density $\dfrac{g}{cm^3}$ | Volume $cm^3$ |
|---|---|---|
| Anhydrite | 3 | 20 |
| Halite | 2 | 15 |
| Hematite | 5 | 12 |

**17.** An ocean liner travels 36 miles per hour for 5 hours. Its destination is 200 miles from its starting point. Use unit analysis to find out how many more miles the ocean liner must travel to reach its destination.

**18.** One group of 6 workers takes 18 hours to build a stone wall. Another group of 4 workers takes 27 hours to build a stone wall. Use unit analysis to calculate the person-hours for each group. Did the same amount of work need to be done for each wall? *Explain.*

**19.** A man runs 6 miles in 1 hour.

   **a.** Write the unit rate as a fraction

   **b.** REASONING Suppose the man maintains this rate for one hour and twenty minutes. *Explain* how to find the number of miles the man runs and state the number of miles.

# Practice

**Copy and complete the statement by finding the missing number or unit.**

1. $\underline{\ ?\ }$ min $\cdot \dfrac{3 \text{ mi}}{1 \text{ min}} = 39$ mi

2. 12 persons $\cdot$ 14 hours $= 168 \underline{\ ?\ }$

3. $\dfrac{5 \text{ g}}{1 \text{ cm}^3} \cdot 25 \underline{\ ?\ } = 125$ g

4. $\dfrac{2 \text{ lb}}{1 \text{ ft}^3} \cdot 28 \text{ ft}^3 = 56 \underline{\ ?\ }$

5. 3 h $\cdot \dfrac{82 \text{ km}}{\underline{\ ?\ }} = 246$ km

6. 24 persons $\cdot$ 30 $\underline{\ ?\ } = 720$ person-days

7. **FIND THE ERROR** Kevin ran at a speed of 11 feet per second for 3 minutes. *Describe* and correct the error in finding the distance he ran.

$d = rt$
$= 11 \cdot 3$
$= 33 \text{ feet}$ ✗

**REASONING Tell whether each answer seems reasonable.** *Explain.*

8. You estimate that the mass of an object with a density of 2 grams per cubic centimeter and a volume of 98 cubic centimeters is about 4 grams.

9. You calculate that you walked 18 miles in 120 minutes yesterday.

**In Exercises 10 and 11, use the table, which shows the density and volume of three element samples. Use the formula** $m = DV$ **and unit analysis to answer the question.**

10. What is the mass of the mercury sample?

11. Compare the masses of the three element samples in the table.

| Sample | Density $\dfrac{g}{1 \text{ cm}^3}$ | Volume $\text{cm}^3$ |
|---|---|---|
| Mercury | 14 | 11 |
| Nickel | 9 | 16 |
| Zinc | 7 | 22 |

12. Workers have started digging a 1 mile long trench for new underground pipes. They can dig a 50 foot section in 1 hour and have been digging for 8 hours. Use unit analysis to find out how much farther the workers must dig to finish the trench.

13. A software company estimates that 48 person-days are needed to evaluate a new video game. Six people evaluate parts of the video game for 5 days, then 3 people are moved to a different project. How long will it take the remaining 3 people to finish evaluating the video game?

14. To raise money for a charity, a group of students forms a relay team to run for 12 hours. The table shows the number of hours each student runs and each student's average speed. The team raises $40 for each mile run. How much money does the team raise?

| Student | Hours | Speed (mi/h) |
|---|---|---|
| Kim | 2 | 7 |
| Reza | 2 | 5 |
| Marta | 3 | 4 |
| Evan | 3 | 5 |
| Mina | 2 | 6 |

# Activity 1.5

## Let's Explore
### Evaluating Expressions

**Goal**
Evaluate an expression that contains variables.

**Materials**
- number cube
- scissors

**QUESTION**  How do you evaluate an expression that contains variables?

**EXPLORE 1**  *Roll a number cube to evaluate expressions*

**1** **Start** with an expression. Players will take turns choosing an expression from the list below. The first expression for player 1 is shown.

**2** **Roll** a number. Each player should roll the number cube. Record the number you roll in a table. Your partner will use a separate table.

**3** **Replace** the variable in your expression with the number you rolled. Record the numerical expression in the table. Evaluate the expression and record your result.

**4** **Repeat** Steps 2 and 3. Take turns choosing an expression from the list below and repeat Steps 2 and 3. Stop when each expression has been used once.

**Player 1**
$3 \times n - 2$

| Turn | Number rolled | Numerical expression | Result |
|------|------|------|------|
| 1 | 5 | $3 \times 5 - 2$ | 13 |
| 2 | ? | ? | ? |
| 3 | ? | ? | ? |
| 4 | ? | ? | ? |

**Expression List**

**A.** $3 \times n - 2$  **B.** $3 + n$  **C.** $17 - 2 \times n$  **D.** $3 \times n \div 3$

**E.** $60 \div n$  **F.** $5 \times n - 4$  **G.** $8 \times n - 5$  **H.** $180 \div (3 \times n)$

**5** **Find** your total score. Add the values from all your turns to get your score. The player with the highest score is the winner.

## Draw Conclusions

**1.** How many different values are possible for each expression above when you use a number cube to choose values for the variable? *Explain* your answer.

**2.** For any given expression, does rolling a high number like 5 always result in a greater value than rolling a low number like 2? *Explain*.

**Gr. 7 AF 1.1 Use variables and appropriate operations to write an expression,** an equation, an inequality, or a system of equations or inequalities **that represents a verbal description (e.g., three less than a number, half as large as area A).**
**Also addresses: Gr. 5 AF 1.0, Gr. 6 AF 1.0**

## EXPLORE 2 *Write an expression from a verbal description*

**1** **Write** each word or phrase shown below on a separate slip of paper.

| | | |
|---|---|---|
| plus | multiplied by | added to |
| times | increased by | squared times |

**2** **Copy** the expression and the table below. Then place slips of paper in the boxes to create different expressions. Record the expressions in the table.

10 [ ? ] *a* [ ? ] *b*

| Expression in words | Expression using symbols |
|---|---|
| 10 multiplied by *a* plus *b* | $10 \cdot a + b$ |
| ? | ? |
| ? | ? |
| ? | ? |
| ? | ? |

**3** **Copy** and complete the table below using the expressions from Step 2. Roll a number cube to find values for *a* and *b*.

| Expression using symbols | Value of *a* | Value of *b* | Numerical expression | Value |
|---|---|---|---|---|
| $10 \cdot a + b$ | ? | ? | ? | ? |
| ? | ? | ? | ? | ? |
| ? | ? | ? | ? | ? |
| ? | ? | ? | ? | ? |
| ? | ? | ? | ? | ? |

## Draw Conclusions

**3.** Tyler has the expression $10 + a \cdot b$ listed in his table. What slips of paper did he use to create his expression?

**4.** For what values of *a* and *b* will the expression $10 + a^2 \cdot b$ have the greatest value?

# Write and Evaluate Algebraic Expressions

## VOCABULARY and CONCEPTS

An **algebraic expression**, or *variable expression*, consists of numbers, operations, at least one variable, and sometimes grouping symbols. To evaluate an algebraic expression, substitute a number for each variable and find the value of the resulting numerical expression.

For example, the expression $3x$ represents the product of 3 and $x$. To evaluate the expression when $x = 2$, substitute 2 for $x$ to get $3(2)$, which is another way of writing $3 \cdot 2$, and carry out the multiplication to get 6.

The table below shows common words and phrases that indicate mathematical operations. You can refer to the table when writing algebraic expressions.

| Addition | Subtraction | Multiplication | Division |
|----------|-------------|----------------|----------|
| plus | minus | times | divided by |
| the sum of | the difference of | the product of | divided into |
| increased by | decreased by | multiplied by | the quotient of |
| total | fewer than | | |
| more than | less than | | |
| added to | subtracted from | | |

**EXAMPLE 1**  *Evaluating Algebraic Expressions*

**Evaluate the expression when $x = 9$ and $y = 3$.**

**a.** $6x - 10 = 6(9) - 10$      **Substitute 9 for $x$.**

$\qquad\qquad = 54 - 10$      **Multiply.**

$\qquad\qquad = 44$      **Subtract.**

**b.** $4x + 7y = 4(9) + 7(3)$      **Substitute 9 for $x$ and 3 for $y$.**

$\qquad\qquad = 36 + 21$      **Multiply.**

$\qquad\qquad = 57$      **Add.**

**c.** $x(5 + y) = 9(5 + 3)$      **Substitute 9 for $x$ and 3 for $y$.**

$\qquad\qquad = 9(8)$      **Add within parentheses.**

$\qquad\qquad = 72$      **Multiply.**

### Practice for Example 1

**Evaluate the expression when $a = 10$ and $b = 4$.**

**1.** $a + 9$      **2.** $8a$      **3.** $a(a - b)$      **4.** $\dfrac{5b}{a}$

**EXAMPLE 2**  *Writing Algebraic Expressions*

| Verbal Phrase | Algebraic Expression |
|---|---|
| **a.** A number increased by 5 | $n + 5$ |
| **b.** 17 less than a number | $n - 17$ |
| **c.** A number divided by 3 | $n \div 3$ or $\dfrac{n}{3}$ |
| **d.** 5 more than twice a number | $2n + 5$ |
| **e.** 4 times the sum of a number and 6 | $4(n + 6)$ |

### Practice for Example 2

**Write the phrase as an algebraic expression using *n*.**

**5.** A number increased by 3

**6.** The quotient of 64 and a number

**EXAMPLE 3**  *Writing and Evaluating Expressions*

There are *n* people signed up to play in a basketball league. You can find the number of 8 person teams there will be in the league by dividing the **number of people by 8**.

**a.** Use *n* to write an expression for the number of teams.

**b.** There are 96 people signed up. How many teams will there be?

### Solution

**a.** The phrase "dividing the number of people by 8" suggests division.

So, an algebraic expression for the number of teams is $n \div 8$ or $\dfrac{n}{8}$.

**b.** Evaluate the expression when $n = 96$.

$$\frac{n}{8} = \frac{96}{8}$$  **Substitute 96 for *n*.**

$$= 12$$  **Divide.**

▸**Answer** There will be 12 teams in the league.

### Practice for Example 3

**7.** Write an algebraic expression for the number of 6 person volleyball teams that can be formed from a group of *n* people. Then find the number of teams that can be formed from a group of 72 people.

# Practice

**Evaluate the expression when $x = 5$.**

**1.** $x + 6$      **2.** $21 - x$      **3.** $9x$      **4.** $\dfrac{20}{x}$

**5.** $12 + x$      **6.** $36 - x$      **7.** $10x$      **8.** $\dfrac{35}{x}$

**9.** $5x - 3$      **10.** $7x + 12$      **11.** $28 - 4x$      **12.** $19 + 3x$

**Evaluate the expression when $a = 4$ and $b = 3$.**

**13.** $a - b$      **14.** $ab$      **15.** $\dfrac{28}{a}$      **16.** $64 - b$

**17.** $3a + 5b$      **18.** $2a - 2b$      **19.** $a(a + b)$      **20.** $\dfrac{8b}{a}$

**21.** $6(a + b)$      **22.** $b(11 - a)$      **23.** $(a + 8) \div b$      **24.** $a \div (b - 1)$

**Write the phrase as an algebraic expression using $n$.**

**25.** The sum of a number and 7      **26.** 11 fewer than a number

**27.** The quotient of a number and 6      **28.** 5 divided into a number

**29.** 6 less than 4 times a number      **30.** The quotient of twice a number and 5

**31.** 9 times the difference of 4 and a number      **32.** 3 times the sum of a number and 12

**FIND THE ERROR** *Describe* and correct the error in evaluating the expression when $x = 4$ and $y = 6$.

**33.**
$$3x - y = 3(6) - 4$$
$$= 14$$

**34.**
$$x(x + y) = 4(4 + 6)$$
$$= 16 + 6$$
$$= 22$$

**35. REASONING** What value of $n$ makes the values of the expressions $3n$ and $n + 6$ equal?

**36.** You can evaluate the expression $112 - p$ to find the number of pencils you have left from a package of 112 pencils after you have distributed $p$ pencils among your classmates. Find the number of pencils left over after distributing 56 pencils.

**In Exercises 37–39, use the double bar graph which shows the scores in an academic competition. A team's final score is the sum of $v$ points for the verbal section and $m$ points for the math section.**

**37.** Write an algebraic expression for a team's final score.

**38.** Find each team's final score.

**39.** Another team earns 175 points for the verbal section. At least how many points must the team earn in the math section to have a higher final score than teams A, B, and C?

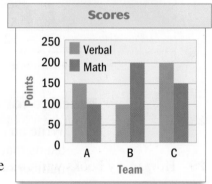

# Practice

**Evaluate the expression when $y = 6$.**

**1.** $\dfrac{24}{y}$

**2.** $20 - y$

**3.** $54 - y$

**4.** $15 - 2y$

**5.** $4y + 7$

**6.** $36 \div 2y$

**7.** $10 + 3y$

**8.** $11(10 - y)$

**Evaluate the expression when $m = 7$, $n = 9$, and $q = 10$.**

**9.** $3m + 2n$

**10.** $3q - 4m$

**11.** $mn + 5$

**12.** $\dfrac{4m + 2}{q}$

**13.** $15(n - m)$

**14.** $q(m + 5)$

**15.** $m \div (q - n)$

**16.** $(m + 2) \div n$

**17.** The diagonals divide the square into 4 triangles of equal area. Write an algebraic expression for the area of one of the labeled triangles.

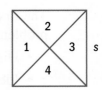

**Write the phrase as an algebraic expression using $n$.**

**18.** 6 fewer than a number

**19.** The quotient of 56 and a number

**20.** 8 more than 6 times a number

**21.** The quotient of 3 times a number and 2

**22.** The product of 12 and the sum of a number and 10

**23.** The quotient of 100 and the difference of 19 and a number

**24.** **REASONING** What value of $n$ makes the values of the expressions $9n$ and $n + 16$ equal?

**25.** Soccer players are ranked by points. Players earn 2 points for each goal scored and 1 point for each assist. Write an expression for the point total earned by a player for $g$ goals and $a$ assists. Mike was the point leader for his soccer team. During the season he scored 21 goals and made 7 assists. Find Mike's point total.

**In Exercises 26–29, use the following information. You join a book club that sells paperback books for $7 each. Your book budget is $350.**

**26.** Copy and complete the table.

| Books | Cost (dollars) | Amount left (dollars) |
|-------|----------------|------------------------|
| 1 | $1 \cdot 7 = 7$ | $350 - 7 = 343$ |
| 2 | $2 \cdot 7 = 14$ | $350 - 14 = 336$ |
| 3 | ? | ? |
| 4 | ? | ? |

**27.** Write an algebraic expression for the cost of $b$ books.

**28.** Write an algebraic expression for the amount left in your budget after buying $b$ books.

**29.** How many books will you be able to buy?

# Let's Explore
## Using Problem Solving Strategies

**Goal**
Use problem solving strategies to solve a problem.

**Materials**
• paper and pencil

**QUESTION** **How can you use given information and problem solving strategies to solve a problem?**

The first step in solving a problem is to read carefully and understand the problem. Consider some of the following actions when reading a problem.

- Distinguish between relevant and irrelevant information.
- Identify missing information.
- Sequence and prioritize information.

**EXPLORE** *Use problem solving strategies* •••••••••••••••••••••

**The problem:** On one day, Tessa walked the Millers' dog, walked the Fearings' dog, and spent some time at a bookstore. She rode her bike between the houses and the bookstore. How many miles did Tessa ride her bike?

**Some facts about Tessa's day:**

- Tessa went directly home after walking the Fearings' dog.

- The distance between the bookstore and the Fearings' house is 5 times the distance between Tessa's house and the Millers' house.

- The distance between the Fearings' house and Tessa's house is 7 miles.

- Tessa arrived at the Millers' house at 1:00 P.M.

- The shortest distance is from Tessa's house to the Miller's house.

- If Tessa rides her bike at an average speed of 12 miles per hour, it takes her 5 minutes to travel the distance between her house and the Millers' house.

- Tessa arrived at the bookstore at 2:30 P.M.

- The distance between the bookstore and the Millers' house is 4 miles less than the distance between Tessa's house and the Fearings' house.

**1** **Find** the *order* in which Tessa visited the Millers' house, the Fearings' house, and the bookstore.

   **a.** Write each fact from the list on a separate slip of paper. Then separate the slips of paper according to whether the fact is relevant or irrelevant to finding the order in which Tessa visited the houses and the bookstore.

| Relevant | Irrelevant |
|----------|------------|
|          |            |

   **b.** Organize your list of relevant information. Write Tessa's stops in order.

**2** **Find** the *distances* Tessa rode her bike.

   **a.** Separate your slips of paper according to whether the fact is relevant or irrelevant to finding the distances that Tessa traveled.

   **b.** Copy and complete the diagram. Use the relevant information to find the distance between consecutive stops.

   **c.** Find the total distance Tessa traveled on her bike.

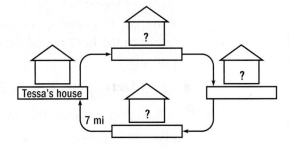

# Draw Conclusions

   **1.** Was there any information in the facts about Tessa's day that was not relevant at all to finding how many miles she rode her bike? If so, which?

   **2.** What are some skills and strategies you used to solve the problem in the activity?

   **3.** Copy and complete the table to show how far Tessa traveled to each stop. What general pattern do your calculations suggest?

| Destination | Total distance traveled |
|-------------|------------------------|
| First stop | ? |
| Second stop | ? + ? = ? |
| Third stop | ? + ? + ? = ? |
| Home | ? + ? + ? + ? = ? |

# Use a Problem Solving Plan

---

## VOCABULARY and CONCEPTS

A **verbal model** describes a real-world situation using words as labels and using math symbols to relate the words.

### Problem Solving Plan

1. **Read and Understand** Read the problem carefully. Identify the question and any important information.
2. **Make a Plan** Decide on a problem solving strategy.
3. **Solve the Problem** Use the problem solving strategy to answer the question.
4. **Look Back** Check that your answer is reasonable.

---

**EXAMPLE 1** *Understanding and Planning* . . . . . . . . . . . . . . . . . .

> **Skills Review**
> Problem solving strategies, p. 496

During a kayak trip, you kayak for 2 hours, break for lunch, kayak for 3 hours, have a short break, and kayak for 2 more hours. During the first part of the trip, you travel 4 miles. You travel at the same rate for the second part of the trip. During the last part of the trip, you travel twice as fast. How many miles did you travel on the kayak trip?

### Step 1 Read and Understand

*What do you know?* You can organize the given information in a diagram.

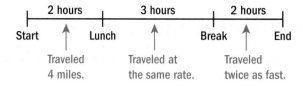

*What do you need to find out?* You need to find the distance traveled after lunch and the distance traveled after the break in order to find the total distance traveled.

### Step 2 Make a Plan

Use what you know to write a verbal model for the total distance traveled.

> | Distance traveled before lunch | + | Distance traveled after lunch | + | Distance traveled after break |

Then calculate the distances needed for the verbal model, substitute the values, and simplify the expression, as in Example 2 on the next page.

Gr. 7 AF 4.2 Solve multistep problems involving rate, average speed, distance, and time or a direct variation.
Gr. 7 MR 1.1 Analyze problems by identifying relationships, distinguishing relevant from irrelevant information, identifying missing information, sequencing and prioritizing information, and observing patterns.

## Practice for Example 1

**1.** How can you determine the distance traveled after lunch?

**2.** How can you determine the distance traveled after the break?

**EXAMPLE 2** *Solving and Looking Back* • • • • • • • • • • • • • • • • • • • • •

Solve the problem in Example 1 by carrying out the plan. Then check your answer.

### Step 3 Solve the Problem

You traveled 4 miles in 2 hours before lunch. Find the rate that you traveled before lunch.

$$\frac{4 \text{ miles}}{2 \text{ hours}} = 2 \text{ miles per hour}$$

This means that you traveled 2 miles per hour after lunch and $2(2) = 4$ miles per hour after the break. Use these rates to find the distance traveled during each part of the trip.

**After Lunch**

$d = rt = 2(3) = 6$

**After Break**

$d = rt = 4(2) = 8$

| Distance traveled before lunch | + | Distance traveled after lunch | + | Distance traveled after break | = |
|---|---|---|---|---|---|
| 4 | + | 6 | + | 8 | = 18 |

▶ **Answer** You traveled a total of 18 miles.

### Step 4 Look Back

Suppose you traveled all 7 hours at a rate of 2 miles per hour. Then you would have traveled $7(2) = 14$ miles. Because you traveled faster during one part of the trip, you traveled more than 14 miles. So, a distance of 18 miles seems reasonable.

## Practice for Example 2

**3.** In Example 2, suppose you traveled twice as fast after lunch as you did before lunch, and you traveled at the same rate after the break as before lunch. How many miles did you travel?

**4.** In Example 2, you traveled 4 miles before lunch, 6 miles after lunch, and 8 miles after a break. If the pattern continued, how many miles would you travel in the next two parts of your trip? Copy and complete the pattern, and then answer the question.

4, 6, 8,  ?  ,  ?

# Practice

Extra Practice
p. 498

**Match the problem solving step with its description.**

1. Read and Understand
2. Make a Plan
3. Solve the Problem
4. Look Back

A. Check that your answer is reasonable.

B. Read the problem carefully. Identify the question and any important information.

C. Decide on a problem solving strategy.

D. Use the problem solving strategy to answer the question.

**Write a verbal model that represents what you have to find to answer the question.**

5. One serving of rice weighs 2 ounces. A bag of rice weighs 90 ounces. How many full servings of rice are in the bag?

6. Your friend lives 3 miles farther away from school than you do. You live 12 miles from school. How far away from school does your friend live?

7. One T-shirt costs $10. How much do 15 T-shirts cost?

8. William is 5 inches shorter than Daniel. Daniel is 67 inches tall. How tall is William?

**In Exercises 9–11, use the following information.**

You volunteered to make 576 muffins for a school bake sale. Each batch makes 36 muffins. You want to know how many batches to mix.

9. Write a verbal model for the problem.

10. Use the model to find the number of batches of muffins you will need to mix.

11. Use estimation to check your answer.

12. Debra has two jobs. She earns $5 per hour baby-sitting and $9 per hour working as a cashier at a grocery store. She will work 13 hours baby-sitting and 23 hours at the grocery store this week. Use a problem solving plan to find how much money she will earn.

13. Jennifer, David, and Latisha walked in a charity walk-a-thon relay. Jennifer walked 6 kilometers in 3 hours, then David walked twice as fast as Jennifer for 4 hours, and then Latisha walked at the same rate as David for 3 hours. How far did the three people walk all together?

14. Copy the pattern below and then draw the next two shapes.

1. **FIND THE ERROR** *Describe* and correct the error made in solving the following problem.

   *You are ordering pizza for a party. One pizza serves 8 people. You expect that there will be 35 people at the party. How many pizzas should you order?*

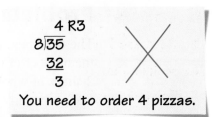

   $$\begin{array}{r} 4\ R3 \\ 8\overline{)35} \\ \underline{32} \\ 3 \end{array}$$

   You need to order 4 pizzas.

2. In a football game, the home team scored 3 touchdowns, 3 extra points, and 2 field goals. The visiting team scored 2 touchdowns, 2 extra points, and 4 field goals. Which team won the game? What was the final score?

   | Method of scoring | Points |
   | --- | --- |
   | Touchdown | 6 |
   | Extra point | 1 |
   | Field goal | 3 |

3. Juanita gets on a train at 12:05 P.M. for a 576 mile trip. Her train travels the entire distance at an average speed of 72 miles per hour. At what time does she arrive at her final destination?

4. Two sections of a patio are located side by side, as shown in the figure. The same paving is used for both sections. How much paving is needed for both sections?

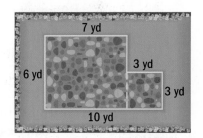

**In Exercises 5–8, copy and complete the pattern.**

5. 4, 13, 22, _?_, _?_

6. 3125, 625, 125, _?_, _?_

7. 82, 71, 60, _?_, _?_

8. 7, 28, 112, _?_, _?_

**In Exercises 9–11, tell whether there is enough information to answer the question. If there is, solve the problem. If there is not, tell what information is needed.**

9. Riley wants to raise $250 for a fundraiser walk. He needs to ask people to pledge money for each mile that he walks. How many people will he need to get pledges from in order to reach his goal?

10. Sal is 4 inches shorter than Derek. Rena is 5 feet, 1 inch tall. Derek is 1 inch taller than Wes. Wes and Lydia are the same height. Lydia is taller than Rena. How tall is Sal?

11. Clark is cooking a 12 pound ham. The ham needs to cook 20 minutes for each pound. Clark wants to serve the ham at 5 P.M. What is the latest time he should place the ham in the oven?

12. Cecilia is training for a marathon. For the first five weeks of training, she runs 12 miles per week. Over the following four weeks, she runs 16 miles per week. During the final three weeks of training she runs twice as many miles per week as her first week of training. Write a verbal model for the problem. How many miles total does she run over the twelve weeks?

# Problem Solving and Reasoning

## Problem

The table below gives nutritional information about various foods. Find the number of calories in a peanut butter and jelly sandwich made with 2 slices of whole wheat bread and 2 tablespoons each of peanut butter and grape jelly. Find the number of grams of fat in a ham sandwich.

| Food | Measure | Calories | Fat (grams) |
|---|---|---|---|
| Bread, white | 1 slice | 80 | 1 |
| Bread, whole wheat | 1 slice | 69 | 2 |
| Creamy peanut butter, reduced fat | 2 tablespoons | 190 | 12 |
| Ham | 2 slices | 56 | 3 |
| Grape jelly | 1 tablespoon | 50 | 0 |

## Solution

**Distinguish relevant from irrelevant information as part of MR 1.1.**

**1** **Find** the relevant data. The table gives the measure, calories, and fat for various foods. To answer the first part, you are interested in the calories in whole wheat bread, peanut butter, and grape jelly. You also need the information about the measure of each of these foods.

Whole wheat bread: 1 slice has 69 calories.

Peanut butter: 2 tablespoons has 190 calories.

Grape jelly: 1 tablespoon has 50 calories.

**Make precise calculations as part of MR 2.8.**

**2** **Write** an expression for the number of calories in a sandwich by multiplying the calories in each food by the number of times each measure is needed. Then evaluate the expression.

$$2 \cdot 69 + 1 \cdot 190 + 2 \cdot 50 = 138 + 190 + 100$$
$$= 428 \text{ calories}$$

**Use estimation to verify reasonableness as part of MR 2.1.**

**3** **Estimate** to check reasonableness. There are about 140 calories in 2 slices of whole wheat bread, about 200 calories in 2 tablespoons of peanut butter, and 100 calories in 2 tablespoons of grape jelly. Because $140 + 200 + 100 = 440$, 428 calories is reasonable.

**Identify missing information as part of MR 1.1.**

**4** **Identify** missing information. For the second part of the problem, you need to find the grams of fat in a ham sandwich.

You do not know how many slices of ham are needed for the sandwich, nor the type of bread and number of slices needed for the sandwich. There is not enough information to find the answer.

# Practice

**1.** Find the area of the figure. *Describe* your procedure. MR 1.3

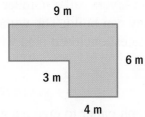
9 m
6 m
3 m
4 m

**2.** For each lettered part below, use the given number of 2s and the operations described to try writing expressions whose values are whole numbers from 0 to 10. In each case, indicate for which of the whole numbers from 0 to 10 you can write expressions. MR 1.1, MR 2.2

   **a.** Use two 2s and the four basic operations.

   **b.** Use three 2s, the four basic operations, and grouping symbols.

   **c.** Use four 2s, the four basic operations, and grouping symbols.

**3.** The shaded region below is formed by two overlapping rectangles. MR 2.5, MR 2.6, MR 3.3

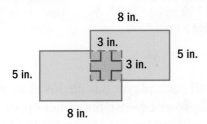
8 in.
3 in.
5 in.
3 in.
5 in.
8 in.

   **a.** Find the area of the shaded region. *Explain* your reasoning.

   **b.** Suppose a region is formed by two rectangles that each have length $\ell$ and width $w$ and that overlap in a square with side length $s$. Write an expression for the area of this region. Draw a region like the one described. Then find its area to show that your expression is correct.

**4.** A *chord* of a circle is a segment whose endpoints are on the circle. In this problem you will draw chords in a circle and find the number of regions formed inside the circle. MR 1.1, MR 2.5

   **a.** In the diagram below, a chord is drawn through the center of the circle. How many regions are formed?

   **b.** Copy the diagram from part (a) and add chords that pass through the center of the circle. For 1 to 5 chords, find the number of regions after each new chord is drawn.

   **c.** *Describe* the pattern in part (b). Use this pattern to find the number of regions formed for 22 chords drawn through the center of a circle.

   **d.** In the diagrams below, chords were drawn so that each chord intersects the other chords at distinct points inside the circle. Put the diagrams in order by the number of chords. Then find the number of regions formed in each diagram. Draw the next circle for this sequence.

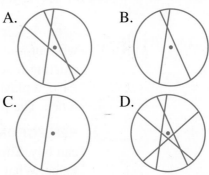
A.
B.
C.
D.

   **e.** *Describe* the pattern in part (d). Find the number of regions formed for 10 chords drawn in the same manner as part (d).

# Chapter ① Review Game

## Don't Fence Me In

**Materials**
- graph paper
- number cubes

**OBJECT OF THE GAME** Play in groups of two. Each player is given a budget of $720 to create an enclosed area on the grid using fencing that costs $12 per foot. In each round, players roll a number cube to determine how much of their fence they can build. The winner of the game is the player who creates the greatest enclosed area without going over the budget.

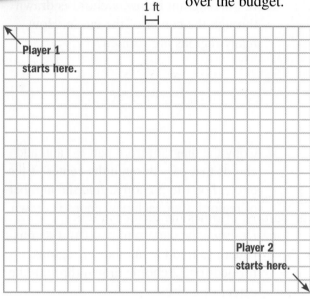

1 ft

Player 1 starts here.

Player 2 starts here.

**HOW TO PLAY**

**Step 1** Use graph paper to create a grid similar to the one shown. The side length of each square on the grid represents 1 foot.

**Step 2** Each player rolls a number cube. The number rolled is the number of feet of fence that a player can build for that round. Players start at opposite ends of the grid and draw part of their fence. The fence must be drawn on the lines of the grid. A new part of the fence must start where existing fence ends. Fencing cannot cross over itself. Players alternate drawing their fence. The player who draws first in a round will draw second in the next round.

**Step 3** Each player calculates the amount of money left in their budget after each round. The verbal model and algebraic expression below represent the new balance.

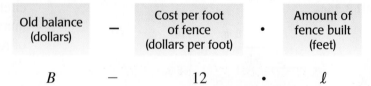

| Old balance (dollars) | − | Cost per foot of fence (dollars per foot) | • | Amount of fence built (feet) |
|---|---|---|---|---|
| $B$ | − | 12 | • | $\ell$ |

**Step 4** Repeat Steps 2 and 3 until each player has enclosed an area without going over the budget. A player can use his or her opponent's existing fence to enclose an area without having to pay for the fence. Also, a player cannot draw his or her fence across the other player's fence. The player with the greatest enclosed area wins.

**REFLECT ON THE GAME** Find the maximum amount of fence you can buy. Suppose you enclose a rectangular area with this amount of fence. What are the dimensions of a rectangle that has the greatest area? Describe how you might play the game differently after answering this question.

# Chapter Summary and Review

@HomeTutor
classzone.com

**VOCABULARY**

- power, p. 6
- base, p. 6
- exponent, p. 6
- numerical expression, p. 12
- grouping symbols, p. 12
- evaluate an expression, p. 12
- order of operations, p. 12
- variable, p. 18
- formula, p. 18
- rate, p. 26
- unit rate, p. 26
- unit analysis, p. 26
- algebraic expression, p. 32
- variable expression, p. 32
- verbal model, p. 38

**Vocabulary Exercises**

1. Copy and complete: A _?_ is a way of writing repeated multiplication.

2. Copy and complete: A _?_ gives a relationship between two or more variables.

## 1.1 Write and Evaluate Powers ................................ pp. 6–9

A power is a way of writing repeated multiplication. In a power, the base is the repeated factor, and the exponent is the number of times the factor is used.

**EXAMPLE** Write 7 · 7 · 7 as a power.

$$7 \cdot 7 \cdot 7 = 7^3$$

**Write the product as a power.**

3. $12 \cdot 12$  
4. $6 \cdot 6 \cdot 6 \cdot 6$  
5. $5 \cdot 5 \cdot 5 \cdot 5 \cdot 5$  
6. $10 \cdot 10 \cdot 10$

**Evaluate the power.**

7. $4^1$  
8. $11^2$  
9. $9^3$  
10. $3^5$

## 1.2 Use Order of Operations ................................ pp. 12–15

1. Evaluate expressions inside grouping symbols.

2. Evaluate powers.

3. Multiply and divide from left to right.

4. Add and subtract from left to right.

**EXAMPLE** Evaluate 2 + 3 × 4.

$$2 + 3 \times 4 = 2 + 12 \quad \textbf{Multiply.}$$
$$= 14 \quad \textbf{Add.}$$

**Evaluate the expression.**

11. $5 + 7 \times 2$  
12. $(7 + 9) \div 4^2$  
13. $5 \cdot 2^2 \div (7 - 3)$

### 1.3 Use Formulas ............................................ pp. 18–21

A formula gives a relationship between two or more variables. Two common formulas are shown below:

| **Distance, Rate, and Time** | **Total Cost** |
|---|---|
| Distance traveled $d$ is equal to the speed (rate of travel) $r$ times the travel time $t$. | The total cost $T$ of $n$ items is the cost $c$ of one item (the *unit cost*) times the number of items. |
| $d = rt$ | $T = cn$ |

**EXAMPLE** Find the distance traveled at a speed of 20 miles per hour for 3 hours.

$$d = rt \qquad \text{Write the formula for distance traveled.}$$
$$= 20 \cdot 3 \qquad \text{Substitute 20 for } r \text{ and 3 for } t.$$
$$= 60 \text{ miles} \qquad \text{Multiply.}$$

**Find the distance traveled for the given rate $r$ and time $t$.**

**14.** $r = 90$ kilometers per hour, $t = 4$ hours  **15.** $r = 18$ feet per second, $t = 30$ seconds

**Find the total cost of $n$ items having unit cost $c$.**

**16.** $c = \$2$ per song, $n = 6$ songs  **17.** $c = \$9$ per ticket, $n = 4$ tickets

### 1.4 Use Unit Analysis ............................................ pp. 26–29

Use unit analysis to make sure that the units used in your answers are correct.
Some units involve products or quotients of quantities measured in different units.

**EXAMPLE** It takes 3 persons 8 days to move the furniture out of a house. How long would it take 4 persons to move the furniture?

Find the number of person-days: 3 persons • 8 days = 24 person-days

Find the number of days for 4 persons: $\dfrac{24 \text{ person-days}}{4 \text{ persons}} = 6$ days

**Use the appropriate formula and unit analysis to answer the question.**

**18.** It takes 8 persons 24 days to build a brick wall. How long would it take 6 persons?

**19.** Sulvanite is a mineral with a density of 4 grams per cubic centimeter. What is the mass of 12 cubic centimeters of Sulvanite?

## 1.5 Write and Evaluate Algebraic Expressions .......... pp. 32–35

To write an algebraic expression, look for common words and phrases that indicate mathematical operations (see page 32). To evaluate an algebraic expression, substitute a number for each variable. Then find the value of the numerical expression.

**EXAMPLE** Write as an algebraic expression using $n$: Three times a number increased by 4. Then evaluate the expression when $n = 2$.

Expression: $3n + 4$

| | |
|---|---|
| $3n + 4 = 3(2) + 4$ | **Substitute 2 for $n$.** |
| $= 6 + 4$ | **Multiply.** |
| $= 10$ | **Add.** |

**Write the phrase as an algebraic expression using $n$.**

**20.** The product of a number and 3      **21.** 36 divided by a number

**Evaluate the expression when $x = 3$ and $y = 5$.**

**22.** $x + 2$      **23.** $\dfrac{15}{y}$      **24.** $4xy$      **25.** $\dfrac{45}{xy}$

## 1.6 Use a Problem Solving Plan .................. pp. 38–41

1. **Read and Understand** Read the problem carefully. Identify the question and any important information.

2. **Make a Plan** Decide on a problem solving strategy.

3. **Solve the Problem** Use the problem solving strategy to answer the question.

4. **Look Back** Check that your answer is reasonable.

**EXAMPLE** Sue drove 300 miles in 5 hours. Due to heavy traffic, her average speed on the return trip was 10 miles per hour less. How long did the return trip take?

You know that Sue drove 300 miles in 5 hours, so her average speed was $\dfrac{300 \text{ mi}}{5 \text{ h}} = 60$ miles per hour. You know that her average speed on the return trip was 10 miles per hour less, or 50 miles per hour. To find the time for the return trip, divide 300 miles by 50 miles per hour to get 6 hours. The answer is reasonable, because driving slower means the trip takes longer.

**26.** A Boston to New York commuter plane leaves Boston every 2 hours and 15 minutes. The earliest plane leaves at 6 A.M. What is the departure time closest to 2 P.M?

# Chapter Test

**Write the product as a power.**

**1.** $2 \cdot 2$

**2.** $6 \cdot 6 \cdot 6$

**3.** $9 \cdot 9 \cdot 9 \cdot 9$

**Write the verbal phrase as a power. Then evaluate.**

**4.** 12 to the second power

**5.** 8 to the third power

**Evaluate the expression.**

**6.** $2 + 3 \times 5$

**7.** $(15 - 8) \times 5$

**8.** $5^2 + 2$

**9.** $\dfrac{9 + 3}{9 - 3}$

**Find the perimeter and area of the rectangle or square.**

**10.**

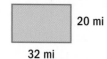

20 mi

32 mi

**11.**

9 m

9 m

**Find the distance traveled for the given rate _r_ and the time _t_.**

**12.** $r = 750$ miles per hour, $t = 4$ hours

**13.** $r = 15$ meters per second, $t = 240$ seconds

**Find the total cost of _n_ items having unit cost _c_.**

**14.** $c = \$3$ per notebook, $n = 4$ notebooks

**15.** $c = \$8$ per movie ticket, $n = 3$ tickets

**Copy and complete the statement by finding the missing number or unit.**

**16.** $\dfrac{40 \text{ mi}}{1 \text{ h}} \times \underline{?} \text{ h} = 120 \text{ mi}$

**17.** $\dfrac{6 \underline{?}}{1 \text{ day}} \times 5 \text{ days} = 30 \text{ classes}$

**18.** $\dfrac{\underline{?} \text{ g}}{1 \text{ cm}^3} \times 2 \text{ cm}^3 = 6 \text{ g}$

**19.** $\dfrac{15 \text{ km}}{1 \text{ h}} \times 5 \text{ h} = 75 \underline{?}$

**Evaluate the expression when _a_ = 7 and _b_ = 3.**

**20.** $4a + 3b$

**21.** $(a - 1) \div b$

**22.** $\dfrac{6a}{2b}$

**23.** $9a \div (b + 6)$

**Write the phrase as an algebraic expression using _n_.**

**24.** A number increased by 10

**25.** The difference of a number and 8

**26.** 3 less than twice a number

**27.** 7 times the sum of a number and 1

**In Exercises 28–30, use the following information.**

You have volunteered to sell 504 tickets for the school play. So far, you have been able to sell 28 tickets per day. You would like to know how many days you will be selling tickets.

**28.** Write a verbal model for the problem.

**29.** Use the model to find the number of days you will be selling tickets.

**30.** Check your answer.

# Multiple Choice Chapter Test

**1.** What is 20 • 20 written as a power?

Ⓐ $2^{20}$  Ⓑ $4^{100}$

Ⓒ $20^2$  Ⓓ $40^2$

**2.** What is $2^6$ written as a verbal phrase?

Ⓐ The product of two and six

Ⓑ The product of six and six

Ⓒ Six to the second power

Ⓓ Two to the sixth power

**3.** What is the value of the expression $2 + 3 \times 4$?

Ⓐ 10  Ⓑ 14

Ⓒ 20  Ⓓ 24

**4.** A rectangular garage has the dimensions shown. What are the perimeter $P$ and the area $A$ of the garage?

6 yd
12 yd

Ⓐ $P = 18$ yd; $A = 18$ yd$^2$

Ⓑ $P = 18$ yd; $A = 72$ yd$^2$

Ⓒ $P = 36$ yd; $A = 18$ yd$^2$

Ⓓ $P = 36$ yd; $A = 72$ yd$^2$

**5.** A plane flew at an average speed of 800 miles per hour for 2 hours. How far did the plane fly?

Ⓐ 400 miles  Ⓑ 800 miles

Ⓒ 1600 miles  Ⓓ 2800 miles

**6.** A school is purchasing 36 textbooks that cost $40 each. What is the total cost?

Ⓐ $360  Ⓑ $900

Ⓒ $1224  Ⓓ $1440

**7.** During a typical bicycle ride, the wheels spin 6 times per second. How many times will the wheels spin during a 15 minute bicycle ride?

Ⓐ 900 times  Ⓑ 3240 times

Ⓒ 3600 times  Ⓓ 5400 times

**8.** What is the value of the expression $3x(y - 1)$ when $x = 4$ and $y = 2$?

Ⓐ 12  Ⓑ 18

Ⓒ 24  Ⓓ 36

**9.** Which phrase is represented by the algebraic expression $5 \div (b + 4)$?

Ⓐ 5 divided into $b + 4$

Ⓑ the quotient of 5 and $b + 4$

Ⓒ $b + 4$ fewer than 5

Ⓓ $b + 4$ divided by 5

**10.** Each side of the triangle shown has the same length $s$. What is an algebraic expression for the perimeter of the triangle?

Ⓐ $s^3$  Ⓑ $s + 3$

Ⓒ $s \div 3$  Ⓓ $3s$

**11.** One package of pens contains 8 pens. What is the least number of packages needed to give 1 pen to each of the 28 students in the class?

Ⓐ 3 packages  Ⓑ 4 packages

Ⓒ 5 packages  Ⓓ 8 packages

**12.** Complete the pattern: 3, 10, 17, 24, __?__

Ⓐ 30  Ⓑ 31

Ⓒ 33  Ⓓ 38

# Fractions

## *Vocabulary for Chapter 2*

### Key Mathematical Vocabulary
- **equivalent fractions, p. 54**
- **least common denominator, p. 54**
- **reciprocals, p. 86**

### Academic Vocabulary
- **explain** Use words to describe the process that you used to solve a problem and why the process worked. For example, see Exercise 33 on page 56.
- **model, p. 52**
- **compare, p. 54**
- **describe, p. 57**
- **check, p. 81**
- **justify, p. 96**
- **make a conjecture, p. 96**
- **estimate, p. 97**

**Calculating distances by multiplying fractions, page 82**

**Gr. 7 NS 1.2** Add, subtract, multiply, and divide rational numbers (integers, **fractions,** and terminating decimals) **and take positive rational numbers to whole-number powers.** **Alg 2.0** Students understand and use such operations as taking the opposite, **finding the reciprocal,** taking a root, and raising to a fractional power. They understand and use the rules of exponents.

# Review Prerequisite Skills

## REVIEW VOCABULARY

- difference, p. 480
- sum, p. 480
- product, p. 481
- quotient, p. 482
- remainder, p. 482
- fraction, p. 483
- greatest common factor, p. 485
- least common multiple, p. 485
- perimeter, p. 488

**VOCABULARY CHECK**

**Copy and complete the statement.**

1. The greatest common factor of 27 and 36 is ? .

2. When you multiply two numbers, the result you get is called the ? .

**SKILLS CHECK**

**Find the greatest common factor of the pair of numbers. (Review p. 484 for 2.1.)**

3. 8, 6      4. 3, 7      5. 12, 36

**Order the numbers from least to greatest. (Review pp. 477–478 for 2.1–2.2.)**

6. 96, 102, 86, 75      7. 2, 0.5, 1, 0.75      8. 52, 5, 5.2, 51.7

**Find the least common multiple of the pair of numbers. (Review p. 484 for 2.2, 2.4.)**

9. 4, 6      10. 20, 16      11. 7, 2

**Find the sum or difference. (Review p. 480 for 2.3–2.4.)**

12. $1276 + 352$      13. $694 - 278$      14. $8427 - 934$

**Find the product. (Review p. 481 for 2.5, 2.7.)**

15. $16 \times 27$      16. $152 \times 18$      17. $632 \times 120$

**Find the quotient. (Review p. 482 for 2.5, 2.7.)**

18. $123 \div 3$      19. $736 \div 4$      20. $858 \div 60$

# Activity 2.1

## Let's Explore
### Modeling Equivalent Fractions

**Goal**
Use models to find equivalent fractions that represent the same number.

**Materials**
• graph paper
• colored pencils

**QUESTION** **How can you use models to find equivalent fractions?**

A unit square is a square that represents one unit. In this activity, you'll draw unit squares on graph paper to find fractions that represent the same number.

**EXPLORE 1** *Use models to find equivalent fractions* .......

Use models to find two fractions equivalent to $\frac{6}{8}$.

**1** **Draw** a unit square that is 8 by 8 on a piece of graph paper.

**2** **Divide** the square into 8 equal parts and shade 6 of the parts.

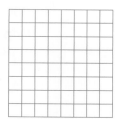

**3** **Look** for other ways of dividing the square into equal parts. Write a fraction to represent each model.

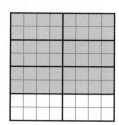

There are 4 equal parts and 3 are shaded: $\frac{3}{4}$.

There are 16 equal parts and 12 are shaded: $\frac{12}{16}$.

**4** **Write** equivalent fractions.

$$\frac{6}{8} = \frac{3}{4} = \frac{12}{16}$$

**Preparing for Gr. 7 NS 1.2** Add, subtract, multiply, and divide rational numbers (integers, fractions, and terminating decimals) and take positive rational numbers to whole-number powers.

# Draw Conclusions

1. Look at the fractions in Step 3. What operation can you perform on both the numerator and denominator of $\frac{6}{8}$ to obtain $\frac{3}{4}$? What operation can you perform on both the numerator and denominator of $\frac{6}{8}$ to obtain $\frac{12}{16}$?

2. In addition to the models shown in Step 3, what is another way of dividing the unit square in Step 1 into equal parts? How many parts should be shaded to model a fraction equivalent to $\frac{6}{8}$?

**Draw a model for the fraction. Then find two equivalent fractions.**

3. $\frac{9}{18}$
4. $\frac{2}{14}$
5. $\frac{4}{5}$
6. $\frac{15}{16}$

**In Exercises 7–10, write the fraction that is represented by the model. Then find two equivalent fractions.**

7.

8.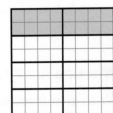

9.

10.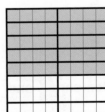

11. How do you know that $\frac{1}{5}$, $\frac{2}{10}$, and $\frac{4}{20}$ all represent the same number?

12. Are $\frac{1}{3}$ and $\frac{3}{6}$ equivalent fractions? Why or why not?

13. Copy the unit square shown.

   a. Can you use the unit square as shown to make a model for the fraction $\frac{2}{3}$? If so, draw the model.

   b. Can you use the unit square as shown to make a model for the equivalent fraction $\frac{20}{30}$? If so, draw the model.

# Lesson 2.1

# Simplify Fractions

## VOCABULARY and CONCEPTS

Fractions that represent the same number are called **equivalent fractions**.

The least common multiple of the denominators of two or more fractions is called the **least common denominator (LCD)**.

A fraction is in **simplest form** if its numerator and denominator have a greatest common factor of 1.

**EXAMPLE 1** *Writing Equivalent Fractions* .............

**Write two fractions that are equivalent to $\frac{6}{9}$.**

Multiply or divide the numerator and denominator by the same nonzero number to find an equivalent fraction.

$$\frac{6}{9} = \frac{6 \cdot 2}{9 \cdot 2} = \frac{12}{18}$$ **Multiply numerator and denominator by 2.**

$$\frac{6}{9} = \frac{6 \div 3}{9 \div 3} = \frac{2}{3}$$ **Divide numerator and denominator by 3, a common factor of 6 and 9.**

### Practice for Example 1

**Write two fractions that are equivalent to the given fraction.**

**1.** $\frac{6}{10}$      **2.** $\frac{12}{16}$      **3.** $\frac{4}{5}$      **4.** $\frac{32}{54}$

**EXAMPLE 2** *Comparing Fractions* .........................

**Skills Review**

Factors and multiples, p. 484

**Compare $\frac{3}{4}$ and $\frac{7}{15}$.**

Rewrite $\frac{3}{4}$ and $\frac{7}{15}$ using the least common denominator, 60.

$$\frac{3}{4} = \frac{3 \cdot 15}{4 \cdot 15} = \frac{45}{60} \qquad \frac{7}{15} = \frac{7 \cdot 4}{15 \cdot 4} = \frac{28}{60}$$

Compare the fractions: $\frac{45}{60} > \frac{28}{60}$, so $\frac{3}{4} > \frac{7}{15}$.

### Practice for Example 2

**Copy and complete the statement using <, >, or =.**

**5.** $\frac{3}{11} \; \underline{?} \; \frac{1}{4}$      **6.** $\frac{7}{10} \; \underline{?} \; \frac{2}{5}$      **7.** $\frac{4}{21} \; \underline{?} \; \frac{8}{42}$      **8.** $\frac{3}{22} \; \underline{?} \; \frac{4}{7}$

**EXAMPLE 3**  *Simplifying Fractions*

**a.** Write $\dfrac{12}{14}$ in simplest form.

$\dfrac{12}{14} = \dfrac{12 \div 2}{14 \div 2}$    **The GCF of 12 and 14 is 2.**

$= \dfrac{6}{7}$    **Simplify.**

**b.** Write $\dfrac{9}{16}$ in simplest form.

$\dfrac{9}{16}$    **The GCF of 9 and 16 is 1.**

The fraction is in simplest form.

**Practice for Example 3**

**Write the fraction in simplest form.**

**9.** $\dfrac{15}{18}$    **10.** $\dfrac{8}{17}$    **11.** $\dfrac{20}{25}$    **12.** $\dfrac{18}{81}$

**EXAMPLE 4**  *Simplifying a Fraction*

Your district's high school baseball team plays a total of 20 regular season games. The team plays 8 home games, that is, games at its home field. Write the number of home games as a fraction in simplest form of the total number of regular season games.

**Solution**

$\dfrac{\text{Number of home games}}{\text{Total number of games played}} = \dfrac{8}{20}$    **Write fraction.**

$= \dfrac{8 \div 4}{20 \div 4}$    **Divide numerator and denominator by GCF, 4.**

$= \dfrac{2}{5}$    **Simplify.**

▶ **Answer** The number of home games is $\dfrac{2}{5}$ of the total number of regular season games played.

**Practice for Example 4**

**13.** In your math class, 12 students participate in after-school clubs. There are 21 students in your math class. Write the number of students who participate in after-school clubs as a fraction of the total number of students. Then write the number of students who do not participate in after-school clubs as a fraction of the total number of students. Write each fraction in simplest form.

**Write two fractions that are equivalent to the given fraction.**

1. $\frac{1}{7}$

2. $\frac{2}{5}$

3. $\frac{8}{12}$

4. $\frac{3}{4}$

5. $\frac{3}{8}$

6. $\frac{6}{12}$

7. $\frac{7}{21}$

8. $\frac{2}{10}$

**Copy and complete the statement using <, >, or =.**

9. $\frac{3}{10} \underline{\ ?\ } \frac{1}{5}$

10. $\frac{21}{36} \underline{\ ?\ } \frac{7}{12}$

11. $\frac{6}{13} \underline{\ ?\ } \frac{2}{3}$

12. $\frac{7}{20} \underline{\ ?\ } \frac{4}{5}$

13. $\frac{6}{56} \underline{\ ?\ } \frac{2}{28}$

14. $\frac{6}{20} \underline{\ ?\ } \frac{2}{7}$

15. $\frac{10}{13} \underline{\ ?\ } \frac{60}{78}$

16. $\frac{1}{4} \underline{\ ?\ } \frac{9}{35}$

**Write the fraction in simplest form.**

17. $\frac{5}{10}$

18. $\frac{6}{8}$

19. $\frac{14}{16}$

20. $\frac{12}{18}$

21. $\frac{16}{20}$

22. $\frac{21}{27}$

23. $\frac{32}{40}$

24. $\frac{21}{56}$

25. $\frac{30}{48}$

26. $\frac{22}{66}$

27. $\frac{42}{105}$

28. $\frac{78}{90}$

29. Kayla lives $\frac{6}{7}$ mile from her school. Rachel lives $\frac{7}{8}$ mile from the school. Which girl lives closer to the school?

30. You are making a snack that includes $\frac{5}{6}$ pound of almonds and $\frac{7}{9}$ pound of cashews. Which is greater, the weight of the almonds or the weight of the cashews?

31. A bag of 24 balloons contains 18 red balloons. A larger bag of 48 balloons contains 36 red balloons. For each bag of balloons, write a fraction in simplest form comparing the number of red balloons with the total number of balloons. Are the fractions equivalent?

32. A company surveys 150 people, asking whether or not they would purchase a new product. Of the people surveyed, 90 people said they would purchase the new product and 60 people said they would not purchase the new product.

    a. What fraction of the people surveyed would purchase the new product? Give your answer in simplest form.

    b. What fraction of the people surveyed would not purchase the new product? Give your answer in simplest form.

33. **REASONING** *Explain* why the fraction $\frac{165}{285}$ is not in simplest form.

34. **REASONING** *Explain* how you would order the numbers $\frac{5}{6}, \frac{7}{8}, \frac{41}{48}$ from least to greatest. Then order the numbers.

**Write two fractions that are equivalent to the given fraction.**

**1.** $\dfrac{28}{44}$  **2.** $\dfrac{42}{60}$  **3.** $\dfrac{45}{90}$  **4.** $\dfrac{5}{14}$

**5.** $\dfrac{7}{16}$  **6.** $\dfrac{18}{20}$  **7.** $\dfrac{22}{34}$  **8.** $\dfrac{14}{35}$

**Copy and complete the statement using <, >, or =.**

**9.** $\dfrac{5}{16}$ ? $\dfrac{11}{32}$  **10.** $\dfrac{2}{9}$ ? $\dfrac{3}{13}$  **11.** $\dfrac{4}{7}$ ? $\dfrac{8}{15}$  **12.** $\dfrac{12}{32}$ ? $\dfrac{3}{8}$

**13.** $\dfrac{11}{12}$ ? $\dfrac{9}{15}$  **14.** $\dfrac{3}{5}$ ? $\dfrac{21}{35}$  **15.** $\dfrac{9}{17}$ ? $\dfrac{2}{3}$  **16.** $\dfrac{6}{11}$ ? $\dfrac{19}{33}$

**Write the fraction in simplest form.**

**17.** $\dfrac{24}{48}$  **18.** $\dfrac{54}{60}$  **19.** $\dfrac{51}{68}$  **20.** $\dfrac{28}{30}$

**21.** $\dfrac{39}{52}$  **22.** $\dfrac{45}{72}$  **23.** $\dfrac{35}{42}$  **24.** $\dfrac{14}{63}$

**25.** On Monday, you spent $\dfrac{1}{8}$ day practicing on the drums. On Tuesday, you spent $\dfrac{1}{12}$ day practicing. On which day did you practice more?

**26.** A copper pipe has a diameter of $\dfrac{3}{4}$ inch. A steel pipe has a diameter of $\dfrac{7}{8}$ inch. Which pipe has the greater diameter?

**27.** Sarah spent 40 minutes of her 3 hour shift at the grocery store stocking shelves. Erika spent 90 minutes of her 4 hour shift stocking shelves. For each girl, write a fraction in simplest form comparing the time spent stocking shelves with the total length of the shift. Are the fractions equivalent?

**28.** You and a friend are taking a 300 mile car trip. You have already traveled 120 miles.

    **a.** What fraction of the trip has been completed? Give your answer in simplest form.

    **b.** What fraction of the trip is left? Give your answer in simplest form.

**29.** **REASONING** *Describe* the following pattern: $\dfrac{3}{8}, \dfrac{6}{16}, \dfrac{9}{24}, \dfrac{12}{32}, \ldots$ Then write the next three fractions.

**30.** **REASONING** Can you find a fraction equivalent to $\dfrac{78}{96}$ with a numerator of 13? *Explain* your answer.

**31.** **REASONING** Can you find a fraction equivalent to $\dfrac{81}{108}$ with a denominator of 24? *Explain* your answer.

## Let's Explore
# Modeling Mixed Numbers and Improper Fractions

**Goal**
Use models to write improper fractions as mixed numbers and mixed numbers as improper fractions.

**Materials**
• paper and pencil

**QUESTION** How can you use models to rewrite improper fractions as mixed numbers and mixed numbers as improper fractions?

A fraction is an *improper fraction* if its numerator is greater than or equal to its denominator. A *mixed number* is a number expressed as a sum of a whole number and a proper fraction.

**EXPLORE 1** *Use a model to rewrite an improper fraction*

Use a model to write $\frac{9}{4}$ as a mixed number.

**1** **Draw** a unit square and divide it into 4 equal parts. Shade all 4 parts to represent 4 fourths. Since the big square is a unit square, it represents 1.

**2** **Draw** another unit square and divide and shade it as in Step 1. You now have a total of 8 fourths. The squares also represent 2.

**3** **Draw** a third square and divide it into 4 equal parts. Shade only 1 part. You now have a total of 9 fourths. You can see that $\frac{9}{4} = 2\frac{1}{4}$.

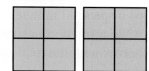

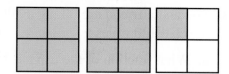

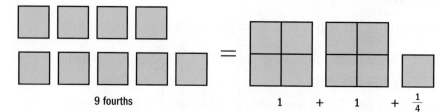

9 fourths $\qquad$ 1 $\quad$ + $\quad$ 1 $\quad$ + $\quad$ $\frac{1}{4}$

## Draw Conclusions
**Write the improper fraction as a mixed number.**

1. $\frac{7}{4}$  2. $\frac{11}{4}$  3. $\frac{19}{8}$  4. $\frac{25}{8}$

**Preparing for Gr. 7 NS 1.2** Add, subtract, multiply, and divide rational numbers (integers, fractions, and terminating decimals) and take positive rational numbers to whole-number powers.

**EXPLORE 2** *Use a model to rewrite a mixed number* . . . . . . . .

Use a model to write $3\frac{3}{4}$ as an improper fraction.

**1** **Draw** four squares.

Shade three whole squares and three-fourths of the last square to represent $3\frac{3}{4}$.

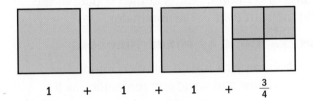

$1 \quad + \quad 1 \quad + \quad 1 \quad + \quad \frac{3}{4}$

**2** **Divide** each square into 4 equal parts.

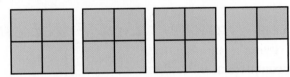

**3** **Count** the number of shaded parts in the model.

There are 15 parts or 15 fourths. So, $3\frac{3}{4}$ can be written as $\frac{15}{4}$.

## Draw Conclusions

**Write the mixed number as an improper fraction.**

**5.** $2\frac{5}{6}$        **6.** $4\frac{4}{5}$        **7.** $1\frac{6}{11}$        **8.** $6\frac{2}{3}$

**Use the model to write a mixed number and an improper fraction.**

**9.**

**10.**

**11.** *Explain* why $1\frac{2}{7} \neq \frac{12}{7}$.

# Mixed Numbers and Improper Fractions

## VOCABULARY and CONCEPTS

A fraction is a **proper fraction** if its numerator is less than its denominator.

A fraction is an **improper fraction** if its numerator is greater than or equal to its denominator.

A **mixed number** is the sum of a whole number and a proper fraction.

### Writing Mixed Numbers as Improper Fractions

To write a mixed number as an improper fraction, multiply the whole number part and the denominator, add the product to the numerator, and write the sum over the denominator.

### Writing Improper Fractions as Mixed Numbers

To write an improper fraction as a mixed number, divide the numerator by the denominator and write any remainder as a fraction.

---

**EXAMPLE 1**  *Writing Mixed Numbers and Fractions* ·······

**a.** Write $4\frac{3}{5}$ as an improper fraction.

$$4\frac{3}{5} = \frac{4 \cdot 5 + 3}{5}$$   **Multiply whole number and denominator. Add product to numerator.**

$$= \frac{23}{5}$$   **Simplify.**

**b.** Write $\frac{27}{7}$ as a mixed number.

**Skills Review**

Dividing whole numbers, p. 482

$$\begin{array}{r} 3 \text{ R6} \\ 7\overline{)27} \\ \underline{21} \\ 6 \end{array}$$   **Divide numerator by denominator.**

$$\frac{27}{7} = 3\frac{6}{7}$$   **Write remainder as a fraction:** $\frac{\text{remainder}}{\text{denominator}}$.

### Practice for Example 1

**Write the number as an improper fraction.**

**1.** $5\frac{8}{9}$     **2.** $6$     **3.** $2\frac{1}{8}$

**Write the number as a mixed number.**

**4.** $\frac{15}{4}$     **5.** $\frac{21}{8}$     **6.** $\frac{19}{6}$

**EXAMPLE 2** *Comparing Mixed Numbers and Fractions* .....

**Compare $\frac{23}{14}$ and $1\frac{7}{8}$.**

Write $1\frac{7}{8}$ as an improper fraction: $1\frac{7}{8} = \frac{15}{8}$.

Rewrite $\frac{23}{14}$ and $\frac{15}{8}$ using the LCD, 56.

$$\frac{23}{14} = \frac{23 \cdot 4}{14 \cdot 4} = \frac{92}{56} \qquad \frac{15}{8} = \frac{15 \cdot 7}{8 \cdot 7} = \frac{105}{56}$$

Compare the fractions: $\frac{92}{56} < \frac{105}{56}$, so $\frac{23}{14} < 1\frac{7}{8}$.

**Practice for Example 2**

**Copy and complete the statement using <, >, or =.**

**7.** $\frac{39}{13}$ _?_ $3\frac{1}{2}$        **8.** $4$ _?_ $\frac{32}{7}$        **9.** $5\frac{1}{3}$ _?_ $\frac{37}{7}$

**EXAMPLE 3** *Ordering Mixed Numbers and Fractions* .......

You are making four types of strawberry smoothies. The amounts of strawberries needed for each recipe are $1\frac{1}{3}$, $2$, $\frac{5}{2}$, and $1\frac{1}{2}$ cups. Order the amounts from least to greatest.

**Solution**

The denominators are 3, 1, and 2. Rewrite each number as an improper fraction using the LCD, 6.

$$1\frac{1}{3} = \frac{4}{3} = \frac{4 \cdot 2}{3 \cdot 2} = \frac{8}{6} \qquad\qquad \frac{5}{2} = \frac{5 \cdot 3}{2 \cdot 3} = \frac{15}{6}$$

$$2 = \frac{2}{1} = \frac{2 \cdot 6}{1 \cdot 6} = \frac{12}{6} \qquad\qquad 1\frac{1}{2} = \frac{3}{2} = \frac{3 \cdot 3}{2 \cdot 3} = \frac{9}{6}$$

▶ **Answer** From least to greatest, the amounts are $1\frac{1}{3}$, $1\frac{1}{2}$, $2$, and $\frac{5}{2}$ cups.

**Practice for Example 3**

**10.** You are making four types of trail mix. You need raisins for each recipe. The amounts of raisins needed for each recipe are $\frac{8}{3}$, $1\frac{5}{6}$, $3$, and $2\frac{1}{4}$ cups. Order the amounts from least to greatest.

**Copy and complete the statement.**

1. In the mixed number $6\frac{3}{4}$, $\frac{3}{4}$ is the ___?___ part of the mixed number.

2. In the mixed number $6\frac{3}{4}$, 6 is the ___?___ part of the mixed number.

3. A fraction whose numerator is greater than or equal to its denominator is a(n) ___?___ fraction.

**Tell whether the number is a *mixed number*, a *proper fraction*, or an *improper fraction*.**

4. $\frac{15}{15}$    5. $\frac{8}{9}$    6. $4\frac{2}{3}$

7. $\frac{7}{1}$    8. $\frac{18}{19}$    9. $\frac{5}{5}$

**Write the number as an improper fraction.**

10. $1\frac{3}{4}$    11. 3    12. $5\frac{1}{3}$

13. 27    14. $5\frac{5}{6}$    15. $7\frac{1}{3}$

**Write the number as a mixed number.**

16. $\frac{5}{2}$    17. $\frac{13}{4}$    18. $\frac{8}{5}$

19. $\frac{11}{10}$    20. $\frac{15}{2}$    21. $\frac{20}{8}$

**Copy and complete the statement using <, >, or =.**

22. $3\frac{1}{4}$ ? $\frac{15}{4}$    23. $\frac{24}{5}$ ? $4\frac{2}{5}$    24. $1\frac{3}{7}$ ? $\frac{9}{7}$

25. $1\frac{5}{6}$ ? $\frac{13}{6}$    26. $8\frac{1}{3}$ ? $\frac{25}{3}$    27. $6$ ? $\frac{25}{4}$

28. A recipe for rye bread calls for $1\frac{1}{3}$ cups of rye flour. You have only a one-third cup measure. How many one-third cups of flour do you need?

29. Natasha buys apples at two different stores. At the first store, she buys $3\frac{1}{2}$ pounds of apples. At the second store, she buys $\frac{17}{5}$ pounds of apples. Which apples weigh more?

30. Three friends helped paint a room. Cheryl worked $\frac{7}{4}$ hours, José worked $2\frac{2}{3}$ hours, and Jade worked $\frac{12}{5}$ hours. Order the lengths of time from least to greatest. Who worked for the longest period of time?

31. **REASONING** Which is greater, an improper fraction or a proper fraction? *Explain.*

# Practice

**Write the number as an improper fraction.**

**1.** $4\frac{1}{4}$      **2.** $3\frac{2}{3}$      **3.** $2\frac{6}{7}$      **4.** $5\frac{5}{6}$

**5.** $5\frac{3}{4}$      **6.** $6\frac{3}{10}$      **7.** $8\frac{2}{15}$      **8.** $7\frac{5}{12}$

**Write the number as a mixed number.**

**9.** $\frac{11}{2}$      **10.** $\frac{15}{4}$      **11.** $\frac{53}{10}$      **12.** $\frac{29}{8}$

**13.** $\frac{23}{3}$      **14.** $\frac{51}{11}$      **15.** $\frac{53}{16}$      **16.** $\frac{49}{15}$

**FIND THE ERROR** *Describe* and correct the error.

**17.**
$$5\frac{4}{9} = \frac{5 \cdot 4 + 9}{9}$$
$$= \frac{29}{9}$$

**18.**
$$\frac{29}{3} = 3\overline{)29}^{\ 9\ R2} \quad \frac{27}{\phantom{2}2}$$
$$\frac{29}{3} = 9\frac{3}{2}$$

**19.** Which number is between $\frac{32}{9}$ and $3\frac{8}{9}$?

     **A.** $\frac{37}{9}$      **B.** $3\frac{7}{9}$      **C.** $3\frac{5}{9}$      **D.** $\frac{31}{9}$

**Order the numbers from least to greatest.**

**20.** $2\frac{2}{5}, \frac{11}{5}, 2\frac{3}{10}, \frac{31}{10}$      **21.** $4\frac{1}{2}, \frac{19}{4}, \frac{37}{8}, 4\frac{3}{16}$      **22.** $\frac{23}{3}, 7\frac{4}{9}, \frac{55}{9}, 7\frac{5}{18}$

**23.** $4\frac{11}{24}, 5\frac{1}{4}, \frac{31}{6}, \frac{57}{12}$      **24.** $1\frac{3}{4}, 2\frac{2}{5}, \frac{21}{10}, \frac{29}{20}$      **25.** $9\frac{1}{6}, 10\frac{1}{4}, \frac{61}{6}, \frac{83}{9}$

**26.** A recipe for rye bread calls for $2\frac{1}{4}$ cups of rye flour. You have only a one-fourth cup measure. How many one-fourth cups of flour do you need?

**27.** The top four distances in the discus throw at a track meet are $97\frac{1}{8}$, $97\frac{3}{5}$, $97\frac{1}{4}$, and $97\frac{2}{9}$ feet. Order the distances from least to greatest.

**28.** Amanda wants to buy a field hockey stick with a length between 3 feet and $3\frac{1}{6}$ feet. Which length should she choose?

     **A.** $\frac{35}{12}$ ft      **B.** $\frac{37}{12}$ ft      **C.** $\frac{13}{4}$ ft      **D.** $\frac{10}{3}$ ft

**29. REASONING** How can you order $3\frac{1}{4}$, $3\frac{3}{4}$, $3\frac{2}{7}$, and $3\frac{1}{8}$ from least to greatest without writing them as improper fractions? *Explain* your reasoning.

# Activity 2.3

## Let's Explore
### Fractions with the Same Denominator

**Goal**
Use models to add and subtract fractions with the same denominator.

**Materials**
- paper
- colored pencils

**QUESTION** **How can you use models to add and subtract fractions with the same denominator?**

You can use models to add and subtract fractions as shown below.

$$\frac{1}{3} + \frac{1}{3} = \frac{2}{3}$$

$$\frac{3}{5} - \frac{1}{5} = \frac{2}{5}$$

**EXPLORE 1** *Use models to add mixed numbers* · · · · · · · · · · ·

Use models to find $2\frac{3}{5} + 1\frac{4}{5}$.

1. **Draw** models representing $2\frac{3}{5}$ and $1\frac{4}{5}$.

2. **Combine** the fraction parts of the models to form a whole number if possible.

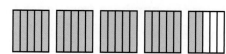

3. **Write** the sum as a mixed number.

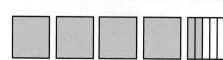

$$2\frac{3}{5} + 1\frac{4}{5} = 4\frac{2}{5}$$

## Draw Conclusions
**Find the sum. Simplify if possible.**

1. $5\frac{3}{5} + 1\frac{1}{5}$      2. $7\frac{1}{2} + 4\frac{1}{2}$      3. $1\frac{2}{7} + 9\frac{6}{7}$      4. $2\frac{1}{6} + 4\frac{5}{6}$

5. $3\frac{2}{3} + 1\frac{1}{3}$      6. $5\frac{1}{4} + 6\frac{1}{4}$      7. $8\frac{3}{8} + 4\frac{7}{8}$      8. $1\frac{4}{9} + 2\frac{8}{9}$

9. When Sue made a model for $\frac{5}{8}$, she noticed that $\frac{5}{8} = \frac{1}{2} + \frac{1}{8}$. *Explain* how this observation could help her find the sum $\frac{5}{8} + \frac{5}{8}$.

**Gr. 7 NS 1.2** Add, **subtract,** multiply, and divide **rational numbers** (integers, **fractions**, and terminating decimals) and take positive rational numbers to whole-number powers.
**Also addresses Gr. 6 NS 2.0, Gr. 6 NS 2.1**

**EXPLORE 2** *Use a model to subtract mixed numbers* . . . . . . .

**Use a model to find** $3\frac{1}{4} - 1\frac{3}{4}$.

**1** **Draw** a model representing $3\frac{1}{4}$.

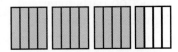

**2** **Use** your model to represent $3\frac{1}{4} - 1\frac{3}{4}$.

**3** **Redraw** your model if necessary to combine remaining fractional parts on the same unit square.

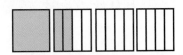

**4** **Write** the difference as a mixed number.
$$3\frac{1}{4} - 1\frac{3}{4} = 1\frac{2}{4}, \text{ or } 1\frac{1}{2}$$

## Draw Conclusions
**Find the difference. Simplify if possible.**

**10.** $3\frac{1}{3} - 1\frac{2}{3}$ **11.** $7\frac{1}{5} - 3\frac{4}{5}$ **12.** $6\frac{1}{6} - 4\frac{5}{6}$ **13.** $5\frac{1}{4} - 2\frac{3}{4}$

**14.** $4\frac{3}{8} - 3\frac{7}{8}$ **15.** $5\frac{2}{9} - 3\frac{7}{9}$ **16.** $9\frac{7}{9} - 3\frac{8}{9}$ **17.** $6\frac{5}{7} - 1\frac{2}{7}$

**18.** *Explain* how you can find the difference $3\frac{1}{4} - 1\frac{3}{4}$ by first rewriting the mixed numbers as improper fractions.

# Add and Subtract Fractions with the Same Denominator

## VOCABULARY and CONCEPTS

- improper fraction, p. 60
- mixed number, p. 60

### Adding and Subtracting Fractions

To add or subtract fractions with the same denominator, write the sum or difference of the numerators over the denominator.

To add or subtract mixed numbers whose fraction parts have the same denominator, write the mixed numbers as improper fractions, then write the sum or difference of the numerators over the denominator. Simplify if possible.

**EXAMPLE 1**  *Adding Fractions*

Find $\frac{4}{9} + \frac{7}{9}$.

$$\frac{4}{9} + \frac{7}{9} = \frac{4+7}{9}$$  Write sum of numerators over common denominator, 9.

$$= \frac{11}{9}$$  Add numerators.

$$= 1\frac{2}{9}$$  Rewrite improper fraction as a mixed number.

### Practice for Example 1

Find the sum.

1. $\frac{7}{10} + \frac{2}{10}$

2. $\frac{2}{9} + \frac{3}{9}$

3. $\frac{4}{5} + \frac{2}{5}$

4. $\frac{2}{7} + \frac{5}{7}$

**EXAMPLE 2**  *Subtracting Fractions*

Find $\frac{5}{6} - \frac{3}{6}$.

$$\frac{5}{6} - \frac{3}{6} = \frac{5-3}{6}$$  Write difference of numerators over common denominator, 6.

$$= \frac{2}{6}$$  Subtract numerators.

$$= \frac{1}{3}$$  Simplify.

### Practice for Example 2

Find the difference.

5. $\frac{4}{5} - \frac{2}{5}$

6. $\frac{5}{8} - \frac{3}{8}$

7. $\frac{5}{7} - \frac{2}{7}$

8. $\frac{8}{9} - \frac{1}{9}$

**EXAMPLE 3** *Adding and Subtracting Mixed Numbers* ......

**a.** $4\frac{1}{6} + 7\frac{5}{6} = \frac{25}{6} + \frac{47}{6}$     **Write as improper fractions.**

$= \frac{72}{6}$     **Add.**

$= 12$     **Simplify.**

**b.** $5\frac{2}{7} - 2\frac{6}{7} = \frac{37}{7} - \frac{20}{7}$     **Write as improper fractions.**

$= \frac{17}{7}$     **Subtract.**

$= 2\frac{3}{7}$     **Write as a mixed number.**

### Practice for Example 3

**Find the sum or difference.**

**9.** $2\frac{5}{11} + 7\frac{3}{11}$     **10.** $2\frac{3}{5} - 1\frac{2}{5}$     **11.** $4\frac{1}{7} - 2\frac{3}{7}$

**EXAMPLE 4** *Solving a Subtraction Problem* ..................

Susan catches a fish that weighs $3\frac{3}{4}$ pounds. Emma catches a fish that weighs $5\frac{1}{4}$ pounds. How much heavier is Emma's fish?

### Solution

$5\frac{1}{4} - 3\frac{3}{4} = \frac{21}{4} - \frac{15}{4}$     **Write as improper fractions.**

$= \frac{6}{4}$     **Subtract.**

$= \frac{3}{2}$     **Simplify.**

$= 1\frac{1}{2}$     **Write as a mixed number.**

▶ **Answer** Emma's fish is $1\frac{1}{2}$ pounds heavier.

### Practice for Example 4

**12.** A tailor cuts a piece of material $4\frac{2}{3}$ inches long from a piece of material that is $10\frac{1}{3}$ inches long. How many inches of material are left?

**Practice**

**Extra Practice**
p. 499

1. What fraction when added to $\frac{1}{8}$ results in a sum of $\frac{1}{4}$?

2. What addition problem does the model below represent?

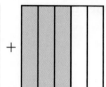

**Find the sum or difference.**

3. $\frac{5}{9} + \frac{1}{9}$

4. $\frac{12}{17} - \frac{8}{17}$

5. $\frac{2}{5} + \frac{4}{5}$

6. $2\frac{1}{4} + \frac{3}{4}$

7. $\frac{19}{21} + \frac{13}{21}$

8. $4\frac{2}{7} - 1\frac{5}{7}$

9. $8\frac{1}{4} - 6\frac{3}{4}$

10. $7\frac{3}{8} - 2\frac{5}{8}$

11. $1\frac{5}{6} + 3\frac{5}{6}$

**In Exercises 12 and 13, use the following information.**
Some friends are walking a $\frac{3}{4}$ mile trail to a creek. They have gone $\frac{1}{4}$ mile so far.

12. Copy and complete the verbal model.

    Distance left to walk = ___?___ − ___?___

13. Find the difference. How far do they have left to walk?

14. Jerome worked $\frac{7}{12}$ hour yesterday. He worked $\frac{8}{12}$ hour today. How much time did he work in all?

15. Yesterday you ran $2\frac{5}{8}$ miles during track practice. Today you ran $3\frac{1}{8}$ miles. How much farther did you run at today's practice than at yesterday's practice?

16. Stacy is making a loaf of bread. The recipe calls for $4\frac{1}{3}$ cups of flour. She decides to add an additional $\frac{2}{3}$ cup of flour. How much flour does she use altogether?

17. Carlos's dog weighed $25\frac{3}{4}$ pounds last month. This month the dog weighs $27\frac{1}{4}$ pounds. How much weight did the dog gain?

18. **REASONING** Can the sum of two fractions that have the same denominator and are each less than 1 be greater than 1? *Explain* your reasoning and provide an example.

# Practice

1. What subtraction problem does the model below represent?

**Find the sum or difference.**

2. $\dfrac{15}{24} + \dfrac{6}{24}$

3. $\dfrac{7}{9} - \dfrac{4}{9}$

4. $\dfrac{11}{12} - \dfrac{5}{12}$

5. $2\dfrac{3}{4} + \dfrac{3}{4}$

6. $4\dfrac{1}{6} + 5\dfrac{5}{6}$

7. $1\dfrac{7}{12} + 2\dfrac{1}{12}$

8. $9\dfrac{3}{8} - 3\dfrac{7}{8}$

9. $3\dfrac{9}{10} + 6\dfrac{3}{10}$

10. $17\dfrac{1}{4} - 3\dfrac{3}{4}$

11. $4\dfrac{5}{12} - 3\dfrac{11}{12}$

12. $5\dfrac{5}{24} - 2\dfrac{11}{24}$

13. $8\dfrac{7}{18} + 6\dfrac{13}{18}$

**Copy and complete the statement.**

14. $\dfrac{a}{c} + \dfrac{b}{c} = \dfrac{? + ?}{c}$

15. $\dfrac{?}{c} - \dfrac{?}{c} = \dfrac{a - b}{c}$

**In Exercises 16–18, use the table, which describes all the types of trees in a park.**

16. What fraction of the trees are elm or maple trees?

17. What fraction of the trees are pine trees?

18. How much greater is the fraction of maple trees than the fraction of pine trees?

| Tree | Fraction of trees |
|------|-------------------|
| Elm | $\dfrac{7}{20}$ |
| Maple | $\dfrac{9}{20}$ |
| Pine | $\dfrac{?}{20}$ |

19. A restaurant serves a steak that weighs $1\dfrac{5}{8}$ pounds. A bone in the steak weighs $\dfrac{7}{8}$ pound. How much does the meat weigh?

20. Matthew worked $2\dfrac{1}{6}$ hours mowing lawns on Sunday. On Monday he mowed for $2\dfrac{5}{6}$ hours, and on Tuesday he mowed for $1\dfrac{5}{6}$ hours. What is the total amount of time Matthew spent mowing lawns on those three days?

21. Sonya's pet cat weighed $10\dfrac{3}{8}$ pounds. Over the last four months, the cat gained $\dfrac{5}{8}$ pound, lost $\dfrac{3}{8}$ pound, gained $\dfrac{7}{8}$ pound, and gained $\dfrac{5}{8}$ pound. How much does the cat now weigh?

22. **REASONING** Can you subtract two fractions with the same denominator and get an answer with a different denominator? *Explain* your reasoning and provide an example.

**VOCABULARY**
- equivalent fractions, p. 54
- least common denominator (LCD), p. 54
- simplest form, p. 54
- proper fraction, p. 60
- improper fraction, p. 60
- mixed number, p. 60

**Vocabulary Exercises**

1. Copy and complete: Fractions that represent the same number are called ___?___ fractions.

2. If a fraction is in simplest form, what is the greatest common factor of its numerator and denominator?

## 2.1 Simplify Fractions ........................................ pp. 54–57

**EXAMPLES**  a. $\dfrac{14}{18} = \dfrac{14 \div 2}{18 \div 2}$   **The GCF of 14 and 18 is 2.**   b. $\dfrac{8}{21}$   **The GCF of 8 and 21 is 1.**

$= \dfrac{7}{9}$   **Simplify.**   The fraction is in simplest form.

**Write the fraction in simplest form.**

3. $\dfrac{19}{38}$        4. $\dfrac{4}{10}$        5. $\dfrac{28}{84}$        6. $\dfrac{56}{92}$

## 2.2 Mixed Numbers and Improper Fractions ........... pp. 60–63

**EXAMPLE**   Write $\dfrac{21}{8}$ as a mixed number.

Divide the numerator by the denominator.

$$\begin{array}{r} 2\ \text{R5} \\ 8\overline{)21} \\ \underline{16} \\ 5 \end{array}$$

$\longrightarrow$   $\dfrac{21}{8} = 2\dfrac{5}{8}$

**Write the number as a mixed number.**

7. $\dfrac{19}{7}$        8. $\dfrac{25}{8}$        9. $\dfrac{16}{3}$        10. $\dfrac{17}{4}$

## 2.3 Add and Subtract Fractions with the Same Denominator  pp. 66–69

**EXAMPLE**   $7\dfrac{3}{5} + 5\dfrac{1}{5} = \dfrac{38}{5} + \dfrac{26}{5}$   **Write as improper fractions.**

$= \dfrac{64}{5} = 12\dfrac{4}{5}$   **Add. Then write as a mixed number.**

**Find the sum or difference.**

11. $3\dfrac{2}{9} + 7\dfrac{5}{9}$     12. $6\dfrac{7}{12} + 9\dfrac{5}{12}$     13. $5\dfrac{1}{5} - 3\dfrac{3}{5}$     14. $7\dfrac{3}{4} - 2\dfrac{1}{4}$

**Write two fractions that are equivalent to the given fraction.**

**1.** $\frac{3}{4}$

**2.** $\frac{7}{10}$

**3.** $\frac{1}{6}$

**4.** $\frac{8}{9}$

**Write the fraction in simplest form.**

**5.** $\frac{6}{21}$

**6.** $\frac{16}{60}$

**7.** $\frac{60}{100}$

**8.** $\frac{15}{51}$

**Tell whether the fraction is a *mixed number*, a *proper fraction*, or an *improper fraction*.**

**9.** $\frac{41}{17}$

**10.** $\frac{100}{29}$

**11.** $\frac{8}{11}$

**12.** $2\frac{4}{5}$

**Write the number as an improper fraction.**

**13.** $1\frac{3}{5}$

**14.** $3\frac{1}{7}$

**15.** $4\frac{8}{9}$

**16.** $12\frac{7}{11}$

**Write the number as a mixed number.**

**17.** $\frac{14}{9}$

**18.** $\frac{11}{7}$

**19.** $\frac{17}{2}$

**20.** $\frac{21}{5}$

**Copy and complete the statement by using <, >, or =.**

**21.** $\frac{1}{4} \underline{\ ?\ } \frac{1}{5}$

**22.** $\frac{3}{7} \underline{\ ?\ } \frac{5}{11}$

**23.** $4\frac{2}{3} \underline{\ ?\ } 4\frac{14}{21}$

**24.** $\frac{1}{3} \underline{\ ?\ } \frac{33}{100}$

**Find the sum or difference.**

**25.** $\frac{5}{8} + \frac{2}{8}$

**26.** $\frac{13}{16} - \frac{5}{16}$

**27.** $5\frac{1}{3} + 18\frac{2}{3}$

**28.** $6\frac{5}{8} - 1\frac{7}{8}$

**In Exercises 29 and 30, find the perimeter of the triangle or square.**

**29.**

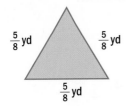

**30.**

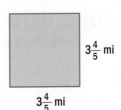

**In Exercises 31 and 32, use the figure, which shows a sheet of paper with printed text and margins.**

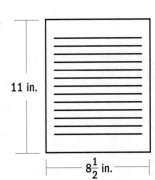

**31.** There are left and right margins that are each $\frac{3}{4}$ inch wide. What is the width of the printed text?

**32.** There are top and bottom margins that are each $1\frac{1}{2}$ inches wide. What is the length of the printed text?

# Activity 2.4

## Let's Explore
### Fractions with Different Denominators

**Goal**
Use models to add and subtract fractions with different denominators.

**Materials**
• paper
• colored pencils

**QUESTION** How can you use models to add and subtract fractions with different denominators?

**EXPLORE 1** *Use models to add fractions* •••••••••••••••••••••

Use models to find $\frac{1}{4} + \frac{2}{3}$.

**1** **Draw** models for $\frac{1}{4}$ and $\frac{2}{3}$ as shown.

**2** **Redraw** to make models that have equal parts.

The least common multiple of 4 and 3 is 12, so each model should have 12 equal parts. You now have models for $\frac{3}{12}$ and $\frac{8}{12}$.

**3** **Combine** the shaded parts to find the sum.

$$\frac{1}{4} + \frac{2}{3} = \frac{3}{12} + \frac{8}{12} = \frac{11}{12}$$

## Draw Conclusions
**Find the sum. Simplify if possible.**

1. $\frac{3}{4} + \frac{1}{6}$

2. $\frac{1}{2} + \frac{2}{7}$

3. $\frac{1}{2} + \frac{1}{3}$

4. $\frac{2}{5} + \frac{1}{4}$

5. $\frac{1}{6} + \frac{5}{8}$

6. $\frac{2}{5} + \frac{3}{10}$

7. $\frac{1}{10} + \frac{2}{5}$

8. $\frac{5}{6} + \frac{1}{12}$

9. $\frac{1}{5} + \frac{3}{10}$

10. Use models to represent $\frac{4}{5}$ and $\frac{9}{10}$. What happens when you combine the shaded parts after redrawing the models so that they have equal parts? What sum does the combined model represent?

**Gr. 7 NS 1.2** Add, subtract, multiply, and divide **rational numbers** (integers, **fractions,** and terminating decimals) and take positive rational numbers to whole-number powers. Also addresses Gr. 6 NS 2.0, Gr. 6 NS 2.1

**EXPLORE 2** *Use models to subtract fractions* · · · · · · · · · · · · · ·

Use models to find $\frac{3}{5} - \frac{1}{2}$.

**1** **Draw** models for $\frac{3}{5}$ and $\frac{1}{2}$ as shown.

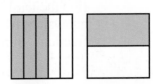

**2** **Redraw** the models so they have the same number of equal parts. The least common multiple of 5 and 2 is 10, so each model should have 10 equal parts. You now have models for $\frac{6}{10}$ and $\frac{5}{10}$.

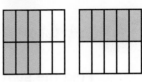

**3** **Remove** 5 shaded parts from the model for $\frac{6}{10}$. This represents subtracting $\frac{5}{10}$ from $\frac{6}{10}$.

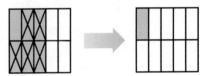

$$\frac{3}{5} - \frac{1}{2} = \frac{6}{10} - \frac{5}{10} = \frac{1}{10}$$

## Draw Conclusions

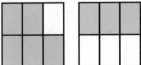

**11.** What subtraction problem do the models at the right represent?

**12.** If you are subtracting $\frac{1}{6}$ from $\frac{5}{9}$, how many equal parts will each model have? How do you know?

**Find the difference.**

**13.** $\frac{2}{3} - \frac{1}{4}$      **14.** $\frac{5}{6} - \frac{2}{5}$      **15.** $\frac{5}{6} - \frac{1}{4}$

**16.** $\frac{3}{4} - \frac{1}{3}$      **17.** $\frac{2}{3} - \frac{1}{2}$      **18.** $\frac{7}{9} - \frac{1}{3}$

**19.** $\frac{5}{6} - \frac{4}{9}$      **20.** $\frac{5}{6} - \frac{1}{3}$      **21.** $\frac{2}{3} - \frac{5}{9}$

**22.** The model at the right shows that $1 - \frac{2}{5}$ is $\frac{3}{5}$. Find $1 - \frac{1}{4}$ using a model.

# Add and Subtract Fractions with Different Denominators

> **VOCABULARY and CONCEPTS**
> • least common denominator (LCD), p. 54
>
> **Adding and Subtracting Fractions**
>
> To add or subtract fractions with different denominators, first find the least common denominator (LCD) of the fractions. Write equivalent fractions using the LCD. Then add or subtract the fractions. Simplify if possible.

**EXAMPLE 1**  *Adding and Subtracting Fractions*

**Find the sum or difference.**

**a.** $\dfrac{17}{45} + \dfrac{3}{5}$

**b.** $\dfrac{11}{15} - \dfrac{5}{12}$

**Solution**

**a.** $\dfrac{17}{45} + \dfrac{3}{5} = \dfrac{17}{45} + \dfrac{27}{45}$    **The LCD is 45. Write an equivalent fraction.**

$\phantom{\dfrac{17}{45} + \dfrac{3}{5}} = \dfrac{17 + 27}{45}$    **Add numerators.**

$\phantom{\dfrac{17}{45} + \dfrac{3}{5}} = \dfrac{44}{45}$    **Simplify.**

**b.** $\dfrac{11}{15} - \dfrac{5}{12} = \dfrac{44}{60} - \dfrac{25}{60}$    **The LCD is 60. Write equivalent fractions.**

$\phantom{\dfrac{11}{15} - \dfrac{5}{12}} = \dfrac{44 - 25}{60}$    **Subtract numerators.**

$\phantom{\dfrac{11}{15} - \dfrac{5}{12}} = \dfrac{19}{60}$    **Simplify.**

**EXAMPLE 2**  *Adding Mixed Numbers*

**Find $3\dfrac{5}{6} + 1\dfrac{7}{9}$.**

$3\dfrac{5}{6} + 1\dfrac{7}{9} = \dfrac{23}{6} + \dfrac{16}{9}$    **Write mixed numbers as improper fractions.**

$\phantom{3\dfrac{5}{6} + 1\dfrac{7}{9}} = \dfrac{69}{18} + \dfrac{32}{18}$    **The LCD is 18. Write equivalent fractions.**

$\phantom{3\dfrac{5}{6} + 1\dfrac{7}{9}} = \dfrac{69 + 32}{18}$    **Add numerators.**

$\phantom{3\dfrac{5}{6} + 1\dfrac{7}{9}} = \dfrac{101}{18} = 5\dfrac{11}{18}$    **Simplify. Then write fraction as a mixed number.**

Gr. 7 NS 1.2 Add, subtract, multiply, and divide **rational numbers** (integers, **fractions**, and terminating decimals) and take positive rational numbers to whole-number powers.
**Also addresses Gr. 6 NS 2.0, Gr. 6 NS 2.1**

**EXAMPLE 3** *Subtracting Mixed Numbers* ·········

**Find $4\frac{3}{4} - 2\frac{2}{3}$.**

$$4\frac{3}{4} - 2\frac{2}{3} = \frac{19}{4} - \frac{8}{3}$$ **Write mixed numbers as improper fractions.**

$$= \frac{57}{12} - \frac{32}{12}$$ **The LCD is 12. Write equivalent fractions.**

$$= \frac{57 - 32}{12}$$ **Subtract numerators.**

$$= \frac{25}{12} = 2\frac{1}{12}$$ **Simplify. Then write fraction as a mixed number.**

## Practice for Examples 1–3

**Find the sum or difference.**

**1.** $\frac{5}{11} + \frac{1}{4}$    **2.** $\frac{7}{8} - \frac{17}{24}$    **3.** $5\frac{1}{4} + 3\frac{1}{6}$    **4.** $6\frac{2}{3} - 1\frac{3}{8}$

**EXAMPLE 4** *Solving a Subtraction Problem* ·············

Mandy is recording songs onto a CD. The first song is $6\frac{2}{3}$ minutes long. The second song is $5\frac{1}{4}$ minutes long. How much longer is the first song?

**Solution**

You need to find $6\frac{2}{3} - 5\frac{1}{4}$.

$$6\frac{2}{3} - 5\frac{1}{4} = \frac{20}{3} - \frac{21}{4}$$ **Write mixed numbers as improper fractions.**

$$= \frac{80}{12} - \frac{63}{12}$$ **The LCD is 12. Write equivalent fractions.**

$$= \frac{17}{12} = 1\frac{5}{12}$$ **Subtract numerators. Then write fraction as a mixed number.**

▶ **Answer** The first song is $1\frac{5}{12}$ minutes longer than the second.

## Practice for Example 4

**5.** The first song on your CD is $5\frac{3}{4}$ minutes long, and the second is $4\frac{1}{6}$ minutes long. How much longer is the first song?

**2.4** Add and Subtract Fractions with Different Denominators

# A Practice

**Extra Practice** p. 499

**Find the LCD of the fractions.**

1. $\frac{3}{4}$ and $\frac{1}{5}$

2. $\frac{2}{7}$ and $\frac{2}{3}$

3. $\frac{7}{12}$ and $\frac{1}{2}$

4. $\frac{5}{6}$ and $\frac{3}{8}$

5. $\frac{5}{8}$ and $\frac{2}{3}$

6. $\frac{4}{9}$ and $\frac{1}{5}$

7. $\frac{7}{12}$ and $\frac{35}{36}$

8. $\frac{6}{11}$ and $\frac{3}{4}$

**Find the sum or difference.**

9. $\frac{3}{8} + \frac{1}{3}$

10. $\frac{7}{10} - \frac{1}{5}$

11. $\frac{5}{7} - \frac{1}{4}$

12. $\frac{4}{11} + \frac{1}{2}$

13. $\frac{7}{20} + \frac{3}{8}$

14. $\frac{7}{8} - \frac{3}{16}$

15. $\frac{1}{6} + \frac{3}{5}$

16. $\frac{13}{15} - \frac{5}{9}$

17. $\frac{2}{5} + \frac{1}{2}$

18. $\frac{9}{11} - \frac{3}{22}$

19. $\frac{6}{7} - \frac{5}{14}$

20. $\frac{5}{6} - \frac{3}{8}$

21. $2\frac{1}{3} + 4\frac{2}{5}$

22. $5\frac{5}{6} - 2\frac{1}{2}$

23. $4\frac{1}{4} + 1\frac{5}{8}$

24. $3\frac{7}{10} + 5\frac{1}{15}$

25. $6\frac{3}{7} - 3\frac{1}{2}$

26. $4\frac{1}{2} - 3\frac{2}{5}$

27. $5\frac{3}{8} - \frac{1}{6}$

28. $2\frac{1}{3} + 2\frac{5}{6}$

29. Carol spends $\frac{1}{2}$ hour weeding her garden and $\frac{4}{5}$ hour mowing her lawn. How much time does she spend working in her yard?

30. Jorge wants to paint his bedroom. He uses $\frac{3}{8}$ can of paint. He started with $\frac{5}{6}$ can of paint. How much paint does he have left over?

31. Tyler makes two long distance phone calls. The first call lasts $6\frac{3}{4}$ minutes. The second phone call lasts $9\frac{1}{2}$ minutes. What is the total time he spends on the phone?

32. Your science teacher assigns $5\frac{1}{2}$ pages to read from your textbook. You have already read $4\frac{2}{5}$ pages. How many more pages do you have left to read?

33. The width of a rectangle is $1\frac{3}{4}$ feet. The rectangle is $2\frac{1}{2}$ feet longer than it is wide. What is the length of the rectangle?

34. The length of a rectangle is $6\frac{1}{6}$ feet. The width is $3\frac{11}{12}$ feet shorter than the length. What is the width of the rectangle?

35. The different species of rattlesnake vary in length from $1\frac{1}{4}$ feet to $8\frac{1}{12}$ feet. By how much do these lengths differ?

36. **REASONING** *Describe* how to obtain each number in the pattern $\frac{1}{8}, \frac{3}{8}, \frac{5}{8}, \frac{7}{8}, \ldots$ from the number before it. Then write the next three fractions in the pattern.

**Find the sum or difference.**

**1.** $\dfrac{7}{12} + \dfrac{7}{10}$

**2.** $\dfrac{8}{9} - \dfrac{10}{21}$

**3.** $\dfrac{4}{17} + \dfrac{3}{5}$

**4.** $\dfrac{3}{4} + \dfrac{5}{18}$

**5.** $\dfrac{1}{6} + \dfrac{9}{22}$

**6.** $\dfrac{11}{12} - \dfrac{7}{15}$

**7.** $\dfrac{9}{20} - \dfrac{3}{16}$

**8.** $\dfrac{5}{14} + \dfrac{9}{10}$

**9.** $\dfrac{2}{3} + \dfrac{1}{11}$

**10.** $\dfrac{5}{6} + \dfrac{8}{9}$

**11.** $\dfrac{13}{15} - \dfrac{2}{9}$

**12.** $\dfrac{21}{24} + \dfrac{4}{9}$

**13.** $5\dfrac{2}{7} + 7\dfrac{1}{6}$

**14.** $4\dfrac{5}{9} - 3\dfrac{2}{15}$

**15.** $2\dfrac{8}{9} + 2\dfrac{5}{6}$

**16.** $1\dfrac{5}{8} + 2\dfrac{1}{5}$

**17.** $1\dfrac{3}{4} + 4\dfrac{3}{14}$

**18.** $6\dfrac{3}{25} + 3\dfrac{1}{2}$

**19.** $4\dfrac{9}{16} - 3\dfrac{3}{10}$

**20.** $1\dfrac{2}{3} + 1\dfrac{4}{11}$

**21.** $8\dfrac{7}{16} - 5\dfrac{5}{6}$

**22.** $4\dfrac{5}{7} - 4\dfrac{2}{9}$

**23.** $9\dfrac{4}{5} - 8\dfrac{7}{8}$

**24.** $4\dfrac{11}{12} + 5\dfrac{7}{8}$

**Find the perimeter of the rectangle.**

**25.** 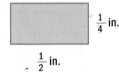 $\frac{1}{4}$ in. $\frac{1}{2}$ in.

**26.** 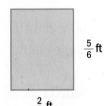 $\frac{5}{6}$ ft $\frac{2}{3}$ ft

**27.** 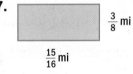 $\frac{3}{8}$ mi $\frac{15}{16}$ mi

**28.** A farmer has three hay fields. The area of one field is $\dfrac{7}{8}$ acre. The area of another field is $\dfrac{5}{6}$ acre. The area of the third field is $\dfrac{11}{12}$ acre. What is the total area of the three fields?

**29.** A baby weighs $7\dfrac{1}{8}$ pounds at birth. After four months, the baby weighs $15\dfrac{2}{3}$ pounds. How much weight did the baby gain?

**30.** In a bag of marbles, $\dfrac{2}{5}$ are red, $\dfrac{2}{7}$ are green, and the rest are blue. What fraction of the marbles are blue?

**31.** An ice sculpture originally had a height of $74\dfrac{3}{4}$ inches. The ice sculpture began to melt, and after several hours the height had decreased by $8\dfrac{7}{16}$ inches. What was the height of the sculpture then?

**32.** **REASONING** Is it possible for the difference of two proper fractions to be a mixed number? *Explain.*

**33.** **REASONING** *Describe* how to obtain each number in the pattern $\dfrac{1}{16}, \dfrac{1}{8}, \dfrac{3}{16}, \dfrac{1}{4}, \ldots$ from the number before it. Then write the next three fractions in the pattern.

# Activity 2.5

## Let's Explore
## Modeling Fraction Multiplication

**Goal**
Use models to multiply fractions.

**Materials**
- paper
- colored pencils

**QUESTION** How can you use a model to multiply fractions?

**EXPLORE 1** *Use a model to multiply fractions* ..............

Use a model to find $\frac{3}{4} \times \frac{1}{3}$.

**1** **Draw** and divide a unit square into 3 equal horizontal parts. Shade 1 of the parts to model $\frac{1}{3}$.

**2** **Further** divide the unit square into 4 equal vertical parts so you can select $\frac{3}{4}$ of the shaded rectangles in the model.

**3** **Select** $\frac{3}{4}$ of $\frac{1}{3}$. Outline 3 of the 4 shaded rectangles within the unit square. You have selected 3 out of a total of 12 equal parts, so $\frac{3}{4} \times \frac{1}{3} = \frac{3}{12}$, or $\frac{1}{4}$.

## Draw Conclusions

Use the model to find the product. Simplify if possible.

**1.** $\frac{1}{2} \times \frac{3}{5}$

**2.** $\frac{1}{4} \times \frac{2}{3}$

Find the product. Simplify if possible.

**3.** $\frac{1}{2} \times \frac{3}{4}$   **4.** $\frac{1}{6} \times \frac{2}{3}$   **5.** $\frac{3}{5} \times \frac{1}{3}$   **6.** $\frac{2}{3} \times \frac{2}{3}$

**7.** $\frac{2}{3} \times \frac{3}{4}$   **8.** $\frac{5}{6} \times \frac{1}{3}$   **9.** $\frac{2}{7} \times \frac{5}{6}$   **10.** $\frac{2}{5} \times \frac{5}{8}$

**11.** You are using a model to find the product of two proper fractions. How is the number of equal parts in the model related to the product of the denominators of the fractions?

Gr. 7 NS 1.2 Add, subtract, **multiply,** and divide **rational numbers** (integers, **fractions,** and terminating decimals) and take positive rational numbers to whole-number powers. Also addresses Gr. 6 NS 2.0, Gr. 6 NS 2.1, Gr. 6 NS 2.2

*Use a model to multiply mixed numbers* ......

**Use a model to find $\frac{1}{2} \times 1\frac{1}{3}$.**

**1**  **Model** $1\frac{1}{3}$. Draw 2 unit squares. Divide each unit square into 3 equal vertical parts.

Shade one of the unit squares and one part of the other unit square to model $1\frac{1}{3}$.

**2**  **Further** divide the unit squares. Divide each of the unit squares into 2 equal horizontal parts.

**3**  **Select** $\frac{1}{2}$ of $1\frac{1}{3}$. Outline 3 of the 6 shaded parts within the first unit square. Then outline 1 of the 2 shaded parts within the second unit square. You have selected $\frac{3}{6}$ and $\frac{1}{6}$, or $\frac{4}{6}$. So, $\frac{1}{2} \times 1\frac{1}{3} = \frac{4}{6}$, or $\frac{2}{3}$.

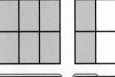

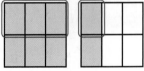

# Draw Conclusions
**Use the model to find the product.**

**12.** $\frac{1}{5} \times 1\frac{1}{5}$

**13.** $\frac{2}{3} \times 1\frac{1}{6}$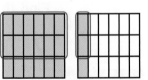

**Find the product. Simplify if possible.**

**14.** $\frac{4}{5} \times 1\frac{1}{2}$

**15.** $\frac{1}{6} \times 1\frac{1}{3}$

**16.** $\frac{3}{4} \times 2\frac{1}{2}$

**17.** $\frac{1}{3} \times 2\frac{1}{4}$

**18.** $\frac{2}{3} \times 1\frac{3}{4}$

**19.** $\frac{1}{4} \times 2\frac{4}{5}$

**20.** $\frac{3}{5} \times 1\frac{1}{6}$

**21.** $\frac{5}{6} \times 2\frac{1}{4}$

**22.** Can the product of a proper fraction and a mixed number ever equal 1? Give an example to show that it's possible, or explain why it's not possible.

# Lesson 2.5

# Multiply Fractions

## VOCABULARY and CONCEPTS

### Multiplying Fractions

**Words**   The product of two or more fractions is equal to the product of the numerators over the product of the denominators.

**Numbers**   $\dfrac{1}{4} \cdot \dfrac{5}{6} = \dfrac{5}{24}$

**Algebra**   $\dfrac{a}{b} \cdot \dfrac{c}{d} = \dfrac{a \cdot c}{b \cdot d}$ $(b, d \neq 0)$

If possible, simplify the product of the fractions.

---

**EXAMPLE 1**   *Multiplying Fractions* .........................

Find $\dfrac{7}{9} \cdot \dfrac{5}{8}$.

$$\dfrac{7}{9} \cdot \dfrac{5}{8} = \dfrac{7 \cdot 5}{9 \cdot 8}$$   **Write product of numerators over product of denominators.**

$$= \dfrac{35}{72}$$   **Multiply.**

### Practice for Example 1

**Find the product.**

**1.** $\dfrac{1}{3} \cdot \dfrac{2}{7}$

**2.** $\dfrac{4}{5} \cdot \dfrac{9}{13}$

**3.** $\dfrac{5}{6} \cdot \dfrac{1}{8}$

---

**EXAMPLE 2**   *Multiplying Whole Numbers and Fractions*

An extra-long submarine sandwich is cut into 6 pieces. Each piece is $\dfrac{7}{12}$ foot long. How long is the sandwich?

**Solution**

$$6 \cdot \dfrac{7}{12} = \dfrac{6}{1} \cdot \dfrac{7}{12}$$   **Write 6 as $\dfrac{6}{1}$.**

$$= \dfrac{42}{12}$$   **Multiply.**

$$= \dfrac{7}{2} = 3\dfrac{1}{2}$$   **Simplify. Then write as a mixed number.**

▶ **Answer**   The sandwich is $3\dfrac{1}{2}$ feet long.

## Practice for Example 2

**4.** In Example 2, show how you can use estimation to check whether the answer is reasonable. Begin by recognizing that $\frac{7}{12} \approx \frac{6}{12} = \frac{1}{2}$.

**5.** You ask 150 people to tell whether or not they have a favorite color. Four-fifths of the people say yes. How many people say yes?

**EXAMPLE 3** *Multiplying Mixed Numbers* ................

**Find $8\frac{1}{4} \cdot 7\frac{1}{3}$.**

$$8\frac{1}{4} \cdot 7\frac{1}{3} = \frac{33}{4} \cdot \frac{22}{3} \qquad \text{Write } 8\frac{1}{4} \text{ and } 7\frac{1}{3} \text{ as improper fractions.}$$

$$= \frac{726}{12} \qquad \text{Multiply.}$$

$$= \frac{726 \div 6}{12 \div 6} \qquad \text{Divide numerator and denominator by GCF, 6.}$$

$$= \frac{121}{2} = 60\frac{1}{2} \qquad \text{Simplify. Then write as a mixed number.}$$

## Practice for Example 3

**Find the product.**

**6.** $3\frac{1}{4} \cdot 2\frac{3}{4}$       **7.** $4\frac{4}{5} \cdot 5\frac{1}{6}$       **8.** $1\frac{2}{3} \cdot 6\frac{3}{7}$

**EXAMPLE 4** *Evaluating a Fraction Raised to a Power* ......

**Evaluate $\left(\frac{2}{3}\right)^4$.**

$$\left(\frac{2}{3}\right)^4 = \frac{2}{3} \cdot \frac{2}{3} \cdot \frac{2}{3} \cdot \frac{2}{3} \qquad \text{Write } \frac{2}{3} \text{ as a factor 4 times.}$$

$$= \frac{2 \cdot 2 \cdot 2 \cdot 2}{3 \cdot 3 \cdot 3 \cdot 3} \qquad \text{Write product of numerators over product of denominators.}$$

$$= \frac{16}{81} \qquad \text{Multiply.}$$

## Practice for Example 4

**Evaluate.**

**9.** $\left(\frac{3}{4}\right)^3$       **10.** $\left(\frac{5}{6}\right)^3$       **11.** $\left(\frac{4}{7}\right)^4$

# Practice

**Extra Practice**
p. 499

**Write the mixed number as an improper fraction.**

1. $8\frac{3}{5}$

2. $5\frac{2}{3}$

3. $10\frac{3}{11}$

4. Which of the following is correct?

   **A.** $\frac{a}{b} \cdot \frac{c}{d} = \frac{a \cdot d}{b \cdot c}$

   **B.** $\frac{a}{b} \cdot \frac{c}{d} = \frac{b \cdot c}{a \cdot d}$

   **C.** $\frac{a}{b} \cdot \frac{c}{d} = \frac{a \cdot c}{b \cdot d}$

**Find the product.**

5. $\frac{1}{3} \cdot \frac{4}{5}$

6. $\frac{5}{6} \cdot \frac{2}{7}$

7. $\frac{1}{4} \cdot 7$

8. $\frac{1}{2} \cdot 18$

9. $3\frac{1}{2} \cdot 1\frac{2}{5}$

10. $1\frac{2}{9} \cdot 4\frac{1}{3}$

**FIND THE ERROR** *Describe* and correct the error.

11.
$$\frac{5}{12} \cdot 3 = \frac{5}{12} \cdot \frac{3}{3}$$
$$= \frac{15}{36} = \frac{5}{12}$$

12.
$$\frac{2}{5} \cdot \frac{3}{5} = \frac{6}{5}$$
$$= 1\frac{1}{5}$$

**Evaluate.**

13. $\left(\frac{2}{9}\right)^3$

14. $\left(\frac{1}{5}\right)^4$

15. $\left(\frac{3}{8}\right)^3$

16. $\left(\frac{4}{5}\right)^3$

**Find the product. Then check your answer using estimation.**

17. $5 \cdot \frac{11}{15}$

18. $3 \cdot \frac{2}{9}$

19. $10 \cdot \frac{3}{20}$

20. $16 \cdot \frac{5}{12}$

**Find the area of the square or rectangle.**

21.
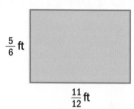
$\frac{5}{6}$ ft

$\frac{11}{12}$ ft

22.
$5\frac{3}{4}$ mi

$5\frac{3}{4}$ mi

23. You can bike 14 miles per hour. How far can you bike in $2\frac{1}{2}$ minutes?

24. A crocodile is $11\frac{3}{4}$ feet long, including its tail. Its tail is one half of its total body length. How long is the tail?

25. You fill $\frac{1}{4}$ of a 5 gallon bucket with water. How many more gallons of water will you need to fill the bucket?

26. **REASONING** Without actually multiplying, tell which product, $\frac{1}{8} \cdot 992$ or $\frac{1}{4} \cdot 992$, is greater. *Explain.*

# Practice

**Find the product.**

**1.** $\frac{1}{8} \cdot \frac{3}{7}$

**2.** $\frac{4}{5} \cdot \frac{10}{11}$

**3.** $\frac{6}{7} \cdot \frac{15}{16}$

**4.** $\frac{7}{10} \cdot \frac{25}{28}$

**5.** $12 \cdot \frac{3}{4}$

**6.** $\frac{5}{6} \cdot 24$

**7.** $2\frac{2}{3} \cdot 1\frac{4}{5}$

**8.** $8\frac{1}{2} \cdot 1\frac{7}{9}$

**9.** $5\frac{3}{4} \cdot 10\frac{2}{3}$

**10.** Which two products have the same value?

**A.** $1\frac{1}{3} \cdot \frac{2}{5}$

**B.** $1\frac{2}{3} \cdot \frac{3}{5}$

**C.** $1\frac{1}{4} \cdot 1\frac{1}{2}$

**D.** $\frac{4}{5} \cdot \frac{2}{3}$

**Evaluate the expression when $x = 4$ and $y = 10$.**

**11.** $\frac{3}{4}x$

**12.** $\frac{5}{7} \cdot \frac{1}{y}$

**13.** $\frac{18}{25} \cdot \frac{3}{x}$

**14.** $\frac{7}{y} \cdot \frac{x}{9}$

**Evaluate.**

**15.** $\left(\frac{9}{11}\right)^3$

**16.** $\left(\frac{7}{8}\right)^4$

**17.** $\left(\frac{2}{5}\right)^6$

**18.** $\left(\frac{3}{4}\right)^4$

**Find the product. Then check your answer using estimation.**

**19.** $4 \cdot \frac{9}{20}$

**20.** $12 \cdot \frac{7}{24}$

**21.** $30 \cdot \frac{21}{60}$

**22.** $16 \cdot \frac{19}{36}$

**Find the area of the triangle.**

**23.**

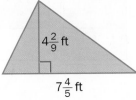

$4\frac{2}{9}$ ft

$7\frac{4}{5}$ ft

**24.**

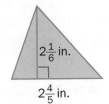

$2\frac{1}{6}$ in.

$2\frac{4}{5}$ in.

**25.** In a survey of 600 families, $\frac{5}{8}$ of the families said that they took a summer vacation. Of those families, $\frac{2}{5}$ said they went on a camping trip. How many families went camping on their summer vacation?

**26.** A rectangular mirror is $13\frac{1}{2}$ inches wide and $21\frac{1}{4}$ inches long. What is the area of the mirror?

**27.** There are 240 calories in 1 cup of low fat ice cream. How many calories are in $1\frac{3}{4}$ cups of low fat ice cream?

**REASONING In Exercises 28–30, copy and complete the statement using *always*, *sometimes*, or *never*.**

**28.** The product of two mixed numbers is ___?___ greater than 1.

**29.** The product of a whole number and a proper fraction is ___?___ less than 1.

**30.** The product of a mixed number and zero is ___?___ greater than 1.

# Let's Explore
## Modeling Reciprocals

**Goal**
Use models to find reciprocals.

**Materials**
- paper
- colored pencils

**QUESTION**  **How can you use models to show that the product of two reciprocals equals 1?**

You know from Lesson 2.5 that the product of $\frac{2}{9}$ and $\frac{9}{2}$ is $\frac{18}{18}$, or 1. Two numbers whose product is 1 are called *reciprocals*.

**EXPLORE 1**  *Use a model to multiply reciprocals* ...........

**Use a model to show that $\frac{2}{3}$ and $\frac{3}{2}$ are reciprocals.**

**1**  **Draw** a model for $\frac{3}{2}$.

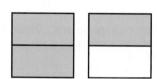

**2**  **Select** $\frac{2}{3}$ of $\frac{3}{2}$. Outline 2 of 3 shaded rectangles in the model. These 2 rectangles form a unit square, so $\frac{2}{3} \cdot \frac{3}{2} = 1$.

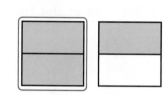

## Draw Conclusions

**1.** *Explain* how the model at the right shows that $\frac{4}{3}$ and $\frac{3}{4}$ are reciprocals.

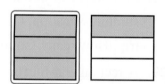

**In Exercises 2–5, show that the numbers are reciprocals.**

**2.** $\frac{2}{7}, \frac{7}{2}$  **3.** $\frac{8}{3}, \frac{3}{8}$  **4.** $\frac{4}{11}, \frac{11}{4}$  **5.** $\frac{5}{2}, \frac{2}{5}$

**6.** What is the reciprocal of 2? How do you know?

**7.** What number is its own reciprocal? *Explain.*

**8.** Why does 0 have no reciprocal?

**EXPLORE 2**  *Use a model to find a reciprocal*

**Find the reciprocal of $\frac{4}{7}$.**

**1** **Draw** a unit square. Divide the unit square horizontally into 7 equal parts. Divide it vertically into 4 equal parts.

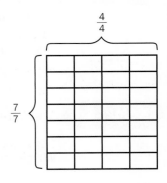

**2** **Rearrange** the small rectangles. Form a rectangle whose vertical dimension is $\frac{4}{7}$.

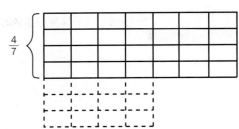

**3** **Determine** the horizontal dimension. The horizontal length of each small rectangle is $\frac{1}{4}$, and there are 7 of them across the rectangle. So, the horizontal dimension is $\frac{7}{4}$.

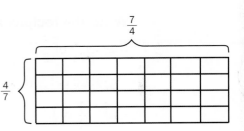

## Draw Conclusions

**9.** What is the area of the large rectangle in Step 3? How does this area show that $\frac{4}{7}$ and $\frac{7}{4}$ are reciprocals?

**10.** Draw and divide a unit square that can be used to find the reciprocal of the fraction $\frac{7}{10}$. Then find the reciprocal.

**Find the reciprocal of the number.**

**11.** $\frac{4}{9}$     **12.** $\frac{3}{5}$     **13.** $\frac{2}{13}$     **14.** $\frac{7}{8}$

**15.** Copy and complete: The reciprocal of $\frac{a}{b}$ where $a \neq 0$ and $b \neq 0$ is ___?___ .

# Find Reciprocals

## VOCABULARY and CONCEPTS

Two nonzero numbers whose product is 1, such as $\frac{2}{9}$ and $\frac{9}{2}$, are **reciprocals**.

Every number except 0 has a reciprocal. To find it, write the number as a fraction, and then switch the numerator and the denominator.

**EXAMPLE 1** *Writing the Reciprocal of a Fraction* · · · · · · · · ·

**Write the reciprocal of $\frac{2}{3}$.**

To write the reciprocal of $\frac{2}{3}$, switch the numerator and denominator.

$$\frac{2}{3} \quad\diagdown\!\!\!\!\times\!\!\!\!\diagup\quad \frac{3}{2}$$

▶ **Check** $\frac{2}{3} \cdot \frac{3}{2} = \frac{6}{6} = 1$

### Practice for Example 1

**Write the reciprocal of the number.**

1. $\frac{5}{6}$     2. $\frac{4}{11}$     3. $\frac{2}{7}$     4. $\frac{8}{5}$

5. $\frac{6}{5}$     6. $\frac{8}{9}$     7. $\frac{19}{17}$     8. $\frac{3}{20}$

**EXAMPLE 2** *Writing the Reciprocal of a Whole Number* · · · ·

**Write the reciprocal of 9.**

$9 = \frac{9}{1}$     **Rewrite whole number as a fraction.**

$$\frac{9}{1} \quad\diagdown\!\!\!\!\times\!\!\!\!\diagup\quad \frac{1}{9}$$     **Switch numerator and denominator.**

▶ **Check** $9 \cdot \frac{1}{9} = \frac{9}{9} = 1$

### Practice for Example 2

**Write the reciprocal of the number.**

9. 2     10. 7     11. 13     12. 1

13. 12     14. 15     15. 19     16. 3

**EXAMPLE 3** *Writing the Reciprocal of a Mixed Number*

**Write the reciprocal of $2\frac{3}{4}$.**

$$2\frac{3}{4} = \frac{11}{4}$$   **Rewrite mixed number as an improper fraction.**

$$\frac{11}{4} \diagup \diagup \frac{4}{11}$$   **Switch numerator and denominator.**

▸ **Check** $\frac{11}{4} \cdot \frac{4}{11} = \frac{44}{44} = 1$

**Practice for Example 3**

**Write the reciprocal of the number.**

**17.** $1\frac{7}{8}$   **18.** $4\frac{2}{9}$   **19.** $10\frac{1}{5}$   **20.** $6\frac{3}{20}$

**21.** $3\frac{5}{6}$   **22.** $7\frac{3}{4}$   **23.** $12\frac{2}{3}$   **24.** $8\frac{9}{10}$

**EXAMPLE 4** *Using Reciprocals*

Your older brother's car gets 25 miles per gallon of gas for highway driving. He plans to travel 200 miles on a highway. How many gallons of gas will the car use?

**Solution**

You can answer the question using unit analysis.

$$\cancel{mi} \cdot \frac{gal}{\cancel{mi}} = gal$$

You are given $\frac{25 \text{ mi}}{1 \text{ gal}}$, so you need to use the reciprocal:

$$200 \; \cancel{mi} \cdot \frac{1 \text{ gal}}{25 \; \cancel{mi}} = 8 \text{ gal}$$

▸ **Answer** Your brother's car will use 8 gallons of gas.

**Practice for Example 4**

**25.** A truck gets 15 miles per gallon of gas for highway driving. The truck will be driven 165 miles on a highway. How many gallons of gas will the truck use?

# Practice

**Extra Practice**
p. 499

**Write the reciprocal of the number.**

**1.** $\frac{6}{7}$

**2.** $\frac{1}{20}$

**3.** 3

**4.** 16

**5.** $\frac{4}{9}$

**6.** 4

**7.** 21

**8.** $\frac{2}{5}$

**9.** $2\frac{1}{6}$

**10.** $9\frac{1}{2}$

**11.** $4\frac{2}{3}$

**12.** $5\frac{3}{7}$

**13.** $12\frac{3}{8}$

**14.** $8\frac{2}{3}$

**15.** $11\frac{2}{5}$

**16.** $20\frac{3}{5}$

**Tell whether the numbers are reciprocals. Show your work.**

**17.** $\frac{9}{10}, \frac{10}{9}$

**18.** $\frac{6}{1}, \frac{1}{6}$

**19.** $\frac{3}{8}, \frac{3}{8}$

**20.** $\frac{8}{7}, \frac{7}{8}$

**21.** $\frac{1}{9}, \frac{19}{1}$

**22.** $1\frac{3}{4}, \frac{7}{4}$

**23.** $1\frac{1}{2}, \frac{2}{3}$

**24.** $2\frac{1}{3}, \frac{3}{7}$

**25.** **FIND THE ERROR** A student wrote the following explanation for finding the reciprocal of $4\frac{2}{3}$. *Describe* and correct the error in the student's work.

$4\frac{2}{3} = 4\frac{3}{2}$     Find the reciprocal of the fraction.

$= \frac{11}{3}$     Change the mixed number to an improper fraction.

$\frac{11}{3} \diagdown \frac{3}{11}$     Switch the numerator and denominator.

$\frac{11}{3} \cdot \frac{3}{11} = \frac{33}{33} = 1$     Check.

**26.** A plane travels at a speed of 590 miles per hour. How long does it take the plane to travel 1770 miles?

**27.** Alexis earns $9 per hour as a waitress. One night Alexis earned $45. For how many hours did she work?

**28.** Jake types 58 words per minute. He types 377 words. How many minutes does he spend typing?

**29.** A family drives 40 miles per hour. They plan to travel 240 miles. How many hours will this take?

**30.** **REASONING** If a number is between 0 and 1, what can you say about its reciprocal?

# B Practice

**Write the reciprocal of the number.**

**1.** $\dfrac{7}{9}$     **2.** $\dfrac{14}{19}$     **3.** 96     **4.** 103

**5.** $\dfrac{1}{80}$     **6.** $\dfrac{6}{25}$     **7.** 1     **8.** 242

**9.** $4\dfrac{2}{15}$     **10.** $30\dfrac{9}{10}$     **11.** $3\dfrac{3}{4}$     **12.** $16\dfrac{4}{5}$

**13.** $17\dfrac{10}{11}$     **14.** $21\dfrac{5}{6}$     **15.** $22\dfrac{1}{12}$     **16.** $100\dfrac{3}{20}$

**Tell whether the numbers are reciprocals. Show your work.**

**17.** $\dfrac{13}{19}, \dfrac{13}{19}$     **18.** $\dfrac{24}{25}, \dfrac{25}{24}$     **19.** $\dfrac{9}{15}, \dfrac{15}{19}$     **20.** $\dfrac{13}{31}, \dfrac{26}{13}$

**21.** $\dfrac{5}{29}, 5\dfrac{4}{5}$     **22.** $7\dfrac{3}{8}, \dfrac{8}{59}$     **23.** $\dfrac{34}{5}, 6\dfrac{4}{5}$     **24.** $9\dfrac{3}{8}, \dfrac{8}{75}$

**REASONING For Exercises 25 and 26, copy and complete the table below.**

| Proper fraction | $\dfrac{1}{1000}$ | $\dfrac{1}{100}$ | $\dfrac{1}{10}$ | $\dfrac{1}{2}$ | $\dfrac{9}{10}$ | $\dfrac{99}{100}$ |
| --- | --- | --- | --- | --- | --- | --- |
| Reciprocal | ? | ? | ? | ? | ? | ? |

**25.** For proper fractions close to 1, what can you say about their reciprocals?

**26.** For proper fractions close to 0, what can you say about their reciprocals?

**27.** You earn $8 per hour stocking shelves at a grocery store. Last week you earned $76. For how many hours did you work?

**28.** Apples cost $2 per pound. You spent $7 on apples. How many pounds of apples did you buy?

**29.** Daniel's family drives 39 miles per hour. They plan to travel 195 miles. How many hours will this take?

**30.** Marshall's car gets 28 miles per gallon of gas for city driving. He plans to travel 4 miles in the city. How many gallons of gas will the car use?

**31.** Michelle earns $8 per hour at her weekend job. She earned $104 last weekend. How many hours did she work?

**REASONING Tell whether the statement is _true_ or _false_. If the statement is false, explain.**

**32.** The reciprocal of a whole number is always a fraction.

**33.** The reciprocal of a proper fraction is always an improper fraction.

# Let's Explore
## Modeling Fraction Division

**Goal**
Use a ruler to investigate dividing by a fraction.

**Materials**
• ruler

**QUESTION** **How can you divide by a fraction?**

**EXPLORE 1** *Use a model to divide fractions* ·················

**1** **Model** $3 \div \frac{3}{8}$. You can use a ruler to divide by a fraction. The diagram below models $3 \div \frac{3}{8}$. Use the ruler shown to find $3 \div \frac{3}{8}$ by counting the number of times $\frac{3}{8}$ fits into 3.

$$\frac{3}{8} \quad \frac{3}{8} \quad \frac{3}{8} \quad \frac{3}{8} \quad \frac{3}{8} \quad \frac{3}{8} \quad \frac{3}{8} \quad \frac{3}{8}$$

| 0 | 1 | 2 | 3 |

**2** **Copy** and complete the left side of the table. Record your answer from Step 1 in the first row of the table where $3 \div \frac{3}{8}$ is shown. Then use the ruler shown in Step 1 to find each quotient in the next two rows.

| Dividend | | Divisor | | Quotient | Dividend | | Multiplier | | Product |
|---|---|---|---|---|---|---|---|---|---|
| 3 | ÷ | $\frac{3}{8}$ | = | ? | 3 | • | $\frac{8}{3}$ | = | ? |
| $2\frac{1}{4}$ | ÷ | $\frac{3}{8}$ | = | ? | $\frac{9}{4}$ | • | $\frac{8}{3}$ | = | ? |
| $\frac{3}{4}$ | ÷ | $\frac{3}{8}$ | = | ? | $\frac{3}{4}$ | • | $\frac{8}{3}$ | = | ? |

**3** **Copy** and complete the right side of the table in Step 2. Use fraction multiplication to find each product. Record your answers in the table.

## Draw Conclusions

**1.** Copy and complete this statement of the *division rule*: "Dividing by a fraction is the same as multiplying by its _?_."

**Gr. 7 NS 1.2** Add, subtract, multiply, and **divide rational numbers** (integers, **fractions**, and terminating decimals) and take positive rational numbers to whole-number powers. Also addresses Gr. 6 NS 2.0, Gr. 6 NS 2.1, Gr. 6 NS 2.2

**EXPLORE 2** *Justify the division rule* ..........................................

Show that dividing $\frac{9}{2}$ by $\frac{3}{8}$ is the same as multiplying $\frac{9}{2}$ by the reciprocal of $\frac{3}{8}$.

**1** **Write** the division expression. You want to divide $\frac{9}{2}$ by $\frac{3}{8}$:

$$\frac{9}{2} \div \frac{3}{8} = ?$$

**2** **Rewrite** as multiplication. You know that you can multiply the quotient and the divisor to get the dividend.

$$\frac{3}{8} \cdot ? = \frac{9}{2}$$

**3** **Find** the unknown quotient and check your answer. Think about how you can turn $\frac{3}{8}$ into $\frac{9}{2}$ through multiplication. If you multiply $\frac{3}{8}$ by its reciprocal, $\frac{8}{3}$, you will get 1. And if you multiply 1 by $\frac{9}{2}$, you will get $\frac{9}{2}$. So the unknown quotient seems to be

$$\frac{8}{3} \cdot \frac{9}{2} = \frac{72}{6} = 12.$$

▶ **Check** $\frac{3}{8} \cdot 12 \stackrel{?}{=} \frac{9}{2}$

$$\frac{36}{8} \stackrel{?}{=} \frac{9}{2}$$

$$\frac{36 \div 4}{8 \div 4} \stackrel{?}{=} \frac{9}{2}$$

$$\frac{9}{2} = \frac{9}{2} ✔$$

## Draw Conclusions
**Repeat the steps of Explore 2 to find the quotient.**

**2.** $\frac{3}{4} \div \frac{6}{7}$      **3.** $\frac{2}{3} \div \frac{4}{5}$      **4.** $\frac{5}{8} \div \frac{3}{4}$

**5.** *Explain* how to use the division rule to find the quotient $\frac{4}{5} \div 2$.

**6.** *Explain* how to divide a number by $2\frac{1}{3}$.

# Divide Fractions

**VOCABULARY and CONCEPTS**

**Division Rule**

**Words**    To divide by any nonzero number, multiply by its reciprocal.

**Numbers**   $\dfrac{3}{4} \div \dfrac{2}{3} = \dfrac{3}{4} \cdot \dfrac{3}{2} = \dfrac{9}{8}$

**Algebra**   $\dfrac{a}{b} \div \dfrac{c}{d} = \dfrac{a}{b} \cdot \dfrac{d}{c} = \dfrac{ad}{bc}$  $(b, c, d \neq 0)$

**EXAMPLE 1**   *Dividing with Fractions*

**Find the quotient.**

**a.** $\dfrac{1}{8} \div \dfrac{3}{4}$        **b.** $\dfrac{6}{7} \div 2$        **c.** $8 \div \dfrac{2}{3}$

**Solution**

**a.** $\dfrac{1}{8} \div \dfrac{3}{4} = \dfrac{1}{8} \cdot \dfrac{4}{3}$    **Use division rule.**

    $= \dfrac{4}{24}$    **Multiply.**

    $= \dfrac{1}{6}$    **Simplify.**

**b.** $\dfrac{6}{7} \div 2 = \dfrac{6}{7} \cdot \dfrac{1}{2}$    **Use division rule.**

    $= \dfrac{6}{14}$    **Multiply.**

    $= \dfrac{3}{7}$    **Simplify.**

**c.** $8 \div \dfrac{2}{3} = \dfrac{8}{1} \cdot \dfrac{3}{2}$    **Use division rule.**

    $= \dfrac{24}{2}$    **Multiply.**

    $= \dfrac{12}{1} = 12$    **Simplify.**

**Practice for Example 1**

**Find the quotient.**

**1.** $\dfrac{1}{6} \div \dfrac{4}{9}$        **2.** $\dfrac{1}{2} \div \dfrac{3}{4}$        **3.** $\dfrac{5}{9} \div 10$

**4.** $\dfrac{14}{15} \div 7$        **5.** $\dfrac{4}{9} \div 2$        **6.** $6 \div \dfrac{1}{2}$

**EXAMPLE 2** *Dividing by a Mixed Number*

You are designing a shopping plaza's parking lot. Two requirements for the parking lot are listed. How many parking spaces are in each row?

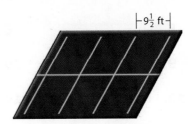

- Each row of parking spaces is 190 feet long.
- Each parking space has a width of $9\frac{1}{2}$ feet.

**Solution**

You can solve this problem by dividing 190 by $9\frac{1}{2}$.

$$190 \div 9\frac{1}{2} = 190 \div \frac{19}{2} \qquad \text{Write } 9\frac{1}{2} \text{ as an improper fraction.}$$

$$= \frac{190}{1} \cdot \frac{2}{19} \qquad \text{Use division rule.}$$

$$= \frac{380}{19} \qquad \text{Multiply.}$$

$$= 20 \qquad \text{Simplify.}$$

▶**Answer** There are 20 parking spaces per row.

**Practice for Example 2**

7. You are cutting strips of cloth from a $33\frac{3}{4}$ inch by 45 inch piece of cloth. You want each strip to be 45 inches long and $3\frac{3}{8}$ inches wide. How many strips can you cut out of the cloth?

**EXAMPLE 3** *Dividing Two Mixed Numbers*

**Find $14\frac{2}{5} \div 4\frac{2}{7}$.**

$$14\frac{2}{5} \div 4\frac{2}{7} = \frac{72}{5} \div \frac{30}{7} \qquad \text{Write } 14\frac{2}{5} \text{ and } 4\frac{2}{7} \text{ as improper fractions.}$$

$$= \frac{72}{5} \cdot \frac{7}{30} \qquad \text{Use division rule.}$$

$$= \frac{504}{150} \qquad \text{Multiply.}$$

$$= \frac{84}{25} = 3\frac{9}{25} \qquad \text{Simplify. Then write as a mixed number.}$$

**Practice for Example 3**

8. Find (**a**) $11\frac{3}{10} \div 6\frac{2}{5}$ and (**b**) $5\frac{5}{6} \div 2\frac{5}{8}$.

**Find the quotient.**

1. $\frac{2}{9} \div \frac{1}{3}$

2. $\frac{3}{4} \div \frac{5}{8}$

3. $\frac{4}{9} \div \frac{9}{20}$

4. $\frac{2}{3} \div \frac{5}{18}$

5. $\frac{9}{14} \div 7$

6. $9 \div 4\frac{2}{3}$

7. $6\frac{3}{4} \div 5\frac{1}{2}$

8. $3\frac{2}{5} \div 8$

9. $4\frac{1}{6} \div 3\frac{2}{5}$

10. $\frac{7}{8} \div 4$

11. $6 \div 2\frac{1}{4}$

12. $3\frac{2}{5} \div 2\frac{1}{5}$

13. $10\frac{3}{4} \div 43$

14. $\frac{2}{3} \div 8$

15. $16 \div \frac{2}{3}$

16. $5\frac{1}{3} \div \frac{8}{15}$

**FIND THE ERROR** *Describe* and correct the error in finding the quotient.

17.
$$\frac{4}{5} \div 3\frac{2}{3} = \frac{4}{5} \div \frac{11}{3}$$
$$= \frac{5}{4} \cdot \frac{11}{3}$$
$$= \frac{55}{12} = 4\frac{7}{12}$$

18.
$$\frac{1}{4} \div \frac{3}{4} = \frac{3}{4} \div \frac{1}{4}$$
$$= \frac{3}{4} \cdot 4$$
$$= 3$$

**Evaluate the expression when $x = \frac{3}{5}$ and $y = 8$.**

19. $x \div y$

20. $y \div x$

21. $1\frac{1}{3} \div x$

22. $y \div \frac{4}{5}$

23. $x \div 1\frac{2}{5}$

24. $\frac{4}{5} \div y$

25. $1\frac{2}{3} \div x$

26. $y \div \frac{1}{5}$

27. You are cutting fabric for placemats that are $14\frac{1}{4}$ inches wide. If you have a piece of fabric that is 114 inches long, how many placemats can you cut from the fabric?

28. A red sea urchin can live as long as 200 years, and it grows during its entire life. The diagram gives the diameter of a red sea urchin at two different ages. How many times as great as the diameter of the sea urchin at age 76 is its diameter at age 172?

Age: 76 years $d = 5\frac{5}{8}$ in.  Age: 172 years $d = 7\frac{5}{16}$ in.

29. A rectangle has an area of $6\frac{9}{10}$ square meters and a width of $1\frac{1}{2}$ meters. Find $6\frac{9}{10} \div 1\frac{1}{2}$ to find the length of the rectangle.

30. A portion of a walkway in a park has a length of 115 yards. A landscaper plants a tree at the beginning of the walkway, then plants another tree every $5\frac{3}{4}$ yards. How many trees will the landscaper plant along the walkway? Be sure to include the tree planted at the beginning of the walkway.

31. **REASONING** If you divide a nonzero whole number by $\frac{1}{2}$, is the result greater or less than the whole number? *Explain.*

# Practice

**Find the quotient.**

**1.** $\frac{4}{9} \div \frac{1}{3}$

**2.** $\frac{4}{5} \div \frac{7}{12}$

**3.** $\frac{5}{9} \div \frac{9}{25}$

**4.** $\frac{4}{5} \div \frac{15}{28}$

**5.** $\frac{8}{15} \div 5$

**6.** $10 \div 3\frac{4}{5}$

**7.** $7\frac{3}{4} \div 4\frac{2}{3}$

**8.** $4\frac{5}{9} \div 14$

**9.** $10\frac{4}{9} \div 3\frac{3}{7}$

**10.** $8 \div 2\frac{4}{5}$

**11.** $4\frac{5}{7} \div 2\frac{1}{5}$

**12.** $10\frac{3}{8} \div 1\frac{1}{12}$

**13.** $6\frac{2}{3} \div \frac{20}{3}$

**14.** $20 \div 6\frac{2}{3}$

**15.** $28 \div \frac{4}{5}$

**16.** $16\frac{1}{2} \div 6\frac{2}{3}$

**Evaluate the expression when $x = \frac{4}{5}$ and $y = 6$.**

**17.** $x \div y$

**18.** $y \div x$

**19.** $2\frac{1}{4} \div x$

**20.** $x \div 1\frac{1}{5}$

**21.** $y \div \frac{2}{3}$

**22.** $\frac{3}{4} \div x$

**23.** $y \div 2\frac{1}{4}$

**24.** $4\frac{1}{2} \div y$

**Evaluate the expression.**

**25.** $\left(3\frac{3}{5} \div \frac{9}{10}\right) \div 1\frac{1}{3}$

**26.** $\left(3\frac{1}{3} - 2\frac{1}{2}\right) \div 2\frac{1}{12}$

**27.** $\left(1\frac{1}{3} + 2\frac{1}{4}\right) \div 1\frac{1}{4}$

**28.** $3\frac{2}{3} \div \left(4\frac{1}{2} - 3\frac{3}{4}\right)$

**29.** $2\frac{1}{3} \div \left(3\frac{1}{2} - \frac{1}{4}\right)$

**30.** $3\frac{1}{3} \div \left(3\frac{1}{4} + \frac{1}{2}\right)$

**31.** The largest and smallest sea stars on record measured about $37\frac{4}{5}$ inches long and $\frac{7}{10}$ inch long. The largest sea star is how many times longer than the smallest sea star?

**32.** The table shows approximations of the populations of six states as a fraction of the total population of the United States in 2005. About how many times as many people lived in California (CA) than in Washington (WA) in 2005?

| State | CA | IL | MA | MI | TX | WA |
|---|---|---|---|---|---|---|
| Fraction of U.S. population | $\frac{3}{25}$ | $\frac{1}{25}$ | $\frac{1}{50}$ | $\frac{3}{100}$ | $\frac{2}{25}$ | $\frac{1}{50}$ |

**33. REASONING** Which operation results in a greater quotient, dividing a number by $\frac{2}{3}$ or dividing the number by $\frac{3}{2}$? *Explain.*

**34. REASONING** Mr. Harris is installing a 126 foot fence across the front of his property. He wants to place a fence post every $7\frac{7}{8}$ feet. How many fence posts will Mr. Harris need?

**35. REASONING** Simplify the expressions below. *Describe* the pattern. *Explain* what happens when you divide a fraction by increasingly greater whole numbers.

$\frac{1}{4} \div 2$ $\qquad$ $\frac{1}{4} \div 3$ $\qquad$ $\frac{1}{4} \div 4$ $\qquad$ $\frac{1}{4} \div 5$

# Problem Solving and Reasoning

## Problem

If two nonzero whole numbers differ by 1, what can you say about the difference of their reciprocals?

### Solution

**1** **Make** a table of nonzero whole numbers that differ by 1. Write the reciprocals of the whole numbers, then find the difference of the reciprocals.

Make precise calculations as part of MR 2.8.

| Whole numbers that differ by 1 | Reciprocals | Difference of reciprocals |
|---|---|---|
| 1, 2 | $1, \frac{1}{2}$ | $1 - \frac{1}{2} = \frac{1}{2}$ |
| 2, 3 | $\frac{1}{2}, \frac{1}{3}$ | $\frac{1}{2} - \frac{1}{3} = \frac{1}{6}$ |
| 3, 4 | $\frac{1}{3}, \frac{1}{4}$ | $\frac{1}{3} - \frac{1}{4} = \frac{1}{12}$ |

Observe a pattern as part of MR 1.1, and formulate a mathematical conjecture as part of MR 1.2.

**2** **Describe** a pattern and make a conjecture. Look for a relationship between the whole numbers and the difference of their reciprocals. Notice that the denominator of the difference of the reciprocals is the same as the product of the two whole numbers. The numerator of each difference is 1.

**Conjecture:** If two nonzero whole numbers differ by 1, then the difference of their reciprocals is the reciprocal of their product.

Use symbols to explain reasoning as part of MR 2.5, and justify a conjecture as part of MR 1.2.

**3** **Justify** your conjecture. Divide a number line between 0 and 1 into $n$ equal parts ($n = 3$ is shown).

Then divide each part into $n + 1$ equal parts for a total of $n(n + 1)$ parts.

Because $\frac{1}{n}$ represents $n + 1$ of the $n(n + 1)$ parts and $\frac{1}{n + 1}$ represents $n$ of the $n(n + 1)$ parts, the difference of $\frac{1}{n}$ and $\frac{1}{n + 1}$ is just 1 of the $n(n + 1)$ parts, or $\frac{1}{n(n + 1)}$.

The difference is the reciprocal of the product.

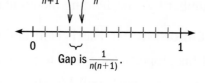

Gap is $\frac{1}{n(n+1)}$.

## Practice

**1.** Consider the difference of the reciprocals of 2 times a nonzero number $n$ and 3 times the number $n$.  **MR 1.1, MR 1.2, MR 2.5**

   **a.** Look for a pattern and make a conjecture.

   **b.** *Justify* your conjecture.

**2.** Your family travels from city A to city B and back. The speeds and times are shown below.  **MR 1.1, MR 3.3**

   **a.** What is your average speed for the round trip, and how do you calculate it?

   **b.** What is a formula for finding average speed for a round trip given time $t_1$ at a speed of $r_1$ for the trip there and $t_2$ at a speed of $r_2$ for the trip back?

   **c.** Is the average speed of the round trip ever the average of the speeds on each part of the trip? If so, under what circumstances?

**3.** A unit square is divided as shown.  **MR 1.1, MR 2.5**

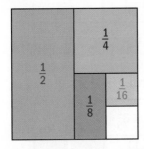

   **a.** What fraction is the next number in the pattern $\frac{1}{2}, \frac{1}{4}, \frac{1}{8}, \frac{1}{16}, \ldots$? How would you you show this number in the diagram?

   **b.** The diagram suggests that the never-ending sum $\frac{1}{2} + \frac{1}{4} + \frac{1}{8} + \frac{1}{16} + \ldots$ is equal to what number?

**4.** A ball dropped from an initial height of 6 feet begins bouncing. The height of each bounce is $\frac{3}{4}$ of the height of the previous bounce.  **MR 1.1, MR 2.5**

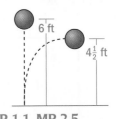

   **a.** Estimate on which bounce the ball will bounce to a height less than $\frac{1}{2}$ of its initial height.

   **b.** Draw a diagram showing the number of bounces and the heights of the bounces. On which bounce does the ball reach a height less than $\frac{1}{2}$ of its initial height?

   **c.** Is knowing the exact height of the ball when it is less than $\frac{1}{2}$ of the initial height necessary to solve part (b)? *Explain.*

**5.** You want to fence the two rectangular areas shown below for your dogs.  **MR 2.1, MR 2.7, MR 2.8**

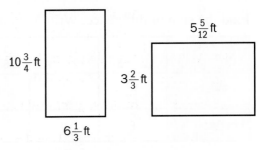

   **a.** Find the exact amount of fencing you will need to buy.

   **b.** Use estimation to check that your answer to part (a) is reasonable.

   **c.** What is the advantage or disadvantage of buying the amount of fencing you estimated instead of the exact amount?

**Materials**
- paper and pencil

## Can you say that again?

**Copy and complete the code puzzle below.**

Justin, a very good math student, came home at 3 P.M. after a day of swimming at the town pool. His mom was quite upset, telling him "You're late! You said you would be home by 11:45." Justin replied,

"$\dfrac{?}{14}$ $\dfrac{?}{75}\dfrac{?}{2}$ $\dfrac{?}{11}\dfrac{?}{14}\dfrac{?}{63}\dfrac{?}{4}\dfrac{?}{45}$ $\dfrac{?}{77}\dfrac{?}{10}$ $\dfrac{?}{45}\dfrac{?}{14}\dfrac{?}{2}\dfrac{?}{8}$! $\dfrac{?}{14}$ $\dfrac{?}{9}\dfrac{?}{75}\dfrac{?}{14}\dfrac{?}{7}$

$\dfrac{?}{14}$ $\dfrac{?}{84}\dfrac{?}{77}\dfrac{?}{20}\dfrac{?}{18}\dfrac{?}{7}$ $\dfrac{?}{3}\dfrac{?}{8}$ $\dfrac{?}{4}\dfrac{?}{77}\dfrac{?}{2}\dfrac{?}{8}$ $\dfrac{?}{3}\dfrac{?}{12}$ $\dfrac{?}{75}$

$\dfrac{?}{1}\dfrac{?}{20}\dfrac{?}{75}\dfrac{?}{11}\dfrac{?}{45}\dfrac{?}{8}\dfrac{?}{11}$ $\dfrac{?}{77}\dfrac{?}{15}$ $\dfrac{?}{45}\dfrac{?}{84}\dfrac{?}{8}\dfrac{?}{18}\dfrac{?}{24}\dfrac{?}{8}$!""

**Find the missing numbers in the boxes. Use your answers to decode Justin's reply.**

**1.** Simplify the fraction.

| Fraction | $\dfrac{132}{144}$ | $\dfrac{49}{84}$ | $\dfrac{30}{195}$ | $\dfrac{92}{300}$ |
|---|---|---|---|---|
| Answer | $\dfrac{?}{12}$ | $\dfrac{7}{?}$ | $\dfrac{?}{13}$ | $\dfrac{23}{?}$ |
| Letter | R | Y | M | A |

**2.** Write the mixed number as an improper fraction.

| Mixed Number | $1\dfrac{9}{14}$ | $3\dfrac{3}{7}$ | $5\dfrac{8}{11}$ | $6\dfrac{6}{13}$ |
|---|---|---|---|---|
| Answer | $\dfrac{23}{?}$ | $\dfrac{?}{7}$ | $\dfrac{?}{11}$ | $\dfrac{?}{13}$ |
| Letter | I | V | G | W |

**3.** Find the sum or difference. Write your answer in simplest form.

| Expression | $\dfrac{1}{2}+\dfrac{7}{8}$ | $\dfrac{1}{2}-\dfrac{1}{4}$ | $3\dfrac{5}{6}+2\dfrac{4}{9}$ | $6\dfrac{2}{3}-4\dfrac{1}{5}$ | $\dfrac{3}{4}+\dfrac{3}{5}$ | $3\dfrac{2}{5}-1\dfrac{1}{4}$ |
|---|---|---|---|---|---|---|
| Answer | $1\dfrac{3}{?}$ | $\dfrac{1}{?}$ | $6\dfrac{5}{?}$ | $2\dfrac{7}{?}$ | $1\dfrac{?}{20}$ | $2\dfrac{3}{?}$ |
| Letter | E | H | L | F | D | U |

**4.** Find the product or quotient. Write your answer in simplest form.

| Expression | $\dfrac{3}{5}\times\dfrac{1}{2}$ | $\dfrac{1}{2}\div\dfrac{2}{3}$ | $2\dfrac{9}{10}\times4\dfrac{1}{8}$ | $10\dfrac{1}{2}\div2\dfrac{1}{3}$ | $1\dfrac{5}{9}\times3\dfrac{2}{5}$ | $2\dfrac{1}{3}\div1\dfrac{1}{2}$ |
|---|---|---|---|---|---|---|
| Answer | $\dfrac{3}{?}$ | $\dfrac{?}{4}$ | $11\dfrac{?}{80}$ | $4\dfrac{?}{2}$ | $5\dfrac{13}{?}$ | $1\dfrac{5}{?}$ |
| Letter | N | B | O | Q | T | S |

# Chapter Summary and Review

@HomeTutor
classzone.com

**VOCABULARY**

- equivalent fractions, p. 54
- least common denominator (LCD), p. 54
- simplest form, p. 54

- proper fraction, p. 60
- improper fraction, p. 60
- mixed number, p. 60
- reciprocals, p. 86

**Vocabulary Exercises**

1. Copy and complete: A fraction is a(n)  ?  if its numerator is greater than or equal to its denominator.

2. Copy and complete: Two numbers whose product is 1 are  ? .

## 2.1 Simplify Fractions ......... pp. 54–57

To simplify a fraction, divide the numerator and denominator by their greatest common factor (GCF).

**EXAMPLE** Write $\dfrac{32}{56}$ in simplest form.

$$\frac{32}{56} = \frac{32 \div 8}{56 \div 8} \qquad \text{The GCF of 32 and 56 is 8.}$$

$$= \frac{4}{7} \qquad \text{Simplify.}$$

**Write the fraction in simplest form.**

3. $\dfrac{12}{16}$  

4. $\dfrac{48}{84}$  

5. $\dfrac{5}{23}$  

6. $\dfrac{60}{132}$

## 2.2 Mixed Numbers and Improper Fractions ......... pp. 60–63

To write a mixed number as an improper fraction, multiply the whole number part and the denominator. Add the product to the numerator. Write the sum over the denominator.

**EXAMPLE** Write $6\dfrac{3}{8}$ as an improper fraction.

$$6\frac{3}{8} = \frac{6 \cdot 8 + 3}{8} \qquad \begin{array}{l}\text{Multiply whole number and denominator.}\\ \text{Add product to numerator.}\end{array}$$

$$= \frac{51}{8} \qquad \text{Simplify.}$$

**Write the number as an improper fraction.**

7. $1\dfrac{3}{4}$  

8. $3\dfrac{5}{12}$  

9. $4$  

10. $5\dfrac{6}{25}$

## Add and Subtract Fractions with the Same Denominator pp. 66–69

To add or subtract fractions with the same denominator, write the sum or difference of the numerators over the denominator. Then simplify, if possible.

**EXAMPLE**
$$\frac{3}{10} + \frac{5}{10} = \frac{3+5}{10}$$ Write sum of numerators over common denominator, 10.

$$= \frac{8}{10}$$ Add numerators.

$$= \frac{4}{5}$$ Simplify.

**Find the sum or difference.**

**11.** $\frac{2}{9} + \frac{5}{9}$    **12.** $\frac{7}{11} - \frac{5}{11}$    **13.** $\frac{5}{6} - \frac{3}{6}$    **14.** $\frac{3}{10} + \frac{7}{10}$

2.4 ## Add and Subtract Fractions with Different Denominators pp. 74–77

To add or subtract fractions with different denominators, first find the least common denominator (LCD) of the fractions. Write equivalent fractions using the LCD. Then add or subtract the fractions. Simplify if possible.

**EXAMPLES**
**a.** $\frac{11}{42} + \frac{5}{12} = \frac{22}{84} + \frac{35}{84}$ The LCD is 84. Write equivalent fractions.

$$= \frac{57}{84}$$ Add numerators.

$$= \frac{19}{28}$$ Simplify.

**b.** $5\frac{5}{6} - 2\frac{1}{4} = \frac{35}{6} - \frac{9}{4}$ Write mixed numbers as improper fractions.

$$= \frac{70}{12} - \frac{27}{12}$$ The LCD is 12. Write equivalent fractions.

$$= \frac{70-27}{12}$$ Subtract numerators.

$$= \frac{43}{12} = 3\frac{7}{12}$$ Simplify. Then write fraction as a mixed number.

**Find the sum or difference.**

**15.** $\frac{1}{4} + \frac{1}{7}$    **16.** $\frac{3}{4} - \frac{2}{5}$    **17.** $\frac{5}{6} + \frac{1}{14}$    **18.** $\frac{7}{10} - \frac{5}{12}$

**19.** $1\frac{3}{4} + 4\frac{1}{8}$    **20.** $5\frac{4}{9} - 2\frac{1}{3}$    **21.** $3\frac{5}{12} + 6\frac{7}{8}$    **22.** $4\frac{1}{6} - 2\frac{7}{15}$

## 2.5 Multiply Fractions ·········· *pp. 80–83*

The product of two or more fractions is equal to the product of the numerators over the product of the denominators.

**EXAMPLE**

$\frac{5}{6} \cdot \frac{3}{4} = \frac{5 \cdot 3}{6 \cdot 4}$  **Write product of numerators over product of denominators.**

$= \frac{15}{24}$  **Multiply.**

$= \frac{5}{8}$  **Simplify.**

**Find the product.**

**23.** $\frac{4}{7} \cdot \frac{2}{3}$  **24.** $\frac{3}{8} \cdot \frac{2}{5}$  **25.** $3\frac{1}{8} \cdot 2\frac{4}{7}$  **26.** $6 \cdot 2\frac{4}{5}$

## 2.6 Find Reciprocals ·········· *pp. 86–89*

To write the reciprocal of a nonzero number, first write the number as a fraction. Then switch the numerator and denominator.

**EXAMPLE**  Write the reciprocal of $3\frac{1}{7}$.

$3\frac{1}{7} = \frac{22}{7}$  **Rewrite mixed number as an improper fraction.**

$\frac{22}{7} \diagdown \frac{7}{22}$  **Switch numerator and denominator.**

The reciprocal of $3\frac{1}{7}$ is $\frac{7}{22}$.

**Find the reciprocal of the number.**

**27.** $\frac{4}{5}$  **28.** $\frac{1}{8}$  **29.** $5$  **30.** $12\frac{1}{2}$

## 2.7 Divide Fractions ·········· *pp. 92–95*

To divide by any nonzero number, multiply by its reciprocal.

**EXAMPLE**

$\frac{4}{5} \div 12 = \frac{4}{5} \cdot \frac{1}{12}$  **Multiply by the reciprocal of 12.**

$= \frac{4}{60} = \frac{1}{15}$  **Multiply, then simplify.**

**Find the quotient.**

**31.** $\frac{1}{6} \div \frac{1}{4}$  **32.** $\frac{2}{3} \div \frac{5}{7}$  **33.** $\frac{4}{21} \div 8$  **34.** $6\frac{4}{5} \div 1\frac{3}{10}$

# Chapter Test

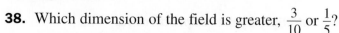

**Write two fractions that are equivalent to the given fraction.**

**1.** $\dfrac{1}{3}$      **2.** $\dfrac{2}{5}$      **3.** $\dfrac{7}{23}$      **4.** $\dfrac{5}{14}$

**Write the number as an improper fraction.**

**5.** $1\dfrac{1}{2}$      **6.** $2\dfrac{4}{5}$      **7.** $8\dfrac{7}{12}$      **8.** $5\dfrac{10}{11}$

**Write the number as a mixed number.**

**9.** $\dfrac{17}{5}$      **10.** $\dfrac{69}{7}$      **11.** $\dfrac{125}{15}$      **12.** $\dfrac{58}{15}$

**Copy and complete the statement using <, >, or =.**

**13.** $\dfrac{1}{9} \,?\, \dfrac{1}{8}$      **14.** $\dfrac{7}{10} \,?\, \dfrac{70}{100}$      **15.** $9\dfrac{1}{5} \,?\, \dfrac{9}{5}$      **16.** $\dfrac{4}{5} \,?\, \dfrac{39}{49}$

**Find the LCD of the fractions.**

**17.** $\dfrac{1}{3}, \dfrac{1}{5}$      **18.** $\dfrac{7}{10}, \dfrac{4}{13}$      **19.** $\dfrac{5}{6}, \dfrac{11}{18}$      **20.** $\dfrac{3}{8}, \dfrac{19}{28}$

**Find the sum or difference.**

**21.** $\dfrac{4}{5} + \dfrac{5}{6}$      **22.** $\dfrac{1}{6} - \dfrac{1}{10}$      **23.** $2\dfrac{1}{10} + 5\dfrac{7}{10}$      **24.** $3\dfrac{5}{24} - 1\dfrac{3}{8}$

**Find the product.**

**25.** $\dfrac{2}{3} \cdot \dfrac{6}{7}$      **26.** $\left(\dfrac{4}{5}\right)^3$      **27.** $3 \cdot 4\dfrac{2}{3}$      **28.** $2\dfrac{1}{4} \cdot 3\dfrac{5}{9}$

**Write the reciprocal of the number.**

**29.** $\dfrac{5}{6}$      **30.** $1\dfrac{3}{8}$      **31.** $\dfrac{56}{57}$      **32.** $2\dfrac{1}{6}$

**Find the quotient.**

**33.** $\dfrac{6}{7} \div \dfrac{5}{8}$      **34.** $\dfrac{11}{12} \div 11$      **35.** $6 \div \dfrac{2}{5}$      **36.** $4\dfrac{3}{4} \div \dfrac{3}{8}$

**37.** A bag contains 5 ounces of popped popcorn. How many $\dfrac{1}{2}$ ounce servings are in the bag?

**In Exercises 38–40, use the diagram, which shows a rectangular field.**

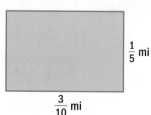

**38.** Which dimension of the field is greater, $\dfrac{3}{10}$ or $\dfrac{1}{5}$?

**39.** Find the perimeter of the field.

**40.** Find the area of the field.

**41.** A bowling ball travels 60 feet from the foul line to the head pin in $2\dfrac{1}{2}$ seconds. What is the average speed of the ball?

1. What is the simplest form of $\frac{32}{72}$?

   (A) $\frac{3}{7}$      (B) $\frac{4}{9}$

   (C) $\frac{8}{18}$      (D) $\frac{16}{36}$

2. Which number is a proper fraction?

   (A) $\frac{17}{18}$      (B) $1\frac{7}{8}$

   (C) $1\frac{8}{7}$      (D) $\frac{17}{8}$

3. Which number is a mixed number?

   (A) $\frac{3}{4}$      (B) $5$

   (C) $\frac{23}{4}$      (D) $5\frac{3}{4}$

4. What improper fraction is equal to $2\frac{37}{100}$?

   (A) $2\frac{370}{1000}$      (B) $\frac{200}{37}$

   (C) $\frac{237}{100}$      (D) $2\frac{9}{25}$

5. What mixed number is equal to $\frac{75}{11}$?

   (A) $6\frac{9}{75}$      (B) $6\frac{2}{11}$

   (C) $6\frac{9}{11}$      (D) $7\frac{2}{11}$

6. What is the LCD of $\frac{5}{6}$ and $\frac{8}{9}$?

   (A) $9$      (B) $18$

   (C) $40$      (D) $54$

7. What fraction is equivalent to $\frac{8}{17}$?

   (A) $\frac{16}{36}$      (B) $\frac{24}{52}$

   (C) $\frac{24}{51}$      (D) $\frac{24}{36}$

8. How long is the plank if $\frac{1}{16}$ inch is removed from each end?

   $24\frac{1}{2}$ in.

   (A) $24\frac{3}{8}$ in.      (B) $24\frac{7}{16}$ in.

   (C) $24\frac{9}{16}$ in.      (D) $24\frac{5}{8}$ in.

9. What is the reciprocal of $8\frac{1}{4}$?

   (A) $\frac{4}{33}$      (B) $\frac{4}{9}$

   (C) $\frac{9}{4}$      (D) $\frac{33}{4}$

10. A school bus travels $5\frac{4}{5}$ miles in $\frac{3}{10}$ hour. What is the average speed of the bus?

    (A) $15\frac{4}{5}$ mi/h      (B) $16\frac{1}{5}$ mi/h

    (C) $17\frac{2}{5}$ mi/h      (D) $19\frac{1}{3}$ mi/h

11. What is the quotient $3\frac{3}{5} \div 2\frac{1}{4}$?

    (A) $1\frac{3}{20}$      (B) $1\frac{7}{20}$

    (C) $1\frac{3}{5}$      (D) $1\frac{13}{20}$

12. What is the area of the square?

    $2\frac{4}{5}$ in.

    (A) $7\frac{3}{5}$ in.$^2$      (B) $7\frac{4}{5}$ in.$^2$

    (C) $7\frac{16}{25}$ in.$^2$      (D) $7\frac{21}{25}$ in.$^2$

# Decimals and Percents

*Vocabulary for Chapter 3* •••••••••••••••••••••••••••

## Key Mathematical Vocabulary

- **terminating decimal,** p. 128
- **repeating decimal,** p. 128
- **percent,** p. 134

## Academic Vocabulary

- **estimate** Perform calculations after choosing easier numbers to work with. For example, see Example 3 on page 109.
- **model,** p. 106
- **check,** p. 107
- **describe,** p. 110
- **explain,** p. 110
- **compare,** p. 113
- **predict,** p. 131
- **approximate,** p. 139

**Comparing the frequencies of guitar strings using decimals, page 122**

Gr. 7 NS 1.2 Add, subtract, multiply, and divide rational numbers (integers, fractions, and terminating decimals) and take positive rational numbers to whole-number powers.
Gr. 7 NS 1.3 Convert fractions to decimals and percents and use these representations in estimations, computations, and applications.

# Review Prerequisite Skills

### REVIEW VOCABULARY

- expression, p. 32
- factor, p. 481
- product, p. 481
- dividend, p. 482
- divisor, p. 482
- quotient, p. 482
- denominator, p. 483
- numerator, p. 483

**VOCABULARY CHECK**

**Copy and complete the statement.**

**1.** In the fraction $\frac{5}{8}$, $\underline{\ ?\ }$ is the numerator and $\underline{\ ?\ }$ is the denominator.

**2.** In the quotient $15 \div 3$, the $\underline{\ ?\ }$ is 15.

**SKILLS CHECK**

**Write the number in expanded form. (Review p. 476 for 3.1–3.7.)**

**3.** 24.32

**4.** 156.058

**5.** 21,037.5

**Round the number to the place value of the red digit. (Review p. 479 for 3.1–3.2.)**

**6.** 342

**7.** 1259.47

**8.** 24.36

**Find the sum or difference. (Review pp. 74 and 480 for 3.1.)**

**9.** $15 + 19 + 23$

**10.** $923 + 892 + 917$

**11.** $12{,}537 - 10{,}837$

**12.** $6912 - 2133$

**13.** $\frac{5}{6} - \frac{1}{3}$

**14.** $4\frac{1}{6} + 2\frac{2}{3}$

**Find the product or quotient. (Review pp. 80, 92, and 481 for 3.2–3.3.)**

**15.** $2342 \times 32$

**16.** $\frac{2}{5} \times \frac{7}{2}$

**17.** $6 \div \frac{4}{3}$

**Order the numbers from least to greatest. (Review p. 60 for 3.4–3.6.)**

**18.** $5, \frac{8}{3}, 2, 2\frac{3}{4}$

**19.** $3\frac{4}{5}, 3\frac{1}{2}, 3, \frac{18}{5}$

**20.** $\frac{1}{3}, \frac{2}{5}, \frac{1}{4}, \frac{2}{3}$

## Let's Explore
## Modeling Decimal Addition and Subtraction

**Goal**
Use models to add and subtract decimals.

**Materials**
• base-ten pieces

**QUESTION** How can you use base-ten pieces to model sums and differences?

The value of each base-ten piece is shown below.

1 one (1 whole): 1          1 tenth: 0.1          1 hundredth: 0.01

**EXPLORE 1** *Use base-ten pieces to model sums* ·············

**1** **Model** the sum 1.25 + 0.98.

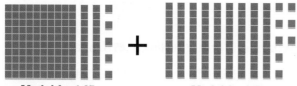

Model for 1.25          Model for 0.98

**2** **Combine** like pieces. Use the fact that 10 tenths = 1 one and 10 hundredths = 1 tenth to replace a group of 10 like pieces.

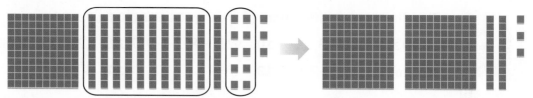

**3** **Copy** and complete the table, then represent the sum.

| Total ones pieces | Total tenths pieces | Total hundredths pieces |
|:---:|:---:|:---:|
| ? | ? | ? |

Use the table to copy and complete the statement: 1.25 + 0.98 = __?__ .

# Draw Conclusions

**Use base-ten pieces to find the sum.**

**1.** $2.1 + 0.9$  **2.** $1.5 + 0.8$  **3.** $2.23 + 1.89$

**4.** Tim added 0.5 and 0.03 and got 0.08. What did he do wrong?

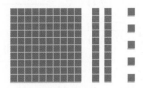 **Use base-ten pieces to model differences** .......

**Find the difference $1.25 - 0.32$.**

**1** **Model** 1.25.

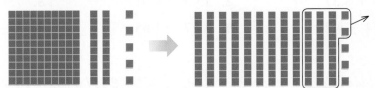

**2** **Remove** pieces representing 0.32. Because there are not 3 tenths pieces to remove, replace the ones piece with 10 tenths pieces first.

**3** **Copy** and complete the table, then represent the difference.

| Remaining ones pieces | Remaining tenths pieces | Remaining hundredths pieces |
|---|---|---|
| ? | ? | ? |

Use the table to copy and complete the statement: $1.25 - 0.32 = \underline{\ ?\ }$.

# Draw Conclusions

**Use base-ten pieces to find the difference.**

**5.** $2.7 - 1.3$  **6.** $1.8 - 0.6$  **7.** $2.65 - 1.21$

**8.** Show how you can use addition to check the answer for the subtraction problem in Explore 2.

# Lesson 3.1 — Add and Subtract Decimals

## VOCABULARY and CONCEPTS

- algebraic expression, p. 32

### Adding and Subtracting Decimals

To add and subtract decimals, line up the decimal points. Then add or subtract as with whole numbers and bring down the decimal point. Use zeros to help line up the digits.

---

**EXAMPLE 1** Adding and Subtracting Decimals

**a.** Find the sum $5.628 + 4.3$.

$$\begin{array}{r} 5.628 \\ + 4.300 \\ \hline 9.928 \end{array}$$

**b.** Find the difference $7 - 3.1$.

$$\begin{array}{r} {}^{6}\overset{1}{7}.0 \\ - 3.1 \\ \hline 3.9 \end{array}$$

Rename 1 as 10 tenths so that you can subtract in the tenths' place.

> **Skills Review**
> Adding and subtracting whole numbers, p. 480

### Practice for Example 1

**Find the sum or difference.**

**1.** $2.5 + 8.37$      **2.** $15.3 + 4.01$      **3.** $7.9 + 12.1$

**4.** $9.74 - 4.2$      **5.** $8.57 - 1.65$      **6.** $6 - 3.52$

---

**EXAMPLE 2** Evaluating Algebraic Expressions

**a.** Evaluate $8.6 + x$ when $x = 6.3$.

$$8.6 + x = 8.6 + 6.3 \qquad \text{Substitute 6.3 for } x.$$
$$= 14.9 \qquad \text{Add.}$$

**b.** Evaluate $x - y$ when $x = 6.3$ and $y = 4.7$.

$$x - y = 6.3 - 4.7 \qquad \text{Substitute 6.3 for } x \text{ and 4.7 for } y.$$
$$= 1.6 \qquad \text{Subtract.}$$

### Practice for Example 2

**Evaluate the expression when $x = 5.2$ and $y = 3.18$.**

**7.** $x + 9.03$      **8.** $5.5 + y$      **9.** $10.45 - y$

**10.** $x - 2.3$      **11.** $8.71 - x$      **12.** $y + x$

**EXAMPLE 3**  *Estimating Sums and Differences*

**a.**
$$6.8 \rightarrow \quad 7 \quad \text{Round 6.8 up to 7.}$$
$$+ 4.3 \rightarrow + 4 \quad \text{Round 4.3 down to 4.}$$
$$\overline{\phantom{+4.3} \quad 11} \quad \text{Add.}$$

▶ **Answer** The sum is about 11.

**b.**
$$11.26 \rightarrow \quad 11 \quad \text{Round 11.26 down to 11.}$$
$$- 5.87 \quad \quad - 6 \quad \text{Round 5.87 up to 6.}$$
$$\overline{\phantom{-5.87} \quad 5} \quad \text{Subtract.}$$

▶ **Answer** The difference is about 5.

### Practice for Example 3

**Use rounding to estimate the sum or difference.**

**13.** $10.4 + 8.5$    **14.** $7.6 - 5.7$    **15.** $5.9 - 2.8$

**16.** $8.63 - 4.7$    **17.** $2.08 + 5.65$    **18.** $11.43 - 6.28$

**EXAMPLE 4**  *Writing a Verbal Model*

Megan jogs to a park that is 1.8 kilometers from her house. She runs a total of 3.5 kilometers in the park, then jogs home. How far does Megan travel altogether?

**Solution**

Write a verbal model to help you find the total distance.

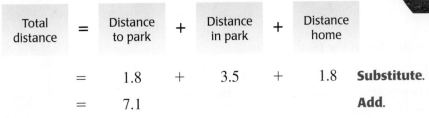

| Total distance | = | Distance to park | + | Distance in park | + | Distance home | |
|---|---|---|---|---|---|---|---|
| | = | 1.8 | + | 3.5 | + | 1.8 | **Substitute.** |
| | = | 7.1 | | | | | **Add.** |

▶ **Answer** Megan travels 7.1 kilometers altogether.

### Practice for Example 4

**19.** On a family trip, you travel 365.4 kilometers the first day. You travel 412.8 kilometers the next day. How far do you travel altogether?

# A Practice

**Extra Practice**
p. 500

**Find the sum or difference.**

**1.** $7.2 + 3.64$    **2.** $8.10 + 7.79$    **3.** $5.61 - 3.28$    **4.** $11.456 + 9.7$

**5.** $0.587 - 0.41$    **6.** $12.841 + 7.23$    **7.** $8.45 - 2.1$    **8.** $3 - 1.48$

**9.** $6.197 + 2.86$    **10.** $0.485 + 4.392$    **11.** $8.75 - 7.19$    **12.** $19 - 8.672$

**Evaluate the expression when $x = 2.49$ and $y = 9.17$.**

**13.** $1.62 + x$    **14.** $y - 3.85$    **15.** $6.02 + y$    **16.** $3.42 - x$

**17.** $8.31 - x$    **18.** $y - x$    **19.** $x + y$    **20.** $10 - y$

**FIND THE ERROR** *Describe* and correct the error in finding the sum or difference.

**21.**

$$\begin{array}{r} 4.6 \\ + 5.7 \\ \hline 9.3 \end{array}$$

**22.**

$$\begin{array}{r} 3.2 \\ - 1.8 \\ \hline 2.4 \end{array}$$

**Use rounding to estimate the sum or difference.**

**23.** $2.2 + 3.1$    **24.** $7.6 - 2.3$    **25.** $13.2 - 9.73$

**26.** $1.9 + 9.6$    **27.** $6.29 - 3.42$    **28.** $6.1 + 10.28$

**29.** $15.27 + 18.83$    **30.** $20.42 - 16.38$    **31.** $24.4 - 6.37$

**Find the perimeter of the rectangle.**

**32.**

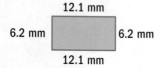

**33.**

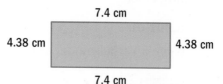

**34.** Find the perimeter of the pool shown.

**35.** You go shopping at the mall and purchase a CD for $15.87. Then you buy a book for $8.99. How much do you spend altogether?

**36.** A tree in your front yard was 9.2 feet tall. You trimmed 1.6 feet off the top to clear it from some wires. How tall is your tree now?

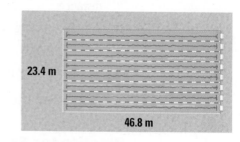

**37.** **REASONING** *Explain* how you can use fractions to find the sum of 2.3 and 4.5.

# Practice

**Find the sum or difference.**

**1.** $2.8 + 3.5$

**2.** $3.15 + 7.27$

**3.** $8.91 - 6.24$

**4.** $22.9167 + 1.0273$

**5.** $3.94 - 0.88$

**6.** $15.79 + 2.68$

**7.** $12.08 - 6.45$

**8.** $19.0670 - 15.287$

**9.** $10.164 + 12.079$

**10.** $7 - 5.097$

**11.** $51.470 - 14.68$

**12.** $62 - 24.8332$

**Evaluate the expression when $x = 3.28$ and $y = 12.46$.**

**13.** $2.49 + x$

**14.** $y - 4.67$

**15.** $9.271 + y$

**16.** $x - 1.23$

**17.** $12.37 - x$

**18.** $y - x$

**19.** $x + y$

**20.** $4.153 - x$

**21.** $24.5 - y$

**22.** $0.361 + x$

**23.** $x - 1.045$

**24.** $y + 4.617$

**Use rounding to estimate the sum or difference.**

**25.** $7.5 + 8.2$

**26.** $9.6 + 2.1$

**27.** $7.1 - 0.2$

**28.** $12.39 + 4.4$

**29.** $5.2 - 2.6$

**30.** $12.81 - 4.36$

**31.** $20.8 - 3.6$

**32.** $3.65 + 18.25$

**33.** $15.96 + 12.87$

**34.** $17.04 - 9.87$

**35.** $103.26 + 51.58$

**36.** $24.19 - 15.26$

**Find the perimeter of the triangle or rectangle.**

**37.**

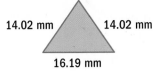

14.02 mm     14.02 mm

16.19 mm

**38.**

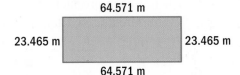

64.571 m

23.465 m        23.465 m

64.571 m

**In Exercises 39–42, use the table, which shows the items you purchased while shopping at the mall with some friends.**

| Item purchased | Cost |
|---|---|
| Sweater | $26.89 |
| CD | $14.99 |
| Pretzel | $2.35 |
| Pair of earrings | $3.45 |
| Shampoo | $2.75 |
| Hat | $7.42 |

**39.** What is the total amount you spent?

**40.** You purchased the CD, shampoo, and a hat at the same store. How much did you spend at that store?

**41.** In Exercise 40, suppose you gave the cashier at the store $30. How much did you get back?

**42.** At a grocery store, you buy a loaf of bread for $1.99, a bag of grapes for $3.99, and a gallon of milk for $2.79. You give the cashier $20. About how much change should you expect to receive? *Explain* your reasoning.

**43.** **REASONING** *Explain* how you can use fractions to find the difference of 3.75 and 0.25.

Let's Explore
## Modeling Decimal Multiplication

**Goal**
Use models to multiply decimals.

**Materials**
• base-ten pieces

**QUESTION** **How can you use base-ten pieces to multiply a decimal and a whole number?**

The value of each base-ten piece is shown below.

**1 one**      **1 tenth**      **1 hundredth**

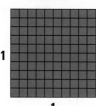    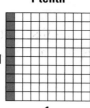   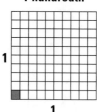

**Area = 1 × 1 = 1**    **Area = 1 × 0.1 = 0.1**    **Area = 0.1 × 0.1 = 0.01**

**EXPLORE 1** *Use base-ten pieces to multiply* ·················

1. **Model** each product. When appropriate, use the fact that
10 hundredths = 1 tenth to replace a group of 10 hundredths.

     1 × 0.04          2 × 0.04            3 × 0.04

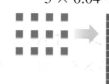

2. **Find** each product in Step 1 by counting the tenths and hundredths pieces
in the corresponding model.

     1 × 0.04 = __?__        2 × 0.04 = __?__        3 × 0.04 = __?__

## Draw Conclusions
**Use base-ten pieces to find the product.**

   **1.** 3 × 0.02      **2.** 3 × 0.2      **3.** 4 × 0.03      **4.** 4 × 0.3

   **5.** The number 3 has 0 decimal places, while the number 0.04 has
2 decimal places. The product of 3 and 0.04 is 0.12, which has
2 decimal places. *Describe* how the number of decimal places in
each of your answers to Exercises 1–4 compares with the number of
decimal places in the factors.

**Gr. 7 NS 1.2** Add, subtract, **multiply,** and divide **rational numbers** (integers, fractions, and **terminating decimals**) and take positive rational numbers to whole-number powers.

## EXPLORE 2 *Use base-ten pieces to multiply decimals* ......

**1** **Model** the product $0.5 \times 2.3$. Use base-ten pieces to form a rectangle with a length of 2.3 and a width of 0.5.

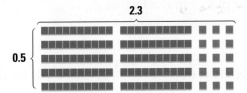

**2** **Combine** like pieces. Use the fact that 10 tenths = 1 one and 10 hundredths = 1 tenth to replace a group of 10 like pieces.

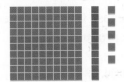

**3** **Find** the product. Copy and complete the statement: $0.5 \times 2.3 = \underline{\ ?\ }$.

## Draw Conclusions

**6.** What multiplication problem does the model at the right represent?

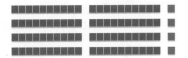

**In Exercises 7–10, use base-ten pieces to find the product.**

**7.** $2.3 \times 0.1$      **8.** $2.3 \times 0.4$      **9.** $2.3 \times 0.9$      **10.** $2.3 \times 1.2$

**11. a.** Find the product $23 \times 9$.

     **b.** How does the product in part (a) compare with your answer for Exercise 9 above? *Explain* why this is true.

**12. a.** Find the product $23 \times 12$.

     **b.** How does the product in part (a) compare with your answer for Exercise 10? *Explain* why this is true.

**13.** How does the product of two decimals compare with the product of the same digits without decimals?

**14.** *Explain* how to find a product of decimals without using base-ten pieces.

# Multiply Decimals

**VOCABULARY and CONCEPTS**

- product, p. 481
- factor, p. 481

**Multiplying Decimals**

Multiply decimals as you do whole numbers. Then place the decimal point. The number of decimal places in the product is the sum of the number of decimal places in the factors.

**EXAMPLE 1** *Multiplying Decimals by Whole Numbers* .....

**a.** Find the product $2 \times 0.4$.

**b.** Find the product $2 \times 0.04$.

**Solution**

**a.** Because 0.4 has 1 decimal place, the product will have 1 decimal place.

$$
\begin{array}{r}
0.4 \\
\times\ \ 2 \\
\hline
0.8
\end{array}
$$

**b.** Because 0.04 has 2 decimal places, the product will have 2 decimal places.

$$
\begin{array}{r}
0.04 \\
\times\ \ 2 \\
\hline
0.08
\end{array}
$$

Write a zero as a placeholder so that the product has 2 decimal places.

**Practice for Example 1**

**Find the product.**

**1.** $6 \times 0.12$

**2.** $0.031 \times 5$

**3.** $4 \times 5.2$

**4.** $0.007 \times 8$

**EXAMPLE 2** *Checking for Reasonableness* ...................

**Skills Review**

Multiplying whole numbers, p. 481

**a.** Find the product $3.04 \times 11$.

**b.** Use estimation to check that the answer is reasonable.

**Solution**

**a.**
$$
\begin{array}{r}
3.04 \\
\times\ \ 11 \\
\hline
3\ 04 \\
30\ 4\ \ \\
\hline
33.44
\end{array}
$$

**b.** $3.04 \times 11 \approx 3 \times 11$

$$= 33$$

▶ **Answer** Because 33.44 is close to 33, the answer is reasonable.

**Practice for Example 2**

**Find the product. Use estimation to check that your answer is reasonable.**

**5.** $8.6 \times 4$

**6.** $7 \times 5.2$

**7.** $0.52 \times 12$

**8.** $9 \times 0.28$

## EXAMPLE 3 — Multiplying Decimals

**a.** Find the product $25 \times 3.34$.

**b.** Evaluate $(0.07)^2$.

**Solution**

**a.**
$$
\begin{array}{r}
3.34 \\
\times\ 25 \\
\hline
1670 \\
668\phantom{0} \\
\hline
83.50
\end{array}
$$

**2 decimal places**
**0 decimal places**

**2 + 0 = 2. So, product has 2 decimal places.**

After you place the decimal point, you can drop any zeros at the end of the product.

▶**Answer** $25 \times 3.34 = 83.5$

**b.**
$$
\begin{array}{r}
0.07 \\
\times 0.07 \\
\hline
0.0049
\end{array}
$$

**2 decimal places**
**2 decimal places**

**2 + 2 = 4. So, product has 4 decimal places.**

Write two zeros before the 4 as placeholders so that the product has 4 decimal places.

▶**Answer** $(0.07)^2 = 0.0049$

### Practice for Example 3

**Find the product or evaluate the power.**

**9.** $0.09 \times 0.72$

**10.** $(0.28)^2$

**11.** $22 \times 7.085$

## EXAMPLE 4 — Multiplying Decimals to Find Area

What is the area of a flag that is 4.75 feet long and 2.5 feet wide?

**Solution**

$$\text{Area} = \ell w$$    Write the formula for the area of a rectangle.

$$= 4.75(2.5)$$    Substitute 4.75 for $\ell$ and 2.5 for $w$.

$$= 11.875$$    Multiply.

▶**Answer** The area of the flag is 11.875 square feet.

### Practice for Example 4

**Find the area of the rectangle.**

**12.**

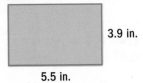

3.9 in.

5.5 in.

**13.**

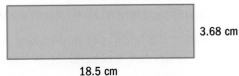

3.68 cm

18.5 cm

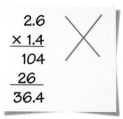

# Practice

**Extra Practice**
p. 500

**Find the product.**

**1.** $6 \times 1.2$    **2.** $7 \times 0.09$    **3.** $4 \times 2.08$

**4.** $13 \times 1.67$    **5.** $24 \times 3.76$    **6.** $34 \times 3.089$

**7.** $5 \times 9.182$    **8.** $10 \times 2.004$    **9.** $16 \times 7.851$

**Tell how many decimal places the product will have.**

**10.** $4.6 \times 3.219$    **11.** $8.045 \times 17.43$    **12.** $0.0271 \times 1.3583$

**13.** $0.159 \times 5.9$    **14.** $21.356 \times 5.687$    **15.** $0.002 \times 0.0034$

**FIND THE ERROR** *Describe* and correct the error in finding the product.

**16.**
$$\begin{array}{r} 2.6 \\ \times\ 1.4 \\ \hline 104 \\ 26\phantom{0} \\ \hline 36.4 \end{array}$$

**17.**
$$\begin{array}{r} 3.2 \\ \times\ 2.1 \\ \hline 32 \\ 64\phantom{0} \\ \hline 0.96 \end{array}$$

**Find the product. Use estimation to check that your answer is reasonable.**

**18.** $0.2 \times 0.7$    **19.** $0.9 \times 1.3$    **20.** $2.64 \times 0.5$

**21.** $3.75 \times 5.4$    **22.** $5.083 \times 4.71$    **23.** $7.009 \times 8.153$

**Evaluate the power.**

**24.** $(0.05)^2$    **25.** $(0.37)^2$    **26.** $(2.2)^2$    **27.** $(0.3)^3$

**Find the area of the square or rectangle.**

**28.**

3.75 cm

3.75 cm

**29.**

4.69 mm

8.1 mm

**30.**
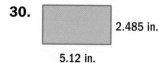
2.485 in.

5.12 in.

**31.** Gas costs $3.39 per gallon. A woman puts 7.6 gallons of gas into her car. How much does she spend on gasoline?

**32.** Fresh pineapple costs $1.99 per pound. You purchase the pineapple shown. How much do you spend?

**33.** You make $5.50 per hour when you baby-sit. You baby-sat for 3.5 hours last weekend. How much money did you make?

**34.** **REASONING** *Explain* how you would use the product of 32 and 145 to find the product of 0.32 and 1.45.

# Practice

**Copy the answer and place the decimal point in the correct location.**

**1.** $9.704 \times 30.6 = 2969424$

**2.** $23.12 \times 8.41 = 1944392$

**3.** $16.483 \times 0.2651 = 43696433$

**4.** $0.18 \times 0.49 = 00882$

**5.** A new car averages 21.6 miles on one gallon of gas. How many miles could you travel on 7.5 gallons of gas?

**6.** A rectangular piece of paper has a length of 4.25 inches and a width of 5.5 inches. What is the total area for writing?

**Find the product. Use estimation to check that your answer is reasonable.**

**7.** $0.4 \times 0.9$

**8.** $0.2 \times 2.3$

**9.** $3.05 \times 1.2$

**10.** $6.04 \times 9.7$

**11.** $7.18 \times 9.408$

**12.** $3.24 \times 1.088$

**13.** $4.709 \times 6.89$

**14.** $7.55 \times 0.008$

**15.** $5.89 \times 3.01$

**Evaluate the power.**

**16.** $(0.06)^2$

**17.** $(2.05)^2$

**18.** $(0.18)^3$

**19.** $(0.8)^4$

**Find the area of the square or rectangle.**

**20.**

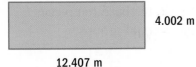

4.002 m

12.407 m

**21.**

9.3 mm

9.3 mm

**Copy and complete the statement with <, >, or =.**

**22.** $7.38 \times 5.1 \underline{\ ?\ } 35$

**23.** $0.05 \times 8.25 \underline{\ ?\ } 0.5$

**24.** $4.2 \times 8.5 \underline{\ ?\ } 35.7$

In Exercises 25–28, use the table, which shows the prices of some items at a mall. To calculate the sales tax, multiply the price of an item by the tax rate. The tax rate that applies is 0.08.

| Item | Cost |
|---|---|
| Jacket | $45.00 |
| Socks | $2.50 |
| Sneakers | $60.00 |
| Belt | $15.75 |
| Poster | $12.75 |

**25.** What is the sales tax on the jacket?

**26.** What is the sales tax on the socks?

**27.** Would you pay more sales tax on the belt or the poster? *Explain.*

**28.** On which item is the sales tax the greatest?

**29. REASONING** Suppose you write 1.8 as $18 \times 0.1$ and 0.25 as $25 \times 0.01$. What is $18 \times 25$? What is $0.1 \times 0.01$? How can you use these results to find $1.8 \times 0.25$?

# Activity 3.3

## Let's Explore
### Modeling Decimal Division

**Goal**
Use models to divide a decimal by a whole number.

**Materials**
• base-ten pieces

**QUESTION** How can you use base-ten pieces to model division involving decimals?

The value of each base-ten piece is shown below.

  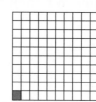

**1 one (1 whole): 1**   **1 tenth: 0.1**   **1 hundredth: 0.01**

**EXPLORE 1** *Use base-ten pieces to model division* ...........

Use base-ten pieces to find the quotient 0.63 ÷ 3.

**1** **Model** 0.63 using 6 tenths pieces and 3 hundredths pieces.

**2** **Divide** the base-ten pieces into 3 equal groups.

**3** **Copy** and complete the table, then represent the quotient.

| Number of tenths pieces in a group | Number of hundredths pieces in a group |
|---|---|
| ? | ? |

Use the table to copy and complete the statement: 0.63 ÷ 3 = __?__.

## Draw Conclusions
**Use base-ten pieces to find the quotient.**

**1.** 4.2 ÷ 2     **2.** 2.68 ÷ 2     **3.** 0.96 ÷ 3     **4.** 0.48 ÷ 4

**Gr. 7 NS 1.2** Add, subtract, multiply, and **divide rational numbers** (integers, fractions, and **terminating decimals**) and take positive rational numbers to whole-number powers.

**EXPLORE 2** *Model division by replacing pieces* · · · · · · · · · ·

**Use base-ten pieces to find the quotient 2.7 ÷ 2.**

**1** **Model** 2.7.

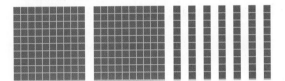

**2** **Divide** the pieces into 2 equal groups. Because you cannot divide the 7 tenths pieces into 2 equal groups, replace 1 tenths piece with 10 hundredths pieces and divide them into 2 equal groups.

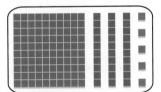 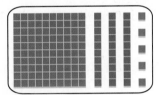

**3** **Copy** and complete the table, then represent the quotient.

| Number of ones pieces in a group | Number of tenths pieces in a group | Number of hundredths pieces in a group |
|:---:|:---:|:---:|
| ? | ? | ? |

Use the table to copy and complete the statement: 2.7 ÷ 2 = _?_ .

## Draw Conclusions

**5.** What division problem does the model below represent?

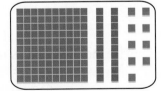 

**Use base-ten pieces to find the quotient.**

**6.** 2.5 ÷ 2          **7.** 0.45 ÷ 3          **8.** 4.28 ÷ 4          **9.** 1.6 ÷ 5

**10.** Show how you can use multiplication to check the answer for the division problem in Explore 2.

# Lesson 3.3

# Divide Decimals

## VOCABULARY and CONCEPTS

- divisor, p. 482
- dividend, p. 482
- quotient, p. 482

### Dividing Decimals

When you divide a decimal by a whole number, place the decimal point in the quotient above the decimal point in the dividend. When you divide by a decimal, multiply both the divisor and the dividend by a power of 10 that will make the divisor a whole number.

## EXAMPLE 1 Dividing a Decimal by a Whole Number

**Skills Review**
Dividing whole numbers, p. 482

**Find the quotient 7)3.99. Then check your answer.**

Place the decimal point.

$$
\begin{array}{r}
. \\
7\overline{)3.99}
\end{array}
$$

Then divide.

$$
\begin{array}{r}
.57 \\
7\overline{)3.99} \\
\underline{3\ 5} \\
49 \\
\underline{49} \\
0
\end{array}
$$

Check by multiplying.

$$
\begin{array}{r}
0.57 \\
\times\ 7 \\
\hline
3.99
\end{array}
$$

▶ **Answer** The quotient is 0.57.

### Practice for Example 1

**Find the quotient. Then check your answer.**

**1.** 3)22.8       **2.** 9)2.16       **3.** 2)23.4

## EXAMPLE 2 Writing Additional Zeros

**Find the quotient 13 ÷ 4.**

Place the decimal points and begin dividing.

$$
\begin{array}{r}
3. \\
4\overline{)13.} \\
\underline{12} \\
1
\end{array}
$$

Write additional zeros in the dividend as needed.

$$
\begin{array}{r}
3.25 \\
4\overline{)13.00} \\
\underline{12} \\
1\ 0 \\
\underline{8} \\
20 \\
\underline{20} \\
0
\end{array}
$$

▶ **Answer** The quotient is 3.25.

**EXAMPLE 3** *Dividing Decimals* •••••••••••••••••••••••••••••••

**a.** Find the quotient $2.68 \div 0.4$.

First multiply the divisor and the dividend by 10, then divide.

$$0.4\overline{)2.6\,8}$$

**Move decimal points 1 place.**

$$
\begin{array}{r}
6.7 \\
4\overline{)26.8} \\
\underline{24} \\
28 \\
\underline{28} \\
0
\end{array}
$$

**b.** Find the quotient $36 \div 0.03$.

First multiply the divisor and the dividend by 100, then divide.

$$0.03\overline{)36.00}$$

**Move decimal points 2 places.**

$$
\begin{array}{r}
1200. \\
3\overline{)3600.} \\
\underline{3} \\
06 \\
\underline{6} \\
0
\end{array}
$$

Fill quotient with zeros up to the decimal point.

## Practice for Examples 2 and 3

**Find the quotient.**

**4.** $58 \div 8$

**5.** $42 \div 5$

**6.** $12.3 \div 5$

**7.** $0.49 \div 0.7$

**8.** $56 \div 0.14$

**9.** $0.448 \div 0.32$

**EXAMPLE 4** *Using Zeros as Placeholders* •••••••••••••••••••••

A volleyball player makes 101 point-scoring hits in 21 games. Find the average number of point-scoring hits per game. Round your answer to the nearest hundredth.

**Solution**

$$
\begin{array}{r}
4.809 \\
21\overline{)101.000} \\
\underline{84}\phantom{.000} \\
17\,0\phantom{00} \\
\underline{16\,8}\phantom{00} \\
200 \\
\underline{189} \\
11
\end{array}
$$

**Write additional zeros in the dividend as needed.**

**Stop when the quotient reaches the thousandths' place.**

> **Skills Review**
> Rounding, p. 479

Round 4.809 to the hundredths' place: 4.81.

▶ **Answer** The average is about 4.81 point-scoring hits per game.

## Practice for Example 4

**10.** A car travels 425 miles on 15 gallons of gas. Find the car's gas mileage to the nearest tenth of a mile per gallon.

# A Practice

**Extra Practice**
p. 500

**Write the letter of the part of the division problem.**

1. divisor
2. dividend
3. quotient

$$\text{B} \longrightarrow 3\overline{)13.5} \longleftarrow \text{C}$$
$$\overset{\overset{\text{A}}{\downarrow}}{4.5}$$

**Find the quotient. Then check your answer.**

| | | |
|---|---|---|
| **4.** $3\overline{)14.1}$ | **5.** $7\overline{)38.5}$ | **6.** $2\overline{)18.6}$ |
| **7.** $4\overline{)25.2}$ | **8.** $5\overline{)41.5}$ | **9.** $3\overline{)23.7}$ |
| **10.** $6\overline{)47.4}$ | **11.** $2\overline{)19.6}$ | **12.** $8\overline{)27.2}$ |

**Find the quotient. Round to the nearest tenth if necessary.**

| | | |
|---|---|---|
| **13.** $5\overline{)27}$ | **14.** $6\overline{)41.8}$ | **15.** $7\overline{)8.43}$ |
| **16.** $4\overline{)105}$ | **17.** $2\overline{)36.14}$ | **18.** $3\overline{)18.21}$ |
| **19.** $6\overline{)35}$ | **20.** $9\overline{)44}$ | **21.** $5\overline{)105.2}$ |

**Find the quotient.**

| | | |
|---|---|---|
| **22.** $12 \div 2.4$ | **23.** $1.25 \div 0.5$ | **24.** $12.8 \div 8$ |
| **25.** $126 \div 1.4$ | **26.** $3.24 \div 0.2$ | **27.** $0.345 \div 0.3$ |
| **28.** $2.244 \div 1.2$ | **29.** $1.0125 \div 2.25$ | **30.** $1.3392 \div 3.6$ |

31. You and 3 friends want to split the cost of a gift for a birthday party. The gift costs $19.96. How much does each of you pay?

32. You earned $31.25 for babysitting 5 hours one night. Find the amount per hour you were paid.

33. An employee had to mail 5 different packages. She spent a total of $24.85. All of the packages cost the same amount to mail. What was the cost of mailing one package?

34. The frequency of the E string on an acoustic guitar is 329.63 Hertz. The frequency of the D string is 146.82 Hertz. How many times greater is the frequency of the E string than the frequency of the D string? Round your answer to the nearest tenth.

35. The local grocery store has a sale on bar soap. A package containing 6 bars of soap costs $5.39. About how much does one bar of soap cost? Round your answer to the nearest cent.

36. **REASONING** Which two quotients are equal? *Explain* your reasoning.

   **A.** $3.84 \div 2.56$     **B.** $384 \div 25.6$     **C.** $3.84 \div 25.6$     **D.** $38.4 \div 2.56$

Organize the steps of dividing a decimal by a whole number in the order in which you should complete them.

**1.** ?          **A.** Divide.

**2.** ?          **B.** Place the decimal point in the quotient above the decimal point in the dividend.

**3.** ?          **C.** Write additional zeros in the dividend as needed.

Find the quotient. Round to the nearest tenth if necessary.

**4.** $9\overline{)12}$          **5.** $3\overline{)147}$          **6.** $6\overline{)29.5}$

**7.** $2\overline{)43.8}$          **8.** $4\overline{)62.3}$          **9.** $5\overline{)74.5}$

**10.** $5\overline{)124.5}$          **11.** $12\overline{)28.13}$          **12.** $13\overline{)129.5}$

Find the quotient. Then check your answer.

**13.** $300.3 \div 42$          **14.** $36 \div 7.2$          **15.** $0.156 \div 1.2$

**16.** $1.89 \div 3.6$          **17.** $4.064 \div 2.54$          **18.** $3.4 \div 1.36$

**19.** $8.91 \div 16.2$          **20.** $25.3 \div 101.2$          **21.** $45.072 \div 125.2$

Find the quotient. Round your answer to the nearest hundredth.

**22.** $0.347 \div 8$          **23.** $25 \div 3.7$          **24.** $11.02 \div 4.25$

**25.** $9.88 \div 4.7$          **26.** $12.5 \div 0.78$          **27.** $61.213 \div 5.6$

Evaluate the expression when $x = 2.5$ and $z = 19.5$.

**28.** $43.875 \div x + z$          **29.** $\frac{z}{x} - 0.23$          **30.** $\frac{2.25}{x} + z$

**31.** You go to a restaurant with 7 of your friends for dessert. The bill totals $41.92. You are going to split the bill evenly. How much does each person pay?

**32.** The area of a rectangular garden is 360.15 square meters. The width of the garden is 15 meters. What is the length of the garden?

**33.** A local grocery store is having a sale on ears of corn. Eight ears of corn cost $1.92. What is the price of each ear of corn? How much do 12 ears of corn cost?

**34.** You have the daily weekday newspaper delivered to your house for 3 months at a cost of $24. What is the cost per month? What is the cost per day? (Assume there are 20 weekdays in a month.) A single newspaper costs $.50 at the newsstand. Is it a better deal to have the paper delivered or to buy it at the newsstand?

**35.** **REASONING** *Explain* why $2.34 \div 6$ is equivalent to $23.4 \div 60$.

# Mid-Chapter Review

**REVIEW VOCABULARY**
- product, p. 481
- dividend, p. 482
- divisor, p. 482
- quotient, p. 482

**Vocabulary Exercises**

1. Copy and complete: When you multiply two or more whole numbers, the result is called the  ?  of the numbers.

2. In the division expression $1.5\overline{)3.25}$, which number is the divisor?

## 3.1 Add and Subtract Decimals ............................ pp. 108–111

**EXAMPLES**

$$\begin{array}{r} 25.16 \\ +\,4.80 \\ \hline 29.96 \end{array}$$ **Line up decimal points.**
**Add zeros, if necessary.**
**Bring down decimal point.**

$$\begin{array}{r} \overset{4\ 111}{5.\cancel{2}3} \\ -\,2.86 \\ \hline 2.37 \end{array}$$ **Line up decimal points.**
**Bring down decimal point.**

**Find the sum or difference.**

3. $9.23 + 3.56$    4. $6.43 + 10.5$    5. $17.44 - 5.32$    6. $8 - 7.51$

## 3.2 Multiply Decimals ................................ pp. 114–117

**EXAMPLE**

$$\begin{array}{r} 5.13 \\ \times\ 0.4 \\ \hline 2.052 \end{array}$$ **2 decimal places**
**1 decimal place**
**$2 + 1 = 3$. So, product has 3 decimal places.**

**Find the product. Use estimation to check that your answer is reasonable.**

7. $5.71 \times 4$    8. $0.8 \times 0.12$    9. $6.03 \times 0.27$    10. $0.55 \times 0.203$

## 3.3 Divide Decimals ................................ pp. 120–123

**EXAMPLE**   **Find the quotient $4.346 \div 0.53$.**

Because $0.53 \times 100 = 53$, multiply the divisor and the dividend by 100. Move the decimal point 2 places to the right. Put the decimal point in the quotient above the decimal point in the dividend.

$$0.53\overline{)4.346} \qquad \Longrightarrow \qquad 53\overline{)434.6}^{\,8.2}$$

**Find the quotient. Then check your answer.**

11. $4.2 \div 1.6$    12. $1.32 \div 0.06$    13. $0.9 \div 2.4$    14. $5.624 \div 3.7$

**Find the sum or difference.**

**1.** 4.56 + 2.7  **2.** 0.32 + 9.45  **3.** 7.2 + 10.39  **4.** 18.4 + 1.63

**5.** 6.18 − 0.74  **6.** 9.14 − 2.65  **7.** 4 − 1.24  **8.** 8 − 6.36

**Use rounding to estimate the sum or difference.**

**9.** 26.781 + 3.19  **10.** 4.036 + 21.68  **11.** 11.173 − 4.092  **12.** 197.4 − 28.25

**Find the product.**

**13.** 28 × 2.5  **14.** 14 × 7.1  **15.** 4.1 × 3.5  **16.** 7.6 × 2.3

**17.** 0.4 × 0.04  **18.** 2.01 × 3.14  **19.** 0.14 × 0.85  **20.** 0.004 × 0.057

**Find (a) the perimeter and (b) the area of the rectangle.**

**21.**
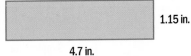
1.15 in.
4.7 in.

**22.**

10.8 ft
17 ft

**Find the product. Use estimation to check that your answer is reasonable.**

**23.** 14.1 × 4.2  **24.** 257 × 11.2  **25.** 1.9 × 3.68  **26.** 16.4 × 24.3

**Find the quotient. Then check your answer.**

**27.** 34.7 ÷ 5  **28.** 391.2 ÷ 16  **29.** 300.3 ÷ 42  **30.** 8.79 ÷ 3

**31.** 59 ÷ 4  **32.** 175 ÷ 8  **33.** 75 ÷ 8  **34.** 22.5 ÷ 15

**In Exercises 35–38, use the information on the poster to answer the question.**

**35.** How much do a hot dog, peanuts, and juice cost altogether?

**36.** How much do 5 T-shirts cost?

**37.** How much more does a hat cost than a pennant?

**38.** How much change would you receive if you bought one of everything and paid using a $50 bill?

Hat:      $12.99
T-shirt:   $ 9.99
Pennant: $ 2.25
Hot dog: $ 3.50
Nachos:  $ 4.00
Peanuts: $ 4.75
Juice:     $ 2.50

**In Exercises 39 and 40, use the grocery receipt, which shows the weight and total price of fruit purchased.**

**39.** How much do the peaches cost per pound?

**40.** Which fruit has the lowest cost per pound? How much does this fruit cost per pound?

| Apples | 7.5 lb | $7.80 |
| Bananas | 4.4 lb | $4.84 |
| Peaches | 4.5 lb | $6.75 |
| Kiwis | 3.5 lb | $8.26 |

# Let's Explore
## Converting Between Fractions and Decimals

**Goal**
Convert between fractions and decimals.

**Materials**
• paper and pencil

**QUESTION** How can you use place values to write decimals as fractions and use equivalent fractions to write fractions as decimals?

**EXPLORE 1** *Write decimals as fractions* •••••••••••••••••••••••

**1** **Copy** the table. Complete the second column of your table. Write each decimal in words.

| Decimal | Words | Fraction | Simplest form |
|---------|-------|----------|---------------|
| 0.03 | three hundredths | $\frac{3}{100}$ | Simplest form |
| 0.65 | ? | ? | ? |
| 0.25 | ? | ? | ? |
| 0.7 | ? | ? | ? |

**2** **Complete** the third column of your table. Write each decimal as a fraction with a denominator that is a power of 10.

**3** **Complete** the fourth column of your table. Write each fraction in simplest form. If the fraction is already in simplest form, write "Simplest form."

## Draw Conclusions
**Write the decimal as a fraction in simplest form.**

**1.** 0.6       **2.** 0.32       **3.** 0.54       **4.** 0.05

**5.** What is the place value of 5 in the decimal 0.125? How would you use the place value to write 0.125 as a fraction with a denominator that is a power of 10? Write 0.125 as a fraction with a denominator that is a power of 10, and as a fraction in simplest form.

**EXPLORE 2** *Write fractions as decimals* · · · · · · · · · · · · · · · · · · ·

**1** **Copy** the table. Complete the second column of your table. Write each fraction as an equivalent fraction with a denominator that is a power of 10.

| Fraction | Equivalent fraction | Words | Decimal |
|----------|---------------------|-------|---------|
| $\frac{2}{5}$ | $\frac{2 \times 2}{5 \times 2} = \frac{4}{10}$ | four tenths | 0.4 |
| $\frac{3}{25}$ | ? | ? | ? |
| $\frac{7}{20}$ | ? | ? | ? |
| $\frac{3}{4}$ | ? | ? | ? |
| $\frac{13}{125}$ | ? | ? | ? |

**2** **Complete** the third column of your table. Write the equivalent fraction from the second column in words.

**3** **Complete** the fourth column of your table. Write each fraction as a decimal.

## Draw Conclusions
**Write the fraction as a decimal.**

**6.** $\frac{4}{5}$

**7.** $\frac{17}{20}$

**8.** $\frac{99}{200}$

**9.** $\frac{26}{125}$

**10.** Would you be able to follow the steps in Explore 2 to write $\frac{4}{15}$ as a decimal? *Explain* your answer.

**11.** In order to write a fraction as a decimal using the method in Explore 2, what must be true about the prime factors of the fraction's denominator? Why?

**12. a.** Divide the numerator of $\frac{12}{25}$ by the denominator.

   **b.** Write the decimal quotient from part (a) as a fraction and simplify. What do you notice?

# Convert Between Fractions and Decimals

## VOCABULARY and CONCEPTS

### Writing Fractions as Decimals

Divide the fraction's numerator by the denominator.

- When a division ends in 0 so that the decimal part of the quotient has a final digit, the quotient is a **terminating decimal**.
- When a division does not end in 0 so that the decimal part of the quotient has one or more digits that repeat without end, the quotient is a **repeating decimal**. Repeating digit(s) can be indicated by bar notation: $0.333\ldots = 0.\overline{3}$.

### Writing Decimals as Fractions

Write the decimal as a fraction with a denominator that is a power of 10. Then simplify the fraction if possible.

## EXAMPLE 1 · Writing Fractions as Terminating Decimals

**a.** Write $\dfrac{9}{25}$ as a decimal.

$$
\begin{array}{r}
0.36 \\
25\overline{)9.00} \\
\underline{7\,5} \\
1\,50 \\
\underline{1\,50} \\
0
\end{array}
$$

**Write zeros in dividend as placeholders.**

**Remainder is 0.**

▸ **Answer** $\dfrac{9}{25} = 0.36$

**b.** Write $4\dfrac{9}{20}$ as a decimal.

$$
\begin{array}{r}
0.45 \\
20\overline{)9.00} \\
\underline{8\,0} \\
1\,00 \\
\underline{1\,00} \\
0
\end{array}
$$

**Write zeros in dividend as placeholders.**

**Remainder is 0.**

▸ **Answer** $4\dfrac{9}{20} = 4 + 0.45 = 4.45$

## EXAMPLE 2 · Writing Fractions as Repeating Decimals

**a.** Write $\dfrac{11}{9}$ as a decimal.

$$
\begin{array}{r}
1.22\ldots \\
9\overline{)11.00} \\
\underline{9} \\
2\,0 \\
\underline{1\,8} \\
20 \\
\underline{18} \\
2
\end{array}
$$

**The digit 2 keeps repeating.**

**Remainder will never be 0.**

▸ **Answer** $\dfrac{11}{9} = 1.\overline{2}$

**b.** Write $\dfrac{26}{99}$ as a decimal.

$$
\begin{array}{r}
0.2626\ldots \\
99\overline{)26.0000} \\
\underline{19\,8} \\
6\,20 \\
\underline{5\,94} \\
260 \\
\underline{198} \\
62
\end{array}
$$

**The digits 2 and 6 keep repeating.**

**Remainder will never be 0.**

▸ **Answer** $\dfrac{26}{99} = 0.\overline{26}$

Gr. 7 NS 1.3 Convert fractions to decimals and percents and use these representations in estimations, computations, and applications.
Gr. 7 NS 1.5 Know that every rational number is either a terminating or a repeating decimal and be able to convert terminating decimals into reduced fractions.

## Practice for Examples 1 and 2

**Write the fraction or mixed number as a decimal.**

**1.** $\dfrac{7}{25}$        **2.** $9\dfrac{3}{20}$        **3.** $\dfrac{10}{11}$

**EXAMPLE 3** *Writing Decimals as Fractions*

**a.** Write 0.72 as a fraction.

$$0.72 = \frac{72}{100}$$
$$= \frac{72 \div 4}{100 \div 4}$$
$$= \frac{18}{25}$$

**2 is in the hundredths' place.**

**b.** Write 5.675 as a mixed number.

$$5.675 = 5\frac{675}{1000}$$
$$= 5\frac{675 \div 25}{1000 \div 25}$$
$$= 5\frac{27}{40}$$

**5 is in the thousandths' place.**

## Practice for Example 3

**Write the decimal as a fraction or mixed number.**

**4.** 0.35        **5.** 0.38        **6.** 3.056

**EXAMPLE 4** *Ordering Numbers*

A fabric store is selling pieces of ribbon. The colors and lengths of the pieces are shown below. Write each length as a decimal. Then order the decimals from least to greatest and tell which piece is the longest.

| Color | Red | Blue | Yellow | Green | Purple |
|---|---|---|---|---|---|
| Length (yards) | $1\dfrac{2}{3}$ | $1\dfrac{5}{8}$ | $1\dfrac{4}{9}$ | $1\dfrac{7}{12}$ | $1\dfrac{5}{16}$ |

### Solution

Red: $1\dfrac{2}{3} = 1.\overline{6}$      Blue: $1\dfrac{5}{8} = 1.625$      Yellow: $1\dfrac{4}{9} = 1.\overline{4}$

Green: $1\dfrac{7}{12} = 1.58\overline{3}$      Purple: $1\dfrac{5}{16} = 1.3125$

▶ **Answer** The order is 1.3125, $1.\overline{4}$, $1.58\overline{3}$, 1.625, and $1.\overline{6}$. Because $1.\overline{6}$ is the greatest decimal, the red piece is the longest.

## Practice for Example 4

**7.** Four friends each bought a bag of trail mix. The bags weighed $1\dfrac{1}{3}$ pounds, $1\dfrac{3}{10}$ pounds, $1\dfrac{5}{16}$ pounds and $1\dfrac{5}{12}$ pounds. Write each weight as a decimal, then order the weights from least to greatest.

**Tell whether the decimal is a *terminating decimal* or a *repeating decimal*.**

**1.** 2.4545

**2.** 4.12125

**3.** 6.767676. . .

**4.** 43.333. . .

**5.** 17.2572

**6.** 8.1919. . .

**Write the fraction or mixed number as a terminating or repeating decimal.**

**7.** $\frac{4}{9}$

**8.** $1\frac{3}{4}$

**9.** $2\frac{1}{3}$

**10.** $5\frac{1}{2}$

**11.** $3\frac{7}{9}$

**12.** $\frac{1}{8}$

**13.** $2\frac{4}{5}$

**14.** $\frac{1}{9}$

**Write the decimal as a fraction or mixed number.**

**15.** 0.7

**16.** 0.35

**17.** 2.375

**18.** 5.125

**19.** 0.1875

**20.** 0.42

**21.** 0.68

**22.** 3.625

**23.** 0.12

**Copy and complete the statement using <, >, or =.**

**24.** $0.75 \underline{\ ?\ } 1\frac{3}{4}$

**25.** $3\frac{1}{2} \underline{\ ?\ } 3.62$

**26.** $2\frac{3}{5} \underline{\ ?\ } 2.6$

**27.** $2.6 \underline{\ ?\ } 2\frac{2}{3}$

**28.** $\frac{3}{50} \underline{\ ?\ } 0.06$

**29.** $\frac{1}{7} \underline{\ ?\ } 0.14$

**Order the numbers from least to greatest.**

**30.** $\frac{1}{2}, 0.3, \frac{2}{5}, 0.6$

**31.** $\frac{3}{4}, 0.6, \frac{13}{20}, 0.7$

**32.** $0.15, \frac{1}{5}, \frac{1}{100}, 0.05$

**33.** $0.30, \frac{1}{3}, 0.35, \frac{1}{4}$

**34.** $0.3, \frac{8}{25}, 0.4, \frac{17}{50}$

**35.** $0.9, \frac{21}{25}, 0.75, \frac{4}{5}$

**36.** Use estimation to approximate 0.24 as a fraction. Use your approximation to compare 0.24 and $\frac{3}{8}$. *Explain* your reasoning.

**37.** At 33.4 miles, the Seikan Tunnel in Japan is one of the world's longest railway tunnels. Write the length as an improper fraction and as a mixed number.

**38.** An athlete threw a shot put $74\frac{1}{4}$ feet. Write the distance as an improper fraction and as a decimal.

**39.** A blueberry bush grows to a height of $\frac{15}{4}$ feet tall. Write the height as a mixed number and as a decimal.

**40.** **REASONING** Find the decimal forms of $\frac{1}{3}, \frac{2}{3}, \frac{3}{3}, \frac{4}{3}, \frac{5}{3}$ and $\frac{6}{3}$. Predict the decimal forms of $\frac{7}{3}, \frac{8}{3}$, and $\frac{9}{3}$.

# Practice

@HomeTutor
classzone.com

**Match the number with its graph on the number line.**

**1.** $2\frac{7}{8}$  **2.** 2.65  **3.** $2.\overline{4}$  **4.** $\frac{61}{20}$

**Write the fraction or mixed number as a decimal. Then tell whether the decimal is a *terminating decimal* or a *repeating decimal*.**

**5.** $\frac{2}{5}$  **6.** $\frac{8}{3}$  **7.** $5\frac{3}{4}$

**8.** $4\frac{2}{9}$  **9.** $\frac{16}{5}$  **10.** $9\frac{11}{20}$

**Rewrite the repeating decimal using bar notation.**

**11.** 0.4444...  **12.** 2.161616...  **13.** 3.67777...  **14.** 4.20303...

**Write the decimal as a fraction or mixed number.**

**15.** 0.6  **16.** 0.18  **17.** 3.25

**18.** 1.375  **19.** 0.125  **20.** 6.34

**Order the numbers from least to greatest.**

**21.** $\frac{2}{5}$, 0.34, $\frac{7}{3}$, 0.3, $0.\overline{3}$  **22.** $\frac{23}{4}$, 5.65, $5\frac{4}{5}$, $5.\overline{6}$  **23.** $\frac{23}{20}$, $1\frac{1}{5}$, 1.01, $1.\overline{15}$

**24.** 3.01, 3.84, $3\frac{41}{50}$, 3.789  **25.** 0.58, $\frac{7}{12}$, 0.67, $\frac{2}{3}$  **26.** 0.1225, $\frac{3}{25}$, $0.1\overline{2}$, $\frac{7}{125}$

**27.** Use estimation and fractions to compare 0.325 and $\frac{7}{15}$. *Explain* your reasoning.

**28.** At 31.35 miles, the English Channel Tunnel is one of the world's longest railway tunnels. Write the length as an improper fraction and as a mixed number.

**29.** You are hiking along the trail shown on the map. You begin at the trailhead and hike to the waterfall. Write a fraction in simplest form that compares the distance from the trailhead to the swinging bridge with the total distance from the trailhead to the waterfall. Then write the fraction as a decimal rounded to the nearest hundredth.

**30. REASONING** Find the decimal forms of $\frac{1}{9}$, $\frac{2}{9}$, $\frac{3}{9}$, and $\frac{4}{9}$. Predict the decimal forms of $\frac{5}{9}$, $\frac{6}{9}$, $\frac{7}{9}$, and $\frac{8}{9}$ based on any pattern you observe. Then check your prediction by calculating the decimal form of each fraction.

## Let's Explore
# Percents, Decimals, and Fractions

**Goal**
Model percents and write percents as decimals and fractions.

**Materials**
- graph paper
- colored pencils

**QUESTION** How can you model percents and write percents as decimals and fractions?

The word *percent* means "per 100." The symbol for percent is %. So 1% represents 1 per 100 or 1 hundredth.

**EXPLORE 1** *Model percents* • • • • • • • • • • • • • • • • • • • • • • •

**1** **Draw** a 10 × 10 grid on graph paper. Think of this as a unit square divided into 100 equal parts.

**2** **Shade** 1 small square. The shaded square represents 1 hundredth or 1%.

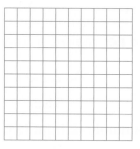

**3** **Shade** 25 small squares. The shaded area represents 25 hundredths or 25%.

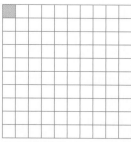

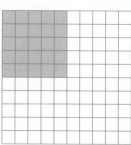

## Draw Conclusions
**Use graph paper to model each percent.**

**1.** 7%          **2.** 13%          **3.** 15%

**4.** How can you model 100%? 200%? *Explain*.

**EXPLORE 2** *Write percents as fractions in simplest form*

**1** **Copy** and complete the table.

| Percent | Words | Fraction | Simplest form |
|---------|-------|----------|---------------|
| 8% | 8 hundredths | $\frac{8}{100}$ | $\frac{2}{25}$ |
| 20% | ? | ? | ? |
| 75% | ? | ? | ? |

## Draw Conclusions

**Write each percent as a fraction in simplest form.**

**5.** 6%                    **6.** 23%                    **7.** 45%

**8.** *Explain* how to write $\frac{1.5}{100}$ with a whole number in the numerator.
Then write 1.5% as a fraction in simplest form.

**EXPLORE 3** *Write percents as decimals* ........................

**1** **Use** the definition of percent to write 3.5% as a fraction.

$$3.5\% = \frac{3.5}{100}$$

**2** **Divide** 3.5 by 100 to write 3.5% as a decimal.

$$
\begin{array}{r}
0.035 \\
100\overline{)3.500} \\
\underline{3\ 00} \\
500 \\
\underline{500} \\
0
\end{array}
$$

3.5% = 0.035

## Draw Conclusions

**Write each percent as a decimal.**

**9.** 53.6%                **10.** 8%                **11.** 70%

**12.** How can you write 3.5% as a decimal by moving the decimal point?

# Write Percents as Fractions and Decimals

## VOCABULARY and CONCEPTS

- A **percent** is a ratio that compares a number to 100. The word *percent* means "per hundred" or "out of 100." The symbol for percent is %. For example, 43% means 43 out of 100.

### Writing Percents as Fractions

Use the definition of percent to write the percent as a fraction with a denominator of 100. Simplify the fraction if possible.

### Writing Percents as Decimals

Write the percent as a fraction with a denominator of 100. Then divide the numerator of the fraction by the denominator.

## EXAMPLE 1  Writing Percents as Fractions

**a.** Write 27% as a fraction.

$$27\% = \frac{27}{100}$$

**b.** Write 45% as a fraction.

$$45\% = \frac{45}{100} = \frac{9}{20}$$

### Practice for Example 1

**Write the percent as a fraction.**

**1.** 17%    **2.** 31%    **3.** 53%

**4.** 2%    **5.** 48%    **6.** 25%

## EXAMPLE 2  Writing Percents as Fractions

**a.** Write 0.5% as a fraction.

$$0.5\% = \frac{0.5}{100}$$
$$= \frac{5}{1000}$$
$$= \frac{1}{200}$$

**b.** Write 135% as a mixed number.

$$135\% = \frac{135}{100}$$
$$= 1\frac{35}{100}$$
$$= 1\frac{7}{20}$$

### Practice for Example 2

**Write the percent as a fraction or mixed number.**

**7.** 125%    **8.** 0.25%    **9.** 240%

**10.** 0.45%    **11.** 0.2%    **12.** 186%

## EXAMPLE 3  Writing a Percent as a Decimal

**Write 15% as a decimal.**

**Method 1**  Write as a fraction first.

$15\% = \dfrac{15}{100}$, so divide 15 by 100.

$$
\begin{array}{r}
0.15 \\
100)\overline{15.00} \\
\underline{10\,0}\phantom{0} \\
5\,00 \\
\underline{5\,00} \\
0
\end{array}
$$

**Method 2**  Move the decimal point. You can obtain the same result as in Method 1 by moving the decimal point 2 places to the left and removing the percent sign.

$15\% = 15\% = 0.15$

▶ **Answer**  $15\% = 0.15$

### Practice for Example 3

**Write the percent as a decimal.**

**13.** 45%          **14.** 160%          **15.** 2.5%

## EXAMPLE 4  Using Circle Graphs with Percents

The circle graph shows the results of a survey of a group of students about which season they prefer. For each season below, write the percent of students preferring that season as a fraction and as a decimal.

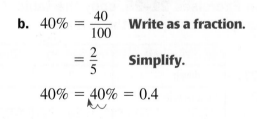

**Favorite Season**
Spring 36%
Summer 18%
Winter 6%
Fall 40%

   **a.** Spring          **b.** Fall

**Solution**

**a.** $36\% = \dfrac{36}{100}$  **Write as a fraction.**

    $= \dfrac{9}{25}$  **Simplify.**

    $36\% = 36\% = 0.36$

**b.** $40\% = \dfrac{40}{100}$  **Write as a fraction.**

    $= \dfrac{2}{5}$  **Simplify.**

    $40\% = 40\% = 0.4$

### Practice for Example 4

**16.** Write the percent of students preferring winter and the percent of students preferring summer as fractions and as decimals.

**Copy and complete the statement.**

1. The word percent means "per _?_ " or "out of _?_ ."

2. To write a percent as a fraction, rewrite the percent as a fraction with a _?_ of 100.

3. To write a percent as a decimal, move the decimal point 2 places to the _?_ and remove the percent sign.

**Match the percent with an equivalent decimal.**

4. 26%                    **A.** 0.0026

5. 260%                   **B.** 0.26

6. 0.26%                  **C.** 2.6

**Write the percent as a fraction or mixed number.**

7. 23%          8. 97%          9. 52%          10. 84%

11. 440%        12. 2.4%        13. 1250%       14. 0.36%

**Write the percent as a decimal.**

15. 65%         16. 245%        17. 37%         18.  0.05%

19. **FIND THE ERROR** *Describe* and correct the error in writing the percent as a fraction.

$$5.5\% = \frac{55}{100}$$
$$= \frac{11}{20}$$

20. In a survey about favorite after-school activities, 33% of the students said that their favorite activity is reading and $\frac{5}{12}$ of the students said that their favorite activity is playing video games. Use estimation to determine which activity is favored by more students. *Explain.*

**In Exercises 21–25, copy the table. Use the circle graph to complete the table.**

|     | Method      | Fraction | Decimal |
|-----|-------------|----------|---------|
| 21. | Are driven  | ?        | ?       |
| 22. | Ride bicycle| ?        | ?       |
| 23. | Take bus    | ?        | ?       |
| 24. | Walk        | ?        | ?       |
| 25. | Other       | ?        | ?       |

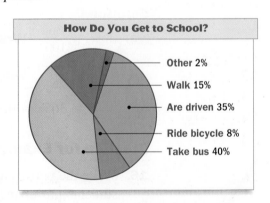

**How Do You Get to School?**

Other 2%
Walk 15%
Are driven 35%
Ride bicycle 8%
Take bus 40%

26. **REASONING** *Explain* how you can write $66\frac{2}{3}\%$ as a decimal by first writing $\frac{2}{3}$ as a decimal.

**Match the percent with an equivalent decimal.**

1. 0.052%
2. 52%
3. 5.2%
4. 0.52%

A. 0.52
B. 0.0052
C. 0.00052
D. 0.052

5. A golfer makes 36% of his putts. Write the percent as a fraction and a decimal.

6. There are 100 employees at a company and 46 are females. What percent of the employees are female? What percent of the employees are not female? *Explain* how you found your answers. Then write each percent as a fraction.

7. Sheila puts 12.5% of her earnings into a savings account. Write the percent as a fraction and a decimal.

**Write the percent as a fraction or mixed number.**

8. 47%
9. 96%
10. 70%
11. 15.5%
12. 235%
13. 110.2%
14. 0.24%
15. 5.2%

**Write the percent as a decimal.**

16. 31%
17. 354%
18. 6.25%
19. 0.98%

20. In a survey about favorite fruits, 27% of the students said that apples are their favorite fruit and $\frac{1}{5}$ of the students said that oranges are their favorite fruit. Use estimation to determine which fruit is favored by more students. *Explain* your reasoning.

**In Exercises 21–25, copy the table. Use the circle graph to complete the table.**

|  | Activity | Fraction | Decimal |
|---|---|---|---|
| 21. | Classes | ? | ? |
| 22. | Studying | ? | ? |
| 23. | Soccer | ? | ? |
| 24. | Softball | ? | ? |
| 25. | Lunch | ? | ? |

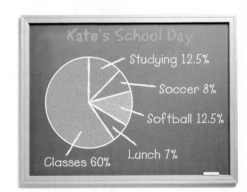

Kate's School Day

Studying 12.5%
Soccer 8%
Softball 12.5%
Lunch 7%
Classes 60%

26. **REASONING** *Explain* how you can write $33\frac{1}{3}\%$ as a fraction by first writing $33\frac{1}{3}$ over 100.

# Let's Explore
## Writing Decimals and Fractions as Percents

**Goal**
Use models to write decimals and
fractions as percents.

**Materials**
• graph paper
• colored pencils

**QUESTION** **How can you use a 10 × 10 grid to write decimals or fractions
as percents?**

In this activity you will shade parts of a 10 × 10 grid (a unit square
divided into 100 equal parts) to represent decimals or fractions, then write
the decimals or fractions as percents.

**EXPLORE 1** *Use a model to write a decimal as a percent*

**Write 0.27 as a percent.**

**1** **Shade** a 10 × 10 grid.
The large square is a unit square,
so each small square represents
1 hundredth. Because 0.27 is
27 hundredths, shade 27 squares.

**2** **Write** a percent.
Each small square represents 1%,
so the shaded area represents 27%.
0.27 = 27%

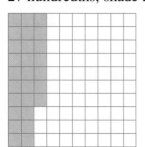
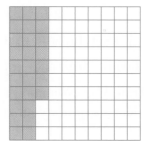

## Draw Conclusions
**Copy and complete the table. Draw a 10 × 10 grid to represent each
decimal.**

| | Decimal | Number of hundredths | Shaded squares | Percent |
|---|---|---|---|---|
| **1.** | 0.04 | ? | ? | ? |
| **2.** | 0.18 | ? | ? | ? |
| **3.** | 0.38 | ? | ? | ? |

**4.** How many small squares would you shade to represent the
number 1? Use your answer to write the number 1 as a percent.

**EXPLORE 2** *Use a model to write a fraction as a percent*

Write the fractions $\frac{1}{2}$, $\frac{2}{5}$, and $\frac{3}{4}$ as percents.

**1** **Use** 10 × 10 grids to represent the fractions.

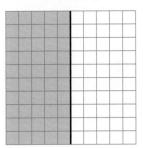 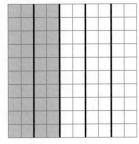 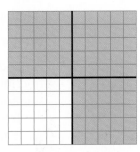

The 10 × 10 grid is divided into 2 equal parts, and 1 part is shaded.

The 10 × 10 grid is divided into 5 equal parts, and 2 parts are shaded.

The 10 × 10 grid is divided into 4 equal parts, and 3 parts are shaded.

**2** **Write** percents. Copy and complete the table using the grids in Step 1.

| Fraction | Squares shaded | Percent |
|----------|----------------|---------|
| $\frac{1}{2}$ | 50 out of 100 | ? |
| $\frac{2}{5}$ | ? | ? |
| $\frac{3}{4}$ | ? | ? |

# Draw Conclusions
**Use a 10 × 10 grid to write the fraction as a percent.**

**5.** $\frac{1}{4}$　　　　**6.** $\frac{4}{5}$　　　　**7.** $\frac{3}{10}$　　　　**8.** $\frac{7}{10}$

**9.** *Explain* why you cannot use the method in Explore 2 to write $\frac{1}{3}$ as a percent.

**10.** Can you use the method in Explore 2 to *approximate* the percent equivalent of $\frac{1}{3}$? *Explain.*

**11.** Explore 2 suggests a method of writing a fraction as a percent using an equivalent fraction. *Describe* this method and give an example.

# Write Decimals and Fractions as Percents

## VOCABULARY and CONCEPTS

- numerator, p. 483
- denominator, p. 483

### Writing Decimals as Percents

First write the decimal as a fraction with a denominator of 100. You may need to multiply or divide both the numerator and denominator of the fraction by a power of 10. Then write the fraction as a percent.

### Writing Fractions as Percents

If the denominator of the fraction is a divisor of 100, rewrite the fraction with a denominator of 100. If the denominator of the fraction is *not* a divisor of 100, write the decimal equivalent of the fraction or a decimal approximation of the fraction first, then write the decimal as a percent.

---

**EXAMPLE 1** *Writing Decimals as Percents*

**Write the decimal as a percent.**

**a.** $0.24 = \dfrac{24}{100}$

$= 24\%$

**b.** $0.3 = \dfrac{3}{10}$

$= \dfrac{30}{100}$

$= 30\%$

**c.** $0.015 = \dfrac{15}{1000}$

$= \dfrac{1.5}{100}$

$= 1.5\%$

You can obtain the same results by moving the decimal point 2 places to the right and adding a percent sign. You may need to add zeros.

$0.24 = 0.24$

$= 24\%$

$0.3 = 0.30$

$= 30\%$

$0.015 = 0.015$

$= 1.5\%$

### Practice for Example 1

**Write the decimal as a percent.**

**1.** 0.53     **2.** 0.7     **3.** 0.0175     **4.** 0.003

---

**EXAMPLE 2** *Writing Fractions as Percents*

**Write the fraction as a percent.**

**a.** $\dfrac{9}{25} = \dfrac{36}{100}$    **Write equivalent fraction.**

$= 36\%$    **Write as a percent.**

**b.** $\dfrac{7}{50} = \dfrac{14}{100}$    **Write equivalent fraction.**

$= 14\%$    **Write as a percent.**

## Practice for Example 2

**Write the fraction as a percent.**

**5.** $\dfrac{1}{4}$      **6.** $\dfrac{7}{100}$      **7.** $\dfrac{7}{20}$      **8.** $\dfrac{2}{5}$

**EXAMPLE 3** *Writing Fractions as Percents* ....................

**Write the fraction as a percent. Round to the nearest tenth of a percent if necessary.**

   **a.** $\dfrac{5}{8} = 0.625$      **Write as a decimal.**

       $= 62.5\%$      **Write as a percent.**

   **b.** $\dfrac{8}{9} \approx 0.889$      **Write as a decimal rounded to the nearest thousandth.**

       $= 88.9\%$      **Write as a percent.**

## Practice for Example 3

**Write the fraction as a percent. Round to the nearest tenth of a percent if necessary.**

**9.** $\dfrac{7}{8}$      **10.** $\dfrac{3}{16}$      **11.** $\dfrac{4}{7}$      **12.** $\dfrac{8}{11}$

**EXAMPLE 4** *Writing Decimals and Fractions as Percents* ....

In a survey of 200 students about favorite pizza toppings, 0.13 of the students said that their favorite topping is cheese, and $\dfrac{1}{8}$ said that their favorite topping is pepperoni. Which group represents a greater percent of those surveyed?

### Solution

Write each number as a percent.

Cheese: $0.13 = 13\%$          Pepperoni: $\dfrac{1}{8} = 0.125 = 12.5\%$

▶ **Answer** Since $13\% > 12.5\%$, the students whose favorite pizza topping is cheese represent a greater percent of those surveyed.

## Practice for Example 4

**13.** In the same survey, 0.24 of the students said that their favorite topping is mushroom, and $\dfrac{1}{5}$ said that their favorite topping is sausage. Which group represents a greater percent of those surveyed?

# Practice

Extra Practice
p. 500

**Match the fraction with the equivalent percent.**

**1.** $\frac{1}{5}$　　　　　　　**A.** 75%

**2.** $\frac{3}{4}$　　　　　　　**B.** 50%

**3.** $\frac{1}{8}$　　　　　　　**C.** 20%

**4.** $\frac{1}{2}$　　　　　　　**D.** 12.5%

**Write the fraction or decimal as a percent. Round percents to the nearest tenth of a percent if necessary.**

**5.** $\frac{27}{50}$ 　　　　**6.** 0.4 　　　　**7.** 0.04 　　　　**8.** $\frac{1}{4}$

**9.** $\frac{9}{10}$ 　　　　**10.** $\frac{13}{25}$ 　　　　**11.** 0.082 　　　　**12.** 0.75

**13.** $\frac{457}{1000}$ 　　**14.** $\frac{163}{1000}$ 　　**15.** $\frac{3}{8}$ 　　　　**16.** $\frac{7}{16}$

**17.** $\frac{5}{9}$ 　　　　**18.** $\frac{7}{15}$ 　　　　**19.** $\frac{3}{11}$ 　　　　**20.** $\frac{9}{16}$

**21.** Three of the five children in a family are girls. What percent of the children are girls?

**22.** A baseball player hit 15 home runs out of the 24 swings he took in a home run derby. What percent of his swings resulted in home runs?

**23.** On an English test you scored $\frac{43}{50}$. Your friend scored 85%. Which score was better?

**24.** Use estimation and percents to compare $\frac{153}{302}$ and 45%. *Explain* your reasoning.

**In Exercises 25–28, use the circle graph, which shows the results of a survey of students' favorite colors.**

**25.** Which color did the greatest percent of students choose?

**26.** Which color did the least percent of students choose?

**27.** Did a greater percent of students choose red or blue?

**28.** Did a greater percent of students choose yellow or purple?

**29.** **REASONING** The fraction $\frac{1}{4}$ is equivalent to 25%. *Explain* how you can use that fact to write $\frac{1}{8}$ as a percent.

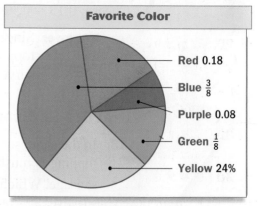

**Favorite Color**

Red 0.18

Blue $\frac{3}{8}$

Purple 0.08

Green $\frac{1}{8}$

Yellow 24%

# Practice

**Write the fraction or decimal as a percent. Round percents to the nearest tenth of a percent if necessary.**

**1.** $\frac{1}{2}$

**2.** 0.2

**3.** 0.37

**4.** $\frac{47}{50}$

**5.** $\frac{17}{20}$

**6.** $\frac{4}{5}$

**7.** 0.146

**8.** 0.02

**9.** $\frac{563}{1000}$

**10.** $\frac{801}{1000}$

**11.** $\frac{4}{1}$

**12.** $\frac{7}{1}$

**13.** $\frac{11}{18}$

**14.** $\frac{19}{45}$

**15.** $\frac{10}{111}$

**16.** $\frac{9}{13}$

**Use a number line to order the numbers from least to greatest.**

**17.** 55%, $\frac{1}{2}$, 0.53

**18.** 0.47, 41%, $\frac{2}{5}$

**19.** $\frac{13}{20}$, 69%, 0.61

**20.** 37%, $\frac{3}{8}$, 0.38

**Each figure is divided into equal parts. Find the percent of the figure that is shaded.**

**21.**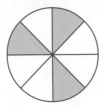

**22.**

**23.**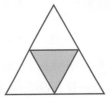

**24.** A group of people were asked their favorite flavor of yogurt from among strawberry, blueberry, and peach. The answers were as follows: strawberry, $\frac{7}{16}$; blueberry, 0.25; peach, $\frac{5}{16}$. Write each fraction or decimal as a percent.

**25.** In a survey of 503 people about favorite household pets, 204 of the people said that their favorite pet is a dog, and 30% said that their favorite pet is a cat. Use estimation to determine which group represents a greater percent of those surveyed. *Explain.*

**In Exercises 26–29, use the circle graph, which shows the results of a survey about museums.**

**26.** Which type of museum was most preferred?

**27.** Which type of museum was least preferred?

**28.** Did a greater percent of those surveyed prefer a natural history museum or a science museum?

**29.** What percent of those surveyed preferred either a science museum or an art museum?

**30.** **REASONING** The fraction $\frac{1}{8}$ is equivalent to 12.5%.

*Explain* how you can use that fact to write $\frac{3}{16}$ as a percent.

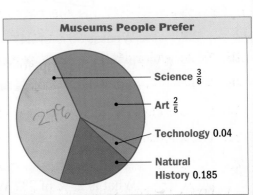

**Museums People Prefer**

Science $\frac{3}{8}$

Art $\frac{2}{5}$

Technology 0.04

Natural History 0.185

# Activity 3.7

## Let's Explore

### Finding a Percent of a Number

**Goal**
Use models to find percents of numbers.

**Materials**
• graph paper
• centimeter ruler

**QUESTION** **How can you use a model to find a percent of a number?**

In this activity, you will make and use percent models. The percent model below represents the number 68. The left end of the model represents 0% of 68, or 0. The right end of the model represents 100% of 68, or 68.

0                                       68

**EXPLORE 1** *Find percents of a number by folding* ..........

**Find 25%, 50%, and 75% of 24.**

**1** **Make** a percent model for the number 24. Use graph paper to cut a strip of paper 24 grid squares long. Number the squares from 1 to 24.

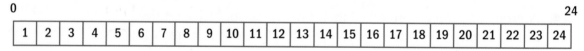

0                                                24

| 1 | 2 | 3 | 4 | 5 | 6 | 7 | 8 | 9 | 10 | 11 | 12 | 13 | 14 | 15 | 16 | 17 | 18 | 19 | 20 | 21 | 22 | 23 | 24 |

What is 0% of 24? What is 100% of 24?

**2** **Fold** the strip in half, then unfold. The fold line represents 50% of 24.

| 1 | 2 | 3 | 4 | 5 | 6 | 7 | 8 | 9 | 10 | 11 | 12 |

What is 50% of 24?

**3** **Refold** the strip, fold the strip in half again, then unfold. The new fold lines represent 25% of 24 and 75% of 24.

What is 25% of 24? What is 75% of 24?

## Draw Conclusions

**1.** Make a percent model for the number 20. Use the model to find 25%, 50%, and 75% of 20.

**2.** On a percent model, 50% is halfway between 0% and 100%, and 25% is halfway between 0% and 50%. *Explain* how to use paper folding to find 12.5% of 24.

**EXPLORE 2** *Find and estimate percents of a number* .......

**Find 30% of 75, and estimate 58% of 75.**

**1** **Draw** a rectangle 10 centimeters long and 1 centimeter high. Divide the rectangle into 10 squares, each 1 centimeter wide. Label the rectangle as shown.

| 0 | | | | | | | | | | 75 |
|---|---|---|---|---|---|---|---|---|---|---|

**2** **Use** the decimal equivalent of 10% to label the model. Since $0.10 \times 75 = 7.5$, 10% of 75 is 7.5. You can use multiples of 7.5 to finish labeling your model. The first few labels are shown. Complete the labels.

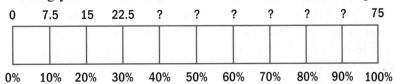

**3** **Use** the model to find or estimate a percent of 75. For example, from the model you can see that 30% of 75 is 22.5. As another example, you can estimate that 58% of 75 is about 60% of 75, or about 45.

## Draw Conclusions

**3.** Use the model in Explore 2 to find 40% of 75 and to estimate 81% of 75.

**4.** Use a percent model to find 60% of 55 and to estimate 19% of 55.

**5.** *Explain* how you could change the model in Steps 1–3 of Explore 2 to find percents of 120 using fractions instead of decimals. Use the model to find 20% of 120.

# Find a Percent of a Number

## VOCABULARY and CONCEPTS

- percent, p. 134

### Finding Percents of Numbers

To find a percent of a number, you can change the percent to a decimal and multiply by the number, or you can change the percent to a fraction and multiply by the number.

| Fifths | Fourths | Thirds |
|---|---|---|
| $20\% = 0.2 = \frac{1}{5}$ | $25\% = 0.25 = \frac{1}{4}$ | $33\frac{1}{3}\% = 0.\overline{3} = \frac{1}{3}$ |
| $40\% = 0.4 = \frac{2}{5}$ | $50\% = 0.5 = \frac{1}{2}$ | $66\frac{2}{3}\% = 0.\overline{6} = \frac{2}{3}$ |
| $60\% = 0.6 = \frac{3}{5}$ | $75\% = 0.75 = \frac{3}{4}$ | (See Ex. 26 on p. 136 and Ex. 26 on p. 137.) |
| $80\% = 0.8 = \frac{4}{5}$ | | |

### Estimating Percents of Numbers

To estimate a percent of a number, you can estimate the percent using a fraction or a decimal. You may also want to round the number.

### Simple Interest Formula

*Interest* is the amount paid for the use of money. The amount owed or borrowed is the *principal*. The *annual interest rate* is the percent of the principal earned or paid per year. Interest paid only on the principal is *simple interest*. A formula for calculating simple interest from the principal $P$, annual interest rate $r$, and time $t$ (in years) is $I = Prt$.

---

**EXAMPLE 1** *Finding a Percent of a Number* · · · · · · · · · · · · · ·

**a.** Find 30% of 50. Use a fraction.

$$30\% \text{ of } 50 = \frac{3}{10} \times 50 = \frac{150}{10} = 15$$

**b.** Find 60% of 35. Use a decimal.

$$60\% \text{ of } 35 = 0.6 \times 35 = 21$$

### Practice for Example 1

**Find the percent of the number. Use a fraction.**

**1.** 25% of 16  **2.** 8% of 60  **3.** 40% of 25  **4.** 60% of 15

**Find the percent of the number. Use a decimal.**

**5.** 75% of 24  **6.** 70% of 80  **7.** 15% of 60  **8.** 4% of 125

**EXAMPLE 2** *Estimating Percents of Numbers* •••••••••••••

**a.** Estimate 65% of 48.

$$65\% \approx 66\frac{2}{3}\% = \frac{2}{3}$$

$$65\% \text{ of } 48 \approx \frac{2}{3} \times 48 = 32$$

**b.** Estimate 21% of 48.

$$21\% \approx 20\% = 0.2$$

$$21\% \text{ of } 48 \approx 0.2 \times 48 = 9.6$$

**EXAMPLE 3** *Finding a Discount* ••••••••••••••••••••••

Your sister buys a shirt that costs $24. She gets a 15% discount. What is the sale price of the shirt?

**Solution**

**Step 1** Find the amount of the discount.

$$15\% \text{ of } \$24.00 = 0.15 \times \$24.00$$
$$= \$3.60$$

**Step 2** Subtract the discount from the cost of the item.

$$\$24.00 - \$3.60 = \$20.40$$

▶ **Answer** The sale price of the shirt is $20.40.

**Practice for Examples 2 and 3**

**9.** Estimate 35% of 63.

**10.** Estimate 39% of 63.

**11.** The price of a video game is $18. Find the cost including a discount of 6%.

**EXAMPLE 4** *Finding Simple Interest* •••••••••••••••••

You deposit $120 in an account that earns simple interest at an annual rate of 3.5%. What amount of interest will you earn on that money in 2 years?

**Solution**

$$I = Prt$$      **Write the simple interest formula.**

$$= 120(0.035)(2)$$      **Substitute values, writing 3.5% as a decimal.**

$$= 8.40$$      **Multiply.**

▶ **Answer** You will earn $8.40 in simple interest in 2 years.

**Practice for Example 4**

**Find the simple interest for the given values.**

**12.** $P = \$230$, $r = 3\%$, $t = 4$ years

**13.** $P = \$190$, $r = 4.5\%$, $t = 5$ years

# A Practice

Extra Practice
p. 500

**Find the percent of the number.**

| | | |
|---|---|---|
| **1.** 20% of 40 | **2.** 15% of 20 | **3.** 30% of 70 |
| **4.** 10% of 90 | **5.** 22% of 50 | **6.** 58% of 25 |
| **7.** 81% of 130 | **8.** $66\frac{2}{3}$% of 36 | **9.** $33\frac{1}{3}$% of 72 |
| **10.** 45% of 30 | **11.** 20% of 95 | **12.** 27% of 60 |

**13.** You deposit $150 in an account that earns simple interest. The annual interest rate is 3.2%. How much interest will you earn in 3 years?

**14.** You are buying a CD that costs $15. There is a 6% sales tax on the CD. What is the tax on your purchase?

**15.** You buy a shirt that is on sale for 30% off the original price. The original price is $17. How much do you save?

**16.** Shannon pays an 8% sales tax on a DVD that costs $22.00. What is the tax on her purchase?

**Estimate the percent of the number.**

| | | |
|---|---|---|
| **17.** 12% of 40 | **18.** 49% of 130 | **19.** 21% of 80 |
| **20.** 9% of 58 | **21.** 75% of 884 | **22.** 88% of 110 |
| **23.** 19% of 61 | **24.** 81.5% of 140 | **25.** 38% of 112 |
| **26.** 19.5% of 375 | **27.** 62% of 230 | **28.** 28% of 160 |

**29.** Angela deposits $500 in an account that earns simple interest at an annual rate of 3.4%. Find the total amount in the account, including the principal and the interest, after 2 years.

**30.** The bill at a restaurant comes to $45.90 for you and four friends. You leave a tip of 20% of the bill. What is the total cost of the meal?

**31.** You want to purchase a new sweater for $28. You have $30 to spend on the sweater. There is also a 5% sales tax. Will you have enough money to pay for the sweater and the sales tax? *Explain.*

**32.** Summer tennis lessons offered by a town's recreation department cost $15 per lesson. If you sign up before May 15, you get a 15% discount. Josh signed up before May 15. How much does he pay for a lesson?

**33.** **REASONING** A shirt that costs $42 is discounted 32%. Dee multiplies the price by $\frac{1}{3}$ to estimate the amount discounted, while Bobby multiplies the price by 0.30. Which estimate is closer to the actual amount of the discount?

**Find the percent of the number.**

1. 10% of 84

2. 5% of 20

3. 25% of 44

4. 37% of 50

5. 72% of 90

6. 12% of 16

7. 61% of 130

8. 15% of 152

9. $66\frac{2}{3}$% of 54

10. 55% of 50

11. 22% of 90

12. 37% of 40

13. You are buying six notebooks that total $10.94. There is a 5% sales tax. What is the amount of the tax?

14. Regina deposits $250 in an account that earns simple interest. The annual interest rate is 2.9%. Estimate the amount of interest she earns in 2 years.

15. The regular price for a pair of jeans is $36. The sale price is 45% off the regular price. How much do you save by buying the jeans on sale?

16. Miguel pays a 7.5% sales tax on a book that costs $14. What is the tax on his purchase?

**A coat costs $150. Find the savings based on the sale described.**

17. 20% off

18. 25% off

19. 50% off

**Estimate the percent of the number.**

20. 8% of 52

21. 76% of 2000

22. 19% of 120

23. 2% of 495

24. 24% of 84

25. 11% of 570

26. 42% of 59

27. 76.5% of 120

28. 68% of 220

29. 31% of 80

30. 89% of 210

31. 5.5% of 1500

32. Larry plans to deposit $800 in an account that earns simple interest. His goal is to have $900 in the account after 3 years. Suppose the annual interest rate is 4%. Will he meet his goal? *Explain.*

33. You and your family eat at a restaurant and the total bill is $62. You have a coupon for 10% off. After taking 10% off, you leave a tip of 20% of the resulting amount. How much do you leave for a tip?

34. Anya wants to purchase a travel bag listed at $45. She receives a discount of 30% off the price before tax. The tax rate is 6%. She has $32 in cash with her. Is that enough to purchase the bag? What is the cost of the bag including tax?

35. **REASONING** Students are asked to estimate 22% of 90. One student multiplies 90 by $\frac{2}{9}$ and another student multiplies 90 by 0.2. Which estimate is closer? *Explain.*

# Problem Solving and Reasoning

## Problem

A person selling an item through an online auction website pays a fee based on the closing price of the item. The person pays 5% of the first $25 of the closing price and 3% of the remaining closing price. Suppose an item has a closing price of $40.

• What percent of the entire closing price does the fee represent?

• Does this percent increase, decrease, or stay the same as the closing price of an item increases? *Explain.*

## Solution

Break a problem into parts as part of MR 1.3, and make precise calculations as part of MR 2.8.

**1** **Calculate** the fee for a closing price of $40. To find the fee, you need to calculate 5% of $25 and add this to 3% of the difference of $40 and $25.

For the first $25:     $0.05 \cdot \$25 = \$1.25$

For the remaining $15:   $0.03 \cdot \$15 = \$.45$

The fee is $\$1.25 + \$.45 = \$1.70$.

**2** **Write** the fee as a percent of the closing price.

$$\frac{1.70}{40} = \frac{17}{400} = 0.0425 = 4.25\%$$

**3** **Find** the percent as the closing price increases. From the table below, you can see that as the closing price increases, the percent of the closing price that the fee represents decreases.

Use a table to explain mathematical reasoning as part of MR 2.5.

| Closing price | 5% of first $25 | 3% of remaining closing price | Fee | Fee as a percent of closing price |
|---|---|---|---|---|
| $40 | $1.25 | $.45 | $1.70 | 4.25% |
| $50 | $1.25 | $.75 | $2.00 | 4.00% |
| $60 | $1.25 | $1.05 | $2.30 | 3.83% |
| $70 | $1.25 | $1.35 | $2.60 | 3.71% |

Check the validity of the results from the context of the problem as part of MR 2.8.

**4** **Check** the validity of the results.

It makes sense that the fee is 4.25% of the $40 closing price because 4.25% is between 3% and 5%.

It also makes sense that the percent of the closing price that the fee represents decreases because as the closing price increases, the 3% is applied to a greater portion of the closing price.

# Practice

1. The rental prices at a video store are given below. You want to rent a console, 3 video games, and 4 controllers. **MR 1.1, MR 2.7**

   | 5-Day Rental Prices | |
   | --- | --- |
   | Movie | $4.88 |
   | Video game | $5.64 |
   | Video game console (with 2 controllers) | $19.95 |
   | Extra controller | $2.29 |

   a. Use estimation to determine the amount of money you should bring to cover your costs. *Explain* how you know that your costs are covered.

   b. Would making an estimate by rounding the prices to the nearest ten cents first give an appropriate answer? Why or why not?

   c. What is an advantage to using estimation in this situation? What is an advantage of finding an exact answer?

2. Suppose a state taxes its residents at a rate of 5% on the first $10,000 of taxable income, then at a rate of 10% on all taxable income over $10,000. Calculate the tax for $30,000 in taxable income. What percent of the entire taxable income does the tax represent? Does this percent increase, decrease, or stay the same as taxable income increases? *Explain.* **MR 1.3, MR 2.5, MR 2.8**

3. Show that $66\frac{2}{3}\% = \frac{2}{3}$. Then write $20\frac{4}{9}\%$ as a fraction in simplest form. **MR 2.6, MR 3.2**

4. At a community center's yard sale, 15% of all sales go to the center. You are selling a lamp that you bought for $20. What is the lowest whole dollar price for which you can sell the lamp and not lose money? *Explain.* **MR 2.5, MR 2.8**

5. A 15% tip can be calculated mentally by finding 10% of a total bill and then adding half of that amount. **MR 2.7, MR 3.2**

   a. Use the method described above to find a 15% tip for a total bill of $64.

   b. How can you mentally calculate a 20% tip for a total bill of $35?

   c. Suppose you want to leave a tip of about 15% for a restaurant bill of $87.85. Approximate the tip and explain your method. Then calculate the tip to the nearest cent to check your approximation.

6. The circle graph shows student participation in fall sports at a middle school. **MR 2.3**

   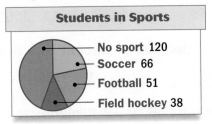

   a. Estimate the percent of students at the middle school who play soccer.

   b. Calculate the percent of students at the middle school who play soccer. How does this percent compare with the estimate you made in part (a)?

7. The original price of a suit at a store is $150. The price is marked down by 20% for a sale. For a final sale, the sale price is marked down by an additional 50%. **MR 1.2, MR 2.5**

   a. Let one paper clip represent $5. Model the original price of the suit using paper clips. Then find the final sale price of the suit using the paper clips.

   b. Can the final sale price of the suit be found by calculating a 70% markdown of the original price? *Explain.*

# Chapter 3 Review Game

## Letter Scramble

Copy the squares below onto graph paper. Then solve the problems below. Write each of your answers in the corresponding blank on a square. Cut out the squares. Pair up sides of squares that have equal or equivalent answers. For example: 0.43 would pair with 43%; $\frac{3}{10}$ would pair with 0.3; $\frac{1}{5}$ would pair with 20%. When you have paired up all the sides, read the words that complete this sentence "I'm at school, and $\underline{?}$ $\underline{?}$ $\underline{?}$."

**Evaluate the expression.**

1. $42.5 - 30.44$
2. $21.02 + 9.32$
3. $3.52 + 8.9$
4. $0.6 \cdot 2.5$
5. $4 \cdot 0.003$
6. $2.3 \cdot 5.4$
7. $0.65 \div 0.25$
8. $12.096 \div 4.2$

**Write the fraction, mixed number, or percent as a decimal.**

9. $\frac{3}{8}$
10. $\frac{5}{8}$
11. $2\frac{3}{5}$
12. $37.5\%$
13. $150\%$
14. $1.2\%$

**Write the decimal or percent as a fraction.**

15. $0.8$
16. $0.26$
17. $80\%$
18. $62.5\%$

**Find the percent of the number.**

19. $67\%$ of 18
20. $82\%$ of 37
21. $24\%$ of 12
22. $25\%$ of 1.04

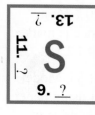

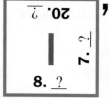

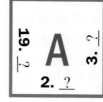

# Chapter Summary and Review

**VOCABULARY**
- terminating decimal, p. 128
- repeating decimal, p. 128

- percent, p. 134

**Vocabulary Exercises**

1. Copy and complete: A __?__ is a ratio that compares a number to 100.

2. Give an example of a fraction that can be written as a terminating decimal.

**3.1** *Add and Subtract Decimals* ........................... *pp. 108–111*

To add and subtract decimals, line up the decimal points. Then add or subtract as with whole numbers and bring down the decimal point. Add zeros to help line up the digits.

**EXAMPLES**

$$\begin{array}{r} 5.23 \\ + 13.60 \\ \hline 18.83 \end{array} \qquad \begin{array}{r} ^7 8.\!^12 7 \\ - 6.45 \\ \hline 1.82 \end{array}$$

**Find the sum or difference.**

3. $1.86 + 0.98$
4. $0.821 + 6.07$
5. $76.1 - 12.4$
6. $3.3 - 2.51$

**Evaluate the expression when $x = 6.75$ and $y = 9.3$.**

7. $35.44 + x$
8. $27.1 - y$
9. $x + y$
10. $y - x$

**3.2** *Multiply Decimals* ........................... *pp. 114–117*

Multiply decimals as you do whole numbers. Then place the decimal point. The number of decimal places in the product is the sum of the number of decimal places in the factors.

**EXAMPLE**

$$\begin{array}{r} 7.04 \quad \text{2 decimal places} \\ \times \ 3.2 \quad \text{1 decimal place} \\ \hline 1408 \\ 2112 \\ \hline 22.528 \quad \text{2 + 1 = 3. So, product has 3 decimal places.} \end{array}$$

**Find the product. Use estimation to check that your answer is reasonable.**

11. $2.7 \times 9.8$
12. $0.25 \times 1.87$
13. $4.22 \times 6.1$
14. $7.3 \times 3.09$

15. Find the area of a rectangle that has a length of 8.04 meters and a width of 3.1 meters.

# Chapter Summary and Review

**3.3** Divide Decimals.........................................pp. 120–123

When you divide a decimal by a whole number, place the decimal point in the quotient above the decimal point in the dividend. When you divide by a decimal, multiply both the divisor and the dividend by a power of 10 that will make the divisor a whole number.

**EXAMPLE**    **Find the quotient 5.22 ÷ 0.6.**

Because $0.6 \times 10 = 6$, multiply the divisor and the dividend by 10. Move the decimal points 1 place.

$$0.6\overline{)5.22} \implies 6\overline{)52.2} \quad \frac{8.7}{}$$

**Find the quotient. Then check your answer.**

**16.** $0.3\overline{)18}$      **17.** $3.2\overline{)64}$      **18.** $49.5 \div 1.5$      **19.** $29.92 \div 4.4$

**3.4** Convert between Fractions and Decimals.........pp. 128–131

**WRITING FRACTIONS AS DECIMALS** Divide the fraction's numerator by the denominator.

**EXAMPLE**    $\dfrac{5}{8} \implies 8\overline{)5.000}\;\dfrac{0.625}{} \implies$ So, $\dfrac{5}{8} = 0.625$.

**WRITING DECIMALS AS FRACTIONS** First write the decimal as a fraction with a denominator that is a power of 10. Then simplify the fraction if possible.

**EXAMPLE**    $0.44 = \dfrac{44}{100} = \dfrac{11}{25}$

**Write the fraction or mixed number as a terminating or repeating decimal.**

**20.** $\dfrac{7}{8}$      **21.** $\dfrac{7}{9}$      **22.** $8\dfrac{3}{20}$      **23.** $4\dfrac{5}{6}$

**Write the decimal as a fraction or mixed number.**

**24.** $0.8$      **25.** $0.55$      **26.** $6.2$      **27.** $1.05$

**3.5** Write Percents as Fractions and Decimals.........pp. 134–137

**WRITING PERCENTS AS FRACTIONS** Use the definition of percent to write the percent as a fraction with a denominator of 100. Simplify the fraction if possible.

**EXAMPLE**    $18\% = \dfrac{18}{100} = \dfrac{9}{50}$

**WRITING PERCENTS AS DECIMALS** Write the percent as a fraction with a denominator of 100. Then divide the numerator of the fraction by the denominator.

**EXAMPLE** $35\% = \dfrac{35}{100}$ ➡ $100\overline{)35.00}^{\,0.35}$ ➡ So, $35\% = 0.35$.

**Write the percent as a fraction or mixed number.**

**28.** 36%          **29.** 4%          **30.** 80%          **31.** 110%

**Write the percent as a decimal.**

**32.** 22%          **33.** 1%          **34.** 125%          **35.** 230%

## 3.6 Write Decimals and Fractions as Percents ...... pp. 140–143

**WRITING DECIMALS AS PERCENTS** First write the decimal as a fraction with a denominator of 100. You may need to multiply or divide both the numerator and denominator of the fraction by a power of 10. Then write the fraction as a percent.

**EXAMPLE** $0.065 = \dfrac{65}{1000} = \dfrac{65 \div 10}{1000 \div 10} = \dfrac{6.5}{100} = 6.5\%$

**WRITING FRACTIONS AS PERCENTS** If the denominator of the fraction is a divisor of 100, rewrite the fraction with a denominator of 100. If the denominator of the fraction is *not* a divisor of 100, write the decimal equivalent of the fraction or a decimal approximation of the fraction first, then write the decimal as a percent.

**EXAMPLE** $\dfrac{7}{10} = \dfrac{7 \times 10}{10 \times 10} = \dfrac{70}{100} = 70\%$

**Write the decimal or fraction as a percent.**

**36.** 0.21          **37.** 0.078          **38.** $\dfrac{33}{50}$          **39.** $\dfrac{1}{8}$

## 3.7 Find a Percent of a Number ..................... pp. 146–149

To find a percent of a number, you can change the percent to a fraction and multiply by the number, or you can change the percent to a decimal and multiply by the number.

**EXAMPLES** $25\%$ of $12 = \dfrac{1}{4} \times 12 = \dfrac{12}{4} = 3$

$8\%$ of $26 = 0.08 \times 26 = 2.08$

**Find the percent of the number.**

**40.** 30% of 180          **41.** 75% of 36          **42.** 42% of 15          **43.** 85% of 140

# Chapter Test

**Find the sum or difference.**

**1.** $3.5 + 4.23$      **2.** $9.15 + 6.59$      **3.** $5 - 2.34$      **4.** $12.391 - 7.47$

**Find the product. Use estimation to check that your answer is reasonable.**

**5.** $3 \times 1.3$      **6.** $5 \times 2.54$      **7.** $0.36 \times 1.24$      **8.** $6.39 \times 5.482$

**Find (a) the perimeter and (b) the area of the rectangle.**

**9.**
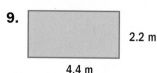
2.2 m

4.4 m

**10.**

2.41 mm

3.36 mm

**Find the quotient. Then check your answer.**

**11.** $12.56 \div 3$      **12.** $9.28 \div 0.5$      **13.** $4.0125 \div 1.25$      **14.** $0.568 \div 0.4$

**Write the fraction or mixed number as a decimal.**

**15.** $\dfrac{5}{8}$      **16.** $3\dfrac{2}{3}$      **17.** $\dfrac{7}{12}$      **18.** $6\dfrac{3}{5}$

**Write the decimal as a fraction or mixed number.**

**19.** $0.9$      **20.** $0.682$      **21.** $5.25$      **22.** $3.45$

**Write the percent as a decimal and as a fraction.**

**23.** $13\%$      **24.** $32\%$      **25.** $0.36\%$      **26.** $124\%$

**Write the fraction or decimal as a percent. Round percents to the nearest tenth of a percent if necessary.**

**27.** $\dfrac{32}{55}$      **28.** $0.025$      **29.** $\dfrac{327}{1000}$      **30.** $0.8348$

**Find the percent of the number.**

**31.** $10\%$ of 45      **32.** $15\%$ of 36      **33.** $48\%$ of 24      **34.** $56\%$ of 140

**In Exercises 35–38, use the information in the advertisement to find the savings based on the sale described.**

**35.** You buy a T-shirt that originally cost $12.

**36.** You buy a sweater that originally cost $44.

**37.** You buy a pair of pants that originally cost $38.

**38.** You buy a sweater that originally cost $25 and two T-shirts that originally cost $15 each.

> **Sale**
> All Sweaters 20% off
> All Pants 15% off
> All T-shirts 45% off

1. You buy two DVDs for $19.98. The sales tax is $1.45. How much change should you receive if you give the cashier $25?

   (A) $2.35     (B) $3.57

   (C) $4.67     (D) $6.47

2. Which list of numbers is in order from least to greatest?

   (A) $\frac{7}{8}, 0.\overline{8}, 0.89, \frac{9}{10}, 0.9\overline{1}$

   (B) $0.\overline{8}, \frac{7}{8}, 0.89, 0.9\overline{1}, \frac{9}{10}$

   (C) $0.9\overline{1}, \frac{9}{10}, 0.89, 0.\overline{8}, \frac{7}{8}$

   (D) $0.\overline{8}, 0.89, \frac{7}{8}, \frac{9}{10}, 0.9\overline{1}$

3. What is the difference of 14.11 and 5.98?

   (A) 7.93     (B) 8.13

   (C) 8.73     (D) 9.43

4. A rectangular park is 1.6 miles long and has an area of 1.44 square miles. What is the width of the park?

   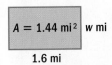

   1.6 mi

   (A) 0.06 mi     (B) 0.09 mi

   (C) 0.6 mi     (D) 0.9 mi

5. Which fraction is equivalent to 0.125?

   (A) $\frac{1}{10}$     (B) $\frac{1}{9}$

   (C) $\frac{1}{8}$     (D) $\frac{1}{7}$

6. What is the product of 12.34 and 0.04?

   (A) 0.4936     (B) 4.936

   (C) 49.36     (D) 493.6

7. A survey asked teenagers to choose the sport they enjoy playing the most. The results are shown in the circle graph below. What percent of the teenagers surveyed enjoy playing soccer?

   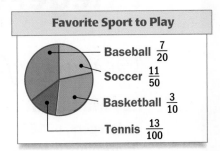

   (A) 20%     (B) 21%

   (C) 22%     (D) 23%

8. Which list of numbers is in order from least to greatest?

   (A) 5.34%, 0.54, 0.5%, 5.34

   (B) 5.34, 0.5%, 0.54, 5.34%

   (C) 0.54, 0.5%, 5.34%, 5.34

   (D) 0.5%, 5.34%, 0.54, 5.34

9. The regular price of a stereo is $185. The sale price is 15% off the regular price. How much money is saved by buying the stereo on sale?

   (A) $2.78     (B) $18.50

   (C) $27.75     (D) $157.25

10. Which percent is equivalent to $\frac{6}{15}$?

    (A) 0.04%     (B) 0.4%

    (C) 4%     (D) 40%

11. What is the sum of 15.64 and 13.88?

    (A) 29.52     (B) 29.92

    (C) 30.22     (D) 30.42

# Integers

## Vocabulary for Chapter 4 · · · · ·

### Key Mathematical Vocabulary

- **integers**, p. 162
- **absolute value**, p. 162
- **opposites**, p. 162

### Academic Vocabulary

- **make a conjecture** Make a general, but unproven, conclusion from specific examples. For example, see Exercise 6 on page 193.
- **compare**, p. 161
- **explain**, p. 164
- **model**, p. 166
- **describe**, p. 170
- **check**, p. 172

**Finding elevation relative to sea level by adding integers, page 171**

**Gr. 7 NS 1.2** Add, subtract, multiply, and divide rational numbers (**integers,** fractions, and terminating decimals) **and take positive rational numbers to whole-number powers.**
**Alg. 2.0** Students understand and use such operations as taking the opposite, finding the reciprocal, taking a root, and raising to a fractional power. They understand and use the rules of exponents.

# Review Prerequisite Skills

## REVIEW VOCABULARY

- whole numbers, p. 476
- number line, p. 477
- difference, p. 480
- sum, p. 480
- factor, p. 481
- quotient, p. 482

### VOCABULARY CHECK

**Copy and complete the statement.**

1. The  ?  are the numbers 0, 1, 2, 3, . . . .

2. When numbers are multiplied together, each number is a  ?  of the product.

3. A  ?  is a line whose points are associated with numbers.

### SKILLS CHECK

**Order the numbers from least to greatest.** (Review pp. 60, 128, and 478 for 4.1.)

4. 14, 5, 0.05, 10

5. 2.7, 0.27, 7, 27

6. 3, 0.03, 0.3, 1.3

7. $7, \frac{7}{2}, 7\frac{1}{2}, 3\frac{1}{3}$

8. $0.55, \frac{1}{2}, 5.5, 5\frac{1}{5}$

9. 21.5, 2.5, 2.15, 2

**Find the sum or difference.** (Review p. 480 for 4.2–4.3.)

10. $12 + 11$

11. $45 + 61$

12. $65 + 25$

13. $22 - 5$

14. $78 - 55$

15. $41 - 15$

**Find the product.** (Review p. 481 for 4.4.)

16. $42 \cdot 15$

17. $32 \cdot 50$

18. $74 \cdot 46$

19. $123 \cdot 250$

20. $2062 \cdot 1000$

21. $34{,}501 \cdot 428$

**Find the quotient.** (Review pp. 120 and 482 for 4.5.)

22. $125 \div 5$

23. $312 \div 13$

24. $182 \div 26$

25. $2052 \div 36$

26. $325 \div 10$

27. $835 \div 15$

## Let's Explore
## Comparing Numbers Using a Number Line

**Goal**
Use a number line to explore positive and negative numbers.

**Materials**
• index cards

**QUESTION** **How can you determine the location of a number on a number line?**

Numbers can be greater than 0 or less than 0. Numbers that are greater than 0 are called positive numbers. Numbers that are less than 0 are called negative numbers. Negative numbers have a negative sign (−) in front of them.

**EXPLORE 1** *Make a number line* • • • • • • • • • • • • • • • • • • • • • • • • • • • •

**1** **Draw** a number line with 21 equally spaced tick marks. Label the middle tick mark 0.

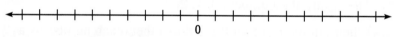

**2** **Draw** an arrow from 0 to the right 5 units slightly above the number line. Label that tick mark 5.

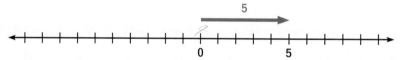

**3** **Draw** another arrow, this one from 0 to the left 5 units. Label that tick mark −5 (read "negative 5").

**4** **Continue** to draw arrows and label tick marks with positive numbers (to the right of 0) and negative numbers (to the left of 0).

## Draw Conclusions
**In Exercises 1 and 2, write the value of *a*, *b*, and *c*.**

**1.**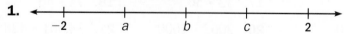

**2.**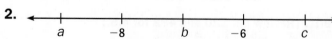

**3.** The *absolute value* of a number *a*, written $|a|$, tells you how far a number is from 0 on a number line. What is $|5|$? What is $|-5|$?

**Preparing for Alg. 2.0** Students understand and use such operations as taking the opposite, finding the reciprocal, taking a root, and raising to a fractional power. They understand and use the rules of exponents.

**EXPLORE 2** *Compare positive and negative numbers* · · · · · · ·

**1** **Write** the following expressions on index cards.

| 7 | 1 | 4 | 0 | 6 | −8 | −9 | −5 |
|---|---|---|---|---|---|---|---|
| −1 | −7 | −4 | $|8|$ | $|-9|$ | $|-5|$ | $|3|$ | $|-2|$ |

**2** **Shuffle** the cards and deal them equally between you and a partner.

**3** **Take** turns doing the following:

   **a.** Lay one of your cards down.

   **b.** Your partner must select a card from his or her hand that has a greater value than your card. (Remember that $a > b$ provided that $a$ is to the right of $b$ on the number line.)

   **c.** If your partner can select such a card, he or she scores a point. Otherwise, no point is scored.

   **d.** Any cards used in this turn are set aside (not to be reused).

**4** **Play** until one person has no cards. The player with more points wins.

## Draw Conclusions

**4.** Which number is greater: 0 or 4? Which number is farther to the right on the number line?

**5.** Which number is farther to the right on the number line: 3 or −7? Which number is greater?

**6.** Which number is greater: 0 or −12? Why?

**7.** Which number is greater: −10 or −8? Why?

**Tell whether the statement is *true* or *false*.**

**8.** −6 is less than 6.      **9.** −6 is less than −8.      **10.** −6 is less than −1.

**Copy and complete the statement using < or >.**

**11.** −1 ? 5      **12.** 0 ? −3      **13.** −5 ? −2      **14.** −6 ? $|-8|$

**Give two values for *x* that make the statement true. The statement $a < x < b$ means *x* is between *a* and *b*.**

**15.** $x < 0$      **16.** $-5 < x < 1$      **17.** $-12 < x < -7$   **18.** $-2 < x < 1$

# Compare and Order Integers

## VOCABULARY and CONCEPTS

The numbers . . . , −4, −3, −2, −1, 0, 1, 2, 3, 4, . . . are called **integers**.
**Negative integers** are less than 0. They lie to the left of 0 on a number line.
**Positive integers** are greater than 0. They lie to the right of 0 on a number line.

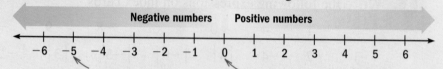

The integer −5 is read "negative 5."     0 is neither positive nor negative.

Two numbers that are the same distance from 0 on a number line but are on opposite sides of 0 are called **opposites**. For example, −3 and 3 are opposites. The opposite of a number $a$ is written $-a$.

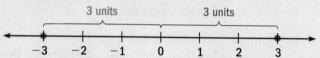

The **absolute value** of a number $a$, written as $|a|$, is the distance between $a$ and 0 on a number line.

**EXAMPLE 1** *Graphing and Ordering Integers* ...............

Below are the temperatures at which various substances freeze. To find which substance has the lowest freezing temperature, graph each integer on a number line.

| Substance | Freezing temperature (°F) |
|---|---|
| Water | 32 |
| Antifreeze and water | −32 |
| Sea water | 28 |
| Gasoline | −36 |

**Solution**

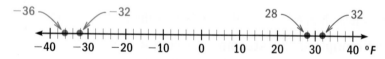

Order the numbers from least to greatest: −36, −32, 28, 32.

▶**Answer** Gasoline has the lowest freezing temperature at −36°F.

## Practice for Example 1

**Order the integers from least to greatest.**

**1.** −8, 5, −2, 0, 6        **2.** −12, 15, 3, 9, −6        **3.** 4, −4, 0, 16, −7

## EXAMPLE 2 · Finding the Opposite of a Number ···········

**a.** If $a = 6$, then $-a = -6$.       **The opposite of a positive is a negative.**

**b.** If $a = -5$, then $-a = -(-5) = 5$.    **The opposite of a negative is a positive.**

## EXAMPLE 3 · Finding the Absolute Value of a Number ······

**a.** If $a = 3$, then $|a| = |3| = 3$.       **The absolute value of a positive is a positive.**

**b.** If $a = -8$, then $|a| = |-8| = 8$.     **The absolute value of a negative is a positive.**

### Practice for Examples 2 and 3
**Write the opposite and the absolute value of the number.**

**4.** 14        **5.** 8        **6.** $-10$        **7.** $-2$

## EXAMPLE 4 · Using Absolute Value ···············

An elevation above sea level is a positive number, while an elevation below sea level is a negative number. The table gives the elevation of a whale at different times. Based on the table, what is the greatest depth the whale reached? How many seconds after diving did the whale return to the surface?

### Solution

Depth indicates a *distance* from the surface of water, so depth is a positive number. The table shows the whale's lowest elevation to be $-8$ meters. Because $|-8| = 8$, the greatest depth the whale reached was 8 meters.

Because the table shows an elevation of 0 meters after 4 seconds, the whale returned to the surface 4 seconds after diving.

| Time (seconds after diving) | Elevation (m) |
|---|---|
| 0 | 0 |
| 1 | $-4$ |
| 2 | $-8$ |
| 3 | $-4$ |
| 4 | 0 |

### Practice for Example 4

**8.** A fish is swimming 7 feet below the surface of a pond. At what elevation relative to the surface is the fish? At what depth is the fish?

**Copy and complete the statement.**

1. The numbers . . . , $-4, -3, -2, -1, 0, 1, 2, 3, 4, \ldots$ are $\underline{\ ?\ }$.

2. Negative integers are $\underline{\ ?\ }$ than 0.

3. Positive integers are $\underline{\ ?\ }$ than 0.

4. Two numbers that are the same distance from 0 on a number line but are on opposite sides of 0 are called $\underline{\ ?\ }$.

5. The absolute value of a number is the distance between $\underline{\ ?\ }$ and $\underline{\ ?\ }$ on a number line.

**Use a number line to order the integers from least to greatest.**

6. $6, 4, -3, -5, -9, -10, 7, 1$

7. $7, -4, 3, 0, -21, -36, 14$

8. $38, -38, -34, -42, 10, -18$

9. $0, -1, -4, -15, -24, 17, 5, 24$

**Write the opposite and the absolute value of the integer.**

10. $12$

11. $-4$

12. $3$

13. $-15$

14. $8$

15. $10$

16. $-6$

17. $-5$

**Copy and complete the statement using < or >.**

18. $-7 \ \underline{\ ?\ } \ 3$

19. $6 \ \underline{\ ?\ } \ -1$

20. $-5 \ \underline{\ ?\ } \ -2$

21. $0 \ \underline{\ ?\ } \ 12$

**Match the numerical expression with the verbal expression.**

22. $-|5|$

23. $|-5|$

24. $-|-5|$

25. $-(-5)$

26. $|5|$

A. the opposite of negative five

B. the absolute value of five

C. the opposite of the absolute value of negative five

D. the absolute value of negative five

E. the opposite of the absolute value of five

**Simplify the expression.**

27. $|-8|$

28. $-(-4)$

29. $-|-14|$

30. $-|-9|$

31. $-[-(-3)]$

32. $-|-10|$

33. A bird is flying 6 feet above the surface of a swimming pool. You are swimming 5 feet below the surface. What are the elevations of the bird and you relative to the surface of the pool? What is your depth in the water? Which of you is closer to the surface of the pool?

34. **REASONING** Is there a value of $a$ that makes the statement $|a| = -2$ true? *Explain* your reasoning.

**Tell whether the given arrow indicates** *positive* **numbers or** *negative* **numbers.**

**1.** A

**2.** B

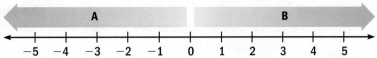

**Order the integers from least to greatest.**

**3.** 17, −24, −16, −8, 7, 2, 23

**4.** −16, −24, −38, 25, 11, −56, 102, −136

**5.** −7, −5, 2, −1, 4, 6, −10, 0

**6.** 8, −15, 17, −39, −51, 73, −84

**Write the opposite and the absolute value of the integer.**

**7.** 7

**8.** −25

**9.** 106

**10.** −241

**Copy and complete the statement using < or >.**

**11.** −6 ? 4

**12.** −2 ? −4

**13.** 0 ? 8

**14.** −11 ? −3

**15.** 31 ? −16

**16.** −24 ? −28

**17.** −4 ? −6

**18.** −10 ? 12

**Match the integer expression with the verbal expression.**

**19.** $-|12|$

**20.** $|-12|$

**21.** $-|-12|$

**22.** $-(-12)$

**23.** $|12|$

**A.** the opposite of negative twelve

**B.** the absolute value of twelve

**C.** the opposite of the absolute value of negative twelve

**D.** the absolute value of negative twelve

**E.** the opposite of the absolute value of twelve

**Simplify the expression.**

**24.** $|-15|$

**25.** $-(-9)$

**26.** $|-16|$

**27.** $-|-6|$

**28.** $-(-|49|)$

**29.** $-[-(-34)]$

**In Exercises 30 and 31, use the following information.**

A cliff diver dives from a cliff 54 feet above the water. He plunges to a depth of 15 feet before returning to the surface.

**30.** During what part of the dive are the diver's elevations relative to the surface of the water positive? During what part of the dive are the diver's elevations negative? When is the diver's elevation 0 feet?

**31.** What is the diver's elevation at the deepest point of the dive? How far is he from the surface at this point? Is there another point at which the diver is this distance from the water's surface? *Explain.*

**32. REASONING** Given that $|a| < 5$, what are several possible positive and negative values of *a*?

# Activity 4.2

## Let's Explore
### Investigating Integer Addition

**Goal**
Use algebra tiles and a number line to investigate adding integers.

**Materials**
• algebra tiles

**QUESTION** **How can you add two integers?**

You can use algebra tiles to model addition of integers. Each **+** represents 1, and each **−** represents −1. Pairing a **+** with a **−** produces a *zero pair*, which has a sum of 0.

**EXPLORE 1** *Use algebra tiles to find a sum* •••••••••••••••••••

**Find the sum −7 + 4.**

**1** **Model** −7 and 4 using algebra tiles.

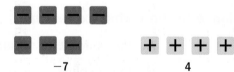

**2** **Form** zero pairs. Count the remaining tiles.

**3** **Complete** the statement: −7 + 4 = __?__ .

## Draw Conclusions
**Use algebra tiles to find the sum.**

| | | | |
|---|---|---|---|
| **1.** 3 + 8 | **2.** 5 + (−1) | **3.** −9 + 6 | **4.** −2 + (−3) |
| **5.** −4 + 4 | **6.** −7 + 5 | **7.** 5 + (−7) | **8.** −6 + 0 |
| **9.** −4 + (−7) | **10.** 8 + (−8) | **11.** −2 + 8 | **12.** −5 + 2 |
| **13.** −2 + 5 | **14.** 7 + (−9) | **15.** 0 + (−4) | **16.** −1 + (−6) |

**17.** When using algebra tiles to add two integers, what must be true in order for the sum to be 0?

**Gr. 7 NS 1.2 Add,** subtract, multiply, and divide **rational numbers** (**integers,** fractions, and terminating decimals) and take positive rational numbers to whole-number powers.
**Also addresses Gr. 6 NS 2.0**

**EXPLORE 2** *Use a number line to find a sum* · · · · · · · · · · · ·

Find the sum 2 + (−3).

**1** **Draw** a number line on a sheet of paper.

**2** **Start** at 0. Move 2 units to the right.

**3** **Move** 3 units to the left.

**4** **Find** your final position on the number line. You are at −1. So, 2 + (−3) = −1.

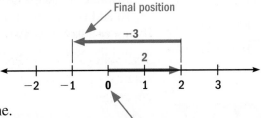

## Draw Conclusions
**Use a number line to find the sum.**

| | | | |
|---|---|---|---|
| **18.** 3 + 6 | **19.** 2 + (−1) | **20.** −4 + 9 | **21.** −5 + (−6) |
| **22.** −8 + 4 | **23.** 2 + (−6) | **24.** −6 + 2 | **25.** −3 + (−9) |
| **26.** −7 + 7 | **27.** 4 + 0 | **28.** −2 + (−3) | **29.** 0 + (−6) |

**In Exercises 30–34, answer the question and give an example from Exercises 1–16 to support your answer.**

**30.** Is the sum of two positive integers *positive* or *negative*?

**31.** Is the sum of two negative integers *positive* or *negative*?

**32.** Is the sum of a positive integer and a negative integer *always* positive?

**33.** What is the sum of an integer and its opposite?

**34.** What is the sum of an integer and 0?

**35.** In Exercises 6 and 7, the two integers being added are the same, but the order is reversed. What does this suggest about the sums $a + b$ and $b + a$ where $a$ and $b$ are integers?

**36.** Does the order in which a positive integer and a negative integer are added affect whether the answer is positive or negative? *Explain.*

# Add Integers

### VOCABULARY and CONCEPTS

- absolute value, p. 162

### Adding Integers

- To add two rational numbers with the *same* sign, add their absolute values. The sum has the same sign as the numbers.
- To add two rational numbers with *different* signs, subtract the lesser absolute value from the greater absolute value. The sum has the same sign as the number with the greater absolute value.

**EXAMPLE 1** *Adding Integers Using a Number Line* .........

**Use a number line to find the sum.**

   **a.** $9 + (-11)$         **b.** $-6 + 14$         **c.** $-3 + (-4)$

**Solution**

  **a.** Starting at 0, move **9** units to the **right**. Then move **11** units to the **left**.

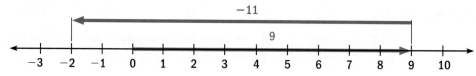

    ▶ **Answer** The final position is $-2$. So, $9 + (-11) = -2$.

  **b.** Starting at 0, move **6** units to the **left**. Then move **14** units to the **right**.

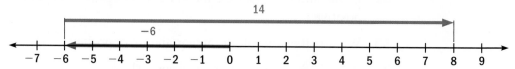

    ▶ **Answer** The final position is 8. So, $-6 + 14 = 8$.

  **c.** Starting at 0, move **3** units to the **left**. Then move **4** units to the **left**.

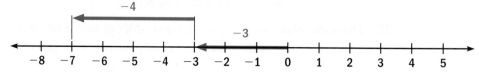

    ▶ **Answer** The final position is $-7$. So, $-3 + (-4) = -7$.

### Practice for Example 1

**Use a number line to find the sum.**

  **1.** $2 + (-5)$     **2.** $-7 + (-6)$     **3.** $-8 + 5$       **4.** $-5 + 9$

**EXAMPLE 2** *Adding Integers Using Absolute Value* ..........

**a.** Find the sum $-4 + (-5)$.

$$-4 + (-5) = -\left(\left|-4\right| + \left|-5\right|\right) \quad \textbf{Rule of same signs}$$
$$= -(4 + 5) \qquad\qquad \textbf{Take absolute values.}$$
$$= -9 \qquad\qquad\quad \textbf{Add.}$$

**b.** Find the sum $-11 + 8$.

$$-11 + 8 = -\left(\left|-11\right| - \left|8\right|\right) \quad \textbf{Rule of different signs}$$
$$= -(11 - 8) \qquad\qquad \textbf{Take absolute values.}$$
$$= -3 \qquad\qquad\quad \textbf{Subtract.}$$

### Practice for Example 2

**Find the sum.**

**5.** $-19 + 18$        **6.** $-5 + 5$        **7.** $26 + (-32)$

**EXAMPLE 3** *Adding More Than Two Integers* ..............

The diagram below shows the results of four plays in a football game. On the first play, the team gained 6 yards. On the second play, the team lost 11 yards. On the third and fourth plays, the team gained 4 yards and then 9 yards. What was the total number of yards the team gained?

**Solution**

$$6 + (-11) + 4 + 9 = -5 + 4 + 9 \quad \textbf{Add 6 and }-11.$$
$$= -1 + 9 \qquad\quad \textbf{Add }-5\textbf{ and 4.}$$
$$= 8 \qquad\qquad\quad \textbf{Add }-1\textbf{ and 9.}$$

▶**Answer** The team gained a total of 8 yards.

### Practice for Example 3

**Find the sum.**

**8.** $25 + (-23) + 4$     **9.** $-11 + 8 + (-14)$     **10.** $-56 + (-12) + 83$

**11.** $(-29) + (-18) + 12$     **12.** $31 + 23 + (-25)$     **13.** $-9 + 33 + (-11)$

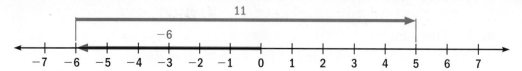
**1.** Write the addition problem represented by the number line. Find the sum.

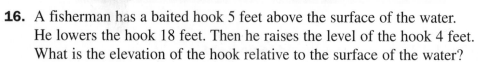

**Use a number line to find the sum.**

**2.** $-2 + 4$

**3.** $7 + (-8)$

**4.** $-6 + (-3)$

**Copy and complete the rule for adding integers.**

**5.** If the integers have the same sign, add the _?_ and use the common sign.

**6.** If the integers have different signs, _?_ the lesser absolute value from the greater absolute value. Use the sign of the number with the _?_ absolute value.

**FIND THE ERROR** *Describe* and correct the error in finding the sum.

**7.**

$-5 + (-2) = -3$  ✕

**8.**

$-9 + (-9) = 18$  ✕

**In Exercises 9–14, find the sum.**

**9.** $-23 + 31$

**10.** $-47 + 0$

**11.** $-38 + (-54)$

**12.** $-49 + (-121)$

**13.** $-15 + 15 + (-23)$

**14.** $-12 + 37 + (-54)$

**15.** You prefer to go snowboarding when the temperature is above 5°F. On Friday, the low temperature was −5°F. On Saturday morning, the temperature is 11°F higher. What is the temperature on Saturday morning? Does this temperature meet your preference?

**16.** A fisherman has a baited hook 5 feet above the surface of the water. He lowers the hook 18 feet. Then he raises the level of the hook 4 feet. What is the elevation of the hook relative to the surface of the water?

**In Exercises 17–20, find the sum.**

**17.** $-18 + 12 + (-35) + 7$

**18.** $25 + 10 + (-20) + (-3)$

**19.** $-29 + (-15) + 8 + (-15)$

**20.** $22 + 30 + (-22) + (-8)$

**21.** Sarah owes $320 for the rent on her apartment. She also owes $45 for her electric bill and $57 for her phone bill. Her paycheck for this week is $415. Will her paycheck be enough to pay the bills? How much will be left over or how much will she still need?

**22. REASONING** Is the sum of two negative integers always negative? *Explain.*

# Practice

1. Write the addition problem represented by the number line. Find the sum.

**Use a number line to find the sum.**

2. $5 + (-4)$

3. $-8 + 3$

4. $-2 + (-7)$

**FIND THE ERROR** *Describe* and correct the error in finding the sum.

5.
$$-9 + (-6) = |-9| + |-6|$$
$$= 15 \quad \times$$

6.
$$-12 + 7 = |-12| - |7|$$
$$= 5 \quad \times$$

**Find the sum.**

7. $-54 + 63$

8. $29 + (-46)$

9. $-38 + (-59)$

10. $-93 + 86$

11. $12 + 38 + (-41)$

12. $-28 + 31 + (-44)$

13. $-101 + 95 + (-37)$

14. $53 + (-19) + (-102)$

15. $-98 + (-91) + 68$

**REASONING** Copy and complete the statement using *always*, *sometimes*, or *never*.

16. The sum of two positive integers is _?_ 0.

17. The sum of 0 and a positive integer is _?_ 0.

18. The sum of 0 and a negative integer is _?_ 0.

19. The sum of a positive integer and a negative integer is _?_ 0.

**In Exercises 20–25, find the sum.**

20. $38 + 51 + (-29) + (-73)$

21. $-34 + (-85) + 63 + 47$

22. $102 + (-173) + 226 + (-185)$

23. $-304 + 246 + (-189) + 107$

24. $-61 + 93 + (-18) + (-14)$

25. $140 + (-60) + (-80) + (-32)$

26. A hot air balloon takes off from a valley that is 12 feet below sea level. The balloon then rises 100 feet, pauses, and descends 14 feet. Find the elevation of the balloon relative to sea level.

27. Yolanda was 8 seconds behind the leader after one lap of a two-mile track race. The same person led the race the entire way and won it. Here is how Yolanda lost or gained time on the leader in each of the remaining laps: lost 9 seconds, lost 3 seconds, gained 1 second, gained 2 seconds, gained 5 seconds, lost 3 seconds, gained 13 seconds. How many seconds behind the leader did Yolanda finish?

# Activity 4.3

## Let's Explore
### Investigating Integer Subtraction

**Goal**
Use algebra tiles and a number line to investigate subtracting integers.

**Materials**
- algebra tiles

**QUESTION** **How can you subtract two integers?**

You have already used algebra tiles to add integers. You can also use algebra tiles to model subtraction of integers. Each **+** represents 1, and each **–** represents −1. Pairing a **+** with a **–** produces a *zero pair*, which has a sum of 0.

**EXPLORE 1** *Use algebra tiles to find a difference*

**Find the difference 3 − (−2).**

**①** **Represent** 3 using alegbra tiles.

**+ + +**

**②** **Introduce** zero pairs. Because there are no negative tiles to subtract, you need to introduce two zero pairs. The zero pairs do not affect the value of the number.

**③** **Remove** 2 negative tiles. The remaining tiles represent the difference 3 − (−2). So, 3 − (−2) = 5.

## Draw Conclusions
**Use algebra tiles to find the difference.**

1. −7 − 4
2. 3 − 6
3. 2 − 8
4. 0 − 5
5. 2 − (−6)
6. −4 − 0
7. 5 − (−3)
8. 1 − 8
9. −4 − (−5)
10. −3 − (−2)
11. 3 − (−7)
12. 5 − (−2)

13. Give an example that shows how you can use addition to check your work when subtracting integers.

**Gr. 7 NS 1.2** Add, **subtract,** multiply, and divide **rational numbers** (**integers,** fractions, and terminating decimals) and take positive rational numbers to whole-number powers.
**Also addresses Gr. 6 NS 2.0**

**EXPLORE 2** *Use a number line to find a difference* • • • • • •

**Find the difference 4 − (−3).**

To find the difference 4 − (−3), let 4 − (−3) = x. If the value of x were added to −3, you would get 4. That is, −3 + x = 4.

**1** **Draw** an arrow from 0 to −3 on a number line.

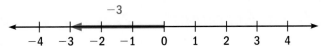

**2** **Draw** an arrow from −3 to 4.

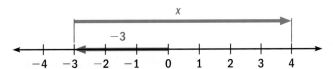

**3** **Identify** the number represented by x. The second arrow you drew is 7 units to the right, so it represents the (positive) number 7. So, x = 7 and 4 − (−3) = 7.

## Draw Conclusions

**Use a number line to find the difference.**

**14.** 0 − (−4)     **15.** 1 − (−3)     **16.** −1 − 6     **17.** −2 − (−8)

**18.** 5 − 8     **19.** 5 − (−6)     **20.** −3 − 6     **21.** −3 − (−4)

**In Exercises 22–25, the number line models the addition of two integers. Write the addition problem and find the sum. Then write a related subtraction problem and find the difference.**

**22.**
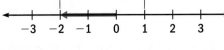

**23.**
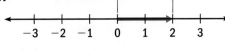

**24.**
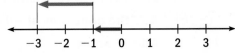

**25.**
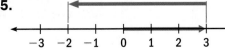

**26.** Can the difference of two negative integers be positive? Can the difference of two negative integers be negative? *Explain* your reasoning and give examples to support your claims.

# Subtract Integers

---

**VOCABULARY and CONCEPTS**

• opposites, p. 162

**Subtraction Rule**

**Words**     To subtract an integer, add its opposite.

**Numbers**   $3 - (-2) = 3 + 2 = 5$

**Algebra**   $a - b = a + (-b)$

---

**EXAMPLE 1** *Subtracting Integers* •••••••••••••••••••••••••••••••

**Find the difference.**

   **a.** $-25 - (-8)$                   **b.** $-18 - 35$

**Solution**

   **a.** $-25 - (-8) = -25 + 8$     **Add the opposite of −8.**
                    $= -17$         **Add −25 and 8.**

   **b.** $-18 - 35 = -18 + (-35)$     **Add the opposite of 35.**
                 $= -53$        **Add −18 and −35.**

**Practice for Example 1**

**Find the difference.**

   **1.** $26 - 32$           **2.** $-9 - 16$           **3.** $36 - (-36)$

   **4.** $-12 - (-52)$       **5.** $-78 - 45$        **6.** $85 - (-2)$

---

**EXAMPLE 2** *Evaluating Algebraic Expressions* ••••••••••••••••

**Evaluate $a - (-b) - 16$ when $a = 21$ and $b = 4$.**

**Solution**

$$a - (-b) - 16 = 21 - (-4) - 16 \quad \textbf{Substitute 21 for } a \textbf{ and 4 for } b.$$
$$= 21 + 4 + (-16) \quad \textbf{Add the opposites of −4 and 16.}$$
$$= 25 + (-16) \quad \textbf{Add 21 and 4.}$$
$$= 9 \quad \textbf{Add 25 and −16.}$$

**Practice for Example 2**

**Evaluate the expression when $x = 11$ and $y = -7$.**

   **7.** $9 - x$            **8.** $y - x$            **9.** $16 - x - y$

**EXAMPLE 3** *Using Integer Subtraction* • • • • • • • • • • • • • • • • • • • • • •

Last year the enrollment at Oakwood School was 568 students. This year the enrollment is 492 students. Find the change in enrollment.

**Solution**

| Change in enrollment | = | Enrollment this year | − | Enrollment last year | **Write verbal model.** |
|---|---|---|---|---|---|

$$= 492 - 568 \qquad \textbf{Substitute value.}$$
$$= 492 + (-568) \qquad \textbf{Subtraction rule}$$
$$= -76 \qquad \textbf{Add.}$$

▸**Answer** The change in enrollment is −76 students (a loss of 76 students).

**EXAMPLE 4** *Using Integer Subtraction* • • • • • • • • • • • • • • • • • • • • • •

A group of friends hiked from Death Valley to Mt. Whitney. Their hike started at an elevation of 282 feet below sea level and ended at an elevation of 14,494 feet above sea level. Find their change in elevation.

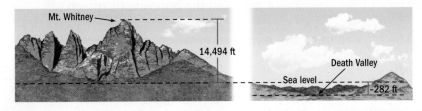

**Solution**

To find the change in elevation, subtract the starting elevation, −282 feet, from the ending elevation, 14,494 feet.

$$14{,}494 - (-282) = 14{,}494 + 282 \qquad \textbf{Subtraction rule}$$
$$= 14{,}776 \qquad \textbf{Add.}$$

▸**Answer** The change in elevation was 14,776 feet.

**Practice for Examples 3 and 4**

**10.** Last week the balance in Jerome's savings account was $312. This week the balance is $280. Find the change in his balance.

**11.** In 1906, the elevation of the surface of California's Salton Sea was 195 feet below sea level. In 1979, the elevation of the surface was 228 feet below sea level. What was the change in elevation during that time period?

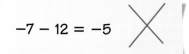

# Practice

**Extra Practice** p. 501

**1.** Copy and complete the statement: $a - b = \underline{\ ?\ } + \underline{\ ?\ }$.

**FIND THE ERROR** *Describe* and correct the error in finding the difference.

**2.**

$$-7 - 12 = -5 \quad \times$$

**3.**

$$-2 - (-14) = -2 + 14$$
$$= -12 \quad \times$$

**Find the difference.**

**4.** $4 - 7$  **5.** $-2 - 5$  **6.** $-3 - (-10)$

**7.** $-13 - 17$  **8.** $15 - 23$  **9.** $-12 - (-14)$

**10.** $-13 - (-13)$  **11.** $-36 - (-21)$  **12.** $16 - 38$

**13.** $25 - 42$  **14.** $21 - 34$  **15.** $-39 - (-46)$

**Write the verbal phrase as a numerical expression and simplify.**

**16.** The difference of negative eight and eleven

**17.** The difference of thirteen and negative four

**18.** The difference of the opposite of nine and the opposite of fifteen

**In Exercises 19–21, evaluate the expression when $a = -7$ and $b = 9$.**

**19.** $12 - a - b$  **20.** $a - 6 - b$  **21.** $b - a - 4 - 8$

**22.** One day in Fairbanks, Alaska, the temperature is $-15°F$. During the night, the temperature decreases by $16°F$. How cold does it get?

**23.** At 8 A.M., the wave height at the beach was 183 centimeters. At 8 P.M., the wave height was 57 centimeters. What was the change in wave height?

**Evaluate the expression.**

**24.** $15 - (-12) - 9$  **25.** $-19 - (-5) - (-18)$  **26.** $28 - (-16) - 7$

**27.** $-7 - (-6) - (-5)$  **28.** $-14 - 6 - (-9)$  **29.** $6 - (-2) - 13$

**30.** $4 - (-11) - (-15)$  **31.** $-31 - (-27) + (-43)$  **32.** $26 + (-18) - 34$

**33.** **REASONING** *Explain* how you can find the distance between the labeled points on the number line using subtraction.

# Practice

**Find the difference.**

1. $7 - 11$
2. $-6 - 9$
3. $-5 - (-12)$

4. $-13 - 8$
5. $-16 - (-11)$
6. $15 - 18$

7. $23 - (-17)$
8. $21 - 35$
9. $-34 - (-18)$

10. $46 - 57$
11. $-61 - (-49)$
12. $-37 - 58$

**Write the verbal phrase as a numerical expression and simplify.**

13. The difference of negative six and nineteen

14. The difference of eight and negative twenty-one

15. The difference of the opposite of fifteen and the opposite of twenty-eight

**FIND THE ERROR** *Describe* and correct the error in evaluating the expression.

16.
$$-16 - (-18) = -16 - 18$$
$$= -34$$

17.
$$14 - 21 = 21 - 14$$
$$= -7$$

**Evaluate the expression.**

18. $35 - 23 - 16$
19. $-35 - 12 - (-18)$
20. $34 - (-46) - 51$

21. $-8 - (-4) - (-7)$
22. $-16 - 10 - (-14)$
23. $63 - 48 - 39$

24. $-34 - (-15) - (-18)$
25. $37 - (-41) - 86$
26. $-54 - 81 - (-47)$

**In Exercises 27–32, evaluate the expression when $a = -5$, $b = 12$, and $c = -8$.**

27. $a - b - 14$
28. $b - c + a$
29. $b - 11 - c$

30. $c - 7 - a$
31. $c - 16 + b$
32. $a - b - c$

33. A scuba diver is 47 feet below the surface of the water. She rises to 31 feet below the surface of the water. What is the change in the diver's elevation?

34. At 2 P.M., the temperature was 9°F. At 11 P.M., the temperature was −11°F. What was the change in temperature?

**REASONING** Copy and complete the statement using *always, sometimes,* or *never.*

35. A positive number minus a positive number is _?_ negative.

36. A negative number minus a positive number is _?_ negative.

# Mid-Chapter Review

> **VOCABULARY**
> - integers, p. 162
> - negative integers, p. 162
> - positive integers, p. 162
> - opposites, p. 162
> - absolute value, p. 162

### Vocabulary Exercises

**1.** Copy and complete: The _?_ of a number $a$ is the distance between $a$ and 0 on a number line.

**2.** What is the sum of a number and its opposite?

### 4.1 Compare and Order Integers · · · · · · · · · · · · · · · · · · · · · · pp. 162–165

**EXAMPLE**   Write the absolute value and the opposite of −7.

If $a = -7$, then $-a = -(-7) = 7$.   **The opposite of a negative is a positive.**

If $a = -7$, then $|a| = |-7| = 7$.   **The absolute value of a negative is a positive.**

**Write the absolute value and the opposite of the number.**

**3.** 13              **4.** 11              **5.** −4              **6.** −7

### 4.2 Add Integers · · · · · · · · · · · · · · · · · · · · · · · · · · · · · · · · · pp. 168–171

**EXAMPLE**   $5 + (-8) + 6 = -3 + 6$   **Add 5 and −8.**
$$= 3 \quad \textbf{Add −3 and 6.}$$

**Find the sum.**

**7.** $9 + (-3) + 4$          **8.** $4 + (-5) + (-6)$          **9.** $-12 + 11 + (-8)$

### 4.3 Subtract Integers · · · · · · · · · · · · · · · · · · · · · · · · · · · · · · pp. 174–177

**EXAMPLE**   **Find the difference.**

$-19 - (-5) = -19 + 5 = -14$   **Add the opposite of −5.**

$-16 - 31 = -16 + (-31) = -47$   **Add the opposite of 31.**

**Find the difference.**

**10.** $-14 - 5$          **11.** $-8 - (-23)$          **12.** $-30 - 26$

**Order the integers from least to greatest.**

**1.** 7, −12, 4, 9, −1

**2.** 3, −2, 0, 8, −5

**3.** 10, 0, −100, 1, −1

**4.** 458, −73, 316, −491, −8

**Write the opposite and the absolute value of the number.**

**5.** 18

**6.** −2

**7.** $|-43|$

**8.** 0

**Copy and complete the statement using <, >, or =.**

**9.** −3 _?_ 8

**10.** 9 _?_ −12

**11.** 0 _?_ −6

**12.** −43 _?_ 57

**13.** −5 _?_ $|-5|$

**14.** 19 _?_ $-|-19|$

**15.** −28 _?_ $-|28|$

**16.** −(−3) _?_ $-[-(-3)]$

**Write the addition problem represented by the number line. Find the sum.**

**17.**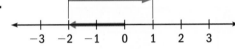

**18.**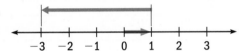

**Find the sum or difference.**

**19.** 5 + (−7)

**20.** −32 + (−17)

**21.** −19 + 27

**22.** −342 + (−5)

**23.** 8 − 13

**24.** −41 − (−19)

**25.** −17 − (−34)

**26.** −59 − 697

**Evaluate the expression when $x = 4$ and $y = -11$.**

**27.** $-7 - x$

**28.** $x - y$

**29.** $-3 - x + |y|$

**30.** $-10 - |x - y|$

**In Exercises 31–33, use the table, which shows temperatures in one town during a winter storm.**

| Time | Temp. (°F) |
|---|---|
| 6 A.M. | −8 |
| Noon | 7 |
| 6 P.M. | −3 |
| Midnight | 5 |

**31.** At what time did the lowest temperature occur?

**32.** Between which two consecutive times was the absolute temperature change the greatest?

**33.** Suppose the temperature dropped 7° by 6 A.M. the next morning. What was the temperature then?

**In Exercises 34–36, use the table, which shows the value of one share of a company's stock for one week.**

| Day | Value ($) |
|---|---|
| Monday | 20 |
| Tuesday | 15 |
| Wednesday | 12 |
| Thursday | 13 |
| Friday | 11 |

**34.** Find the change in value of one share of the stock from day to day over the entire business week.

**35.** Between which two consecutive days did the stock have the greatest absolute change in value?

**36.** Find the change in value of one share of the stock from Monday to Friday.

# Activity 4.4

## Let's Explore
## Investigating Integer Multiplication

**Goal**
Investigate integer multiplication.

**Materials**
• paper and pencil

**QUESTION** **How can you multiply integers?**

**EXPLORE 1** *Show that a(−1) = −a for a > 0* ...............

1. **Write** products as repeated addition.

   Copy and complete the table by treating multiplication by a positive integer as repeated addition.

   | Product | Repeated addition | Sum |
   |---------|-------------------|-----|
   | 2(−1) | −1 + (−1) | −2 |
   | 3(−1) | ? | ? |
   | 4(−1) | ? | ? |
   | 5(−1) | ? | ? |

2. **Generalize** the result.

   Copy and complete: If $a$ is any positive integer, then $a(-1) = \underline{?}$.

## Draw Conclusions
**Copy and complete using the result from Step 2 of Explore 1.**

1. $10(-1) = \underline{?}$
2. $-6 = (\underline{?})(-1)$
3. $\underline{?} = 7(-1)$
4. $8(-1) = \underline{?}$
5. $-32 = (\underline{?})(-1)$
6. $\underline{?} = 11(-1)$
7. $9(-1) = \underline{?}$
8. $-7 = (\underline{?})(-1)$
9. $\underline{?} = 20(-1)$
10. $14(-1) = \underline{?}$

11. Suppose you extend the result from Step 2 to $a = -1$. Copy and complete: $(-1)(-1) = -(-1) = \underline{?}$.

12. The result from Step 2 allows you to write −1 as the product of what two integers?

**Gr. 7 NS 1.2** Add, subtract, **multiply,** and divide **rational numbers** (**integers**, fractions, and terminating decimals) and take positive rational numbers to whole-number powers.
**Also addresses Gr. 6 NS 2.0**

**EXPLORE 2** *Use the rule a(−1) = −a to find products* ......

**1** **Find** the product $2(-3)$.

$$2(-3) = 2(3)(-1) \qquad \text{Apply the rule } -a = a(-1) \text{ to } -3.$$
$$= 6(-1) \qquad \text{Multiply 2 and 3.}$$
$$= -6 \qquad \text{Apply the rule } a(-1) = -a.$$

**2** **Find** the product $-2(3)$.

$$-2(3) = 2(-1)(3) \qquad \text{Apply the rule } -a = a(-1) \text{ to } -2.$$
$$= 2(3)(-1) \qquad \text{Rearrange factors.}$$
$$= 6(-1) \qquad \text{Multiply 2 and 3.}$$
$$= -6 \qquad \text{Apply the rule } a(-1) = -a.$$

**3** **Find** the product $(-2)(-3)$.

$$(-2)(-3) = 2(-1)(3)(-1) \qquad \text{Apply the rule } -a = a(-1) \text{ to both } -2 \text{ and } -3.$$
$$= (-1)(-1)(2)(3) \qquad \text{Rearrange factors.}$$
$$= 1(2)(3) \qquad \text{Apply the rule } (-1)(-1) = 1 \text{ (see Ex. 11).}$$
$$= 6 \qquad \text{Multiply 1, 2, and 3.}$$

## Draw Conclusions
**Find the product.**

**13.** $(-4)(-2)$       **14.** $4(-2)$       **15.** $3(-5)$

**16.** $-3(4)$       **17.** $-2(-7)$       **18.** $6(-2)$

**19.** $(-6)(-4)$       **20.** $-2(10)$       **21.** $3(-15)$

**22.** $-9(9)$       **23.** $-5(-8)$       **24.** $-4(-9)$

**25.** $13(-2)$       **26.** $(-6)(-5)$       **27.** $-3(11)$

**28.** $(-9)(-2)$       **29.** $8(-2)$       **30.** $-12(-3)$

**31.** $-16(10)$       **32.** $(-4)(-7)$       **33.** $7(-3)$

**34.** When two numbers are both positive or both negative, is their product positive or negative?

**35.** When one number is positive and another number is negative, is their product positive or negative?

# Multiply Integers

## VOCABULARY and CONCEPTS

- integers, p. 162

### Multiplying Two Integers

- The product of two non-zero integers with the *same* sign is positive.
- The product of two non-zero integers with *different* signs is negative.
- The product of 0 and any integer is 0.

### Multiplying More Than Two Non-Zero Integers

- A product is positive if it has an even number of negative factors.
- A product is negative if it has an odd number of negative factors.

**EXAMPLE 1** *Multiplying Integers* . . . . . . . . . . . . . . . . . . . .

**a.** $-6(-9) = 54$      **Same sign, so product is positive.**

**b.** $-7(3) = -21$      **Different signs, so product is negative.**

**c.** $-5(0) = 0$      **The product of 0 and any integer is 0.**

### Practice for Example 1

**Find the product.**

**1.** $-5(6)$     **2.** $-12(-1)$     **3.** $-7(-11)$     **4.** $-5(0)$

**EXAMPLE 2** *Multiplying More Than Two Integers* . . . . . . . . .

**a.** $3(-2)(-5) = (-6)(-5)$   **Multiply 3 and −2. Product is negative.**

$= 30$   **Multiply −6 and −5. Product is positive.**

**b.** $-9(-4)(-3) = 36(-3)$   **Multiply −9 and −4. Product is positive.**

$= -108$   **Multiply 36 and −3. Product is negative.**

**c.** $7(-10)(2) = -70(2)$   **Multiply 7 and −10. Product is negative.**

$= -140$   **Multiply −70 and 2. Product is negative.**

### Practice for Example 2

**Find the product.**

**5.** $-3(2)(-4)$     **6.** $5(68)(0)$     **7.** $-16(-1)(-3)$     **8.** $7(-2)(4)$

**EXAMPLE 3** *Comparing Integer Products* .........................

**a.** $3(-4) \underline{?} (-3)(-4)$
$\quad -12 \ < \ 12$      **Find each product. Then compare.**

**b.** $5 \cdot |-7| \underline{?} |-6| \cdot (-8)$
$\quad 5 \cdot 7 \underline{?} 6 \cdot (-8)$      **Evaluate absolute values.**
$\quad 35 \ > \ -48$      **Find each product. Then compare.**

**EXAMPLE 4** *Evaluating Variable Expressions with Integers*

**Evaluate $2a - b^2$ when $a = -12$ and $b = -4$.**

$2a - b^2 = 2(-12) - (-4)^2$      **Substitute $-12$ for $a$ and 4 for $b$.**

$\qquad\quad = -24 - 16$      **Evaluate the power, and multiply 2 and $-12$.**

$\qquad\quad = -24 + (-16) = -40$      **Use the subtraction rule. Then add.**

### Practice for Examples 3 and 4

**Copy and complete the statement using < or >.**

**9.** $-10(-3) \underline{?} (4)(-11)$           **10.** $-3 \cdot |5| \underline{?} 5 \cdot |-3|$

**Evaluate the expression when $a = -2$, $b = -1$, and $c = 5$.**

**11.** $a - bc$         **12.** $ac - b$         **13.** $b - a^2$         **14.** $ab - c^2$

**EXAMPLE 5** *Using Integer Multiplication* .....................

A store sells 200 notebooks at a below-cost price to attract customers. The loss on each notebook is 9 cents. This can also be represented as a negative profit, $-9$ cents. Find the store's profit on the sale of the 200 notebooks.

Find the profit by multiplying the number of notebooks by the profit per notebook.

$$\text{Profit} = 200(-9) = -1800$$

▶ **Answer** The store's profit was $-1800$ cents, or a loss of \$18.

### Practice for Example 5

**15.** An airplane descends 4 feet per second as it lands. Find the change in the airplane's altitude after 8 seconds.

# A Practice

Extra Practice
p. 501

**Match the expression with its value.**

1. $5(-8)$
2. $-4(-10)$
3. $8(-6)$
4. $-3(-16)$

A. 48
B. 40
C. $-40$
D. $-48$

**Find the product.**

5. $3(-8)$
6. $-7(-6)$
7. $0(-14)$
8. $5(-10)$
9. $-11(-3)$
10. $-12(-13)$
11. $-14(7)$
12. $8(-19)$
13. $-15(16)$
14. $-2(4)(-8)$
15. $6(-8)(-9)$
16. $-7(-7)(-3)$
17. $|-7| \cdot 3$
18. $-6 \cdot |15|$
19. $-3(-9) \cdot |-5|$

**FIND THE ERROR** *Describe* and correct the error in finding the product.

20.
$$4(-2)(-3) = (-8)(-3)$$
$$= -24$$

21.
$$5 \cdot |-5| \cdot (-2) = (-25)(-2)$$
$$= 50$$

**Copy and complete the statement using < or >.**

22. $2(-3) \underline{\ ?\ } (-2)(-3)$
23. $(-7)(-6) \underline{\ ?\ } 6(-7)$
24. $(-9)(-2) \underline{\ ?\ } (-3)(-7)$
25. $4(-4) \underline{\ ?\ } 8 \cdot |-2|$
26. $-4 \cdot |6| \underline{\ ?\ } -2 \cdot (-13)$
27. $-10 \cdot |4| \underline{\ ?\ } -2 \cdot |-21|$

**Evaluate the expression when $x = -8$, $y = -5$, and $z = -3$.**

28. $4xy$
29. $7xz^2$
30. $xy^2 - z$
31. $yz + x^2$
32. $9xyz$
33. $-3xy + 2xz$

34. While hiking down a mountain, your rate of descent is $-500$ feet per hour. Your descent begins at an elevation of 3000 feet. What is your elevation after 3 hours of hiking?

35. A crew needs to dig a well 108 feet deep. They can drill at a rate of $-6$ feet per hour. How many more feet do they need to drill after 7 hours of work?

36. Marie has $400 in a savings account. She withdraws $30 each week for 6 weeks to pay for piano lessons. How much money is left in her savings account?

37. A man goes on a diet and loses 3 pounds each month for 8 months. What is the total change in the man's weight?

38. **REASONING** Does $(-2)^2$ equal $-2^2$? *Explain* your reasoning.

# Practice

**Find the product.**

**1.** $4(-9)$

**2.** $-5(-7)$

**3.** $-12(0)$

**4.** $-9(-11)$

**5.** $-12(8)$

**6.** $-13(-20)$

**7.** $-17(18)$

**8.** $-4(-9)(8)$

**9.** $6(-5)(7)$

**10.** $-9(-8)(11)$

**11.** $42(-3)(0)$

**12.** $-5(-7)(-13)$

**13.** $|-12| \cdot 4$

**14.** $-7 \cdot |9|$

**15.** $-4(-8) \cdot |-5|$

**FIND THE ERROR** *Describe* and correct the error in finding the product.

**16.**
$$4(-8)(-2) = (32)(-2)$$
$$= -64$$

**17.**
$$-3 \cdot |-6| \cdot 1 = 18 \cdot 1$$
$$= 18$$

**Copy and complete the statement using < or >.**

**18.** $9(-3) \underline{\ ?\ } (-9)(-3)$

**19.** $(6)(-6) \underline{\ ?\ } 4(-8)$

**20.** $5 \cdot |-3| \underline{\ ?\ } 2(-9)$

**21.** $(-6)(-5) \underline{\ ?\ } 3 \cdot |-11|$

**22.** $-12 \cdot |3| \underline{\ ?\ } 3 \cdot |-12|$

**23.** $-7 \cdot |-9| \underline{\ ?\ } -6 \cdot |10|$

**Evaluate the expression when $x = -9$, $y = -7$, and $z = -11$.**

**24.** $2xy$

**25.** $-6yz$

**26.** $yz - 4x^2$

**27.** $xy^2 + 3z$

**28.** $7xyz$

**29.** $5xy - 7zx$

**30.** The water in a swimming pool is being drained at a rate of $-8$ inches per hour. The initial depth of the water was 96 inches. How many inches of water will be left after 9 hours of draining?

**31.** A football team starts with the ball at its own 20 yard line. The team makes two 6 yard gains in a row, then the team has three 5 yard losses in a row. What yard line is the ball on at this point?

**In Exercises 32–34, evaluate the expression when $x = -6$ and $y = -13$.**

**32.** $-xy$

**33.** $xy^2$

**34.** $[y + (-x)y]^2$

**35.** There is an old saying that goes, "Every time I go one step forward, I get bumped two steps backward." Taken literally, what would a person's forward progress be after going through this process 23 times?

**36.** You went to the department store for back-to-school shopping and picked out 6 shirts and 4 pairs of pants having a total cost of $170. When you paid for the clothes, the cashier took $3 off the price of each shirt and $5 off the price of each pair of pants. There was no sales tax. How much did you have to pay?

**37.** **REASONING** What must be true about $n$ in the expression $(-1)^n = -1$?

## Activity 4.5

### Let's Explore

# Investigating Integer Division

**Goal**
Investigate integer division by relating it to integer multiplication.

**Materials**
• paper and pencil

**QUESTION** **How can you divide integers?**

Every product has two related quotients. For example, $2 \cdot 7 = 14$ tells you that $14 \div 2 = 7$ and $14 \div 7 = 2$.

**EXPLORE 1** *Write a product as a related quotient* ..........

Write two related quotients for the product $(-3)(5) = -15$.

$$\textbf{Quotient 1: } -15 \div (-3) = 5 \text{ or } \frac{-15}{-3} = 5$$

$$\textbf{Quotient 2: } -15 \div 5 = -3 \text{ or } \frac{-15}{5} = -3$$

## Draw Conclusions
**Write two related quotients for the given product.**

**1.** $(-7)(3) = -21$      **2.** $11(-6) = -66$      **3.** $(-10)(-5) = 50$

**4.** $(-1)(-3) = 3$      **5.** $(-5)(-6) = 30$      **6.** $20(-5) = -100$

**7.** $(-9)(5) = -45$      **8.** $(-7)(-6) = 42$      **9.** $12(-5) = -60$

**10.** If you divide a positive integer by a positive integer, is the quotient *positive* or *negative*?

**11.** If you divide a negative integer by a negative integer, is the quotient *positive* or *negative*?

**12.** If you divide a positive integer by a negative integer, is the quotient *positive* or *negative*?

**13.** If you divide a negative integer by a positive integer, is the quotient *positive* or *negative*?

**14.** State two simple rules that tell you when the quotient of two integers will be positive and when it will be negative.

**15.** Compare your rules from Exercise 11 with the rules for multiplying integers from Lesson 4.4. What do you notice?

**Gr. 7 NS 1.2** Add, subtract, multiply, and **divide rational numbers** (integers, fractions, and terminating decimals) and take positive rational numbers to whole-number powers.
**Also addresses Gr. 6 NS 2.0**

**EXPLORE 2** *Find a quotient* ......................................

**Find the quotient 10 ÷ (−5).**

**1** **Divide** using the absolute values of the dividend and divisor.

$10 \div 5 = 2$

**2** **Determine** the sign of the quotient.

Based on your observations from Explore 1, you know that the quotient of a positive number and a negative number is negative.

$10 \div (-5) = -2$

**3** **Check** the answer using multiplication.

$(-5)(-2) = 10 \checkmark$

**Find the quotient −32 ÷ (−4).**

**1** **Divide** using the absolute value of the dividend and divisor.

$32 \div 4 = 8$

**2** **Determine** the sign of the quotient.

Based on your observations from Explore 1, you know that the quotient of two negative numbers is positive.

$-32 \div (-4) = 8$

**3** **Check** the answer using multiplication.

$-4(8) = -32 \checkmark$

## Draw Conclusions

**Find the quotient.**

**16.** $-9 \div 3$      **17.** $-6 \div (-2)$      **18.** $8 \div (-4)$      **19.** $18 \div (-3)$

**20.** $-14 \div 2$      **21.** $56 \div (-8)$      **22.** $-45 \div (-9)$      **23.** $16 \div (-4)$

**Without actually evaluating the expression, tell whether the value of the expression is *positive* or *negative*.**

**24.** $\dfrac{3(-4)}{-6(-2)}$      **25.** $\dfrac{43(16)}{-56(-34)}$      **26.** $\dfrac{-7(8)}{5(-2)}$      **27.** $\dfrac{-55(20)}{13(65)}$

# Divide Integers

## VOCABULARY and CONCEPTS

- The **mean**, also called the *average*, is the sum of the numbers in a set of data divided by the number of items in the set.
- The **average rate of change** of one quantity with respect to another is the change in the first quantity divided by the change in the second quantity.

### Dividing Integers

- The quotient of two integers with the *same* sign is positive.
- The quotient of two integers with *different* signs is negative.
- The quotient of 0 and any nonzero integer is 0.

**EXAMPLE 1**  *Dividing Integers*

a. $\dfrac{-36}{-12} = 3$  **Same sign, so quotient is positive.**

b. $\dfrac{-56}{8} = -7$  **Different signs, so quotient is negative.**

c. $\dfrac{45}{-9} = -5$  **Different signs, so quotient is negative.**

d. $\dfrac{0}{-18} = 0$  **The quotient of zero and any nonzero integer is 0.**

**EXAMPLE 2**  *Finding a Mean*

**Find the mean of the numbers: 21, −53, −46, 32, −14.**

$$\text{Mean} = \frac{21 + (-53) + (-46) + 32 + (-14)}{5}$$  **Write sum divided by 5.**

$$= \frac{-60}{5}$$  **Add.**

$$= -12$$  **Divide.**

▶ **Answer** The mean of the numbers is −12.

### Practice for Examples 1 and 2

**Find the quotient.**

**1.** $\dfrac{-58}{-1}$  **2.** $\dfrac{38}{-2}$  **3.** $\dfrac{-72}{6}$  **4.** $\dfrac{0}{-9}$

**Find the mean of the numbers.**

**5.** 25, −26, −25, 46, −55  **6.** −3, 0, 4, 5, −2, 8

**EXAMPLE 3**

## Finding the Mean of Data

The table shows the average monthly high temperature for the coldest months in Barrow, Alaska. What is the mean high temperature for these months?

| Month | Temp. (°F) |
|---|---|
| November | 5 |
| December | −4 |
| January | −8 |
| February | −10 |
| March | −7 |
| April | 6 |

**Solution**

$$\text{Mean} = \frac{5 + (-4) + (-8) + (-10) + (-7) + 6}{6}$$

$$= \frac{-18}{6}$$

$$= -3$$

▶ **Answer** The mean high temperature is −3°F.

### Practice for Example 3

**7.** At McMurdo Base in Antarctica, the average monthly temperatures for January through April are 27°F, 15°F, −1°F, and −5°F. What is the mean average temperature for those months?

**EXAMPLE 4**

## Finding the Average Rate of Change

A hot air balloon flying at an altitude of 1500 feet descended to an altitude of 616 feet in 34 minutes. What was the average rate of change in altitude in feet per minute?

**Solution**

To find the change in altitude, subtract the starting altitude from the ending altitude.

$$616 - 1500 = -884$$

Divide by the time it took the balloon to descend to find the rate of change.

$$\frac{-884 \text{ ft}}{34 \text{ min}} = -26 \text{ ft/min}$$

▶ **Answer** The balloon's altitude changed at an average rate of −26 feet per minute.

### Practice for Example 4

**8.** A scuba diver swimming at an elevation of −105 feet relative to the surface of the water rises to an elevation of −15 feet in 3 minutes. What is the average rate of change in the diver's elevation in feet per minute?

# A Practice

Extra Practice
p. 501

**Tell whether the statement is *true* or *false*.**

1. The quotient of two integers with the same sign is negative.

2. The quotient of two integers with different signs is negative.

3. The quotient of zero and any nonzero integer is zero.

4. The mean of a set of data is the number of items in the set of data divided by the sum of the numbers in the set.

**Find the quotient.**

5. $\dfrac{-35}{7}$

6. $\dfrac{-63}{-9}$

7. $\dfrac{-21}{3}$

8. $\dfrac{40}{-8}$

9. $\dfrac{0}{16}$

10. $\dfrac{-72}{9}$

11. $\dfrac{-12}{3}$

12. $\dfrac{-24}{-6}$

13. $\dfrac{45}{-5}$

14. $\dfrac{0}{-46}$

15. $\dfrac{-33}{11}$

16. $\dfrac{64}{-8}$

17. $\dfrac{60}{-12}$

18. $\dfrac{-39}{-13}$

19. $\dfrac{-55}{11}$

20. $\dfrac{110}{-10}$

**Evaluate the expression when $x = 16$, $y = -4$, and $z = -8$.**

21. $\dfrac{x}{z}$

22. $\dfrac{x}{y}$

23. $\dfrac{x}{z - y}$

24. $\dfrac{z - x}{y}$

25. $\dfrac{z^2}{y}$

26. $\dfrac{2z}{y}$

27. $\dfrac{z}{y}$

28. $\dfrac{-2x}{y}$

**In Exercises 29–32, find the mean of the numbers.**

29. $7, -6, 8, -10, -8, 4, 5$

30. $-5, -4, -7, -8, 1, 2, -6, 3$

31. $-4, 6, -15, -7, 4, -8$

32. $-8, 7, 4, 2, -3, 9, 3$

33. One winter, the low temperatures for 5 consecutive days in Buffalo, New York, were $-5°F$, $-8°F$, $-12°F$, $-9°F$, and $-6°F$. What was the mean low temperature in Buffalo over the 5 days?

34. Over the past 6 weeks, the value (in dollars) of one share of a company's stock has changed as follows: $-1, +2, +3, +4, -1, -1$. Find the mean of the changes in value of one share of the company's stock.

35. The aerial tramway in Palm Springs, California, takes passengers up and down the side of Mt. San Jacinto. Suppose a tramcar starts at the top station at an elevation of 8516 feet and after 2 minutes descends to an elevation of 7342 feet. What is the average rate of change in elevation in feet per minute?

36. **REASONING** Is the mean of a set of negative integers *always*, *sometimes*, or *never* negative? *Explain* your reasoning.

**190** Chapter 4 Integers

# Practice

**Find the quotient.**

1. $\dfrac{-64}{-8}$

2. $\dfrac{-32}{4}$

3. $\dfrac{50}{-10}$

4. $\dfrac{0}{-29}$

5. $\dfrac{0}{-65}$

6. $\dfrac{-36}{3}$

7. $\dfrac{30}{-15}$

8. $\dfrac{56}{-7}$

9. $\dfrac{-36}{4}$

10. $\dfrac{-48}{-6}$

11. $\dfrac{42}{-2}$

12. $\dfrac{-60}{-12}$

**Evaluate the expression when $a = -24$, $b = -6$, and $c = -12$.**

13. $\dfrac{a}{b}$

14. $\dfrac{bc}{a}$

15. $\dfrac{-c}{b}$

16. $\dfrac{ac}{b}$

17. $\dfrac{c^2}{a}$

18. $\dfrac{a + c}{b}$

19. $\dfrac{-2a}{c}$

20. $\dfrac{c^2}{ab}$

**Find the mean of the numbers.**

21. $8, 5, -4, 9, -3, 11, 2$

22. $-7, -13, 5, 2, -8, -9$

23. $-16, 2, -18, 4, -11, -8, -6, 5$

24. $-4, 11, -6, 14, -3, 7, 2$

**In Exercises 25–28, use the table at the right and the information below.**

The table shows the final golf scores, relative to *par*, of the top 10 golfers at the 2006 Masters Tournament. *Par* indicates the number of strokes needed to play a golf course based on the distance to each hole and other factors.

| Player | Final |
|--------|-------|
| P. Mickelson | −7 |
| T. Clark | −5 |
| F. Couples | −4 |
| C. Campbell | −4 |
| T. Woods | −4 |
| R. Goosen | −4 |
| J. Olazabal | −4 |
| V. Singh | −3 |
| A. Cabrera | −3 |
| S. Cink | −2 |

25. Calculate the mean score of the golfers.

26. Par for the tournament's course was 288 strokes. Find the actual number of strokes taken by each of the golfers. (For example, Mickelson's number of strokes was $288 + (-7) = 281$.)

27. What was the mean number of strokes taken in the tournament by the 10 golfers?

28. **REASONING** Convert the mean score found in Exercise 25 to a number of strokes. Why is this number the same as the mean you found in Exercise 27?

**In Exercises 29 and 30, use the table below, which shows the beginning and ending elevations and the completion times for two riders on different bobsled tracks.**

29. Find each rider's average rate of change in elevation in feet per second.

30. Which person had the greater absolute rate of change in elevation?

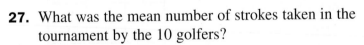

| Rider | Beginning elevation (ft) | Ending elevation (ft) | Time (sec) |
|-------|--------------------------|-----------------------|------------|
| Pat | 7320 | 6984 | 48 |
| Julia | 7143 | 6984 | 53 |

# Problem Solving and Reasoning

## Problem

In a $3 \times 3$ magic square, the row, column, and diagonal sums are all equal. Complete a magic square using each of the numbers 1, 2, 3, 4, 5, 6, 7, 8, and 9 only once.

## Solution

**Identify relationships as part of MR 1.1.**

**1** **Replace** the given numbers with a related set of numbers that is easier to work with. Because opposites have a sum of 0, consider subtracting 5 from each of the numbers 1, 2, 3, 4, 5, 6, 7, 8, and 9 so that the new set of numbers includes 4 pairs of opposites and 0.

| Original numbers | | New numbers |
|---|---|---|
| 1, 2, 3, 4, 5, 6, 7, 8, 9 | **Subtract 5.** | −4, −3, −2, −1, **0**, 1, 2, 3, 4 |

**Sequence information as part of MR 1.1.**

**2** **Construct** a magic square using the new numbers by placing 0 in the center of the square. Then arrange the 4 pairs of opposites around 0 as shown. The sum of each row, column, and diagonal will be equal to 0.

| 3 | −2 | −1 |
|---|---|---|
| −4 | **0** | 4 |
| 1 | 2 | −3 |

**Apply strategies and results from simpler problems as part of MR 2.2.**

**3** **Complete** a square using the original numbers by adding back 5 to each number in the square from Step 2.

| 8 | 3 | 4 |
|---|---|---|
| 1 | 5 | 9 |
| 6 | 7 | 2 |

**Check the validity of the result as part of MR 2.8.**

**4** **Check** that the square in Step 3 is a magic square by finding the sum of each row, column, and diagonal.

| Row sums | Column sums | Diagonal sums |
|---|---|---|
| $8 + 3 + 4 = 15$ | $8 + 1 + 6 = 15$ | $8 + 5 + 2 = 15$ |
| $1 + 5 + 9 = 15$ | $3 + 5 + 7 = 15$ | $4 + 5 + 6 = 15$ |
| $6 + 7 + 2 = 15$ | $4 + 9 + 2 = 15$ | |

The square is a magic square.

## Practice

1. Suppose you want to complete a 3 × 3 magic square. **MR 1.1, MR 2.2**

   |   |   |   |
   |---|---|---|
   | ? | ? | ? |
   | ? | ? | ? |
   | ? | ? | ? |

   a. *Describe* a strategy that you can use to complete the square using each of the numbers 2, 4, 6, 8, 10, 12, 14, 16, and 18 only once.

   b. Complete the square. Is the square you found the only possible square? *Explain.*

2. Is it possible to form a 2 × 2 magic square using each of the numbers 1, 2, 3, and 4 only once? *Explain.* **MR 2.5, MR 3.2**

3. In a 5 × 5 magic square, the row, column, and diagonal sums are all equal.
   **MR 2.2, MR 2.5, MR 3.3**

   |   |   |   |   |   |
   |---|---|---|---|---|
   | ? | ? | ? | ? | ? |
   | ? | ? | ? | ? | ? |
   | ? | ? | ? | ? | ? |
   | ? | ? | ? | ? | ? |
   | ? | ? | ? | ? | ? |

   a. Complete a 5 × 5 magic square using each of the integers from −12 to 12 only once. Start by using the 3 × 3 magic square from Step 2 on the previous page as the center of the square.

   b. Suppose every number in the square that you found in part (a) is increased by 13. Is the square still a magic square? *Explain* your reasoning.

4. The product of 0 and any integer is always equal to 0. Use this fact to explain why the quotient of any nonzero integer and 0 is always undefined.
   **MR 1.2, MR 2.5, MR 2.6**

5. To convert temperatures in degrees Celsius to degrees Fahrenheit, multiply the number of degrees Celsius by 9, divide the result by 5, and add 32. **MR 1.1, MR 2.5, MR 2.8**

   a. Convert 5°C to degrees Fahrenheit.

   b. Convert −5°C to degrees Fahrenheit.

   c. How can you convert a temperature in degrees Fahrenheit to degrees Celsius? *Explain* your reasoning.

6. Recall that the first power of a number is the number itself: $a^1 = a$. **MR 2.4, MR 2.6**

   a. Let $a$ be a negative integer. Make conjectures about the sign of $a^n$ for each of the following values of $n$: 1, 2, 3, and 4. Test your conjectures. For which values of $n$ is $a^n$ positive? negative?

   b. *Explain* how the value of $n$ determines whether the $n$th power of a negative integer is positive or negative.

7. On a game show, teams buy antique items at a market and then put the items up for auction. For each item, a team's score is the difference of the auction price and the market price the team paid. A team's total score is the sum of the scores of all their items. The table lists the prices (in dollars) of a team's antiques. **MR 2.1, MR 2.8**

   | Item | Market price | Auction price |
   |------|------|------|
   | Cabinet | 154 | 170 |
   | Chair | 120 | 100 |
   | Clock | 75 | 80 |
   | Vase | 49 | 60 |

   a. Find the team's total score.

   b. Use estimation to check that your answer to part (a) is reasonable.

# Chapter 4 Review Game

### Materials
• index cards

## Integer Game

**GETTING GOING** Make a copy of the table below (leaving the table cells with question marks blank). This will be your score sheet.

Write the integers 1 through 12 and −12 through −1 on index cards to make a deck of 24 cards. Shuffle the cards and place the pile face down on a desk.

Then, on a piece of paper write "1st integer" and on another piece of paper write "2nd integer." Place them on the desk.

| 1st integer | ? | ? | ? | ? | ? | ? | ? | ? | ? | ? | ? | ? | |
| Operation | + | + | + | − | − | − | × | × | × | ÷ | ÷ | ÷ | |
| 2nd integer | ? | ? | ? | ? | ? | ? | ? | ? | ? | ? | ? | ? | |
| Result | ? | ? | ? | ? | ? | ? | ? | ? | ? | ? | ? | ? | ? |

**Grand Total (Sum of results)** ↑

**HOW TO PLAY THE GAME** A player draws one card from the pile and places it face up on the paper labeled "1st integer" and draws another card and places it face up on the paper labeled "2nd integer."

Each player decides into which column on the score sheet to enter the integers. The "1st integer" must be entered into the row labeled "1st integer" and the "2nd integer" must be entered into the row labeled "2nd integer." Both integers must be entered in the same column.

Apply the operation in the column to the two integers to obtain the result for the column. If necessary when dividing, round your result to the nearest tenth.

The objective is to enter the integers into a column that gives the greatest result possible.

Now the next player draws a "1st integer" and a "2nd integer" and places them on the desk as before. Play continues in this way until all cards have been used and the score sheets are filled.

**WINNING THE GAME** Add all of your results to obtain your grand total. The player with the greatest grand total wins.

# Chapter Summary and Review

**@HomeTutor**
**classzone.com**

**VOCABULARY**
- integers, p. 162
- negative integers, p. 162
- positive integers, p. 162
- opposites, p. 162
- absolute value, p. 162
- mean, p. 188
- average rate of change, p. 188

**Vocabulary Exercises**

1. Copy and complete: The  ?  of one quantity with respect to another is the change in the first quantity divided by the change in the second quantity.

2. Explain how to find the mean of a set of numbers.

**4.1** *Compare and Order Integers* •••••••••••••••••••••• **pp. 162–165**

To arrange a list of numbers from least to greatest, graph each integer on a number line. Then read the numbers from left to right.

**EXAMPLE** **Order the integers from least to greatest: 24, −22, −24, 18.**

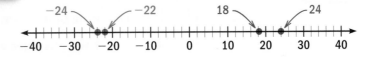

From least to greatest, the numbers are −24, −22, 18, and 24.

Two numbers that are the same distance from 0 on a number line but are on opposite sides of 0 are called opposites. The opposite of $a$ is written $-a$.

**EXAMPLE** If $a = 7$, then $-a = -7$.  **The opposite of a positive is a negative.**

If $a = -2$, then $-a = -(-2) = 2$.  **The opposite of a negative is a positive.**

The absolute value of a number $a$ is the distance between $a$ and 0 on a number line, written as $|a|$.

**EXAMPLE** If $a = 9$, then $|a| = |9| = 9$.  **The absolute value of a positive is a positive.**

If $a = -4$, then $|a| = |-4| = 4$.  **The absolute value of a negative is a positive.**

**Order the integers from least to greatest.**

3. $-3, 1, -4, 0, 9$

4. $19, 7, -2, -17, 4$

5. $7, -3, 0, 15, -8$

6. $5, -12, -3, 18, -6$

# Chapter Summary and Review

Write the opposite and the absolute value of the number.

**7.** 12 **8.** 3 **9.** $-27$ **10.** $|4|$

**4.2** *Add Integers* • • • • • • • • • • • • • • • • • • • • • • • • • • • • • *pp. 168–171*

To add two integers with the *same* sign, add their absolute values. The sum has the same sign as the integers.

**EXAMPLE** Find the sum $-2 + (-3)$.

$$-2 + (-3) = -(|-2| + |-3|) \quad \text{Rule of same signs.}$$
$$= -(2 + 3) \quad \text{Take absolute values.}$$
$$= -5 \quad \text{Add.}$$

To add two integers with *different* signs, subtract the lesser absolute value from the greater absolute value. The sum has the same sign as the number with the greater absolute value.

**EXAMPLE** Find the sum $-7 + 4$.

$$-7 + 4 = -(|-7| - |4|) \quad \text{Rule of different signs.}$$
$$= -(7 - 4) \quad \text{Take absolute values.}$$
$$= -3 \quad \text{Subtract.}$$

Find the sum.

**11.** $3 + (-5)$ **12.** $-2 + 6$ **13.** $-4 + (-7)$

**14.** $-11 + 8$ **15.** $23 + (-17)$ **16.** $-19 + 19$

**4.3** *Subtract Integers* • • • • • • • • • • • • • • • • • • • • • • • • • • • • *pp. 174–177*

To subtract an integer, add its opposite.

**EXAMPLE** Find the difference $-12 - (-5)$.

$$-12 - (-5) = -12 + 5 \quad \text{Add the opposite of } -5.$$
$$= -7 \quad \text{Add } -12 \text{ and } 5.$$

**EXAMPLE** Find the difference $-9 - 41$.

$$-9 - 41 = -9 + (-41) \quad \text{Add the opposite of } 41.$$
$$= -50 \quad \text{Add } -9 \text{ and } -41.$$

Find the difference.

**17.** $2 - 9$ **18.** $6 - (-6)$ **19.** $21 - 43$

**20.** $-8 - (-21)$ **21.** $-35 - (-35)$ **22.** $-53 - 100$

## 4.4 Multiply Integers ........................... pp. 182–185

**EXAMPLE**

a. $(-7)(-6) = 42$    **Same sign, so product is positive.**

b. $5(-3) = -15$    **Different signs, so product is negative.**

c. $-14(0) = 0$    **The product of 0 and any integer is 0.**

**Find the product.**

**23.** $-8(4)$      **24.** $-5(-2)$      **25.** $-7(0)$

**26.** $-12(-3)$      **27.** $9(-7)$      **28.** $-40(6)$

## 4.5 Divide Integers ........................... pp. 188–191

**EXAMPLE**

a. $\dfrac{-36}{-9} = 4$    **Same sign, so quotient is positive.**

b. $\dfrac{54}{-9} = -6$    **Different signs, so quotient is negative.**

c. $\dfrac{0}{-27} = 0$    **The quotient of 0 and any nonzero integer is 0.**

The mean, also called the average, is the sum of the numbers in a set of data divided by the number of items in the set.

**EXAMPLE**    **Find the mean of the numbers: 1, 9, 7, −5, 3.**

$$\text{Mean} = \frac{1 + 9 + 7 + (-5) + 3}{5} \quad \textbf{Write sum divided by 5.}$$

$$= \frac{15}{5} \quad \textbf{Add.}$$

$$= 3 \quad \textbf{Divide.}$$

**Find the quotient.**

**29.** $\dfrac{28}{-7}$      **30.** $\dfrac{-63}{9}$      **31.** $\dfrac{-30}{-6}$      **32.** $\dfrac{-96}{6}$

**33.** $\dfrac{56}{-4}$      **34.** $\dfrac{0}{-15}$      **35.** $\dfrac{-65}{5}$      **36.** $\dfrac{-77}{-7}$

**Find the mean of the numbers.**

**37.** $5, 3, -7, 1, 8$          **38.** $-16, 12, 3, 8, -6, 5$

# Chapter Test

**Order the integers from least to greatest.**

**1.** 6, −9, 1, 5, 3

**2.** −1, −7, 4, 0, −2

**3.** 87, −78, −98, 10, 71

**4.** 95, −44, −45, −75, −89

**Write the opposite and the absolute value of the number.**

**5.** 31

**6.** −9

**7.** $|-29|$

**8.** $-|-47|$

**Write the addition problem represented by the number line.
Find the sum.**

**9.**

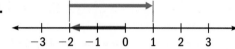

**10.**

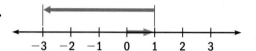

**Find the sum or difference.**

**11.** $9 + (-5) + 4$

**12.** $31 + (-37)$

**13.** $-147 + 219$

**14.** $-861 + (-5) + 71$

**15.** $7 - 18$

**16.** $1000 - 463$

**17.** $-29 - (-53)$

**18.** $-347 + 63 - (-4)$

**Evaluate the expression when $a = 12$ and $b = -5$.**

**19.** $7 - a$

**20.** $a - b$

**21.** $-23 - a + |b|$

**22.** $4 + |b - a|$

**Find the product.**

**23.** $-4(7)$

**24.** $5(-12)(-2)$

**25.** $-2|-1|(-23)$

**26.** $-|-4| \cdot 3$

**Copy and complete the statement using <, >, or =.**

**27.** $-5 \underline{\ ?\ } -10$

**28.** $-3(-2) \underline{\ ?\ } 0$

**29.** $8(-3) \underline{\ ?\ } -6(-4)$

**30.** $-12 \cdot 5 \underline{\ ?\ } 20 \cdot |-3|$

**Find the quotient.**

**31.** $\dfrac{-18}{6}$

**32.** $\dfrac{40}{-5}$

**33.** $\dfrac{0}{-27}$

**34.** $\dfrac{-56}{-8}$

**35.** $\dfrac{-32}{-4}$

**36.** $\dfrac{-36}{3}$

**37.** $\dfrac{48}{2}$

**38.** $\dfrac{45}{-9}$

**In Exercises 39–43, use the table, which shows the daily high
temperature for a major city.**

| Day | Temp. (°C) |
|-----|-----------|
| Monday | 5 |
| Tuesday | −2 |
| Wednesday | 3 |
| Thursday | −7 |
| Friday | −4 |

**39.** Which day of the week was coldest?

**40.** On which day was the temperature closest to 0°C?

**41.** What was the temperature change from Monday to Tuesday?

**42.** What was the difference between the highest and lowest temperatures?

**43.** Find the mean temperature for the week.

1. Which list of integers is in order from least to greatest?

   (A) $|-7|, -5, -1, 0, 3$

   (B) $-5, -1, 0, 3, |-7|$

   (C) $|-7|, 3, 0, -1, -5$

   (D) $0, -1, 3, -5, |-7|$

2. What number is the opposite of $-4$?

   (A) $-4$  (B) $-|-4|$

   (C) $-|4|$  (D) $4$

3. Which addition problem is represented by the number line?

   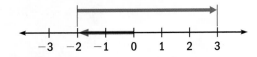

   (A) $2 + 3 = 5$  (B) $-3 + (-2) = -5$

   (C) $-2 + 5 = 3$  (D) $5 + (-3) = 2$

4. What is the sum $-12 + 7 + (-4)$?

   (A) $-23$  (B) $-9$

   (C) $-1$  (D) $15$

5. Amy will wear her favorite winter coat if the outside temperature is below $-5°C$. Today the outside temperature is $-8°C$. Will Amy wear her favorite winter coat today?

   (A) Yes, today is warmer than $-5°C$.

   (B) No, today is warmer than $-5°C$.

   (C) Yes, today is colder than $-5°C$.

   (D) No, today is colder than $-5°C$.

6. What is $3 - (-14) - (-8)$?

   (A) $-19$  (B) $-3$

   (C) $9$  (D) $25$

7. Which is the value of the expression $3x - y^2$ when $x = -2$ and $y = -4$?

   (A) $-22$  (B) $-15$

   (C) $10$  (D) $14$

8. What is the product $(-4)(-5)$?

   (A) $-20$  (B) $-9$

   (C) $9$  (D) $20$

9. On each of 4 successive days, the stock market dropped 5 points. By how many points did the stock market change in that time?

   (A) $-20$ points  (B) $-5$ points

   (C) $5$ points  (D) $20$ points

10. What is the quotient $\frac{24}{-4}$?

    (A) $-96$  (B) $-6$

    (C) $-2$  (D) $20$

11. What is the mean of the numbers $-1, 0, 4, 7, -3, 5$?

    (A) $2$  (B) $4$

    (C) $5$  (D) $6$

12. A jet plane starts at an altitude of 32,000 feet. After 4 minutes, it has descended to an altitude of 28,800 feet. What is the average rate of change in altitude in feet per minute?

    (A) $-3200$ ft/min  (B) $-800$ ft/min

    (C) $4200$ ft/min  (D) $28,800$ ft/min

13. What is the difference $-27 - (-35)$?

    (A) $-62$  (B) $-8$

    (C) $8$  (D) $62$

# Rational Numbers and Their Properties

*Vocabulary for Chapter 5*

## Key Mathematical Vocabulary

- **rational number,** p. 204
- **terms,** p. 236
- **coefficient,** p. 236

## Academic Vocabulary

- **justify** Give an argument using mathematical facts to show that a statement is true. For example, see Example 3 on page 217.
- **model,** p. 202
- **explain,** p. 203
- **compare,** p. 212
- **describe,** p. 223
- **check,** p. 231
- **make a conjecture,** p. 240

**Finding the rate of change in the amount of oxygen left in an astronaut's space suit, page 226**

**Gr. 7 NS 1.5** Know that every rational number is either a terminating or a repeating decimal and be able to convert terminating decimals into reduced fractions.
**Gr. 7 AF 1.3** Simplify numerical expressions by applying properties of rational numbers (e.g., identity, inverse, distributive, associative, commutative) and justify the process used.

# Review Prerequisite Skills

## REVIEW VOCABULARY

- variable, p. 18
- expression, p. 32
- reciprocals, p. 86
- opposites, p. 162
- absolute value, p. 162

**VOCABULARY CHECK**

**Copy and complete the statement.**

1. The variable in the algebraic expression $16x + 4$ is __?__.

2. The reciprocal of $\frac{1}{5}$ is __?__.

**SKILLS CHECK**

**Order the integers from least to greatest. (Review p. 162 for 5.1.)**

3. $-3, -8, -15, -2, 0, 4, -11$

4. $-7, -77, 17, 72, -27, 7$

5. $-4, 0, -5, 2, 1, -10, 5$

6. $-102, 120, -12, -120, 102$

**Write the opposite and the absolute value of the number. (Review p. 162 for 5.1–5.2.)**

7. $22$

8. $-5$

9. $0$

10. $-13$

**Find the sum or difference. (Review pp. 66, 74, 108, 168, and 174 for 5.2–5.6.)**

11. $\frac{9}{11} - \frac{3}{11}$

12. $\frac{4}{5} + \frac{5}{6}$

13. $4.1 + 1.8$

14. $9.4 + 1.86$

15. $-3 + (-7)$

16. $5 - (-2)$

**Find the product. (Review pp. 80, 114, and 182 for 5.2–5.6.)**

17. $2\frac{4}{5} \times \frac{2}{7}$

18. $15 \cdot 2.4$

19. $-20 \cdot 14$

**Find the quotient. (Review pp. 92, 120, and 188 for 5.2–5.6.)**

20. $\frac{5}{12} \div \frac{1}{6}$

21. $0.9 \div 4.5$

22. $-309 \div (-3)$

# Activity 5.1

## Let's Explore
### Identifying Numbers on a Number Line

**Goal**
Associate numbers with points on a number line.

**Materials**
- rope
- clothespins
- index cards

**QUESTION**  How can you associate numbers with points on a number line?

**EXPLORE**  *Identify numbers on a number line* . . . . . . . . . . . .

**1** **Model** a number line using rope. Two students go to the front of the class and each holds an end of a rope. A third student writes "−1" on an index card and uses a clothespin to clip it to the left end of the rope so it is visible to the class. That student then writes "1" on an index card and clips it to the right end of the rope.

**2** **Locate** the number 0 on the number line. Another student writes "0" on an index card and uses a clothespin to clip it onto the rope at the correct position. Describe how to find the correct position.

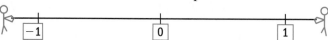

**3** **Divide** the number line between 0 and 1. Using three clothespins, another student divides the section of the rope between 0 and 1 into four sections of equal length.

**4** **Divide** the number line between −1 and 0. Using three clothespins, another student divides the section of the rope between −1 and 0 into four sections of equal length. Now the rope should be divided into 8 sections of equal length. Make a copy of this number line on a piece of paper.

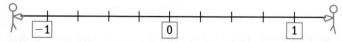

**5** **Identify** numbers on the number line. Your teacher will have an index card with a "?" written on it. Your teacher will think of a particular number, and clip the card on the rope. Write down the number that the "?" card represents at the appropriate position on your copy of the number line. Give the number in both decimal and fraction form. Your teacher will then ask someone in the class to state the number and explain how he or she determined what the number is.

**Gr. 7 NS 1.5** Know that every rational number is either a terminating or a repeating decimal and be able to convert terminating decimals into reduced fractions. Also addresses Gr. 6 NS 1.1

6. **Repeat** Step 5. Your teacher will continue to move the "?" card to new locations on the number line and ask for the number that the card represents.

# Draw Conclusions

1. Tom identified the unknown number on the number line below as $-\frac{1}{3}$. Do you agree or disagree? *Explain.*

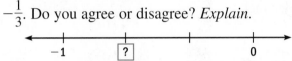

**In Exercises 2–4, identify the values of *a*, *b*, and *c*.**

2.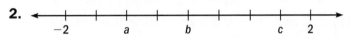

3.

4.

**In Exercises 5 and 6, make a copy of the number line and locate the given numbers on it.**

5. $-0.5, -0.7, 1.2$

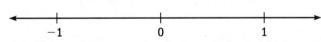

6. $-3\frac{2}{3}, -4\frac{1}{2}, -2$

7. Draw a number line and graph the numbers $-7.5$, $-7\frac{1}{3}$, and $-7\frac{7}{10}$. Then order the numbers from least to greatest.

8. Three numbers are graphed on a number line. How can you tell which is the least? the greatest?

9. Describe how to locate $1\frac{2}{3}$ on a number line. Describe how to locate $-1\frac{2}{3}$ on the same number line.

10. What number is a third of the way from $-4$ to $-5$ (moving from right to left)? What number is a third of the way from $-5$ to $-4$ (moving from left to right)?

# Lesson 5.1

# Compare and Order Rational Numbers

**VOCABULARY and CONCEPTS**

- terminating decimal, p. 128
- repeating decimal, p. 128

**Rational Numbers**

- A **rational number** is a number that can be written as $\frac{a}{b}$ where $a$ and $b$ are integers and $b \neq 0$.
- Every rational number can also be written either as a terminating decimal or a repeating decimal.

**EXAMPLE 1**  *Identifying Rational Numbers*

**Show that (a) 1.9 and (b) −8.25 are rational numbers.**

**a.** $1.9 = 1\frac{9}{10}$   **Write as mixed number.**

$= \frac{19}{10}$   **Write as improper fraction.**

**b.** $-8.25 = -8\frac{1}{4}$   **Write as mixed number.**

$= \frac{-33}{4}$   **Write as improper fraction.**

Both numbers are rational numbers because they are quotients of two integers.

**Practice for Example 1**

**Show that the number is a rational number by writing it as a quotient of two integers.**

**1.** 0.4        **2.** 1.15        **3.** −1.2        **4.** −2.6

**EXAMPLE 2**  *Graphing and Comparing Rational Numbers*

**Graph −3.9 and $-\frac{7}{2}$ on a number line. Then tell which is greater.**

The number −3.9 is nine-tenths to the left of −3 on the number line.

The number $-\frac{7}{2}$ is equal to −3.5, which is five-tenths to the left of

−3 on the number line.

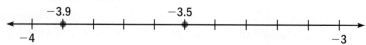

On the number line, $-\frac{7}{2}$ is to the right of −3.9. So, $-\frac{7}{2} > -3.9$.

**Practice for Example 2**

**Graph the numbers on a number line. Then tell which number is greater.**

**5.** $\frac{2}{5}$ and −0.3        **6.** $-\frac{11}{8}$ and −4.2        **7.** −7.1 and $-\frac{29}{4}$

**EXAMPLE 3** *Ordering Rational Numbers* .....................

**Order the rational numbers 2.2, −1.7, $\frac{2}{5}$, 0, and −$\frac{1}{3}$ from least to greatest.**

Begin by graphing the numbers on a number line.

From least to greatest, the numbers are $-1.7$, $-\frac{1}{3}$, $0$, $\frac{2}{5}$, and $2.2$.

## Practice for Example 3

**Order the rational numbers from least to greatest.**

**8.** $2, 1.5, -3, -0.5$

**9.** $0, -0.3, -0.6, -0.1$

**10.** $-3.2, 1, 2.5, -\frac{1}{2}$

**11.** $\frac{1}{5}, -\frac{2}{3}, \frac{2}{5}, -1\frac{1}{2}$

**EXAMPLE 4** *Comparing Data Values* ..............

The table shows the change in temperature every hour during a winter snowstorm.

| Hour | 1 | 2 | 3 | 4 | 5 | 6 |
|---|---|---|---|---|---|---|
| Change in temperature (°F) | −0.8 | 1.2 | −1.6 | −2.9 | 0.5 | −1.3 |

**a.** Which hour shows the greatest increase in temperature?

**b.** Which hour shows the greatest absolute decrease in temperature?

### Solution

**a.** Hour 2 shows the greatest increase in temperature, because 1.2 is the greatest positive number.

**b.** The negative number that has the greatest absolute value is −2.9, so hour 4 shows the greatest absolute decrease in temperature.

## Practice for Example 4

**12.** In Example 4, does hour 2 or hour 5 show the greater increase in temperature?

**13.** In Example 4, does hour 3 or hour 6 show the greater absolute decrease in temperature?

# Practice

**Extra Practice**
p. 502

**Show that the number is a rational number by writing it as a quotient of two integers.**

**1.** $0.8$    **2.** $-0.35$    **3.** $5.6$    **4.** $2.7$

**5.** $-2.4$    **6.** $3.25$    **7.** $-2.5$    **8.** $-4.8$

**Graph the numbers on a number line. Then tell which number is greater.**

**9.** $0$ and $-\dfrac{2}{5}$    **10.** $-\dfrac{8}{5}$ and $-1.75$    **11.** $-2\dfrac{1}{3}$ and $-2.3$

**12.** $3\dfrac{2}{5}$ and $-3.25$    **13.** $-7.4$ and $-7\dfrac{4}{9}$    **14.** $-1.25$ and $-1\dfrac{1}{5}$

**Write the fraction in decimal form and tell whether the decimal form of the rational number *repeats* or *terminates*.**

**15.** $\dfrac{1}{2}$    **16.** $-\dfrac{2}{3}$    **17.** $-\dfrac{3}{4}$    **18.** $\dfrac{4}{9}$

**19.** $-\dfrac{3}{5}$    **20.** $-\dfrac{4}{15}$    **21.** $\dfrac{1}{9}$    **22.** $-\dfrac{9}{16}$

**Order the rational numbers from least to greatest.**

**23.** $\dfrac{1}{4}, -1, 0$    **24.** $4.5, -3, \dfrac{1}{2}$    **25.** $\dfrac{1}{8}, -7, 3.5$    **26.** $-2.8, \dfrac{2}{3}, 209$

**Write the opposite and the absolute value of the number.**

**27.** $3.5$    **28.** $4\dfrac{7}{8}$    **29.** $-2\dfrac{1}{7}$    **30.** $-0.09$

**Evaluate the expression when $x = -\dfrac{4}{5}$.**

**31.** $-x$    **32.** $|x|$    **33.** $|x| + 2$    **34.** $|x| - \dfrac{1}{5}$

**35.** A small store's monthly profits for 6 months of a year are shown in the table.

| Month | July | Aug. | Sept. | Oct. | Nov. | Dec. |
|---|---|---|---|---|---|---|
| Profit | $1889.44 | $2318.19 | $2044.94 | $812.70 | $-$49.85 | $-$125.50 |

    **a.** In which month did the store make the greatest profit?

    **b.** In which month did the store make the least profit?

**36.** You record your transactions from September 14 to September 29 in your checkbook. Payments are negative amounts and deposits are positive amounts. On which day did you make the biggest payment? On which day did you make the biggest deposit?

| RECORD ALL CREDITS AND CHARGES THAT AFFECT YOUR ACCOUNT | | | | | |
|---|---|---|---|---|---|
| Check Number | Date | Transaction Description | Payment (−) | | Deposit (+) |
| 102 | 9/14 | Team T-shirt | $12 | 95 | |
| | 9/15 | Deposit | | | $20 50 |
| 103 | 9/21 | Bus pass | $24 | 50 | |
| | 9/29 | Deposit | | | $30 81 |

**37. REASONING** If $a$ is a positive integer, which is greater, $-\dfrac{1}{a}$ or $-\dfrac{1}{a+1}$? *Explain* your reasoning.

**Show that the number is a rational number by writing it as a quotient of two integers.**

**1.** 1.12　　　　　**2.** −0.04　　　　　**3.** 8.6　　　　　**4.** 0.85

**5.** −5.5　　　　　**6.** 0.025　　　　　**7.** −0.03　　　　　**8.** −2.06

**Write the fraction in decimal form and tell whether the decimal form of the rational number *repeats* or *terminates*.**

**9.** $\dfrac{7}{5}$　　　　　**10.** $-\dfrac{2}{15}$　　　　　**11.** $-\dfrac{19}{9}$　　　　　**12.** $\dfrac{10}{11}$

**13.** $-\dfrac{5}{6}$　　　　　**14.** $-\dfrac{1}{12}$　　　　　**15.** $-\dfrac{7}{8}$　　　　　**16.** $-\dfrac{11}{6}$

**Graph the numbers on a number line. Then tell which number is greater.**

**17.** $-2\dfrac{1}{2}$ and −2.4　　　　**18.** −3.75 and $-\dfrac{37}{10}$　　　　**19.** −3.6 and $-3\dfrac{1}{3}$

**20.** −1.3 and $-1\dfrac{1}{4}$　　　　**21.** $-3\dfrac{1}{8}$ and −3.2　　　　**22.** $-4\dfrac{2}{3}$ and −4.8

**Order the rational numbers from least to greatest.**

**23.** $-1.9, \dfrac{3}{4}, 0.8, -3$　　**24.** $1.3, -2, \dfrac{1}{2}, 0$　　**25.** $4.7, \dfrac{1}{5}, \dfrac{3}{4}, -2$　　**26.** $2.5, -\dfrac{7}{8}, -0.5, \dfrac{1}{3}$

**Evaluate the expression when *x* = −2.5.**

**27.** $-x$　　　　　**28.** $|x| + 3$　　　　　**29.** $|x| - 4$　　　　　**30.** $|x| + 1.5$

**31.** The daily gains and losses in the value of a share of stock during a week are shown in the table. Which day showed the greatest gain? Which day showed the greatest absolute loss?

| Day | Monday | Tuesday | Wednesday | Thursday | Friday |
|---|---|---|---|---|---|
| Gain or loss | $.02 | −$.05 | −$.12 | −$.08 | −$.01 |

**32.** The activity in your bank account during a week-long period is shown in the table. A positive amount indicates a deposit and a negative amount indicates a withdrawal. Which transaction increased the amount in your account the most? Which transaction decreased the amount in your account the most? *Explain* your reasoning.

| Transaction number | 1 | 2 | 3 | 4 | 5 | 6 |
|---|---|---|---|---|---|---|
| Amount | $150.52 | −$57.87 | $212.15 | −$75.41 | −$52.98 | $210.41 |

**33. REASONING** If *a* is a positive integer, which is greater, $-\dfrac{1}{a}$ or $-\dfrac{1}{2a}$? *Explain* your reasoning.

# Activity 5.2

## Let's Explore
## Adding Rational Numbers Using a Ruler

**Goal**
Add rational numbers by using rulers.

**Materials**
• graph paper
• scissors

**QUESTION**

**How can you use rulers to model addition of rational numbers?**

Use graph paper and scissors to construct two rulers with identical markings as shown below.

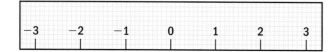

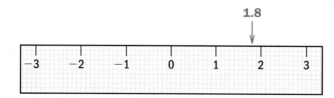

**EXPLORE**

*Model addition of rational numbers* · · · · · · · · · · ·

**Find the sum 1.8 + (−2.7).**

**1** **Locate** the first number, 1.8, on the first ruler.

1.8

**2** **Place** the second ruler above the first ruler so that the tick mark for 0 is directly above 1.8.

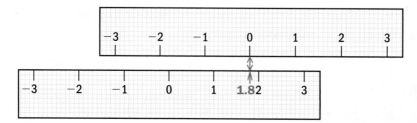

**3** **Locate** the second number, −2.7, on the top ruler. The sum of the two numbers is the corresponding number on the bottom ruler.

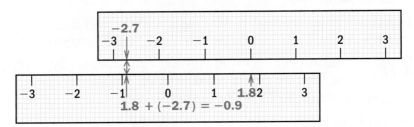

# Draw Conclusions

**1.** Repeat Steps 1–3 of the Explore, but this time start with −2.7 and add 1.8 to it. What do you observe?

**Use rulers to find the sum.**

**2.** 0.9 + 1.5        **3.** −2.6 + 2.9        **4.** 0.1 + (−2.7)

**5.** −1.1 + (−1.3)        **6.** −0.8 + 2.6        **7.** −2.1 + 1.8

**8.** To find the difference 0.8 − (−1.7), let 0.8 − (−1.7) = x. If −1.7 is added to the value of x, you would get 0.8. That is, −1.7 + x = 0.8.

  **a.** As shown below, locate −1.7 on the bottom ruler. Then line up 0 on the top ruler with −1.7 on the bottom ruler.

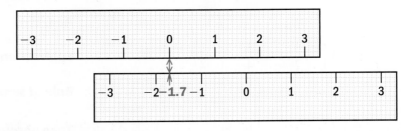

  **b.** Locate 0.8 on the bottom ruler. What number x on the top ruler is directly above 0.8?

**Use rulers to find the difference.**

**9.** 2.3 − 2.9        **10.** −0.5 − 1.2        **11.** 1.8 − (−1.1)

**12.** −3 − (−1.6)        **13.** −0.7 − (−1.3)        **14.** −1.3 − 0.8

**15.** You know from your work with integers that a − b = a + (−b). Does this rule apply when a and b are rational numbers in decimal form? *Explain*.

# Add and Subtract Rational Numbers

## VOCABULARY and CONCEPTS

- absolute value, p. 162
- opposites, p. 162

### Rules of Addition

- To add two rational numbers with the *same* sign, add their absolute values. The sum has the same sign as the numbers.
- To add two rational numbers with *different* signs, subtract the lesser absolute value from the greater absolute value. The sum has the same sign as the number with the greater absolute value.

### Subtraction Rule

To subtract $b$ from $a$, add the opposite of $b$ to $a$:
$$a - b = a + (-b)$$

**EXAMPLE 1** *Adding and Subtracting Rational Numbers*

**a.** $\dfrac{1}{5} + \left(-\dfrac{4}{5}\right) = -\left(\left|-\dfrac{4}{5}\right| - \left|\dfrac{1}{5}\right|\right)$ **Rule of different signs**

$\qquad\qquad = -\left(\dfrac{4}{5} - \dfrac{1}{5}\right)$ **Take absolute values.**

$\qquad\qquad = -\dfrac{3}{5}$ **Subtract.**

**b.** $-1.3 + (-5.8) = -\left(\left|-1.3\right| + \left|-5.8\right|\right)$ **Rule of same signs**

$\qquad\qquad = -(1.3 + 5.8)$ **Take absolute values.**

$\qquad\qquad = -7.1$ **Add.**

**c.** $-1\dfrac{3}{4} - \dfrac{1}{2} = -1\dfrac{3}{4} + \left(-\dfrac{1}{2}\right)$ **Subtraction rule**

$\qquad\qquad = -\left(\left|-1\dfrac{3}{4}\right| + \left|-\dfrac{1}{2}\right|\right)$ **Rule of same signs**

$\qquad\qquad = -\left(1\dfrac{3}{4} + \dfrac{1}{2}\right)$ **Take absolute values.**

$\qquad\qquad = -\left(\dfrac{7}{4} + \dfrac{2}{4}\right)$ **Write improper fraction and use common denominator.**

$\qquad\qquad = -\dfrac{9}{4} = -2\dfrac{1}{4}$ **Add. Write as a mixed number.**

## Practice for Example 1

**Find the sum or difference.**

**1.** $5.3 + (-9)$      **2.** $-0.2 + (-0.6)$      **3.** $-11.2 - (-14.6)$

**4.** $-\dfrac{1}{3} + \dfrac{7}{8}$      **5.** $1\dfrac{2}{5} + \left(-\dfrac{3}{5}\right)$      **6.** $-9\dfrac{1}{2} - 3\dfrac{3}{4}$

**EXAMPLE 2** *Evaluating an Algebraic Expression* ..........

**Evaluate the expression** $x - 5.1 - y$ **when** $x = 3.7$ **and** $y = -2.3$.

**Solution**

$$
\begin{aligned}
x - 5.1 - y &= 3.7 - 5.1 - (-2.3) && \text{Substitute 3.7 for } x \text{ and } -2.3 \text{ for } y. \\
&= 3.7 + (-5.1) + 2.3 && \text{Add the opposites of 5.1 and } -2.3. \\
&= 0.9 && \text{Add.}
\end{aligned}
$$

**Practice for Example 2**

**Evaluate the expression when** $x = -\dfrac{3}{8}$ **and** $y = \dfrac{1}{2}$.

**7.** $x + y - \dfrac{1}{3}$

**8.** $\dfrac{3}{4} - y - x$

**9.** $x - \left(2\dfrac{1}{3} - y\right)$

**EXAMPLE 3** *Evaluating Change* .........................

A man was at the top of a mountain at an elevation of 513.4 meters. He rappelled down to an elevation of 485.9 meters. What was the change in elevation?

**Solution**

**Step 1** Write a verbal model.

$$
\boxed{\text{Change in elevation}} = \boxed{\text{Ending elevation}} - \boxed{\text{Starting elevation}}
$$

**Step 2** Find the change in elevation.

$$
\begin{aligned}
\text{Change in elevation} &= 485.9 - 513.4 && \text{Substitute values.} \\
&= 485.9 + (-513.4) && \text{Subtraction rule} \\
&= -27.5 && \text{Add.}
\end{aligned}
$$

▶ **Answer** The change in elevation was −27.5 meters.

**Practice for Example 3**

**Find the change in temperature.**

**10.** From 12.5°C to −2.1°C

**11.** From $-50\dfrac{3}{4}$°F to −51°F

**12.** From 57.7°C to 49.4°C

**13.** From $-8\dfrac{1}{5}$°F to $-21\dfrac{1}{2}$°F

**Write the absolute value of the number.**

**1.** $\frac{2}{3}$

**2.** $-6.25$

**3.** $-\frac{1}{2}$

**Find the sum or difference.**

**4.** $1.9 - (-8.1)$

**5.** $-\frac{1}{4} + \frac{3}{8}$

**6.** $-40.6 - 56.7$

**7.** $-\frac{7}{9} + \frac{2}{3}$

**8.** $0.7 - (-0.1)$

**9.** $-\frac{1}{2} - \left(-\frac{9}{10}\right)$

**10.** $77.8 + (-79.1)$

**11.** $\frac{2}{11} - \frac{17}{22}$

**12.** $-13.4 - (-19.5)$

**13.** $\frac{2}{5} + \left(-\frac{2}{5}\right)$

**14.** $-3.5 - (-0.6)$

**15.** $5\frac{5}{6} - \left(-1\frac{1}{3}\right)$

**Evaluate the expression when $x = 2.5$ and $y = -34.7$.**

**16.** $y - x$

**17.** $x - y$

**18.** $y - x + 3$

**19.** $y - 8 - x$

**20.** $-y + 12 + x$

**21.** $10.5 - x - y$

**22.** $x + 3.5 - y$

**23.** $4.5 - x - y$

**24.** $y + 4 - (-x)$

**Find the change in temperature or elevation.**

**25.** From $-4\frac{1}{2}°F$ to $-10°F$

**26.** From $-56.6°C$ to $-52.2°C$

**27.** From 124.1 meters to $-10.2$ meters

**28.** From $-2$ yards to $-1\frac{1}{4}$ yards

**29.** The highest elevation in Long Beach, California, is 109.7 meters. The lowest elevation in Long Beach is $-2.1$ meters. What is the difference in elevations?

**30.** The average daytime temperature on the surface of the moon is $224\frac{3}{5}°F$, and the average nighttime temperature on the surface of the moon is $-243\frac{2}{5}°F$. What is the average change in temperature from nighttime to daytime?

**31.** You are scuba diving at an elevation of $15\frac{1}{5}$ feet below sea level. Thirty minutes later, you are at an elevation of $12\frac{1}{2}$ feet below sea level. What is your change in elevation? Did you go up or down?

**32.** The table shows the average weekly prices (in dollars) of a gallon of regular gasoline during a month at a gas station. Determine the change in the price per gallon from week to week. Then find the sum of these changes. Compare the sum with the change from week 1 to week 4.

| Week | 1 | 2 | 3 | 4 |
|---|---|---|---|---|
| Price per gallon (dollars) | 2.10 | 2.15 | 2.09 | 2.11 |

**33.** **REASONING** *Describe* a method for finding the sum of $-\frac{4}{5}$ and 0.6. Then find the sum.

**Find the sum or difference.**

**1.** $1.9 - (-0.1)$

**2.** $-\frac{1}{7} + \frac{3}{8}$

**3.** $-400.6 - 506.7$

**4.** $-\frac{5}{9} + \frac{2}{11}$

**5.** $0.7 - (-20.1)$

**6.** $-\frac{1}{6} - \left(-\frac{19}{10}\right)$

**7.** $547.8 + (-79.1)$

**8.** $-\frac{3}{5} - \frac{17}{22}$

**9.** $-36.4 - (-19.5)$

**10.** $-3\frac{2}{5} - \left(-\frac{17}{5}\right)$

**11.** $-300.5 - (-120.6)$

**12.** $2\frac{5}{6} - \left(-1\frac{1}{4}\right)$

**Evaluate the expression when $x = -6\frac{2}{5}$ and $y = 10\frac{4}{5}$.**

**13.** $y - x$

**14.** $x - (-y)$

**15.** $x - y$

**16.** $-y - x$

**17.** $x - y - 2\frac{3}{5}$

**18.** $y - 5\frac{2}{5} - x$

**19.** $-7\frac{3}{10} - x + y$

**20.** $6\frac{2}{5} + y - x$

**21.** $10\frac{4}{5} - x - y$

**22.** $y - (-x) + 6\frac{2}{5}$

**23.** $7\frac{1}{5} + y - x$

**24.** $4\frac{1}{4} - x - y$

**Find the change in temperature or elevation.**

**25.** From $-8.5°C$ to $2°C$

**26.** From $-23\frac{4}{5}$ feet to $-24\frac{7}{10}$ feet

**27.** From $-7\frac{1}{2}$ yards to $-11\frac{1}{4}$ yards

**28.** From $4.3$ meters to $-3.1$ meters

**29.** A manned submersible used in deep sea exploration moved $20\frac{3}{4}$ feet below its initial elevation of $-7\frac{1}{3}$ feet. What was the new elevation of the submersible?

**30.** The table shows the weekly prices (in dollars) of a pound of bananas during a month at a local supermarket. Determine the change in the price per pound from week to week. Then find the sum of these changes. Compare the sum with the change from week 1 to week 4.

| Week | 1 | 2 | 3 | 4 |
|---|---|---|---|---|
| Price per pound (dollars) | 0.49 | 0.49 | 0.39 | 0.49 |

**31.** The table shows the record high and low temperatures for several states. Find the difference between the record high and low temperatures for each state. For which two states is the difference the greatest?

| State | Alaska | North Dakota | Wyoming | Virginia | Nevada |
|---|---|---|---|---|---|
| High temperature (°C) | 37.8°C | 49.4°C | 46.1°C | 43.3°C | 51.7°C |
| Low temperature (°C) | −62.2°C | −51.1°C | −54.4°C | −34.4°C | −45.6°C |

**32.** **REASONING** Using rational numbers, give an example that satisfies the given conditions. If it is not possible, explain why.

**a.** positive − negative = negative

**b.** negative − negative = positive

**c.** negative − positive = positive

**d.** positive − positive = negative

# Activity 5.3

## Let's Explore

## Investigating Addition Properties

**Goal**
Investigate the ordering and grouping properties of addition and subtraction.

**Materials**
• paper and pencil

**QUESTION** How does changing the order of numbers or the grouping of numbers affect the value of an expression?

**EXPLORE 1** *Change the order of numbers* •••••••••••••••••••

**1** **Write** two fractions or mixed numbers, at least one of which should be negative. Let $a$ represent the first number and $b$ represent the second number.

|  | Original order | Reverse order |
|---|---|---|
| Addition | $a + b = ?$ | $b + a = ?$ |
| Subtraction | $a - b = ?$ | $b - a = ?$ |

**2** **Copy** the table and complete the *Original order* column by finding the sum $a + b$ and the difference $a - b$.

**3** **Complete** the *Reverse order* column by finding the sum $b + a$ and the difference $b - a$.

**4** **Write** two terminating decimals, at least one of which should be negative. Let $a$ represent the first number and $b$ represent the second number. Repeat Steps 2 and 3.

## Draw Conclusions

**In Exercises 1–6, tell whether the statement is *true* or *false*.**

**1.** $5 - 4.5 = 4.5 - 5$

**2.** $-\frac{11}{14} + 9 = 9 + \left(-\frac{11}{14}\right)$

**3.** $-\frac{1}{3} - 3 = 3 - \left(-\frac{1}{3}\right)$

**4.** $\frac{4}{11} + (-2) = -2 + \frac{4}{11}$

**5.** $\frac{2}{3} + \frac{1}{2} = \frac{1}{2} + \frac{2}{3}$

**6.** $-3.2 - 1.8 = 1.8 - (-3.2)$

**7.** What can you conclude about the order in which you add or subtract two numbers?

**Gr. 7 AF 1.3** Simplify numerical expressions by applying properties of rational numbers (e.g., identity, inverse, distributive, **associative**, **commutative**) and justify the process used.

**EXPLORE 2** *Change the grouping of numbers*

**1** **Write** three fractions or mixed numbers, at least one of which should be negative. Let $a$ represent the first number, $b$ the second number, and $c$ the third number.

|  | Original grouping | New grouping |
|---|---|---|
| Addition | $(a + b) + c = ?$ | $a + (b + c) = ?$ |
| Subtraction | $(a - b) - c = ?$ | $a - (b - c) = ?$ |

**2** **Copy** the table and complete the *Original grouping* column by finding the value of $(a + b) + c$ and $(a - b) - c$.

**3** **Complete** the *New grouping* column by finding the value of $a + (b + c)$ and $a - (b - c)$.

**4** **Write** three terminating decimals, at least one of which should be negative. Let $a$ represent the first number, $b$ the second number, and $c$ the third number. Repeat Steps 2 and 3.

## Draw Conclusions

**In Exercises 8–11, tell whether the statement is *true* or *false*.**

**8.** $-4.3 - (3.9 - 11.8) = (-4.3 - 3.9) - 11.8$

**9.** $-1 + \left(1\frac{1}{5} + \frac{4}{5}\right) = \left(-1 + 1\frac{1}{5}\right) + \frac{4}{5}$

**10.** $\left(\frac{1}{2} - 3\right) - 4\frac{2}{5} = \frac{1}{2} - \left(3 - 4\frac{2}{5}\right)$

**11.** $(-7 + 2.2) + 13.1 = -7 + (2.2 + 13.1)$

**In Exercises 12 and 13, tell whether each statement is *always true* or *not always true*.**

**12.** $a + (b + c) = (a + b) + c$

**13.** $a - (b - c) = (a - b) - c$

**14.** For any statement in Exercises 12 and 13 that is not always true, provide values for $a$, $b$, and $c$ that make the statement true as well as values for $a$, $b$, and $c$ that make the statement false. *Explain* your reasoning.

# Use the Properties of Addition

### VOCABULARY and CONCEPTS

- opposites, p. 162

### Properties of Addition

| Property | Words | Algebra |
|---|---|---|
| **Commutative Property** | The order in which you add two numbers does not change the sum. | $a + b = b + a$ |
| **Associative Property** | The way you group three numbers when adding does not change the sum. | $(a + b) + c = a + (b + c)$ |
| **Identity Property** | The sum of a number and 0 is the number. The number 0 is called the **additive identity**. | $a + 0 = a$ |
| **Inverse Property** | The opposite of a number $a$, written $-a$, is also called the **additive inverse** of $a$. The sum of a number and its additive inverse is 0. | $a + (-a) = 0$ |

**EXAMPLE 1** *Identifying the Properties of Addition* • • • • • • • • •

**Identify the property illustrated.**

| Statement | Property Illustrated |
|---|---|
| **a.** $-15 + 0 = -15$ | **Identity property of addition** |
| **b.** $12 + (-17) = -17 + 12$ | **Commutative property of addition** |
| **c.** $-\frac{2}{3} + 0 = -\frac{2}{3}$ | **Identity property of addition** |
| **d.** $-1\frac{3}{4} + 1\frac{3}{4} = 0$ | **Inverse property of addition** |

### Practice for Example 1

**Identify the property illustrated.**

**1.** $-1.5 + 2.4 = 2.4 + (-1.5)$   **2.** $\frac{1}{3} + \left(-\frac{1}{3}\right) = 0$

**3.** $\frac{2}{9} + (6 + 0.5) = \left(\frac{2}{9} + 6\right) + 0.5$   **4.** $0 + 44.6 = 44.6$

**Gr. 7 AF 1.3** Simplify numerical expressions by applying properties of rational numbers (e.g., identity, inverse, distributive, associative, commutative) and justify the process used.
Also addresses Gr. 2 AF 1.1

**EXAMPLE 2** *Using the Properties of Addition*

You used your computer for 57 minutes on Monday, 91 minutes on Tuesday, and 73 minutes on Wednesday. Find the total time you spent using your computer.

**Solution**

The total time is the sum of the three times.

**Method 1** Use order of operations.

$$57 + 91 + 73 = 148 + 73 \qquad \textbf{Add 57 and 91.}$$
$$= 221 \qquad \textbf{Add 148 and 73.}$$

**Method 2** Use mental math. The properties of addition allow you to group together terms that are easy to add mentally.

$$57 + 91 + 73 = 91 + (57 + 73) \qquad \textbf{Commutative and associative properties}$$
$$= 91 + (130) \qquad \textbf{Add 57 and 73 mentally.}$$
$$= 221 \qquad \textbf{Add 91 and 130 mentally.}$$

▶**Answer** The total time is 221 minutes.

**Practice for Example 2**

5. Jason did volunteer work for $1\frac{1}{2}$ hours on Monday, $\frac{3}{4}$ hour on Tuesday, and $\frac{1}{2}$ hour on Wednesday. Find the total time he spent doing volunteer work.

**EXAMPLE 3** *Simplifying Algebraic Expressions*

**Simplify the expression. Justify your steps.**

$$2.1 - 3.8y + 3 = 2.1 + (-3.8y) + 3 \qquad \textbf{Subtraction rule}$$
$$= \left[2.1 + (-3.8y)\right] + 3 \qquad \textbf{Use order of operations.}$$
$$= \left[(-3.8y) + 2.1\right] + 3 \qquad \textbf{Commutative property of addition}$$
$$= -3.8y + (2.1 + 3) \qquad \textbf{Associative property of addition}$$
$$= -3.8y + 5.1 \qquad \textbf{Add 2.1 and 3.}$$

**Practice for Example 3**

**Simplify the expression. Justify your steps.**

6. $-\dfrac{1}{6} + x + 1$

7. $-8.9 - 10x + 8.9$

**Extra Practice**
p. 502

**Identify the property illustrated.**

**1.** $4.5 + (-4.5) = 0$

**2.** $\frac{4}{7} + 0 = \frac{4}{7}$

**3.** $3 + (-9) = -9 + 3$

**4.** $6 + (-9w + 7.7) = (6 + (-9w)) + 7.7$

**5.** $2k + (-2k) = 0$

**6.** $-34.9 + 0 = -34.9$

**7.** $\frac{1}{3} + (-x) = -x + \frac{1}{3}$

**8.** $5\frac{1}{8} + \left(-1 + \frac{6}{7}\right) = \left(5\frac{1}{8} + (-1)\right) + \frac{6}{7}$

**9.** $7z + 0 = 7z$

**10.** $(23 + 39.7) + 41 = (39.7 + 23) + 41$

**Evaluate the expression using mental math. Justify your steps.**

**11.** $23.5 + 9 + (-3.5)$

**12.** $\frac{3}{7} + \frac{4}{5} + \left(-\frac{3}{7}\right)$

**13.** $4.6 + 0 + 44.6$

**14.** $\frac{1}{6} + \left(-\frac{2}{3}\right) + \left(-\frac{1}{3}\right)$

**15.** $0.8 + (-1.9) + 0.2$

**16.** $5\frac{2}{5} + \left(-2\frac{1}{5}\right) + \left(-5\frac{2}{5}\right)$

**Simplify the expression. Justify your steps.**

**17.** $2.9 + y + 7.8$

**18.** $x + (-x) + \frac{10}{13}$

**19.** $\frac{11}{4} + \left(-\frac{1}{2} + m\right)$

**20.** $6y + (-29.7) - 19.8$

**21.** $-4\frac{5}{6} + \left(-\frac{1}{7}z\right) - 4$

**22.** $24.6y - 45.6 - (-95.1)$

**23.** John walks from his house 0.6 mile east to school. After school, he walks 0.2 mile west to the library and then 1.4 miles east to the post office. When he is at the post office, how far and in what direction is his house?

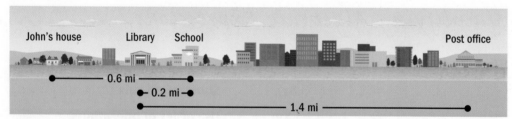

**24.** During a recent school football game, your quarterback was sacked and lost $8\frac{1}{2}$ yards on the first down. On the second down, a $15\frac{1}{4}$ yard pass was completed. On the third down, your team rushed for $3\frac{3}{4}$ yards. How many net yards did your team gain? *Justify* your steps.

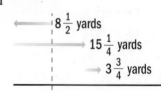

**25.** **REASONING** *Explain* why there is no commutative property of subtraction.

**Identify the property illustrated.**

**1.** $84.5 + (-84.5) = 0$

**2.** $0.02 + (-0.09) = -0.09 + 0.02$

**3.** $5x + (-3 + 7) = (5x + (-3)) + 7$

**4.** $-2\frac{6}{7} + 0 = -2\frac{6}{7}$

**5.** $\frac{3}{4}w + \left(-\frac{3}{4}w\right) = 0$

**6.** $\frac{1}{3} + (-9x) = -9x + \frac{1}{3}$

**7.** $5\frac{1}{8} + \left(-1 + \frac{6}{7}\right) = \left(5\frac{1}{8} + (-1)\right) + \frac{6}{7}$

**8.** $-934.9 = -934.9 + 0$

**9.** $(2z - 1) + 0 = 2z - 1$

**10.** $(38 + 2r) + 7.1 = (2r + 38) + 7.1$

**Evaluate the expression using mental math. Justify your steps.**

**11.** $-8.5 + 6 - 3.5$

**12.** $\frac{3}{7} + \frac{4}{7} - \left(-\frac{3}{7}\right)$

**13.** $4.61 + 0 - 44.86$

**14.** $\left(-\frac{2}{3}\right) + 1 + \left(-\frac{2}{3}\right)$

**15.** $0.08 + (-1.09) + 0.02$

**16.** $9\frac{3}{5} + \left(-2\frac{1}{5}\right) + 5\frac{2}{5}$

**Simplify the expression. Justify your steps.**

**17.** $24.9 + y - 7.8$

**18.** $7x + \frac{10}{13} + (-7x)$

**19.** $1\frac{1}{4} + (-1.25 + m)$

**20.** $3x + (-21.4) - 14.8$

**21.** $-3\frac{5}{6} + \left(-\frac{1}{7}z\right) - 4\frac{1}{6}$

**22.** $17.3y - 11.3 - (-89.1)$

**23.** You have a part-time job walking dogs during the summer. The home of the first dog is 3.5 miles west of your house. The home of the second dog is 3.25 miles east of the home of the first dog. The home of the last dog is 5.5 miles west of the home of the second dog. How far away and in what direction from your house are you after you walk the last dog?

**24.** The graph shows the profits earned by a small company during the first six months of the year. Did the company gain or lose money for the first six months? If so, how much? *Explain* your reasoning.

**25.** **REASONING** *Explain* why there is no associative property of subtraction.

**26.** **REASONING** State the reasons that justify the steps in $(a + b) + (-b) = a + (b + (-b)) = a + 0 = a$.

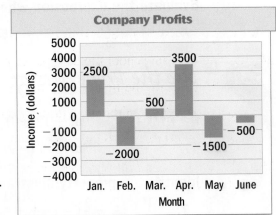

# Mid-Chapter Review

**Vocabulary Exercise**

**1.** Copy and complete: A _?_ is a number that can be written as $\frac{a}{b}$ where $a$ and $b$ are integers and $b \neq 0$.

**5.1** *Compare and Order Rational Numbers* . . . . . . . . . . . . *pp. 204–207*

**EXAMPLE** Order 1.8, $-1.7$, $-\frac{3}{4}$, and 0 from least to greatest.

Begin by graphing the numbers on a number line.

From least to greatest, the numbers are $-1.7$, $-\frac{3}{4}$, 0, and 1.8.

**Order the rational numbers from least to greatest.**

**2.** $0.4, 0, -1.1, 1\frac{1}{3}$

**3.** $-0.9, \frac{9}{10}, -2\frac{1}{2}, 1.7$

**5.2** *Add and Stubract Rational Numbers* . . . . . . . . . . . . *pp. 210–213*

**EXAMPLE** Evaluate $x - 4.8 - y$ when $x = 2.9$ and $y = -1.5$.

$$
\begin{aligned}
x - 4.8 - y &= 2.9 - 4.8 - (-1.5) &&\text{Substitute.} \\
&= 2.9 + (-4.8) + 1.5 &&\text{Subtraction rule} \\
&= -0.4 &&\text{Add.}
\end{aligned}
$$

**Evaluate the expression when $x = -\frac{4}{5}$ and $y = \frac{1}{4}$.**

**4.** $x + y - \frac{1}{5}$

**5.** $\frac{9}{10} - y - x$

**6.** $x - \left(1\frac{1}{2} - y\right)$

**5.3** *Use the Properties of Addition* . . . . . . . . . . . . . . . . . *pp. 216–219*

**EXAMPLES**

**a.** $-12 + 0 = -12$     **Identity property of addition**

**b.** $6 + (-9) = -9 + 6$     **Commutative property of addition**

**Identify the property illustrated.**

**7.** $-\frac{1}{5} + \left(\frac{2}{5} + \frac{3}{4}\right) = \left(-\frac{1}{5} + \frac{2}{5}\right) + \frac{3}{4}$

**8.** $-3\frac{4}{5} + 3\frac{4}{5} = 0$

**Show that the number is a rational number by writing it as a quotient of two integers.**

**1.** $0.3$      **2.** $1.72$      **3.** $-2.4$      **4.** $-4.75$

**Order the rational numbers from least to greatest.**

**5.** $1.8, \frac{1}{8}, -2.6, -\frac{2}{3}$      **6.** $0.2, -0.03, 0.004, -0.0005$    **7.** $\frac{2}{3}, -\frac{3}{4}, \frac{4}{5}, -\frac{5}{6}$

**Find the sum or difference.**

**8.** $-1.8 + 2.7$      **9.** $-4.7 + (-0.6)$      **10.** $2\frac{1}{8} - \frac{3}{4}$

**11.** $-1\frac{3}{4} - 2\frac{2}{3}$      **12.** $-2.3 - (-1.2)$      **13.** $-\frac{5}{8} + \frac{1}{6}$

**Evaluate the expression when $x = \frac{1}{2}$ and $y = -\frac{3}{5}$.**

**14.** $x + y - \frac{1}{4}$      **15.** $\frac{5}{6} - y - x$      **16.** $x - \left(1\frac{1}{2} + y\right)$

**17.** $x - y - \frac{3}{4}$      **18.** $y + x - 2\frac{3}{8}$      **19.** $-3\frac{2}{5} - \left(y + 1\frac{1}{5}\right)$

**Simplify the expression.**

**20.** $6.8 + w + (-w)$      **21.** $4.6 - 1.7r + 3$      **22.** $\frac{7}{4} - \frac{3}{2} + j$

**Identify the property illustrated.**

**23.** $-2\frac{3}{8} + 2\frac{3}{8} = 0$      **24.** $-5 + 0 = -5$      **25.** $\frac{5}{8} + \left(-\frac{3}{4}\right) = -\frac{3}{4} + \frac{5}{8}$

**26.** The table shows the weekly prices (in dollars) of a pound of apples during a month at a local supermarket.

| Week | 1 | 2 | 3 | 4 |
|---|---|---|---|---|
| Price per pound (dollars) | 0.59 | 0.39 | 0.49 | 0.59 |

     **a.** Determine the change in the price per pound from week to week. Find the sum of these changes.

     **b.** Find the change in price from week 1 to week 4. Compare the sum from part (a) with the change from week 1 to week 4.

**27.** Sharon walks from her house 0.4 mile east to school. After school, she walks 0.1 mile west to the store and then 2.3 miles east to the library.

     **a.** Draw a diagram to illustrate Sharon's path.

     **b.** When Sharon is at the library, how far and in what direction is her house?

# Activity 5.4

## Let's Explore
### A Rational Number Game

**Goal**
Multiply and divide rational numbers.

**Materials**
• index cards

**QUESTION** **How do you multiply and divide rational numbers?**

The rules you learned for multiplying and dividing integers in Chapter 4 also apply to multiplying and dividing rational numbers. This game gives you an opportunity to practice multiplying and dividing positive and negative fractions and mixed numbers.

**EXPLORE** *Multiply and divide rational numbers* . . . . . . . . .

**1** **Create** 24 game cards like the ones shown by writing the given rational numbers on index cards.

$$\frac{3}{8} \quad \frac{2}{5} \quad 3 \quad \frac{7}{8} \quad \frac{17}{2} \quad 1\frac{1}{8} \quad \frac{1}{10} \quad 1\frac{1}{2}$$

$$\frac{1}{2} \quad \frac{3}{4} \quad \frac{7}{3} \quad \frac{11}{4} \quad -1 \quad -\frac{1}{2} \quad -\frac{1}{5} \quad -1\frac{1}{9}$$

$$-1\frac{1}{2} \quad -3 \quad -\frac{8}{22} \quad -\frac{3}{7} \quad -\frac{17}{2} \quad -5 \quad -\frac{9}{8} \quad -2\frac{1}{4}$$

**2** **Copy** the table. Complete the table as you play the game.

| Round | Number 1 | Number 2 | Product or Quotient | Points |
|-------|----------|----------|---------------------|--------|
| 1 | ? | ? | ? | ? |
| 2 | ? | ? | ? | ? |
| 3 | ? | ? | ? | ? |
| 4 | ? | ? | ? | ? |
| 5 | ? | ? | ? | ? |
| 6 | ? | ? | ? | ? |

**3** **Play** the game with a partner. Begin by shuffling the cards and spreading them out face up. Each player takes turns choosing two cards. You want to choose two numbers that, when multiplied or divided, will earn the most points. The number of points you score depends on the product or quotient of the numbers on the cards. Scoring is as follows:

| Product or quotient is: | Number of points earned is: |
|---|---|
| Greater than 1 | 1 |
| Between 0 and 1, including 1 | 4 |
| Between 0 and −1 | 3 |
| Less than −1, including −1 | 2 |
| Incorrect or incomplete | 0 |

Decide which player chooses first. The first player chooses any two cards, then the second player chooses two cards. Each of you should record the numbers on the cards in the table for Round 1 under the *Number 1* and *Number 2* columns. Then, each of you should choose to take either the product or the quotient of the two numbers and write the result in the *Product or Quotient* column. Repeat this process until all cards have been chosen.

**4** **Exchange** tables. Check each other's results and then find the number of points your partner has earned. The player who scores more points wins.

## Draw Conclusions
**Find the product or quotient.**

1. $\frac{1}{2} \cdot (-4)$

2. $\frac{2}{3} \div \frac{1}{6}$

3. $1\frac{1}{2} \cdot \frac{2}{3}$

4. $-\frac{5}{6} \div \frac{5}{2}$

5. $2\frac{1}{4} \cdot (-2)$

6. $-1\frac{1}{8} \div \frac{4}{3}$

7. If you want the product or quotient of two numbers to be positive and one number is positive, what sign should the other number be? *Explain* your reasoning.

8. If you want the product or quotient of two numbers to be positive and one number is negative, what sign should the other number be? *Explain* your reasoning.

9. *Describe* a strategy you might use to win the game.

# Multiply and Divide Rational Numbers

## VOCABULARY and CONCEPTS

- reciprocal, p. 86
- average rate of change, p. 188

### Division Rule

To divide a number $a$ by a nonzero number $b$, multiply $a$ by the reciprocal of $b$: $a \div b = a \cdot \dfrac{1}{b}$.

### The Sign of a Product

- The product of two rational numbers with the *same* sign is positive.
- The product of two rational numbers with *different* signs is negative.

### The Sign of a Quotient

- The quotient of two rational numbers with the *same* sign is positive.
- The quotient of two rational numbers with *different* signs is negative.

**EXAMPLE 1** *Multiplying and Dividing Rational Numbers*

**Find the product or quotient.**

a. $(-2.8)(-3)$

b. $4\left(-\dfrac{5}{6}\right)\left(-\dfrac{3}{5}\right)$

c. $-24 \div \dfrac{2}{3}$

d. $\dfrac{3}{7} \div \left(-\dfrac{1}{2}\right)$

**Solution**

a. $(-2.8)(-3) = 8.4$     **Same signs; product is positive.**

b. $4\left(-\dfrac{5}{6}\right)\left(-\dfrac{3}{5}\right) = \left(-\dfrac{10}{3}\right)\left(-\dfrac{3}{5}\right)$     **Multiply 4 and $-\dfrac{5}{6}$; product is negative.**

$\qquad = 2$     **Same signs; product is positive.**

c. $-24 \div \dfrac{2}{3} = -24 \cdot \dfrac{3}{2}$     **Division rule**

$\qquad = -36$     **Different signs; product is negative.**

d. $\dfrac{3}{7} \div \left(-\dfrac{1}{2}\right) = \dfrac{3}{7} \cdot (-2)$     **Division rule**

$\qquad = -\dfrac{6}{7}$     **Different signs; product is negative.**

### Practice for Example 1

**Find the product or quotient.**

**1.** $-10.4(0.5)$     **2.** $-\dfrac{1}{4}(-2)$     **3.** $7.4 \div (-1.85)$     **4.** $-1\dfrac{1}{2} \div \dfrac{3}{5}$

**EXAMPLE 2** *Evaluating an Algebraic Expression* • • • • • • • • • • •

Evaluate the expression $2x \div y$ when $x = -\dfrac{4}{5}$ and $y = -8$.

$2x \div y = 2 \cdot \left(-\dfrac{4}{5}\right) \div (-8)$  **Substitute** $-\dfrac{4}{5}$ **for** $x$ **and** $-8$ **for** $y$.

$\quad = -\dfrac{8}{5} \div (-8)$  **Different signs; product is negative.**

$\quad = -\dfrac{8}{5} \cdot \left(-\dfrac{1}{8}\right)$  **Division rule**

$\quad = \dfrac{1}{5}$  **Same signs; product is positive.**

### Practice for Example 2

Evaluate the expression when $x = -\dfrac{3}{4}$ and $y = \dfrac{4}{7}$.

**5.** $x \cdot y$       **6.** $x \div (-2y)$       **7.** $-3y \div x$

**EXAMPLE 3** *Finding a Rate of Change* • • • • • • • • • • • • • • • • • •

A camper fills a lantern with 1.8 pints of fuel. After 2.5 hours of use, there is only 0.5 pint of fuel left in the lantern. Find the average rate of change in the amount of fuel over this time period.

**Solution**

$\text{Rate of change} = \dfrac{\text{Final amount} - \text{Initial amount}}{\text{Time}}$  **Write verbal model.**

$\quad = \dfrac{0.5 - 1.8}{2.5}$  **Substitute values.**

$\quad = \dfrac{-1.3}{2.5}$  **Subtract.**

$\quad = -0.52$  **Divide.**

▶ **Answer** The rate of change is $-0.52$ pint per hour.

### Practice for Example 3

**Find the rate of change.**

**8.** Will the lantern in Example 3 operate for another hour? *Explain.*

**9.** When Sue went to bed, the temperature outside was 63°F. When she woke up 8 hours later, the temperature outside was 59°F. What was the average rate of change in temperature overnight?

# Practice

**Extra Practice**
p. 502

**Find the reciprocal of the number.**

**1.** $-22$

**2.** $5$

**3.** $-4$

**4.** $-\dfrac{1}{4}$

**5.** $\dfrac{1}{3}$

**6.** $-\dfrac{5}{6}$

**7.** $-2$

**8.** $\dfrac{2}{5}$

**Find the product or quotient.**

**9.** $-14\left(\dfrac{5}{7}\right)$

**10.** $-\dfrac{1}{2} \div \left(-\dfrac{1}{4}\right)$

**11.** $-36 \div (-1.5)$

**12.** $-\dfrac{9}{10}\left(\dfrac{5}{7}\right)$

**13.** $10(-3.6)$

**14.** $-1\dfrac{1}{2}\left(-\dfrac{3}{4}\right)$

**15.** $6.5 \div (-0.2)$

**16.** $-6.1(-10.4)$

**17.** $-0.4 \div (-10)$

**18.** $24 \div \left(-\dfrac{1}{3}\right)$

**19.** $\dfrac{5}{3} \div (-5)$

**20.** $-\dfrac{3}{8} \div \left(-\dfrac{1}{4}\right)$

**21.** $-2\dfrac{2}{3}\left(\dfrac{7}{8}\right)$

**22.** $-0.25 \div 5$

**23.** $-2\dfrac{2}{5} \cdot \dfrac{1}{2}$

**24.** $-12 \div (-2.4)$

**25.** $\dfrac{6}{7} \div (-4)$

**26.** $-\dfrac{3}{8} \div \left(\dfrac{9}{10}\right)$

**27.** $-12\dfrac{1}{4} \div 4\dfrac{2}{3}$

**28.** $8.2 \div (-0.4)$

**29.** $3\dfrac{3}{4} \div \left(-2\dfrac{1}{2}\right)$

**30.** $3.4(-21.1)$

**31.** $-2\dfrac{1}{6}\left(-\dfrac{3}{4}\right)$

**32.** $-\dfrac{2}{5} \div \dfrac{3}{4}$

**Evaluate the expression when $x = -\dfrac{2}{5}$ and $y = -\dfrac{7}{10}$.**

**33.** $xy$

**34.** $-5xy$

**35.** $x \div y$

**36.** $y \div x$

**Evaluate the expression when $x = 4.8$ and $y = -0.5$.**

**37.** $x \div y$

**38.** $x \div 2y$

**39.** $xy \div (-5)$

**40.** $3 \div xy$

**41. REASONING** *Describe* the steps you would take to divide 0.8 by $-\dfrac{2}{5}$.

**42.** During a space walk, an astronaut's space suit provides the astronaut with oxygen. While working in the space suit for 1.5 hours, the astronaut's oxygen level dropped from 1.017 pounds to 0.717 pound. Find the average rate of change in the amount of oxygen in the astronaut's space suit.

**43.** The imbalance in the federal budget is the difference of the government's revenue and its expenses. In 1974, the imbalance was $-6.1$ billion dollars. In 2004, the imbalance was $-412.7$ billion dollars. The imbalance in 2004 was how many times the imbalance in 1974? Round your answer to the nearest tenth.

**44.** The gas tank in Eva's car contained 13.3 gallons of gas. After a 3 hour trip she had 4.6 gallons of gas left. Find the average rate of change in the amount of gas in the tank over the 3 hours.

**45.** During a 4 year period, the area of a beach decreased by 5.8 square miles due to erosion. Find the average rate of change (in square miles per year) in the area of the beach over the 4 year period.

# Practice

**Find the reciprocal of the number.**

**1.** $\frac{2}{3}$

**2.** $-0.2$

**3.** $-4$

**4.** $2.5$

**5.** $1\frac{1}{3}$

**6.** $-2\frac{3}{4}$

**7.** $1.5$

**8.** $0.8$

**Find the product or quotient.**

**9.** $-15(4.3)$

**10.** $-28 \div \left(-\frac{4}{7}\right)$

**11.** $-3.1(-11.4)$

**12.** $-\frac{5}{8} \div 4$

**13.** $-6.25(9.1)$

**14.** $-\frac{7}{10} \div (-5)$

**15.** $-9(-3)(-2.4)$

**16.** $-50.4 \div (-10)$

**17.** $\frac{1}{9} \div \left(-\frac{7}{9}\right)$

**18.** $14\left(-\frac{3}{5}\right)\left(-\frac{5}{7}\right)$

**19.** $-\frac{5}{6}\left(-\frac{2}{5}\right)\left(-\frac{9}{4}\right)$

**20.** $26\left(-\frac{21}{13}\right)\left(\frac{5}{6}\right)$

**21.** $-3\frac{1}{3} \div \frac{4}{9}$

**22.** $-\frac{3}{8} \div \left(-\frac{5}{4}\right)$

**23.** $-\frac{5}{6}\left(-1\frac{4}{5}\right)$

**24.** $-\frac{5}{2} \div \frac{5}{7}$

**25.** $-\frac{3}{7} \div \left(-\frac{7}{3}\right)$

**26.** $-3\frac{3}{8}\left(-\frac{2}{3}\right)$

**27.** $-\frac{1}{12} \div \frac{7}{4}$

**28.** $-\frac{9}{10} \div \frac{3}{2}$

**29.** $\frac{3}{8} \div \left(-\frac{5}{4}\right)$

**30.** $-\frac{3}{8}\left(\frac{4}{9}\right)$

**31.** $-3\frac{1}{3} \div \left(-\frac{2}{3}\right)$

**32.** $-4\frac{1}{4}\left(\frac{10}{3}\right)$

**Evaluate the expression when $x = -\frac{2}{5}$ and $y = -\frac{7}{10}$.**

**33.** $\frac{x}{y}$

**34.** $-5xy \div 2$

**35.** $x \div (2y)$

**36.** $y \div (3x)$

**Evaluate the expression when $x = 4.8$ and $y = -0.5$.**

**37.** $-10x \div y$

**38.** $0.25xy$

**39.** $xy \div (-6)$

**40.** $9 \div xy$

**41. REASONING** Is the reciprocal of a negative number positive or negative? *Explain* your reasoning.

**42.** You are descending from the top of a climbing wall. It takes you 5 minutes to move down 11.5 feet. Find your average rate of descent.

**43.** A can of frozen orange juice is set out to thaw. Its temperature changes from $-1.1°C$ to $4.5°C$ in 20 minutes. Find the average rate of change in the temperature of the juice over the 20 minutes.

**44.** Some people conserve water by collecting rain water in barrels and using this water to water their vegetable gardens. A full 55 gallon water barrel gets a small leak and is losing water at an average rate of $-0.03$ gallon per hour. If it doesn't rain for 5 days, how much water is in the barrel after this time?

**45.** The table below shows the difference between the money in a store's cash drawer and the daily receipts during a 5 day period. Find the average amount (in dollars per day) the drawer is off during the 5 day period.

| Day | Monday | Tuesday | Wednesday | Thursday | Friday |
|---|---|---|---|---|---|
| Difference (dollars) | 4.50 | −3.75 | −0.80 | 2.10 | −0.25 |

# Activity 5.5

## Let's Explore
### Investigating Multiplication

**Goal**
Investigate the ordering and grouping properties of multiplication and division.

**Materials**
• paper and pencil

**QUESTION** How does changing the order of numbers or the grouping of numbers affect the value of an expression?

**EXPLORE 1** *Change the order of numbers* ........................

**1** **Write** two fractions or mixed numbers, at least one of which should be negative. Let $a$ represent the first number and $b$ represent the second number.

|  | Original order | Reverse order |
|---|---|---|
| Multiplication | $a \cdot b = ?$ | $b \cdot a = ?$ |
| Division | $a \div b = ?$ | $b \div a = ?$ |

**2** **Copy** the table and complete the *Original order* column by finding the product $a \cdot b$ and the quotient $a \div b$.

**3** **Complete** the *Reverse order* column by finding the product $b \cdot a$ and the quotient $b \div a$.

**4** **Write** two terminating decimals, at least one of which should be negative. Let $a$ represent the first number and $b$ represent the second number. Repeat Steps 2 and 3.

## Draw Conclusions
**In Exercises 1–4, tell whether the statement is *true* or *false*.**

**1.** $-4.5 \div (0.15) = 0.15 \div (-4.5)$

**2.** $-\frac{12}{5}(10) = 10\left(-\frac{12}{5}\right)$

**3.** $\frac{3}{7}(-2) = (-2)\left(\frac{3}{7}\right)$

**4.** $22 \div (-2.2) = -2.2 \div (22)$

**5.** What can you conclude about the order in which you multiply or divide two numbers?

### EXPLORE 2 · *Change the grouping of numbers* ·········

**1** **Write** three fractions or mixed numbers, at least one of which should be negative. Let $a$ represent the first number, $b$ the second number, and $c$ the third number.

|  | Original grouping | New grouping |
|---|---|---|
| Multiplication | $(a \cdot b) \cdot c = ?$ | $a \cdot (b \cdot c) = ?$ |
| Division | $(a \div b) \div c = ?$ | $a \div (b \div c) = ?$ |

**2** **Copy** the table and complete the *Original grouping* column by finding the value of $(a \cdot b) \cdot c$ and $(a \div b) \div c$.

**3** **Complete** the *New grouping* column by finding the value of $a \cdot (b \cdot c)$ and $a \div (b \div c)$.

**4** **Write** three terminating decimals, at least one of which should be negative. Let $a$ represent the first number, $b$ the second number, and $c$ the third number. Repeat Steps 2 and 3.

## Draw Conclusions

**In Exercises 6 and 7, tell whether the statement is *true* or *false*.**

**6.** $-\frac{1}{2}(3 \cdot 4) = \left(-\frac{1}{2} \cdot 3\right)4$

**7.** $-14 \div (3.5 \div 0.5) = (-14 \div 3.5) \div 0.5$

**In Exercises 8 and 9, tell whether the statement is *always true* or *not always true*.**

**8.** $a \cdot (b \cdot c) = (a \cdot b) \cdot c$

**9.** $a \div (b \div c) = (a \div b) \div c$

**10.** For any statement in Exercises 8 and 9 that is not always true, provide values for $a$, $b$, and $c$ that make the statement true, as well as values for $a$, $b$, and $c$ that make the statement false. *Explain* your reasoning.

# Use the Properties of Multiplication

## VOCABULARY and CONCEPTS

- reciprocal, p. 86

### Properties of Multiplication

| Property | Words | Algebra |
|---|---|---|
| Commutative Property | The order in which you multiply two numbers does not change the product. | $ab = ba$ |
| Associative Property | The way you group three numbers when multiplying does not change the product. | $(ab)c = a(bc)$ |
| Identity Property | The product of a number and 1 is the number. The number 1 is called the **multiplicative identity**. | $a \cdot 1 = a$ |
| Inverse Property | The reciprocal of a nonzero number $a$, written $\frac{1}{a}$, is also called the **multiplicative inverse** of $a$. The product of a nonzero number and its multiplicative inverse is 1. | $a \cdot \frac{1}{a} = 1$ |
| Property of Zero | The product of a number and 0 is 0. | $a \cdot 0 = 0$ |
| Property of −1 | The product of a number and −1 is the opposite of the number. | $a \cdot (-1) = -a$ |

**EXAMPLE 1**  *Identifying the Properties of Multiplication*

**Identify the property illustrated.**

| Statement | Property Illustrated |
|---|---|
| **a.** $x \cdot \frac{1}{3} = \frac{1}{3} \cdot x$ | Commutative property of multiplication |
| **b.** $-\frac{5}{6} \cdot (-1) = \frac{5}{6}$ | Multiplicative property of −1 |
| **c.** $(-3 \cdot x) \cdot 2.7 = -3 \cdot (x \cdot 2.7)$ | Associative property of multiplication |
| **d.** $-\frac{3}{7} \cdot 0 = 0$ | Multiplicative property of zero |
| **e.** $8 \cdot \frac{1}{8} = 1$ | Inverse property of multiplication |
| **f.** $9.8 \cdot 1 = 9.8$ | Identity property of multiplication |

### Practice for Example 1

**Identify the property illustrated.**

**1.** $-x \cdot 1 = -x$     **2.** $\left(-\frac{5}{7} \cdot \frac{2}{3}\right) \cdot \frac{3}{8} = -\frac{5}{7} \cdot \left(\frac{2}{3} \cdot \frac{3}{8}\right)$     **3.** $0 \cdot (-21.5) = 0$

**EXAMPLE 2** *Simplifying Algebraic Expressions*

**Simplify $(-3x) \cdot \left(-\frac{1}{3}\right)$. Justify your steps.**

$$(-3x) \cdot \left(-\frac{1}{3}\right) = \left(-\frac{1}{3}\right) \cdot (-3x) \qquad \text{Commutative property of multiplication}$$

$$= \left[-\frac{1}{3} \cdot (-3)\right]x \qquad \text{Associative property of multiplication}$$

$$= 1 \cdot x \qquad \text{Inverse property of multiplication}$$

$$= x \qquad \text{Identity property of multiplication}$$

**EXAMPLE 3** *Using the Identity Property*

The African elephant is the largest living land animal. Its average weight is 4.54 metric tons. What is the African elephant's average weight in pounds?

**Skills Review**

Converting units of measurement, p. 486

Converting between metric units and customary units, p. 487

**Step 1** Use the fact that 1 metric ton = 1000 kilograms and 1 kilogram ≈ 2.2 pounds to write conversion factors.

$$\frac{1000 \text{ kg}}{1 \text{ t}} = 1 \qquad \text{and} \qquad \frac{2.2 \text{ lb}}{1 \text{ kg}} \approx 1$$

**Step 2** Multiply 4.54 metric tons by the conversion factors and use unit analysis. Because each conversion factor is equal to (or almost equal to) 1, the identity property tells you that you are not changing the weight, just the units.

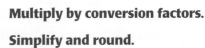

$$4.54 \text{ t} \approx 4.54 \, t \cdot \frac{1000 \text{ kg}}{1 \, t} \cdot \frac{2.2 \text{ lb}}{1 \, kg} \qquad \text{Multiply by conversion factors.}$$

$$\approx 10,000 \text{ lb} \qquad \text{Simplify and round.}$$

▶**Answer** The average weight of the African elephant is about 10,000 pounds.

▶**Check** To check reasonableness, round 4.54 and 2.2 and use mental math.

$$4.54(1000)(2.2) \approx 4.5(1000)(2) \qquad \text{Round 4.54 and 2.2.}$$

$$= 4.5(2)(1000) \qquad \text{Commutative property of multiplication}$$

$$= 9(1000) \qquad \text{Multiply 4.5 and 2.}$$

$$= 9000 \qquad \text{Multiply 9 and 1000.}$$

**Practice for Examples 2 and 3**

**Find the product. Justify your steps.**

**4.** $(-0.9 + 0.9) \cdot x$

**5.** $\left(-\frac{3}{7} \cdot x\right) \cdot 2\frac{1}{3}$

**6.** $\frac{2}{5} \cdot \left(\frac{9}{2} \cdot x\right) \cdot (-1)$

**7.** Use a conversion factor to convert $3\frac{1}{4}$ years to months.

**Identify the property illustrated.**

1. $-\dfrac{1}{2} \cdot 0 = 0$

2. $-x \cdot (-1) = x$

3. $-2.8 \cdot x = x \cdot (-2.8)$

4. $(3 \cdot 4) \cdot y = 3 \cdot (4 \cdot y)$

5. $(2x) \cdot 1 = 2x$

6. $-\dfrac{1}{2} \cdot (-2) = 1$

7. $(8y) \cdot 7 = 7 \cdot (8y)$

8. $(x + 1) \cdot 0 = 0$

9. $-1\dfrac{3}{5} \cdot (-1) = 1\dfrac{3}{5}$

**Simplify the expression. Justify your steps.**

10. $x\left(\dfrac{1}{3}\right)(3)$

11. $(-7 + 0)(1)(x)$

12. $\dfrac{1}{2}(-6m)$

13. $6y(-2.5)$

14. $8\left(-\dfrac{1}{2}x\right)$

15. $4.2x(-3)(-1)$

16. $6 \cdot x \cdot (-1.5)$

17. $5[x + (-x) + 1]$

18. $-\dfrac{3}{2}\left(\dfrac{1}{4}m\right)\left(\dfrac{2}{3}\right)$

19. $(-0.25)(x)(4)(24)$

20. $z(3)(-1)\left(\dfrac{1}{3}\right)$

21. $\dfrac{4}{5}(-1)[2p + (-2p)]$

**Use a conversion factor to perform the indicated conversion. Round your answer to the nearest hundredth if necessary.**

22. 30.6 minutes to hours

23. $2\dfrac{1}{2}$ miles to feet

24. 20.5 ounces to pounds

25. 15.7 millimeters to centimeters

26. $1\dfrac{1}{2}$ inches to millimeters

27. 98 kilograms to pounds

28. The trunk shown is a rectangular prism with a length of 5 feet, a width of $2\dfrac{2}{5}$ feet, and a height of 2 feet. The formula for the volume of a rectangular prism is $V = \ell wh$. Use the properties of multiplication and mental math to find the volume of the trunk.

2 ft

$2\dfrac{2}{5}$ ft

5 ft

29. The surface of the table shown has an area of 28.75 square feet. Use conversion factors to find the length and width of the table in meters and use these dimensions to find the area of the surface of the table in square meters. Then compare your result with the area given in square feet. Round your answer to the nearest hundredth.

4.6 ft

6.25 ft

30. The end zone of a football field has four identical pylons, each a rectangular prism, to mark the four corners. Each pylon has the dimensions shown. The formula for the volume of a rectangular prism is $V = \ell wh$. Find the volume of a pylon in cubic centimeters.

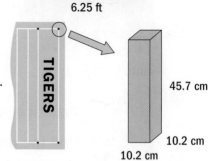

TIGERS

45.7 cm

10.2 cm

10.2 cm

31. **REASONING** From Lesson 2.6 you know that if $a \neq 0$ and $b \neq 0$, then the reciprocal of the fraction $\dfrac{a}{b}$ is $\dfrac{b}{a}$. In this lesson you learned that the reciprocal of a nonzero number $a$ is $\dfrac{1}{a}$. Show that if $a \neq 0$ and $b \neq 0$, then $\dfrac{1}{\frac{a}{b}} = \dfrac{b}{a}$.

# Practice

**Identify the property illustrated.**

**1.** $(-5x) \cdot 0 = 0$

**2.** $(y - 3) \cdot 1 = y - 3$

**3.** $8 \cdot w = w \cdot 8$

**4.** $(2x \cdot 7) \cdot 8 = 2x \cdot (7 \cdot 8)$

**5.** $(9w) \cdot 1 = 9w$

**6.** $-1\frac{1}{2}\left(-\frac{2}{3}\right) = 1$

**7.** $(x + 2) \cdot 3 = 3 \cdot (x + 2)$

**8.** $-170(0) = 0$

**9.** $-3k \cdot (-1) = 3k$

**Simplify the expression. Justify your steps.**

**10.** $-5.5(0)(2.6)$

**11.** $(-7x)(3.5)(2x)$

**12.** $\left(-\frac{3}{4}x\right)\left(\frac{2}{3}\right)(-5)$

**13.** $\frac{2}{3}\left(\frac{3}{2} \cdot x\right)(-60)$

**14.** $-7(-y)(-1)(15)$

**15.** $\frac{1}{2}(336 \cdot x)$

**16.** $6.5 \cdot y \cdot (-1.2)$

**17.** $5\left(-\frac{3}{2}\right)(-x)\left(-\frac{4}{5}\right)$

**18.** $\left(-\frac{m}{4}\right)\left(\frac{6}{5} - \frac{6}{5}\right)$

**19.** $(-1.1)(a)(2)(-4.5)$

**20.** $\left(-\frac{1}{3}\right)(-z)\left(-\frac{5}{3}\right)\left(\frac{1}{2}\right)$

**21.** $(-1)(2p - 2p + 1)\left(\frac{5}{7}\right)$

**Use a conversion factor to perform the indicated conversion.**

**22.** $3\frac{1}{3}$ yards to feet

**23.** 1.6 kilometers to meters

**24.** 12.6 seconds to minutes

**25.** 112.8 ounces to pounds

**26.** 2.9 pints to cups

**27.** 21.5 gallons to quarts

**28.** The square infield of the college softball field shown has a side length of 60 feet.

    **a.** Find the area of the field in square feet.

    **b.** Use a conversion factor to find the side length of the infield in meters. Round to the nearest tenth of a meter. Then find the area of the field to the nearest square meter.

    **c.** Convert your answer in part (a) to the nearest square meter. Compare the result with your answer in part (b).

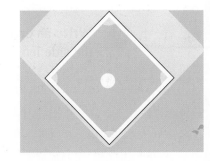

**29.** The wooden box shown is a rectangular prism. The formula for the volume of a rectangular prism is $V = \ell wh$. Find the volume of the box in cubic meters.

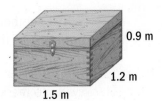

0.9 m

1.2 m

1.5 m

**30.** Ivan has a job that pays $25 per hour. He works 37.5 hours per week. Use the properties of multiplication and mental math to find the total amount Ivan earns in 4 weeks.

**31.** A square playground has an area of 40.96 square meters. Use a conversion factor to find the area in square feet. Round your answer to the nearest square foot.

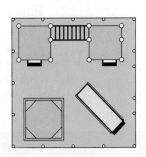

**32.** **REASONING** Use the multiplicative property of $-1$ to show that $-\frac{a}{b} = \frac{-a}{b} = \frac{a}{-b}$ for any integer $a$ and nonzero integer $b$.

# Activity 5.6

## Let's Explore
## Modeling the Distributive Property

**Goal**
Model the distributive property.

**Materials**
- graph paper
- scissors

**EXPLORE 1** *Model* $a(b + c)$ •••••••••••••••••••••••••••••••••••••••••••

**①** **Cut** a $9 \times 9$ square from a piece of graph paper. Then fold a $3 \times 3$ flap at each corner of the square and cut off the flaps. The result is an 8-sided figure with four sides of length $a$ and four sides of length $b$.

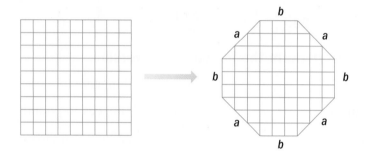

**②** **Write** an expression for the perimeter of the figure using the grouping of the side lengths shown below.

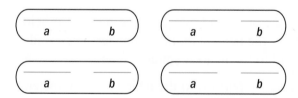

**③** **Write** another expression for the perimeter of the figure using the new grouping of the side lengths shown below.

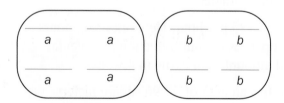

## Draw Conclusions

1. What conclusion can you draw about the expressions from Steps 2 and 3? *Explain* your reasoning.

2. The figure shown is a rectangle with its corners cut off so that the figure has two sides of length *a*, two sides of length *b*, two sides of length *c*, and two sides of length *d*. Write two different expressions for the perimeter of the figure by using groupings similar to those in Steps 2 and 3. What can you conclude about the expressions?

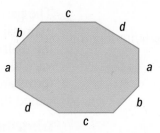

**EXPLORE 2** *Explore 2 Model a(b − c)* ·····················

**1** **Draw** a $9 \times 9$ square on a piece of graph paper. Then draw two horizontal and two vertical lines to divide the square into nine $3 \times 3$ squares. Shade the center square within each of the nine $3 \times 3$ squares to indicate its removal. Let *A* represent the area of each of the $3 \times 3$ squares (before the shaded squares are removed), and let *B* represent the area of each of the shaded squares.

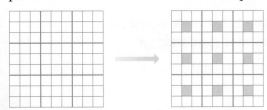

**2** **Use** the grouping shown below to write an expression for the area of the original square with the shaded squares removed.

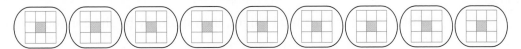

**3** **Use** the grouping shown below to write another expression for the area of the original square with the shaded squares removed.

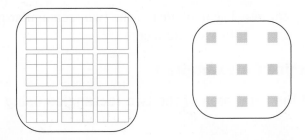

## Draw Conclusions

3. What conclusions can you draw about the expressions from Steps 2 and 3? *Explain* your reasoning.

# Use the Distributive Property

## VOCABULARY and CONCEPTS

The parts of an expression that are added together are the **terms** of the expression. A term that has no variable part is a **constant term**. You can use the distributive property to combine *like terms*. **Like terms** have identical variable parts with corresponding variables raised to the same power. Constant terms are also like terms. The number part of a term with a variable part is called the **coefficient** of the term.

### Distributive Property

**Words**   The product of a number and the sum (or difference) of two other numbers is equal to the sum (or difference) of the products of the number and each other number.

**Algebra**   $a(b + c) = ab + ac$      $a(b - c) = ab - ac$

---

**EXAMPLE 1**   *Finding a Combined Area*

**Find the total area of the two rectangular gardens.**

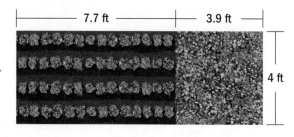

**Method 1** Find the area of each rectangle, then find the total area.

$$\text{Area} = 7.7(4) + 3.9(4)$$
$$= 30.8 + 15.6$$
$$= 46.4 \text{ square feet}$$

**Method 2** Find the total length, then multiply by the common width.

$$\text{Area} = 4(7.7 + 3.9)$$
$$= 4(11.6)$$
$$= 46.4 \text{ square feet}$$

▶ **Answer** The total area of the two rectangular gardens is 46.4 square feet.

### Practice for Example 1

**Find the total area of the two rectangles using two different methods.**

1.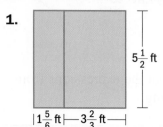

2.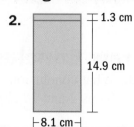

### EXAMPLE 2  Using the Distributive Property

**a.** $-3.2(x - 5) = -3.2(x) - (-3.2)(5)$  **Distributive property**
$$= -3.2x - (-16) \quad \textbf{Multiply.}$$
$$= -3.2x + 16 \quad \textbf{Subtraction rule}$$

**b.** $4\left(\dfrac{3}{4} - x - \dfrac{7}{2}y\right) = 4\left(\dfrac{3}{4}\right) - 4(x) - 4\left(\dfrac{7}{2}y\right)$  **Distributive property**
$$= 3 - 4x - 14y \quad \textbf{Multiply.}$$

### Practice for Example 2

**Use the distributive property to write an equivalent expression.**

**3.** $-3(x + 2.4)$　　　**4.** $-\dfrac{3}{4}(-16x - 12y)$　　　**5.** $6(8.7m - 2.2)$

**6.** $2\left(w - 9\dfrac{1}{2}\right)$　　　**7.** $-0.8(7 - y)$　　　**8.** $-0.5(3z + 2)$

### EXAMPLE 3  Combining Like Terms

**a.** $7x + 5x = (7 + 5)x$  **Distributive property**
$$= 12x \quad \textbf{Add.}$$

**b.** $-6y + 8y + 9 = (-6 + 8)y + 9$  **Distributive property**
$$= 2y + 9 \quad \textbf{Add.}$$

### EXAMPLE 4  Simplifying Expressions

$3(7 - x) + 4x = 21 - 3x + 4x$  **Distributive property**
$$= 21 + (-3x) + 4x \quad \textbf{Subtraction rule}$$
$$= 21 + (-3 + 4)x \quad \textbf{Distributive property}$$
$$= 21 + x \quad \textbf{Simplify.}$$

### Practice for Examples 3 and 4

**Simplify the expression by combining like terms.**

**9.** $r + \dfrac{1}{4}r - \dfrac{3}{4}r$　　　　　　**10.** $1.7w - w - 3.2w - 12.9w$

**Simplify the expression.**

**11.** $-5(8x + 2) - 3$　　　　　　**12.** $r + \dfrac{1}{2}(4r - 10)$

**Match the expression with its simplified expression.**

**1.** $6(x + 8)$      **A.** $6x - 48$

**2.** $8(x + 6)$      **B.** $6x + 48$

**3.** $2(3x - 24)$      **C.** $8x + 48$

**4.** $2(4x - 24)$      **D.** $8x - 48$

**Use the distributive property to write an equivalent expression.**

**5.** $-6(4x + 3.5)$      **6.** $0.8(9 + 4y)$      **7.** $\frac{1}{2}(6x + 7y)$

**8.** $-4.9(x + 3)$      **9.** $5\left(\frac{2}{3} + x\right)$      **10.** $\frac{1}{6}\left(x - \frac{1}{3}\right)$

**Simplify the expression by combining like terms.**

**11.** $m + 4m$      **12.** $8x + 7y + 2x$      **13.** $15m + 11p - p$

**14.** $2.7c + 11d - 0.3c - 4d$      **15.** $-\frac{1}{2}x - \frac{1}{3}y + 2x - y$      **16.** $1.6x - y + 6.8x - 1.3y - 8.4$

**Find the total area of the two rectangles using two different methods.**

**17.**
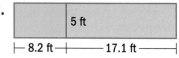
5 ft
├─ 8.2 ft ─┼──── 17.1 ft ────┤

**18.**
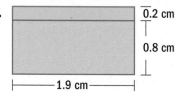
0.2 cm
0.8 cm
├──── 1.9 cm ────┤

**In Exercises 19–24, simplify the expression.**

**19.** $\frac{1}{2}(x - y) + x$      **20.** $4x + 3(x - 5)$      **21.** $7x - (3 + 9x)$

**22.** $8\left(\frac{1}{2}d + 4\right) - 3d$      **23.** $\frac{2}{5}p - (p - 4p)$      **24.** $9(3g - 5) + 6$

**25.** You and three friends go bowling. You each pay \$2.75 for games and \$1.50 to rent bowling shoes.

     **a.** Write and evaluate an expression in which the total cost for *one* person is calculated and then multiplied by 4.

     **b.** Write and evaluate an expression in which the total costs of games and shoes for everyone are calculated separately and then added together.

     **c.** Compare your answers to parts (a) and (b). *Explain* how the result illustrates the distributive property.

**26.** **REASONING** Show that $a(b + c + d) = ab + ac + ad$. Start by writing $a(b + c + d)$ as $a[(b + c) + d]$ and applying the distributive property twice.

# Practice

**Use the distributive property to write an equivalent expression.**

**1.** $-\frac{1}{3}(y + 3)$

**2.** $0.4(1.1 + 0.6y)$

**3.** $-\frac{1}{2}\left(\frac{3}{5} + \frac{1}{4}m\right)$

**4.** $-3.1(2.4x + 1.2)$

**5.** $\frac{1}{3}(z - 6)$

**6.** $4\left(\frac{1}{2}d + 2\right)$

**7.** $\frac{3}{4}(w - 8)$

**8.** $0.3(2x + 5.4)$

**9.** $\frac{3}{4}\left(8x - \frac{4}{9}\right)$

**Simplify the expression by combining like terms.**

**10.** $c + \frac{7}{8}c + \frac{4}{5}d$

**11.** $\frac{1}{4}m + \frac{1}{3}k + \frac{1}{2}m + \frac{1}{9}k$

**12.** $0.8s + 1.6t - (-0.5s) - 0.2t$

**13.** $\frac{1}{2}\left(d + \frac{3}{4}d\right) - \frac{1}{4}d$

**14.** $-1.6g + 3.3h - 1.9h - 2.4g$

**15.** $8.3x + 5.3y + 11.2x - 2.4y$

**Find the total area of the two rectangles using two different methods.**

**16.**

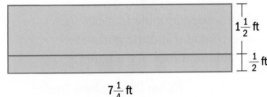

$1\frac{1}{2}$ ft

$\frac{1}{2}$ ft

$7\frac{1}{4}$ ft

**17.**

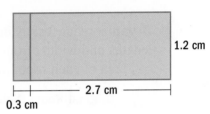

1.2 cm

2.7 cm

0.3 cm

**FIND THE ERROR** *Describe* and correct the error.

**18.**
$$4(\tfrac{1}{2}d - 2) = 4(\tfrac{1}{2}d) + 4(2)$$
$$= 2d + 8$$

**19.**
$$0.2(5 + x) = 0.2(5) + x$$
$$= 1 + x$$

**Simplify the expression.**

**20.** $\frac{2}{3}(8n - 12) + 5$

**21.** $12 + 1.5(3y + 2)$

**22.** $5z - \frac{1}{2}(3z + 8)$

**23.** $0.7(d + 6d) - 19.3d$

**24.** $1.3p - (2.8p + 3.7p) - 4.3p$

**25.** $\frac{11}{3}\left(\frac{1}{2}g - \frac{1}{4}\right) + \frac{1}{12} - \frac{1}{6}g$

**In Exercises 26–28, use the table, which shows costs of school supplies.**

| Item | Cost ($) |
|---|---|
| Notebook | 3.98 |
| Pen | 1.99 |
| Ruler | 2.97 |

**26.** You buy 5 notebooks for $3.98 each. Think of 3.98 as $4.00 - 0.02$. *Describe* how you can use the distributive property and mental math to find the total cost. Then find the total cost.

**27.** Find the total cost of 6 pens.

**28.** Find the total cost of 3 rulers.

**29. REASONING** Show how $a(b - c) = ab - ac$ is a consequence of $a(b + c) = ab + ac$. Start by writing $a(b - c)$ as $a[b + (-c)]$.

# Problem Solving and Reasoning

## Problem

Jamie is installing wall-to-wall carpet in a room with a length of $\ell$ meters and a width of $w$ meters. The edges of the carpet are held in place by using strips of carpet tack. How do the amounts of carpet tack and carpeting Jamie needs change for a room whose length and width are $k$ times those of the original room?

## Solution

**1** **Draw** floor plans for several rooms and label the lengths and widths. Find the perimeter and area of each room.

*Break a problem into parts as part of MR 1.3.*

**2** **Organize** your results in a table. Make a second table that has the lengths and widths from the first table tripled. Find the perimeter and area of each room in the second table and look for a pattern.

*Solve a simpler problem first as part of MR 2.2 and look for a pattern as part of MR 1.1.*

| Original Room Dimensions | | | | Room Dimensions Tripled | | | |
|---|---|---|---|---|---|---|---|
| Length | Width | Perimeter | Area | Length | Width | Perimeter | Area |
| 4 | 3 | 14 | 12 | 12 | 9 | 42 | 108 |
| 5 | 4 | 18 | 20 | 15 | 12 | 54 | 180 |
| 6 | 5 | 22 | 30 | 18 | 15 | 66 | 270 |

**3** **Make** a conjecture that when each dimension is multiplied by $k$, the perimeter is multiplied by $k$, and the area is multiplied by $k^2$. Write expressions for the perimeter and area of a room that has a length of $k\ell$ meters and a width of $kw$ meters to test the conjecture.

*Make and test a conjecture as part of MR 2.4.*

| | |
|---|---|
| Perimeter $= 2(k\ell) + 2(kw)$ | **Formula for the perimeter of a rectangle** |
| $= (2k)\ell + (2k)w$ | **Associative property of multiplication** |
| $= 2k(\ell + w)$ | **Distributive property** |
| $= k \cdot 2(\ell + w)$ | **Commutative property of multiplication** |
| $= k \cdot (2\ell + 2w)$ | **Distributive property** |

| | |
|---|---|
| Area $= (k\ell) \cdot (kw)$ | **Formula for the area of a rectangle** |
| $= (k \cdot k)(\ell w)$ | **Commutative and associative properties** |
| $= k^2 \cdot \ell w$ | **Definition of a power** |

*Express the solution clearly and support the solution with evidence as part of MR 2.6.*

Jamie needs $k$ times as much carpet tack and $k^2$ times as much carpet for the new room, because the perimeter is $k$ times as great and the area is $k^2$ times as great. The table in Step 2 supports this result.

# Practice

**1.** The crew of a sailboat is measuring the elevation of the sea floor below the boat by lowering a weighted rope with evenly spaced knots.

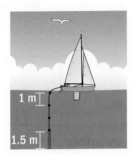

When the weight at the end of the rope hits the sea floor, 30 knots are beneath the surface of the water. The 31st knot is just barely touching the surface. What is the elevation of the sea floor? **MR 2.5, MR 3.3**

**2.** The steps below demonstrate that $a - b = -(b - a)$. Provide the justification for each step (The first step has been done for you.) **MR 2.5**

$$a - b = a + (-b) \qquad \textbf{Subtraction rule}$$
$$= -b + a \qquad \underline{\textbf{?}}$$
$$= -1(b) + -1(-a) \qquad \underline{\textbf{?}}$$
$$= -1[b + (-a)] \qquad \underline{\textbf{?}}$$
$$= -1(b - a) \qquad \underline{\textbf{?}}$$
$$= -(b - a) \qquad \underline{\textbf{?}}$$

**3.** A building rises $257\frac{2}{3}$ feet above the ground. The bottom of the first floor is $18\frac{1}{3}$ feet below ground level. Each floor is $11\frac{1}{2}$ feet tall. **MR 2.1**

**a.** How many floors does the building have?

**b.** Round each of the numbers given to the nearest multiple of 10. Then use estimation to check your answer to part (a).

**4.** Use the method described on the previous page to determine how the circumference and area of a circle with radius $r$ change when the radius is increased by a factor of $k$. **MR 3.2**

**5.** Chris has two types of bolts with two different diameters. Each type has five different lengths. The lengths (in inches) of the bolts with a diameter of $\frac{5}{16}$ inch and the lengths (in millimeters) of the bolts with a diameter of 8 millimeters are given. **MR 1.1, MR 2.6**

| Diameter | Length |
|---|---|
| $\frac{5}{16}$ in. | $1\frac{1}{4}, 1\frac{3}{4}, 2, 2\frac{1}{2}, 2\frac{3}{4}$ |
| 8 mm | 25, 35, 50, 55, 70 |

**a.** Which type of bolt has the greater diameter? (1 inch = 25.4 millimeters)

**b.** Order the 10 bolts from shortest to longest. *Describe* the method you used to order the bolts.

**6.** The stem-and-leaf plot shows one city's monthly rainfall last year relative to its normal monthly rainfall. **MR 2.3**

```
-2 | 45 89
-1 | 04 17 28 59
-0 | 77 91
 0 | 09            Key: 1 | 37 =
 1 | 37 60 92           1.37 in.
```

**a.** *Explain* how you can determine without calculation whether the city had more or less rain than normal for the given year.

**b.** The normal yearly amount of rain for the city is 40 inches. How much rain did the city receive last year?

# Chapter 5 Review Game

**Materials**
- paper and pencil

## Math Bingo

Copy the table below. Use the list of answers in the answer box below to make a bingo card. Write 16 answers on your bingo card in any order. Your teacher will choose one of the 21 problems. Solve the problem or identify the property and put an X on the answer if it is written on your bingo card. When you have 4 X's in a row, horizontally, diagonally, or vertically, you have Math Bingo! Whoever gets bingo first is the winner.

| M | A | T | H |
|---|---|---|---|
| ? | ? | ? | ? |
| ? | ? | ? | ? |
| ? | ? | ? | ? |
| ? | ? | ? | ? |

**1.** $-\dfrac{1}{5} + \dfrac{2}{5} = $ _?_

**2.** $-4\dfrac{1}{7} + \dfrac{3}{7} = $ _?_

**3.** $\dfrac{1}{6} - \dfrac{5}{6} + \dfrac{2}{6} = $ _?_

**4.** $3\dfrac{3}{4} + \left(-5\dfrac{1}{5}\right) = $ _?_

**5.** $-\dfrac{3}{5} - \dfrac{1}{8} = $ _?_

**6.** $-\dfrac{2}{3} \cdot \left(-\dfrac{1}{4}\right) = $ _?_

**7.** $9 \cdot \left(-2\dfrac{1}{10}\right) = $ _?_

**8.** $-\dfrac{4}{17} \div 3 = $ _?_

**9.** $2\dfrac{2}{7} \div \left(-\dfrac{1}{2}\right) = $ _?_

**10.** $-10.7 + 2.78 = $ _?_

**11.** $-11.32 - 8.51 = $ _?_

**12.** $-4.07 - 2.31 = $ _?_

**13.** $-12 \div (-0.24) = $ _?_

**14.** $15.7 \cdot (-5.3) = $ _?_

**15.** $-56.32 \div 16$

**16.** $2x \cdot (-1) = -1 \cdot 2x$

**17.** $7k + (-7k) = 0$

**18.** $(x + y) + 0 = x + y$

**19.** $3 + (4 + x) = (3 + 4) + x$

**20.** $\left(-\dfrac{3}{7}\right)(0) = 0$

**21.** $\left(-1\dfrac{8}{9}\right)(-1) = 1\dfrac{8}{9}$

**Answers**

| | | | |
|---|---|---|---|
| Inverse property of addition | $-3.52$ | $-3\dfrac{5}{7}$ | $-18\dfrac{9}{10}$ |
| Multiplicative property of $-1$ | $-1\dfrac{9}{20}$ | $-\dfrac{1}{3}$ | $-19.83$ |
| Commutative property of multiplication | $-7.92$ | $\dfrac{1}{6}$ | $-\dfrac{29}{40}$ |
| Identity property of addition | $\dfrac{1}{5}$ | $-6.38$ | $-4\dfrac{4}{7}$ |
| Associative property of addition | $-\dfrac{4}{51}$ | $-83.21$ | $50$ |
| Multiplicative property of 0 | | | |

# Chapter Summary and Review

**@HomeTutor**
**classzone.com**

---

**VOCABULARY**

- rational number, p. 204
- additive identity, p. 216
- additive inverse, p. 216
- multiplicative identity, p. 230
- multiplicative inverse, p. 230
- terms, p. 236
- constant term, p. 236
- like terms, p. 236
- coefficient, p. 236

## Vocabulary Exercises

**1.** Copy and complete: The opposite of a number $a$, written $-a$, is also called the  ?  of $a$.

**2.** Copy and complete: The parts of an expression that are added together are the  ? .

---

**5.1** *Compare and Order Rational Numbers* ·········· **pp. 204–207**

A rational number is a number that can be written as $\dfrac{a}{b}$ where $a$ and $b$ are integers and $b \neq 0$.

**EXAMPLES** Show that (a) 2.7 and (b) −4.6 are rational by writing each as a quotient of two integers.

**a.** $2.7 = 2\dfrac{7}{10}$  **Write as mixed number.**

$= \dfrac{27}{10}$  **Write as improper fraction.**

**b.** $-4.6 = -4\dfrac{3}{5}$  **Write as mixed number.**

$= \dfrac{-23}{5}$  **Write as improper fraction.**

To order rational numbers from least to greatest, graph the numbers on a number line.

**EXAMPLE** Order 1.5, $\dfrac{2}{3}$, −2.1, 0, and $-\dfrac{4}{5}$ from least to greatest.

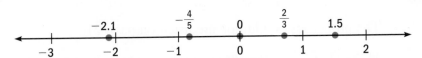

From least to greatest, the numbers are $-2.1$, $-\dfrac{4}{5}$, $0$, $\dfrac{2}{3}$, and $1.5$.

**Show that the number is a rational number by writing it as a quotient of two integers.**

**3.** 0.9  **4.** 4.16  **5.** −0.375  **6.** −1.7

**Order the rational numbers from least to greatest.**

**7.** $0.8, \dfrac{1}{5}, -1.3, -\dfrac{3}{4}$  **8.** $-\dfrac{7}{8}, 1.5, \dfrac{1}{2}, -2.6$  **9.** $0.2, -\dfrac{1}{3}, -0.4, -\dfrac{1}{5}$

**5.2** *Add and Subtract Rational Numbers* .................. pp. 210–213

To add two rational numbers with the *same* sign, add the absolute values. The sum has the same sign as the numbers.

**EXAMPLE** $-1\frac{1}{2} + \left(-\frac{3}{4}\right) = -\left(\left|-1\frac{1}{2}\right| + \left|-\frac{3}{4}\right|\right)$   **Rule of same signs**

$= -\left(1\frac{1}{2} + \frac{3}{4}\right)$   **Take absolute values**

$= -\left(\frac{6}{4} + \frac{3}{4}\right)$   **Write improper fraction and use common denominator.**

$= -\frac{9}{4} = -2\frac{1}{4}$   **Add. Write as a mixed number.**

To subtract two rational numbers with *different* signs, subtract the lesser absolute value from the greater absolute value. The sum has the same sign as the number with the greater absolute value.

**EXAMPLE** $\frac{1}{7} + \left(-\frac{5}{7}\right) = -\left(\left|-\frac{5}{7}\right| - \left|\frac{1}{7}\right|\right)$   **Rule of different signs**

$= -\left(\frac{5}{7} - \frac{1}{7}\right)$   **Take absolute values.**

$= -\frac{4}{7}$   **Subtract.**

**Find the sum or difference.**

**10.** $-4.8 + 6.2$     **11.** $-5.3 - (-7.9)$   **12.** $-\frac{1}{5} + \frac{3}{8}$     **13.** $-2\frac{4}{7} + 1\frac{3}{4}$

**5.3** *Use the Properties of Addition* .................. pp. 216–219

The properties of addition are listed on page 216.

**EXAMPLE** **Simplify the expression. Justify your steps.**

$p + 5 + (-p) = [p + 5] + (-p)$   **Use order of operations.**

$= (-p) + [p + 5]$   **Commutative property of addition**

$= [(-p) + p] + 5$   **Associative property of addition**

$= 0 + 5$   **Additive inverse**

$= 5$   **Identity property of addition**

**Simplify the expression.**

**14.** $y + (-y) + 0.7$     **15.** $-3 - 8v + 3$     **16.** $-\frac{1}{3} + d + 2$

### 5.4 Multiply and Divide Rational Numbers · · · · · · · · · pp. 224–227

The product of two rational numbers with the *same* sign is positive.
The product of two rational numbers with *different* signs is negative.

**EXAMPLE**   $(-4.6)(-3) = 13.8$    **Same signs; product is positive.**

The quotient of two rational numbers with the *same* sign is positive.
The quotient of two rational numbers with *different* signs is negative.

**EXAMPLE**   $-36 \div \dfrac{3}{4} = -36 \cdot \dfrac{4}{3}$    **Division rule**

$\qquad\qquad\quad = -48$    **Different signs; quotient is negative.**

**Find the product or quotient**

**17.** $5.6 \div (-7)$    **18.** $-40 \div \left(-\dfrac{2}{5}\right)$    **19.** $4 \cdot \left(-\dfrac{3}{8}\right)$    **20.** $(-3.5)(-2.7)$

### 5.5 Use the Properties of Multiplication · · · · · · · · · · pp. 230–233

The properties of multiplication are listed on page 230.

**EXAMPLE**   **Find the product. Justify your steps.**

$\dfrac{2}{3}(-12k) = \left[\dfrac{2}{3} \cdot (-12)\right]k$    **Associative property of multiplication**

$\qquad\quad = -8k$    **Multiply.**

**Find the product. Justify your steps.**

**21.** $5(-2r)$    **22.** $36\left(-\dfrac{1}{9}c\right)$    **23.** $\left(\dfrac{1}{4}t\right)4$    **24.** $(18x)\left(-\dfrac{1}{9}\right)$

### 5.6 Use the Distributive Property · · · · · · · · · · · · · · · · pp. 236–239

**DISTRIBUTIVE PROPERTY**   The product of a number and the sum (or difference) of two other numbers is equal to the sum (or difference) of the products of the number and each other number: $a(b + c) = ab + ac$ and $a(b - c) = ab - ac$.

**EXAMPLE**   $3(5 - u) = 3(5) - 3(u)$    **Distributive property**

$\qquad\qquad = 15 - 3u$    **Simplify.**

**Use the distributive property to write an equivalent expression.**

**25.** $4(s - 0.7)$    **26.** $-9.8(h - 4)$    **27.** $\dfrac{3}{5}\left(x - \dfrac{1}{7}\right)$    **28.** $7\left(w - \dfrac{3}{2}\right)$

# Chapter Test

**Show that the number is a rational number by writing it as a quotient of two integers.**

**1.** 0.9　　　　　**2.** 2.35　　　　　**3.** −4.8　　　　　**4.** −1.3

**Order the rational numbers from least to greatest.**

**5.** $1.3, \frac{1}{4}, -2.1, -\frac{5}{7}$　　　**6.** $0.5, -0.06, 0.007, -0.0008$　**7.** $-\frac{1}{3}, \frac{2}{5}, -\frac{4}{7}, \frac{8}{9}$

**Find the sum or difference.**

**8.** $-2.7 + 5.3$　　**9.** $-6.4 + (-0.9)$　**10.** $-3\frac{2}{5} + \frac{1}{2}$　　**11.** $-1\frac{1}{2} - 2\frac{5}{8}$

**Find the product or quotient.**

**12.** $(-2.4)(-4)$　　**13.** $6(-1.2)$　　**14.** $-40 \div \frac{4}{5}$　　**15.** $1\frac{1}{2} \div \left(-\frac{2}{3}\right)$

**Find the total area of the two rectangles using two different methods.**

**16.**
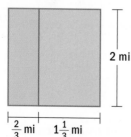

**17.**
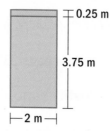

**18.**
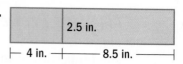

**Use the distributive property to write an equivalent expression.**

**19.** $\frac{3}{5}(2x - 10)$　　　**20.** $0.4(-m + 5)$　　　**21.** $-\frac{2}{3}(6t - 1)$

**Simplify the expression.**

**22.** $-\frac{2}{3} + \frac{1}{3}(p + 2)$　　**23.** $n + \frac{2}{5}(n - 10)$　　**24.** $t + 5(2.4t - 3)$

**Identify the property illustrated.**

**25.** $-\frac{5}{3} + x = x + \left(-\frac{5}{3}\right)$　**26.** $7 \cdot \frac{1}{7} = 1$　　　**27.** $(-2 \cdot n) \cdot 8 = -2 \cdot (n \cdot 8)$

**28.** $-\frac{7}{12} \cdot 0 = 0$　　**29.** $5 + \left(12 + \frac{3}{8}\right) = (5 + 12) + \frac{3}{8}$ **30.** $43.6 + 0 = 43.6$

**In Exercises 31–33, use the table, which shows the temperature at various elevations on a mountain.**

| Elevation (m) | Temperature (°C) |
|---|---|
| 0 | 24.0 |
| 100 | 23.4 |
| 200 | 22.8 |
| 300 | 22.2 |

**31.** *Describe* how the temperature changes when the elevation increases by 100 meters.

**32.** Given the pattern in the table, will the temperature at 400 meters be greater or less than the temperature at 300 meters?

**33.** What would be the temperature change from an elevation of 0 meters to an elevation of 500 meters?

1. Which expression shows that $2\frac{3}{8}$ is a rational number?

   (A) $2 + \frac{3}{8}$

   (B) $\frac{19}{8}$

   (C) $2 + \frac{375}{1000}$

   (D) $2.375$

2. Which list of rational numbers is in order from least to greatest?

   (A) $-0.2, -0.4, -0.6, -0.8$

   (B) $-\frac{1}{4}, -\frac{1}{3}, \frac{1}{5}, \frac{1}{6}$

   (C) $-0.3, -\frac{1}{5}, -0.7, -\frac{1}{9}$

   (D) $-0.7, -\frac{1}{6}, 0.05, \frac{1}{4}$

3. The table below shows the daily change in the value of a share of stock. Which day shows the greatest absolute decrease in value?

   | Day | 1 | 2 | 3 | 4 | 5 |
   |---|---|---|---|---|---|
   | Change in price ($) | −0.2 | 1.4 | −3.9 | −3.2 | 0.6 |

   (A) Day 2

   (B) Day 3

   (C) Day 4

   (D) Day 5

4. What is the value of the expression $\frac{1}{2} - y - x$ when $x = -\frac{1}{4}$ and $y = \frac{2}{3}$?

   (A) $-\frac{7}{12}$

   (B) $-\frac{5}{12}$

   (C) $\frac{1}{12}$

   (D) $\frac{11}{12}$

5. What is the change in temperature from $-11.7°C$ to $-9.3°C$?

   (A) $-2.6°C$

   (B) $-2.4°C$

   (C) $2.4°C$

   (D) $21°C$

6. What is the quotient $-72 \div \frac{3}{4}$?

   (A) $-96$

   (B) $-54$

   (C) $54$

   (D) $96$

7. What is the simplified form of the expression $w + \frac{4}{9} + 3w - \frac{1}{3}$?

   (A) $w + \frac{1}{9} + 3w$

   (B) $4w + \frac{1}{9}$

   (C) $w - \frac{1}{9} + 3w$

   (D) $4w + \frac{4}{9} - \frac{1}{3}$

8. Which equation illustrates the associative property of multiplication?

   (A) $2 \cdot \frac{1}{2} = 1$

   (B) $2 \cdot (3 \cdot 4) = (3 \cdot 4) \cdot 2$

   (C) $2 \cdot (3 \cdot 4) = (2 \cdot 3) \cdot 4$

   (D) $2 \cdot (3 + 4) = 2 \cdot 3 + 2 \cdot 4$

9. What is the total area of the two rectangles?

   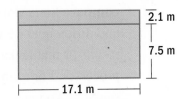

   (A) $92.34$ m$^2$

   (B) $128.25$ m$^2$

   (C) $153.9$ m$^2$

   (D) $164.16$ m$^2$

10. An elevator starts moving at an elevation of 840 feet above the ground and stops 12 seconds later at an elevation of 804 feet. Find the rate of change in the elevation relative to the ground over the 12 seconds.

    (A) $-36$ feet/second

    (B) $-3$ feet/second

    (C) $3$ feet/second

    (D) $36$ feet/second

11. What is the simplified form of $3.7m + 1.1 - 2.5(m + 4.6)$?

    (A) $1.2m - 10.4$

    (B) $1.2m + 12.6$

    (C) $1.2m + 5.7$

    (D) $1.2m - 3.5$

# Exponents

## Vocabulary for Chapter 6

### Key Mathematical Vocabulary
- **zero exponent, p. 266**
- **negative exponents, p. 266**
- **scientific notation, p. 266**

### Academic Vocabulary
- **compare** State similarities and differences between results or mathematical processes. For example, see Step 2 on page 250.
- **describe, p. 250**
- **explain, p. 251**
- **approximate, p. 255**

**Rewriting lengths of molecule bonds using scientific notation, page 268**

**Gr. 7 NS 2.1** Understand negative whole-number exponents. Multiply and divide expressions involving exponents with a common base.
**Alg 2.0** Students understand and use such operations as taking the opposite, finding the reciprocal, taking a root, and raising to a fractional power. **They understand and use the rules of exponents.**

# Review Prerequisite Skills

## REVIEW VOCABULARY

- exponent, p. 6
- base, p. 6
- power, p. 6
- reciprocal, p. 86
- area, p. 488
- surface area, p. 492
- volume, p. 492

**VOCABULARY CHECK**

**Copy and complete the statement.**

**1.** In the expression $12^8$, 12 is the _?_ and 8 is the _?_.

**2.** A(n) _?_ is a way of writing repeated multiplication.

**SKILLS CHECK**

**Evaluate the power.** (Review pp. 6, 80 and 114 for 6.1–6.4.)

**3.** $10^5$

**4.** $2^6$

**5.** $3^4$

**6.** $(1.3)^2$

**7.** $\left(\dfrac{1}{7}\right)^2$

**8.** $\left(\dfrac{2}{5}\right)^3$

**Find the area of the rectangle.** (Review p. 488 for 6.1.)

**9.**
9 ft
14 ft

**10.**
3 m
12 m

**11.**

18 in.
20 in.

**Write the fraction in simplest form.** (Review p. 54 for 6.2, 6.4.)

**12.** $\dfrac{4}{12}$

**13.** $\dfrac{8}{20}$

**14.** $\dfrac{33}{44}$

**Write the number in standard form.** (Review p. 476 for 6.3.)

**15.** $4 \times 100 + 8 \times 10 + 3 \times 1$

**16.** $1 \times 1000 + 5 \times 100 + 6 \times 10 + 2 \times 1$

**17.** $9 \times 100 + 7 \times 10 + 5 \times 1 + 1 \times 0.1$

## Let's Explore

### Investigating Products of Powers

**Goal**
Multiply powers with the same base.

**Materials**
• number cube

**QUESTION** How can you find the product of powers with the same base?

**EXPLORE 1** *Find products of powers*

**1** **Copy** and complete the table.

The first row has been completed for you.

| Expression | Expanded expression | Number of factors | Product as a power |
|---|---|---|---|
| $2^2 \cdot 2^4$ | $(2 \cdot 2) \cdot (2 \cdot 2 \cdot 2 \cdot 2)$ | 6 | $2^6$ |
| $3^3 \cdot 3^1$ | $(3 \cdot 3 \cdot 3) \cdot 3$ | ? | ? |
| $7^2 \cdot 7^3$ | ? | ? | ? |
| $(-5)^4 \cdot (-5)^4$ | ? | ? | ? |
| $(-4)^5 \cdot (-4)^2$ | ? | ? | ? |
| $(-2)^3 \cdot (-2)^5$ | ? | ? | ? |

**2** **Compare** exponents.

*Describe* how the exponents of the factors in the first column and the exponent of the power in the last column are related.

## Draw Conclusions
**Write the product as a single power.**

**1.** $3^4 \cdot 3^3$ **2.** $6^5 \cdot 6^{11}$ **3.** $10^7 \cdot 10^{13}$

**4.** $(-7)^2 \cdot (-7)^9$ **5.** $(-9)^3 \cdot (-9)^6$ **6.** $(-11)^6 \cdot (-11)^7$

**7.** Copy and complete: If $a$ is a real number and $m$ and $n$ are positive integers, then $a^m \cdot a^n = \underline{?}$.

**8.** Let $m$ and $n$ be positive integers. What has to be true about $m$ and $n$ for $(-5)^m \cdot (-5)^n$ to be a positive number? to be a negative number?

Gr. 7 NS 2.1 Understand negative whole-number exponents. **Multiply** and divide expressions involving exponents with a common base.
**Alg. 2.0 Students** understand and use such operations as taking the opposite, finding the reciprocal, taking a root, and raising to a fractional power. They **understand and use the rules of exponents.**

**EXPLORE 2** *Use products of powers* · · · · · · · · · · · · · · · · · · · · · ·

**Play the following game in a group of 2 or 3 students.**

**1** **Copy** the table below. Each player should make a separate copy of the table.

| Expression | Expression with value of $m$ from number cube | Product as a power | Value |
|---|---|---|---|
| $4^2 \cdot 4^m$ | ? | ? | ? |
| $(-5)^2 \cdot (-5)^m$ | ? | ? | ? |
| $10^m \cdot 10^m$ | ? | ? | ? |
| $(-2)^m \cdot (-2)^5$ | ? | ? | ? |
| $7^4 \cdot 7^m$ | ? | ? | ? |
| $1^m \cdot 1^5$ | ? | ? | ? |

**2** **Choose** a player to go first. The player should do the following:

- Roll a number cube, then choose an expression from the table and replace $m$ with the number rolled.
- Next, write the expression as a single power, then find the value of the power.
- Repeat these steps for 5 more rolls, choosing a different expression for each roll.

After 6 rolls, find the sum of the values in the last column of the table. The goal is to have the greatest sum compared with the other players in your group.

**3** **Repeat** Step 2 until each player has rolled the number cube 6 times and completed the table. The player with the greatest sum wins!

## Draw Conclusions
**Evaluate the expression for $m = 2$, $n = 3$, and $p = 4$.**

**9.** $4^5 \cdot 4^m$        **10.** $7^n \cdot 7^3$        **11.** $2^9 \cdot 2^p$

**12.** $(-4)^m \cdot (-4)^4$        **13.** $5^2 \cdot 5^n$        **14.** $10^n \cdot 10^m$

**15.** Suppose you roll a 6 while playing the game. If all 6 expressions are available, which one would you choose? *Explain.*

**16.** Without actually simplifying, do you think $4^2 \cdot 4^4$ is less than or greater than $(-5)^2 \cdot (-5)^4$? *Explain* your reasoning.

# Multiply Powers with the Same Base

## VOCABULARY and CONCEPTS
- power, p. 6
- exponent, p. 6
- base, p. 6

**Product of Powers Property**

**Words**     To multiply powers having the same base, add the exponents.

**Numbers**   $2^3 \cdot 2^4 = 2^{3+4} = 2^7$

**Algebra**     $a^m \cdot a^n = a^{m+n}$ where $a$ is a real number and $m$ and $n$ are integers.

**EXAMPLE 1**   *Using the Product of Powers Property* •••••••••

**Simplify the expression. Write your answer using exponents.**

   **a.** $2^6 \cdot 2^8$                         **b.** $(-3)^7 \cdot (-3)$

   **c.** $(-7)^3 \cdot (-7) \cdot (-7)^4$            **d.** $m \cdot m^5 \cdot m^6$

**Solution**

   **a.** $2^6 \cdot 2^8 = 2^{6+8}$                                   **Product of powers property**

                 $= 2^{14}$                                        **Add exponents.**

   **b.** $(-3)^7 \cdot (-3) = (-3)^7 \cdot (-3)^1$            **Write $(-3)$ as $(-3)^1$.**

                      $= (-3)^{7+1}$                **Product of powers property**

                      $= (-3)^8$                   **Add exponents.**

   **c.** $(-7)^3 \cdot (-7) \cdot (-7)^4 = (-7)^3 \cdot (-7)^1 \cdot (-7)^4$   **Write $(-7)$ as $(-7)^1$.**

                            $= (-7)^{3+1+4}$         **Product of powers property**

                            $= (-7)^8$                 **Add exponents.**

   **d.** $m \cdot m^5 \cdot m^6 = m^1 \cdot m^5 \cdot m^6$           **Write $m$ as $m^1$.**

                   $= m^{1+5+6}$                **Product of powers property**

                   $= m^{12}$                   **Add exponents.**

## Practice for Example 1

**Simplify the expression. Write your answer using exponents.**

   **1.** $8^3 \cdot 8^{11}$           **2.** $y^3 \cdot y^6 \cdot y^2$           **3.** $(-10)^2 \cdot (-10) \cdot (-10)^5$

**EXAMPLE 2** *Simplifying Expressions* • • • • • • • • • • • • • • • •

**Simplify $13x^7 \cdot 4x^4$.**

### Solution

$$13x^7 \cdot 4x^4 = 13 \cdot 4 \cdot x^7 \cdot x^4 \qquad \text{Commutative property of multiplication}$$
$$= 13 \cdot 4 \cdot x^{7+4} \qquad \text{Product of powers property}$$
$$= 13 \cdot 4 \cdot x^{11} \qquad \text{Add exponents.}$$
$$= 52x^{11} \qquad \text{Multiply.}$$

### Practice for Example 2

**Simplify the expression.**

**4.** $11x^3 \cdot 4x^7$

**5.** $9a^5 \cdot 8a^8$

**6.** $4y \cdot 3y^9 \cdot 4y^5$

**7.** $5k^3 \cdot 3k^{12} \cdot 4k^8$

**EXAMPLE 3** *Solving a Real-World Problem* • • • • • • • • • • • •

The sun evaporates about $10^{12}$ tons of water on Earth each day. Find the weight of water evaporated by the sun in $10^3$ days.

### Solution

Write a verbal model to help you find the weight.

| Tons of water evaporated in $10^3$ days | = | Tons of water evaporated in 1 day | • | Number of days |
|---|---|---|---|---|

$$= 10^{12} \cdot 10^3 \qquad \text{Substitute values.}$$
$$= 10^{12+3} \qquad \text{Product of powers property}$$
$$= 10^{15} \qquad \text{Add exponents.}$$

▸ **Answer** The sun evaporates about $10^{15}$ tons of water in $10^3$ days.

### Practice for Example 3

**8.** A rectangular field has a length of $2^9$ meters and a width of $2^7$ meters. What is the area of the field? Write your answer using exponents.

# Practice

**Extra Practice**
p. 503

1. Copy and complete: To multiply powers with the same base, _?_ their _?_.

**Tell whether the product of powers property can be used to simplify the expression.**

2. $7^3 \cdot 7^2$

3. $5^4 \cdot 4^5$

4. $m^6 \cdot n^3$

5. $z^3 \cdot z^9$

**Simplify the expression. Write your answer using exponents.**

6. $3^2 \cdot 3^4$

7. $2^3 \cdot 2^3$

8. $5^4 \cdot 5^3 \cdot 5^2$

9. $4 \cdot 4^8 \cdot 4^7$

10. $9^7 \cdot 9$

11. $8^5 \cdot 8^6$

12. $(-9)^7 \cdot (-9)^4$

13. $(-13)^3 \cdot (-13)^{12}$

14. $(-4) \cdot (-4)^3 \cdot (-4)^5$

**Simplify the expression.**

15. $a^3 \cdot a^2$

16. $b^6 \cdot b^7$

17. $x^9 \cdot x^3$

18. $y^8 \cdot y^5$

19. $3g^4 \cdot g^5$

20. $4h^3 \cdot 5h^4 \cdot h^2$

**FIND THE ERROR** *Describe* and correct the error in simplifying the expression.

21.
$$2x^3 \cdot 2x^6 = 2x^{3+6}$$
$$= 2x^9$$

22.
$$c^7 \cdot d^{12} = cd^{7+12}$$
$$= cd^{19}$$

**Find the missing exponent.**

23. $f^? \cdot f^6 = f^{17}$

24. $w^6 \cdot w^? = w^9$

25. $j^? \cdot j^9 = j^{13}$

26. **REASONING** Write three products of powers that are equivalent to $18x^{10}$.

**In Exercises 27 and 28, use the table showing the populations of two states in 1870.**

27. Copy and complete the table by writing the power of 10 that best approximates the population.

28. In 1870, the population of Wisconsin was about 10 times as great as the population of Oregon. Use the powers of 10 in the table to estimate the population of Oregon in 1870.

| State | Wisconsin | Nebraska |
|---|---|---|
| Population | 1,054,670 | 122,993 |
| Power of 10 | ? | ? |

29. There are about $10^{27}$ water molecules in 1 cubic foot of water. Lake Huron holds about $10^{14}$ cubic feet of water. About how many water molecules are in Lake Huron? Write your answer using an exponent.

**Tell whether the product of powers property can be used to simplify the expression.**

**1.** $8^4 \cdot 8^7$        **2.** $2^3 \cdot 3^2$        **3.** $x^2 \cdot y^5$        **4.** $p^4 \cdot p^6$

**Simplify the expression. Write your answer using exponents.**

**5.** $5^{10} \cdot 5^{11}$        **6.** $4^8 \cdot 4^9$        **7.** $6^7 \cdot 6^2 \cdot 6^8$

**8.** $8^2 \cdot 8^{14} \cdot 8^3$        **9.** $9^{12} \cdot 9^{13}$        **10.** $10^7 \cdot 10^{13}$

**11.** $(-6)^7 \cdot (-6)^{11}$        **12.** $(-11)^9 \cdot (-11) \cdot (-11)^4$        **13.** $(-15)^{12} \cdot (-15)^{12}$

**Simplify the expression.**

**14.** $d^4 \cdot d^4$        **15.** $3h^5 \cdot 4h^6$        **16.** $5g^2 \cdot g^{16}$

**17.** $8e^9 \cdot 7e^{10}$        **18.** $9w^3 \cdot 2w^4 \cdot w^2$        **19.** $5v^6 \cdot 2v^4 \cdot 2v^3$

**20.** $4p^2 \cdot 4p^6$        **21.** $11f^8 \cdot 11f^3$        **22.** $6a^3b^5 \cdot 6a^4b^4$

**Find the missing exponent.**

**23.** $u^{22} \cdot u^? = u^{40}$        **24.** $d^? \cdot d^{13} = d^{24}$        **25.** $f^8 \cdot f^? = f^{33}$

**26. REASONING** Write a product of powers that is equivalent to $(-10)x^{11}$.

**27.** Find the area of the rectangle.

**28.** Find the area of the triangle.

**29.** Find the volume of the prism.

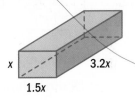

**30.** Hot Springs National Park in Arkansas covers an area of about 10 square miles. Kenai Fjords National Park in Alaska covers an area that is about $10^2$ times the area of Hot Springs National Park. Find the approximate area of Kenai Fjords National Park. Write your answer using exponents.

**31.** In 2005, approximately $10^3$ metric tons of silver were mined in the United States. The amount of copper mined in the United States in 2005 was approximately $10^3$ times the amount of silver mined. About how many metric tons of copper were mined in the United States in 2005?

**32.** An earthquake of magnitude 6.7 releases $32^2$ times the energy that an earthquake of magnitude 4.7 does. An earthquake of magnitude 4.7 releases $32^2$ times the energy that an earthquake of magnitude 2.7 does. How many times as great as the energy of an earthquake of magnitude 2.7 is the energy of an earthquake of magnitude 6.7? Write your answer using an exponent.

Let's Explore
## Investigating Quotients of Powers

**Goal**
Divide powers with the same base.

**Materials**
• index cards

**QUESTION** **How can you find a quotient of powers with the same base?**

**EXPLORE 1** *Find quotients of powers* . . . . . . . . . . . . . . . . . . . . . . . . . . .

1. **Copy** and complete the table.

The first row has been completed for you.

| Expression | Expanded expression | Simplified expression | Number of factors | Quotient as a power |
|---|---|---|---|---|
| $\dfrac{2^8}{2^3}$ | $\dfrac{2 \cdot 2 \cdot 2 \cdot 2 \cdot 2 \cdot 2 \cdot 2 \cdot 2}{2 \cdot 2 \cdot 2}$ | $2 \cdot 2 \cdot 2 \cdot 2 \cdot 2$ | 5 | $2^5$ |
| $\dfrac{3^5}{3^3}$ | ? | ? | ? | ? |
| $\dfrac{5^7}{5^6}$ | ? | ? | ? | ? |
| $\dfrac{(-7)^5}{(-7)^2}$ | ? | ? | ? | ? |

2. **Compare** exponents.

*Describe* how the exponents of the expression in the first column relate to the exponent of the expression in the last column.

## Draw Conclusions
**Write the quotient as a single power.**

1. $\dfrac{7^8}{7^3}$

2. $\dfrac{6^9}{6^8}$

3. $\dfrac{(-5)^{10}}{(-5)^2}$

4. $\dfrac{4^8}{4^3}$

5. $\dfrac{(-3)^7}{(-3)^4}$

6. $\dfrac{9^9}{9^2}$

7. Copy and complete: If $a$ is a nonzero real number and $m$ and $n$ are positive integers with $m > n$, then $\dfrac{a^m}{a^n} = \underline{\ ?\ }$.

8. Let $m$ and $n$ be positive integers where $m > n$. What has to be true about $m$ and $n$ for $\dfrac{(-5)^m}{(-5)^n}$ to be a positive number? a negative number?

**Gr. 7 NS 2.1** Understand negative whole-number exponents. Multiply and **divide expressions involving exponents with a common base.**
**Alg. 2.0 Students** understand and use such operations as taking the opposite, finding the reciprocal, taking a root, and raising to a fractional power. They **understand and use the rules of exponents.**

**EXPLORE 2**   *Use quotients of powers*

**Play the following game in a group of 2 or 3 students.**

**1**   **Copy** each expression below on a separate index card.

$$\frac{4^6}{4^2} \qquad \frac{4^9}{4^3} \qquad \frac{(-4)^4}{(-4)^3} \qquad -4 \qquad \frac{4^5}{4^2} \qquad 4$$

$$\frac{4^7}{4^4} \qquad \frac{4^{11}}{4^6} \qquad \frac{4^8}{4^5} \qquad \frac{(-4)^{12}}{(-4)^3} \qquad \frac{(-4)^5}{(-4)^6} \qquad \frac{(-4)^2}{-4}$$

**2**   **Choose** a player to go first. Copy the table below. Then shuffle the cards from Step 1 and place them face down. Next, select a card and write the expression from the card in the first row of the *Card 1* column of the table. Select a second card and write the expression in the first row of the *Card 2* column of the table. Using the symbol in the first row, tell whether the statement is true or false. The other players in your group will then determine whether your answer is correct or not. Score points as follows:

**1 point:** saying a true statement is true or a false statement is false
**0 points:** saying a true statement is false or a false statement is true

Continue filling out rows of the table until all cards have been used.

| Card 1 | Symbol | Card 2 | True or false? | Points |
|--------|--------|--------|----------------|--------|
| ? | > | ? | ? | ? |
| ? | = | ? | ? | ? |
| ? | < | ? | ? | ? |
| ? | > | ? | ? | ? |
| ? | = | ? | ? | ? |
| ? | < | ? | ? | ? |
| | | | Total points → | ? |

**3**   **Repeat** Step 2 until each player has completed his or her table.

## Draw Conclusions
**Copy and complete using <, >, or =.**

**9.** $\dfrac{(-3)^2}{-3} \ \underline{?} \ \dfrac{(-3)^5}{(-3)^4}$    **10.** $\dfrac{7^9}{7^2} \ \underline{?} \ \dfrac{7^8}{7^3}$    **11.** $\dfrac{12^{12}}{12^{10}} \ \underline{?} \ 12$

**12.** Is it true that $\dfrac{a^m}{a^n} = \dfrac{a^{m+1}}{a^{n+1}}$ for any nonzero real number $a$ and integers $m$ and $n$ with $m > n$? *Explain.*

# Divide Powers with the Same Base

## VOCABULARY and CONCEPTS

- power, p. 6   • exponent, p. 6   • base, p. 6

### Quotient of Powers Property

**Words**   To divide powers having the same base, subtract the exponents.

**Numbers**   $\dfrac{2^5}{2^3} = 2^{5-3} = 2^2$

**Algebra**   $\dfrac{a^m}{a^n} = a^{m-n}$ for any nonzero real number $a$ and positive integers $m$ and $n$ with $m > n$.

**EXAMPLE 1**   *Using the Quotient of Powers Property* • • • • • • • •

**Simplify the expression. Write your answer using exponents.**

**a.** $\dfrac{7^{13}}{7^8} = 7^{13-8}$   **Quotient of powers property**

$= 7^5$   **Subtract exponents.**

**b.** $\dfrac{(-1)^6}{(-1)^2} = (-1)^{6-2}$   **Quotient of powers property**

$= (-1)^4$   **Subtract exponents.**

**c.** $\dfrac{1}{y^7} \cdot y^{18} = \dfrac{1}{y^7} \cdot \dfrac{y^{18}}{1}$   **Write $y^{18}$ as $\dfrac{y^{18}}{1}$.**

$= \dfrac{y^{18}}{y^7}$   **Multiply.**

$= y^{18-7}$   **Quotient of powers property**

$= y^{11}$   **Subtract exponents.**

**d.** $\dfrac{x^6}{x} = \dfrac{x^6}{x^1}$   **Write $x$ as $x^1$.**

$= x^{6-1}$   **Quotient of powers property**

$= x^5$   **Subtract exponents.**

## Practice for Example 1

**Simplify the expression. Write your answer using exponents.**

**1.** $\dfrac{12^{15}}{12^6}$

**2.** $\dfrac{1}{w^{16}} \cdot w^{21}$

**3.** $\dfrac{x^9}{x^6}$

**Gr. 7 NS 2.1** Understand negative whole-number exponents. Multiply and **divide expressions involving exponents with a common base.**
**Alg. 2.0 Students** understand and use such operations as taking the opposite, finding the reciprocal, taking a root, and raising to a fractional power. They understand and use the rules of exponents.

**EXAMPLE 2**  *Using the Quotient of Powers Property* · · · · · · · · ·

**Simplify the expression.**

**a.** $\dfrac{5x^{11}}{20x^8} = \dfrac{5x^{11-8}}{20}$    **Quotient of powers property**

$= \dfrac{5x^3}{20}$    **Subtract exponents.**

$= \dfrac{x^3}{4}$    **Divide numerator and denominator by their GCF, 5.**

**b.** $\dfrac{x^5 \cdot y^{12}}{x^2} = x^{5-2}y^{12}$    **Quotient of powers property**

$= x^3y^{12}$    **Subtract exponents.**

## Practice for Example 2

**Simplify the expression.**

**4.** $\dfrac{8m^8}{12m^2}$    **5.** $\dfrac{a^3b^9}{a}$    **6.** $\dfrac{x^6y^{13}}{y^7}$

**EXAMPLE 3**  *Solve a Real-World Problem* · · · · · · · · · · · · · · · ·

The mean, or average, distance from the sun to Eris, a dwarf planet in the solar system, is about $10^{10}$ kilometers. The mean distance from the sun to the planet Venus is about $10^8$ kilometers. About how many times as far from the sun is Eris as Venus?

### Solution

$\dfrac{\text{Distance from the sun to Eris}}{\text{Distance from the sun to Venus}} = \dfrac{10^{10}}{10^8}$

$= 10^{10-8}$

$= 10^2$

▶ **Answer** Eris is about $10^2$ times as far from the sun as Venus.

## Practice for Example 3

**7.** The mean distance from the sun to Saturn is about $10^{12}$ meters. The mean distance from the sun to Venus is about $10^{11}$ meters. About how many times as far from the sun is Saturn as Venus?

**1.** Copy and complete: To simplify a quotient of two powers with the same base, subtract the exponent of the _?_ from the exponent of the _?_ .

**Tell whether the quotient of powers property can be used to simplify the expression.**

**2.** $\dfrac{5^2}{(-5)^2}$  **3.** $\dfrac{6^4}{6^2}$  **4.** $\dfrac{b^8}{b^3}$  **5.** $\dfrac{m^5}{n^4}$

**Simplify the expression. Write your answer using exponents.**

**6.** $\dfrac{2^{14}}{2^9}$  **7.** $\dfrac{5^9}{5^8}$  **8.** $\dfrac{3^{15}}{3^6}$

**9.** $\dfrac{12^4}{12^3}$  **10.** $\dfrac{9^{13}}{9^7}$  **11.** $\dfrac{8^8}{8^6}$

**12.** $\dfrac{(-9)^{11}}{(-9)^7}$  **13.** $\dfrac{(-13)^{15}}{(-13)^{12}}$  **14.** $\dfrac{(-19)^{21}}{(-19)^{17}}$

**Simplify the expression.**

**15.** $\dfrac{k^9}{k^7}$  **16.** $\dfrac{m^{14}}{m^3}$  **17.** $\dfrac{1}{y^5} \cdot y^{11}$

**18.** $z^3 \cdot \dfrac{1}{z^2}$  **19.** $\dfrac{1}{n^4} \cdot n^8$  **20.** $\dfrac{8w^{13}}{w^7}$

**21.** $\dfrac{32d^5}{8d^3}$  **22.** $\dfrac{18s^5 \cdot t^2}{15s^4}$  **23.** $\dfrac{16w^6 \cdot t^4}{12t^2}$

**Find the missing exponent.**

**24.** $\dfrac{c^?}{c^5} = c^3$  **25.** $\dfrac{v^?}{v^4} = v^7$  **26.** $\dfrac{z^{12}}{z^?} = z^8$

**27. REASONING** Name a pair of integers $c$ and $d$ that make the statement $\dfrac{7^c}{7^d} = 7$ true. Are there other pairs of integers $c$ and $d$ that will also make the statement true? *Explain.*

**28.** The table shows the approximate numbers of Internet users in selected countries in 2005.

| Country | China | Guyana | Laos | Mexico |
|---|---|---|---|---|
| Internet users | $10^8$ | $10^5$ | $10^4$ | $10^7$ |

   **a.** In 2005, how many times as great as the number of users from Guyana was the number of users from Mexico?

   **b.** How many times as great as the number of users from Laos was the number of users from China?

# Practice

**Simplify the expression. Write your answer using exponents.**

**1.** $\dfrac{3^{16}}{3^8}$

**2.** $\dfrac{7^{20}}{7^{14}}$

**3.** $\dfrac{11^{19}}{11^{15}}$

**4.** $\dfrac{13^5}{13^2}$

**5.** $\dfrac{16^8}{16^5}$

**6.** $\dfrac{20^9}{20^7}$

**7.** $\dfrac{(-10)^{10}}{(-10)^9}$

**8.** $\dfrac{(-18)^{15}}{(-18)^8}$

**9.** $\dfrac{(-25)^{21}}{(-25)^{15}}$

**Simplify the expression.**

**10.** $\dfrac{x^{15}}{x^9}$

**11.** $\dfrac{v^{11}}{v^3}$

**12.** $\dfrac{y^{18}}{y^2}$

**13.** $\dfrac{1}{y^9} \cdot y^{15}$

**14.** $z^{16} \cdot \dfrac{1}{z^7}$

**15.** $m^5 \cdot \dfrac{1}{m}$

**16.** $\dfrac{a^6 \cdot b^3}{a^4}$

**17.** $\dfrac{15x^5z^{10}}{z^5}$

**18.** $\dfrac{11p^4q^4}{q}$

**19.** $\dfrac{63m^8}{7m^4}$

**20.** $\dfrac{42u^{10}}{12u^2}$

**21.** $\dfrac{36d^{11}}{14d^8}$

**22.** $\dfrac{24q^{20}}{52q^{17}}$

**23.** $\dfrac{34t^{18}v^9}{72t^{15}v^7}$

**24.** $\dfrac{45z^{21}a^{10}}{81z^{16}a^4}$

**FIND THE ERROR** *Describe* and correct the error in simplifying the expression.

**25.**
$$\dfrac{12r^6}{3r^2} = \dfrac{12r^3}{3}$$
$$= 4r^3$$

**26.**
$$\dfrac{35b^{16}c^8}{7c^4} = \dfrac{35b^{16}c^{12}}{7}$$
$$= 5b^{16}c^{12}$$

**27.** **REASONING** *Explain* how you could show a friend that $\dfrac{4^7}{4^3} = 4^4$ without using the quotient of powers property.

**28.** A file on the hard drive of a computer is $3^2$ kilobytes. Another file is $3^7$ kilobytes. How many times as large as the first file is the second file? Write your answer using an exponent.

**29.** The table below shows the approximate number of cell phone subscribers in various countries in 2004.

| Country | Sudan | Romania | Palau |
|---|---|---|---|
| Cell phone subscribers | $10^6$ | $10^7$ | $10^3$ |

**a.** In 2004, how many times as great as the number of cell phone subscribers in Palau was the number of subscribers in Sudan?

**b.** How many times as great as the number of cell phone subscribers in Palau was the number of subscribers in Romania?

# Mid-Chapter Review

> **REVIEW VOCABULARY**
> - power, p. 6
> - base, p. 6
> - exponent, p. 6

**Vocabulary Exercise**

**1.** Copy and complete: A(n) _?_ is a way of writing repeated multiplication.

## 6.1 Multiply Powers with the Same Base ............ *pp. 252–255*

**EXAMPLES** Simplify the expression. Write your answer using exponents.

**a.** $(-5)^3 \cdot (-5)^5 = (-5)^{3+5} = (-5)^8$     **Product of powers property**

**b.** $11x^3 \cdot 3x^8 = 11 \cdot 3 \cdot x^3 \cdot x^8$     **Commutative property of multiplication**

$\qquad\qquad = 11 \cdot 3 \cdot x^{3+8}$     **Product of powers property**

$\qquad\qquad = 11 \cdot 3 \cdot x^{11}$     **Add exponents.**

$\qquad\qquad = 33x^{11}$     **Multiply.**

Simplify the expression. Write your answer using exponents.

**2.** $3^6 \cdot 3^3$     **3.** $m^6 \cdot m^2$     **4.** $6x^5 \cdot 7x^{11}$     **5.** $3y^{10} \cdot 9y^4$

## 6.2 Divide Powers with the Same Base ............ *pp. 258–261*

**EXAMPLES** Simplify the expression. Write your answer using exponents.

**a.** $\dfrac{8^{15}}{8^4} = 8^{15-4} = 8^{11}$     **Quotient of powers property**

**b.** $\dfrac{1}{y^4} \cdot y^{12} = \dfrac{1}{y^4} \cdot \dfrac{y^{12}}{1}$     **Write $y^{12}$ as $\dfrac{y^{12}}{1}$.**

$\qquad\qquad = \dfrac{y^{12}}{y^4}$     **Multiply.**

$\qquad\qquad = y^{12-4}$     **Quotient of powers property**

$\qquad\qquad = y^8$     **Subtract exponents.**

Simplify the expression. Write your answer using exponents.

**6.** $\dfrac{12^{10}}{12^5}$     **7.** $\dfrac{1}{y^9} \cdot y^{15}$     **8.** $\dfrac{x^8}{x}$     **9.** $z^{13} \cdot \dfrac{1}{z^8}$

# Mid-Chapter Test

**Simplify the expression. Write your answer using exponents.**

**1.** $2^4 \cdot 2^3$

**2.** $(-3)^2 \cdot (-3)^5$

**3.** $a^6 \cdot a^4$

**4.** $r^7 \cdot r$

**5.** $7^5 \cdot 7^2 \cdot 7^3$

**6.** $12^3 \cdot 12^3 \cdot 12^3$

**7.** $(-n)^4 \cdot (-n)^5 \cdot (-n)^2$

**8.** $(-c)^2 \cdot (-c)^7 \cdot (-c)$

**9.** $\dfrac{6^4}{6^2}$

**10.** $\dfrac{(-8)^7}{(-8)^3}$

**11.** $\dfrac{u^{13}}{u^6}$

**12.** $\dfrac{(-q)^{12}}{(-q)^3}$

**13.** $\dfrac{1}{y^6} \cdot y^{13}$

**14.** $n^8 \cdot \dfrac{1}{n^5}$

**15.** $\dfrac{9x^4 \cdot y^2}{12x^3}$

**16.** $\dfrac{10m^5 \cdot n^4}{25n^2}$

**In Exercise 17–19, find the missing exponent.**

**17.** $b^7 \cdot b^? = b^{15}$

**18.** $\dfrac{z^{11}}{z^?} = z^2$

**19.** $\dfrac{r^?}{r^6} = r^{13}$

**20.** Find the area of the square. **21.** Find the area of the triangle. **22.** Find the volume of the prism.

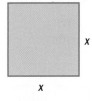

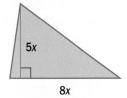

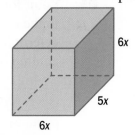

**23.** Write three products of powers that are equivalent to $24x^9$.

**24.** Name a pair of integers $b$ and $c$ that make the statement $\dfrac{9^b}{9^c} = 9^2$ true.

**In Exercises 25 and 26, use the table showing the 2005 population estimates of two locations.**

| Location | Antioch, CA | Lindsay, CA |
|---|---|---|
| Population | 103,339 | 10,767 |
| Power of 10 | ? | ? |

**25.** Copy and complete the table by writing the power of 10 that best approximates the population.

**26.** The 2005 population estimate for Dallas, Texas, was about 10 times as great as the population estimate for Antioch. Use the powers of 10 in the table to estimate the population of Dallas in 2005.

**27.** Lake Iliamna in Alaska covers an area of about 1000 square miles. The Great Lakes cover an area that is about $10^2$ times the area of Lake Iliamna. Find the approximate area of the Great Lakes. Write your answer using exponents.

**28.** The table shows some units of length in the metric system.

| Unit | Gigameter | Megameter | Kilometer | Dekameter |
|---|---|---|---|---|
| Length (in meters) | $10^9$ | $10^6$ | $10^3$ | $10^1$ |

**a.** How many times as long as a kilometer is a gigameter?

**b.** How many times as long as a dekameter is a megameter?

# Activity 6.3

## Let's Explore

### Zero and Negative Exponents

**Goal**
Simplify expressions with zero and negative exponents.

**Materials**
• pencil and paper

**QUESTION** How do you evaluate expressions with zero or negative exponents?

**EXPLORE 1** *Investigate zero and negative exponents* ......

1. **Look** for a pattern in each of the tables below. Identify what happens to the exponents as you read down the left column of each table. Then determine how to obtain one value from the previous value in the right column of each table.

| Table 1 | |
|---|---|
| **Power** | **Value** |
| $2^4$ | 16 |
| $2^3$ | 8 |
| $2^2$ | 4 |
| $2^1$ | 2 |
| $2^0$ | ? |
| $2^{-1}$ | ? |
| $2^{-2}$ | ? |
| $2^{-3}$ | ? |

| Table 2 | |
|---|---|
| **Power** | **Value** |
| $3^4$ | 81 |
| $3^3$ | 27 |
| $3^2$ | 9 |
| $3^1$ | 3 |
| $3^0$ | ? |
| $3^{-1}$ | ? |
| $3^{-2}$ | ? |
| $3^{-3}$ | ? |

| Table 3 | |
|---|---|
| **Power** | **Value** |
| $4^4$ | 256 |
| $4^3$ | 64 |
| $4^2$ | 16 |
| $4^1$ | 4 |
| $4^0$ | ? |
| $4^{-1}$ | ? |
| $4^{-2}$ | ? |
| $4^{-3}$ | ? |

2. **Use** the pattern from Step 1 to copy and complete the tables.

## Draw Conclusions

1. Compare the value of $2^3$ with the value of $2^{-3}$. Compare the value of $3^1$ with $3^{-1}$. If two powers have the same base but their exponents are opposites, how are their values related?

2. Suppose $a$ is a nonzero number. Make a prediction about the value of $a^n$ when $n = 0$.

Gr. 7 AF 2.1 Interpret positive whole-number powers as repeated multiplication and **negative whole-number powers as repeated division or multiplication by the multiplicative inverse.** Simplify and evaluate expressions that include exponents.
Gr. 7 NS 2.1 Understand negative whole-number exponents. Multiply and divide expressions involving exponents with a common base.

**EXPLORE 2** *Define zero and negative exponents* . . . . . . . . . . .

**1** **Develop** the definition of zero exponent by copying and completing the statements in the *Algebra* column in the table below. Use the equivalent statements in the *Numbers* column as a guide.

| Numbers | Algebra |
|---|---|
| Consider the expression $\dfrac{2^5}{2^5}$. | Consider the expression $\dfrac{a^n}{a^n}$ where $a \neq 0$ and $n > 0$. |
| The value of $\dfrac{2^5}{2^5}$ is 1. | The value of $\dfrac{a^n}{a^n}$ is _?_ . |
| Using the quotient of powers property, you can write $\dfrac{2^5}{2^5}$ as $2^{5-5} = 2^0$. | Using the quotient of powers property, you can write _?_ as _?_ = _?_ . |
| Because $\dfrac{2^5}{2^5} = 1$ and $\dfrac{2^5}{2^5} = 2^0$, it makes sense to define $2^0$ as equal to 1. | ? |

**2** **Develop** the definition of negative exponents by copying and completing the statements in the *Algebra* column in the table below. Use the equivalent statements in the *Numbers* column as a guide.

| Numbers | Algebra |
|---|---|
| Consider the expression $2^{-4} \cdot 2^4$. | Consider the expression $a^{-n} \cdot a^n$ where $a \neq 0$ and $n > 0$. |
| Using the product of powers property, you can write: $\begin{aligned} 2^{-4} \cdot 2^4 &= 2^{-4+4} \\ &= 2^0 \\ &= 1 \end{aligned}$ | Using the product of powers property, you can write: $\begin{aligned} a^{-n} \cdot a^n &= \underline{\ ?\ } \\ &= \underline{\ ?\ } \\ &= \underline{\ ?\ } \end{aligned}$ |
| Because $2^{-4} \cdot 2^4 = 1$, $2^{-4}$ is the reciprocal of $2^4$. So, you can define $2^{-4}$ as $\dfrac{1}{2^4}$. | ? |

# Draw Conclusions

**3.** Copy and complete: $a^0 = \underline{\ ?\ }$, $a \neq 0$.

**4.** Copy and complete: $a^{-n} = \dfrac{1}{\underline{\ ?\ }}$, $a \neq 0$.

**5.** Why is $a^0$ not defined when $a = 0$?

## VOCABULARY and CONCEPTS

### Definition of Zero and Negative Exponents

- A nonzero number $a$ to the zero power is 1: $a^0 = 1$ where $a \neq 0$.
- For a nonzero number $a$, $a^{-n}$ is the reciprocal of $a^n$: $a^{-n} = \dfrac{1}{a^n}$ where $a \neq 0$.

### Powers of 10

You can use the definitions of zero and negative exponents to express powers of 10 in fraction form and decimal form. The following table lists some examples.

| Power | $10^0$ | $10^{-1}$ | $10^{-2}$ | $10^{-3}$ |
|---|---|---|---|---|
| Fraction | 1 | $\dfrac{1}{10}$ | $\dfrac{1}{100}$ | $\dfrac{1}{1000}$ |
| Decimal | 1 | 0.1 | 0.01 | 0.001 |

### Scientific Notation

A number is written in **scientific notation** when it is of the form $c \times 10^n$ where $c$ is greater than or equal to 1 and less than 10 and $n$ is an integer.

| Number | Standard form | Scientific notation |
|---|---|---|
| Four million | 4,000,000 | $4 \times 10^6$ |
| Seven hundredths | 0.07 | $7 \times 10^{-2}$ |

---

**EXAMPLE 1** Using Zero and Negative Exponents

**a.** $2^{-3} = \dfrac{1}{2^3}$     **Definition of negative exponent**

      $= \dfrac{1}{8}$     **Simplify.**

**b.** $15^0 = 1$     **Definition of zero exponent**

### Practice for Example 1

**Evaluate the expression.**

**1.** $(-10)^0$      **2.** $5^{-4}$      **3.** $9^{-3}$      **4.** $(-6)^{-2}$

---

**EXAMPLE 2** Writing Decimals Using Powers of 10

**Skills Review**

Place value, p. 476

**a.** Write 0.25 in expanded form using powers of 10.

$$0.25 = \dfrac{2}{10} + \dfrac{5}{100}$$

$$= 2 \times 10^{-1} + 5 \times 10^{-2}$$

**b.** Write $3 \times 10^1 + 9 \times 10^0 + 7 \times 10^{-1}$ in standard form.

$$3 \times 10^1 + 9 \times 10^0 + 7 \times 10^{-1} = 30 + 9 + \dfrac{7}{10}$$

$$= 39.7$$

### Practice for Example 2

**5.** Write 68.2 in expanded form using powers of 10.

**6.** Write $1 \times 10^0 + 5 \times 10^{-1} + 4 \times 10^{-2}$ in standard form.

**EXAMPLE 3** *Using Scientific Notation*

**a.** Write $4.52 \times 10^6$ in standard form.

$$4.52 \times 10^6 = 4,520,000$$

To multiply by $10^6$, move the decimal point 6 places to the right.

**b.** Write $1.8 \times 10^{-7}$ in standard form.

$$1.8 \times 10^{-7} = 0.00000018$$

To multiply by $10^{-7}$, move the decimal point 7 places to the left.

**c.** Write 7500 in scientific notation.

$$7500 = 7.5 \times 10^3$$

Move the decimal point 3 places to the left and multiply by $10^3$.

**d.** Write 0.000053 in scientific notation.

$$0.000053 = 5.3 \times 10^{-5}$$

Move the decimal point 5 places to the right and multiply by $10^{-5}$.

### Practice for Example 3

**7.** Write $8.4 \times 10^{-6}$ in standard form.

**8.** Write 0.021 in scientific notation.

**EXAMPLE 4** *Comparing Numbers in Scientific Notation*

The mass of an oxygen atom and the mass of a hydrogen atom are shown. Which atom has a greater mass?

**Oxygen atom**

Mass $\approx 2.657 \times 10^{-23}$ g

**Hydrogen atom**

Mass $\approx 1.6735 \times 10^{-24}$ g

#### Solution

To compare numbers written in scientific notation, first compare the exponents. If the exponents are equal, then compare the decimal parts.

Oxygen:   $2.657 \times 10^{-23}$
Hydrogen: $1.6735 \times 10^{-24}$

Because $-23 > -24$, $2.657 \times 10^{-23} > 1.6735 \times 10^{-24}$.

▸**Answer** The oxygen atom has a greater mass.

### Practice for Example 4

**9.** The mass of a nitrogen atom is $2.3259 \times 10^{-23}$ gram. Does a nitrogen atom have a greater mass than an oxygen atom? *Explain.*

# Practice

**Extra Practice**
p. 503

**Copy and complete the statement.**

**1.** $a^{-n}$ is equal to $\dfrac{1}{\underline{?}}$.

**2.** If $a$ is a nonzero number, then $a^0 = \underline{\ ?\ }$.

**Evaluate the expression.**

**3.** $6^{-2}$

**4.** $(-3)^{-5}$

**5.** $7^{-3}$

**6.** $13^0$

**7.** $3^{-3}$

**8.** $4^{-6}$

**9.** $158^0$

**10.** $(-4)^{-2}$

**Write the number in expanded form using powers of 10.**

**11.** $18.4$

**12.** $9.8$

**13.** $27.3$

**14.** $6.9$

**Write the number in standard form.**

**15.** $6 \times 10^0 + 5 \times 10^{-1} + 3 \times 10^{-2}$

**16.** $3 \times 10^1 + 5 \times 10^0 + 6 \times 10^{-1} + 5 \times 10^{-2}$

**17.** $1 \times 10^1 + 9 \times 10^0 + 8 \times 10^{-1} + 9 \times 10^{-2}$

**18.** $4 \times 10^1 + 1 \times 10^0 + 6 \times 10^{-1} + 7 \times 10^{-2}$

**Tell whether the number is expressed in scientific notation.**

**19.** $6.43 \times 10^6$

**20.** $17.08 \times 10^2$

**21.** $0.08 \times 10^{-5}$

**Write the number in standard form.**

**22.** $7.61 \times 10^{-3}$

**23.** $4.39 \times 10^{-9}$

**24.** $1.09 \times 10^{-5}$

**25.** $7.65 \times 10^7$

**26.** $5.49 \times 10^2$

**27.** $8.87 \times 10^{11}$

**Write the number in scientific notation.**

**28.** $416,000$

**29.** $9300$

**30.** $7,500,000,000$

**31.** $0.04219$

**32.** $0.0000065$

**33.** $0.0000000083$

**34.** In the molecule shown, the carbon-carbon bond length is 0.1535 nanometer. Write the carbon-carbon bond length in meters using scientific notation. Use the fact that 1 nanometer is $10^{-9}$ meter.

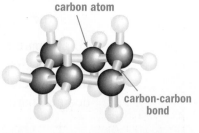

carbon atom

carbon-carbon bond

**In Exercises 35–38, use the table to determine which ant has a greater length.**

**35.** Carpenter ant or white-footed house ant

**36.** Bulldog ant or carpenter ant

**37.** Bulldog ant or white-footed house ant

**38.** **REASONING** Without using standard form, do you know if a white-footed house ant is shorter than a carpenter ant? *Explain.*

| Type of ant | Length |
| --- | --- |
| Carpenter | $1.1 \times 10^{-2}$ m |
| White-footed house | $2.7 \times 10^{-3}$ m |
| Bulldog | $1.5 \times 10^{-2}$ m |

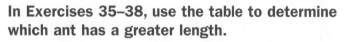
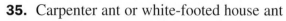
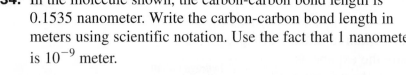

# B Practice

**Evaluate the expression.**

**1.** $5^{-4}$     **2.** $(-8)^{-6}$     **3.** $4^{-5}$     **4.** $15^0$

**5.** $(-3)^{-4}$     **6.** $11^{-1}$     **7.** $537^0$     **8.** $7^{-2}$

**Write the number in expanded form using powers of 10.**

**9.** 11.4     **10.** 0.013     **11.** 0.63     **12.** 5.18

**Write the number in standard form.**

**13.** $5 \times 10^2 + 2 \times 10^1 + 7 \times 10^0$     **14.** $9 \times 10^0 + 8 \times 10^{-1} + 1 \times 10^{-2}$

**15.** $2 \times 10^2 + 3 \times 10^1 + 7 \times 10^0 + 5 \times 10^{-1}$     **16.** $5 \times 10^{-1} + 8 \times 10^{-2} + 2 \times 10^{-3}$

**Write the number in standard form.**

**17.** $8.04 \times 10^{-5}$     **18.** $5.26 \times 10^{-9}$     **19.** $1.39 \times 10^{-2}$

**20.** $4.11 \times 10^3$     **21.** $7.61 \times 10^6$     **22.** $7.45 \times 10^8$

**Write the number in scientific notation.**

**23.** 730,000     **24.** 6,100     **25.** 8,915,000,000

**26.** 0.0000748     **27.** 0.00093     **28.** 0.000000056

**FIND THE ERROR** *Describe* and correct the error.

**29.** $0.0048 = 4.8 \times 10^3$ ✕

**30.** $(-2)^{-3} = \dfrac{1}{2^3}$ ✕

**31. REASONING** When a number greater than 1 is written in scientific notation, what do you know about the exponent?

**In Exercises 32–34, use the table, which show the amounts (in pounds) of some elements in the body of a 150 pound person.**

| Element | Oxygen | Chlorine | Cobalt | Sodium | Hydrogen |
|---|---|---|---|---|---|
| **Standard form (lb)** | 97.5 | ? | 0.00024 | ? | ? |
| **Scientific notation (lb)** | ? | $3 \times 10^{-1}$ | ? | $1.65 \times 10^{-1}$ | $1.5 \times 10^1$ |

**32.** Order the given weights of chlorine, sodium, and hydrogen from least to greatest.

**33.** Copy and complete the table.

**34.** Order the standard-form weights of chlorine, sodium, and hydrogen from least to greatest. Does this order agree with your answer to Exercise 32?

## Let's Explore
## Investigating Expressions Involving Exponents

**Goal**
Show that the properties of exponents can be used with negative exponents.

**Materials**
• paper and pencil

**QUESTION**

**How can you show that the properties of exponents can be used with powers that have negative exponents?**

Recall that a power is a way of writing repeated multiplication.

$$6^4 = 6 \cdot 6 \cdot 6 \cdot 6$$

Using the definition of negative exponents and the definition of a power, you can express $6^{-4}$ as follows:

$$6^{-4} = \frac{1}{6^4} = \frac{1}{6 \cdot 6 \cdot 6 \cdot 6}$$

**EXPLORE 1** *Extend the product of powers property* .........

1. **Copy** and complete the statements in the *Algebra* column in the table.
Use the equivalent statements in the *Numbers* column as a guide.

| Numbers | Algebra |
|---|---|
| Consider the expression $3^4 \cdot 3^{-2}$. | Consider the expression $a^4 \cdot a^{-2}$ where $a \neq 0$. |
| Using the definitions of power and negative exponents, you can write $3^4 \cdot 3^{-2}$ as: $$3 \cdot 3 \cdot 3 \cdot 3 \cdot \frac{1}{3 \cdot 3}$$ | Using the definitions of power and negative exponents, you can write $a^4 \cdot a^{-2}$ as: $$\underline{\;?\;}$$ |
| Using the multiplication rule for fractions, you can rewrite the expression as: $$3 \cdot 3 \cdot 3 \cdot 3 \cdot \frac{1}{3} \cdot \frac{1}{3}$$ | Using the multiplication rule for fractions, you can rewrite the expression as: $$\underline{\;?\;}$$ |
| Using the associative property of multiplication and the inverse property of multiplication, you can write the expression as: $$3 \cdot 3 \cdot \left(3 \cdot \frac{1}{3}\right) \cdot \left(3 \cdot \frac{1}{3}\right) = 3 \cdot 3 \cdot 1 \cdot 1$$ $$= 3^2 \cdot 1^2 = 3^2$$ | $?$ |

2. **Simplify** the expression $3^4 \cdot 3^{-2}$ using the product of powers property.
Do you get the same result as in Step 1?

**Gr. 7 AF 2.1** Interpret positive whole-number powers as repeated multiplication and negative whole-number powers as repeated division or multiplication by the multiplicative inverse. Simplify and evaluate expressions that include exponents.
**Gr. 7 NS 2.1** Understand negative whole-number exponents. **Multiply and divide expressions involving exponents with a common base.**

## Draw Conclusions

**Simplify the expression. Write your answer using positive exponents.**

**1.** $7^{-6} \cdot 7^7$  **2.** $x^{13} \cdot x^{-10}$  **3.** $3^8 \cdot 3^{-3}$  **4.** $y^{-8} \cdot y^{15}$

**5.** *Describe* the method you used to complete Exercises 1–4.

**EXPLORE 2**    *Extend the quotient of powers property* •••••••

**①** **Copy** and complete the statements in the *Algebra* column in the table. Use the equivalent statements in the *Numbers* column as a guide.

| Numbers | Algebra |
|---|---|
| Consider the expression $\dfrac{10^2}{10^{-3}}$, or $10^2 \div 10^{-3}$. | Consider the expression $\dfrac{a^2}{a^{-3}}$, or $a^2 \div a^{-3}$, where $a \neq 0$. |
| Using the definitions of power and negative exponents, you can write $\dfrac{10^2}{10^{-3}}$ as: <br><br> $10 \cdot 10 \div \left(\dfrac{1}{10 \cdot 10 \cdot 10}\right)$ | Using the definitions of power and negative exponents, you can write $\dfrac{a^2}{a^{-3}}$ as: <br><br> $\underline{\quad ? \quad}$ |
| You can use the multiplicative inverse of $\dfrac{1}{10 \cdot 10 \cdot 10}$ to simplify the expression as: <br><br> $10 \cdot 10 \div \left(\dfrac{1}{10 \cdot 10 \cdot 10}\right) = 10 \cdot 10 \cdot (10 \cdot 10 \cdot 10)$ | You can use the multiplicative inverse of $\underline{\;?\;}$ to simplify the expression as: <br><br> $\underline{\quad ? \quad}$ |
| You can write the product as a power as: <br><br> $10 \cdot 10 \cdot 10 \cdot 10 \cdot 10 = 10^5$ | $?$ |

**②** **Simplify** the expression $\dfrac{10^2}{10^{-3}}$ using the quotient of powers property. Do you get the same result as in Step 1?

## Draw Conclusions

**Simplify the expression. Write your answer using positive exponents.**

**6.** $\dfrac{4^2}{4^{-5}}$  **7.** $\dfrac{x^9}{x^{-2}}$  **8.** $\dfrac{9^8}{9^{-7}}$  **9.** $\dfrac{y^6}{y^{-6}}$

**10.** *Describe* the method you used to complete Exercises 6–9.

# Simplify Expressions Involving Exponents

## VOCABULARY and CONCEPTS

- zero exponent, p. 266
- negative exponents, p. 266

### Properties of Exponents

The properties of exponents you learned in Lessons 6.1 and 6.2 can also be used with negative or zero exponents.

**Product of powers property** $\quad a^m \cdot a^n = a^{m+n}$

**Quotient of powers property** $\quad \dfrac{a^m}{a^n} = a^{m-n}, a \neq 0$

Notice that the quotient of powers property no longer has the restriction that $m > n$. In this lesson, $a^{m-n}$ is defined even when $m = n$ or $m < n$.

**EXAMPLE 1** *Evaluating Exponential Expressions* • • • • • • • • • • •

**Evaluate the expression.**

**a.** $13^{16} \cdot 13^{-14}$ **b.** $(-5)^{-2} \cdot (-5)^9 \cdot (-5)^{-7}$ **c.** $\dfrac{2^6}{2^{10}}$

**Solution**

**a.** $13^{16} \cdot 13^{-14} = 13^{16 + (-14)}$      **Product of powers property**

$\qquad\qquad\quad\; = 13^2$      **Add exponents.**

$\qquad\qquad\quad\; = 169$      **Evaluate power.**

**b.** $(-5)^{-2} \cdot (-5)^9 \cdot (-5)^{-7} = (-5)^{-2 + 9 + (-7)}$      **Product of powers property**

$\qquad\qquad\qquad\qquad\qquad = (-5)^0$      **Add exponents.**

$\qquad\qquad\qquad\qquad\qquad = 1$      **Definition of zero exponent**

**c.** $\dfrac{2^6}{2^{10}} = 2^{6-10}$      **Quotient of powers property**

$\qquad\; = 2^{-4}$      **Subtract exponents.**

$\qquad\; = \dfrac{1}{2^4}$      **Definition of negative exponents**

$\qquad\; = \dfrac{1}{16}$      **Evaluate power.**

### Practice for Example 1

**Evaluate the expression.**

**1.** $10^{10} \cdot 10^{-8}$    **2.** $(-3)^{-3} \cdot (-3)^7 \cdot (-3)^{-5}$    **3.** $\dfrac{4^3}{4^5}$      **4.** $16^{-7} \cdot 16^9$

**EXAMPLE 2** *Using Both Properties of Powers* . . . . . . . . . . . . . . .

**Simplify the expression. Write your answer using positive exponents.**

$$\frac{18n^8 \cdot n^{-3}}{81n^9} = \frac{18n^{8 + (-3)}}{81n^9}$$  **Product of powers property**

$$= \frac{18n^5}{81n^9}$$  **Add exponents.**

$$= \frac{18n^{5-9}}{81}$$  **Quotient of powers property**

$$= \frac{18n^{-4}}{81}$$  **Subtract exponents.**

$$= \frac{18}{81n^4}$$  **Definition of negative exponents**

$$= \frac{2}{9n^4}$$  **Divide numerator and denominator by their GCF, 9.**

## Practice for Example 2

**Simplify the expression. Write your answer using positive exponents.**

**5.** $\dfrac{a \cdot a^7}{a^{11}}$  **6.** $\dfrac{b^7}{b^2 \cdot b^3}$  **7.** $\dfrac{15x^5 \cdot x^4}{90x^{12}}$  **8.** $\dfrac{4z^{13} \cdot 5z^{18}}{25z^5 \cdot z^{12}}$

**EXAMPLE 3** *Solving a Real-World Problem* . . . . . . . . . . . . . . . . . .

A typical snowflake is made of $10^2$ snow crystals. Each snow crystal contains about $10^{18}$ water molecules. Each water molecule has a mass of about $3 \times 10^{-23}$ gram. Find the mass of a typical snowflake.

### Solution

To find the mass, multiply the number of snow crystals in a snowflake by the number of water molecules in a snow crystal, and then by the mass of a water molecule.

$$10^2 \times 10^{18} \times (3 \times 10^{-23}) = 3 \times 10^{2 + 18 + (-23)}$$  **Product of powers property**

$$= 3 \times 10^{-3}$$  **Add exponents.**

▶**Answer** A typical snowflake has a mass of $3 \times 10^{-3}$ gram. That is 0.003 gram, or 3 milligrams.

## Practice for Example 3

**9.** The diameter of a rock climbing rope is $10^{-2}$ meter, which is $10^2$ times as great as the diameter of a human hair. Find the diameter of a human hair.

# Practice

Extra Practice
p. 503

**Match the expression with an equivalent expression.**

**1.** $3^5 \cdot 3^{-2}$

**2.** $3^{-6} \cdot 3^2$

**3.** $\dfrac{3^{-10}}{3^{-7}}$

**A.** $3^{-4}$

**B.** $3^{-3}$

**C.** $3^3$

**Evaluate the expression.**

**4.** $6^3 \cdot 6^{-2}$

**5.** $11^2 \cdot 11^{-4}$

**6.** $\dfrac{(-7)^2}{(-7)^{-2}}$

**7.** $15^5 \cdot 15^{-5}$

**8.** $\dfrac{10^{-4}}{10^{-2}}$

**9.** $\dfrac{(-2)^3}{(-2)^{-3}}$

**10.** $\dfrac{12^{-3}}{12^{-5}}$

**11.** $4^{-7} \cdot 4^5$

**Tell whether the expression is equivalent to $x^3 \cdot x^{-7}$.**

**12.** $x^{-4}$

**13.** $\dfrac{1}{x^4}$

**14.** $\dfrac{x^7}{x^3}$

**15.** $\dfrac{x^3}{x^7}$

**Simplify the expression. Write your answer using positive exponents.**

**16.** $x^{-7} \cdot x^4$

**17.** $w^6 \cdot w^{-6}$

**18.** $\dfrac{s^{-3}}{s^5}$

**19.** $\dfrac{f^{-4}}{f^6}$

**20.** $a^{-2} \cdot a^{-3} \cdot a^{-6}$

**21.** $z^5 \cdot z^2 \cdot z^{-7}$

**22.** $\dfrac{24t^{-5}}{6t^2}$

**23.** $\dfrac{m^{-3} \cdot m^9}{m^{14}}$

**24.** $\dfrac{w^{-3}y^{13}}{w^{11}y^{-6}}$

**25.** $\dfrac{h^6}{h^3 \cdot h^{-5}}$

**26.** $\dfrac{3x^{-6}}{18x^{-3}}$

**27.** $\dfrac{k^{11}m^{-8}}{k^{-9}m^{13}}$

**Find the missing exponent.**

**28.** $x^? \cdot x^{-2} = x^7$

**29.** $\dfrac{w^5}{w^?} = w^{10}$

**30.** $b^? \cdot b^4 = \dfrac{1}{b^9}$

**31.** $\dfrac{m^?}{m^4} = \dfrac{1}{m^{11}}$

**32.** $u^{-5} \cdot u^? = \dfrac{1}{u^{18}}$

**33.** $\dfrac{f^{-7}}{f^?} = \dfrac{1}{f^{14}}$

**34. REASONING** Simplify $\dfrac{12b^{-4} \cdot b^2}{b^{-9}}$ using the product of powers property first. Then simplify the expression using the quotient of powers property first. Does the order in which you apply the properties matter? *Explain.*

**In Exercises 35–37, use the table, which shows the approximate masses of an elephant, a dog, a koi (a type of fish), and an ant.**

| Animal | Mass |
|---|---|
| Elephant | $10^3$ kg |
| Dog | 10 kg |
| Koi | $10^{-1}$ kg |
| Ant | $10^{-6}$ kg |

**35.** How many times as great as the mass of a koi is the mass of an elephant?

**36.** How many times as great as the mass of an ant is the mass of a dog?

**37.** Suppose the mass of a human is $10^8$ times as great as the mass of an ant. Find the mass of a human.

**Evaluate the expression.**

1. $9^7 \cdot 9^{-5}$

2. $12^{-8} \cdot 12^7$

3. $13^2 \cdot 13$

4. $\dfrac{(-15)^{11}}{(-15)^8}$

5. $\dfrac{2^{-3}}{2^{-6}}$

6. $\dfrac{(-10)^{-1}}{(-10)^{-2}}$

7. $16^{10} \cdot 16^{-12}$

8. $\dfrac{9^{-6}}{9^{-9}}$

**Tell whether the expression is equivalent to $a^{-9} \cdot a^8$.**

9. $\dfrac{a^8}{a^9}$

10. $\dfrac{a^9}{a^8}$

11. $a^{-1}$

12. $\dfrac{1}{a}$

**Simplify the expression. Write your answer using positive exponents.**

13. $g^{-5} \cdot g^8$

14. $y^{12} \cdot y^{-12}$

15. $\dfrac{c^{-11}}{c^3}$

16. $\dfrac{m^{-3}}{m^6}$

17. $b^8 \cdot b^{-6} \cdot b^{-9}$

18. $j^{-5} \cdot j^{-3} \cdot j^{-8}$

19. $\dfrac{15d^{-8}}{5d^3}$

20. $\dfrac{a^7 \cdot a^{-4}}{a^{-2}}$

21. $\dfrac{x^{-4}z^{-2}}{x^2z^7}$

22. $\dfrac{12b^{-9}}{16b^{-6}}$

23. $5g^7 \cdot g^{-3} \cdot 7g^{-4}$

24. $\dfrac{9x^{-5}}{6x^7}$

**FIND THE ERROR** *Describe* and correct the error in simplifying the expression.

25.
$$\dfrac{25b^{-9}}{5b^3} = \dfrac{25b^{-3}}{5}$$
$$= \dfrac{25}{5b^3}$$
$$= \dfrac{5}{b^3}$$

26.
$$\dfrac{k^{-8}m^3}{k^7m^{-13}} = \dfrac{k^{-15}m^3}{m^{-13}}$$
$$= k^{-15}m^{-16}$$
$$= \dfrac{1}{k^{15}m^{16}}$$

**Find the missing exponent.**

27. $\dfrac{g^?}{g^7} = \dfrac{1}{g^{15}}$

28. $w^{-8} \cdot w^? = \dfrac{1}{w^{17}}$

29. $\dfrac{h^{-16}}{h^?} = \dfrac{1}{h^{24}}$

30. **REASONING** *Describe* how to write the product of $6 \times 10^{-2}$ and $3 \times 10^{-3}$ in scientific notation. Then find the product in scientific notation.

31. The diameter of an atom is about $10^{-8}$ centimeter. The diameter of the nucleus of the atom is about $10^{-12}$ centimeter. How many times as great as the diameter of the nucleus of the atom is the diameter of the atom?

**In Exercises 32–34, use the table showing units of length.**

32. How many times as long as a picometer is a nanometer?

33. How many times as long as a picometer is a micrometer?

34. A portable MP3 player is $10^4$ micrometers thick. Find the thickness of the MP3 player in meters.

| Unit | Length |
|------------|---------------|
| Micrometer | $10^{-6}$ m |
| Nanometer | $10^{-9}$ m |
| Picometer | $10^{-12}$ m |

# Problem Solving and Reasoning

## Problem

A closed cubical box and a cubical box with no top have the same edge length. Find the following ratios for the closed box:

- outer surface area to edge length
- volume to edge length
- outer surface area to volume

Will the ratios for the closed box be the same for the box with no top? If not, explain how the ratios will change.

Closed cubical box    Cubical box with no top

## Solution

*Use symbols to explain mathematical reasoning as part of MR 2.5.*

**1** **Find** the outer surface area and the volume of the closed box. Use the formulas for surface area and volume of a cube. Let $x$ be the outer edge length of the closed box.

$$\text{Surface area: } S = 6x^2 \qquad \text{Volume: } V = x^3$$

*Make precise calculations as part of MR 2.8.*

**2** **Find** the ratios.

$$\frac{\text{Surface area}}{\text{Edge length}} = \frac{6x^2}{x} \qquad \frac{\text{Volume}}{\text{Edge length}} = \frac{x^3}{x} \qquad \frac{\text{Surface area}}{\text{Volume}} = \frac{6x^2}{x^3}$$

$$= 6x^{2-1} \qquad\qquad = x^{3-1} \qquad\qquad = 6x^{2-3}$$

$$= 6x \qquad\qquad\quad = x^2 \qquad\qquad\quad = 6x^{-1} \text{ or } \frac{6}{x}$$

**3** **Decide** whether the ratios will be the same for the box with no top.

*Use a chart to explain mathematical reasoning as part of MR 2.5.*

| Measure | Will the closed box and the box with no top have the same measure? | What ratios are affected? |
|---|---|---|
| Surface Area | No. The surface area of the box with no top is the sum of the areas of 5 faces, which is less than the 6 faces considered for the surface area of the closed box. | Surface area to edge length Surface area to volume |
| Volume | Yes. Because both boxes have the same edge length, they have the same volume. | None |

**4** **Explain** how the ratios will change.

Because the outer surface area of the box with no top is less than the outer surface area of the closed box and the edge lengths are the same, the ratio of surface area to edge length will decrease.

*Express the solution clearly as part of MR 2.6.*

Because the outer surface area of the box with no top is less than the outer surface area of the closed box and the volumes are the same, the ratio of surface area to volume will decrease.

## Practice

1. Find the ratios listed below for the cubical box with no top in the problem on the previous page. Use $x$ for the outer edge length. Then use the ratios to check the solution to the problem on the previous page. **MR 2.8, MR 3.1**

   - outer surface area to edge length
   - volume to edge length
   - outer surface area to volume

2. The formula for the area $A$ of a circle is $A = \pi r^2$ where $r$ is the radius of the circle. The radii of three circles are given below. **MR 2.4, MR 3.2**

   Circle 1: $r = 3$ cm
   Circle 2: $r = 3^2$ cm
   Circle 3: $r = 3^3$ cm

   a. Find the area of each circle. Write the area using powers.

   b. How many times as great as the area of circle 1 is the area of circle 2? How many times as great as the area of circle 2 is the area of circle 3?

   c. Predict how many times as great as the area of circle 3 is the area of a circle with a radius of $3^4$ centimeters. *Explain.*

3. Copy and complete the steps below to show that $(8x)^3 = 8^3 x^3$. **MR 1.1**

   $(8x)^3 = 8x \cdot \underline{\ ?\ } \cdot \underline{\ ?\ }$
   $\qquad = (8 \cdot \underline{\ ?\ } \cdot \underline{\ ?\ }) \cdot (x \cdot \underline{\ ?\ } \cdot \underline{\ ?\ })$
   $\qquad = \underline{\ ?\ }$

4. Use the relationship shown in Exercise 3 to help evaluate $(3xy)^6 \cdot (2x)^3$. **MR 1.3, MR 2.2**

5. There are about $2 \times 10^5$ species of flowering plants. The orchid family contains about $2 \times 10^4$ species. About what percent of species of flowering plants are species of orchids? *Explain* how you found your answer. **MR 2.5, MR 2.6**

6. The side length of the larger square below is three times as great as the side length of the smaller square. **MR 2.6, MR 3.2**

   a. For the smaller square, find the ratio of its area to its side length.

   b. Will the ratio that you calculated in part (a) be the same for the larger square? If not, explain how the ratio will change.

7. The table below gives the distances of three stars from Earth. **MR 2.7, MR 3.3**

   | Star | Distance from Earth (km) |
   |------|--------------------------|
   | Sirius | $8.1 \times 10^{13}$ |
   | Vega | $2.4 \times 10^{14}$ |
   | Rigel | $7.3 \times 10^{15}$ |

   a. Find the time in seconds it takes for light to travel from each star to Earth given that light travels about $3 \times 10^5$ kilometers per second. Round your answers to the nearest power of 10.

   b. Repeat part (a), but round each distance and the speed of light to the nearest power of 10 before making any calculations.

   c. Compare your answers from part (a) with your answers from part (b). If you need to find the time it takes for light to travel from other stars to Earth, should you use the method from part (a) or part (b)? *Explain.*

8. Consider the power $a^n$ where $a$ is a negative integer and $n$ is a positive integer. Is the value of $a^n$ always negative? *Explain.* **MR 1.2**

# Chapter 6 Review Game

## Math History

Solve each exercise below. Find the answer from among those given. Copy and complete what's in the blue box at the bottom of the page by placing the letter associated with each answer on the line with the exercise number. You'll get the answer to the following question.

**Who was the first mathematician to use exponential notation the way we use it today?**

### EXERCISES

1. Simplify: $x^3 \cdot x^5$.

2. Write in scientific notation: 31,009,100.

3. Simplify: $18x^4 \cdot y^0$.

4. Simplify: $\dfrac{x^6}{x^3}$.

5. Simplify: $x^3 \cdot x^{-2} \cdot x^{-6}$.

6. Simplify: $-3x \cdot 6x^3$.

7. Write in standard form: $9.87 \times 10^{-5}$.

8. Simplify: $\dfrac{1}{y^4} \cdot y^{16}$.

9. Write in standard form:
   $9 \times 10^{-1} + 8 \times 10^{-2} + 7 \times 10^{-3}$.

10. Simplify: $6y^2 \cdot y^9 \cdot y^4$.

11. Simplify: $\dfrac{15x^8y^4}{3x^6}$.

12. Write in expanded form using powers of ten: 3.1.

13. Simplify: $\dfrac{6y \cdot y^{-2}}{y^7}$.

### ANSWERS

(S) $\dfrac{6}{y^8}$

(F) $x^2$

(R) $x^8$

(S) 0.0000987

(E) $3 \times 10^0 + 1 \times 10^{-1}$

(E) $-18x^4$

(L) $6y^8$

(B) 0

(A) 0.987

(N) $18x^4$

(T) $5x^2y^4$

(D) $\dfrac{1}{x^5}$

(K) 987,000

(E) $x^3$

(R) $6y^{15}$

(P) $x^{15}$

(U) $x^5$

(C) $y^{12}$

(E) $3.10091 \times 10^7$

| **1** | **2** | **3** | **4** |
|---|---|---|---|
| ? | ? | ? | ? |

| **5** | **6** | **7** | **8** | **9** | **10** | **11** | **12** | **13** |
|---|---|---|---|---|---|---|---|---|
| ? | ? | ? | ? | ? | ? | ? | ? | ? |

# Chapter Summary and Review

**VOCABULARY**
- zero exponent, p. 266
- negative exponents, p. 266
- scientific notation, p. 266

**Vocabulary Exercises**

1. Copy and complete: A nonzero number $a$ to the _?_ power is 1.

2. Copy and complete: A number is written in _?_ when it is of the form $c \times 10^n$ where $c$ is greater than or equal to 1 and less than 10 and $n$ is an integer.

## 6.1 Multiply Powers with the Same Base .............. pp. 252–255

To multiply powers having the same base, add the exponents.
So, $a^m \cdot a^n = a^{m+n}$ for a real number $a$ and positive integers $m$ and $n$.

**EXAMPLE**

$$5^2 \cdot 5^4 = 5^{2+4} \qquad \text{Product of powers property}$$
$$= 5^6 \qquad \text{Add exponents.}$$

**Simplify the expression. Write your answer using exponents.**

3. $4^3 \cdot 4^2$

4. $(-12)^3 \cdot (-12)^7$

5. $y^5 \cdot y^3$

6. $p^2 \cdot p$

7. $2^3 \cdot 2^4 \cdot 2^2$

8. $16^4 \cdot 16^6 \cdot 16^3$

9. $(-r)^3 \cdot (-r)^7 \cdot (-r)^4$

10. $(-m)^{10} \cdot (-m)^7 \cdot (-m)$

## 6.2 Divide Powers with the Same Base .................. pp. 258–261

To divide powers having the same base, subtract the exponents.
So, $\dfrac{a^m}{a^n} = a^{m-n}$ for a nonzero real number $a$ and positive integers $m$ and $n$ with $m > n$.

**EXAMPLE**

$$\frac{3^{12}}{3^7} = 3^{12-7} \qquad \text{Quotient of powers property}$$
$$= 3^5 \qquad \text{Subtract exponents.}$$

**Simplify the expression. Write your answer using exponents.**

11. $\dfrac{7^5}{7^2}$

12. $\dfrac{(-6)^8}{(-6)^3}$

13. $\dfrac{a^{11}}{a^4}$

14. $\dfrac{(-k)^{13}}{(-k)^5}$

15. $\dfrac{y^8}{y^3}$

16. $\dfrac{m^{18}}{m^9}$

17. $\dfrac{(-11)^{20}}{(-11)^{12}}$

18. $\dfrac{x^6}{x^5}$

# Chapter Summary and Review

## 6.3 Use Zero and Negative Exponents

pp. 266–269

A nonzero number $a$ to the zero power is 1: $a^0 = 1$ where $a \neq 0$.

**EXAMPLE** $5^0 = 1$ **Definition of zero exponent**

For a nonzero number $a$, $a^{-n}$ is the reciprocal of $a^n$: $a^{-n} = \frac{1}{a^n}$ where $a \neq 0$.

**EXAMPLE** $3^{-4} = \frac{1}{3^4}$ **Definition of negative exponent**

$= \frac{1}{81}$ **Simplify.**

You can use the definitions of zero and negative exponents to express powers of 10 in decimal form and fraction form. This, in turn, allows you to write numbers in expanded or standard form.

**EXAMPLES** **a.** $3.18 = 3 + \frac{1}{10} + \frac{8}{100}$

$= 3 \times 10^0 + 1 \times 10^{-1} + 8 \times 10^{-2}$

**b.** $6 \times 10^1 + 2 \times 10^0 + 5 \times 10^{-1} = 60 + 2 + \frac{5}{10}$

$= 62.5$

A number is written in scientific notation when it is of the form $c \times 10^n$ where $c$ is greater than or equal to 1 and less than 10 and $n$ is an integer.

**EXAMPLES** **a.** $632 = 6.32 \times 10^2$

**b.** $5.01 \times 10^{-3} = 0.00501$

**Evaluate the expression.**

**19.** $6^0$      **20.** $10^0$      **21.** $(-4)^0$      **22.** $(-29)^0$

**23.** $2^{-4}$      **24.** $12^{-2}$      **25.** $(-5)^{-3}$      **26.** $(-7)^{-4}$

**Write the number in expanded form using powers of 10.**

**27.** 5.31      **28.** 9.46      **29.** 21.7      **30.** 0.1208

**Write the number in standard form.**

**31.** $3 \times 10^1 + 7 \times 10^0 + 5 \times 10^{-1}$      **32.** $2 \times 10^{-1} + 3 \times 10^{-2} + 6 \times 10^{-3}$

**Write the number in scientific notation.**

**33.** 0.03      **34.** 0.00754      **35.** 36,000,000      **36.** 2,200,000

**37.** 1,000,000      **38.** 0.1536      **39.** 5900      **40.** 0.009

## 6.4 *Simplify Expressions Involving Exponents* ........ pp. 272–275

The properties of exponents you learned in Lessons 6.1 and 6.2 can also be used with negative or zero exponents.

**Product of powers property**  $a^m \cdot a^n = a^{m+n}$

**Quotient of powers property**  $\dfrac{a^m}{a^n} = a^{m-n}$

**EXAMPLE**

$$2^{-4} \cdot 2^0 = 2^{-4+0} \qquad \text{Product of powers property}$$

$$= 2^{-4} \qquad \text{Add exponents.}$$

$$= \frac{1}{16} \qquad \text{Simplify.}$$

**EXAMPLE**

$$\frac{42x^4 \cdot x^{-2}}{56x^7} = \frac{42x^{4+(-2)}}{56x^7} \qquad \text{Product of powers property}$$

$$= \frac{42x^2}{56x^7} \qquad \text{Add exponents.}$$

$$= \frac{42x^{2-7}}{56} \qquad \text{Quotient of powers property}$$

$$= \frac{42x^{-5}}{56} \qquad \text{Subtract exponents.}$$

$$= \frac{42}{56x^5} \qquad \text{Definition of negative exponents}$$

$$= \frac{3}{4x^5} \qquad \text{Simplify.}$$

**Evaluate the expression.**

**41.** $7^0 \cdot 7^2$  **42.** $4^{-2} \cdot 4^0$  **43.** $\dfrac{2^0}{2^{-3}}$  **44.** $\dfrac{(-3)^2}{(-3)^{-2}}$

**45.** $5^{-3} \cdot 5^2$  **46.** $\dfrac{2^5}{2^{-2}}$  **47.** $4^1 \cdot 4^0$  **48.** $8^{-7} \cdot 8^7$

**Simplify the expression. Write your answer using positive exponents.**

**49.** $\dfrac{t^{-2} \cdot t^3}{t^{-5}}$  **50.** $\dfrac{j^3 \cdot j^0}{j^{-2}}$  **51.** $\dfrac{12m^3 \cdot m^{-4}}{108m^6}$  **52.** $\dfrac{28y^2}{48y^7 \cdot y^{-4}}$

**53.** $\dfrac{w^4 \cdot w^2}{w^7}$  **54.** $\dfrac{-3y^3 \cdot y^4}{12y^2}$  **55.** $\dfrac{x^5 \cdot 16x^3}{4x}$  **56.** $\dfrac{z^{-2} \cdot z^5}{-z^{-3} \cdot z^2}$

# Chapter Test

**Simplify the expression. Write your answer using exponents.**

**1.** $7^3 \cdot 7^2$

**2.** $s^7 \cdot s^4$

**3.** $9^2 \cdot 9^4 \cdot 9^7$

**4.** $d^2 \cdot d \cdot d^3$

**5.** $(-5)^4 \cdot (-5)^3$

**6.** $(-x)^2 \cdot (-x)^4$

**7.** $(-12)^2 \cdot (-12) \cdot (-12)^5$

**8.** $(-v)^4 \cdot (-v)^6 \cdot (-v)^3$

**9.** $15x^8 \cdot 3x^{11}$

**10.** $\dfrac{9^7}{9^3}$

**11.** $(-4)^{10} \cdot \dfrac{1}{(-4)^7}$

**12.** $\dfrac{1}{k^9} \cdot k^{14}$

**13.** $\dfrac{n^{11}}{n^8}$

**14.** $\dfrac{8^3}{8^1}$

**15.** $\dfrac{3^3}{3^{-4}}$

**16.** $(-6)^{-3} \cdot \dfrac{1}{(-6)^2}$

**17.** $\dfrac{y^6}{y^{-4}}$

**18.** $\dfrac{1}{x^8} \cdot x^5$

**Evaluate the expression.**

**19.** $9^{-2}$

**20.** $(-2)^{-4}$

**21.** $3^0$

**22.** $(-10)^0$

**Write the number in expanded form using powers of 10.**

**23.** 9.74

**24.** 23.5

**25.** 0.36

**26.** 407

**Write the number in standard form.**

**27.** $2 \times 10^1 + 9 \times 10^0 + 8 \times 10^{-1}$

**28.** $5 \times 10^2 + 3 \times 10^1 + 1 \times 10^0$

**29.** $6 \times 10^{-1} + 0 \times 10^{-2} + 2 \times 10^{-3}$

**30.** $8 \times 10^1 + 5 \times 10^0 + 0 \times 10^{-1} + 4 \times 10^{-2}$

**Write the number in scientific notation.**

**31.** 0.09

**32.** 0.00487

**33.** 3570

**34.** 1,420,000

**Simplify the expression. Write your answer using positive exponents.**

**35.** $2k^7 \cdot 3k^{-9}$

**36.** $6x^4 \cdot 5x^{-4}$

**37.** $\dfrac{12p^3 \cdot p^4}{48p^{10}}$

**38.** $\dfrac{5y \cdot y^6}{60y^5}$

**39.** A byte is a unit of computer memory. Other units are based on the number of bytes they represent. The table shows the number of bytes in certain units.

| Unit | Number of bytes |
|---|---|
| Kilobyte | $2^{10}$ |
| Megabyte | $2^{20}$ |
| Gigabyte | $2^{30}$ |
| Terabyte | $2^{40}$ |
| Petabyte | $2^{50}$ |

**a.** How many times greater is a gigabyte than a kilobyte?

**b.** How many times greater is a petabyte than a megabyte?

**c.** How many gigabytes are in 1 terabyte?

# Multiple Choice Chapter Test

1. What is the volume of the figure?

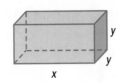

   **(A)** $x + 2y$      **(B)** $xy$

   **(C)** $x + y^2$      **(D)** $xy^2$

2. What is the product $5u^3 \cdot 3u^2 \cdot 6u^4$?

   **(A)** $90u^9$      **(B)** $90u^{10}$

   **(C)** $90u^{11}$      **(D)** $90u^{24}$

3. What is the quotient $\dfrac{8^5}{8}$?

   **(A)** $8^{-6}$      **(B)** $8^{-4}$

   **(C)** $8^4$      **(D)** $8^6$

4. What number is $(-5)^0$ equal to?

   **(A)** $-5$      **(B)** $-1$

   **(C)** $0$      **(D)** $1$

5. What number is $(-3)^{-2}$ equal to?

   **(A)** $-9$      **(B)** $-\dfrac{1}{9}$

   **(C)** $\dfrac{1}{9}$      **(D)** $9$

6. What is the expanded form of 2.07?

   **(A)** $2 \times 10^{-2} + 0 \times 10^{-1} + 7 \times 10^0$

   **(B)** $2 \times 10^{-1} + 0 \times 10^0 + 7 \times 10^1$

   **(C)** $2 \times 10^0 + 0 \times 10^{-1} + 7 \times 10^{-2}$

   **(D)** $2 \times 10^1 + 0 \times 10^0 + 7 \times 10^{-1}$

7. What is the standard form of $1 \times 10^2 + 4 \times 10^1 + 6 \times 10^0$?

   **(A)** 14      **(B)** 41

   **(C)** 146      **(D)** 641

8. What is 0.00523 in scientific notation?

   **(A)** $5.23 \times 10^{-2}$      **(B)** $5.23 \times 10^{-3}$

   **(C)** $5.23 \times 10^{-4}$      **(D)** $5.23 \times 10^{-5}$

9. In the night sky, the star nearest to Earth is about 25,000,000,000,000 miles away. What is this distance in scientific notation?

   **(A)** $25 \times 10^4 \, \text{mi}$      **(B)** $2.5 \times 10^{12} \, \text{mi}$

   **(C)** $25 \times 10^{12} \, \text{mi}$      **(D)** $2.5 \times 10^{13} \, \text{mi}$

10. A computer running a video game performs about $10^9$ calculations per second. An outdated model of the same computer performs $10^8$ calculations per second. The updated computer is about how many times faster than the outdated computer?

    **(A)** 10      **(B)** $9 \times 10^8$

    **(C)** $10^{17}$      **(D)** $10^{72}$

11. What number is $\dfrac{(-2)^3}{(-2)^{-3}}$ equal to?

    **(A)** 1      **(B)** 16

    **(C)** 36      **(D)** 64

12. What is the simplified form of $\dfrac{t}{t^4 \cdot t^{-2}}$?

    **(A)** $\dfrac{1}{t}$      **(B)** $\dfrac{1}{t^3}$

    **(C)** $\dfrac{1}{t^5}$      **(D)** $\dfrac{1}{t^7}$

13. What is the simplified form of $\dfrac{120w^5 \cdot x^0}{36w^3}$?

    **(A)** 0      **(B)** 1

    **(C)** $\dfrac{10}{3w^2}$      **(D)** $\dfrac{10w^2}{3}$

14. What is the simplified form of $\dfrac{w^9}{w}$?

    **(A)** $w^{10}$      **(B)** $\dfrac{1}{w^8}$

    **(C)** $w^8$      **(D)** $w^{-9}$

# Square Roots and the Pythagorean Theorem

## Vocabulary for Chapter 7

### Key Mathematical Vocabulary
- **square root, p. 288**
- **real numbers, p. 294**
- **right triangle, p. 302**

### Academic Vocabulary
- **approximate** Perform calculations using given numbers that are not exact, rounding the result to reflect the inaccuracy of the given numbers. For example, see Example 1 on page 294.
- **describe, p. 286**
- **explain, p. 287**
- **check, p. 293**
- **make a conjecture, p. 300**
- **compare, p. 300**
- **predict, p. 312**

Calculating an animal's maximum walking speed using square roots, page 296

# Review Prerequisite Skills

## REVIEW VOCABULARY

- integers, p. 162
- rational numbers, p. 204
- round, p. 479
- area, 488
- perimeter, p. 488
- triangle, p. 488

## VOCABULARY CHECK

**Copy and complete the statement.**

1. Numbers that can be written in the form $\frac{a}{b}$ where $a$ and $b$ are integers and $b \neq 0$ are called  ? .

2. When you approximate a number to a given place value, you are  ? the number.

3. The numbers . . . , $-3, -2, -1, 0, 1, 2, 3, \ldots$ are called  ? .

## SKILLS CHECK

**Find the area of the square or rectangle. (Review pp. 114 and 488 for 7.1–7.2.)**

4.
1 m
1 m

5.
3.3 ft
5.5 ft

6.
4 in.
4 in.

**Evaluate the expression. (Review pp. 80, 114, and 182 for 7.1–7.2.)**

7. $(-5)^2$

8. $\left(\frac{1}{2}\right)^2$

9. $0.25^2$

**Order the numbers from least to greatest. (Review pp. 60 and 204 for 7.2.)**

10. $12, 11\frac{1}{5}, 11.3, \frac{121}{10}$

11. $-3, \frac{1}{3}, -\frac{10}{3}, -2\frac{2}{3}$

12. $2.9, 2\frac{8}{7}, -2.25, \frac{2}{5}$

**Evaluate the expression. (Review p. 12 for 7.3–7.4.)**

13. $5^2 + 3^2$

14. $6^2 + 2^2$

15. $1^2 + 9^2$

# Let's Explore
## Finding Side Lengths of Squares

**Goal**
Find the side length of a square if you know its area.

**Materials**
• graph paper

**QUESTION** How can you find the side length of a square if you know its area?

**EXPLORE 1** *Draw diagrams and use a table to find side lengths*

1. **Draw** four squares with areas 1, 4, 9, and 16.

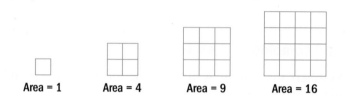

Area = 1     Area = 4     Area = 9     Area = 16

2. **Look** for a pattern in your drawings in Step 1. Copy and complete the areas and side lengths in the table below.

| Area of square (square units) | 1 | 4 | 9 | 16 | 25 | 36 | 49 | 64 | 100 | 400 |
|---|---|---|---|---|---|---|---|---|---|---|
| Side length (units) | 1 | ? | ? | ? | ? | ? | ? | ? | ? | ? |

3. **Write** a formula that gives the relationship between a square's side length $s$ and its area $A$.

## Draw Conclusions

1. Does the square shown confirm one of the entries in your table from Step 2? *Explain.*

2. Draw a square with an area of 36 square units. What side length must you use?

3. *Describe* how you could use the area formula you wrote in Step 3 to find the length of a side of a square if you know its area.

4. The area of a square is 81 square units. Substitute 81 for $A$ in the area formula you wrote in Step 3. What is the length of a side of this square? How do you know?

**EXPLORE 2** *Find positive and negative square roots* .......

Any number you square to get a number *a* is called a *square root of a.* Because $10^2 = 100$ and $(-10)^2 = 100$, 10 and $-10$ are square roots of 100.

**1** **Find** a positive number, if one exists, that you can square to get each value of *a* listed in the table. Copy the table and complete the second row.

| Value of *a* | 1 | 4 | 9 | 16 |
|---|---|---|---|---|
| Positive number whose square is *a* | ? | ? | ? | ? |

**2** **Find** a negative number, if one exists, that you can square to get each value of *a* listed in the table. Add and complete the third row of the table.

| Value of *a* | 1 | 4 | 9 | 16 |
|---|---|---|---|---|
| Positive number whose square is *a* | ? | ? | ? | ? |
| Negative number whose square is *a* | ? | ? | ? | ? |

## Draw Conclusions

**In Exercises 5–7, write the number as (a) the square of a positive integer and (b) the square of a negative integer.**

**5.** 9 **6.** 49 **7.** 121

**8.** Notice that in Exercises 5–7, each number can be written as the square of two integers, so each number has two *square roots.* In Exercise 4, you wrote a formula for the area of a square whose area was 81 square inches. Are there two side lengths in that situation? How is Exercise 4 different from Exercises 5–7?

**9.** In Exercises 5–7, you saw that a positive number *a* has two square roots.

 **a.** Consider the case when *a* is 0. How many square roots does 0 have?

 **b.** Consider the case when *a* is negative. When you square a positive number, is the result positive or negative? When you square a negative number, is the result positive or negative? Will you ever get a square that is negative? Can a negative number have a square root? *Explain.*

# Find Square Roots of Perfect Squares

## VOCABULARY and CONCEPTS

- A **square root** of a real number $a$ is a real number $b$ such that $b^2 = a$.
- The square of an integer is called a **perfect square**.

### Square Roots

- A square root is written with the symbol $\sqrt{\phantom{x}}$.
- Any positive number $a$ has two square roots, a positive (principal) square root, $\sqrt{a}$, and a negative square root, $-\sqrt{a}$.
- Zero has one square root: $\sqrt{0} = 0$.
- Negative numbers have no real square roots.
- The two square roots of a positive number can be written together with the symbol $\pm$ (plus or minus): You can read $\pm\sqrt{36}$ as *the positive and negative square roots of 36.*

**EXAMPLE 1** *Finding Square Roots* • • • • • • • • • • • • • • • • • • • • • • • • • • •

**Find the two square roots of the number.**

**a.** 49

**b.** 169

**Solution**

**a.** Because $7^2 = 49$ and $(-7)^2 = 49$, the two square roots of 49 are 7 and −7.

**b.** Because $13^2 = 169$ and $(-13)^2 = 169$, the two square roots of 169 are 13 and −13.

**EXAMPLE 2** *Using Square Root Symbols* • • • • • • • • • • • • • • • • • • • • • • •

**Evaluate the expression.**

**a.** $\sqrt{400}$

**b.** $-\sqrt{16}$

**c.** $\pm\sqrt{81}$

**Solution**

**a.** $\sqrt{400} = 20$      The positive square root of 400 is 20.

**b.** $-\sqrt{16} = -4$      The negative square root of 16 is −4.

**c.** $\pm\sqrt{81} = \pm9$      The positive and negative square roots of 81 are 9 and −9.

### Practice for Examples 1 and 2

**1.** What are the two square roots of 144?

**Evaluate the expression.**

**2.** $\sqrt{289}$

**3.** $-\sqrt{100}$

**4.** $\pm\sqrt{441}$

**5.** $\sqrt{0}$

**EXAMPLE 3** *Finding a Side Length* • • • • • • • • • • • • • • • • •

**The area of a square is 900 square inches. Find the side length of the square.**

$s^2 = A$          **Formula for area of a square**

$s^2 = 900$         **Substitute 900 for *A*.**

$s = \pm\sqrt{900}$      **Definition of square root**

$s = 30$          **Choose positive square root; length is nonnegative.**

▸ **Answer** The side length of the square is 30 inches.

**EXAMPLE 4** *Using Area to Find Perimeter* • • • • • • • • • • • • • • • •

A landscaper wants to put fencing around two square gardens that are next to each other as shown. The areas of the gardens are 64 m² and 100 m². What is the length of fencing that will be needed?

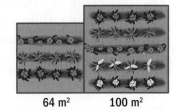

64 m²     100 m²

**Solution**

Notice that the perimeter is formed by three sides of the small square, three sides of the large square, and part of the fourth side of the large square.

The areas of the squares are 64 m² and 100 m². Use the area formula to find the side lengths of the small garden and of the large garden.

             **Small garden**              **Large garden**

               $s^2 = 64$               $s^2 = 100$

               $s = 8$                 $s = 10$

The distance around 3 sides of the small garden is $8 + 8 + 8 = 24$ m. The distance around 3 sides of the large garden is $10 + 10 + 10 = 30$ m. The remaining part of the perimeter has length $10 - 8 = 2$ m.

▸ **Answer** The distance around the figure is $24 + 30 + 2 = 56$, so 56 meters of fencing will be needed.

### Practice for Examples 3 and 4

**Find the side length of a square with the given area.**

  **6.** 25 square miles                **7.** 400 square meters

  **8.** Suppose the area of the small garden in Example 4 is increased to 81 m² instead. How much fencing will be needed now?

# Practice

**Extra Practice**
p. 504

**Find the two square roots of the number.**

**1.** 4        **2.** 25        **3.** 81        **4.** 100

**5.** 36        **6.** 121        **7.** 16        **8.** 196

**Evaluate the expression.**

**9.** $\sqrt{49}$      **10.** $-\sqrt{4}$      **11.** $-\sqrt{25}$      **12.** $-\sqrt{1600}$

**13.** $\sqrt{81}$      **14.** $-\sqrt{121}$      **15.** $\pm\sqrt{16}$      **16.** $\pm\sqrt{225}$

**17.** $-\sqrt{9}$      **18.** $\sqrt{400}$      **19.** $\sqrt{169}$      **20.** $-\sqrt{100}$

**21.** $\pm\sqrt{64}$      **22.** $\sqrt{144}$      **23.** $-\sqrt{36}$      **24.** $-\sqrt{256}$

**25.** You are considering buying a square area rug that has an area of 25 square feet. Find the side length of the area rug.

**26.** The infield of a baseball field is a square, as shown in the figure. If its area is 8100 square feet, what is the distance from first base to second base?

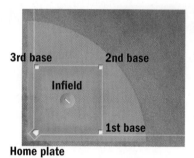

**27.** A square ice skating rink has an area of 2500 square feet. What is the perimeter of the rink?

**28.** You are going to put carpet binding on all four sides of a square piece of leftover carpet. The area of the carpet is 9 square feet. What length of carpet binding do you need?

**29.** The U.S. Department of Transportation determines the sizes of the traffic control signs that you see along the roadways. If you ignore the rounded corners, the square Alabama state route sign at the right has an area of 576 square inches. Find the side length of the sign.

**In Exercises 30–33, use the following information.**

Elisa wants to build a sandbox for her cousins. She wants the sandbox to be in the shape of a square with an area of 121 square feet. Elisa has several boards with a combined length of 45 feet to use as sides.

**30.** Find the side length (in feet) of the sandbox.

**31.** Find the perimeter of the sandbox.

**32.** Does Elisa have enough boards to make the sides of the sandbox? *Explain.*

**33.** Elisa wants to use boards that are 6 inches high and fill the sand to the top of the boards. What will the volume of the sandbox be?

**34.** **REASONING** Evaluate each expression. *Describe* the pattern.

$$\sqrt{1}, \sqrt{1+3}, \sqrt{1+3+5}, \sqrt{1+3+5+7}, \sqrt{1+3+5+7+9}, \ldots$$

# Practice

**Find the two square roots of the number.**

**1.** 9 **2.** 400 **3.** 121 **4.** 225

**5.** 3600 **6.** 576 **7.** 289 **8.** 676

**Evaluate the expression.**

**9.** $\sqrt{900}$ **10.** $-\sqrt{2500}$ **11.** $-\sqrt{196}$ **12.** $\sqrt{324}$

**13.** $-\sqrt{16}$ **14.** $\sqrt{784}$ **15.** $\pm\sqrt{81}$ **16.** $\pm\sqrt{25}$

**17.** $-\sqrt{400}$ **18.** $\sqrt{625}$ **19.** $\sqrt{4900}$ **20.** $\pm\sqrt{169}$

**21.** $-\sqrt{841}$ **22.** $\sqrt{1225}$ **23.** $\sqrt{961}$ **24.** $\pm\sqrt{2025}$

**Find the two square roots of the number.**

**25.** 0.36 **26.** 2.25 **27.** 4.41 **28.** 3.24

**29.** $\sqrt{0.25}$ **30.** $\sqrt{0.81}$ **31.** $\sqrt{1.21}$ **32.** $\sqrt{2.56}$

**Evaluate the expression for the given value of *x*.**

**33.** $14 + \sqrt{x}$ when $x = 16$ **34.** $\sqrt{x} - 5.5$ when $x = 4$

**35.** $-9 \cdot \sqrt{x}$ when $x = 25$ **36.** $2\sqrt{x} - 1$ when $x = 100$

**37.** A community garden is in the shape of a square and covers an area of 3600 square feet. Find the side length of the garden.

**38.** The first, second, and third bases on a baseball field are square canvas bags that each have an area of 225 square inches. What is the side length of a base?

**39.** You are considering buying a square wall poster that has an area of 6.25 square feet. Find the side length of the wall poster.

**40.** You are building a square shadow box whose front has an area of 36 square inches. The box will be divided into 9 square compartments of equal size. What is the side length of each compartment?

**41.** The area inside the square picture frame shown is 100 square inches. The area of the space for a square photograph is 25 square inches. The frame creates a uniform border all around the photograph. What is the width of the border?

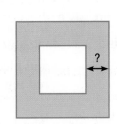

**42.** A park occupies one square-shaped city block. The city wants to put a fence around the park. The park has an area of 960,400 square feet. The city already has 3000 feet of fencing. How much more will the city need to purchase?

**43.** **REASONING** For a nonnegative value of *a*, what is $(\sqrt{a})^2$? *Explain* your reasoning.

# Activity 7.2

## Let's Explore
## Using Squares to Approximate Square Roots

**Goal**
Use a model to approximate a square root.

**Materials**
- graph paper
- tape
- scissors
- colored pencils

**QUESTION** How can you use unit squares to approximate a square root?

You can build squares using unit squares.

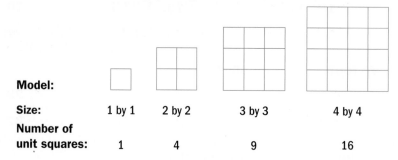

| | | | | |
|---|---|---|---|---|
| **Model:** | | | | |
| **Size:** | 1 by 1 | 2 by 2 | 3 by 3 | 4 by 4 |
| **Number of unit squares:** | 1 | 4 | 9 | 16 |

The length of a side of any square is the positive square root of the number of unit squares the square contains.

**EXPLORE** *Use a model to approximate a square root* . . . . . . . . . .

You can build squares that have areas close to 14 unit squares. The lengths of the sides of these squares will be approximations of √14.

**1** **Build** the largest square that you can using 14 unit squares. The 14 squares are more than 9 squares (3 by 3) and less than 16 squares (4 by 4). So, the largest square you can build is 3 by 3, with 5 unit squares left over.

**2** **Imagine** building a slightly larger square with an area of 14 by cutting up the leftover squares and placing them along two sides to fill the red region shown.

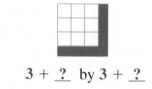

3 + _?_ by 3 + _?_

**3** **Divide** the 5 leftover squares into 2 • 3 = 6 equal pieces and place them on the red region as shown. (You may need to turn some of the pieces.) A small corner of the red region will be left uncovered.

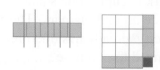

**292** Chapter 7 Square Roots and the Pythagorean Theorem

**4** **Repeat** Steps 2 and 3, but this time divide the 5 leftover squares into 6 + 1 = 7 equal pieces and place them on the red region as shown. The seventh piece can be used to fill the small corner, but some of this piece will be left over.

# Draw Conclusions

**Use your results from the Explore section. Write your answers using fractions and mixed numbers.**

1. In Step 3, you divided 5 unit squares into 6 equal pieces. The length of each piece is still 1 unit. What is the width of each piece?

2. What is the size of the square in Step 3?
   Copy and complete:  ? + ?  by  ? + ?

3. In Step 4, you divided 5 unit squares into 7 equal pieces. The length of each piece is still 1 unit. What is the width of each piece?

4. What is the size of the square in Step 4?
   Copy and complete:  ? + ?  by  ? + ?

5. Use the side length you found in Exercise 2. Square the length to find the area of the square. You may need to write the mixed number as an improper fraction. Is this area *greater than* or *less than* 14?

6. Use the side length you found in Exercise 4. Square the length to find the area of the square. You may need to write the mixed number as an improper fraction. Is this area *greater than* or *less than* 14?

7. Use your answers in Exercises 5 and 6. Copy and complete the statement using *overestimate* or *underestimate*. *Explain* your reasoning.

   a. The side length of the square formed in Step 3 is an  ?  for $\sqrt{14}$.

   b. The side length of the square formed in Step 4 is an  ?  for $\sqrt{14}$.

8. *Explain* how you know that the actual value of $\sqrt{14}$ is between the side lengths you found in Exercise 2 and Exercise 4.

9. Give another mixed number as an approximation of $\sqrt{14}$. Choose a number between the values you found in Exercise 2 and Exercise 4.

   a. Check your approximation by squaring.

   b. Is your choice an *overestimate* or an *underestimate* for $\sqrt{14}$?

   c. Which do you think is the best approximation for $\sqrt{14}$: the length in Exercise 2, the length in Exercise 4, or your choice here in Exercise 9? *Explain* your reasoning.

# Approximate Square Roots

## VOCABULARY and CONCEPTS

- An **irrational number** is a number that cannot be written as a quotient of two integers. The decimal form of an irrational number neither terminates nor repeats.
- The set of **real numbers** consists of all rational and irrational numbers. Every real number can be represented on the real number line.

### Irrational Numbers

- $\sqrt{3}$ is irrational because 3 is not a perfect square.
- 2.353353335. . . is irrational because it neither terminates nor repeats.

---

**EXAMPLE 1** *Approximating to the Nearest Integer*..........

**Approximate $\sqrt{13}$ to the nearest integer.**

Make a list of integers that are perfect squares:

$$0, 1, 4, 9, 16, 25, \ldots.$$

$$9 < 13 < 16 \qquad \text{Identify perfect squares closest to 13.}$$
$$\sqrt{9} < \sqrt{13} < \sqrt{16} \qquad \text{Take positive square root of each number.}$$
$$3 < \sqrt{13} < 4 \qquad \text{Evaluate square roots.}$$

▶**Answer** The average of 3 and 4 is 3.5, and $(3.5)^2 = 12.25$. Because $13 > 12.25$, $\sqrt{13}$ is closer to 4 than to 3. So, $\sqrt{13} \approx 4$.

### Practice for Example 1

**Approximate the square root to the nearest integer.**

**1.** $\sqrt{10}$      **2.** $\sqrt{17}$      **3.** $\sqrt{28}$      **4.** $-\sqrt{66}$

---

**EXAMPLE 2** *Approximating to the Nearest Tenth*..........

**Approximate $\sqrt{13}$ to the nearest tenth.**

You know from Example 1 that $\sqrt{13}$ is between 3 and 4. Make a list of squares of 3.1, 3.2, . . . , 3.9. From the list, you can see that 13 is between $3.6^2$ and $3.7^2$. So, $\sqrt{13}$ is between 3.6 and 3.7.

▶**Answer** The average of 3.6 and 3.7 is 3.65, and $(3.65)^2 = 13.3225$. Because $13 < 13.3225$, $\sqrt{13}$ is closer to 3.6 than to 3.7. So, $\sqrt{13} \approx 13.6$.

| |
|---|
| $3.1^2 = 9.61$ |
| $\vdots$ |
| $3.5^2 = 12.25$ |
| $3.6^2 = 12.96$ |
| $3.7^2 = 13.69$ |
| $3.8^2 = 14.44$ |
| $3.9^2 = 15.21$ |

## Practice for Example 2

**Approximate the square root to the nearest tenth.**

**5.** $\sqrt{19}$        **6.** $\sqrt{30}$        **7.** $\sqrt{85}$        **8.** $-\sqrt{112}$

**EXAMPLE 3**   *Graphing and Ordering Real Numbers* .........

**Order the numbers from least to greatest: $\frac{3}{5}$, $\sqrt{16}$, $-2.2$, $-\sqrt{12}$, $\sqrt{6}$.**

Begin by graphing the numbers on a real number line.

Approximate $-\sqrt{12}$ and $\sqrt{6}$: $-\sqrt{12} \approx -3.5$ and $\sqrt{6} \approx 2.4$.

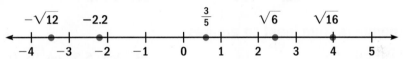

Read the numbers from left to right: $-\sqrt{12}$, $-2.2$, $\frac{3}{5}$, $\sqrt{6}$, $\sqrt{16}$.

## Practice for Example 3

**9.** Order the following numbers from least to greatest:

$\sqrt{10}$, $-\frac{1}{2}$, $-\sqrt{8}$, $-2$, $1.3$

**EXAMPLE 4**   *Finding a Distance* ..................

When you are at a height $h$, the distance $d$ to the horizon can be approximated using the equation $d = 3.57\sqrt{h}$. The distance $d$ is measured in kilometers and the height $h$ is measured in meters. Approximate the distance to the horizon if you are at the top of a lighthouse that is 52 meters high.

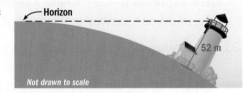

| | |
|---|---|
| $d = 3.57\sqrt{h}$ | **Write formula.** |
| $= 3.57\sqrt{52}$ | **Substitute 52 for $h$.** |
| $\approx 3.57(7.2)$ | **To the nearest tenth, $\sqrt{52} \approx 7.2$.** |
| $= 25.704$ | **Multiply.** |

▶ **Answer** The distance to the horizon is about 26 kilometers.

## Practice for Example 4

**10.** Use the formula in Example 4. Find the approximate distance to the horizon if you are at the top of a building that is 77 meters high.

**Identify the two integers closest to the number.**

**1.** $\sqrt{15}$  **2.** $\sqrt{28}$  **3.** $-\sqrt{45}$  **4.** $-\sqrt{19}$

**Approximate the square root to the nearest integer.**

**5.** $\sqrt{5}$  **6.** $\sqrt{19}$  **7.** $-\sqrt{28}$  **8.** $\sqrt{17}$

**9.** $-\sqrt{53}$  **10.** $-\sqrt{11}$  **11.** $\sqrt{70}$  **12.** $\sqrt{39}$

**13.** $\sqrt{23}$  **14.** $\sqrt{82}$  **15.** $-\sqrt{141}$  **16.** $\sqrt{78}$

**Approximate the square root to the nearest tenth.**

**17.** $\sqrt{3}$  **18.** $\sqrt{7}$  **19.** $-\sqrt{11}$  **20.** $\sqrt{18}$

**21.** $\sqrt{75}$  **22.** $-\sqrt{39}$  **23.** $\sqrt{142}$  **24.** $\sqrt{210}$

**Order the numbers from least to greatest.**

**25.** $\sqrt{64}, -5, \sqrt{9}, 2$  **26.** $\sqrt{3}, 5.5, -\sqrt{16}, 0$

**27.** $\frac{2}{3}, \sqrt{4}, -3.6, -\sqrt{1}$  **28.** $-\sqrt{6}, \frac{5}{2}, 7, -4$

**29.** You buy 134 square feet of linoleum to cover the floor in a square kitchen. There are 8 square feet of linoleum left over. Approximate the side length of the kitchen to the nearest foot.

**30.** You are using railroad ties to build a square flower bed like the one shown. You want to place a railroad tie on the diagonal to form two triangular beds. Find the length of the diagonal by using the expression $\sqrt{2s^2}$ where $s$ is the side length of the flower bed. Round your answer to the nearest tenth.

**31.** Computer screens are measured according to their diagonal length. The diagonal length of a computer screen is $\sqrt{2362}$ centimeters. Approximate the diagonal length to the nearest tenth.

├── 5 ft ──┤

**REASONING** The Venn diagram shows the relationships among various sets of numbers. Copy the diagram and place the given number in the appropriate part of the diagram. Then list all sets to which the given number belongs.

**32.** $\frac{1}{2}$  **33.** $-7$

**34.** $\sqrt{2}$  **35.** $3$

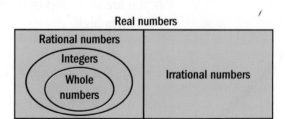

**36.** An animal's maximum walking speed $s$ (in feet per second) can be calculated using the formula $s = 5.66\sqrt{\ell}$ where $\ell$ is the animal's leg length (in feet). What is the maximum walking speed for an elephant with a leg length of 8 feet?

**Approximate the square root to the nearest integer.**

**1.** $\sqrt{15}$      **2.** $-\sqrt{48}$      **3.** $\sqrt{79}$      **4.** $\sqrt{140}$

**5.** $-\sqrt{29}$      **6.** $\sqrt{108}$      **7.** $-\sqrt{53}$      **8.** $\sqrt{73}$

**9.** $\sqrt{138}$      **10.** $-\sqrt{55}$      **11.** $\sqrt{640}$      **12.** $-\sqrt{211}$

**FIND THE ERROR** *Describe* **and correct the error in approximating the square root to the nearest integer.**

**13.**

$\sqrt{39}$

39 falls between 36 and 49.
Because 39 is closer to 36,
$\sqrt{39} \approx 36$.

**14.**

$\sqrt{19}$

19 falls between 16 and 25.
Because 19 is closer to 25,
$\sqrt{19} \approx \sqrt{25} = 5$.

**Approximate the square root to the nearest tenth.**

**15.** $\sqrt{27}$      **16.** $-\sqrt{65}$      **17.** $\sqrt{92}$      **18.** $\sqrt{110}$

**19.** $\sqrt{130}$      **20.** $\sqrt{162}$      **21.** $-\sqrt{231}$      **22.** $\sqrt{189}$

**Order the numbers from least to greatest.**

**23.** $7.4, \sqrt{53}, -8, -8.15$

**24.** $\sqrt{64}, 8.2, \sqrt{137}, -3$

**25.** $-\sqrt{21}, -\sqrt{\frac{2}{5}}, -4.7, -\frac{5}{9}$

**26.** $3.64, \sqrt{4.8}, \sqrt{8.61}, \frac{12}{5}$

**27.** An A1 sheet of paper has a width of 594 millimeters. The length of an A1 sheet of paper is $\sqrt{2}$ times its width. Approximate the length of an A1 sheet of paper to the nearest millimeter.

**28.** The maximum speed $s$ (in knots, or nautical miles per hour) for a sailboat using wind power can be found using the formula $s = 1.34\sqrt{\ell}$ where $\ell$ is the length of the boat's waterline (in feet). What is the maximum speed of a 34 foot sailboat to the nearest knot?

**29.** The radius $r$ of a circle with area $A$ is given by the formula $r = \sqrt{\frac{A}{\pi}}$. Find the radius of a circle that has an area of 31.4 square centimeters. Use 3.14 for $\pi$. Round your answer to the nearest tenth.

**REASONING Tell whether the number is *rational* or *irrational*. *Explain*.**

**30.** $\sqrt{360}$      **31.** $\frac{2}{11}$      **32.** $0.3$      **33.** $\sqrt{15}$

**REASONING Give an example of the real number being described.**

**34.** Integer

**35.** Rational number that is not an integer

**36.** Irrational number in square root form

**37.** Irrational number in decimal form

# Mid-Chapter Review

> **VOCABULARY**
> - square root, p. 288
> - perfect square, p. 288
> - irrational number, p. 294
> - real numbers, p. 294

## Vocabulary Exercises

1. Copy and complete: A _?_ of a real number $a$ is a real number $b$ such that $b^2 = a$.

2. Give three examples of irrational numbers.

3. Give three examples of numbers that are perfect squares.

### 7.1

## Find Square Roots of Perfect Squares · · · · · · · · · · · · **pp. 288–291**

**EXAMPLE** Evaluate the expression.

a. $\sqrt{100} = 10$     **The positive square root of 100 is 10.**

b. $-\sqrt{25} = -5$     **The negative square root of 25 is −5.**

c. $\pm\sqrt{49} = \pm7$     **The positive and negative square roots of 49 are 7 and −7.**

**Evaluate the expression.**

4. $\sqrt{256}$            5. $-\sqrt{9}$            6. $\pm\sqrt{64}$

7. $-\sqrt{625}$         8. $\pm\sqrt{324}$       9. $\sqrt{841}$

### 7.2

## Approximate Square Roots · · · · · · · · · · · · · · · · · · · · · · · **pp. 294–297**

**EXAMPLE** Approximate $\sqrt{7}$ to the nearest integer.

Make a list of integers that are perfect squares: 0, 1, 4, 9, . . . .

$4 < 7 < 9$     **Identify the perfect squares closest to 7.**

$\sqrt{4} < \sqrt{7} < \sqrt{9}$     **Take the positive square root of each number.**

$2 < \sqrt{7} < 3$     **Evaluate the square roots.**

Because 7 is closer to 9 than to 4, $\sqrt{7}$ is closer to $\sqrt{9} = 3$.
So, to the nearest integer, $\sqrt{7} \approx 3$.

**Approximate the square root to the nearest integer.**

10. $\sqrt{23}$           11. $\sqrt{39}$           12. $\sqrt{78}$

13. $\sqrt{44}$           14. $-\sqrt{85}$        15. $-\sqrt{119}$

# Chapter 7

## Mid-Chapter Test

**Find the two square roots of the number.**

1. 361
2. 484
3. 324
4. 441
5. 289
6. 256
7. 400
8. 2500

**Evaluate the expression.**

9. $\sqrt{36}$
10. $-\sqrt{121}$
11. $\pm\sqrt{676}$
12. $\sqrt{1}$
13. $\pm\sqrt{25}$
14. $-\sqrt{49}$
15. $-\sqrt{144}$
16. $\pm\sqrt{256}$
17. $-\sqrt{81}$
18. $\pm\sqrt{900}$
19. $-\sqrt{169}$
20. $\pm\sqrt{100}$

**Approximate the square root to the nearest integer.**

21. $\sqrt{5}$
22. $\sqrt{60}$
23. $\sqrt{33}$
24. $\sqrt{70}$
25. $-\sqrt{93}$
26. $\sqrt{107}$
27. $-\sqrt{520}$
28. $-\sqrt{444}$
29. $\sqrt{129}$
30. $-\sqrt{251}$
31. $-\sqrt{173}$
32. $\sqrt{197}$

**Approximate the square root to the nearest tenth.**

33. $\sqrt{2}$
34. $\sqrt{43}$
35. $\sqrt{105}$
36. $\sqrt{222}$
37. $\sqrt{6}$
38. $-\sqrt{63}$
39. $-\sqrt{105}$
40. $-\sqrt{83}$
41. $-\sqrt{123}$
42. $\sqrt{311}$
43. $\sqrt{236}$
44. $-\sqrt{262}$

**Order the numbers from least to greatest.**

45. $-\sqrt{8}, \frac{2}{3}, 4.7, \sqrt{6}$
46. $\sqrt{5}, -7, \frac{4}{3}, 3$
47. $\sqrt{3}, 2\frac{3}{5}, -\sqrt{14}, -5$
48. $-\sqrt{13}, \frac{13}{8}, \sqrt{5}, -3.$

49. A school has an athletic practice field in the shape of a square with an area of 10,000 square feet. Find the side length of the field.

50. Jerome is designing a flower garden. He wants the garden to be square and to be bordered by a decorative fence. The garden will have an area of 64 square feet. How many feet of fence does Jerome need?

51. A stained-glass window is in the shape of a square with an area of 2304 square inches. What is the perimeter of the window?

52. You buy a bag of grass seed that covers an area of 650 square meters. You spread the entire bag over an area in the shape of a square. Find the side length of the square to the nearest tenth.

53. A person's maximum running speed $s$ (in meters per second) can be approximated using the formula $s = \sqrt{16\ell}$ where $\ell$ is the person's leg length in meters. Find the maximum running speed of a person with a leg length of 0.75 meter. Round your answer to the nearest tenth.

# Activity 7.3

## Let's Explore
### Investigating Right Triangles

**Goal**
Examine the relationship among the lengths of the sides of a right triangle.

**Materials**
• graph paper
• scissors

**QUESTION** **How are the lengths of the sides of a right triangle related to each other?**

A right triangle has one right angle (90°) and three sides. The side opposite the right angle is called the *hypotenuse*. The two sides that form the right angle are called the *legs*.

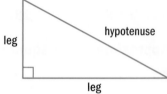

**EXPLORE 1** *Examine the hypotenuse of a right triangle* · · · · · · ·

**1** **Draw** a right triangle with legs of length 3 units and 4 units on graph paper.

For each leg, draw a square that has a leg as one side. What is the sum of the areas of these two squares?

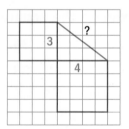

**2** **Measure** the hypotenuse using graph paper. If you draw a square with the hypotenuse as one side, what is its area?

**3** **Compare** the sum of the areas you found in Step 1 with the area you found in Step 2. What do you notice?

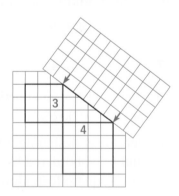

## Draw Conclusions
**Repeat Steps 1–3 for right triangles with legs of the given lengths.**

**1.** 5, 12        **2.** 6, 8        **3.** 8, 15

**4.** Let the lengths of the legs of a right triangle be *a* and *b*, and let the length of the hypotenuse be *c*. Make a conjecture about the relationship between the lengths of the legs and the length of the hypotenuse.

**EXPLORE 2** *Examine the area of a right triangle* • • • • • • • •

**1** **Make** right triangles.
Cut a right triangle out of graph paper.
Make three copies of it.

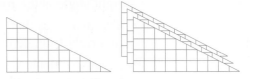

**2** **Arrange** the right triangles to form a square within a square, as shown.

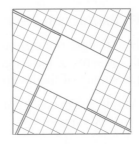

## Draw Conclusions

**5.** How is the area of the inner square related to the area of the outer square?

**In Exercises 6–9, let *a*, *b*, and *c* be the lengths of the sides of a right triangle with *a* < *b* < *c*, as shown.**

**6.** Write an expression for the area of one of the triangles in terms of *a* and *b*.

**7.** Write an expression for the area of the outer square in terms of *c*.

**8.** *Explain* why the length of each side of the inner square is $b - a$.

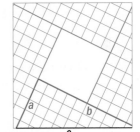

**9.** A way to write the area of the inner square is $(b - a) \cdot (b - a)$, or $b^2 - 2ab + a^2$ once you use the distributive property to find the product.

Use the relationships you have determined in Exercises 5–8 to create a formula that relates *a*, *b*, and *c*. Copy and complete the steps.

$$c^2 = (\underline{?}) \left( \frac{1}{2}ab \right) + (b^2 - 2ab + a^2)$$

$$= \underline{?} + b^2 - 2ab + a^2$$

$$= \underline{?} + \underline{?}$$

Simplify by combining like terms to write the formula.

# Use the Pythagorean Theorem

## VOCABULARY and CONCEPTS

- A **right triangle** is a triangle with one right angle.
- In a right triangle, the side opposite the right angle is the **hypotenuse.**
- The two sides that form the right angle in a right triangle are the **legs.**
- When a statement is written in **if-then form**, the *if* part contains the hypothesis and the *then* part contains the conclusion.

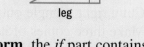

## Pythagorean Theorem

If a triangle is a right triangle, then the sum of the squares of the lengths of the legs equals the square of the length of the hypotenuse.

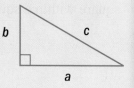

**Algebra** For the right triangle shown, $a^2 + b^2 = c^2$.

---

**EXAMPLE 1** *Writing If-Then Statements*

**Write each statement in if-then form and identify the hypothesis and conclusion.**

**a.** The longest side in a right triangle is the hypotenuse.

▶ **Answer** If a side of a right triangle is the longest side, then it is the hypotenuse.
*Hypothesis:* a side of a right triangle is the longest side
*Conclusion:* the side is the hypotenuse

**b.** Negative numbers are less than zero.

▶ **Answer** If a number is negative, then it is less than zero.
*Hypothesis:* a number is negative
*Conclusion:* the number is less than zero

### Practice for Example 1

**Write the statement in if-then form.**

**1.** Even numbers are divisible by 2.

**2.** All integers are rational numbers.

**3.** Identify the hypothesis and the conclusion in the statement of the Pythagorean theorem.

**EXAMPLE 2** *Finding the Length of a Hypotenuse* • • • • • • • • • • •

**For the right triangle shown, find the length of the hypotenuse.**

$$a^2 + b^2 = c^2 \quad \text{Pythagorean theorem}$$
$$18^2 + 24^2 = c^2 \quad \text{Substitute 18 for } a \text{ and 24 for } b.$$
$$324 + 576 = c^2 \quad \text{Evaluate powers.}$$
$$900 = c^2 \quad \text{Add.}$$
$$\pm\sqrt{900} = c \quad \text{Definition of square root}$$
$$30 = c \quad \text{Choose positive square root; length is nonnegative.}$$

▶ **Answer** The length of the hypotenuse is 30 centimeters.

**EXAMPLE 3** *Approximating the Length of a Hypotenuse*

A rectangular table measures 72 inches by 36 inches. What is the length of the diagonal from one corner of the table to the opposite corner? Round your answer to the nearest tenth of an inch.

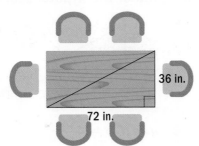

**Solution**

The diagonal divides the rectangle into two identical right triangles. Find the length of the hypotenuse of either triangle.

$$a^2 + b^2 = c^2 \quad \text{Pythagorean theorem}$$
$$72^2 + 36^2 = c^2 \quad \text{Substitute 72 for } a \text{ and 36 for } b.$$
$$6480 = c^2 \quad \text{Simplify.}$$
$$\sqrt{6480} = c \quad \text{Definition of square root}$$
$$80.5 \approx c \quad \text{Approximate square root.}$$

▶ **Answer** The diagonal of the table is about 80.5 inches long.

**Practice for Examples 2 and 3**

**Find the length of the hypotenuse.**

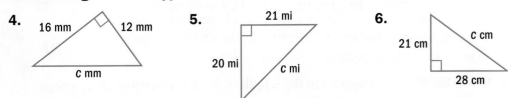

**4.** 16 mm, 12 mm, *c* mm

**5.** 21 mi, 20 mi, *c* mi

**6.** 21 cm, *c* cm, 28 cm

**7.** A television screen is measured by the length of its diagonals. A rectangular television screen is 9 inches wide and 12 inches long. What is the length of its diagonal?

**Write the statement in if-then form and identify the hypothesis and the conclusion.**

1. A glass that is $\frac{3}{5}$ full is 60% full.

2. $x = 2.3$ and $y = 1.2$, so $xy = 2.76$.

3. $a = -4$, so $a^2 = 16$.

4. **FIND THE ERROR** *Describe* and correct the error in finding the length of the hypotenuse.

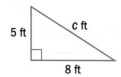

5 ft    c ft

8 ft

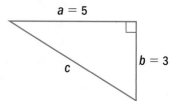

$c^2 = a^2 + b^2$
$c^2 = 5 + 8$
$c^2 = 13$     The length of the
$c = \sqrt{13}$    hypotenuse is
$c \approx 3.6$     about 3.6 feet.

**Let $a$ and $b$ represent the lengths of the legs of a right triangle. Find the length $c$ of the hypotenuse. Round to the nearest tenth if necessary.**

5.
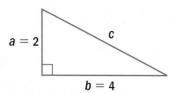

$a = 2$    $c$

$b = 4$

6.
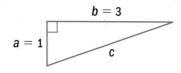

$b = 3$

$a = 1$    $c$

7.
$a = 5$

$c$

$b = 3$

8. $a = 6, b = 4$

9. $a = 3, b = 7$

10. $a = 5, b = 5$

11. $a = 9, b = 12$

12. $a = 5, b = 6$

13. $a = 4, b = 8$

**Find the length $c$ of the hypotenuse. Round to the nearest tenth if necessary.**

14.
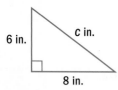

6 in.    c in.

8 in.

15.
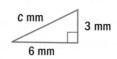

c mm    3 mm

6 mm

16.
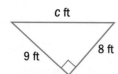

c ft

9 ft    8 ft

17. The Greens have a rectangular pool that is 23 feet long and 20 feet wide. Find the length of a diagonal of the pool to the nearest tenth.

18. A tree is 16 feet tall and casts a shadow 24 feet long. Find the distance between the top of the tree and the tip of the tree's shadow to the nearest foot.

19. **REASONING** What happens to the length of the hypotenuse of a right triangle when you double the lengths of the legs? Give an example to support your conclusion.

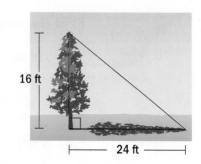

16 ft

24 ft

# B Practice

**Write the statement in if-then form and identify the hypothesis and the conclusion.**

1. A fish tank that is 80% full is $\frac{4}{5}$ full.

2. $x = 2 + 5$, so $x = 5 + 2$.

3. $a = 0$, so $a^2 = 0$.

4. **FIND THE ERROR** *Describe* and correct the error in finding the length of the hypotenuse.

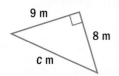

$$c^2 = 8^2 + 9^2$$
$$c^2 = 64 + 81$$
$$c = 145$$

The length of the hypotenuse is 145 meters.

**Let *a* and *b* represent the lengths of the legs of a right triangle. Find the length *c* of the hypotenuse. Round to the nearest tenth if necessary.**

5. $a = 1, b = 5$

6. $a = 8, b = 4$

7. $a = 6, b = 6$

8. $a = 4, b = 15$

9. $a = 2, b = 7$

10. $a = 10, b = 20$

11. $a = 30, b = 40$

12. $a = 15, b = 20$

13. $a = 11, b = 22$

14. You are trying to determine the distance across a pond. You put posts into the ground at points *A*, *B*, and *C* so that angle *B* is a right angle. You measure and find that the distance *AB* is 18 feet and the distance *CB* is 28 feet. How wide is the pond from *A* to *C*? Round your answer to the nearest foot.

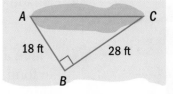

15. Drywall comes in 4 feet by 8 feet sheets. To get the sheets of drywall through a small window of an upper-level apartment, the workers must pass the sheets diagonally through the window. The window is a rectangle that is 3 feet wide and 4 feet tall. Will the workers be able to pass the drywall through the window? *Explain.*

16. To find the length of segment *AB* shown, draw dashed line segments to form a right triangle with segment *AB* as the hypotenuse. Then follow these steps:

    a. Count grid squares to find the lengths of the legs of the right triangle.

    b. Use the Pythagorean theorem to find the length of the segment to the nearest tenth.

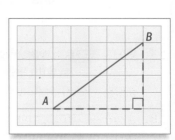

17. **REASONING** What happens to the length of the hypotenuse in a right triangle when you make the lengths of the legs half of their original lengths? Give an example to support your conclusion.

# Activity 7.4

## Let's Explore
## Investigating Sides and Angles of Triangles

**Goal**
Examine the relationship between the lengths of the sides of a triangle and the measures of the angles of the triangle.

**Materials**
- graph paper
- scissors
- colored pencils

**QUESTION** How can you use the side lengths of a triangle to decide whether it is a right triangle?

**EXPLORE 1** *Build a right triangle* ...................................

1. **Cut** out strips of graph paper as follows.

   Cut 3 strips that are 3 units long.
   Cut 1 strip that is 5 units long.
   Cut 4 strips that are 4 units long.
   Cut 1 strip that is 6 units long.

2. **Shade** one long edge of each strip in red.

3. **Place** a 4 unit strip next to a 3 unit strip as shown to form a corner of a triangle. Take another 4 unit strip and form a corner at the other end of the 3 unit strip.

4. **Move** the strips so that they form a triangle with side lengths 3, 4, and 4.

5. **Repeat** Steps 3 and 4 with other strips to form a triangle with side lengths 3, 4, and 5 and a triangle with side lengths 3, 4, and 6.

6. **Take** the corner of a piece of paper and lay it against each corner of each triangle. The piece of paper is a rectangle and so has right angles at its corners. Which of the triangles has a right angle at one of its corners?

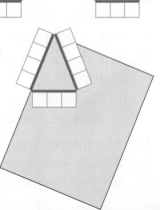

## Draw Conclusions

1.  Consider the triangle you chose in Step 6 of Explore 1. Show that the side lengths of that triangle satisfy the relationship $a^2 + b^2 = c^2$ where $a$, $b$, and $c$ are the side lengths with $c$ being the length of the longest side.

2.  Copy and complete this conjecture: If the side lengths $a$, $b$, and $c$ of a triangle satisfy the relationship $a^2 + b^2 = c^2$, then the triangle must be a _?_ triangle.

**EXPLORE 2** *Find Pythagorean triples* •••••••••••••••••••••••••••

A *Pythagorean triple* is a set of three positive integers $a$, $b$, and $c$ such that $a^2 + b^2 = c^2$.

The numbers 3, 4, and 5 form a Pythagorean triple. In Explore 1, you showed that a triangle with side lengths 3, 4, and 5 is a right triangle. You can find other Pythagorean triples and show that they also form right triangles.

**①** **Choose** any two positive integers $m$ and $n$ such that $m < n$.

**②** **Use** formulas to generate a Pythagorean triple.
Use your values for $m$ and $n$ to find $a$, $b$, and $c$ as follows:

$$a = n^2 - m^2 \qquad b = 2mn \qquad c = n^2 + m^2$$

**③** **Show** that $a^2 + b^2 = c^2$ is true for the numbers you generated. That is, show that they form a Pythagorean triple.

## Draw Conclusions

3.  Use the Pythagorean triple $a$, $b$, and $c$ you found in Explore 2.

    a.  Use the method from Explore 1, Steps 1–4, to create a triangle with side lengths $a$, $b$, and $c$.

    b.  Use Step 6 of Explore 1 to show that the triangle you created is a right triangle.

4.  Use the formulas in Explore 2 to generate two more Pythagorean triples.

5.  If the numbers $a$, $b$, and $c$ form a Pythagorean triple, what do you expect is true about $2a$, $2b$, and $2c$? Give an example to test your conjecture.

# Lesson 7.4

# Use the Converse of the Pythagorean Theorem

## VOCABULARY and CONCEPTS

- The **converse** of a statement written in if-then form is formed by switching the hypothesis and conclusion of the statement. The converse of a true statement is not necessarily true. In the case of the Pythagorean theorem, the converse is true.

### Converse of the Pythagorean Theorem

If the sum of the squares of the lengths of two sides of a triangle equals the square of the length of the third (longest) side, then the triangle is a right triangle.

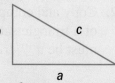

**Algebra** For the triangle shown, if $a^2 + b^2 = c^2$, then the triangle is a right triangle.

---

**EXAMPLE 1** *Writing Converses* •••••••••••••••••••••••••••••••

**Write the converse of the if-then statement. Tell whether the converse is *true* or *false*.**

**a.** If you are a guitar player, then you are a musician.

▶ **Answer** If you are a musician, then you are a guitar player. *False.* A violinist who does not play the guitar is still a musician.

**b.** If $x$ is odd, then $3x$ is odd.

▶ **Answer** If $3x$ is odd, then $x$ is odd. *True.* If the product of two numbers is odd and one of the numbers is odd, then the other number must be odd.

---

**EXAMPLE 2** *Identifying a Right Triangle* •••••••••••••••••••

Use the converse of the Pythagorean theorem to determine whether a triangle with side lengths $a = 5$, $b = 12$, and $c = 13$ is a right triangle.

**Solution**

| | |
|---|---|
| $a^2 + b^2 \stackrel{?}{=} c^2$ | **Converse of Pythagorean theorem** |
| $5^2 + 12^2 \stackrel{?}{=} 13^2$ | **Substitute 5 for $a$, 12 for $b$, and 13 for $c$.** |
| $25 + 144 \stackrel{?}{=} 169$ | **Evaluate powers.** |
| $169 = 169$ ✓ | **Add.** |

▶ **Answer** The triangle is a right triangle.

**EXAMPLE 3**   *Showing That a Triangle is Not a Right Triangle*

**Show that a triangle with sides of length 6 inches, 10 inches, and 12 inches is not a right triangle.**

The length of the longest side is 12 inches, so let $c = 12$.

$$a^2 + b^2 \stackrel{?}{=} c^2 \qquad \textbf{Converse of Pythagorean theorem}$$

$$6^2 + 10^2 \stackrel{?}{=} 12^2 \qquad \textbf{Substitute 6 for } a\textbf{, 10 for } b\textbf{, and 12 for } c.$$

$$136 \neq 144 \qquad \textbf{Evaluate powers and add.}$$

▶ **Answer**  The triangle is not a right triangle, because together the Pythagorean theorem and its converse say that *only* right triangles satisfy $a^2 + b^2 = c^2$.

## Practice for Examples 1, 2, and 3

**1.** Write the converse of this statement: If $n$ is an even number, then $2n$ is an even number. Tell whether the converse is *true* or *false*. If it is false, explain why.

**Determine whether the triangle with the given side lengths is a right triangle.**

**2.** 7, 24, 25        **3.** 8, 20, 25        **4.** 3, 5, $\sqrt{34}$

**EXAMPLE 4**   *Verifying a Right Triangle* ·······················

**A door is braced with a diagonal crosspiece. Are the identical triangles formed in the door right triangles?** *Explain.*

Use the converse of the Pythagorean theorem.

$$a^2 + b^2 \stackrel{?}{=} c^2 \qquad \textbf{Converse of Pythagorean theorem}$$

$$132^2 + 224^2 \stackrel{?}{=} 260^2 \qquad \textbf{Substitute 132 for } a\textbf{, 224 for } b\textbf{, and 260 for } c.$$

$$67{,}600 = 67{,}600 \checkmark \quad \textbf{Evaluate powers and add.}$$

▶ **Answer**  Yes, the diagonal crosspiece and the sides of the door form two right triangles because the given lengths satisfy the converse of the Pythagorean theorem.

132 cm

260 cm   224 cm

## Practice for Example 4

**5.** A rectangular picture frame is 15 inches wide and 36 inches long. On the back, there is a 39 inch diagonal crosspiece for support. Are the triangles formed in the frame right triangles? *Explain.*

# Practice

**A**

**Extra Practice**
p. 504

**Write the converse of the if-then statement. Tell whether the converse is *true* or *false*. If it is false, explain why.**

1. If you are a soccer player, then you are an athlete.

2. If a number is negative, then the number is less than zero.

3. If an animal is a whale, then the animal is a mammal.

4. If $a \div 4 = 3$, then $a \div 3 = 4$.

**Determine whether the triangle with the given side lengths is a right triangle.**

5. $a = 35, b = 21, c = 40$

6. $a = 39, b = 52, c = 65$

7. $a = 20, b = 21, c = 29$

8. $a = 16, b = 24, c = 26$

9. $a = 1.44, b = 0.36, c = 1.69$

10. $a = 3.6, b = 4.8, c = 6$

11. $a = 9.2, b = 3.4, c = 10$

12. $a = 45, b = 108, c = 117$

**Tell whether the triangle is a right triangle.**

13.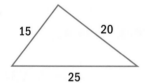

14.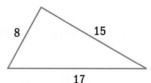

15.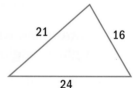

**Determine whether the triangle with the given side lengths is a right triangle.**

16. $6, \sqrt{117}, 9$

17. $5.2, 3.5, 2.6$

18. $6, 2, \sqrt{42}$

19. $7, 9, 2.4$

20. $12, \sqrt{225}, 9$

21. $64, \sqrt{196}, 76$

22. A sail has the shape of a triangle. The lengths of the sides are 146 inches, 131 inches, and 84 inches. Is the sail a right triangle? *Explain.*

23. Nicole is making a picture frame that is 12 inches long by 10 inches wide. She measures and finds that the length of a diagonal is 16 inches. Are the angles opposite the diagonal right angles? *Explain.*

24. A rectangular banner is 2.5 feet wide and 6 feet long. The banner has a diagonal line 6.5 feet long that separates the banner into two triangles. Can you tell from the given lengths whether the triangles formed in the banner are right triangles? *Explain.*

25. **REASONING** A worker builds a wooden frame to hold wet cement while it dries. The frame *appears* to be a rectangle. *Explain* how the worker can use a tape measure to know for sure that the corners of the frame are right angles.

**310** Chapter 7 Square Roots and the Pythagorean Theorem

**Write the converse of the if-then statement. Tell whether the converse is *true* or *false*. If it is false, explain why.**

**1.** If an animal is a lizard, then the animal is a reptile.

**2.** If $x = 1$, then $xy = y$.

**3.** If it is snowing, then the temperature is below freezing.

**4.** If $12 \div \frac{3}{4} = 16$, then $12 \times \frac{4}{3} = 16$.

**Determine whether the triangle with the given side lengths is a right triangle.**

**5.** $a = 24, b = 10, c = 26$

**6.** $a = 34, b = 44, c = 48$

**7.** $a = 17, b = 23, c = 29$

**8.** $a = 54, b = 72, c = 90$

**9.** $a = 0.36, b = 0.48, c = 0.60$

**10.** $a = 1.27, b = 3.46, c = 4.55$

**11.** $a = 7.56, b = 8.49, c = 9.88$

**12.** $a = 228, b = 95, c = 247$

**Tell whether the triangle is a right triangle.**

**13.**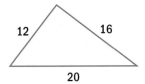

**14.**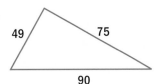

**15.**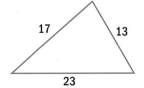

**Determine whether the triangle with the given side lengths is a right triangle.**

**16.** $26, \sqrt{961}, 26$

**17.** $6.1, 2.6, 5.2$

**18.** $\sqrt{1225}, 28, 21$

**19.** $15, \sqrt{289}, 8$

**20.** $\sqrt{576}, 13, 14$

**21.** $2.6, 3.2, 4.2$

**22.** Show that a triangle with sides of length 8 inches, 9 inches, and 13 inches is not a right triangle.

**23.** Each wilderness troop at a camping outing has created its own flag. Your troop's flag is triangular with side lengths of 15 inches, 18 inches, and 23 inches. Is the flag a right triangle? *Explain.*

**24.** You are building a tool shed. The framing for the floor measures 12 feet by 7 feet. To ensure the floor is "square," you measure the diagonal and find it to be 15 feet long. (Carpenters consider the framing to be "square" when the angles measure 90°.) Does the framing form a rectangle? *Explain.*

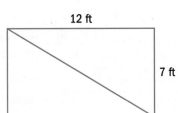

**25.** **REASONING** *Explain* the difference between the Pythagorean theorem and the converse of the Pythagorean theorem. Give an example to show how each is used.

## Problem

A square has a side length of 4 inches. The midpoints of the sides of the square are connected to form a square within the original square. The midpoints of this square are then connected to form a third square. How is the side length of the innermost square related to the side length of the original square? Suppose this procedure is repeated using the innermost square as the starting square. Predict the side length of the new innermost square.

### Solution

*Use a diagram to explain mathematical reasoning as part of MR 2.5.*

**1** **Draw** the three squares as described in the problem. Label the side length of the outermost square as 4 inches. Each side of the second square is the hypotenuse of a right triangle with legs of length 2 inches.

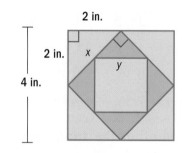

*Make precise calculations as part of MR 2.8.*

**2** **Find** the the side length $x$ of the second square. Use the Pythagorean theorem.

$$x^2 = 2^2 + 2^2$$
$$x^2 = 4 + 4$$
$$x^2 = 8$$
$$x = \sqrt{8} \text{ inches}$$

**3** **Find** the side length $y$ of the third square. Each side of the third square is the hypotenuse of a right triangle with legs of length $\frac{x}{2}$, or $\frac{\sqrt{8}}{2}$ inches. Use the Pythagorean theorem to find $y$.

$$y^2 = \left(\frac{\sqrt{8}}{2}\right)^2 + \left(\frac{\sqrt{8}}{2}\right)^2$$
$$y^2 = \frac{8}{4} + \frac{8}{4}$$
$$y^2 = 4$$
$$y = 2 \text{ inches}$$

*Develop generalizations of the results obtained as part of MR 3.3.*

**4** **Predict** the side length of the new innermost square by generalizing the relationship between the side lengths.

The side length of the innermost square, 2 inches, is half the side length of the original square, 4 inches. If the procedure were repeated using the innermost square as the starting square, the new innermost square would have a side length that is half of 2 inches, or 1 inch.

## Practice

1. Semicircles with areas *A*, *B*, and *C* are constructed on the sides of a right triangle as shown. Make and test a conjecture about the relationship between $A + B$ and $C$. **MR 2.4, MR 3.2**

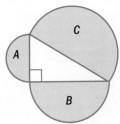

2. An approximately square region with an area of about 256 square miles is being sprayed with pesticide to reduce the mosquito population. Suppose the center of town A is in the spray zone. If the center of town B is 20 miles from the center of town A, is it possible for the center of town B to be in the spray zone? *Explain.* **MR 2.5, MR 2.6**

3. Using the number line shown below, estimate a number between $\sqrt{11}$ and $\sqrt{12}$. Then actually find a number between $\sqrt{11}$ and $\sqrt{12}$ without using a calculator. *Explain* your reasoning. **MR 2.3, MR 2.5**

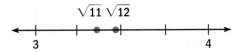

4. A painter needs a ladder to reach from a point on the ground 7 feet from the base of a house to a height of 23 feet on the house. The painter's ladder is able to extend from 14 feet to 25 feet. **MR 2.1, MR 2.7**

   **a.** To the nearest foot, calculate the length the ladder needs to be extended. Can the painter use the ladder? *Explain* why it is not necessary to find an exact distance.

   **b.** Use estimation to check that your answer to part (a) is reasonable.

5. A 30 foot tall utility pole stands between a sidewalk and a street. A guy wire connects the top of the pole to the ground to increase the stability of the pole. The wire runs through the end of a bar extended from the pole as shown to protect people on the sidewalk. **MR 1.3, MR 2.4**

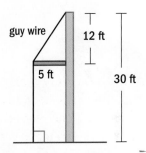

   **a.** How much wire is used?

   **b.** If the bar were lowered, would the amount of wire used increase, decrease, or stay the same? *Explain* your reasoning.

6. Write a formula for the perimeter *P* of a square in terms of its area *A*. If a square has an area equal in value to its perimeter, what is the side length of the square? *Explain* how you found your answer. **MR 1.1, MR 2.5**

7. Tim wants to build a skateboard ramp that is 100 centimeters long and 28 centimeters high. The base and height of the ramp must form a right angle. **MR 2.5, MR 2.6**

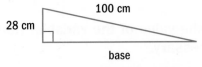

   **a.** *Explain* why the base of the ramp cannot be 90 centimeters long.

   **b.** How long should Tim make the base of the ramp? *Explain* your reasoning. (*Hint:* Use your answer to part (a) as a starting point.)

# Chapter 7 Review Game

**Materials**
- paper
- pencil

## Leap Frog

Complete the exercises below to find the path the frog takes to get to the rock. Each answer can be found on a lily pad along with a letter. Copy the letter onto your paper to answer this question: What was the nationality of Pythagoras?

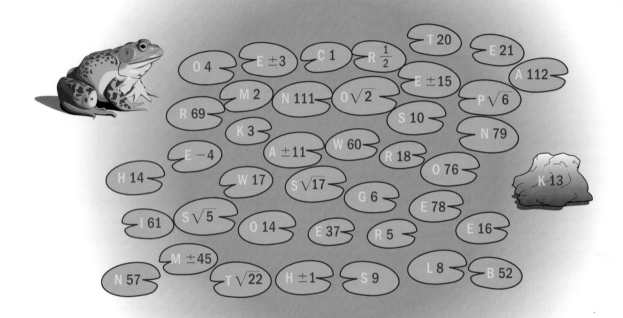

**Evaluate the expression.**

1. $\sqrt{196}$
2. $-\sqrt{16}$
3. $\sqrt{289}$
4. $\pm\sqrt{121}$

5. What is the side length of a square with area 17 square units?

6. Evaluate $\sqrt{x+4}$ when $x = 32$.

**Find the value of the variable. Round to the nearest whole number if necessary.**

7.

8.
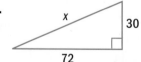

9.
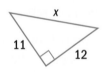

10. The lengths of the sides of a triangle are 5, 12, and $c$ with $c$ being the greatest length. What value of $c$ is needed for the triangle to be a right triangle?

**VOCABULARY**
- square root, p. 288
- perfect square, p. 288
- irrational number, p. 294
- real numbers, p. 294
- right triangle, p. 302
- hypotenuse, p. 302
- legs, p. 302
- if-then form, p. 302
- converse, p. 308

## Vocabulary Exercises

**1.** Copy and complete: The set of _?_ consists of all rational and irrational numbers.

**2.** Copy and complete: The _?_ of a statement written in if-then form is formed by switching the hypothesis and conclusion of the statement.

### 7.1 Find Square Roots of Perfect Squares • • • • • • • • • • • • *pp. 288–291*

A square root of a real number $a$ is a real number $b$ such that $b^2 = a$.

**EXAMPLE**

**a.**  $\sqrt{36} = 6$     **The positive square root of 36 is 6.**

**b.**  $-\sqrt{100} = -10$     **The negative square root of 100 is −10.**

**c.**  $\pm\sqrt{64} = \pm 8$     **The positive and negative square roots of 64 are 8 and −8.**

**Evaluate the expression.**

**3.** $\sqrt{225}$     **4.** $-\sqrt{49}$     **5.** $\pm\sqrt{529}$     **6.** $\sqrt{1}$

**7.** $-\sqrt{81}$     **8.** $\pm\sqrt{121}$     **9.** $\sqrt{441}$     **10.** $\sqrt{361}$

### 7.2 Approximate Square Roots • • • • • • • • • • • • • • • • • • • • *pp. 294–297*

**EXAMPLE**

Approximate $\sqrt{24}$ to the nearest integer.

Make a list of integers that are perfect squares: 0, 1, 4, 9, 25, . . .

$16 < 24 < 25$     **Identify perfect squares closest to 24.**

$\sqrt{16} < \sqrt{24} < \sqrt{25}$     **Take positive square root of each number.**

$4 < \sqrt{24} < 5$     **Evaluate square roots.**

The average of 4 and 5 is 4.5, and $(4.5)^2 = 20.25$. Because $24 > 20.25$, $\sqrt{24}$ is closer to 5 than to 4. So, $\sqrt{24} \approx 5$.

**Approximate the square root to the nearest integer.**

**11.** $\sqrt{8}$     **12.** $\sqrt{50}$     **13.** $-\sqrt{12}$     **14.** $-\sqrt{200}$

**15.** $-\sqrt{3}$     **16.** $-\sqrt{137}$     **17.** $-\sqrt{79}$     **18.** $\sqrt{150}$

**7.3** *Use the Pythagorean Theorem* .................... **pp. 302–305**

When a statement is written in if-then form, the *if* part contains the hypothesis and the *then* part contains the conclusion.

> **EXAMPLE** Write the following statement in if-then form and identify the hypothesis and conclusion: A square is a figure with four sides.
>
> ▶ **Answer** If a figure is a square, then it has four sides.
>
> *Hypothesis:* a figure is a square
>
> *Conclusion:* the figure has four sides

**PYTHAGOREAN THEOREM** If a triangle is a right triangle, then the sum of the squares of the lengths of the legs equals the square of the length of the hypotenuse.

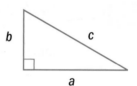

For the right triangle shown, $a^2 + b^2 = c^2$.

> **EXAMPLE** Find the length of the hypotenuse.
>
> $a^2 + b^2 = c^2$    **Pythagorean theorem**
>
> $15^2 + 16^2 = c^2$    **Substitute 15 for *a* and 16 for *b*.**
>
> $225 + 256 = c^2$    **Evaluate powers.**
>
> $481 = c^2$    **Add.**
>
> $\pm\sqrt{481} = c$    **Definition of square root**
>
> $21.9 \approx c$    **Choose positive square root; length is nonnegative.**

**Write the statement in if-then form. Identify the hypothesis and conclusion.**

**19.** The length of either leg of a right triangle is less than the length of the hypotenuse.

**20.** An integer whose last digit is 0 is divisible by 10.

**21.** The hypotenuse of a right triangle is opposite the right angle.

**Find the length of the hypotenuse. Round to the nearest tenth if necessary.**

**22.**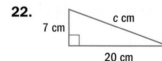

**23.**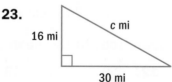

**24.**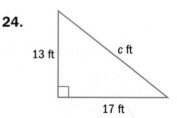

**7.4** *Use the Converse of the Pythagorean Theorem* • • • • pp. 308–311

The converse of a statement written in if-then form is formed by switching the hypothesis and conclusion of the statement. The converse of a true statement is not necessarily true.

**EXAMPLE**   **Write the converse of the following if-then statement:**
**If $x = 3$, then $x^2 = 9$.**
**Tell whether the converse is *true* or *false*.**

▶ **Answer**   If $x^2 = 9$, then $x = 3$.

*False.* Another possible value of $x$ is $-3$.

**CONVERSE OF THE PYTHAGOREAN THEOREM**  If the sum of the squares of the lengths of two sides of a triangle equals the square of the length of the third (longest) side, then the triangle is a right triangle.

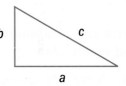

For the triangle shown, if $a^2 + b^2 = c^2$, then the triangle is a right triangle.

**EXAMPLE**   **Show that a triangle with sides of length 28, 45, and 53 is a right triangle.**

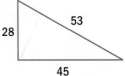

$$a^2 + b^2 \stackrel{?}{=} c^2 \qquad \text{Converse of Pythagorean theorem}$$
$$28^2 + 45^2 \stackrel{?}{=} 53^2 \qquad \text{Substitute 28 for } a, \text{ 45 for } b, \text{ 53 for } c.$$
$$784 + 2025 \stackrel{?}{=} 2809 \qquad \text{Evaluate powers.}$$
$$2809 = 2809 \checkmark \qquad \text{Add.}$$

▶ **Answer**   The triangle is a right triangle.

**Write the converse of the if-then statement. Tell whether the converse is *true* or *false*. If it is false, explain why.**

**25.** If $x$ is an even number, then $x + 1$ is an odd number.

**26.** If an integer is divisible by 2, then it is even.

**27.** If $x$ is greater than 4, then $x$ is greater than 3.

**28.** For positive numbers $a$ and $b$, if $a$ and $b$ are both less than 1, then $ab$ is less than 1.

**Determine whether the triangle with the given side lengths is a right triangle.**

**29.** 15, 20, 25   **30.** 3, 7, 9   **31.** 65, 72, 97   **32.** 21, 42, 47

**Evaluate the expression.**

1. $\sqrt{64}$  2. $-\sqrt{81}$  3. $\pm\sqrt{576}$  4. $\sqrt{0}$

5. $-\sqrt{169}$  6. $\pm\sqrt{1}$  7. $-\sqrt{361}$  8. $\pm\sqrt{256}$

**Approximate the square root to the nearest integer.**

9. $\sqrt{10}$  10. $\sqrt{80}$  11. $-\sqrt{125}$  12. $-\sqrt{999}$

13. $\sqrt{128}$  14. $-\sqrt{71}$  15. $\sqrt{103}$  16. $-\sqrt{161}$

**Order the numbers from least to greatest.**

17. $\sqrt{2}, 1.2, \dfrac{5}{12}, -1.9, -\dfrac{3}{4}, -\sqrt{3}$  18. $4.3, \dfrac{5}{7}, \sqrt{8}, -2.9, -\sqrt{20}, -\dfrac{2}{5}$

**Write the statement in if-then form and identify the hypothesis and conclusion.**

19. A rational number in decimal form is a terminating decimal.

20. An irrational number is a real number.

**For the right triangle shown, find the length of the hypotenuse. Round to the nearest tenth if necessary.**

21.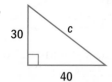

22.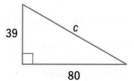

23.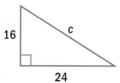

**Write the converse of each if-then statement. Tell whether the converse is *true* or *false*. If it is false, explain why.**

24. If you are adding two negative integers, then the sum is negative.

25. If a number is an integer, then it is rational.

**Determine whether the triangle with the given side lengths is a right triangle.**

26. 12, 15, 16  27. 12, 16, 20  28. 16, 40, 43  29. 33, 56, 65

30. 30, 18, 22  31. $\sqrt{9}$, 5, 4  32. 17, $\sqrt{16}$, 20  33. 40, 27, $\sqrt{225}$

34. Refer to the diagram of a ladder leaning against a chimney. How long is the ladder?

35. A ramp is extended from the back of a truck to help workers unload a refrigerator. The ramp touches the ground at a point 8 feet behind the truck. The height from the top of the ramp to the ground is 4 feet. How long is the ramp? Round your answer to the nearest tenth.

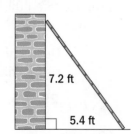

7.2 ft

5.4 ft

1. What is the value of $-\sqrt{16}$?

   (A) $-4$      (B) $\pm4$

   (C) $-256$      (D) $\pm256$

2. Which integer is a perfect square?

   (A) 10      (B) 11

   (C) 99      (D) 100

3. A square field has the area shown. What length of fencing is needed around the field?

   Area = 400 m²

   (A) 20 m      (B) 40 m

   (C) 80 m      (D) 400 m

4. What is the value of $\sqrt{40}$ to the nearest integer?

   (A) 2      (B) 6

   (C) 7      (D) 20

5. Which list of numbers is in order from least to greatest?

   (A) $-2, -\frac{1}{2}, -0.2, \sqrt{2}, 2$

   (B) $-\frac{3}{8}, -0.38, -3.8, -38, \sqrt{3.8}$

   (C) $-\frac{1}{4}, -0.4, -4, 1.4, \sqrt{14}$

   (D) $-5, -\frac{1}{15}, -\frac{1}{5}, 0.5, \sqrt{5}$

6. The equation $t = 0.45\sqrt{h}$ gives the time $t$ (in seconds) that an object falling from a height of $h$ meters takes to reach the ground. A golf ball is dropped from a height of 20 meters. In about how many seconds does it reach the ground?

   (A) 0.45 sec      (B) 2 sec

   (C) 9 sec      (D) 20 sec

7. What is the if-then form of the statement "A polygon that has three sides is a triangle"?

   (A) If a polygon is a triangle, then it has three sides.

   (B) If a triangle has three sides, then it is a polygon.

   (C) If a polygon has three sides, then it is a triangle.

   (D) If a polygon is not a triangle, then it does not have three sides.

8. What is the length of the hypotenuse in the triangle shown?

   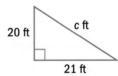

   20 ft    c ft    21 ft

   (A) 20.5 ft      (B) 22 ft

   (C) 24.5 ft      (D) 29 ft

9. What is the converse of the statement "If $n$ is an even number, then $2n$ is even"?

   (A) If $n$ is not an even number, then $2n$ is not even.

   (B) If $n$ is an even number, then $2n$ is odd.

   (C) If $2n$ is an even number, then $n$ is even.

   (D) If $2n$ is not an even number, then $n$ is not even.

10. Which of the following are the side lengths of a right triangle?

    (A) $a = 9, b = 40, c = 41$

    (B) $a = 19, b = 40, c = 49$

    (C) $a = 10, b = 45, c = 50$

    (D) $a = 15, b = 15, c = 25$

# Equations in One Variable

## Vocabulary for Chapter 8

### Key Mathematical Vocabulary

- **equation, p. 324**
- **inverse operation, p. 324**
- **equivalent equations, p. 324**

### Academic Vocabulary

- **model** Represent a mathematical relationship using words, symbols, diagrams, or physical objects. For example, see Explore 1 on page 322.
- **check, p. 322**
- **describe, p. 323**
- **explain, p. 329**
- **estimate, p. 353**
- **predict, p. 360**

**Determining who wins a race using the formula for distance traveled, page 360**

# Review Prerequisite Skills

### REVIEW VOCABULARY

- least common denominator, p. 54
- reciprocal, p. 86
- like terms, p. 236

## VOCABULARY CHECK

**Copy and complete the statement.**

1. The reciprocal of $\frac{2}{3}$ is _?_ .

2. The like terms in the expression $3x + 5 + (-2x)$ are _?_ .

3. The _?_ of $\frac{3}{4}$ and $\frac{1}{6}$ is 12.

## SKILLS CHECK

**Write the phrase as an algebraic expression.** (Review p. 32 for 8.1–8.4.)

4. Three times a number plus five

5. The difference of a number divided by four and two

6. Two thirds of perimeter $P$

**Find the sum or difference.** (Review pp. 74, 168, and 210 for 8.1–8.6.)

7. $-5 - 0.5$

8. $-4 + 12 - 3$

9. $\frac{2}{3} + \frac{1}{4}$

**In Exercises 10–18, evaluate the expression for $x = -2$ and $y = 0.25$.** (Review pp. 210, 224, and 236 for 8.1–8.6.)

10. $14 - x$

11. $-8 + x$

12. $y + 5 - x$

13. $\frac{x}{y}$

14. $xy$

15. $-3x$

16. $xy + 5$

17. $2(x + 3)$

18. $x(6 - y) + 1$

19. A car travels at a speed of 45 miles per hour for 3 hours. Find the total distance traveled by the car. (Review p. 18 for 8.6.)

# Activity 8.1

## Let's Explore
## Equations Involving Addition or Subtraction

**Goal**
Use algebra tiles to solve equations involving addition or subtraction.

**Materials**
• algebra tiles

**QUESTION** **How can you use algebra tiles to solve equations involving addition or subtraction?**

An *equation* is a mathematical sentence formed by placing an equal sign between two expressions. A *solution of an equation* in one variable is a number that produces a true statement when substituted for the variable in the equation.

You can use algebra tiles to model and solve equations.

| x-tile | 1-tile | –1-tile |
|--------|--------|---------|
| **+** | **+** | **—** |
| Represents the variable *x*. | Represents positive 1. | Represents negative 1. |

Pairing  and **—** results in a *zero pair*, which has a sum of 0.

**EXPLORE 1** *Use algebra tiles to solve an addition equation*

**Use algebra tiles to solve the equation *x* + 3 = 7.**

**1** **Model** the equation *x* + 3 = 7 using one *x*-tile and ten 1-tiles.

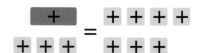

**2** **Remove** three 1-tiles from each side. By removing the same quantity from each side, you keep the two sides equal.

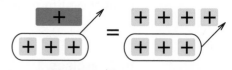

**3** **Identify** the solution. One *x*-tile is equal to four 1-tiles. So, the solution of *x* + 3 = 7 is *x* = 4.

▶ **Check** 4 + 3 = 7 ✓

## Draw Conclusions
**Write the equation that the model represents, then solve the equation.**

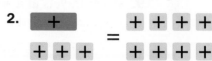

**Use algebra tiles to solve the equation.**

**3.** $x + 2 = 3$    **4.** $x + 3 = 6$    **5.** $x + 1 = 4$      **6.** $x + 4 = 8$

**7.** $1 + x = 7$    **8.** $4 + x = 7$    **9.** $2 + x = 9$    **10.** $3 + x = 5$

**11.** *Describe* how you can solve equations like those in Exercises 3–10 without using algebra tiles.

**EXPLORE 2**   *Solve a subtraction equation* .......................

**Use algebra tiles to solve the equation $x - 2 = 25$.**

**1**   **Rewrite** the equation as an addition equation.     $x - 2 = -5$
Adding the opposite of 2 is the same as           $x + (-2) = -5$
subtracting 2.

**2**   **Model** the equation $x - 2 = -5$ using
one $x$-tile and seven $-1$-tiles.

**3**   **Add** two 1-tiles to each side. Then
remove zero pairs.

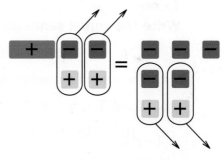

**4**   **Identify** the solution. One $x$-tile is
equal to three $-1$-tiles. So, the solution
of the equation $x - 2 = -5$ is $x = -3$.

▶ **Check** $-3 - 2 = -5$ ✓

## Draw Conclusions
**Use algebra tiles to solve the equation.**

**12.** $x - 3 = -7$   **13.** $x - 2 = -9$   **14.** $x - 1 = -9$    **15.** $-10 = x - 4$

**16.** $-7 = x - 5$   **17.** $-6 = x - 3$   **18.** $x - 3 = -10$   **19.** $-8 = x - 4$

**20.** *Describe* how you can solve equations like those in Exercises 12–19 without using algebra tiles.

# Solve Equations Involving Addition or Subtraction

## VOCABULARY and CONCEPTS

- An **inverse operation** is an operation that "undoes" another operation.
- An **equation** is a mathematical sentence formed by placing an equal sign between two expressions.
- A **solution of an equation** in one variable is a number that produces a true statement when substituted for the variable in the equation.
- **Equivalent equations** are equations that have the same solution.

### Solving Equations Using Properties of Equality

Because addition and subtraction are inverse operations, you can solve an equation like $x + 6 = -15$ using the *subtraction property of equality*, and you can solve an equation like $12 = y - 5$ using the *addition property of equality*.

**Subtraction property of equality** Subtracting the same number from each side of an equation produces an equivalent equation.

**Addition property of equality** Adding the same number to each side of an equation produces an equivalent equation.

**EXAMPLE 1** *Translating Verbal Sentences* . . . . . . . . . . . . . . . . . . . . . . .

Write the verbal sentence as an equation.

| Verbal Sentence | Equation |
|---|---|
| **a.** The sum of a number and 13 is 20. | $n + 13 = 20$ |
| **b.** The difference of 15 and a number is 7. | $15 - n = 7$ |
| **c.** $-10$ is 6 less than a number. | $-10 = n - 6$ |

### Practice for Example 1

Write the verbal sentence as an equation. Let *n* represent the number.

**1.** The difference of a number and 3 is 9.  **2.** $-12$ is 5 more than a number.

**3.** 4 more than a number is 20.  **4.** The sum of a number and 4 is $-9$.

**EXAMPLE 2** *Solving an Addition Equation* . . . . . . . . . . . . . . . . . . . . . . .

Solve $x + 6 = -15$.

| | |
|---|---|
| $x + 6 = -15$ | **Write original equation.** |
| $x + 6 - 6 = -15 - 6$ | **Subtract 6 from each side.** |
| $x = -21$ | **Simplify.** |

Gr 7 AF 1.1 Use variables and appropriate operations to write an expression, **an equation**, an inequality, or a system of equations or inequalities **that represents a verbal description (e.g., three less than a number, half as large as area A).** **Preparing for Gr. 7 AF 4.1** Solve two-step linear equations and inequalities in one variable over the rational numbers, interpret the solution or solutions in the context from which they arose, and verify the reasonableness of the results.
Also addresses Gr. 4 AF 2.0, Gr. 4 AF 2.1, Gr. 6 AF 1.0, Gr. 6 AF 1.1

**EXAMPLE 3** *Solving a Subtraction Equation*

**Solve $12 = y - 5$.**

| | |
|---|---|
| $12 = y - 5$ | Write original equation. |
| $12 + 5 = y - 5 + 5$ | Add 5 to each side. |
| $17 = y$ | Simplify. |
| ▶ **Check** $\quad 12 = y - 5$ | Write original equation. |
| $12 \overset{?}{=} 17 - 5$ | Substitute 17 for y. |
| $12 = 12 \checkmark$ | Solution checks. |

**Practice for Examples 2 and 3**

**Solve the equation. Check your solution.**

**5.** $a + 9 = 4$    **6.** $3 + b = 8$    **7.** $5.2 = c + 2.1$

**8.** $r - 2 = 8$    **9.** $-13 = s - 13$    **10.** $7.5 = t - 4.4$

**EXAMPLE 4** *Writing and Solving an Equation*

An unknown amount of salt is in a glass salt shaker. The mass of the shaker when it is empty is 134.40 grams. The mass of the shaker with the salt is 243.05 grams. What is the mass of the salt?

**Solution**

Write a verbal model. Let $s$ represent the unknown mass of the salt.

| Mass of shaker with salt | = | Mass of empty shaker | + | Mass of salt |
|---|---|---|---|---|

| | |
|---|---|
| $243.05 = 134.40 + s$ | Write an equation. |
| $243.05 - 134.40 = 134.40 - 134.40 + s$ | Subtract 134.40 from each side. |
| $108.65 = s$ | Simplify. |

▶ **Answer** The salt has a mass of 108.65 grams.

**Practice for Example 4**

**11.** Anthony wants to buy a CD that is on sale for $13.49. This is $2 less than the regular price. Write and solve an equation to find the regular price of the CD.

**Write the verbal sentence as an equation. Let *n* represent the number.**

1. The sum of a number and 3 equals 7.

2. The difference of 4 and a number is 9.

3. $-8$ is 5 less than a number.

4. $-6$ is equal to the sum of 2 and a number.

**Tell whether the given value of the variable is a solution of the equation.**

5. $x + 9 = 23; x = 14$

6. $b - 5 = 12; b = 7$

7. $m - 7 = 15; m = 8$

8. $b - 14 = -6; b = -20$

9. $d + 9 = 11; d = 2$

10. $t - 12 = 7; t = -19$

11. Copy and complete the steps for solving the equation $x + 16 = 17$.

$$x + 16 = 17 \qquad \text{Write original equation.}$$
$$x + 16 - \underline{?} = 17 - \underline{?} \qquad \underline{?} \text{ from each side.}$$
$$x = \underline{?} \qquad \text{Simplify.}$$

**Solve the equation. Check your solution.**

12. $n + 5 = 11$

13. $y + 13 = -6$

14. $9 + s = 4$

15. $12 + x = 3$

16. $a + 7 = 11$

17. $b + 17 = 16$

18. Copy and complete the steps for solving the equation $-8 = y - 14$.

$$-8 = y - 14 \qquad \text{Write original equation.}$$
$$-8 + \underline{?} = y - 14 + \underline{?} \qquad \underline{?} \text{ to each side.}$$
$$\underline{?} = y \qquad \text{Simplify.}$$

**Solve the equation. Check your solution.**

19. $a - 4 = 25$

20. $z - 15 = -12$

21. $r - 21 = 14$

22. $m - 9 = 12$

23. $c - 16 = 4$

24. $f - 23 = 21$

25. A paperback version of a book costs $7.95. This cost is $5.45 less than the cost of the hardcover version of the book. Write and solve an equation to find the cost of the hardcover version of the book.

26. During a recent trip to the gym, you worked out on a weight machine and shot baskets. You shot baskets for 25 minutes of the 75 minutes you spent at the gym. Write and solve an equation to find the number of minutes you spent working out on a weight machine.

27. The Hawks won 5 more games than the Wildcats. The Hawks won 21 games. Write and solve an equation to find the number of games that the Wildcats won.

28. **REASONING** Write an addition equation and a subtraction equation that each have 0 as the solution.

# Practice

**Tell whether the given value of the variable is a solution of the equation.**

**1.** $x + 15 = 20; x = 5$     **2.** $a - 12 = 13; a = 1$     **3.** $7 + m = -31; m = 24$

**Solve the equation. Check your solution.**

**4.** $y + 6 = 15$     **5.** $n + 23 = -14$     **6.** $18 = r + 7$

**7.** $a - 12 = 28$     **8.** $z - 24 = -9$     **9.** $20 = s - 35$

**10.** $3.6 + m = 2.5$     **11.** $c - 2.1 = 6.7$     **12.** $4.2 + x = 7.5$

**13.** $t - \dfrac{1}{5} = \dfrac{3}{10}$     **14.** $\dfrac{6}{7} = a + 1$     **15.** $-\dfrac{1}{2} + x = -\dfrac{5}{6}$

**FIND THE ERROR** *Describe* and correct the error in solving the equation.

**16.**
$$1.8 + a = -4.5$$
$$1.8 + a - 1.8 = -4.5 - 1.8$$
$$a = 2.7$$

**17.**
$$19 = y - 16$$
$$19 = y - 16 + 16$$
$$19 = y$$

**Write the verbal sentence as an equation. Then solve the equation.**

**18.** The difference of a number and 8 is $-15$.

**19.** 9 more than a number is 24.

**20.** A number decreased by 5 is 12.

**21.** A number minus 15 is 7.

**Write and solve an equation to find the unknown side length.**

**22.** Perimeter: 12 ft     **23.** Perimeter: 11.3 mm     **24.** Perimeter: 12.3 in.

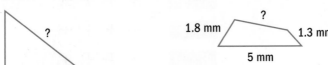

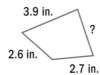

**25.** Your teacher wants to fill a bus for a field trip. A bus holds 54 people. Only 37 people have signed up for the trip. Write and solve an equation to find the number of additional people needed to fill the bus.

**26.** You are purchasing materials to make a decorative pillow. You have $25 to spend. To make the outer surface of the pillow, you buy $\dfrac{3}{4}$ yard of solid-color fabric at $8 per yard and $\dfrac{3}{4}$ yard of printed fabric at $12 per yard. You also buy 2 packages of stuffing at $3 per package. Write and solve an equation to find how much you can spend on beads to trim the pillow.

**27.** **REASONING** *Describe* how you can solve the equation $x + 3 = 7$ by using the addition property of equality rather than the subtraction property of equality.

# Activity 8.2

## Let's Explore
### Equations Involving Multiplication

**Goal**
Use algebra tiles to solve equations involving multiplication.

**Materials**
• algebra tiles

**QUESTION** How can you use algebra tiles to solve equations involving multiplication?

You can use algebra tiles to model and solve equations.

| *x*-tile | –*x*-tile | 1-tile | –1-tile |
|---|---|---|---|
| **+** | **—** | **+** | **—** |
| Represents the variable *x*. | Represents the opposite of *x*. | Represents positive 1. | Represents negative 1. |

Pairing **+** and **—** or + and — results in a *zero pair*, which has a sum of 0.

**EXPLORE 1** *Solve an equation with a positive x-coefficient*

**Use algebra tiles to solve the equation 4*x* = 16.**

**1** **Model** the equation $4x = 16$ using four *x*-tiles and sixteen 1-tiles.

**2** **Divide** the *x*-tiles and 1-tiles into 4 equal groups.

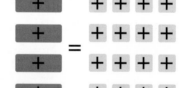

**3** **Identify** the solution. One *x*-tile is equal to four 1-tiles. So, the solution of the equation $4x = 16$ is $x = 4$.

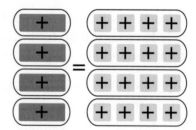

▶ **Check** $4(4) = 16$ ✓

**EXPLORE 2** *Solve an equation with a negative x-coefficient*

**Use algebra tiles to solve the equation $-2x = 4$.**

**①** **Model** the equation $-2x = 4$ using two $-x$-tiles and four 1-tiles.

**②** **Divide** the $-x$-tiles and 1-tiles into 2 equal groups.

**③** **Notice** that one $-x$-tile is equal to two 1-tiles. This is *not* the solution because you need to identify the value of $x$ rather than the value of $-x$.

**④** **Add** one $x$-tile and two $-1$-tiles to each side, then remove zero pairs.

**⑤** **Identify** the solution. One $x$-tile is equal to two $-1$-tiles. So, the solution of the equation $-2x = 4$ is $x = -2$.

▶ **Check** $-2(-2) = 4$ ✓

# Draw Conclusions

**Write the equation that the model represents, then solve the equation.**

1.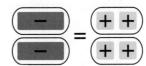

2.

**Use algebra tiles to model and solve the equation.**

**3.** $5x = 15$      **4.** $2x = 4$      **5.** $4x = -8$

**6.** $5x = 20$      **7.** $3x = -18$      **8.** $7x = 21$

**9.** $-2x = 12$      **10.** $-9x = -18$      **11.** $-3x = 12$

**12.** $-3x = 15$      **13.** $-4x = -24$      **14.** $-7x = 28$

**15.** **REASONING** *Describe* how you can solve equations like those in Exercises 3–14 without using algebra tiles.

# Lesson 8.2

## Solve Equations Involving Multiplication or Division

### VOCABULARY and CONCEPTS

- reciprocal, p. 86
- equivalent equations, p. 324

**Solving Equations Using Properties of Equality**

Because multiplication and division are inverse operations, you can solve an equation like $7x = -63$ using the *division property of equality*, and you can solve an equation like $\frac{x}{4} = 2.25$ using the *multiplication property of equality*.

**Division property of equality** Dividing each side of an equation by the same nonzero number produces an equivalent equation.

**Multiplication property of equality** Multiplying each side of an equation by the same nonzero number produces an equivalent equation.

---

**EXAMPLE 1** *Solving a Multiplication Equation* · · · · · · · · · · · · ·

**Solve $7x = -63$.**

$$7x = -63 \qquad \text{Write original equation.}$$
$$\frac{7x}{7} = \frac{-63}{7} \qquad \text{Divide each side by 7.}$$
$$x = -9 \qquad \text{Simplify.}$$

▶ **Check** $\qquad 7x = -63 \qquad$ Write original equation.

$$7(-9) \stackrel{?}{=} -63 \qquad \text{Substitute } -9 \text{ for } x.$$
$$-63 = -63 \checkmark \qquad \text{Solution checks.}$$

---

**EXAMPLE 2** *Solving a Division Equation* · · · · · · · · · · · · · · · · · · · ·

**Solve $\frac{x}{4} = 2.25$.**

$$\frac{x}{4} = 2.25 \qquad \text{Write original equation.}$$
$$4 \cdot \frac{x}{4} = 4 \cdot 2.25 \qquad \text{Multiply each side by 4.}$$
$$x = 9 \qquad \text{Simplify.}$$

### Practice for Examples 1 and 2

Solve the equation. Check your solution.

1. $9a = 45$
2. $-6b = 36$
3. $7 = 2c$
4. $\frac{r}{4} = 8$
5. $\frac{s}{3} = -15$
6. $1.5 = \frac{t}{3}$

**Gr. 7 AF 1.1** Use variables and appropriate operations to write an expression, **an equation**, an inequality, or a system of equations or inequalities **that represents a verbal description (e.g., three less than a number, half as large as area A).**

**Preparing for Gr 7 AF 4.1** Solve two-step linear equations and inequalities in one variable over the rational numbers, interpret the solution or solutions in the context from which they arose, and verify the reasonableness of the results. **Also addresses Gr. 4 AF 2.0, Gr. 4 AF 2.2, Gr. 6 AF 1.0, Gr. 6 AF 1.1**

**EXAMPLE 3** *Solving an Equation Using a Reciprocal*

**Solve** $\frac{2}{7}x = 4.$

| | |
|---|---|
| $\frac{2}{7}x = 4$ | **Write original equation.** |
| $\frac{7}{2} \cdot \frac{2}{7}x = \frac{7}{2} \cdot 4$ | **Multiply each side by $\frac{7}{2}$.** |
| $x = 14$ | **Simplify.** |

**Practice for Example 3**

**Solve the equation. Check your solution.**

**7.** $\frac{5}{6}x = 5$

**8.** $\frac{3}{4}y = -1$

**9.** $6 = \frac{3}{2}z$

**EXAMPLE 4** *Solving a Real-World Problem*

Arlene bought 6 identical flowers for her garden. The total cost of the flowers was $10.74 before tax. What was the cost of each flower?

**Solution**

Write a verbal model. Let $f$ represent the unknown cost of each flower.

| Total cost | = | Number of flowers | × | Cost of each flower |
|---|---|---|---|---|

| | |
|---|---|
| $10.74 = 6f$ | **Write an equation.** |
| $\frac{10.74}{6} = \frac{6f}{6}$ | **Divide each side by 6.** |
| $1.79 = f$ | **Simplify.** |

▶**Answer** The cost of each flower was $1.79.

**Practice for Example 4**

**10.** The area of a rectangle is 224 square inches. The width of the rectangle is 14 inches. What is the length of the rectangle?

**11.** Keisha charged her neighbors $63 for babysitting their children 9 times. She charged the same amount each time. How much did she charge each time?

**12.** You are helping your aunt plan her daughter's wedding. There are 176 people attending the wedding. There are 8 chairs to a table at the reception. How many tables are needed?

# Practice

A

Extra Practice
p. 505

**Tell whether the given value of the variable is a solution of the equation.**

**1.** $9a = 108$; $a = 12$  **2.** $\dfrac{x}{4} = 16$; $x = 4$  **3.** $\dfrac{2}{3}m = 2$; $m = 3$

**4.** $7x = 84$; $x = 12$  **5.** $\dfrac{b}{5} = 8$; $b = 45$  **6.** $\dfrac{3}{4}d = 4$; $d = 3$

**Match the equation with its solution.**

**7.** $6x = 30$  **A.** $x = \dfrac{1}{180}$

**8.** $\dfrac{x}{6} = 30$  **B.** $x = \dfrac{1}{5}$

**9.** $30x = 6$  **C.** $x = 5$

**10.** $6x = \dfrac{1}{30}$  **D.** $x = 180$

**FIND THE ERROR** *Describe* and correct the error in solving the equation.

**11.**
$$-6a = 42$$
$$\dfrac{-6a}{-6} = \dfrac{42}{-6}$$
$$a = 7$$

**12.**
$$\dfrac{3}{5}x = 15$$
$$\dfrac{3}{5} \cdot \dfrac{3}{5}x = \dfrac{3}{5} \cdot 15$$
$$x = 9$$

**Solve the equation. Check your solution.**

**13.** $12w = 48$  **14.** $7b = -56$  **15.** $-20r = -420$

**16.** $\dfrac{c}{5} = 11$  **17.** $\dfrac{n}{4} = -13$  **18.** $\dfrac{2}{3}s = -8$

**19.** $-5b = 40$  **20.** $\dfrac{2}{9}a = 4$  **21.** $\dfrac{2}{3}g = -6$

**22.** $7x = 15.75$  **23.** $\dfrac{y}{3} = 2.5$  **24.** $\dfrac{4}{5}g = -4$

**25. REASONING** Is it possible to solve the equation $3x = 35$ by *multiplying* each side of the equation by the same number? *Explain* your reasoning.

**26.** You purchase 5 packages of notebook paper. You pay a total of $15 for all of the paper. Write a multiplication equation that you can use to find $p$, the cost of a package of paper. Then solve the equation.

**27.** A salesperson starts with a full tank of gas, drives her car 363 miles, and then refuels. It takes 11 gallons of gas to fill the car's tank. Write and solve an equation to find the number of miles per gallon her car gets.

**28.** In a survey about favorite book categories, $\dfrac{1}{3}$ of the total number of people surveyed, or 53 people, responded that science fiction was their favorite category. Write and solve an equation to find the total number of people surveyed.

**B** Practice

@HomeTutor
classzone.com

**Tell whether the given value of the variable is a solution of the equation.**

**1.** $-5r = 125;\ r = -15$      **2.** $4.2a = -21;\ a = -5$      **3.** $\dfrac{n}{-6} = -84;\ n = -14$

**4.** $13b = -52;\ b = -4$      **5.** $-0.5q = -8;\ q = 16$      **6.** $\dfrac{5}{8} = \dfrac{2}{3}x;\ x = \dfrac{5}{12}$

**Solve the equation. Check your solution. Round the solution to the nearest hundredth if necessary.**

**7.** $4p = 48$      **8.** $2.3y = -20.7$      **9.** $-\dfrac{1}{5}c = 7$

**10.** $-9d = -76.5$      **11.** $\dfrac{m}{7} = -43$      **12.** $\dfrac{z}{6.2} = 4.5$

**13.** $\dfrac{a}{-8} = 3.6$      **14.** $-9.8 = \dfrac{w}{-2.3}$      **15.** $-6 = \dfrac{3}{8}r$

**16.** $\dfrac{5}{3}t = 30$      **17.** $5.3q = 1.431$      **18.** $5b = 8$

**19.** $\dfrac{3}{4}d = -9$      **20.** $-3.7k = 14.8$      **21.** $\dfrac{f}{7} = 1.2$

**FIND THE ERROR** *Describe* and correct the error in solving the equation.

**22.**
$$\frac{3}{5}d = -30$$
$$\frac{5}{3} \cdot \frac{3}{5}d = \frac{3}{5} \cdot (-30)$$
$$d = -18 \quad \times$$

**23.**
$$\frac{x}{4} = 8$$
$$\frac{1}{4} \cdot \frac{x}{4} = \frac{1}{4} \cdot 8$$
$$x = 2 \quad \times$$

**In Exercises 24–26, write the verbal sentence as an equation. Then solve the equation.**

**24.** The quotient of a number and 6 is 8.7.

**25.** Three times a number equals 14.4.

**26.** The product of $-2.2$ and a number is 13.2.

**27.** **REASONING** *Describe* how you can solve $\dfrac{2x}{3} = 6$ in two steps. Then describe how you can solve the equation in just one step.

**28.** At a part-time job, Marcus earns \$8.50 per hour. Write and solve an equation to find the number of hours he has to work to earn \$102.

**29.** You pay \$4.80 for 3.2 pounds of peanuts. Write and solve an equation to find the cost of 1 pound of peanuts.

**30.** Josh works at a grocery store part-time. Josh estimates that he spends $\dfrac{3}{5}$ of his time each week, or 12 hours, stocking shelves. Write and solve an equation to find the total time he works each week.

# Activity 8.3

## Let's Explore
## Modeling Two-Step Equations

**Goal**
Use algebra tiles to solve two-step equations.

**Materials**
• algebra tiles

**QUESTION** How can you use algebra tiles to solve two-step equations?

A *two-step equation* is an equation you solve using two operations. You can use algebra tiles to model and solve two-step equations.

| *x*-tile | 1-tile | −1-tile |
|:---:|:---:|:---:|
|  | + | − |
| Represents the variable x. | Represents positive 1. | Represents negative 1. |

Pairing  with  results in a *zero pair*, which has a sum of 0.

**EXPLORE 1** *Model a two-step equation involving addition*

**Model and solve 2*x* + 3 = 7.**

**1** **Model** the equation 2*x* + 3 = 7.

**2** **Remove** three 1-tiles from each side.

**3** **Divide** the *x*-tiles and 1-tiles into 2 equal groups.

**4** **Identify** the solution. One *x*-tile is equal to two 1-tiles. So, the solution of the equation 2*x* + 3 = 7 is *x* = 2.

▶ **Check** $2(2) + 3 \stackrel{?}{=} 7$
$4 + 3 \stackrel{?}{=} 7$
$7 = 7 ✓$

**EXPLORE 2** *Model a two-step equation involving subtraction*

**Model and solve $3x - 4 = 5$.**

**①** **Model** the equation $3x - 4 = 5$ by thinking of it as $3x + (-4) = 5$.

**②** **Add** four 1-tiles to each side. Then remove zero pairs.

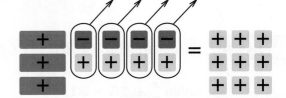

**③** **Divide** the $x$-tiles and the 1-tiles into 3 equal groups.

**④** **Identify** the solution. One $x$-tile is equal to three 1-tiles. So, the solution of the equation $3x - 4 = 5$ is $x = 3$.

▶ **Check** $3(3) - 4 \stackrel{?}{=} 5$

$\qquad 9 - 4 \stackrel{?}{=} 5$

$\qquad\quad 5 = 5 \checkmark$

# Draw Conclusions
**Use algebra tiles to solve the equation.**

**1.** $3x + 1 = 7$  **2.** $2x + 4 = 10$  **3.** $2x + 3 = 5$  **4.** $4x + 1 = 9$

**5.** $3x - 6 = 6$  **6.** $2x - 3 = 7$  **7.** $4x - 2 = -10$  **8.** $2x - 5 = -9$

**9.** *Describe* the steps you would take to solve a two-step equation involving addition without using algebra tiles.

**10.** *Describe* the steps you would take to solve a two-step equation involving subtraction without using algebra tiles.

# Solve Two-Step Equations

> **VOCABULARY and CONCEPTS**
>
> • inverse operation, p. 324
>
> **Solving a Two-Step Equation Using Inverse Operations**
>
> For an equation where an expression containing the variable involves two operations, such as multiplying by 3 and adding 2 in the equation $3x + 2 = 11$, you must perform two inverse operations to solve the equation.
>
> Check your solution by substituting the value into the original equation.

**EXAMPLE 1**  *Solving a Two-Step Equation*

**Solve $\frac{x}{3} + 16 = 31$.**

| | |
|---|---|
| $\frac{x}{3} + 16 = 31$ | **Write original equation.** |
| $\frac{x}{3} + 16 - 16 = 31 - 16$ | **Subtract 16 from each side.** |
| $\frac{x}{3} = 15$ | **Simplify.** |
| $\frac{x}{3} \cdot 3 = 15 \cdot 3$ | **Multiply each side by 3.** |
| $x = 45$ | **Simplify.** |

**Practice for Example 1**

**Solve the equation.**

**1.** $\frac{x}{4} - 21 = 30$    **2.** $\frac{z}{7} + 12 = 19$    **3.** $3t + 2 = 34$

**EXAMPLE 2**  *Solving an Equation with Negative Coefficients*

**Solve $20 = 3 - 9z$.**

| | |
|---|---|
| $20 = 3 - 9z$ | **Write original equation.** |
| $20 - 3 = 3 - 9z - 3$ | **Subtract 3 from each side.** |
| $17 = -9z$ | **Simplify.** |
| $\frac{17}{-9} = \frac{-9z}{-9}$ | **Divide each side by $-9$.** |
| $-1\frac{8}{9} = z$ | **Simplify.** |

**Practice for Example 2**

**Solve the equation.**

**4.** $15 - z = 21$    **5.** $24 - 2w = 33$    **6.** $-6x + 18 = 6$

**EXAMPLE 3** *Writing and Solving a Two-Step Equation* ......

**The difference of 9 times a number and 5 is 49. What is the number?**

Let $n$ represent the number.

| | |
|---|---|
| $9n - 5 = 49$ | **Write an equation.** |
| $9n - 5 + 5 = 49 + 5$ | **Add 5 to each side.** |
| $9n = 54$ | **Simplify.** |
| $\dfrac{9n}{9} = \dfrac{54}{9}$ | **Divide each side by 9.** |
| $n = 6$ | **Simplify.** |

### Practice for Example 3

**7.** The sum of 4 times a number and $-15$ is 22. What is the number?

**EXAMPLE 4** *Solving a Real-World Problem* .......

A class of 130 students is going on a field trip. Twelve students will ride in the school's van. How many of the school's buses, which can each hold 40 students, are needed to transport the rest of the students?

**Solution**

Write a verbal model. Let $b$ represent the number of buses needed.

| Capacity of a bus | × | Number of buses | + | Number of students in van | = | Number of students on trip |
|---|---|---|---|---|---|---|

| | |
|---|---|
| $40b + 12 = 130$ | **Write an equation.** |
| $40b = 118$ | **Subtract 12 from each side.** |
| $b = 2\dfrac{19}{20}$ | **Divide each side by 40.** |

▶ **Answer** The number of buses must be a whole number, so 3 buses are needed.

### Practice for Example 4

**8.** In Example 4, suppose only 1 bus is available, but the school has a fleet of vans that each hold 12 students. How many vans are needed to transport the 130 students?

**Solve the equation. Check your solution.**

1. $5x + 3 = 13$
2. $4t - 8 = 12$
3. $7 + 3m = 22$
4. $-3z - 8 = -26$
5. $15 = 5 + \dfrac{p}{3}$
6. $42 = 3x + 12$
7. $26 = 14 - \dfrac{m}{2}$
8. $7h - 27 = 36$
9. $96 - 5g = 51$
10. $8m - 3 = 7$
11. $\dfrac{x}{7} - 3 = 4$
12. $-4 + \dfrac{f}{5} = 6$
13. $9 = 3 + \dfrac{g}{3}$
14. $5 + \dfrac{d}{4} = 10$
15. $7 - 3c = 15$
16. $6 = 27 - 9y$
17. $20 - 8q = -14$
18. $-13 = 7 + \dfrac{a}{4}$

**FIND THE ERROR** *Describe* and correct the error in solving the equation.

19.
$$63 = 48 - 6n$$
$$63 - 48 = 48 - 6n - 48$$
$$15 = -6n$$
$$\dfrac{15}{6} = \dfrac{-6n}{6}$$
$$2\tfrac{1}{2} = n$$

20.
$$15 = 5x - 2$$
$$\dfrac{15}{5} = \dfrac{5x - 2}{5}$$
$$3 = x - 2$$
$$3 + 2 = x - 2 + 2$$
$$5 = x$$

21. **REASONING** Is it possible to solve $\dfrac{x}{2} + 3 = 5$ by multiplying each side by 2 first rather than by subtracting 3 from each side first? *Explain.*

**In Exercises 22–24, write the verbal sentence as an equation. Then solve the equation.**

22. Six added to the quotient of a number and 3 is 8.

23. The sum of 3 and 7 times a number is 45.

24. 15 decreased by 6 times a number is $-9$

25. You want to buy a ring and some bracelets. The ring costs $3.18, and each bracelet costs $2.90. You can spend $20. Write and solve an equation to find the number of bracelets you can buy if you buy the ring.

26. A take-out restaurant charges $2.50 per delivery plus $3 per pound of food. Your bill was $8.50. Write and solve an equation to find how many pounds of food you purchased.

27. A plumber charges $45 for a service call plus $60 per hour of work time. The plumber charged the Garcias $225 to repair a drain. Write and solve an equation to find the number of hours the plumber took to do the job.

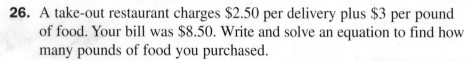

**Solve the equation. Check your solution.**

**1.** $7x + 3 = 31$

**2.** $5t - 9 = 26$

**3.** $12 + \dfrac{r}{2} = 112$

**4.** $-3z - 7 = 23$

**5.** $36 = 8 - 14p$

**6.** $63 = 3x + 9$

**7.** $28 = 16 - 4m$

**8.** $8 - \dfrac{h}{3} = 28$

**9.** $124 - 8g = 36$

**10.** $6m + 15 = 12$

**11.** $\dfrac{x}{4} - 7 = 9$

**12.** $7 + \dfrac{d}{6} = 19$

**13.** $11 - 4c = 18$

**14.** $4 = 23 - 7y$

**15.** $35 - 7q = -8$

**16.** $67 = 13 + \dfrac{u}{9}$

**17.** $-94 = 25 + \dfrac{a}{7}$

**18.** $\dfrac{k}{8} - 37 = -5$

**FIND THE ERROR** *Describe* and correct the error in solving the equation.

**19.**

$$\frac{n}{5} - 12 = 32$$

$$\frac{n}{5} - 12 - 12 = 32 - 12$$

$$\frac{n}{5} = 20$$

$$\frac{n}{5} \cdot 5 = 20 \cdot 5$$

$$n = 100$$

**20.**

$$2y - 11 = 11$$

$$2y - 11 + 11 = 11 + 11$$

$$2y = 22$$

$$2y \cdot 2 = 22 \cdot 2$$

$$y = 44$$

**21.** **REASONING** *Describe* how solving $\dfrac{x + 1}{2} = 3$ is different than solving $\dfrac{x}{2} + 1 = 3$.

**In Exercises 22–24, write the verbal sentence as an equation. Then solve the equation.**

**22.** The difference of the product of 4 times a number and $\dfrac{2}{3}$ is $\dfrac{34}{3}$.

**23.** 9.8 increased by the quotient of a number and 5 is 10.4.

**24.** The sum of 5 and 3 times a number is $-10$.

**25.** At the grocery store, you bought 4 identical boxes of cereal and a carton of strawberries. The carton of strawberries costs $2.89. The total cost was $12.25. Write and solve an equation to find the cost of one box of cereal.

**26.** You have $80 in birthday money. You want to take some friends to a concert. You can order tickets for $14 each, and there is a $2 handling charge for the entire order. Write and solve an equation to find how many people can go.

**27.** Jessica is printing invitations to the opening of a museum. She needs to print 260 invitations, one per sheet of paper. She was able to purchase only 5 packages of 25 sheets of paper at the store. Write and solve an equation to find how many more packages of paper she needs in order to print the rest of the invitations.

**VOCABULARY**
- equation, p. 324
- equivalent equations, p. 324
- inverse operation, p. 324
- solution of an equation, p. 324

**Vocabulary Exercise**

1. Copy and complete: A(n) _?_ is a mathematical sentence formed by placing an equal sign between two expressions.

## 8.1 Solve Equations Involving Addition or Subtraction   pp. 324–327

**EXAMPLE**

$$x + 8 = -13 \quad \text{Original equation}$$
$$x + 8 - 8 = -13 - 8 \quad \text{Subtract 8 from each side.}$$
$$x = -21 \quad \text{Simplify.}$$

**Solve the equation. Check your solution.**

2. $a + 5 = 6$

3. $7 + b = 10$

4. $r - 4 = 4$

## 8.2 Solve Equations Involving Multiplication or Division  pp. 330–333

**EXAMPLE**

$$5x = -35 \quad \text{Original equation}$$
$$\frac{5x}{5} = \frac{-35}{5} \quad \text{Divide each side by 5.}$$
$$x = -7 \quad \text{Simplify.}$$

**Solve the equation. Check your solution.**

5. $6a = 42$

6. $-4b = 16$

7. $\frac{r}{6} = 9$

## 8.3 Solve Two-Step Equations   pp. 336–339

**EXAMPLE**

$$\frac{x}{5} + 4 = 24 \quad \text{Original equation}$$
$$\frac{x}{5} + 4 - 4 = 24 - 4 \quad \text{Subtract 4 from each side.}$$
$$\frac{x}{5} \cdot 5 = 20 \cdot 5 \quad \text{Multiply each side by 5.}$$
$$x = 100 \quad \text{Simplify.}$$

**Solve the equation. Check your solution.**

8. $\frac{x}{2} - 14 = 26$

9. $\frac{z}{9} + 14 = 23$

10. $11 - n = 18$

**Write the verbal sentence as an equation. Let *n* represent the number.**

**1.** The sum of a number and 4 is 10.

**2.** The difference of a number and 6 is 15.

**3.** −7 is equal to the sum of 3 and a number.

**4.** −8 is 2 less than a number.

**5.** Six times a number is 96.

**6.** 6 equals a number divided by 7.

**Solve the equation. Check your solution.**

**7.** $t + 3 = 11$

**8.** $5 + c = 15$

**9.** $4.1 = p + 1.8$

**10.** $k - 7.3 = 3.9$

**11.** $-7 = x - 5$

**12.** $5.6 = b - 6.6$

**13.** $6c = 30$

**14.** $-4j = 36$

**15.** $\frac{n}{4} = 3$

**16.** $\frac{q}{7} = 1.2$

**17.** $\frac{2}{3}v = 6$

**18.** $\frac{7}{8}a = -42$

**19.** $\frac{y}{5} + 8 = 11$

**20.** $\frac{m}{6} - 7 = -5$

**21.** $12f - 45 = -54$

**22.** $-1 = \frac{1}{2}m + 9$

**23.** $6 - 3x = 21$

**24.** $2 + \frac{a}{6} = 5$

**Write the verbal sentence as an equation. Then solve the equation.**

**25.** Four more than twice a number is 8.

**26.** One less than four times a number is 11.

**27.** Three more than four times a number is 15.

**28.** Five less than twice a number is 7.

**29.** Nine more than twice a number is 3.

**30.** Four less than a number divided by 3 is 9.

**In Exercises 31 and 32, use the information from the ad shown for an online music store.**

**31.** Amanda has $24 to spend on CDs. Write and solve an equation to find the number of CDs that she can buy for $4 each.

**32.** Brandon spent a total of $19 for 3 CDs. How much did Brandon pay for each CD?

**33.** To weigh her cat, Sue steps on a scale while holding the cat. Together, they weigh 132 pounds. Sue alone weighs 124 pounds. Write and solve an equation to find how much the cat weighs.

**34.** You bought 4 identical greeting cards and paid for them with a $10 bill. You received $2.04 in change. Write and solve an equation to find the cost of each greeting card.

**35.** Lucas is taking a trip that is 224 miles long. He has already driven a total of 59 miles. Suppose he drives the rest of the way at an average speed of 55 miles per hour. How many hours will he need to drive to finish the trip?

## Let's Explore
# Solving Equations with Fractions and Decimals

**Goal**
Investigate clearing fractions and decimals from an equation.

**Materials**
• paper and pencil

**QUESTION** How can you clear fractions and decimals from an equation?

**EXPLORE 1** *Clear fractions from an equation* . . . . . . . . . . . . . . . .

**①** **Copy** and complete the table.
Consider the equations in each row of the table. Multiply each side of the equation by the number described in the second column. Write the simplified equation in the last column.

| Equation | Multiply by | Simplified equation |
| --- | --- | --- |
| $\frac{3}{5}x + \frac{2}{3} = \frac{8}{3}$ | LCD of $\frac{3}{5}, \frac{2}{3}$, and $\frac{8}{3}$ | ? |
| $\frac{1}{6}x + \frac{1}{10} = \frac{29}{30}$ | LCD of $\frac{1}{6}, \frac{1}{10}$, and $\frac{29}{30}$ | ? |
| $\frac{3}{4}x - \frac{1}{6} = \frac{2}{9}$ | LCD of $\frac{3}{4}, \frac{1}{6}$, and $\frac{2}{9}$ | ? |

**②** **Solve** the simplified equations.
Solve each of the simplified equations you wrote in Step 1.

**③** **Check** your solutions.
For each equation from Step 1, substitute the value you found for $x$ into the original equation and simplify the left side. Is the solution of the simplified equation the solution of the original equation?

## Draw Conclusions

1. What property of equality are you using when you clear an equation of fractions?

2. Suppose you want to clear fractions in an equation.

   **a.** Could you multiply each side of the equation by the product of the denominators of the fractions? *Explain.*

   **b.** What is the advantage of multiplying each side of the equation by the least common denominator of the fractions?

**Solve the equation by first clearing the fractions.**

**3.** $\frac{3}{4}x + \frac{1}{6} = \frac{1}{3}$

**4.** $\frac{3}{7}x + \frac{3}{14} = \frac{19}{42}$

**5.** $\frac{3}{4}x - \frac{5}{8} = -\frac{7}{12}$

**EXPLORE 2** *Clear decimals from an equation*

**1** **Copy** and complete the table.
Consider the equations in each row of the table. Multiply each side of the equation by the number described in the second column. Write the simplified equation in the last column.

| Equation | Multiply by | Simplified equation |
| --- | --- | --- |
| $3.5x = 2.45$ | $10^2$ | ? |
| $2.5x = 2.4$ | $10$ | ? |
| $0.0004x = 0.05$ | $10^4$ | ? |
| $3.35 = 0.002x + 2.1$ | $10^3$ | ? |

**2** **Determine** the decimal places.
For each equation in Step 1, determine the greatest number of decimal places in any decimal. How does this number relate to the number you multiplied by to simplify the equation?

**3** **Solve** the simplified equations.
Solve each of the simplified equations you wrote in Step 1. Substitute the value of $x$ into the original equation and confirm that it is a solution of the original equation.

## Draw Conclusions

**6.** You want to clear the decimals in the equation $5.5x = 2.55$.

**a.** Will multiplying each side by 10 clear the decimals? *Explain.*

**b.** Will multiplying each side by 100 clear the decimals? *Explain.*

**c.** Will multiplying each side by 1000 clear the decimals? *Explain.*

**Solve the equation by first clearing the decimals.**

**7.** $1.5x = 1.2$

**8.** $0.25x = 1.5$

**9.** $3.5 = 0.0025x$

**10.** $3.5 = 1.25x - 2.7$

**11.** $0.6x + 0.24 = 3.84$

**12.** $2.28 = 0.004x + 2.1$

# Solve Equations with Fractions and Decimals

---

## VOCABULARY and CONCEPTS

- least common denominator (LCD), p. 54

**Clearing Fractions and Decimals to Solve Equations**

- To clear fractions in an equation, multiply each side of the equation by the LCD of the fractions.
- To clear decimals in an equation, multiply each side of the equation by 10 raised to the power equal to the greatest number of decimal places in any decimal.

---

**EXAMPLE 1** *Solving an Equation by Clearing Fractions* ......

Solve $\dfrac{9}{10}x - \dfrac{11}{15} = -\dfrac{12}{25}$.

| | |
|---|---|
| $\dfrac{9}{10}x - \dfrac{11}{15} = -\dfrac{12}{25}$ | Write original equation. |
| $150\left(\dfrac{9}{10}x - \dfrac{11}{15}\right) = 150\left(-\dfrac{12}{25}\right)$ | Multiply each side by LCD of fractions. |
| $150\left(\dfrac{9}{10}x\right) - 150\left(\dfrac{11}{15}\right) = 150\left(-\dfrac{12}{25}\right)$ | Use distributive property. |
| $135x - 110 = -72$ | Simplify. |
| $135x - 110 + 110 = -72 + 110$ | Add 110 to each side. |
| $135x = 38$ | Simplify. |
| $\dfrac{135x}{135} = \dfrac{38}{135}$ | Divide each side by 135. |
| $x = \dfrac{38}{135}$ | Simplify. |

---

**EXAMPLE 2** *Solving an Equation by Clearing Decimals* ......

Solve $4.263 = 2 - 0.31x$.

| | |
|---|---|
| $4.263 = 2 - 0.31x$ | Write original equation. |
| $1000(4.263) = 1000(2 - 0.31x)$ | Multiply each side by $10^3$, or 1000. |
| $4263 = 2000 - 310x$ | Use distributive property. Simplify. |
| $4263 - 2000 = 2000 - 310x - 2000$ | Subtract 2000 from each side. |
| $2263 = -310x$ | Simplify. |
| $\dfrac{2263}{-310} = \dfrac{-310x}{-310}$ | Divide each side by $-310$. |
| $-7.3 = x$ | Simplify. |

---

Gr 7 AF 1.1 Use variables and appropriate operations to write an expression, an equation, an inequality, or a system of equations or inequalities that represents a verbal description (e.g., three less than a number, half as large as area *A*).
Gr 7 AF 4.1 Solve two-step linear equations and inequalities in one variable over the rational numbers, interpret the solution or solutions in the context from which they arose, and verify the reasonableness of the results.

### Practice for Examples 1 and 2

**Solve the equation by first clearing the fractions or decimals.**

**1.** $\frac{5}{6}x - \frac{2}{3} = \frac{1}{4}$

**2.** $-\frac{26}{45}x + \frac{3}{10} = -\frac{8}{9}$

**3.** $1.2a - 3.65 = -2.57$

**4.** $-0.18b + 11.2 = 12.856$

**EXAMPLE 3** *Writing and Solving an Equation* ················

A camping expedition company has $3000 to spend on new equipment. It will spend $1167.90 on tents. It will also buy backpacks at $185 each and sleeping bags at $110.50 each. The company wants to buy an equal number of backpacks and sleeping bags. How many of each can it afford to buy?

**Solution**

Write a verbal model. Let *n* represent the number of backpacks and the number of sleeping bags.

| Cost of backpacks | + | Cost of sleeping bags | + | Cost of tents | = | Total budget |
|---|---|---|---|---|---|---|

$185.00n + 110.50n + 1167.90 = 3000$      **Write an equation.**

$295.50n + 1167.90 = 3000$      **Combine like terms.**

$295.50n + 1167.90 - 1167.90 = 3000 - 1167.90$    **Subtract 1167.90 from each side.**

$295.50n = 1832.10$      **Simplify.**

$\dfrac{295.50n}{295.50} = \dfrac{1832.10}{295.50}$      **Divide each side by 295.50.**

$n = 6.2$      **Simplify.**

▶ **Answer** The company cannot buy a fraction of a backpack or a sleeping bag, and the total cost cannot exceed the company's budget, so you must round down. The company can afford to buy 6 backpacks and 6 sleeping bags.

### Practice for Example 3

**5.** You have $70 to spend on clothing for a winter camping trip. You will buy ear warmers for $20.72 and an equal number of pairs of liner socks at $4.40 per pair and outer socks at $11 per pair. How many pairs of liner socks and outer socks can you buy?

**Tell what number you would multiply each side of the equation by to clear the decimals or fractions.**

**1.** $4.2x + 5.0 = 6.4$     **2.** $8.35b - 9.16 = 9.21$     **3.** $3.4y - 5y = 4.88$

**4.** $\frac{4}{5}w + 2 = -\frac{3}{5}$     **5.** $\frac{1}{6}m + \frac{1}{4} = \frac{2}{3}$     **6.** $\frac{4}{5}g - \frac{5}{8}g = 7$

**Solve the equation by first clearing the fractions.**

**7.** $-\frac{2}{3}x + \frac{1}{2} = \frac{1}{3}$     **8.** $\frac{7}{11}a + \frac{13}{22} = \frac{6}{11}$     **9.** $\frac{17}{27}n + \frac{16}{27} = \frac{5}{9}$

**10.** $\frac{7}{12} = -\frac{3}{4}z - \frac{2}{3}$     **11.** $\frac{7}{9}t + \frac{13}{18} = \frac{2}{3}$     **12.** $\frac{11}{18} = \frac{1}{3} - \frac{13}{18}b$

**13.** $\frac{1}{4} - \frac{2}{3}c = -\frac{1}{3}$     **14.** $\frac{11}{46} = \frac{10}{23} - \frac{12}{23}x$     **15.** $\frac{17}{40} = \frac{4}{5} - \frac{9}{10}m$

**16.** $h - \frac{7}{8}h = \frac{1}{5}$     **17.** $\frac{1}{9}w + \frac{2}{7}w = 1$     **18.** $\frac{11}{12}t - \frac{3}{4}t = -\frac{5}{6}$

**FIND THE ERROR** *Describe* and correct the error in solving the equation.

**19.**

$20 = 0.8y - 0.4$
$20 = 10(0.8y - 0.4)$
$20 = 8y - 4$
$24 = 8y$ ✗
$3 = y$

**20.**

$\frac{4}{5}x - 1 = \frac{3}{4}$
$20\left(\frac{4}{5}x\right) - 1 = 20\left(\frac{3}{4}\right)$
$16x - 1 = 15$ ✗
$16x = 16$
$x = 1$

**Solve the equation by first clearing the decimals.**

**21.** $6g + 9.6 = 24$     **22.** $12.2 = 6.1d + 18.3$     **23.** $10.5z - 1.9 = 19.1$

**24.** $5.5p + 18.7 = 46.75$     **25.** $54 = 7.2x + 21.6$     **26.** $2.6a - 8.32 = 20.8$

**27.** $6.75 = 8.1 - 2.7y$     **28.** $-6.9 = -2.76 - 4.6q$     **29.** $9.75 = 3.9 - 1.5r$

**30.** $0.3f + 9.4 + 0.8f = -3.8$     **31.** $m - 2.3 - 0.7m = 1.6$     **32.** $4.3 = 4.1g - 1.9 - g$

**33.** A restaurant features a family dinner for four for $25.50 including tip. The Tylers ordered the family dinner along with an equal number of servings of fruit cobbler at $1.30 each and rice pudding at $1.20 each. The Tylers gave the cashier $30. Write and solve an equation to find the number of servings of each dessert that they ordered.

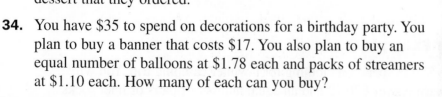

**34.** You have $35 to spend on decorations for a birthday party. You plan to buy a banner that costs $17. You also plan to buy an equal number of balloons at $1.78 each and packs of streamers at $1.10 each. How many of each can you buy?

**35. REASONING** *Describe* two different ways you could solve $0.5x - \frac{1}{2} = \frac{1}{2}$.

# Practice

**Solve the equation by first clearing the fractions.**

**1.** $-\dfrac{17}{31}t + \dfrac{7}{31} = \dfrac{15}{31}$

**2.** $\dfrac{1}{12} - \dfrac{2}{3}m = \dfrac{1}{3}$

**3.** $\dfrac{8}{17}x + \dfrac{5}{34} = \dfrac{6}{17}$

**4.** $\dfrac{2}{3} = \dfrac{7}{9}z + \dfrac{11}{36}$

**5.** $\dfrac{1}{6} - \dfrac{1}{3}h = \dfrac{2}{3}$

**6.** $\dfrac{6}{11} = \dfrac{1}{4} + \dfrac{7}{11}n$

**7.** $\dfrac{2}{3}p - \dfrac{1}{6} = \dfrac{2}{7}$

**8.** $\dfrac{7}{20} = \dfrac{1}{6} + \dfrac{1}{2}w$

**9.** $\dfrac{5}{16} = \dfrac{1}{6} - \dfrac{7}{12}b$

**10.** $g - \dfrac{2}{3}g = -\dfrac{5}{6}$

**11.** $\dfrac{1}{4}a - \dfrac{4}{9} + \dfrac{5}{6}a = \dfrac{2}{9}$

**12.** $\dfrac{7}{8}r + \dfrac{1}{4} - \dfrac{3}{8}r = \dfrac{3}{4}$

**FIND THE ERROR** *Describe* and correct the error in solving the equation.

**13.**
$$\dfrac{2}{3}x - \dfrac{1}{2} = \dfrac{3}{4}$$
$$6\left(\dfrac{2}{3}x - \dfrac{1}{2}\right) = 4\left(\dfrac{3}{4}\right)$$
$$4x - 3 = 3$$
$$4x = 6$$
$$x = 1\dfrac{1}{2}$$

**14.**
$$2.25x - 6.1 = 14.15$$
$$100(2.25x - 6.1) = 100(14.15)$$
$$225x - 61 = 1415$$
$$225x = 1476$$
$$x = 6.56$$

**Solve the equation by first clearing the decimals.**

**15.** $2.3x + 9.2 = 23$

**16.** $9.6 - 2.4q = -24$

**17.** $-3.9 = 2.6d + 1.56$

**18.** $6.1c + 20.74 = -51.85$

**19.** $26.4 = 6.6v + 10.56$

**20.** $4.5g + 15.3 = -38.25$

**21.** $1.55 = -3.1z - 0.62$

**22.** $81.9 = 32.76 + 9.1r$

**23.** $-0.24 = 0.96 - 0.6p$

**24.** $m + 6.74 + 0.7m = -3.8$ **25.** $3.4w - 2.6 - w = 16.6$

**26.** $8.89k - 9.36k - 1.021 = 1$

**27.** A pet store owner has \$250 to spend on new pet supplies. She will spend \$86.10 on pet toys. She will also buy bags of cat food at \$6.95 per bag and bags of dog food at \$7.95 per bag. She plans to buy an equal number of bags of cat food and dog food. Write and solve an equation to find how many of each she can afford to buy.

**28.** Vanessa has \$100 to spend on clothes for summer camp. She will spend \$10.20 for sneakers. She wants to buy an equal number of shorts and T-shirts to make sets. Shorts cost \$12.50 each and T-shirts cost \$9.95 each. Write and solve an equation to find how many shorts and T-shirts she can buy.

**29.** Greta has 32.45 Australian dollars, and she needs 50 Australian dollars. She has a bunch of U.S. \$1 bills. She can get 1.308 Australian dollars for each U.S. dollar bill. Write and solve an equation to find the number of U.S. dollar bills she must exchange so that she will have as much Australian money as she needs.

**30.** **REASONING** *Describe* two different ways to solve $0.75 = 0.25 + \dfrac{1}{4}x$.

# Activity 8.5

## Let's Explore
## Modeling Multi-Step Equations

**Goal**
Use algebra tiles to solve an equation with like terms or parentheses.

**Materials**
• algebra tiles

**QUESTION** How can you use algebra tiles to solve an equation with like terms or parentheses?

Sometimes you need to simplify one side of an equation before you can solve the equation. Using algebra tiles can help you solve such equations.

An $x$-tile represents $x$.   A 1-tile represents 1.

**EXPLORE 1** *Use algebra tiles to solve an equation* .........

**Use algebra tiles to solve $2x + 4 + x = 10$.**

**1** **Represent** the equation $2x + 4 + x = 10$ using algebra tiles.

**2** **Combine** the $x$-tiles on the left side of the equation to rewrite the equation as $3x + 4 = 10$.

**3** **Remove** four 1-tiles from each side.

**4** **Divide** the $x$-tiles and the 1-tiles into 3 equal groups.

**5** **Identify** the solution. One $x$-tile is equal to two 1-tiles. So, the solution of the equation $2x + 4 + x = 10$ is $x = 2$.

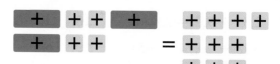
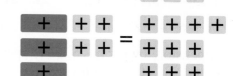

## Draw Conclusions
**Use algebra tiles to model and solve the equation.**

**1.** $x + 3 + 2x = 9$

**2.** $2x + 1 + 3x = 16$

**3.** $4x + 3 + 2x = 9$

**4.** $2x + 2 + 3x = 17$

**5.** In Lesson 8.3, you learned how to solve two-step equations. How is solving the equation in Explore 1 different from solving a two-step equation?

**EXPLORE 2** *Use algebra tiles to solve an equation* . . . . . . . . . . . .

**Use algebra tiles to solve $3(x + 1) = 12$.**

**1** **Represent** the equation $3(x + 1) = 12$ using algebra tiles. To model $3(x + 1)$, use an $x$-tile and a 1-tile to model the expression $x + 1$. Repeat the model two more times to obtain the expression $3x + 3$.

**2** **Remove** three 1-tiles from each side.

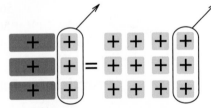

**3** **Divide** the $x$-tiles and the 1-tiles into 3 equal groups.

**4** **Identify** the solution. One $x$-tile is equal to three 1-tiles. So, the solution of $3(x + 1) = 12$ is $x = 3$.

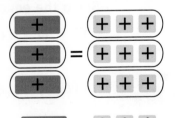

## Draw Conclusions
**Use algebra tiles to model and solve the equation.**

**6.** $5(x + 2) = 15$

**7.** $2(2 + x) = 18$

**8.** $4(x + 1) + 5 = 21$

**9.** $2 + 2(x + 1) = 20$

**10.** How is solving the equation in Explore 2 different from solving a two-step equation?

# Solve Equations Using the Distributive Property

**VOCABULARY and CONCEPTS**

• like terms, p. 236

**Using the Distributive Property**

When an equation contains parentheses, you should use the distributive property and combine like terms to simplify one or both sides of the equation before using the properties of equality (see Lessons 8.1 and 8.2) to solve the equation.

**EXAMPLE 1** *Using the Distributive Property* ...............

Solve $-8(5 - 7c) = 184$.

| | |
|---|---|
| $-8(5 - 7c) = 184$ | **Write original equation.** |
| $-40 + 56c = 184$ | **Distributive property** |
| $-40 + 56c + 40 = 184 + 40$ | **Add 40 to each side.** |
| $56c = 224$ | **Simplify.** |
| $\dfrac{56c}{56} = \dfrac{224}{56}$ | **Divide each side by 56.** |
| $c = 4$ | **Simplify.** |

**Practice for Example 1**

Solve the equation. Check your solution.

**1.** $-2(7 - 11v) = 96$     **2.** $12(4 - 3g) = -132$     **3.** $-5(c - 1) = -50$

**EXAMPLE 2** *Using the Distributive Property* ...............

Solve $4(x + 3) + 2(x - 1) = 22$.

| | |
|---|---|
| $4(x + 3) + 2(x - 1) = 22$ | **Write original equation.** |
| $4x + 12 + 2x - 2 = 22$ | **Distributive property** |
| $6x + 10 = 22$ | **Combine like terms.** |
| $6x = 12$ | **Subtract 10 from each side.** |
| $x = 2$ | **Divide each side by 6.** |

**Practice for Example 2**

Solve the equation. Check your solution.

**4.** $3(x - 4) + 4(x + 1) = 13$       **5.** $-2(x + 1) - 7(3x - 1) = 28$

**Alg. 4.0** Students simplify expressions before solving linear equations and inequalities **in one variable, such as** $3(2x - 5) + 4(x - 2) = 12.$
**Alg. 5.0** Students solve multistep problems, including word problems, involving linear equations and linear inequalities **in one variable and provide justification for each step.**

**EXAMPLE 3** *Solving an Equation* • • • • • • • • • • • • • • • • • • • • • •

**Solve $11(y - 3) = 7(y + 1)$.**

| | |
|---|---|
| $11(y - 3) = 7(y + 1)$ | **Write original equation.** |
| $11y - 33 = 7y + 7$ | **Distributive property** |
| $11y - 33 - 7y = 7y + 7 - 7y$ | **Subtract 7y from each side.** |
| $4y - 33 = 7$ | **Simplify.** |
| $4y - 33 + 33 = 7 + 33$ | **Add 33 to each side.** |
| $4y = 40$ | **Simplify.** |
| $\dfrac{4y}{4} = \dfrac{40}{4}$ | **Divide each side by 4.** |
| $y = 10$ | **Simplify.** |

**EXAMPLE 4** *Writing and Solving an Equation* • • • • • • • • • • • • • • •

Three friends went on an 8 day (192 hours) backpacking trip and traveled 80 miles. The friends hiked at an average rate of 2 miles per hour. How many hours of the trip were they *not* hiking?

**Solution**

Write a verbal model. Let $t$ be the amount of time the friends were *not* hiking. Then $192 - t$ is the amount of time the friends were hiking.

| Distance (miles) | = | Rate (miles per hour) | · | Time spent hiking (hours) |
|---|---|---|---|---|

| | |
|---|---|
| $80 = 2(192 - t)$ | **Write an equation.** |
| $80 = 384 - 2t$ | **Distributive property** |
| $-304 = -2t$ | **Subtract 384 from each side.** |
| $152 = t$ | **Divide each side by −2.** |

▶ **Answer** The friends were not hiking for 152 hours of the trip.

**Practice for Examples 3 and 4**

**Solve the equation. Check your solution.**

**6.** $6(n - 2) = 4(n + 1)$    **7.** $9(m + 3) = 3(m + 7)$

**8.** In Example 4, suppose the friends take 6 days (144 hours) to hike the 80 miles. How many hours of the trip were they *not* hiking?

**Tell whether the given value of x is a solution of the equation.**

**1.** $6x + 1 - 5x = 7$; $x = 2$   **2.** $7 + 2(x - 4) = 3$; $x = 1$   **3.** $\frac{1}{2}(8x - 6) = 1$; $x = 1$

**State the first step in solving the equation.**

**4.** $13y + 7y - 6 = 11$   **5.** $5(a - 4) = 44$   **6.** $\frac{1}{3}(m - 4) = 5$

**7.** $7 + 6(w - 3) = 31$   **8.** $8d - 4 - 6d = 22$   **9.** $7 - 3(p + 6) = 27$

**Solve the equation. Check your solution.**

**10.** $3(6 - x) = 27$   **11.** $-2(x + 7) = 16$   **12.** $-40 = 4(x - 10)$

**13.** $20 = -5(x + 7)$   **14.** $-6(2x + 3) = 44$   **15.** $2 + 3(x + 1) = 17$

**16.** $15 + 4(m - 2) = 21$   **17.** $2(p + 3) + 2(p - 4) = 22$   **18.** $5(a + 2) - 3(a + 4) = 6$

**19.** $6(w + 5) = 2(w - 2) + 4$   **20.** $7(h + 2) = 9(h + 4) - 24$   **21.** $3(b - 3) = -2(b + 2) + 21$

**Find the value of x for the figure.**

**22.** Perimeter = 17 feet

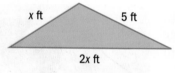

x ft   5 ft
2x ft

**23.** Perimeter = 18 meters

x m
2x m

**24.** Perimeter = 81 kilometers

18 km
x km   16 km
32 km

**25.** Perimeter = 4.75 miles

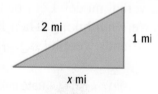

2 mi   1 mi
x mi

**26. REASONING** Are the equations $2(x + 3) - x = 5$ and $x + 3 = 5$ equivalent? *Explain* your reasoning.

**27.** The Donati family went on a 3 day trip and traveled 330 miles. They drove at an average rate of 55 miles per hour. How many hours of the trip were they *not* driving?

**28.** The target heart rate is the number of heartbeats per minute at which your heart should be beating during aerobic exercise. The target heart rate for a person exercising at 70% intensity is given by the equation $r = 0.7(220 - a)$ where $r$ is the target heart rate in beats per minute and $a$ is the person's age in years.

**a.** How old is a person with a target heart rate of 126 beats per minute?

**b.** How old is a person with a target heart rate of 112 beats per minute?

**Solve the equation. Check your solution.**

**1.** $9 + 4(x + 1) = 25$

**2.** $7(d + 5) - 12 = -5$

**3.** $10a + 5(a - 3) = 15$

**4.** $19a - 3(a - 6) = 66$

**5.** $6(c + 3) - 2(c - 2) = 10$

**6.** $4(d - 1) - 5(d + 2) = -3$

**7.** $10(n - 1) + 10(n - 2) = 30$

**8.** $9(w + 9) + 8(w - 2) = 116$

**9.** $6.4 + 2.1(z - 2) = 8.5$

**10.** $4.5 - 1.5(6m + 2) = 6$

**Find the value of $x$ for the figure.**

**11.** Perimeter = 23 feet

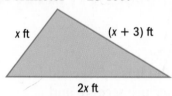

**12.** Perimeter = 24 meters

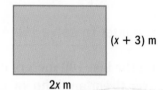

**13.** Perimeter = 29 yards

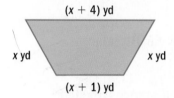

**14.** Perimeter = 62 inches

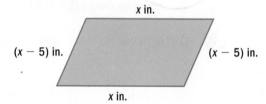

**15. REASONING** Are the equations $3(x + 4) + 5(x - 2) = 18$ and $8x + 2 = 18$ equivalent? *Explain* your reasoning.

**16.** You need 70 inches of ribbon to wrap a ribbon around the box shown and make a bow. The bow takes 32 inches of ribbon. The width of the box is 14 inches. What is the height of the box?

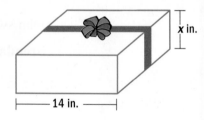

**17.** Maya drove to a vacation spot that is 1500 miles away. The trip took 42 hours. She estimated that she drove at an average speed of 50 miles per hour. How many hours was she *not* driving?

**18.** You have quarters and nickels saved in a piggy bank. The total value of the coins is $3.45, and there are 9 more nickels than quarters.

    **a.** Use the verbal model below to write an equation that you can use to find the number of quarters and nickels in your piggy bank. Let $q$ represent the number of quarters.

| Value of 1 quarter | · | Number of quarters | + | Value of 1 nickel | · | Number of nickels | = | Total amount in piggy bank |
|---|---|---|---|---|---|---|---|---|

    **b.** How many quarters and nickels are in the piggy bank?

## Modeling Rate Problems

| **Goal** | **Materials** |
| --- | --- |
| Use a model to solve a rate problem. | • graph paper <br> • colored pencils |

**QUESTION** How can you use a model to solve a rate problem in which one person overtakes another?

**EXPLORE** *Use a model to solve a rate problem* . . . . . . . . . . . .

Use a model to solve the following problem.

During the last 100 meters of a swimming race, John has a 5 second lead over Brendan. John swims at a speed of 0.4 meter per second, and Brendan swims at a speed of 0.5 meter per second. How long will it take Brendan to overtake John?

**1** **Determine** how far John swims in 5 seconds and how far Brendan swims in 5 seconds.

| **John:** | $d = rt$ | **Formula for distance traveled** |
| --- | --- | --- |
| | $= 0.4 \cdot 5$ | **Substitute 0.4 for *r* and 5 for *t*.** |
| | $= 2$ | **Multiply.** |

John swims 2 meters in 5 seconds.

| **Brendan:** | $d = rt$ | **Formula for distance traveled** |
| --- | --- | --- |
| | $= 0.5 \cdot 5$ | **Substitute 0.5 for *r* and 5 for *t*.** |
| | $= 2.5$ | **Multiply.** |

Brendan swims 2.5 meters in 5 seconds.

**2** **Copy** the two grids below onto a piece of graph paper. Label the first grid "John" and the second grid "Brendan." Make sure the grids are lined up as shown below. Each square represents 0.5 meter.

John

  1   2   3   4   5   6   7   8   9   10  11  12 (meters)

Brendan

**3** **Use** red to represent the first 5 seconds. John swims 2 meters in the first 5 seconds, so shade 4 squares on John's grid. John has a 5 second lead over Brendan, so don't shade any squares on Brendan's grid.

This represents the distance that John swam in 5 seconds.

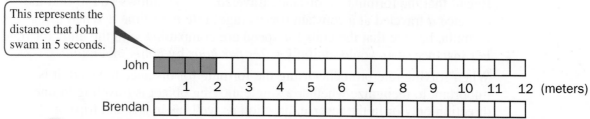

**4** **Use** blue to represent the next 5 seconds. During these 5 seconds John swims 2 more meters, so shade 4 more squares on John's grid. Brendan swims 2.5 meters during these 5 seconds, so shade 5 squares on Brendan's grid.

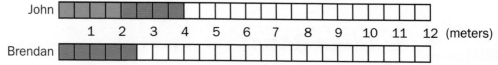

**5** **Repeat** Step 4 using a different color for each period of 5 seconds until John and Brendan have traveled the same distance.

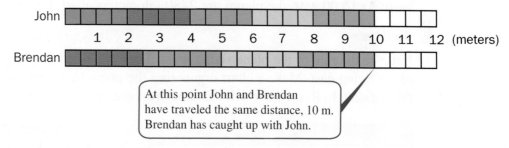

At this point John and Brendan have traveled the same distance, 10 m. Brendan has caught up with John.

**6** **Solve** the original problem. Each color represents a period of 5 seconds. After how many seconds does Brendan overtake John? There are four 5 second periods shaded on Brendan's grid, so Brendan overtakes John after 4(5) seconds, or 20 seconds.

## Draw Conclusions

**1.** Suppose John and Brendan start at opposite ends of a pool 18 meters long and swim toward each other. If they start at the same time, when will they meet?

Start with a *single* grid. Color each person's progress from each end after 5 seconds, after 5 more seconds, and so on until the colors meet.

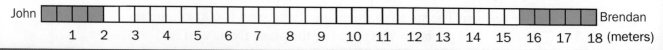

## VOCABULARY and CONCEPTS

- rate, p. 26

### Solving Rate Problems

Recall that the formula for distance traveled, $d = rt$, allows you to find the distance $d$ traveled at a constant (or average) rate $r$ for time $t$. When using this formula, be sure that the units for speed are compatible with the units for time. For instance, you would multiply *miles per hour* by *hours*, not *minutes*.

When solving rate problems using the formula for distance traveled, it is important to recognize whether a single moving object is traveling in one direction only or in the reverse direction as well (as in a round trip) or whether two moving objects are traveling in the same direction or in opposite directions. Drawing a diagram should make the direction of motion clear and help you to write an equation based on the distance(s) traveled.

**EXAMPLE 1** *Finding Rates* •••••••••••••••••••••••••••••••••••••

Two jets leave St. Louis at 8:00 A.M., one flying east at a speed that is 40 kilometers per hour greater than the speed of the other, which is traveling west. At 10:00 A.M. the planes are 2480 kilometers apart. Find their speeds.

### Solution

Let $r$ be the rate of the plane flying west. Then $r + 40$ is the rate of the plane flying east. Make a chart organizing the given facts and use it to label a sketch. Remember that east and west are *opposite directions*.

| Jet | Rate | × Time | = Distance |
|-----|------|--------|------------|
| Eastbound | $r + 40$ | 2 | $2(r + 40)$ |
| Westbound | $r$ | 2 | $2r$ |

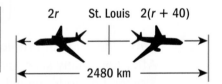

The distance between two objects moving in *opposite directions* is the sum of the separate distances traveled, which is 2480 kilometers.

| | |
|---|---|
| $2r + 2(r + 40) = 2480$ | **Write equation.** |
| $2r + 2r + 80 = 2480$ | **Distributive property** |
| $4r + 80 = 2480$ | **Combine like terms.** |
| $4r = 2400$ | **Subtract 80 from each side.** |
| $r = 600$ | **Divide each side by 4.** |

▶ **Answer** The speed of the plane flying west is 600 kilometers per hour. The speed of the plane flying east is $600 + 40 = 640$ kilometers per hour.

## Practice for Example 1

**1.** Two jets leave Ontario at the same time, one flying east at a speed 20 kilometers per hour greater than the speed of the other, which is flying west. After 4 hours, the planes are 6000 kilometers apart. Find their speeds.

**EXAMPLE 2** *Finding a Time* •••••••••••••••••••••••••••••••••

A small plane leaves an airport and flies north at 240 miles per hour. A jet leaves the airport 30 minutes later and follows the small plane at 360 miles per hour. How long does it take the jet to overtake the small plane?

### Solution

Let $t$ be the jet's flying time. Then $t + \frac{1}{2}$ is the small plane's flying time. Make a chart organizing the given facts and use it to label a sketch. Notice that 30 minutes must be written as $\frac{1}{2}$ hour.

| Plane | Rate | × Time | = Distance |
|---|---|---|---|
| Small plane | 240 | $t + \frac{1}{2}$ | $240\left(t + \frac{1}{2}\right)$ |
| Jet | 360 | $t$ | $360t$ |

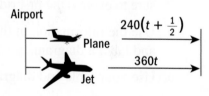

When the jet overtakes the small plane, the distances will be equal.

$$360t = 240\left(t + \frac{1}{2}\right)$$  **Write equation.**

$$360t = 240t + 120$$  **Distributive property**

$$120t = 120$$  **Subtract 240t from each side.**

$$t = 1$$  **Divide each side by 1.**

▶ **Answer** The jet overtakes the small plane in 1 hour.

## Practice for Example 2

**2.** A car left from Memphis headed toward Little Rock at the rate of 60 kilometers per hour. A second car left from the same point 2 hours later and drove along the same route at 75 kilometers per hour. How long did it take the second car to overtake the first car?

**3.** Two cars are 350 kilometers apart and drive toward each other. One car is moving at 65 kilometers per hour, and the other car is moving at 75 kilometers per hour. How long does it take for the two cars to meet?

# Practice

**Extra Practice**
p. 505

1. Two cars leave a baseball stadium at the same time, one driving north at a speed that is 10 kilometers per hour greater than the speed of the other, which is traveling south. After 2 hours the cars are 220 kilometers apart. Find their speeds.

2. Two cars leave an airport at 6:00 P.M. One drives west at a speed that is 5 kilometers per hour greater than the speed of the other, which is traveling east. After 3 hours the cars are 351 kilometers apart. Find their speeds.

3. Two camper vans leave Arrowhead Lake at the same time, one traveling north at a speed that is 10 kilometers per hour greater than the speed of the other, which is traveling south. After 3 hours, the camper vans are 420 kilometers apart. Find their speeds.

4. A bike rider leaves a park and rides east at 6 miles per hour. A second bike rider leaves the park 45 minutes later and follows the first bike rider at 9 miles per hour. How far do the bike riders travel before the second rider overtakes the first rider?

   a. Let $t$ be the second rider's riding time in hours. Copy and complete the table. Be sure to express the first rider's time in hours.

   | Bike rider | Rate × | Time | = Distance |
   |---|---|---|---|
   | First | ? | ? | ? |
   | Second | ? | $t$ | ? |

   b. Use the information in the table to draw and label a diagram.

   c. Use your table and diagram to write an equation for the problem.

   d. Solve the equation you wrote in part (c) to find how long it takes the second rider to overtake the first rider.

   e. Notice that finding the time that it takes the second rider to overtake the first does not answer the question in the problem. Answer the question and then check your answer.

5. At 10:00 A.M. a car left a service station on Route 209 heading south at 80 kilometers per hour. At 10:30 A.M. another car left the station and headed south at 86 kilometers per hour. How long did it take the second car to overtake the first car?

6. Jenny's house is 7 kilometers from Karen's house. Each girl left her house at the same time heading toward the other's house. Jenny walked, Karen rode her bike, and the two met in just half an hour. If Karen's speed was 1 kilometer per hour less than twice Jenny's speed, how far did Karen travel?

7. **REASONING** Two objects are a fixed distance apart and start moving toward each other, one at twice the speed of the other. Predict where the objects will meet. *Explain* your reasoning.

1. Two vans leave a warehouse at 7.30 A.M., one driving north at a speed that is 7 kilometers per hour greater than the speed of the other, which is traveling south. At 1:30 P.M. the vans are 738 kilometers apart. Find their speeds.

2. Two planes 1350 miles apart are flying toward each other at different assigned altitudes. One is flying at 250 miles per hour and the other at 290 miles per hour. How long will it take the planes to pass each other?

3. Two trains left a station at the same time and traveled in opposite directions. One train traveled for 78 minutes. The other train traveled for 144 minutes at a rate that was 5 kilometers per hour faster than the speed of the first train. The faster train went twice as far as the slower train. How far did each train travel?

   a. Let *r* be the slower train's speed in kilometers per hour. Copy and complete the table. Since the rate is given in kilometers per hour, express the times in hours using decimals.

   | Train | Rate | × Time | = Distance |
   |-------|------|--------|------------|
   | Slower train | r | ? | ? |
   | Faster train | ? | ? | ? |

   b. Use the information in the table to draw and label a diagram.

   c. Use your table and diagram to write an equation for the problem.

   d. Solve the equation you wrote in part (c) to find each train's speed.

   e. Notice that finding the trains' speeds does not answer the question in the problem. Answer the question and then check your answer.

4. The average speeds of two runners are 4 yards per second and 5 yards per second. The slower runner was given a $7\frac{1}{2}$ second head start in a race that ended in a tie. What distance did they race?

5. A tourist bus leaves Richmond at 1:00 P.M. for New York City. Exactly 24 minutes later, a truck sets out in the same direction. The tourist bus travels 60 kilometers per hour. The truck travels at 80 kilometers per hour. How long does it take the truck to overtake the tourist bus?

6. Exactly 20 minutes after Alex left home, his sister Alison set out to overtake him. Alex drove at 48 miles per hour, and Alison drove at 54 miles per hour. How long did it take Alison to overtake Alex?

7. The McLeans drove to Dayton at 75 kilometers per hour. When they returned, they drove at 50 kilometers per hour. It took them 1 hour longer to return than to go. How long did it take them to drive home?

8. **REASONING** One runner can run 10% faster than another runner, who runs at a rate *r*. How much of a head start should the slower runner get so that the runners finish a race in the same time *t*? Give your answer in terms of *r* and *t*. *Explain* your reasoning.

## Problem

Lydia can run at a rate of 8 yards per second. Her younger sister, Hannah, can run at a rate of 6 yards per second. Lydia and Hannah agree to race for 100 yards. Lydia gives Hannah a 30 yard head start. Who wins the race?

### Solution

**1** **Graph** the distance traveled every 3 seconds for each sister.

Write ordered pairs in the form (time $t$, distance $d$) for each sister.

Hannah has a 30 yard head start, so plot the point (0, 30).
Lydia starts at (0, 0).

Find the distance each sister travels every 3 seconds.

*Make precise calculations as part of MR 2.8.*

| **Hannah** | **Lydia** |
|---|---|
| $d = rt$ | $d = rt$ |
| $= 6(3)$ | $= 8(3)$ |
| $= 18$ | $= 24$ |

Use these distances to write ordered pairs for the total distance traveled by each sister after 3, 6, and 9 seconds.

**Hannah**
(3, 48)
(6, 66)  — Add 18 yards to the $d$-coordinate for every 3 second increase in the $t$-coordinate.
(9, 84)

**Lydia**
(3, 24)
(6, 48)  — Add 24 yards to the $d$-coordinate for every 3 second increase in the $t$-coordinate.
(9, 72)

Plot the ordered pairs.

*Use a graph to estimate as part of MR 2.3.*

**2** **Use** the graph to predict who wins the race.

Notice that since each sister travels at a constant speed, each set of points lies on a line. Draw a line through each set of points. Then draw a horizontal line at $d = 100$ to represent the end of the race.

Because the line for Hannah crosses the line at $d = 100$ first, it appears that Hannah wins the race.

*Check the reasonableness of the solution in the context of the problem as part of MR 3.1.*

**3** **Check** the reasonableness of the result.

Hannah has 70 yards to run. Running at 6 yards per second, she covers the distance in a little less than 12 seconds because $70 \div 6 < 12$.

Lydia has 100 yards to run. Running at 8 yards per second, she covers the distance in a little more than 12 seconds because $100 \div 8 > 12$.

# Practice

1. Evan and Colby are both saving for a video game. Evan already has $15 and Colby already has $10. Each week Evan saves an additional $2 and Colby saves an additional $3. **MR 2.3, MR 3.1, MR 3.2**

> ### Game Land
>
> Video Games $50
> Hand-Held Game Systems $75
> Game Systems $150

   **a.** Use a graph to estimate the number of weeks until Colby's savings equals Evan's savings. Will Colby be able to buy the game first? Check that your answer is reasonable.

   **b.** How is the process you used to solve this problem similar to that used in the problem on the previous page?

2. Show how the equation $ax + b = c$ where $a \neq 0$ can be solved for $x$. Then show how the solution you obtain can be used to find the solution of $3x + 2 = 14$. **MR 3.3**

3. Keri can run at a rate of 8 yards per second and Andy can run at a rate of 9 yards per second. Andy gives Keri a 3 second head start and they race a distance of 200 yards. **MR 2.8, MR 3.1**

   **a.** Write an equation to model when Andy catches up to Keri.

   **b.** Use the equation you wrote in part (a) to determine after how many seconds Andy catches up with Keri.

   **c.** Determine who wins the race. *Explain* your reasoning.

   **d.** Check your answer for reasonableness.

4. Solve the equations $2x + 1 = 3$, $2x + 1 = 5$, and $2x + 1 = 7$, then predict the solution of $2x + 1 = 9$. *Explain* your reasoning. **MR 1.1**

5. John is saving money by placing all of his spare dimes in a jar. The jar, when half full, weighs 2 pounds. When empty, the jar weighed 0.2 pound. When the jar is full, how many dimes will John have? **MR 1.1, MR 1.3, MR 2.2**

180 pennies weigh 1 pound.    200 dimes weigh 1 pound.

90 nickels weigh 1 pound.    80 quarters weigh 1 pound.

6. A fitness center offers yoga classes for $10 per class and sells yoga mats for $19.95. Shonda paid a total of $139.95 to the fitness center for yoga classes and a mat. **MR 2.5, 2.6**

   **a.** Part of a table showing the number of classes and the total cost, including one mat, is shown below. *Explain* how you could use the table to find the number of yoga classes Shonda took.

| Number of classes | Total cost (dollars) |
|---|---|
| 0 | 19.95 |
| 1 | 29.95 |
| 2 | 39.95 |
| 3 | 49.95 |

   **b.** *Explain* how you could solve this problem using an equation. Then solve the problem using an equation.

## Materials
- paper
- pencil

## Riddle

Solve each of the equations below.

Copy the boxes at the bottom of the page. Then locate the solution of each equation and cross out the box containing the solution.

Unscramble the remaining letters in the boxes to find the answer to the following riddle:

**What did the computer do at lunchtime?**

**1.** $5x = -25$

**2.** $x + 9.6 = 7.8$

**3.** $3x - 8 = 16$

**4.** $\frac{x}{4} + 2 = -3$

**5.** $x - 2(x + 4) = 10$

**6.** $\frac{2}{3}(4x - 1) = -22$

**7.** $2(5x + 8) = -(x + 17)$

**8.** $29 - 15x = -46$

**9.** $\frac{x}{3} - 4 = -2$

**10.** $4(x + 9) = 12$

**11.** $5(x + 8) = 3(2x + 4)$

**12.** $36 = 0.96x$

**13.** $6(x - 3) = 4x$

**14.** $2.3x + 4.5 = 0.3 - 0.5x$

**15.** $4.7x - 2.5 + 2.7x = 12.8 - 1.6x$

**16.** $\frac{3}{4}x + \frac{1}{8}(x - 5) = \frac{1}{4}$

**17.** $\frac{1}{2}(x - 1) = 3$

**18.** $-10 = \frac{x}{8} - 15$

**19.** $4(2x + 3) = 6(2 - x)$

**20.** $4.9 = 0.25x$

**21.** $3x + 8(x - 1.9) = 7.9$

**22.** $-4x + 20 = 12x + 36$

| $x = 4$ | $x = -20$ | $x = 7.1$ | $x = 5$ | $x = 8$ | $x = -9$ |
|---|---|---|---|---|---|
| Y | X | B | V | P | A |
| $x = 1.7$ | $x = 2.8$ | $x = 37.5$ | $x = 40$ | $x = 7$ | $x = 9$ |
| C | E | F | L | K | S |
| $x = 1$ | $x = 2.1$ | $x = -5$ | $x = 35$ | $x = -8$ | $x = 19.6$ |
| J | O | M | H | W | R |
| $x = 3$ | $x = -3$ | $x = 1.5$ | $x = -1.8$ | $x = -1$ | $x = -1.5$ |
| T | I | D | O | P | U |
| $x = -18$ | $x = 0$ | $x = 6$ | $x = 28$ | $x = 18$ | $x = -6$ |
| R | N | G | Z | A | Q |

$\underline{\phantom{?}}$ $\underline{?}$ $\underline{\phantom{?}}$ $\underline{?}$ $\underline{\phantom{?}}$ $\underline{?}$ $\underline{\phantom{?}}$ $\underline{?}$ $\underline{\phantom{?}}$ $\underline{?}$ $\underline{\phantom{?}}$ $\underline{?}$ $\underline{\phantom{?}}$ $\underline{?}$ $\underline{\phantom{?}}$ $\underline{?}$ !

> **VOCABULARY**
> - equation, p. 324
> - equivalent equations, p. 324
> - inverse operation, p. 324
> - solution of an equation, p. 324

## Vocabulary Exercises

1. Copy and complete: An operation that "undoes" another operation is called a(n)  ? .

2. Copy and complete: A number that produces a true statement when substituted for the variable in an equation is called a(n)  ? .

## 8.1 Solve Equations Involving Addition or Subtraction pp. 324–327

**EXAMPLES**   Solve (a) $r + 3 = -14$ and (b) $m - 2 = -1$.

a.
$$r + 3 = -14 \qquad \text{Write original equation.}$$
$$r + 3 - 3 = -14 - 3 \qquad \text{Subtract 3 from each side.}$$
$$r = -17 \qquad \text{Simplify.}$$

b.
$$m - 2 = -1 \qquad \text{Write original equation.}$$
$$m - 2 + 2 = -1 + 2 \qquad \text{Add 2 to each side.}$$
$$m = 1 \qquad \text{Simplify.}$$

Solve the equation. Check your solution.

3. $y + 5 = 12$

4. $h - 3 = -10$

5. $-9 = s + 7$

## 8.2 Solve Equations Involving Multiplication or Division pp. 330–333

**EXAMPLES**   Solve (a) $6p = -18$ and (b) $\dfrac{q}{6} = -2$.

a. $6p = -18$    Write original equation.

$$\frac{6p}{6} = \frac{-18}{6} \qquad \text{Divide each side by 6.}$$

$$p = -3 \qquad \text{Simplify.}$$

b. $\dfrac{q}{6} = -2$    Write original equation.

$$6\left(\frac{q}{6}\right) = 6(-2) \qquad \text{Multiply each side by 6.}$$

$$q = -12 \qquad \text{Simplify.}$$

Solve the equation. Check your solution.

6. $\dfrac{w}{4} = 8$

7. $\dfrac{d}{8} = 1.25$

8. $0.25z = -1.75$

**8.3** *Solve Two-Step Equations* ..................................... **pp. 336–339**

**EXAMPLE**

| | |
|---|---|
| $4t + 9 = 1$ | Original equation |
| $4t + 9 - 9 = 1 - 9$ | Subtract 9 from each side. |
| $4t = -8$ | Simplify. |
| $t = -2$ | Divide each side by 4. |

**Solve the equation. Check your solution.**

**9.** $3n + 5 = 7$ **10.** $\dfrac{k}{2} - 8 = -5$ **11.** $-6f + 14 = 32$

**8.4** *Solve Equations with Fractions and Decimals* .... **pp. 344–347**

To clear fractions, multiply each side of the equation by the LCD of the fractions.

**EXAMPLE**

| | |
|---|---|
| $\dfrac{3}{4}x + \dfrac{1}{6} = -\dfrac{1}{3}$ | Original equation |
| $12\left(\dfrac{3}{4}x + \dfrac{1}{6}\right) = 12\left(-\dfrac{1}{3}\right)$ | Multiply each side by LCD of fractions. |
| $12\left(\dfrac{3}{4}x\right) + 12\left(\dfrac{1}{6}\right) = 12\left(-\dfrac{1}{3}\right)$ | Use distributive property. |
| $9x + 2 = -4$ | Simplify. |
| $9x + 2 - 2 = -4 - 2$ | Subtract 2 from each side. |
| $9x = -6$ | Simplify. |
| $\dfrac{9x}{9} = \dfrac{-6}{9}$ | Divide each side by 9. |
| $x = -\dfrac{2}{3}$ | Simplify. |

To clear decimals, multiply each side of the equation by 10 raised to the power equal to the greatest number of decimal places in any decimal.

**EXAMPLE**

| | |
|---|---|
| $4.17 = 2 - 0.35m$ | Original equation |
| $100(4.17) = 100(2 - 0.35m)$ | Multiply each side by $10^2$, or 100. |
| $417 = 200 - 35m$ | Use distributive property. Simplify. |
| $417 - 200 = 200 - 35m - 200$ | Subtract 200 from each side. |
| $217 = -35m$ | Simplify. |
| $\dfrac{217}{-35} = \dfrac{-35m}{-35}$ | Divide each side by $-35$. |
| $-6.2 = m$ | Simplify. |

**Solve the equation by first clearing the fractions or decimals.**

**12.** $\dfrac{2}{3}q - \dfrac{5}{12} = \dfrac{13}{20}$ **13.** $-0.2h + 1.4 = 2.3$ **14.** $\dfrac{5}{6}s - \dfrac{7}{8} = -\dfrac{11}{4}$

## 8.5 Solve Equations Using the Distributive Property pp. 350–353

**EXAMPLE** Solve $4(5d - 7) = -88$.

| | |
|---|---|
| $4(5d - 7) = -88$ | Write original equation. |
| $20d - 28 = -88$ | Distributive property |
| $20d - 28 + 28 = -88 + 28$ | Add 28 to each side. |
| $20d = -60$ | Simplify. |
| $\dfrac{20d}{20} = \dfrac{-60}{20}$ | Divide each side by 20. |
| $d = -3$ | Simplify. |

**Solve the equation. Check your solution.**

**15.** $3(4 - u) = 6$      **16.** $2(g + 5) = 10$      **17.** $-7 + 4(b - 1) = 3$

## 8.6 Solve Rate Problems ........................ pp. 356–359

Recall that the formula for distance traveled, $d = rt$, allows you to find the distance $d$ traveled at a constant (or average) rate $r$ for time $t$.

**EXAMPLE** Two planes left Chicago at the same time flying in opposite directions. One plane flew at 540 miles per hour, and the other plane flew at 720 miles per hour. After how many hours were the planes 1890 miles apart?

Make a chart organizing the given facts and use it to label a sketch.

| Plane | Rate | × Time | = Distance |
|---|---|---|---|
| Slower | 540 | $t$ | $540t$ |
| Faster | 720 | $t$ | $720t$ |

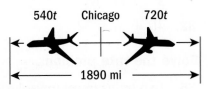

The distance between two objects moving in *opposite directions* is the sum of the separate distances traveled.

| | |
|---|---|
| $540t + 720t = 1890$ | Write equation. |
| $1260t = 1890$ | Combine like terms. |
| $t = 1.5$ | Divide each side by 1260. |

▶ **Answer** The planes were 1890 miles apart after 1.5 hours.

**Solve the following rate problem.**

**18.** A hiker walks westward from camp at 3 miles per hour. At the same time, another hiker walks eastward from camp at 2 miles per hour. After how many hours will the hikers be 12.5 miles apart?

# Chapter Test

**Write the verbal sentence as an equation. Then solve the equation.**

**1.** The sum of a number and 7 is 16.

**2.** The difference of a number and 12 is 5.

**3.** Four times a number equals 72.

**4.** The quotient of a number and 7 is 12.

**Tell whether the given value of the variable is a solution of the equation.**

**5.** $x + 6 = 21; x = 15$

**6.** $b - 8 = 15; b = 22$

**7.** $m - 12 = 36; m = 48$

**8.** $11a = 45; a = 4$

**9.** $\frac{x}{7} = 14; x = 98$

**10.** $\frac{3}{4}m = 9; m = 16$

**Solve the equation. Check your solution.**

**11.** $d + 7 = 4$

**12.** $-12 = u - 8$

**13.** $5.6 = k - 3.8$

**14.** $5r = 40$

**15.** $-3w = 12$

**16.** $\frac{g}{8} = 6$

**17.** $\frac{4}{3}b = 16$

**18.** $\frac{2}{5}f = -8$

**19.** $3 = \frac{3}{4}j$

**20.** $3c + 2 = 14$

**21.** $\frac{m}{9} + 3 = 7$

**22.** $\frac{h}{7} - 3 = 9$

**Tell what number you would multiply each side of the equation by to clear the decimals or fractions.**

**23.** $2.9x + 3 = 5.6$

**24.** $9.16b - 1.28b = 12.2$

**25.** $6.9y - 2y = 12.5$

**26.** $\frac{2}{3}w + 4 = \frac{1}{3}$

**27.** $\frac{1}{4}m + \frac{5}{6}m = \frac{11}{2}$

**28.** $\frac{5}{6}y - \frac{1}{5}y = 10$

**Solve the equation. Check your solution.**

**29.** $\frac{2}{3}y - \frac{1}{4} = \frac{5}{6}$

**30.** $-\frac{1}{2}n + \frac{4}{5} = \frac{7}{10}$

**31.** $6.2z + 2.8 = 3.73$

**32.** $4(t + 3) = 32$

**33.** $6(5a - 3) = 42$

**34.** $5(11 - 2v) = 135$

**Solve the rate problem.**

**35.** Two trains travel toward each other from points that are 200 miles apart. The eastbound train travels at 45 miles per hour, and the westbound train travels at 55 miles per hour. If the trains start at the same time, in how many hours will they meet?

| Train | Rate | × Time | = Distance |
|---|---|---|---|
| Eastbound | 45 | $t$ | $45t$ |
| Westbound | 55 | $t$ | $55t$ |

**36.** Mandi and Nina leave a movie theater at the same time, but travel in opposite directions. Mandi is walking home, and Nina is taking the bus. Nina's speed is 9 times Mandi's speed. After $\frac{1}{4}$ hour, they are 5 miles apart. What is Nina's speed?

| Person | Rate | × Time | = Distance |
|---|---|---|---|
| Mandi | $r$ | $\frac{1}{4}$ | $\frac{1}{4}t$ |
| Nina | $9r$ | $\frac{1}{4}$ | $\frac{9}{4}t$ |

1. What equation represents the following verbal sentence?
   The sum of 3 and a number is $-8$.

   Ⓐ $3 = -8 + n$   Ⓑ $3 + n = -8$

   Ⓒ $n = -8 + 3$   Ⓓ $3n = -8$

2. Ann's heart rate is 125 beats per minute when jogging. This is 55 beats per minute more than her resting heart rate. Which equation can be used to find Ann's resting heart rate $r$?

   Ⓐ $55r = 125$   Ⓑ $r + 55 = 125$

   Ⓒ $r - 55 = 125$   Ⓓ $\frac{r}{55} = 125$

3. What is the solution of $4r = -16$?

   Ⓐ $r = -64$   Ⓑ $r = -4$

   Ⓒ $r = 4$   Ⓓ $r = 64$

4. Which equation can be used to find the value of $x$ in the figure below?

   $A = 1.8$ in.$^2$   0.3 in.

   $x$ in.

   Ⓐ $x - 0.3 = 1.8$   Ⓑ $0.3 = 1.8x$

   Ⓒ $0.3 + x = 1.8$   Ⓓ $1.8 = 0.3x$

5. What number is the solution of $0.5a - 1.5 = -5$?

   Ⓐ $a = -1.75$   Ⓑ $a = 1.75$

   Ⓒ $a = -7$   Ⓓ $a = 13$

6. A used softcover book costs $16 less than the new hardcover book. The softcover book costs $9. Which equation can be used to find the cost $c$ of the hardcover book?

   Ⓐ $c + 16 = 9$   Ⓑ $c + 9 = 16$

   Ⓒ $16 - c = 9$   Ⓓ $c - 16 = 9$

7. What is the solution of $\frac{4}{5}u = 10$?

   Ⓐ $u = 4$   Ⓑ $u = 8$

   Ⓒ $u = 12\frac{1}{2}$   Ⓓ $u = 25$

8. Jake has $115 to buy a baseball bat and balls. He buys a bat for $83.50. Each ball costs $4.50. How many balls does Jake buy?

   Ⓐ 7   Ⓑ 8

   Ⓒ 9   Ⓓ 10

9. Two cars leave a rest area at the same time. One drives east at a speed that is 15 miles per hour greater than the speed of the other, which is traveling west. After 2 hours, the cars are 230 miles apart. What is the speed of the slower car?

   Ⓐ 35 mi/h   Ⓑ 50 mi/h

   Ⓒ 60 mi/h   Ⓓ 65 mi/h

10. What is the solution of
    $-3x + 4 + 5x = -6$?

    Ⓐ $x = -12$   Ⓑ $x = -5$

    Ⓒ $x = -1.25$   Ⓓ $x = -1$

11. Barry begins biking on a trail and travels at a rate of 8 miles per hour. Ariel leaves from the same location 15 minutes later and travels at a rate of 10 miles per hour. How long will it take for Ariel to overtake Barry?

    | Rider | Rate | × | Time | = | Distance |
    |-------|------|---|------|---|----------|
    | Barry | 8 | | $t + \frac{1}{4}$ | | $8\left(t + \frac{1}{4}\right)$ |
    | Ariel | 10 | | $t$ | | $10t$ |

    Ⓐ $\frac{1}{2}$ hour   Ⓑ 1 hour

    Ⓒ $1\frac{1}{2}$ hours   Ⓓ 2 hours

# Inequalities in One Variable

## Vocabulary for Chapter 9

### Key Mathematical Vocabulary
- **inequality, p. 372**
- **graph of an inequality, p. 372**
- **equivalent inequalities, p. 378**

### Academic Vocabulary
- **check** Examine the solution of a problem and determine whether the solution is correct or reasonable. For example, see Example 2 on page 378.
- **explain, p. 371**
- **describe, p. 380**
- **compare, p. 385**

Calculating the number of paintings you need to sell to make a profit, page 395

**Gr. 7 AF 4.1** Solve two-step linear equations and inequalities in one variable over the rational numbers, interpret the solution or solutions in the context from which they arose, and verify the reasonableness of the results.

**Gr. 7 AF 1.1** Use variables and appropriate operations to write an expression, an equation, an inequality, or a system of equations or inequalities that represents a verbal description (e.g., three less than a number, half as large as area A).

# Review Prerequisite Skills

### REVIEW VOCABULARY

- inverse operations, p. 324
- equivalent equations, p. 324
- solution of an equation, p. 324

## VOCABULARY CHECK

**Copy and complete the statement.**

1. A(n) _?_ in one variable is a number that produces a true statement when substituted for the variable in the equation.

2. Two equations that have the same solution are _?_.

3. _?_ are operations that "undo" each other.

## SKILLS CHECK

**Copy and complete the statement using <, >, or =. (Review pp. 162 and 204 for 9.1–9.4)**

4. $-5$ _?_ $-3$

5. $3.02$ _?_ $-3.2$

6. $-\dfrac{4}{3}$ _?_ $-1\dfrac{1}{3}$

**Solve the equation. Check your solution. (Review p. 324 for 9.2.)**

7. $y + 22 = 7$

8. $n - 15 = 24$

9. $x + 8 = -11$

10. $a - 9 = 17$

11. $32 + r = 5$

12. $w - 18 = -8$

**Solve the equation. Check your solution. (Review p. 330 for 9.3.)**

13. $5b = 35$

14. $\dfrac{r}{3} = 14$

15. $\dfrac{x}{-7} = 9$

16. $-8a = 48$

17. $-15w = 5$

18. $\dfrac{y}{10} = -2$

**Solve the equation. Check your solution. (Review p. 336 for 9.4.)**

19. $8m - 4 = 12$

20. $\dfrac{x}{5} + 10 = 13$

21. $8 - 7n = -41$

22. $8 = -40 + 6y$

23. $-5p + 25 = 20$

24. $\dfrac{r}{-9} + 15 = 20$

# Let's Explore
## Investigating Solutions of Simple Inequalities

**Goal**
Identify and write simple inequalities.

**Materials**
• index cards

**QUESTION** How can you recognize solutions of and write a simple inequality?

An *inequality* is a mathematical sentence formed by placing an inequality symbol between two expressions.

| Symbol | Meaning |
|--------|---------|
| < | is less than |
| ≤ | is less than or equal to |
| > | is greater than |
| ≥ | is greater than or equal to |

**EXPLORE 1** *Identify the solutions of simple inequalities*

**1** **Write** the integers from −5 to 5 on index cards and display them in numerical order as shown below. Also write three dots on two index cards and place the cards at each end of the display as shown.

... −5 −4 −3 −2 −1 0 1 2 3 4 5 ...

**2** **Determine** whether each integer is a solution of $x \leq 2$. If the integer is *not* a solution, turn over the card. Which numbers are left face up?

... −5 −4 −3 −2 −1 0 1 2 ...

**3** **Turn** all the cards face up. Repeat Step 2 for the inequality $x < 2$. How are the solutions of $x < 2$ different from those of $x \leq 2$ in Step 2?

... −5 −4 −3 −2 −1 0 1 ...

## Draw Conclusions

**1.** Is 2 a solution of the inequality $x < 0$? *Explain* your reasoning.

**2.** Is $-1$ a solution of the inequality $x \geq -4$? *Explain* your reasoning.

**3.** Is 3 a solution of the inequality $x < 3$, the inequality $x \leq 3$, or both? *Explain* your reasoning.

**4.** Is $-4$ a solution of the inequality $x \geq -4$, the inequality $x > -4$, or both? *Explain* your reasoning.

**5.** Based on your answers to Exercises 3 and 4, explain the difference between $\geq$ and $>$ (or $\leq$ and $<$).

**EXPLORE 2** *Write simple inequalities* ............................

**1** **Work** with a partner. Using the ordered, face-up index cards from Step 1 of Explore 1, one of you should turn over a series of consecutive cards starting at either the left or right end.

$$\ldots \quad -5 \quad -4 \quad -3 \quad -2 \quad \ldots$$

**2** **Write** an inequality. The other partner should write a simple inequality using $\leq$ or $\geq$ to represent the numbers shown.

$$x \leq -2$$

**3** **Switch** roles and repeat Steps 1 and 2.

## Draw Conclusions
**Write a simple inequality using $\geq$ or $\leq$.**

**6.**

$$\ldots \qquad\qquad 0 \quad 1 \quad 2 \quad 3 \quad 4 \quad 5 \quad \ldots$$

**7.**

$$\ldots \quad -5 \quad -4 \quad -3 \quad -2 \quad -1 \quad 0 \quad 1 \quad 2 \quad 3 \qquad \ldots$$

**8.** Carl wrote the inequality $x > 1$ for the numbers shown below.

$$\ldots \qquad\qquad\qquad 1 \quad 2 \quad 3 \quad 4 \quad 5 \quad \ldots$$

Is he correct? *Explain* your reasoning.

# Write and Graph Simple Inequalities

## VOCABULARY and CONCEPTS

- An **inequality** is a mathematical sentence formed by placing an inequality symbol between two expressions.

- A **solution of an inequality** in one variable is a number that produces a true statement when substituted for the variable in the inequality.

- The **graph of an inequality** in one variable is the set of points on a number line that represents the solutions of the inequality.

### Interpreting and Graphing Inequalities

Use the table below to become familiar with the meaning of each inequality symbol and to recognize commonly used phrases that indicate inequality.

| Symbol | Meaning | Commonly used phrases |
|--------|---------|----------------------|
| $<$ | is less than | fewer than; under |
| $\leq$ | is less than or equal to | at most; no more than; up to |
| $>$ | is greater than | more than; over |
| $\geq$ | is greater than or equal to | at least; no less than; from |

When graphing an inequality, an *open dot* is used to show that a point is not included in the solution. A *closed dot* is used to show that a point is included. Use an open dot if the inequality symbol is $<$ or $>$. Use a closed dot if the inequality symbol is $\leq$ or $\geq$.

---

**EXAMPLE 1** *Graphing Inequalities*

| Inequality | Graph | Verbal Phrase |
|------------|-------|---------------|
| **a.** $x > 8$ | | All numbers greater than 8 |
| **b.** $y \leq -1$ | | All numbers less than or equal to $-1$ |
| **c.** $h < 4\frac{1}{2}$ | | All numbers less than $4\frac{1}{2}$ |
| **d.** $q \geq -3$ | | All numbers greater than or equal to $-3$ |

### Practice for Example 1

**Graph the inequality.**

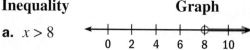

**1.** $m > -2$      **2.** $n \leq 3$      **3.** $k < -5.5$      **4.** $y \geq -\frac{1}{2}$

**EXAMPLE 2** *Writing an Inequality from a Graph*

**Write an inequality represented by the graph.**

a.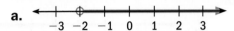

b.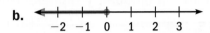

**Solution**

a. The graph shows all numbers greater than $-2$. Because there is an open dot at $-2$, use the $>$ symbol. An inequality represented by the graph is $x > -2$.

b. The graph shows all numbers less than or equal to 0. Because there is a closed dot at 0, use the $\leq$ symbol. An inequality represented by the graph is $x \leq 0$.

**EXAMPLE 3** *Writing an Inequality from a Common Phrase*

**Write the common phrase as an inequality.**

| Verbal Phrase | Inequality |
|---|---|
| a. No more than 5 | $x \leq 5$ |
| b. 1 or more | $x \geq 1$ |

**EXAMPLE 4** *Solving a Real-World Problem*

A travel agency advertises vacations to the Caribbean starting from $499 per person. Write an inequality that represents the possible vacation costs $C$ for one person.

**Solution**

The cost $C$ starts at $499, which is the lowest possible cost for the vacation. Use the greater than or equal to symbol ($\geq$) to show that the cost is at least $499. The inequality that represents the possible costs is $C \geq 499$.

**Practice for Examples 2, 3, and 4**

5. Write an inequality represented by the graph.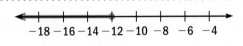

6. Write the common phrase "fewer than 12" as an inequality.

7. The temperature in Millerstown stayed above 42°F during the summer. Write an inequality that represents the temperature $T$.

# Practice

**Extra Practice**
p. 506

**Graph the inequality.**

**1.** $x < -2$  **2.** $a \leq 1\frac{1}{2}$  **3.** $m \geq 0$  **4.** $y > 3\frac{1}{2}$

**Write an inequality represented by the graph.**

**5.**

**6.**

**7.**

**8.**

**Match the inequality with its graph.**

**9.** $x < -4$  **A.**

**10.** $x \leq -4$  **B.**

**11.** $x > -4$  **C.**

**12.** $x \geq -4$  **D.**

**Write the common phrase as an inequality.**

**13.** 10 or more

**14.** No less than 2

**15.** Fewer than 5

**16.** No more than 4

**Match the inequality with its verbal phrase.**

**17.** $x < 7$  **A.** All numbers less than or equal to 7

**18.** $x > 7$  **B.** All numbers greater than 7

**19.** $x \leq 7$  **C.** All numbers greater than or equal to 7

**20.** $x \geq 7$  **D.** All numbers less than 7

**Write an inequality to represent the situation. Then graph the inequality.**

**21.** To ride an amusement park ride, you must be 48 inches tall or taller.

**22.** A restaurant can hold at most 40 people.

**23.** To be president of the United States, you must be at least 35 years old.

**24.** You have less than $3.25 in your pocket.

**25.** Lisa ran more than 2.2 miles.

**26.** **REASONING** You are given the inequality $m < 1$. Must a solution of the inequality be a negative number? *Explain.*

# Practice

**Graph the inequality.**

**1.** $x > -9.1$     **2.** $a \geq \dfrac{1}{2}$     **3.** $m \leq -0.3$     **4.** $y < 73$

**Write an inequality represented by the graph.**

**5.**

$$\text{0  1  2  3  4  5  6  7  8}$$

**6.**

$$-5 \;\; -4 \;\; -3 \;\; -2 \;\; -1 \;\; 0 \;\; 1 \;\; 2 \;\; 3$$

**7.**

$$-15 \;\; -10 \;\; -5 \;\; 0 \;\; 5 \;\; 10 \;\; 15 \;\; 20 \;\; 25$$

**8.**

$$-9 \;\; -8 \;\; -7 \;\; -6 \;\; -5 \;\; -4 \;\; -3 \;\; -2 \;\; -1$$

**Match the inequality with its graph.**

**9.** $x < 0$  **A.**
$$-2 \;\; -1 \;\; 0 \;\; 1 \;\; 2$$

**10.** $x \leq 0$  **B.**
$$-2 \;\; -1 \;\; 0 \;\; 1 \;\; 2$$

**11.** $x \geq 0$  **C.**
$$-2 \;\; -1 \;\; 0 \;\; 1 \;\; 2$$

**12.** $x > 0$  **D.**
$$-2 \;\; -1 \;\; 0 \;\; 1 \;\; 2$$

**Write the common phrase as an inequality.**

**13.** 6 or less

**14.** No more than 3

**15.** No less than 2

**16.** 8 or more

**Match the inequality with its verbal phrase.**

**17.** $x < \dfrac{3}{2}$   **A.** All numbers greater than $\dfrac{3}{2}$

**18.** $x \geq \dfrac{3}{2}$   **B.** All numbers greater than or equal to $\dfrac{3}{2}$

**19.** $x > \dfrac{3}{2}$   **C.** All numbers less than $\dfrac{3}{2}$

**20.** $x \leq \dfrac{3}{2}$   **D.** All numbers less than or equal to $\dfrac{3}{2}$

**Write an inequality to represent the situation. Then graph the inequality.**

**21.** To ride an amusement park ride, you must be 52 inches tall or taller.

**22.** A restaurant can hold at most 45 people.

**23.** In most states, you must be at least 16 years old to drive a motor vehicle.

**24.** Mac has more than $6.75 in his wallet.

**25.** The temperature is below 65°F.

**26.** **REASONING** You are given the inequality $x < a$ where $a$ is a real number. If a solution of the inequality cannot be positive, what do you know about $a$?

## Let's Explore
# Inequalities Involving Addition or Subtraction

**Goal**
Investigate inequalities having the same solutions.

**Materials**
• paper and pencil

**QUESTION** **How can you determine whether two inequalities have the same solutions?**

Two inequalities that have the same solutions are called *equivalent*.

**EXPLORE 1** *Determine whether inequalities are equivalent*

**1** **Make** a table like the one shown. Use the table to determine if each value of
$x$ is a solution of $x + 1 \geq -2$.

| $x + 1 \geq -2$ | | |
|---|---|---|
| $x$ | Substitute. | Solution? |
| $-5$ | $-5 + 1 \overset{?}{\geq} -2$ | No, $-4 \ngeq -2$ |
| $-4$ | ? | ? |
| $-3$ | ? | ? |
| $-2$ | ? | ? |
| $-1$ | ? | ? |
| $0$ | ? | ? |

**2** **Repeat** Step 1 for the inequality $x \geq -3$.

| $x \geq -3$ | | |
|---|---|---|
| $x$ | Substitute. | Solution? |
| $-5$ | $-5 \overset{?}{\geq} -3$ | No, $-5 \ngeq -3$ |
| $-4$ | ? | ? |
| $-3$ | ? | ? |
| $-2$ | ? | ? |
| $-1$ | ? | ? |
| $0$ | ? | ? |

## Draw Conclusions

**1.** For the given values of $x$, do the inequalities in Explore 1 have the
same solutions? *Explain.*

**2.** How can you transform the inequality $x + 1 \geq -2$ to obtain $x \geq -3$?

**Gr. 7 AF 1.1** Use variables and appropriate operations to write an expression, an equation, **an inequality**, or a system of equations or inequalities that represents a verbal description (e.g., three less than a number, half as large as area A).
**Preparing for Gr. 7 AF 4.1** Solve two-step linear equations and inequalities in one variable over the rational numbers, interpret the solution or solutions in the context from which they arose, and verify the reasonableness of the results.

**Determine whether the inequalities have the same solutions.**

**3.** $x + 1 \geq 4$ and $x \geq 3$     **4.** $y + 5 \leq -6$ and $y \leq -11$    **5.** $4 \leq w + 2$ and $w \geq 6$

**EXPLORE 2** *Determine whether inequalities are equivalent*

**1** **Make** a table like the one shown. Use the table to determine if each value of $x$ is a solution of $x - 4 \leq -5$.

| $x - 4 \leq -5$ | | |
|---|---|---|
| $x$ | Substitute. | Solution? |
| $-3$ | $-3 - 4 \overset{?}{\leq} -5$ | Yes, $-7 \leq -5$ |
| $-2$ | ? | ? |
| $-1$ | ? | ? |
| $0$ | ? | ? |
| $1$ | ? | ? |
| $2$ | ? | ? |

**2** **Repeat** Step 1 for the inequality $x \leq -1$.

| $x \leq -1$ | | |
|---|---|---|
| $x$ | Substitute. | Solution? |
| $-3$ | $-3 \overset{?}{\leq} -1$ | Yes, $-3 \leq -1$ |
| $-2$ | ? | ? |
| $-1$ | ? | ? |
| $0$ | ? | ? |
| $1$ | ? | ? |
| $2$ | ? | ? |

## Draw Conclusions

**6.** For the given values of $x$, do the inequalities in Explore 2 have the same solutions? *Explain.*

**7.** How can you transform the inequality $x - 4 \leq -5$ to obtain $x \leq -1$?

**Determine whether the inequalities have the same solutions.**

**8.** $x - 2 \leq 3$ and $x \leq 5$     **9.** $y - 4 \geq -1$ and $y \geq -3$   **10.** $5 \geq z - 2$ and $z \leq 7$

**11.** If two inequalities have the same graph, do they have the same solutions? *Explain.*

**12.** Write two inequalities that have the graph shown.

$\begin{array}{ccccc} \leftarrow & | & | & \diamond & | & | & \rightarrow \\ & -4 & -3 & -2 & -1 & 0 \end{array}$

# Lesson 9.2

## Solve Inequalities Involving Addition or Subtraction

### VOCABULARY and CONCEPTS

- **Equivalent inequalities** are inequalities that have the same solutions.

**Addition Property of Inequality**

Adding the same number to both sides of an inequality produces an equivalent inequality.

**Subtraction Property of Inequality**

Subtracting the same number from both sides of an inequality produces an equivalent inequality.

**EXAMPLE 1** *Verifying a Solution of an Inequality* . . . . . . . . . . . .

**Tell whether $x = 6$ is a solution of the inequality $x - 4 \leq 1$.**

Substitute $x = 6$ into the inequality.

$$x - 4 \leq 1 \qquad \text{Write the original inequality.}$$
$$6 - 4 \stackrel{?}{\leq} 1 \qquad \text{Substitute 6 for } x.$$
$$2 \leq 1 \; \text{✗} \qquad \text{Subtract.}$$

Because $2 \leq 1$ is not true, $x = 6$ is not a solution.

#### Practice for Example 1

**Tell whether $x = 2$ is a solution of the inequality.**

**1.** $x + 4 < 0$        **2.** $x - 1 \geq -3$        **3.** $-1.5 \leq x - 2.5$

**EXAMPLE 2** *Solving an Inequality Using Addition* . . . . . . . . .

**Solve $x - 1.3 < 2.8$. Graph your solution.**

$$x - 1.3 < 2.8 \qquad \text{Write original inequality.}$$
$$x - 1.3 + 1.3 < 2.8 + 1.3 \qquad \text{Add 1.3 to each side.}$$
$$x < 4.1 \qquad \text{Simplify.}$$

The solutions are all real numbers less than 4.1. Check by substituting a number less than 4.1 for $x$ in the original inequality.

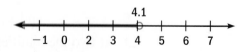

▸ **Check** $\qquad x - 1.3 < 2.8 \qquad$ **Write original inequality.**

$$3 - 1.3 \stackrel{?}{<} 2.8 \qquad \text{Substitute 3 for } x.$$
$$1.7 < 2.8 \; \text{✓} \qquad \text{Solution checks.}$$

**Gr.7 AF 1.1 Use variables and appropriate operations to write** an expression, an equation, **an inequality,** or a system of equations or inequalities **that represents a verbal description** (e.g., three less than a number, half as large as area A).
**Preparing for Gr. 7 AF 4.1** Solve two-step linear equations and inequalities in one variable over the rational numbers, interpret the solution or solutions in the context from which they arose, and verify the reasonableness of the results.

**EXAMPLE 3** *Solving an Inequality Using Subtraction*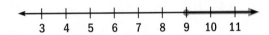

**Solve $13 \leq x + 4$. Graph your solution.**

| | |
|---|---|
| $13 \leq x + 4$ | **Write original inequality.** |
| $13 - 4 \leq x + 4 - 4$ | **Subtract 4 from each side.** |
| $9 \leq x$ | **Simplify.** |

You can rewrite $9 \leq x$ as $x \geq 9$. The solutions are all real numbers greater than or equal to 9.

$$3 \quad 4 \quad 5 \quad 6 \quad 7 \quad 8 \quad 9 \quad 10 \quad 11$$

### Practice for Examples 2 and 3

**Solve the inequality. Graph your solution.**

**4.** $x - 7 \leq -3$  **5.** $z + 9 < -1$  **6.** $6 \leq w + 1.5$

**EXAMPLE 4** *Solving Inequalities* 

An airline lets you check in up to 65 pounds of luggage. You want to check two suitcases. One suitcase weighs 48 pounds. How much must the second suitcase weigh?

**Solution**

Write a verbal model. Let $w$ represent the weight of the second suitcase.

| Weight of suitcase 1 | + | Weight of suitcase 2 | $\leq$ | Total weight allowed |
|---|---|---|---|---|

| | |
|---|---|
| $48 + w \leq 65$ | **Write the inequality.** |
| $48 - 48 + w \leq 65 - 48$ | **Subtract 48 from each side.** |
| $w \leq 17$ | **Simplify.** |

▶**Answer** The second suitcase must weigh 17 pounds or less.

### Practice for Example 4

**7.** You are saving to buy a bicycle that will cost at least $110. Your parents give you $65 toward the bicycle. Write an inequality to find how much money you will have to save. Then solve the inequality.

1. Tell whether $x = 3$ is a solution of $1 - x < -4$.

2. Tell whether $y = -5$ is a solution of $1 > y + 5$.

3. Tell whether $m = 5.7$ is a solution of $3.6 - m \leq 2.4$.

**Solve the inequality. Graph your solution.**

4. $x + 3 > 6$
5. $7 \geq m - 4$
6. $p + 10 < 5$

7. $17 < 8 + f$
8. $11 \leq a - 6$
9. $9 + y > 4$

10. $q + 5 \geq -3$
11. $-36 + v \leq -48$
12. $-28 > j - 35$

13. $x + 17 < 10$
14. $10\frac{1}{2} \geq m + 1\frac{1}{2}$
15. $25 < y + 25$

16. $a - 18.8 \leq -7.3$
17. $v + (-1.1) > -2.1$
18. $-5\frac{1}{4} \geq -7\frac{3}{4} + p$

**FIND THE ERROR** *Describe* and correct the error in solving the inequality.

19.

$$x + 7 > -4$$
$$x + 7 - 7 > -4 + 7$$
$$x > 3$$

20.

$$p - 1.5 \geq 0.1$$
$$p - 1.5 + 1.5 \geq 0.1$$
$$p \geq 0.1$$

21. To be accepted at a particular college, you must score at least 170 points on an entrance exam. The exam consists of two sections, an English section and a mathematics section. You score 80 points on the mathematics section. Write and solve an inequality to represent the possible scores that you must have on the English section to be accepted at the college.

22. The difference between Amy's height and Anna's height is less than 4 inches. Anna is 57 inches tall, and Amy is taller. Write and solve an inequality that can be used to find Amy's possible heights.

23. Shannon is buying an airplane ticket to fly from San Francisco to Orlando. Prices start from $348.50. She has earned a flight credit of $100. Write and solve an inequality that represents the amount she will pay for a flight.

24. The difference between Erin's age and her brother Brendan's age is more than 3 years. Brendan is 12, and Erin is older. Write and solve an inequality that can be used to find Erin's possible ages.

25. **REASONING** Are $x - 2 \leq 4$ and $6 \geq x$ equivalent inequalities? *Explain* your reasoning.

1. Tell whether $x = 0$ is a solution of $-4 < x - 3$.

2. Tell whether $y = 2$ is a solution of $-6 > y - 4$.

3. Tell whether $c = -5$ is solution of $c + 6.5 > 1$.

**Solve the inequality. Graph your solution.**

4. $x + 8 > 9$

5. $10 \geq m - 3$

6. $p + 4 < 2$

7. $13 > 5 + f$

8. $7 \leq a - 9$

9. $6 + y > 4$

10. $q + 8 \geq -5$

11. $-29 + v \leq -51$

12. $-32 > j - 29$

13. $x - 1\frac{3}{5} > -1$

14. $y \geq 4 + \left(-4\frac{1}{3}\right)$

15. $m - 1.09 \leq 3.16$

16. $-9.8 > k + (-3.4)$

17. $-20.9 \leq 4 + c$

18. $-12.6 > a - 9.1$

**FIND THE ERROR** *Describe* and correct the error in solving the inequality.

19.
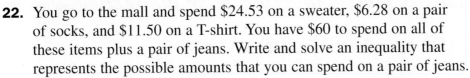
$$y + 2.8 > -3.6$$
$$y + 2.8 - 2.8 > -3.6 - 2.8$$
$$y > -0.8$$

20.
$$4.8 \geq w - 12.6$$
$$w - 12.6 \geq 4.8$$
$$w - 12.6 + 12.6 \geq 4.8 + 12.6$$
$$w \geq 17.4$$

21. You are trying to run 5 miles in less than 30 minutes. You run the first mile in 5 minutes, the second mile in 7 minutes, the third mile in 8 minutes, and the fourth mile in 6 minutes. Write and solve an inequality that represents the time in which you must run the last mile in order to run 5 miles in less than 30 minutes.

22. You go to the mall and spend $24.53 on a sweater, $6.28 on a pair of socks, and $11.50 on a T-shirt. You have $60 to spend on all of these items plus a pair of jeans. Write and solve an inequality that represents the possible amounts that you can spend on a pair of jeans.

23. Andris can travel with up to 50 pounds of luggage. He has two suitcases that weigh 8.5 pounds each and he has packed 25.5 pounds of clothes and accessories in the suitcases. He wants to buy some gifts to pack in the suitcases. Write and solve an inequality that represents the weight of the gifts he can buy.

24. Rebecca has $8.50 for lunch at the deli. She orders a sandwich for $5.25 and an apple for $.95. Write and solve an inequality that represents the amount of money she can spend on a drink.

25. **REASONING** Does the number line show the solution of $-1 \leq x - 3$? *Explain* your reasoning.

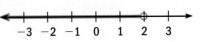

**VOCABULARY**
- inequality, p. 372
- solution of an inequality, p. 372
- graph of an inequality, p. 372
- equivalent inequalities, p. 378

### Vocabulary Exercises

**1.** Copy and complete: A(n) _?_ in one variable is a number that produces a true statement when substituted for the variable in the inequality.

**2.** Give three solutions of $x < 9$.

**3.** Are $x > 10$ and $x - 5 > 5$ equivalent inequalities? *Explain.*

## 9.1 Write and Graph Simple Inequalities ................. pp. 372–375

**EXAMPLE**   Graph (a) $x > 5$ and (b) $y \le -4$.

a.   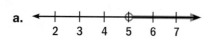   Use an open dot at 5 because 5 is not a solution.

b.   Use a closed dot at $-4$ because $-4$ is a solution.

**Graph the inequality.**

**4.** $m > -3$     **5.** $n \le 1$     **6.** $k < -2.5$     **7.** $y \ge \dfrac{1}{2}$

## 9.2 Solve Inequalities Involving Addition or Subtraction pp. 378–381

**EXAMPLE**   Solve $x - 2.5 < 3.6$. Graph your solution.

$$x - 2.5 < 3.6$$   **Write original inequality.**

$$x - 2.5 + 2.5 < 3.6 + 2.5$$   **Add 2.5 to each side.**

$$x < 6.1$$   **Simplify.**

The solutions are all real numbers less than 6.1.

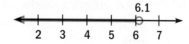

**Solve the inequality. Graph your solution.**

**8.** $x - 5 \le -6$     **9.** $z + 6 < -4$     **10.** $10 \le w + 3.5$     **11.** $14 > b - 6.5$

**Graph the inequality.**

1. $x \le \dfrac{2}{3}$

2. $z < -3.25$

3. $t < 5\dfrac{1}{4}$

4. $m \ge -\dfrac{5}{3}$

**Write an inequality represented by the graph.**

5. ![number line with open circle at -3, arrow left; marks -5 -4 -3 -2 -1]
   $-5 \quad -4 \quad -3 \quad -2 \quad -1$

6. ![number line with closed point at 2.5; marks 0 1 2 3 4]
   $2.5$
   $0 \quad 1 \quad 2 \quad 3 \quad 4$

7. ![number line with closed point at 6; marks 4 5 6 7 8]
   $4 \quad 5 \quad 6 \quad 7 \quad 8$

8. ![number line with open circle at 0; marks -3 -2 -1 0 1]
   $-3 \quad -2 \quad -1 \quad 0 \quad 1$

**Write the common phrase as an inequality.**

9. No more than 15

10. 8 or more

11. At most 20

12. Fewer than 9

**In Exercises 13–15, write an inequality to represent the situation. Then graph the inequality.**

13. The cost of flying from Seattle to San Diego starts from \$139 per person.

14. The gym can hold at most 650 people.

15. Average rainfall for the month of April is at least 5 inches.

16. Tell whether $y = 5$ is a solution of the inequality $y - 5 \ge 10$.

17. Tell whether $x = \dfrac{2}{3}$ is a solution of the inequality $x - 1 < 0$.

18. Tell whether $z = -3.5$ is solution of the inequality $z + 5 < 1.5$.

**Solve the inequality. Graph your solution.**

19. $x + 2 > -5$

20. $8 \le z + 5$

21. $-1 > m - 3.5$

22. $12 > 5 + n$

23. $9 > a - 2$

24. $y + 2.6 \le 3.5$

25. $b + (-8) \ge 11$

26. $q - 7.2 > -10$

27. $9.3 \ge h - 3.7$

28. The difference between Anthony's height and Aidan's height is less than 4 inches. Aidan is 65 inches tall, and Anthony is taller. Write and solve an inequality that can be used to find Anthony's possible heights.

29. Marc can spend up to \$45 to buy gifts for his family. He buys a set of art supplies for \$16.45 for his younger brother. Write and solve an inequality that can be used to find the possible amounts he can spend on the remaining gifts.

30. Natalie wants to read at least 15 books over summer vacation. She has read 8 books during the first half of summer vacation. Write and solve an inequality that can be used to find the possible numbers of books she should read during the second half of summer vacation.

# Let's Explore

## Inequalities Involving Multiplication or Division

**Goal**
Solve inequalities using
multiplication or division.

**Materials**
• index cards

**QUESTION**  How can you solve inequalities involving multiplication
or division?

**EXPLORE 1**  *Solve inequalities involving multiplication* . . . . . .

Your teacher will select 9 students for the following activity. Each student
will receive an index card with one of the following integers on it:
$-4, -3, -2, -1, 0, 1, 2, 3, 4$.

**1** **Arrange** a human number line using a row of chairs. Each student sitting in
a chair holds an index card that represents an integer on the number line. The
numbers should be in order from left to right when viewed by the class.

**2** **Check** whether the index card you are holding contains a solution of the
inequality $5x \leq 10$.

**3** **Stand** if the number on your card is a solution of the inequality. Remain
seated if the number on your card is not a solution of the inequality. Everyone
should graph the real-number solutions of the inequality on a piece of paper.

**4** **Repeat** Steps 1–3 for the inequality $-5x \leq 10$.

## Draw Conclusions

**1.** What solutions of $5x \leq 10$ are suggested based on the students who
stood up in Step 3?

**2.** What solutions of $-5x \leq 10$ are suggested based on the students who
stood up in Step 4?

**3.** Compare the inequalities $5x \leq 10$ and $x \leq 2$. *Explain* how you can
transform the inequality $5x \leq 10$ to obtain $x \leq 2$.

**4.** Compare the inequalities $-5x \leq 10$ and $x \geq -2$. *Explain* how you
can transform the inequality $-5x \leq 10$ to obtain $x \geq -2$.

**5.** What is the difference in transforming the two inequalities in
Exercises 3 and 4?

**Gr. 7 AF 1.1 Use variables and appropriate operations to write** an expression, an equation, **an inequality**, or a system of equations or inequalities that represents a verbal description (e.g., three less than a number, half as large as area A).
**Preparing for Gr. 7 AF 4.1** Solve two-step linear equations and inequalities in one variable over the rational numbers, interpret the solution or solutions in the context from which they arose, and verify the reasonableness of the results.

**EXPLORE 2** *Solve inequalities involving division* ·········

Your teacher will select 9 other students. Each student will receive one of the index cards from Explore 1.

**1** **Arrange** another human number line using a row of chairs.

**2** **Check** whether the index card you are holding contains a solution of the inequality $\frac{x}{2} \geq 1$.

**3** **Stand** if the number on your card is a solution of the inequality. Remain seated if the number on your card is not a solution of the inequality. Everyone should graph the real-number solutions of the inequality on a piece of paper.

**4** **Repeat** Steps 1–3 for the inequality $\frac{x}{-2} \geq 1$.

## Draw Conclusions

**6.** What solutions of $\frac{x}{2} \geq 1$ are suggested based on the students who stood up in Step 3?

**7.** What solutions of $\frac{x}{-2} \geq 1$ are suggested based on the students who stood up in Step 4?

**8.** Compare the inequalities $\frac{x}{2} \geq 1$ and $x \geq 2$. *Explain* how you can transform the inequality $\frac{x}{2} \geq 1$ to obtain $x \geq 2$.

**9.** Compare the inequalities $\frac{x}{-2} \geq 1$ and $x \leq -2$. *Explain* how you can transform the inequality $\frac{x}{-2} \geq 1$ to obtain $x \leq -2$.

**10.** What is the difference in transforming the two inequalities in Exercises 8 and 9?

**Match the inequality with the graph of its solution.**

**11.** $3x \leq -6$

A. ![number line -3 -2 -1 0 1 2 3]

**12.** $\frac{x}{-2} \leq 1$

B. ![number line -3 -2 -1 0 1 2 3]

**13.** $-3x \geq -6$

C. ![number line -3 -2 -1 0 1 2 3]

**14.** $\frac{x}{2} \geq 1$

D. ![number line -3 -2 -1 0 1 2 3]

> **VOCABULARY and CONCEPTS**
>
> • equivalent inequalities, p. 378
>
> **Multiplication Property of Inequality**
>
> Multiplying each side of an inequality by a *positive* number produces an equivalent inequality.
>
> Multiplying each side of an inequality by a *negative* number and *reversing the direction of the inequality symbol* produces an equivalent inequality.
>
> **Division Property of Inequality**
>
> Dividing each side of an inequality by a *positive* number produces an equivalent inequality.
>
> Dividing each side of an inequality by a *negative* number and *reversing the direction of the inequality symbol* produces an equivalent inequality.

**EXAMPLE 1** *Solving an Inequality Using Multiplication*

**Solve the inequality. Graph your solution.**

a. $\dfrac{x}{7} > 3$
b. $\dfrac{x}{-2} \le 5$

**Solution**

a.
$$\dfrac{x}{7} > 3 \qquad \text{Write original inequality.}$$

$$7 \cdot \dfrac{x}{7} > 7 \cdot 3 \qquad \text{Multiply each side by 7.}$$

$$x > 21 \qquad \text{Simplify.}$$

The solutions are all real numbers greater than 21. Check by substituting a number greater than 21 in the original inequality.

$$
\begin{array}{ccccccccc}
\leftarrow & | & | & | & | & \oplus & | & | & | & | & \rightarrow \\
 & 17 & 18 & 19 & 20 & 21 & 22 & 23 & 24 & 25
\end{array}
$$

b.
$$\dfrac{x}{-2} \le 5 \qquad \text{Write original inequality.}$$

$$-2 \cdot \dfrac{x}{-2} \ge -2 \cdot 5 \qquad \text{Multiply each side by } -2. \text{ Reverse inequality symbol.}$$

$$x \ge -10 \qquad \text{Simplify.}$$

The solutions are all real numbers greater than or equal to $-10$. Check by substituting a number greater than or equal to $-10$ in the original inequality.

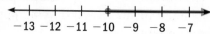

**EXAMPLE 2** *Solving an Inequality Using Division* ...........

**Solve $6x > -36$. Graph your solution.**

$$6x > -36 \quad \textbf{Write original inequality.}$$

$$\frac{6x}{6} > \frac{-36}{6} \quad \textbf{Divide each side by 6.}$$

$$x > -6 \quad \textbf{Simplify.}$$

The solutions are all real numbers greater than $-6$. Check by substituting a number greater than $-6$ in the original inequality.

**Practice for Examples 1 and 2**

**Solve the inequality. Graph your solution.**

**1.** $\frac{m}{4} < -3$        **2.** $\frac{n}{-6} \le 4$        **3.** $\frac{p}{-1.2} > -8$

**4.** $-3x \le 9$        **5.** $18 \ge 9x$        **6.** $6x < 12$

**EXAMPLE 3** *Writing and Solving an Inequality* .............

A wheelchair racer's average racing speed is 15 miles per hour. The racer practices racing for at least 12 miles on Saturday. Write and solve an inequality for the possible amounts of time $t$ (in hours) that the racer practices on Saturday.

**Solution**

The distance that the racer travels is $15t$. Write a verbal model. Then write an inequality.

$$\text{distance} \ge 12 \quad \textbf{Write a verbal model.}$$

$$15t \ge 12 \quad \textbf{Write the inequality.}$$

$$t \ge \frac{12}{15} \quad \textbf{Divide each side by 15.}$$

$$t \ge 0.8 \quad \textbf{Write as a decimal.}$$

The racer should practice for at least 0.8 hour (48 minutes).

**Practice for Example 3**

**7.** A small library has $120 to spend on books that cost $8 each. Write and solve an inequality to find the possible numbers of books the library can buy.

**Match the inequality with the graph of its solution.**

**1.** $-5x \geq -10$

**2.** $5x \geq -10$

**3.** $-5x \geq 10$

**4.** $\dfrac{x}{5} \leq 10$

**5.** $\dfrac{x}{-5} \leq 10$

**A.**

$$-4 \quad -3 \quad -2 \quad -1 \quad 0 \quad 1 \quad 2 \quad 3 \quad 4$$

**B.**

$$-75 \quad -50 \quad -25 \quad 0 \quad 25 \quad 50 \quad 75$$

**C.**

$$-4 \quad -3 \quad -2 \quad -1 \quad 0 \quad 1 \quad 2 \quad 3 \quad 4$$

**D.**

$$-75 \quad -50 \quad -25 \quad 0 \quad 25 \quad 50 \quad 75$$

**E.**

$$-4 \quad -3 \quad -2 \quad -1 \quad 0 \quad 1 \quad 2 \quad 3 \quad 4$$

**Solve the inequality. Then graph your solution.**

**6.** $\dfrac{m}{5} > 1$

**7.** $\dfrac{h}{-5} \geq 2$

**8.** $\dfrac{y}{-8} \leq 36$

**9.** $\dfrac{p}{4} < -12$

**10.** $5g < 30$

**11.** $28 \geq -7n$

**12.** $10k < -120$

**13.** $-4q \leq 60$

**14.** $2 > \dfrac{-u}{9}$

**15.** $-8c \geq 72$

**16.** $\dfrac{b}{-6} < 43$

**17.** $-54 \leq -18j$

**18.** You need at least $250 for a plane ticket to fly to see your grandmother. You earn $10 for each game you work as a softball umpire. What are the possible numbers of games that you will need to umpire to have enough money for the ticket?

**19.** You go to the mall to buy CDs with $38.00. Each CD cost $9.50. Write and solve an inequality that represents the number of CDs you can buy.

**20.** A class needs to rent a bus for a field trip. The cost to rent a bus is $187. Each student who goes on the trip will pay $8.50 towards the bus rental. What are the possible numbers of students who go on the field trip to cover the cost of the bus?

**21.** You want to save at least $180 to purchase a skateboard. You can save $15 each week. How many weeks will it take you to save enough to purchase the skateboard?

**22.** **FIND THE ERROR** *Describe* and correct the error in solving $15x > -45$.

$$15x > -45$$
$$x < \frac{-45}{15}$$
$$x < -3$$

**23.** **REASONING** What number do you have to divide each side of the inequality $-x \geq 0$ by to solve the inequality? *Explain* your reasoning.

**Solve the inequality. Then graph your solution.**

**1.** $\dfrac{m}{6} \geq 2$

**2.** $\dfrac{h}{8} \leq 9$

**3.** $\dfrac{y}{-5} \leq 29$

**4.** $\dfrac{p}{3} < -17$

**5.** $7g < 42$

**6.** $36 \geq -9n$

**7.** $15k < -165$

**8.** $-8q \leq 64$

**9.** $9 > \dfrac{u}{-12}$

**10.** $-13c \geq 104$

**11.** $\dfrac{b}{-7} < 61$

**12.** $-68 \leq -17j$

**FIND THE ERROR** *Describe* and correct the error in solving the inequality.

**13.**
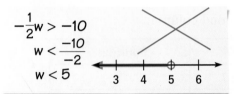
$$-\frac{1}{2}w > -10$$
$$w < \frac{-10}{-2}$$
$$w < 5$$

**14.**
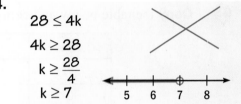
$$28 \leq 4k$$
$$4k \geq 28$$
$$k \geq \frac{28}{4}$$
$$k \geq 7$$

**15.** A college student expects that her textbooks for next semester will cost at least $350. She wants to save enough money over the next 4 months from her part-time job to pay for the books. Write and solve an inequality that gives the possible amounts she needs to save each month.

**16.** Mark's previous job paid $363 per week. He earns $8.25 per hour at his new job. What are the possible numbers of hours that Mark must work to make as much as or more per week than at his previous job?

**17.** You are in charge of purchasing helium balloons for a school carnival. You have been given $40 to buy the balloons. The balloons cost $1.60 each. Write and solve an inequality that gives the possible numbers of balloons you can buy.

**18.** You want to improve your reading speed to at least 300 words per minute. You have been working on reading faster and want to test yourself by reading for 5 minutes. Write and solve an inequality that gives the possible numbers of words you must read in 5 minutes to meet your goal.

**19.** A group of four friends plans to rent a car for a road trip. The group budget is $300. The group decides to split the cost of the rental equally. Write and solve an inequality that gives the possible costs that each person will pay.

**20.** **REASONING** What number do you have to multiply each side of the inequality $0.25x \geq -6$ by to solve the inequality? *Explain* your reasoning.

**21.** **REASONING** *Describe* two ways to solve the inequality $-\frac{1}{2}x > 1$.

## Let's Explore
### Using Tables to Solve Two-Step Inequalities

**Goal**
Investigate how to solve inequalities requiring two steps.

**Materials**
• paper and pencil

**QUESTION** How can you use a table to solve a two-step inequality?

**EXPLORE 1** *Use a table to solve an inequality*

**1** **Copy** the table below and complete the second column.

| $x$ | $2x + 3 \geq 7$ | Solution? |
|---|---|---|
| $-1$ | $2(-1) + 3 \overset{?}{\geq} 7$ | ? |
| 0 | ? | ? |
| 1 | ? | ? |
| 2 | ? | ? |
| 3 | ? | ? |
| 4 | ? | ? |

**2** **Complete** the third column of the table.

| $x$ | $2x + 3 \geq 7$ | Solution? |
|---|---|---|
| $-1$ | $2(-1) + 3 \overset{?}{\geq} 7$ | No, $1 \not\geq 7$ |
| 0 | ? | ? |
| 1 | ? | ? |
| 2 | ? | ? |
| 3 | ? | ? |
| 4 | ? | ? |

**3** **Use** the table to graph the real-number solutions of the inequality $2x + 3 \geq 7$.

**4** **Use** the graph from Step 3 to write a simple inequality that describes the solutions.

## Draw Conclusions
**1.** How can you transform the inequality $2x + 3 \geq 7$ to obtain the inequality in Step 4?

**Gr. 7 AF 1.1 Use variables and appropriate operations to write** an expression, an equation, **an inequality**, or a system of equations or inequalities that represents a verbal description (e.g., three less than a number, half as large as area A).
**Gr. 7 AF 4.1 Solve two-step linear** equations and **inequalities in one variable over the rational numbers,** interpret the solution or solutions in the context from which they arose, and verify the reasonableness of the results.

**Solve the inequality.**

**2.** $3x + 1 \geq 4$

**3.** $\frac{x}{2} + 1 \geq 3$

**4.** $14 + 2x \leq 38$

**EXPLORE 2** *Use a table to solve an inequality* •••••••••••••••

**1** **Copy** the table below and complete the second column.

| x | $-4x + 5 \leq 1$ | Solution? |
|---|---|---|
| −1 | $-4(-1) + 5 \overset{?}{\leq} 1$ | ? |
| 0 | ? | ? |
| 1 | ? | ? |
| 2 | ? | ? |
| 3 | ? | ? |
| 4 | ? | ? |

**2** **Complete** the third column of the table.

| x | $-4x + 5 \leq 1$ | Solution? |
|---|---|---|
| −1 | $-4(-1) + 5 \overset{?}{\leq} 1$ | No, $9 \nleq 1$ |
| 0 | ? | ? |
| 1 | ? | ? |
| 2 | ? | ? |
| 3 | ? | ? |
| 4 | ? | ? |

**3** **Use** the table to graph the real-number solutions of the inequality $-4x + 5 \leq 1$.

**4** **Use** the graph from Step 3 to write a simple inequality that describes the solutions.

## Draw Conclusions

**5.** How can you transform the inequality $-4x + 5 \leq 1$ to obtain the inequality from Step 4?

**Solve the inequality.**

**6.** $-4x + 1 \geq 17$

**7.** $-10x + 30 \geq -40$

**8.** $\frac{x}{-7} - 14 \leq -35$

# Solve Two-Step Inequalities

**VOCABULARY and CONCEPTS**

- equivalent inequalities, p. 378

**Solving Two-Step Inequalities**

When solving two-step inequalities, you will need to apply two of the properties of inequality from Lessons 9.2 and 9.3.

**EXAMPLE 1** *Solve a Two-Step Inequality* · · · · · · · · · · · · · · · · · ·

**Solve $-4x + 3 > 15$. Graph your solution.**

$$-4x + 3 > 15 \quad \textbf{Write original inequality.}$$
$$-4x > 12 \quad \textbf{Subtract 3 from each side.}$$
$$x < -3 \quad \textbf{Divide each side by } -4. \textbf{ Reverse inequality symbol.}$$

The solution is all real numbers less than $-3$. Check by substituting a number less than $-3$ in the original inequality.

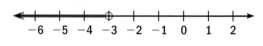

▶ **Check** $-4x + 3 > 15$     **Write original inequality.**

$$-4(-5) + 3 \stackrel{?}{>} 15 \quad \textbf{Substitute } -5 \textbf{ for } x.$$
$$23 > 15 \checkmark \quad \textbf{Solution checks.}$$

**EXAMPLE 2** *Solve a Two-Step Inequality* · · · · · · · · · · · · · · · · · ·

**Solve $\frac{x}{4} - 5 > 1$. Graph your solution.**

$$\frac{x}{4} - 5 > 1 \quad \textbf{Write original inequality.}$$
$$\frac{x}{4} > 6 \quad \textbf{Add 5 to each side.}$$
$$x > 24 \quad \textbf{Multiply each side by 4.}$$

The solution is all real numbers greater than 24. Check by substituting a number greater than 24 in the original inequality.

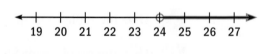

▶ **Check** $\frac{x}{4} - 5 > 1$     **Write original inequality.**

$$\frac{28}{4} - 5 > 1 \quad \textbf{Substitute 28 for } x.$$
$$2 > 1 \checkmark \quad \textbf{Solution checks.}$$

## Practice for Examples 1 and 2

**Solve the inequality. Graph your solution.**

**1.** $7x + 8 > 22$       **2.** $\frac{x}{2} + 7 > 4$       **3.** $2 \le \frac{x}{-3} - 0.5$

**Gr 7 AF 1.1** Use variables and appropriate operations to write an expression, an equation, **an inequality**, or a system of equations or inequalities **that represents a** verbal description (e.g., three less than a number, half as large as area A).
**Gr. 7 AF 4.1** Solve two-step linear equations and inequalities in one variable over the rational numbers, interpret the solution or solutions in the context from which they arose, and verify the reasonableness of the results.

**EXAMPLE 3** *Write and Solve a Two-Step Inequality*

Write the verbal sentence as an inequality. Then solve the inequality.
"Four more than twice a number is greater than −6."

### Solution

"Four more than twice a number" can be written $2x + 4$. This expression is greater than −6. So, the inequality is $2x + 4 > -6$.

$$2x + 4 > -6 \qquad \text{Write original inequality.}$$
$$2x > -10 \qquad \text{Subtract 4 from each side.}$$
$$x > -5 \qquad \text{Divide each side by 2.}$$

**EXAMPLE 4** *Write and Solve a Two-Step Inequality*

James has $100 to buy a tennis racket and some cans of tennis balls. The tennis racket costs $85.30, and a can of tennis balls costs $3.15. What are the possible numbers of cans of tennis balls that James can buy?

### Solution

Write a verbal model. Let $c$ represent the number of cans of tennis balls James can buy.

| Cost of tennis racket | + | Cost of a can of tennis balls | · | Number of cans of tennis balls | ≤ | Total amount of money |
|---|---|---|---|---|---|---|

$$85.30 + 3.15c \leq 100 \qquad \text{Write the inequality.}$$
$$85.30 + 3.15c - 85.30 \leq 100 - 85.30 \qquad \text{Subtract 85.30 from each side.}$$
$$\frac{3.15c}{3.15} \leq \frac{14.70}{3.15} \qquad \text{Divide each side by 3.15.}$$
$$c \leq 4\frac{2}{3} \qquad \text{Simplify.}$$

▶ **Answer** Because James cannot buy a fraction of a can of tennis balls, he can buy at most 4 cans.

### Practice for Examples 3 and 4

**In Exercise 4 and 5, write the verbal sentence as an inequality. Then solve the inequality.**

4. When the quotient of a number and 5 is decreased by 9, the result is greater than 2.

5. Six more than 1.5 times a number is less than 7.5.

6. Check the reasonableness of the solution in Example 4. *Explain.*

**State the first step you would take to solve the inequality.**

**1.** $8x + 6 < 1$

**2.** $-10 > 3a - 5$

**3.** $7y - 4 \le -6$

**4.** $0.5 \ge m + 1.97$

**5.** $\dfrac{x}{2} + \dfrac{1}{2} \ge 4$

**6.** $-9.8 < 2.2 + \dfrac{k}{3}$

**Solve the inequality. Graph your solution.**

**7.** $-2x - 1 < 5$

**8.** $0 \le 3x - 6$

**9.** $1.9 \ge 2x - 0.5$

**10.** $0.5c + 9 > -4.5$

**11.** $\dfrac{y}{-2} - 3 \le 4$

**12.** $\dfrac{n}{-4} + 3 < -10$

**13.** $-12 \ge 11 + \dfrac{x}{2}$

**14.** $2 + \dfrac{a}{-6} \ge 7$

**15.** $3.2 + (-10b) < 4.6$

**16.** $-11.3 \ge -5.3 + (-2x)$

**17.** $0 > -9 + \dfrac{c}{-4}$

**18.** $-4.7 \ge -4.7 + \dfrac{x}{10}$

**Match the verbal sentence with the correct inequality.**

**19.** The sum of $2x$ and 3 is greater than 5.

**A.** $2x + 3 > 5$

**20.** The sum of $3x$ and 2 is greater than 5.

**B.** $2x - 3 < 5$

**21.** The difference of $2x$ and 3 is less than 5.

**C.** $3x - 2 < 5$

**22.** The difference of $3x$ and 2 is less than 5.

**D.** $3x + 2 > 5$

**Write the verbal sentence as an inequality. Then solve the inequality and graph your solution.**

**23.** When 5 is added to the product of 3 and a number, the result is less than 8.

**24.** When 2.5 is subtracted from the quotient of a number and 2, the result is greater than or equal to 5.

**25.** When 1 is subtracted from the product of $-3.2$ and a number, the result is less than or equal to 5.4.

**26. REASONING** Is $x = -4.2$ a solution of $-2 \le 3x - 4$? *Explain.*

**27. REASONING** Is $x = \dfrac{3}{4}$ a solution of $4x - 5 < 10$? *Explain.*

**28.** Carly received scores of 74, 83, 96, 87, and 78 for five of six tests she has taken for a class. She wants an average of at least 85 on her six test scores. Write and solve an inequality that gives the possible scores she can get on her last test to achieve this.

**29.** Your club is in charge of making pins that students can buy to show their school spirit for the upcoming football game. You have made 220 pins so far, and you only have 2 hours left to make the rest of the pins. You need to make at least 400 pins. Write and solve an inequality that gives the possible numbers of pins that you have to make per minute in order to meet your goal.

**State the first step you would take to solve the inequality.**

**1.** $2x + 4 \geq -3$

**2.** $-6 + \dfrac{y}{3} > 1$

**3.** $1.09 + 3.7p \geq -4.6$

**4.** $27p - 13 \leq -91$

**5.** $\dfrac{m}{-2} - 15 \leq 26$

**6.** $-17.8 > 14.3 + \dfrac{q}{0.4}$

**Solve the inequality. Graph your solution.**

**7.** $-3 + 4x < 5$

**8.** $2.5x + 7 \geq 22$

**9.** $-55 > -5w + 25$

**10.** $4 + (-2y) > 28$

**11.** $\dfrac{c}{5} - 2 < 1$

**12.** $4m - \dfrac{1}{2} \geq \dfrac{3}{2}$

**13.** $-11 > 1 + 0.2w$

**14.** $-4 + 0.25q < 1.5$

**15.** $-10x + 1 \leq 121$

**16.** $5 > -\dfrac{1}{2}p + 2$

**17.** $\dfrac{x}{9} - 3 < -4$

**18.** $\dfrac{y}{-6} + 10 \geq 5$

**Match the verbal sentence with the correct inequality.**

**19.** The sum of $-2x$ and 3 is greater than 9.

**A.** $2x + 9 < -3$

**20.** The difference of $9x$ and 2 is less than or equal to $-3$.

**B.** $9x - 2 \leq -3$

**21.** The sum of $2x$ and 9 is less than $-3$.

**C.** $-2x + 3 > 9$

**22.** The difference of $2x$ and 9 is greater than or equal to $-3$.

**D.** $2x - 9 \geq -3$

**Write the verbal sentence as an inequality. Then solve the inequality and graph your solution.**

**23.** Six more than 5 times a number is greater than or equal to 31.

**24.** Three less than a number divided by 4 is less than 2.

**25.** Ten more than $-2$ times a number is less than 8.

**26.** REASONING Is $a = -11.5$ a solution of $-2a + 3.8 < -2.7$? *Explain.*

**27.** REASONING Is $k = -20$ a solution of $-5 \leq \dfrac{k}{4} + 2$? *Explain.*

**28.** Sara subscribes to a telephone plan that charges a $4.48 monthly fee and $.08 for every minute that she uses her phone. She does not want her monthly phone bill to exceed $20. Write and solve an inequality that gives the possible numbers of minutes that she can use her phone and stay within her budget.

**29.** You spend $34 on supplies to make small paintings for a fundraiser. You sell the paintings for $7.50 each. Write and solve an inequality that gives the possible numbers of paintings you need to sell to make at least $50.

**30.** You currently have 8 neon tetra fish in your 25 gallon aquarium. The general rule is that each fish needs at least 2 gallons of water. Write and solve an inequality that can be used to find the possible numbers of fish that you can add to your aquarium.

# Problem Solving and Reasoning

## Problem

A supermarket makes deposits to its bank account by dropping off deposits in the depository box at its bank. The fees for this service are given in the table, along with the fees being advertised by a new bank.

| | Yearly fee for using depository box | Fee for processing each deposit |
|---|---|---|
| **Current bank** | $25 | $1.20 |
| **New bank** | $20 | $1.30 |

If the supermarket has a budget of $475 for a deposit service and makes a maximum of 365 deposits in a year, should the supermarket switch to the deposit service offered by the new bank? *Explain.*

## Solution

*Use symbols to explain mathematical reasoning as part of MR 2.5.*

**1** **Write** and solve an inequality for the possible numbers of deposits at each bank for a maximum of $475. Let $x$ represent the number of deposits.

| **Current bank** | **New bank** |
|---|---|
| $25 + 1.2x \leq 475$ | $20 + 1.3x \leq 475$ |
| $1.2x \leq 450$ | $1.3x \leq 455$ |
| $x \leq 375$ | $x \leq 350$ |

*Use a graph to explain mathematical reasoning as part of MR 2.5.*

**2** **Graph** the solutions. Because the maximum number of deposits the supermarket makes in a year is 365, locate that number on each of the graphs.

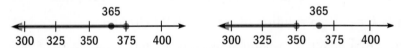

**3** **Decide** whether the supermarket should switch to the new bank.

The supermarket should not switch to the new bank because it can make a maximum of only 350 deposits at the new bank and it needs to have a maximum of 365 deposits.

*Check the reasonableness of the solution in the context of the problem as part of MR 3.1.*

**4** **Check** your solution by substituting 365 for $x$ in each of the inequalities from Step 2.

**Current bank:** $25 + 1.2(365) \overset{?}{\leq} 475 \longrightarrow 463 \leq 475$ ✔

**New bank:** $20 + 1.3(365) \overset{?}{\leq} 475 \longrightarrow 494.5 \leq 475$ ✗

The fees for making 365 deposits at the new bank are greater than the supermarket's budget of $475.

# Practice

1. In the problem on the previous page, what are the possible numbers of deposits a business can make for which the deposit service offered by the new bank would be a better deal? *Explain.* MR 3.3

2. A delivery company's charges for two types of courier service are given below. MR 2.5, MR 3.2

| Service | Base cost | Cost per mile |
|---|---|---|
| Standard | $5.00 | $1.00 |
| Rush | $6.00 | $1.25 |

   a. A business wants to spend no more than $20 each on packages to be delivered locally. For each type of delivery service, write and solve an inequality for the possible numbers of miles a courier can travel at a total cost of $20 or less.

   b. Graph the inequalities from part (a). Use the graphs to explain when to select standard or rush delivery.

3. A small farm uses raised rectangular gardening beds to grow vegetables. The table below lists the maximum number of winter squash plants that can be planted in beds with the given dimensions. MR 1.1, MR 3.3

| Length of bed (ft) | Width of bed (ft) | Maximum number of squash plants |
|---|---|---|
| 8 | 1 | 2 |
| 8 | 2 | 4 |
| 8 | 3 | 6 |

   a. Use the information in the table to determine the minimum number of square feet needed for each squash plant.

   b. Write and solve an inequality to find the possible numbers of plants that can be planted in a raised bed that has a length of 8 feet and a width of 6 feet.

4. You are given a $20 gift card for an online music store. You purchase an album for $14.99. MR 2.8

   a. You decide to purchase individual songs that cost $.99 each with the remaining money. Write and solve an inequality for the possible numbers of individual songs you can purchase.

   b. Copy and complete the table below. Then continue the table to check your answer to part (a).

| Individual songs | Total |
|---|---|
| 0 | $14.99 |
| 1 | $14.99 + ? = ? |

5. The student membership fees for a town pool are shown. Students who have a school-year membership have to pay $3 for each day they use the pool during the summer. MR 3.1

| Pool Membership Fees | |
|---|---|
| Full-year membership | $119 |
| School-year membership | $105 |

   a. Write and solve an inequality for the possible numbers of days you can use the pool during the summer so that the money you spend for using the pool does not exceed the cost of a full-year membership.

   b. What is the maximum number of days you can use the pool during the summer? *Explain.*

6. Consider the inequality $ax + b > c$ where $a$, $b$, and $c$ are integers and $a \neq 0$. Is $x > \dfrac{c - b}{a}$ always true? *Explain.* MR 1.2

**Problem Solving and Reasoning**

# Chapter ⑨ Review Game

## Matching Inequalities

**Step 1** Write the inequalities shown in the table on separate cards.

| Inequality Cards | | | |
|---|---|---|---|
| $\frac{x}{2} < 5$ | $x + 10 \leq 4$ | $\frac{x}{2} - 3 \geq 11$ | $x - 9 > -3$ |
| $2x - 4 < -2$ | $2x + 3 < -3$ | $-7x - 4 \leq -25$ | $-2x > 10$ |
| $\frac{x}{3} + 4 > -6$ | $12x - 3 \leq -39$ | $\frac{x}{-5} + 9 > 15$ | $3x - 7 \geq -25$ |

**Step 2** The solutions of the inequalities in Step 1 are shown in the table below. Write the solutions on separate cards.

| Solution Cards | | | |
|---|---|---|---|
| $x \leq -6$ | $x \geq 28$ | $x > -30$ | $x < -3$ |
| $x > 6$ | $x < 1$ | $x \leq -3$ | $x \geq 3$ |
| $x < 10$ | $x < -5$ | $x \geq -6$ | $x < -30$ |

**Step 3** Shuffle the inequality cards and place them face down in a row. Shuffle the solution cards and place them face down in another row.

**Step 4** One player selects a card from the inequality cards and a card from the solution cards. If the cards match, that player keeps the two cards and takes another turn. If they do not match, the cards are turned face down again and the next player selects two cards.

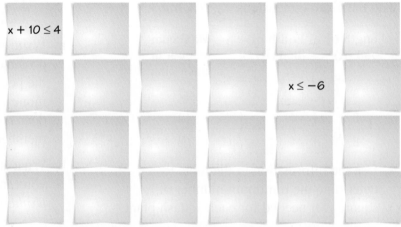

**A match! Keep these cards and take another turn.**

**Step 5** Play continues until all cards have been matched. The player with the most matches wins.

**VOCABULARY**
- inequality, p. 372
- solution of an inequality, p. 372
- graph of an inequality, p. 372
- equivalent inequalities, p. 378

**Vocabulary Exercises**

1. Copy and complete: A(n) _?_ is a mathematical sentence formed by placing an inequality symbol between two expressions.

2. Copy and complete: _?_ are inequalities that have the same solutions.

## 9.1 *Write and Graph Simple Inequalities* •••••••••••• pp. 372–375

When graphing an inequality, an *open dot* is used to show that a point is not included in the solution. A *closed dot* is used to show that a point is included. Use an open dot if the inequality symbol is < or >. Use a closed dot if the inequality symbol is ≤ or ≥ .

**EXAMPLES**  Graph (a) *x* > 4 and (b) *k* ≤ −1.

a.    Use an open dot at 4 and shade to the right.

b.    Use a closed dot at −1 and shade to the left.

**EXAMPLES**  Write an inequality represented by the graph.

a.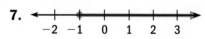

b.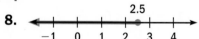

a.  All numbers less than $3\frac{1}{2}$ are graphed, so $x < 3\frac{1}{2}$.

b.  All numbers greater than or equal to 5 are graphed, so $x \geq 5$.

**Graph the inequality.**

3. $s < 6$
4. $y \leq \frac{1}{2}$
5. $n > 0$
6. $t \geq -2.5$

**Write an inequality represented by the graph.**

7.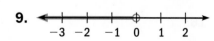

8.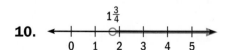

9.

10.

**9.2** *Solve Inequalities Involving Addition or Subtraction* pp. 378–381

**EXAMPLE** Solve $x - 5.2 > 7.8$. Graph your solution.

$$x - 5.2 > 7.8 \qquad \text{Write original inequality.}$$
$$x - 5.2 + 5.2 > 7.8 + 5.2 \qquad \text{Add 5.2 to each side.}$$
$$x > 13 \qquad \text{Simplify.}$$

The solutions are all real numbers greater than 13.

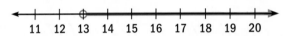

Check by substituting a number greater than 13 for $x$ in the original inequality.

$$x - 5.2 > 7.8 \qquad \text{Write original inequality.}$$
$$14 - 5.2 \overset{?}{>} 7.8 \qquad \text{Substitute 14 for } x.$$
$$8.8 > 7.8 \; \checkmark \qquad \text{Solution checks.}$$

**EXAMPLE** Solve $x + 7 \le 10$. Graph your solution.

$$x + 7 \le 10 \qquad \text{Write original inequality.}$$
$$x + 7 - 7 \le 10 - 7 \qquad \text{Subtract 7 from each side.}$$
$$x \le 3 \qquad \text{Simplify.}$$

The solutions are all real numbers less than or equal to 3.

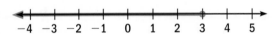

Check by substituting a number less than or equal to 3 for $x$ in the original inequality.

$$x + 7 \le 10 \qquad \text{Write original inequality.}$$
$$0 + 7 \overset{?}{\le} 7 \qquad \text{Substitute 0 for } x.$$
$$7 \le 10 \; \checkmark \qquad \text{Solution checks.}$$

**Solve the inequality. Graph your solution.**

**11.** $z - 2 < 6$

**12.** $q + 5.1 \ge 4.5$

**13.** $a + \dfrac{1}{2} > 2\dfrac{3}{4}$

**14.** $t - 1 \le -5$

**15.** $m + 1.7 \ge 14.2$

**16.** $c + \dfrac{1}{2} < -8$

**9.3** *Solve Inequalities Involving Multiplication or Division* pp. 386–389

Multiplying or dividing each side of an inequality by a *positive* number produces an equivalent inequality. Multiplying or dividing each side of an inequality by a *negative* number and *reversing the direction of the inequality symbol* produces an equivalent inequality.

**EXAMPLES**  Solve (a) $\frac{x}{6} < 4$ and (b) $-5x < -35$. Graph each solution.

a.       $\frac{x}{6} < 4$       **Write original inequality.**

$\frac{x}{6} \cdot 6 < 6 \cdot 4$   **Multiply each side by 6.**

$x < 24$       **Simplify.**

The solutions are all real numbers less than 24.

$$\text{20  21  22  23  24  25}$$

b.   $-5x < -35$       **Write original inequality.**

$\frac{-5x}{-5} > \frac{-35}{-5}$   **Divide each side by −5.**
**Reverse inequality symbol.**

$x > 7$       **Simplify.**

The solutions are all real numbers greater than 7.

$$\text{6  7  8  9  10  11}$$

**Solve the inequality. Graph your solution.**

**17.** $\frac{v}{2} > 8$   **18.** $7d \geq 6.3$   **19.** $\frac{t}{7} < 1$

**20.** $-14k > 42$   **21.** $\frac{y}{-0.35} \leq -20$   **22.** $16f \geq -88$

**9.4** *Solve Two-Step Inequalities*  pp. 392–395

**EXAMPLE**  Solve $3x + 2 > 17$. Graph your solution.

$3x + 2 > 17$   **Write original inequality.**

$3x > 15$   **Subtract 2 from each side.**

$x > 5$   **Divide each side by 3.**

The solutions are all real numbers greater than 5.

$$\text{2  3  4  5  6  7}$$

**Solve the inequality. Graph your solution.**

**23.** $\frac{p}{3} - 2\frac{1}{7} \leq 3\frac{6}{7}$   **24.** $4.7j + 0.2 < 19$   **25.** $-32h + 5 \geq -11$

**Graph the inequality.**

**1.** $x \le \dfrac{5}{2}$
**2.** $z > -5.25$
**3.** $t > 2\dfrac{1}{3}$
**4.** $c \le -\dfrac{13}{4}$

**Write an inequality represented by the graph.**

**5.**

**6.**

**7.**

**8.**

**In Exercises 9 and 10, write the common phrase as an inequality.**

**9.** No less than $-8$

**10.** At most 20

**11.** Tell whether $x = -2.5$ is a solution of the inequality $x + 5 \ge 1.5$.

**12.** Tell whether $x = \dfrac{5}{2}$ is a solution of the inequality $x - 7 < -5$.

**Solve the inequality. Graph your solution.**

**13.** $z - 3 < -7$
**14.** $x + 8 > -2$
**15.** $-5 \le y + 2.5$

**16.** $\dfrac{x}{3} < 7$
**17.** $\dfrac{y}{-4} \ge 8$
**18.** $\dfrac{p}{-2.4} > -2$

**19.** $3x \ge 12$
**20.** $-2 > -3x$
**21.** $5x \le 15$

**22.** $5x - 7 < 8$
**23.** $-2z + 9 \ge 21$
**24.** $4y + 2.3 > 1.5$

**25.** $3 \le \dfrac{x}{-4} - 4$
**26.** $\dfrac{m}{3} + 8 > -3$
**27.** $\dfrac{z}{-3} + 2 \ge \dfrac{1}{6}$

**In Exercises 28 and 29, write the verbal sentence as an inequality. Then solve the inequality and graph your solution.**

**28.** Five more than 3 times a number is at most $-6$.

**29.** When 3.5 is subtracted from the quotient of a number and 6, the result is greater than $-2$.

**30.** The cost of flying from San Francisco to Los Angeles starts from $109 per person. Write an inequality that represents the possible costs for one person.

**31.** The difference between Paula's height and Sheila's height is at least 2.5 inches. Sheila is 62 inches tall, and Paula is taller. Write and solve an inequality that can be used to find Paula's possible heights.

**32.** George has $150 to buy a compact disc player and some CDs. The player that he wants costs $45.95, and each CD costs $10. What are the possible numbers of CDs that George can buy?

# Multiple Choice Chapter Test

**1.** What inequality does the graph represent?

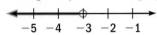

     −5   −4   −3   −2   −1

  **A** $x > -3$       **B** $x \geq -3$

  **C** $x < -3$       **D** $x \leq -3$

**2.** What inequality represents the verbal phrase "no more than 5"?

  **A** $x > 5$       **B** $x \geq 5$

  **C** $x < 5$       **D** $x \leq 5$

**3.** The daytime temperature of a town during the month of July was always above 78°F. What inequality represents the daytime temperature?

  **A** $T > 78$       **B** $T \geq 78$

  **C** $T < 78$       **D** $T \leq 78$

**4.** Which value of $x$ is *not* a solution of the inequality $x - 5 < -3$?

  **A** $x = 1$       **B** $x = 0$

  **C** $x = -1$       **D** $x = 2$

**5.** Which inequality is equivalent to $-3 < y - 6$?

  **A** $y > -9$       **B** $y > -3$

  **C** $y < -3$       **D** $y > 3$

**6.** Nikolai has saved $255 to buy a video game system that costs at least $395. What inequality describes the possible amounts of money he needs to save?

  **A** $s - 255 \geq 395$

  **B** $s + 255 \geq 395$

  **C** $s - 395 \leq 255$

  **D** $s + 395 \leq 255$

**7.** Which inequality is equivalent to $\frac{x}{-8} < -3$?

  **A** $x > -24$       **B** $x < -24$

  **C** $x < 24$       **D** $x > 24$

**8.** Julia walks 3 miles per hour. She walks at least 15 miles each week. What inequality describes the amounts of time $t$ (in hours) she spends walking each week?

  **A** $3t \geq 15$       **B** $3t \leq 15$

  **C** $15t \geq 3$       **D** $15t \leq 3$

**9.** What is the solution of the inequality $-2x + 5 > -3$?

  **A** $x < 4$       **B** $x > -1$

  **C** $x < -4$       **D** $x < 1$

**10.** Which graph represents the solution of $\frac{x}{3} - 5 \leq 2$?

  **A**    19   20   21   22   23

  **B**    19   20   21   22   23

  **C**    19   20   21   22   23

  **D**    19   20   21   22   23

**11.** Liza has $26.50 to buy cleaning supplies. She buys various cleansers for $18.25 and decides to spend the rest on sponges. Each sponge costs $1.10. Which describes the possible number of sponges Liza can buy?

  **A** She can buy at most 6 sponges.

  **B** She can buy at most 7 sponges.

  **C** She can buy at most 8 sponges.

  **D** She can buy at most 9 sponges.

# Linear Equations in Two Variables

*Vocabulary for Chapter 10* .............

## Key Mathematical Vocabulary

- **coordinate plane, p. 408**
- **linear equation, p. 414**

- **slope, p. 434**
- **direct variation, p. 446**

## Academic Vocabulary

- **predict** Use a pattern or relationship to determine an unknown value of a variable. For example, see Exercise 24 on page 454.
- **describe, p. 406**
- **compare, p. 411**
- **estimate, p. 411**
- **explain, p. 413**
- **check, p. 418**
- **model, p. 418**
- **make a conjecture, p. 457**

**Finding the distance hikers can walk if they are walking at a constant rate, page 454**

**Gr. 7 AF 3.3** Graph linear functions, noting that the vertical change (change in *y*-value) per unit of horizontal change (change in *x*-value) is always the same and know that the ratio ("rise over run") is called the slope of a graph.
**Gr. 7 AF 3.4** Plot the values of quantities whose ratios are always the same (e.g., cost to the number of an item, feet to inches, circumference to diameter of a circle). Fit a line to the plot and understand that the slope of the line equals the ratio of the quantities.
**Gr. 7 AF 4.2** Solve multistep problems involving rate, average speed, distance, and time or a direct variation.

# Review Prerequisite Skills

## REVIEW VOCABULARY

- integer, p. 162
- equation, p. 324
- solution of an equation, p. 324
- number line, p. 477
- ratio, p. 483

### VOCABULARY CHECK

**Copy and complete the statement.**

1. A(n) _?_ uses division to compare two numbers.

2. The solution of the equation $2x = -6$ is _?_ .

### SKILLS CHECK

**Use a number line to order the integers from least to greatest.**
**(Review p. 162 for 10.1.)**

3. $-5, 7, 3, -2, 0, 4, 9, -1$

4. $-12, -8, -27, 38, 6, -15, 27$

**Solve the equation. (Review p. 336 for 10.2–10.4.)**

5. $2x - 17 = 13$

6. $4 = 15x - 11$

7. $-6x + 30 = 0$

8. $7x - 3x = -16$

9. $-3 = x + 5x$

10. $7x + 17 = -25$

**Write the fraction in simplest form. (Review p. 54 for 10.5.)**

11. $\dfrac{15}{45}$

12. $\dfrac{6}{20}$

13. $\dfrac{32}{56}$

14. $\dfrac{25}{90}$

**Write the specified ratio in three ways. (Review p. 483 for 10.5–10.8)**

15. 5 apples to 8 pears

16. 12 boys to 20 girls

17. 13 pens to 26 pencils

18. 2 wins to 7 losses

19. A mountain trail has a vertical change in elevation of 1800 feet. On average, a hiker gains 7.5 feet in elevation per minute of walking. How long does the hiker take to reach the top of the mountain?
**(Review p. 330 for 10.5–10.8.)**

405

# Let's Explore
## Using a Map

**Goal**
Use a grid to describe a location on a map.

**Materials**
• graph paper

**QUESTION**  How can you use a grid to describe a particular location on a map?

**EXPLORE 1**  *Give directions from one point to another* . . . . .

Describe how to walk from the intersection of West 4th Avenue and North 3rd Street to the intersection of East 2nd Avenue and South 1st Street.

**1** **Find** the intersections on the map. On graph paper, copy the map at the right. Label the intersection of West 4th Avenue and North 3rd Street as point *A*. Then label the intersection of East 2nd Avenue and South 1st Street as point *B*.

**2** **Find** a route from point *A* to point *B*. A *block* is the distance between an intersection and an adjacent intersection. One way to walk from point *A* to point *B* would be to walk 4 blocks south and 6 blocks east.

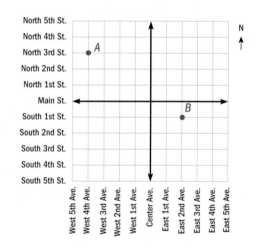

## Draw Conclusions
Use your map from Explore 1 to complete the exercises.

1. Plot and label point *C* at the intersection of East 2nd Avenue and North 2nd Street. Plot and label point *D* at the intersection of West 2nd Avenue and South 3rd Street. Plot and label point *E* at the intersection of West 3rd Avenue and North 1st Street.

2. Describe how to walk from point *B* to point *C*.

3. Describe how to walk from point *C* to point *D*. Then describe how to walk back from point *D* to point *C* using the same route.

4. Describe how to walk from point *D* to point *E*. Then describe how to walk back from point *E* to point *D* using a different route.

**5.** Main Street and Center Avenue divide the city into four sections: northwest, northeast, southwest, and southeast. In which section of the city is point *A* located?

**6.** Some friends tell you to meet them at the intersection of 1st Avenue and 1st Street. What additional information do you need to find them?

**EXPLORE 2** *Find an unknown point using distance* ........

**1** **Choose** a hidden location.
Choose a partner for this hide-and-seek game. One player will be the hider and one player will be the seeker. The hider chooses a location on the map from Explore 1 and notes the location without telling the seeker where it is.

**2** **Guess** the hidden location.
The seeker chooses a location on the map. If the location is incorrect, the hider must tell the seeker the least number of blocks the seeker would have to move in order to get from the guessed location to the hidden one.

**3** **Continue** guessing until the location is found.
The seeker continues to choose locations, and the hider continues to tell the least number of blocks between the guessed and hidden locations until the seeker finds the hidden location.

**4** **Switch** roles.
Switch roles so that the seeker becomes the hider and vice versa. Repeat Steps 1–3.

## Draw Conclusions
**Use the map from Explore 1 to complete the exercises.**

**7.** Name all the intersections that are one block away from the intersection of Main Street and Center Avenue. What do these streets and avenues have in common?

**8.** Which location is 3 blocks west and 4 blocks south from the intersection of Main Street and Center Avenue? How are the street names in the intersection related to the distance from the intersection of Main Street and Center Avenue?

# Graph in the Coordinate Plane

## VOCABULARY and CONCEPTS

A **coordinate plane** is formed by the intersection of a horizontal number line called the **x-axis** and a vertical number line called the **y-axis**. The axes meet at the point $O$ called the **origin** and divide the coordinate plane into four **quadrants**.

Each point in a coordinate plane is represented by a pair of numbers $(x, y)$ called an **ordered pair**. The first number is the **x-coordinate**, and the second number is the **y-coordinate**. The point $P$ shown has coordinates $(-4, 2)$. The origin $O$ has coordinates $(0, 0)$.

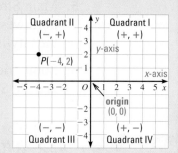

**EXAMPLE 1** *Naming Points in a Coordinate Plane* • • • • • • • • • •

**Give the coordinates of points A and B.**

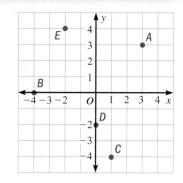

a. Point $A$ is 3 units to the right of the origin and 3 units up. The x-coordinate is 3, and the y-coordinate is 3. The coordinates are $(3, 3)$.

b. Point $B$ is 4 units to the left of the origin and 0 units up or down. The x-coordinate is $-4$, and the y-coordinate is 0. The coordinates are $(-4, 0)$.

### Practice for Example 1

Use the coordinate plane in Example 1. Give the coordinates of the point.

**1.** $C$         **2.** $D$         **3.** $E$

**EXAMPLE 2** *Plotting Points in a Coordinate Plane* • • • • • • • • • •

**Plot the points A(−1, 3) and B(0, −3). Describe each point's location.**

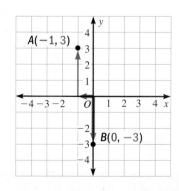

a. To graph $A(-1, 3)$, start at $(0, 0)$. Move 1 unit to the left and 3 units up. Point $A$ is in Quadrant II.

b. To graph $B(0, -3)$, start at $(0, 0)$. Move 3 units down. Point $B$ is on the y-axis.

## Practice for Example 2

**Graph the point and describe its location.**

**4.** $A(0, 2)$          **5.** $B(2, 3)$          **6.** $C(2, -2)$

**7.** $D(3, 0)$          **8.** $E(-2, 3)$          **9.** $F(0, -1)$

**EXAMPLE 3**  *Finding Lengths in a Coordinate Plane* ·········

A map of a city park is shown in a coordinate plane. The park has two main paths. Points $A$, $B$, $C$, and $D$ are at the end of the paths. The units are feet. What are the lengths of the two paths?

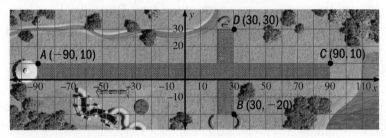

### Solution

To find the length of the longer path, find the distance between points $A$ and $C$, written $AC$.

$$AC = |x\text{-coordinate of } A - x\text{-coordinate of } C|$$
$$= |-90 - 90| = |-180| = 180$$

To find the length of the shorter path, find the distance between points $B$ and $D$, written $BD$.

$$BD = |y\text{-coordinate of } B - y\text{-coordinate of } D|$$
$$= |-20 - 30| = |-50| = 50$$

▶**Answer** The lengths of the two paths are 180 feet and 50 feet.

## Practice for Example 3

**10.** A work crew is clearing a rectangular area for a tiny tot playground in the city park from Example 3. The following points represent the corners of the playground.

$F(50, -5)$, $G(80, -5)$, $H(50, -25)$, and $J(80, -25)$

What will the perimeter of the playground be?

# Practice

**Extra Practice**
p. 507

**Give the coordinates of the point.**

**1.** $A$              **2.** $B$              **3.** $C$

**4.** $D$              **5.** $E$              **6.** $F$

**Plot the point and describe its location.**

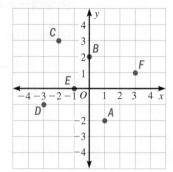

**7.** $G(3, -2)$        **8.** $H(0, 4)$        **9.** $I(7, 6)$

**10.** $J(1, -5)$        **11.** $K(-3, 7)$        **12.** $L(-4, -8)$

**Plot the points. Connect them in the order given, and connect the last point with the first. Then identify the resulting figure and find its perimeter and area.**

**13.** $(2, 0), (2, -3), (4, -3), (4, 0)$        **14.** $(7, 2), (7, 6), (2, 6), (2, 2)$

**15.** $(1, 5), (-3, 5), (-3, 1), (1, 1)$        **16.** $(-4, -1), (2, -1), (2, 2), (-4, 2)$

**FIND THE ERROR** *Describe* and correct the error in plotting the point.

**17.**

> To plot $(-3, 4)$, move
> 3 units to the right of the
> origin and 4 units up.

**18.**

> To plot $(-7, 5)$, move 7 units
> to the left of the origin and
> 5 units down.

**19.** To plot point $A$, you start at the origin, move 5 units to the left and 4 units up. Then to plot point $B$, you start at point $A$ and move 3 units to the right and 2 units down. What are the coordinates of point $B$?

**20.** Pat wants to create a flower garden in her yard. She makes a scale drawing on a coordinate plane with each unit representing 1 foot. Points $A$, $B$, $C$, and $D$ represent the corners of the garden.

$A(-4, 7)$, $B(6, 7)$, $C(6, 1)$, and $D(-4, 1)$

What will the perimeter of Pat's garden be? What will the area be?

**21.** On the map shown, each unit represents 1 mile. Julia drives from point $A$ to point $B$ using the roads shown.

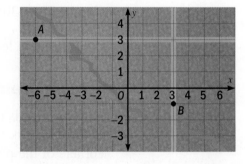

    **a.** Give the coordinates of points $A$ and $B$.

    **b.** What is the distance from $A$ to the intersection of the roads? What is the distance from $B$ to the intersection of the roads?

    **c.** How many miles does Julia drive?

**22.** **REASONING** *Write* a rule for determining in which quadrant a point is located using the $x$- and $y$-coordinates of the point. Assume $x \neq 0$ and $y \neq 0$.

**Give the coordinates of the point.**

**1.** *A*

**2.** *B*

**3.** *C*

**4.** *D*

**5.** *E*

**6.** *F*

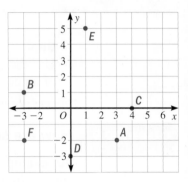

**Plot the point and describe its location.**

**7.** $G(-5, 3)$

**8.** $H(1, -3)$

**9.** $I(0, -1)$

**10.** $J(3, 7)$

**11.** $K(-6, 0)$

**12.** $L(-8, -5)$

**Plot the points. Connect them in the order given, and connect the last point with the first. Then identify the resulting figure and find its perimeter and area.**

**13.** $(-1, 0), (-1, 4), (-4, 4), (-4, 0)$

**14.** $(3, -5), (3, 3), (-2, 3), (-2, -5)$

**15.** $(-6, -3), (-6, 2), (-1, 2), (-1, -3)$

**16.** $(-2, -2), (3, -2), (3, 2), (-2, 2)$

**FIND THE ERROR** *Describe* and correct the error in finding the distance between the points.

**17.**

Distance between $G(-2, 3)$ and
$H(4, 3)$:
$GH = |-2 - 3|$
$= |-5| = 5$ units

**18.**

Distance between $J(-4, 3)$ and
$K(-4, 5)$:
$JK = |3 - 5|$
$= -2$ units

**19.** Amanda wants to create a vegetable garden. She makes a scale drawing on a coordinate plane with each unit representing 1 foot. Points *A*, *B*, *C*, and *D* represent the corners of the garden.

$A(-2, 2), B(11, 2), C(11, -15),$ and $D(-2, -15)$

What will the perimeter of Amanda's garden be? What will the area be?

**20.** A coordinate plane with units in feet is used to show the location of items from a shipwreck.

**a.** What are the coordinates of the anchor, cup, belt buckle, and sword?

**b.** Use the Pythagorean theorem to estimate the distance between the anchor and the cup. Round your answer to the nearest tenth.

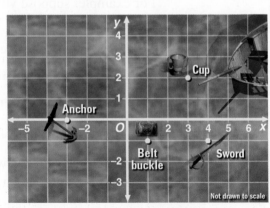

**21.** **REASONING** Draw a rectangle in a coordinate plane. Multiply the coordinates of each corner point by 2 and draw a new rectangle. *Compare* the perimeter of the new rectangle with the perimeter of the original rectangle. What do you notice?

# Activity 10.2

## Let's Explore
## Modeling Graphs of Equations in Two Variables

**Goal**
Use the classroom to model the graph of an equation in two variables.

**Materials**
• graph paper

**QUESTION**  **How are solutions of equations in two variables related on a graph?**

An example of an equation in two variables is $x - y = 1$. A *solution of an equation in two variables, x and y,* is an ordered pair $(x, y)$ that produces a true statement when the values of $x$ and $y$ are substituted into the equation.

**EXPLORE**  *Graph equations in two variables* ..............

**Use your classroom to model the graph of $x - y = 1$.**

**1**  **Define** the coordinate plane. Turn your class into a coordinate plane. Your teacher will assign each student in the class an ordered pair. Record your ordered pair.

**2**  **Substitute** values into the equation. Check whether your ordered pair is a solution of the equation $x - y = 1$ by substituting for $x$ and $y$ and then simplifying. If the result is a true statement, stand up. If it is false, remain seated.

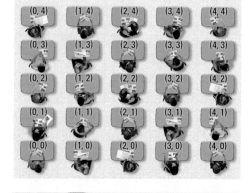

For example, suppose your ordered pair is (3, 2):

$x - y = 1$    **Write original equation.**

$3 - 2 \stackrel{?}{=} 1$    **Substitute.**

$1 = 1$    **Statement is true.**

In this case, you should stand up.

Notice that the students who are standing represent points on a line. The line is the graph of $x - y = 1$.

**Gr. 7 AF 3.3 Graph linear functions,** noting that the vertical change (change in *y*-value) per unit of horizontal change (change in *x*-value) is always the same and know that the ratio ("rise over run") is called the slope of a graph.
**Also addresses Gr. 4 MG 2.0, Gr. 4 MG 2.1**

**3** **Record** the model.
Using graph paper, draw a coordinate plane for the classroom, plot the ordered pairs for the students standing, and draw a line through the points.

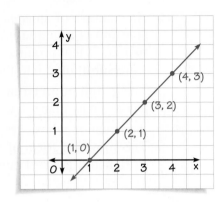

**4** **Model** other equations.
Your teacher will give you other equations. Repeat Steps 1–3.

# Draw Conclusions

### In Exercises 1–4, use the line shown in Step 3.

1. Is the ordered pair $\left(\frac{3}{2}, \frac{1}{2}\right)$ a solution of the equation $x - y = 1$? *Explain*.

2. What point on the *y*-axis is part of the line?

3. Name three points in Quadrant III that are on the line.

4. Are there any points on the line that are in Quadrant II? in Quadrant IV? If so, give an example.

### In Exercises 5–10, tell whether the ordered pair is a solution of the equation $x - y = 15$.

5. $(25, 10)$     6. $(14, 1)$     7. $(18, 3)$

8. $(-2, -17)$     9. $\left(17\frac{3}{4}, 2\frac{3}{4}\right)$     10. $(0.25, -12.75)$

11. Which ordered pair is a solution of $2x + 3y = 18$?

   **A.** $(4, 3)$     **B.** $(8, 3)$     **C.** $(3, 4)$     **D.** $(0, 4)$

12. Which ordered pair is a solution of $3x + 2y = 8$?

   **A.** $\left(-\frac{1}{2}, 7\right)$     **B.** $(7, -2)$     **C.** $\left(\frac{2}{3}, 3\right)$     **D.** $\left(-1, -5\frac{1}{2}\right)$

### Tell which quadrants the graph of the equation passes through. *Explain* your reasoning.

13. $4x - 3y = 9$     14. $y - 2x = 0$     15. $-5x + 6y = 30$

16. $-3x + y = 4$     17. $-3x + 2y = 6$     18. $2x - 4y = 12$

## Lesson 10.2

# Graph Linear Equations in Standard Form

> **VOCABULARY and CONCEPTS**
>
> An example of an *equation in two variables* is $2x - y = 5$. A **solution of an equation in two variables**, $x$ and $y$, is an ordered pair $(x, y)$ that produces a true statement when the values of $x$ and $y$ are substituted into the equation.
>
> The **graph of an equation in two variables** is the set of points in a coordinate plane that represent all the solutions of the equation.
>
> An equation whose graph is a line is called a **linear equation**. The **standard form of a linear equation** is $Ax + By = C$ where $A$, $B$, and $C$ are real numbers and $A$ and $B$ are not both zero.

**EXAMPLE 1** *Checking a Solution* • • • • • • • • • • • • • • • • • • • • • • • • • •

**Tell whether $(-1, 19)$ is a solution of $5x + 6y = 100$.**

| | |
|---|---|
| $5x + 6y = 100$ | **Write original equation.** |
| $5(-1) + 6(19) \stackrel{?}{=} 100$ | **Substitute $-1$ for $x$ and $19$ for $y$.** |
| $109 \neq 100$ | **Simplify.** |

▶ **Answer** $(-1, 19)$ is not a solution of $5x + 6y = 100$.

**EXAMPLE 2** *Finding Solutions of an Equation* • • • • • • • • • • • • • • •

**List four solutions of the equation $5x + y = 12$.**

Solve for $y$ and then find $y$-values for several $x$-values.

**Step 1** Solve the equation for $y$.  **Step 2** Find $y$-values for several $x$-values.

$5x + y = 12$

$y = 12 - 5x$

| $x$ | $y = 12 - 5x$ | $(x, y)$ |
|---|---|---|
| $-1$ | $y = 12 - 5(-1) = 17$ | $(-1, 17)$ |
| $0$ | $y = 12 - 5(0) = 12$ | $(0, 12)$ |
| $1$ | $y = 12 - 5(1) = 7$ | $(1, 7)$ |
| $2$ | $y = 12 - 5(2) = 2$ | $(2, 2)$ |

▶ **Answer** Four solutions are $(-1, 17)$, $(0, 12)$, $(1, 7)$, and $(2, 2)$.

### Practice for Examples 1 and 2

**1.** Tell whether $(-8, 7)$ is a solution of $3x + y = -17$.

**List four solutions of the equation.**

**2.** $-5x + y = 2$        **3.** $4x + y = 10$        **4.** $6x - y = 2$

**EXAMPLE 3** *Graphing a Linear Equation*

**Graph the equation $x - 2y = 2$.**

**Step 1** Solve the equation for *y*, then make a table by choosing a few values for *x* and finding the values of *y*.

$$x - 2y = 2$$
$$-2y = -x + 2$$
$$y = \frac{1}{2}x - 1$$

| x | −2 | 0 | 2 | 4 |
|---|----|---|---|---|
| y | −2 | −1 | 0 | 1 |

**Step 2** Plot the points. Draw a line through them.

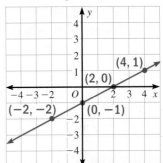

**EXAMPLE 4** *Graphing a Real-World Model*

Ms. Kay has \$120 to spend on *x* shawls at \$30 each and *y* scarves at \$15 each as gifts. The equation $30x + 15y = 120$ is a model of the situation. Graph the model. What combinations of shawls and scarves can she buy?

**Solution**

Solve the equation $30x + 15y = 120$ for *y*.

$$30x + 15y = 120$$
$$15y = 120 - 30x$$
$$y = -2x + 8$$

Make a table of values, then graph the model.

| x | 0 | 1 | 2 | 3 | 4 |
|---|---|---|---|---|---|
| y | 8 | 6 | 4 | 2 | 0 |

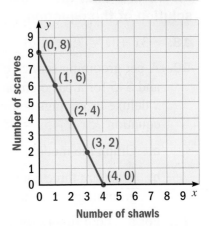

▶ **Answer** She can buy 0 shawls and 8 scarves, 1 shawl and 6 scarves, 2 shawls and 4 scarves, 3 shawls and 2 scarves, or 4 shawls and 0 scarves.

**Practice for Examples 3 and 4**

**5.** Graph the equation $-2x + y = 1$.

**6.** *Explain* why no other combinations of shawls and scarves are possible in Example 4.

# Practice

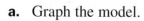

**Extra Practice**
p. 507

**Tell whether the ordered pair is a solution of $3x + y = 9$.**

**1.** $(2, 3)$  **2.** $(3, 1)$  **3.** $(1, 3)$  **4.** $(-3, 18)$

**Tell whether the ordered pair is a solution of the equation.**

**5.** $-3x + y = 7; (-2, 1)$  **6.** $2x - y = 5; (4, 3)$

**7. FIND THE ERROR** *Describe* and correct the error in determining whether $(1, 2)$ is a solution of $4x + 2y = 8$.

$$4x + 2y = 8$$
$$4(2) + 2(1) \overset{?}{=} 8$$
$$10 \neq 8$$

$(1, 2)$ is not a solution of $4x + 2y = 8$.

**Use the equation to find the value of $y$ when $x$ has the given value.**

**8.** $-3x + y = 8; x = 4$  **9.** $-4x + y = -12; x = 6$

**10.** $-6x + y = 8; x = -3$  **11.** $5x + 2y = 22; x = 2$

**Graph the equation.**

**12.** $-x + y = 4$  **13.** $x + y = 2$  **14.** $-2x + y = -1$

**15.** $-\frac{1}{2}x + y = 4$  **16.** $2x - y = -4$  **17.** $-2x + y = 6$

**REASONING Find the value of $a$ that makes the ordered pair a solution of the equation.**

**18.** $-3x + y = 7; (-3, a)$  **19.** $7x + y = 11; (a, -10)$

**20.** A pet grooming service charges \$75 for a deluxe grooming and \$45 for a basic grooming. On a certain day, sales of $x$ deluxe groomings and $y$ basic groomings totaled \$450. The equation $75x + 45y = 450$ is a model of this situation.

   **a.** Graph the model.

   **b.** What are three combinations of deluxe and basic groomings that total \$450?

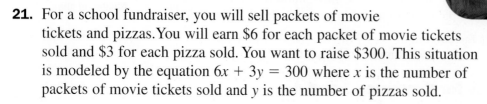

**21.** For a school fundraiser, you will sell packets of movie tickets and pizzas. You will earn \$6 for each packet of movie tickets sold and \$3 for each pizza sold. You want to raise \$300. This situation is modeled by the equation $6x + 3y = 300$ where $x$ is the number of packets of movie tickets sold and $y$ is the number of pizzas sold.

   **a.** Graph the model.

   **b.** What are four combinations of packets of movie tickets and pizzas that you could sell to meet your goal?

**Tell whether the ordered pair is a solution of the equation.**

**1.** $5x + y = -17$; $(3, -6)$

**2.** $-4x + y = 9$; $(-2, 1)$

**3.** $4x - 5y = 1$; $(4, 3)$

**4.** $-3x + 7y = 11$; $(5, 8)$

**5.** $4x - 3y = 2$; $(2, -2)$

**6.** $-2x - 5y = 13$; $(-4, -1)$

**Use the equation to find the value of *y* when *x* has the given value.**

**7.** $-3x + y = 120$; $x = 62$

**8.** $-5x + y = 40$; $x = 40$

**9.** $8x - 2y = 40$; $x = 6$

**10.** $4.5x + 2.25y = 54$; $x = -2$

**11.** $1.5x - 2y = 3$; $x = 4$

**12.** $3.8x - 2y = 20$; $x = 5$

**13.** **FIND THE ERROR** *Describe* and correct
the error in finding a solution of the equation
$2x + y = 4$.

$2x + y = 4$
$y = 4 - 2x$
Evaluate for x = −1.

$y = 4 - 2(-1)$
$y = 6$
One solution is (6, −1).

**Graph the equation.**

**14.** $-x + y = -3$

**15.** $x + y = 8$

**16.** $\frac{1}{3}x + y = 2$

**17.** $-2x + y = 2$

**18.** $2x + y = 4$

**19.** $2x + y = -6$

**20.** $-x + 2y = 4$

**21.** $3x - 2y = 6$

**22.** $x - 3y = -6$

**REASONING Find the value of *a* that makes the ordered pair a
solution of the equation.**

**23.** $2x + 4y = 14$; $(-5, a)$

**24.** $9x - 5y = -9$; $(a - 1, 9)$

**25.** You have $480 to buy flowers for tables at an awards banquet. You will
buy *x* dozen tulips at $30 per dozen and *y* dozen daffodils at $24 per
dozen. The equation $30x + 24y = 480$ is a model of this situation.

   **a.** Graph the model.

   **b.** What are four combinations of tulips and daffodils that you can buy?

**26.** You are in charge of buying salads for a picnic. You will spend $20
for *x* pounds of potato salad at $1.25 per pound and *y* pounds of pasta
salad at $2.50 per pound. The equation $1.25x + 2.50y = 20$ is a model
of this situation.

   **a.** Graph the model.

   **b.** What are four combinations of potato salad and pasta salad that you
   can purchase?

## Let's Explore
## Modeling Graphs of Horizontal and Vertical Lines

**Goal**
Use the classroom to model graphs of horizontal and vertical lines.

**Materials**
• graph paper

**QUESTION** How can you graph a horizontal or vertical line on a coordinate plane?

**EXPLORE 1** *Model the graph of a vertical line* ............

Use your classroom to model the graph of $x = 2$.

**1** **Define** the coordinate plane.

Turn your class into a coordinate plane. Your teacher will assign each student in the class an ordered pair. Record your ordered pair.

**2** **Substitute** values into the equation.

Check whether your ordered pair is a solution of the equation $x = 2$ by substituting the $x$-coordinate for $x$. If the result is a true statement, stand up. If it is false, remain seated.

**3** **Record** the model.

Using graph paper, draw a coordinate plane for the classroom, plot the points represented by the students standing, and draw a line through the points.

**4** **Model** other equations.

Your teacher will give you other equations of the form $x = a$. Repeat Steps 1–3.

## Draw Conclusions

**1.** Compare the ordered pairs for the students standing when $x = 2$ is graphed. What do you notice?

**Graph the equation on a coordinate plane.**

**2.** $x = 6$      **3.** $x = -4$      **4.** $x = 3$      **5.** $x = -2$

**Gr. 7 AF 3.3** **Graph linear functions,** noting that the vertical change (change in y-value) per unit of horizontal change (change in x-value) is always the same and know that the ratio ("rise over run") is called the slope of a graph.
**Also addresses Gr. 4 MG 2.0, Gr. 4 MG 2.1**

**EXPLORE 2** *Model the graph of a horizontal line* •••••••••

**Use your classroom to model the graph of y = 4.**

**1** **Define** the coordinate plane.

Use the same coordinate plane as in Step 1 of Explore 1.

**2** **Substitute** values into the equation.

Check whether your ordered pair is a solution of the equation $y = 4$ by substituting the $y$-coordinate for $y$. If the result is a true statement, stand up. If it is false, remain seated.

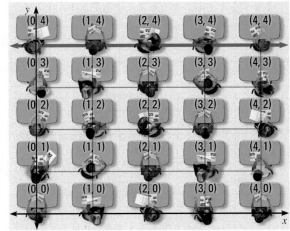

**3** **Record** the model.

Using graph paper, draw a coordinate plane for the classroom, plot the points represented by the students standing, and draw a line through the points.

**4** **Model** other equations.

Your teacher will give you other equations of the form $y = b$. Repeat Steps 1–3.

## Draw Conclusions

**6.** Compare the ordered pairs for the students standing when $y = 4$ is graphed. What do you notice?

**Graph the equation on a coordinate plane.**

**7.** $y = 3$      **8.** $y = -2$      **9.** $y = 6$      **10.** $y = -4$

**In Exercises 11–14, give an equation of the line that passes through the given points.**

**11.** $(-1, 0), (-1, 1), (-1, 2), (-1, 3)$      **12.** $(1, 5), (2, 5), (3, 5), (4, 5)$

**13.** $(2, -3), (5, -3), (9, -3), (11, -3)$      **14.** $(5, -2), (5, -1), (5, 0), (5, 1)$

**15.** Show that the equation $x = 2$ (from Explore 1) and the equation $y = 4$ (from Explore 2) can be written in standard form. (Recall that the standard form of a linear equation is $Ax + By = C$ where $A$ and $B$ are not both zero.)

# Graph Horizontal and Vertical Lines

### VOCABULARY and CONCEPTS

In a coordinate plane, lines that are parallel to the *x*-axis are *horizontal lines*. Lines that are parallel to the *y*-axis are *vertical lines*.

The graph of the equation $x = a$ is a vertical line.
The graph of the equation $y = b$ is a horizontal line.

**EXAMPLE 1**  *Checking a Solution* ...........................

**Tell whether (−12, 19) is a solution of $x = 14$.**

| | |
|---|---|
| $x = 14$ | **Write original equation.** |
| $-12 \stackrel{?}{=} 14$ | **Substitute the *x*-coordinate, −12, for *x*.** |
| $-12 \neq 14$ | **Compare.** |

▶ **Answer**  (−12, 19) is not a solution of $x = 14$.

### Practice for Example 1

**Tell whether the ordered pair is a solution of the equation.**

1. Equation: $x = 3$
   Ordered pair: (3, −4)

2. Equation: $y = 6$
   Ordered pair: (−15, 6)

3. Equation: $y = 7$
   Ordered pair: (13, −7)

**EXAMPLE 2**  *Graphing an Equation of the Form $x = a$* .....

**Graph $x = -1$.**

All points on the graph of $x = -1$ must have an *x*-coordinate of −1, such as (−1, 0), (−1, 2), and (−1, −3). Plot the points, then draw a vertical line through them.

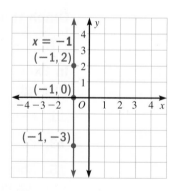

### Practice for Example 2

**Graph the equation on a coordinate plane.**

4. $x = 3$

5. $x = 4$

6. $x = -3$

**EXAMPLE 3** *Graphing an Equation of the Form $y = b$* ......

**Graph $y = 5$.**

All points on the graph of $y = 5$ must have a *y*-coordinate of 5, such as $(0, 5)$, $(-2, 5)$, and $(3, 5)$. Plot the points, then draw a horizontal line through them.

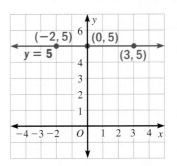

### Practice for Example 3

**Graph the equation on a coordinate plane.**

**7.** $y = 1$          **8.** $y = 2$          **9.** $y = -2$

**EXAMPLE 4** *Solving a Real-World Problem* ....................

Mr. Gray is laying sod. The boundaries of the area to be sodded can be modeled by the graphs of $x = 5$, $y = 5$, $x = 35$, and $y = 20$, where all the distances are in yards. How much sod does Mr. Gray need?

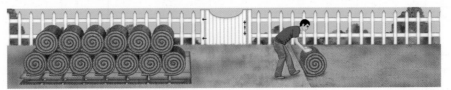

### Solution

Graph the equations as shown. The boundaries form a rectangle with corner points at $(5, 5)$, $(5, 20)$, $(35, 5)$, and $(35, 20)$. Find the area.

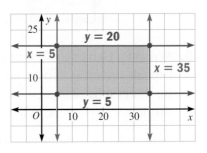

Length $= |35 - 5| = |30| = 30$
Width $= |20 - 5| = |15| = 15$
Area $= 30 \cdot 15 = 450$

▸ **Answer** Mr. Gray needs 450 square yards of sod.

### Practice for Example 4

**10.** Ms. Gonzales is buying carpeting. The boundaries of the room can be modeled by the graphs of $x = 6$, $y = 4$, $x = 16$, and $y = 16$, where all the distances are in feet. How many square feet of carpeting are needed?

# Practice

Extra Practice
p. 507

**Match the equation with the description of its graph.**

**1.** $y = -8$  **A.** Vertical line

**2.** $x = 15$  **B.** Horizontal line

**3.** $y = x + 3$  **C.** Neither horizontal nor vertical line

**Tell whether the ordered pair is a solution of the equation.**

**4.** Equation: $x = -5$  **5.** Equation: $y = -8$  **6.** Equation: $y = 2$
Ordered pair: $(9, -4)$      Ordered pair: $(-8, 6)$      Ordered pair: $(10, 2)$

**Write three ordered pairs that are solutions of the equation.**

**7.** $x = -25$  **8.** $y = -23$  **9.** $y = 12$  **10.** $x = -11$

**11.** $y = 59$  **12.** $x = -29$  **13.** $y = -17$  **14.** $x = 32$

**Graph the equation on a coordinate plane.**

**15.** $x = -5$  **16.** $y = -3$  **17.** $y = 5$  **18.** $y = -5$

**19.** $x = 6$  **20.** $x = 2$  **21.** $x = -2$  **22.** $y = -4$

**In Exercises 23 and 24, write an equation of the line.**

**23.** 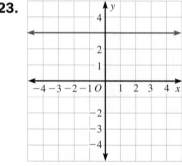  **24.**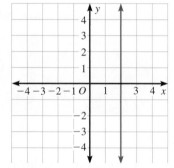

**25.** Wilson's Driveway Construction is preparing the ground to put in an asphalt driveway. The boundaries of the driveway can be modeled by the graphs of $x = 10$, $y = 5$, $x = 25$, and $y = 30$, where all the distances are in feet. What is the area of the driveway?

**26.** A farm has a field of hay to be harvested. The boundaries of the field can be modeled by the graphs of $x = 100$, $y = 100$, $x = 700$, and $y = 900$, where all the distances are in yards. What is the area of the field?

**27.** **REASONING** Consider the equation $Ax + By = C$.

  **a.** What must be true of the equation if its graph is a vertical line?

  **b.** What must be true of the equation if its graph is a horizontal line?

# Practice

**Match the equation with the description of its graph.**

1. $x = -3$
2. $y = 8$
3. $y = x - 4$

A. Vertical line

B. Horizontal line

C. Neither horizontal nor vertical line

**Tell whether the ordered pair is a solution of the equation.**

4. Equation: $x = -29$
   Ordered pair: $(15, -29)$

5. Equation: $y = -13$
   Ordered pair: $(12, -13)$

6. Equation: $y = -2.5$
   Ordered pair: $(9, -16)$

**Write three ordered pairs that are solutions of the given equation.**

7. $x = -32$
8. $y = 85$
9. $y = -56$
10. $x = -2.5$
11. $x = -0.2$
12. $y = -11$
13. $y = 0$
14. $x = 15$

**Graph the equation on a coordinate plane.**

15. $x = -4$
16. $y = 6$
17. $y = 12$
18. $y = -9$
19. $x = -11$
20. $x = 16$
21. $x = 6$
22. $y = 3$

**In Exercises 23 and 24, write an equation of the line.**

23.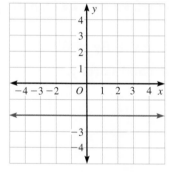

24.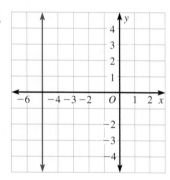

25. **REASONING** Graph the equations $x = 5$ and $y = -2$ in the same coordinate plane. Then write the coordinates of the point where the lines intersect. *Explain* how you can find the coordinates of this point without graphing. Then tell at what point the graphs of $x = -7$ and $y = -6$ would intersect.

26. A mason is laying a brick patio. The boundaries of the patio can be modeled by the graphs of $x = 10$, $y = 30$, $x = 20$, and $y = 10$, where all the distances are in feet. What is the area of the patio?

27. A homeowner is putting ceramic tiles on a tabletop. The tabletop can be modeled by the graphs of $x = 15$, $y = 5$, $x = 35$, and $y = 30$, where all the distances are in inches. What is the area of the tabletop?

**VOCABULARY**
- coordinate plane, p. 408
- *x*-axis, p. 408
- *y*-axis, p. 408
- origin, p. 408
- quadrants, p. 408
- ordered pair, p. 408
- *x*-coordinate, p. 408
- *y*-coordinate, p. 408
- solution of an equation in two variables, p. 414
- graph of an equation in two variables, p. 414
- linear equation, p. 414
- standard form of a linear equation, p. 414

**1.** Copy and complete: The __?__ of $(-2, 3)$ is $-2$.

## 10.1 Graph in the Coordinate Plane ········································· pp. 408–411

**EXAMPLE** Plot the points $A(-2, 3)$ and $B(3, -1)$.

To plot $A(-2, 3)$, start at $(0, 0)$. Move 2 units left and 3 units up. Point $A$ is in Quadrant II. To plot $B(3, -1)$, start at $(0, 0)$. Move 3 units right and 1 unit down. Point $B$ is in Quadrant IV.

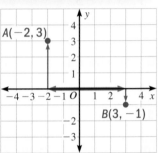

**2.** Plot $C(-1, -2)$ and describe its location.

## 10.2 Graph Linear Equations in Standard Form ············· pp. 414–417

**EXAMPLE** Tell whether $(-4, 12)$ is a solution of $3x + 8y = 82$.

$$3(-4) + 8(12) \stackrel{?}{=} 82 \quad \textbf{Substitute } -4 \textbf{ for } x \textbf{ and } 12 \textbf{ for } y.$$

$$84 \neq 82 \quad \textbf{Simplify.}$$

$(-4, 12)$ is not a solution of $3x + 8y = 82$.

**3.** Tell whether $(3, 19)$ is a solution of $6x + 3y = 75$.

## 10.3 Graph Horizontal and Vertical Lines ····················· pp. 420–423

**EXAMPLE** Graph $x = -2$.

All points on the graph of $x = -2$ must have an $x$-coordinate of $-2$, such as $(-2, 3)$, $(-2, 1)$, and $(-2, -2)$. Plot the points and draw a vertical line through them.

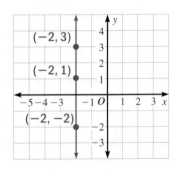

Graph the equation on a coordinate plane.

**4.** $x = 4$ **5.** $y = -4$ **6.** $y = 3$ **7.** $x = -3$

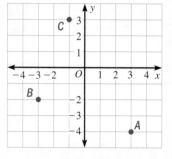

**Give the coordinates of the point.**

**1.** $A$  **2.** $B$  **3.** $C$

**Plot the point and describe its location.**

**4.** $D(-3, 2)$  **5.** $E(3, 4)$  **6.** $F(0, -3)$

**Tell whether the ordered pair is a solution of the equation.**

**7.** $-2x + y = 6; (-3, 1)$  **8.** $x - 3y = -5; (-2, 1)$  **9.** $2x - 3y = 7; (-4, -5)$

**10.** $5x - 2y = 7; (2, -1)$  **11.** $x = -5; (-2, -5)$  **12.** $y = 7; (-3, 7)$

**Use the equation to find the value of y when x has the given value.**

**13.** $3x + y = 5; x = 2$  **14.** $-x + 3y = 2; x = 7$  **15.** $3x - 2y = 11; x = 5$

**Graph the equation.**

**16.** $3x + y = 3$  **17.** $x - 3y = 6$  **18.** $2x - y = 4$

**19.** $-x + y = 3$  **20.** $\frac{1}{2}x - y = 4$  **21.** $2x + y = -1$

**22.** $y = -1$  **23.** $x = -2$  **24.** $x - \frac{3}{2}y = 1$

**25.** $5x - 2y = 10$  **26.** $\frac{4}{3}x + y = 4$  **27.** $y = 2$

**28.** Andrea wants to build a sandbox in her backyard. She makes a scale drawing on a coordinate plane with each unit representing 1 foot. Points $A(-1, 3)$, $B(3, 3)$, $C(3, -2)$, and $D(-1, -2)$ represent the corners of the sandbox. What will the perimeter and area of the sandbox be?

**29.** A barber shop charges $15 for an adult haircut and $10 for a child haircut. On a certain day, income from $x$ adult haircuts and $y$ child haircuts totaled $450. The equation $15x + 10y = 450$ is a model of this situation.

   **a.** Graph the model.

   **b.** What are four combinations of adult and child haircuts that can total $450?

**30.** Michelle sold two types of coupon books. She sold $x$ coupon books for $25 each and $y$ coupon books for $40 each. She sold them for a total of $400. The equation $25x + 40y = 400$ models this situation.

   **a.** Graph the model.

   **b.** What are three combinations of $25 and $40 coupon books that total $400?

**31.** A garden has boundaries that can be modeled by the graphs of $x = -3$, $y = 2$, $x = 2$, and $y = 5$, where all the distances are in yards. What is the area of the garden?

# Let's Explore
## Using Intercepts

**Goal**
Investigate graphing lines using intercepts.

**Materials**
- graph paper
- straightedge

**QUESTION** **How do intercepts help you graph an equation?**

The *x*-coordinate of a point where a graph crosses the *x*-axis is called an *x-intercept*. The *y*-coordinate of a point where a graph crosses the *y*-axis is called a *y-intercept*. For a linear equation whose graph is neither horizontal nor vertical, there is one *x*-intercept and one *y*-intercept.

**EXPLORE 1** *Use a lattice to solve a problem* • • • • • • • • • • • • • • •

**Work in a group. Your teacher will tell your group how much money you have to buy CDs at a music store. The store sells new CDs for $16 and used CDs for $8. Find the possible combinations of new and used CDs you can buy.**

**1** **Draw** a lattice like the one shown.
Copy and extend the lattice so that it contains all the combinations of CDs you can buy with the full amount your group has to spend. For example, the cost of buying 2 new CDs and 2 used CDs is 2 · 16 + 2 · 8 = $48, so write "$48" at the lattice point (2, 2).

*(lattice diagram)*

Used CDs (vertical axis), New CDs (horizontal axis)

| | 0 | 1 | 2 | 3 |
|---|---|---|---|---|
| 3 | $24 | $40 | $56 | $72 |
| 2 | $16 | $32 | ? | $64 |
| 1 | $8 | $24 | $40 | $56 |
| 0 | $0 | $16 | $32 | $48 |

**2** **Identify** the solutions.
Circle all the numbers on the lattice that equal the amount of money your group has to spend. Then draw a line through the circled numbers.

**3** **Compare** your line with the lines of other groups. Draw the lines from all groups on one lattice.

## Draw Conclusions

1. Let *x* be the number of new CDs you buy, and let *y* be the number of used CDs you buy. What is the *x*-intercept of the graph you drew in Step 2? What is the *y*-intercept?

2. From Step 3, what do you notice about the intercepts of the graphs as the amount of money spent on CDs increases?

**EXPLORE 2** *Use intercepts to solve a problem*

**You have $48 to spend for the CDs from Explore 1. Use a graph to find the possible combinations of CDs that you can buy.**

**1** **Plot** a point on the *x*-axis.

Draw and label a coordinate plane like the one shown.

If you buy 0 used CDs, you can buy $48 ÷ $16 = 3 new CDs. In the coordinate plane, plot the point (3, 0) to represent this combination.

**2** **Plot** a point on the *y*-axis.

If you buy 0 new CDs, you can buy $48 ÷ $8 = 6 used CDs. In the coordinate plane, plot the point (0, 6) to represent this combination.

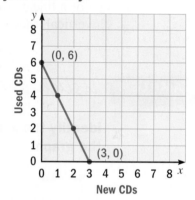

**3** **Draw** a line through the points from Steps 1 and 2.

Look for points where the line passes through an intersection of grid lines. In this case, the points are (1, 4) and (2, 2) which means that you can buy 1 new CD and 4 used CDs or 2 new CDs and 2 used CDs.

## Draw Conclusions

**3.** Which method is simpler, the lattice used in Explore 1 or the intercepts used in Explore 2? *Explain.*

**4.** Two points define a line in a coordinate plane. Why were the two points chosen in Steps 1 and 2 good choices to use in drawing the graph?

**5.** Refer to the graph in Explore 2. Does it make sense to consider points that are not located at an intersection of grid lines? *Explain.*

**6.** A used bookstore sells paperback books for $4 and hardcover books for $6. Copy and complete the graph to find possible combinations of paperback and hardcover books that you can buy for $36. Name three combinations.

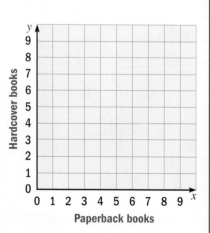

# Graph Linear Equations Using Intercepts

> **VOCABULARY and CONCEPTS**
>
> The *x*-coordinate of a point where a graph crosses the *x*-axis is an
> **x-intercept**.
>
> The *y*-coordinate of a point where a graph crosses the *y*-axis is a
> **y-intercept**.
>
> For a linear equation whose graph is neither horizontal nor
> vertical, there is one *x*-intercept and one *y*-intercept.

**EXAMPLE 1** *Using a Graph to Find Intercepts* · · · · · · · · · · · ·

**Identify the *x*-intercept and *y*-intercept of
the graph.**

**Solution**

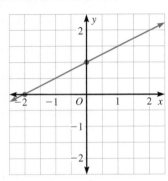

To find the *x*-intercept, observe where the
graph crosses the *x*-axis. The *x*-intercept is −2.

To find the *y*-intercept, observe where the
graph crosses the *y*-axis. The *y*-intercept is 1.

**EXAMPLE 2** *Finding x- and y-Intercepts* · · · · · · · · · · · · · · · ·

**Find the *x*-intercept and *y*-intercept of the graph of
$7x - 3y = 21$.**

**Solution**

To find the *x*-intercept, substitute 0 for *y* and solve for *x*.

$$7x - 3y = 21 \qquad \text{Write original equation.}$$

$$7x - 3(0) = 21 \qquad \text{Substitute 0 for } y.$$

$$x = \frac{21}{7} = 3 \qquad \text{Solve for } x.$$

To find the *y*-intercept, substitute 0 for *x* and solve for *y*.

$$7x - 3y = 21 \qquad \text{Write original equation.}$$

$$7(0) - 3y = 21 \qquad \text{Substitute 0 for } x.$$

$$y = \frac{21}{-3} = -7 \qquad \text{Solve for } y.$$

The *x*-intercept is 3, and the *y*-intercept is −7.

## Practice for Examples 1 and 2

**1.** For the graph shown, identify the *x*-intercept and *y*-intercept.

**Find the *x*-intercept and *y*-intercept of the graph of the equation.**

**2.** $-4x + 3y = 24$      **3.** $5x - y = 15$

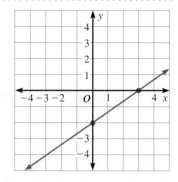

---

**EXAMPLE 3** *Using Intercepts to Graph a Real-World Model*

General admission tickets for a football game cost $6 each and student tickets cost $4 each. Len spent $48 on tickets. An equation that models this situation is $6x + 4y = 48$ where *x* is the number of general admission tickets and *y* is the number of student tickets. What are the possible combinations of tickets Len bought?

### Solution

Find the *x*-intercept and *y*-intercept of the graph.

| ***x*-intercept** | ***y*-intercept** |
|---|---|
| $6x + 4(0) = 48$ | $6(0) + 4y = 48$ |
| $6x = 48$ | $4y = 48$ |
| $x = 8$ | $y = 12$ |

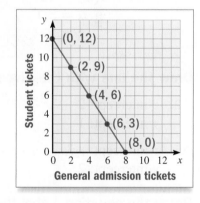

Plot the points (8, 0) and (0, 12), then draw a line connecting them.

Find all points where the line passes through an intersection of grid lines: (0, 12), (2, 9), (4, 6), (6, 3) and (8, 0).

▶ **Answer**  Possible combinations of tickets Len bought are: 0 general and 12 student tickets, 2 general and 9 student tickets, 4 general and 6 student tickets, 6 general and 3 student tickets, or 8 general and 0 student tickets.

## Practice for Example 3

**4.** Small posters cost $4 each and large posters cost $5 each. You plan to spend $40 on posters. This situation can be modeled by $4x + 5y = 40$. Draw a graph and find three possible combinations of posters you can buy for exactly $40.

# Practice

Extra Practice
p. 507

**Identify the *x*-intercept and *y*-intercept of the graph.**

1. 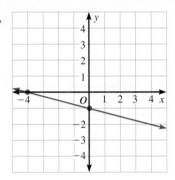   2. 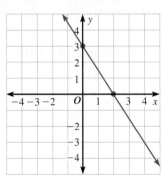   3.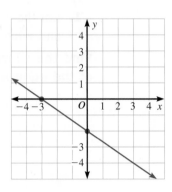

**Find the *x*-intercept and *y*-intercept of the graph of the equation.**

4. $x - y = 4$    5. $2x + 3y = 12$    6. $3y - 7x = 42$

7. $12x - 4y = 24$    8. $-8x + 4y = 64$    9. $3x - 5y = 15$

**FIND THE ERROR *Describe* and correct the error in finding the *y*-intercept of the graph of the equation.**

10.
$$3x + 5y = 30$$
$$3x + 5(0) = 30$$
$$3x = 30$$
$$x = 10$$

11.
$$2y - 3x = 12$$
$$2y - 3(0) = 12 \cdot 0$$
$$2y = 0$$
$$y = 0$$

**Draw the line with the given intercepts.**

12. *x*-intercept: 2
    *y*-intercept: 1

13. *x*-intercept: −4
    *y*-intercept: 3

14. *x*-intercept: 3
    *y*-intercept: −5

15. *x*-intercept: −3
    *y*-intercept: 2

16. *x*-intercept: −1
    *y*-intercept: −2

17. *x*-intercept: 4
    *y*-intercept: 4_

**Graph the equation. Label the points where the graph crosses the axes.**

18. $x - y = -6$    19. $2x - 3y = 6$    20. $2x - y = -8$

21. $x - 4y = -4$    22. $-3x - y = -3$    23. $x - y = 5$

24. **REASONING** Can the graph of a nonhorizontal line have two *x*-intercepts? *Explain.*

25. The drama club has $240 to spend on wigs for a play. Long-hair wigs cost $40 and short-hair wigs cost $30. This situation can be modeled by the equation $40x + 30y = 240$ where *x* is the number of long-hair wigs and *y* is the number of short-hair wigs. Graph the equation and find three possible combinations of wigs the club can buy for exactly $240.

# Practice

**Identify the *x*-intercept and *y*-intercept of the graph.**

**1.**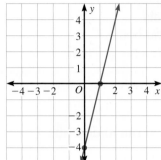
**2.**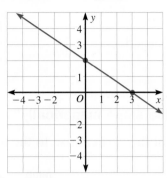
**3.**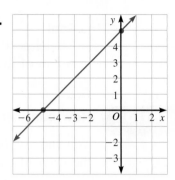

**Find the *x*-intercept and *y*-intercept of the graph of the equation.**

**4.** $x - y = -5$
**5.** $2x - y = -1$
**6.** $x + 2y = 6$

**FIND THE ERROR** *Describe* and correct the error in finding the *x*-intercept of the graph of the equation.

**7.**
$$4x + 5y = 20$$
$$4(0) + 5y = 20$$
$$5y = 20$$
$$y = 4$$

**8.**
$$-2x + 5y = 10$$
$$-2x + 5(0) = 10$$
$$-2x = 10$$
$$x = 5$$

**Draw the line with the given intercepts.**

**9.** *x*-intercept: 4
*y*-intercept: 5

**10.** *x*-intercept: −1
*y*-intercept: 6

**11.** *x*-intercept: 2
*y*-intercept: −3

**Graph the equation. Label the points where the graph crosses the axes.**

**12.** $2x - 3y = -12$
**13.** $x - y = 6$
**14.** $-2x - 3y = 6$

**15.** $x - 5y = -5$
**16.** $-4x - y = 4$
**17.** $2x - y = 6$

**18.** Jim burns 10 calories per minute while mountain biking and 7.5 calories per minute while in-line skating. His goal is to burn 420 calories daily by biking and in-line skating. This situation can be modeled by $10x + 7.5y = 420$ where *x* is the number of minutes spent mountain biking and *y* is the number of minutes spent in-line skating. Draw a graph and find three possible combinations of times spent mountain biking and in-line skating that burn 420 calories.

**19.** **REASONING** If you know that the *x*-intercept of a nonvertical line is 0, what can you say about the *y*-intercept? *Explain.*

# Let's Explore
## Modeling Slopes of Lines

| Goal | Materials |
|---|---|
| Model positive and negative slopes of lines. | • several books<br>• two rulers |

**QUESTION** **How can you describe slope numerically?**

You can use the ratio of the vertical rise to the horizontal run to describe the *slope* of a ramp.

$$\text{slope} = \frac{\text{rise}}{\text{run}}$$

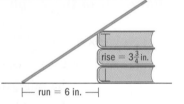

**EXPLORE 1** *Calculate the slopes of ramps* . . . . . . . . . . . . . . . . . . .

**①** **Make** a ramp.
Make a stack of three books. Use a ruler as a ramp. Use another ruler to measure the rise and run of the ramp. Record them in a table. Calculate and record the slope of the ramp.

| Rise | Run | Slope |
|---|---|---|
| $3\frac{3}{4}$ | 6 | $3\frac{3}{4} \div 6 = \frac{15}{4} \times \frac{1}{6} = \frac{15}{24} = \frac{5}{8}$ |

**②** **Change** the run.
Without changing the rise, make three ramps with different runs by moving the lower end of the ruler. Measure and record the rise and run of each ramp. Calculate and record each slope.

**③** **Change** the rise.
Without changing the run, make three ramps with different rises by adding or removing books. Measure and record the rise and run of each ramp. Calculate and record each slope.

## Draw Conclusions
**Describe how the slope of the ramp changes for the given condition. Give three examples that support your answer.**

**1.** The run of the ramp increases, and the rise stays the same.

**2.** The rise of the ramp increases, and the run stays the same.

**Gr. 7 AF 3.3** Graph linear functions, noting that the vertical change (change in *y*-value) per unit of horizontal change (change in *x*-value) is always the same and **know that the ratio ("rise over run") is called the slope of a graph.**

In Exercises 3–5, describe the relationship between the rise and the run of the ramp.

3. A ramp with a slope of 1

4. A ramp with a slope greater than 1

5. A ramp with a slope less than 1 but greater than 0

6. Ramp A has a rise of 6 feet and a run of 2 feet. Ramp B has a rise of 10 feet and a run of 4 feet. Which ramp is steeper? How do you know?

**EXPLORE 2** *Calculate the slopes of escalators* •••••••••••••••••

**Determine the slopes of the escalators described below.**

Inside a department store, you are standing in front of a pair of escalators. Both escalators will move you forward 20 feet. One escalator takes you up 12 feet to the next higher level of the store, while the other takes you down 12 feet to the next lower level.

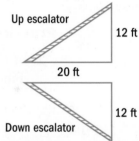

**①** **Draw** a diagram.

Copy the coordinate plane and sketch the up and down escalators as shown.

**②** **Calculate** the slopes.

For the down escalator, the rise is negative because your vertical change in position is negative. Copy and complete the following.

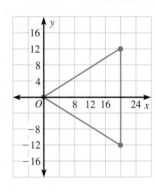

Slope of up escalator = ?

Slope of down escalator = ?

# Draw Conclusions

7. Compare the slopes for the up and down escalators.

8. Many airports have moving walkways. People stand on the walkway and the walkway moves them forward along the floor. What is the slope of a moving walkway? *Explain* your reasoning.

9. Can you find the slope of the path that an elevator takes? *Explain.*

# Find Slopes of Lines

## VOCABULARY and CONCEPTS

The **slope** $m$ of a nonvertical line is the ratio of the vertical change, called the *rise*, to the horizontal change, called the *run*, between any two points on the line. The rise is the difference of the *y*-coordinates of the points, and the run is the difference of the *x*-coordinates.

**EXAMPLE 1** *Finding Slope* • • • • • • • • • • • • • • • • • • • • • • • •

Find the slope of a ladder leaning against a house if the base is 6 feet from the house and the top is 22 feet above the ground.

$$\text{slope} = \frac{\text{rise}}{\text{run}} = \frac{22}{6} = \frac{11}{3}$$

▶ **Answer** The ladder has a slope of $\frac{11}{3}$.

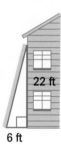

22 ft

6 ft

### Practice for Example 1

1. A railing on a staircase has a rise of 15 feet and a run of 10 feet. Find the slope of the railing.

**EXAMPLE 2** *Finding Positive and Negative Slopes* • • • • • • • • • •

**Find the slope of the line shown.**

**a.** $m = \dfrac{\text{rise}}{\text{run}} = \dfrac{\text{difference of } y\text{-coordinates}}{\text{difference of } x\text{-coordinates}}$

$\qquad = \dfrac{4 - (-2)}{1 - (-1)}$

$\qquad = \dfrac{6}{2}$

$\qquad = 3$

▶ **Answer** The slope is 3.

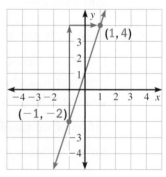

**b.** $m = \dfrac{\text{rise}}{\text{run}} = \dfrac{\text{difference of } y\text{-coordinates}}{\text{difference of } x\text{-coordinates}}$

$\qquad = \dfrac{-4 - (-2)}{3 - 0}$

$\qquad = \dfrac{-2}{3}$

$\qquad = -\dfrac{2}{3}$

▶ **Answer** The slope is $-\dfrac{2}{3}$.

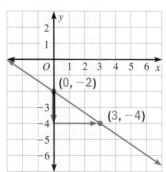

**EXAMPLE 3** *Finding Zero and Undefined Slope* •••••••••••

**Find the slope of the line shown.**

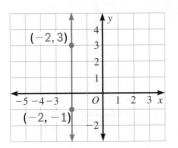

$(-2, 3)$

$(-2, -1)$

**a.** $m = \dfrac{\text{rise}}{\text{run}} = \dfrac{\text{difference of } y\text{-coordinates}}{\text{difference of } x\text{-coordinates}}$

$= \dfrac{3 - (-1)}{-2 - (-2)}$

$= \dfrac{4}{0}$   **Division by zero is undefined.**

▶ **Answer** The slope is undefined.

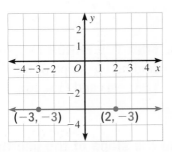

$(-3, -3)$     $(2, -3)$

**b.** $m = \dfrac{\text{rise}}{\text{run}} = \dfrac{\text{difference of } y\text{-coordinates}}{\text{difference of } x\text{-coordinates}}$

$= \dfrac{-3 - (-3)}{2 - (-3)} = \dfrac{0}{5} = 0$

▶ **Answer** The slope is 0.

**EXAMPLE 4** *Interpreting Slope as a Rate of Change* •••••••••

The slope of the line shown gives the number of calories burned while swimming per unit of time, which is the *rate of change* in calories burned with respect to time. Find this rate of change.

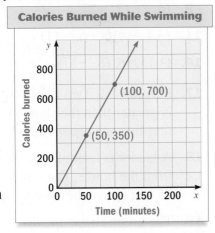

**Calories Burned While Swimming**

$(100, 700)$

$(50, 350)$

Calories burned

Time (minutes)

**Solution**

$m = \dfrac{\text{rise}}{\text{run}} = \dfrac{\text{difference of } y\text{-coordinates}}{\text{difference of } x\text{-coordinates}}$

$= \dfrac{700 \text{ Cal} - 350 \text{ Cal}}{100 \text{ min} - 50 \text{ min}} = \dfrac{350 \text{ Cal}}{50 \text{ min}} = 7 \text{ Cal/min}$

▶ **Answer** Swimming burns 7 calories per minute.

### Practice for Examples 2–4

**In Exercises 2–5, find the slope of the line through the given points.**

**2.** $(-3, 3), (2, -1)$  **3.** $(5, 6), (-3, 6)$  **4.** $(-3, -3), (9, 7)$  **5.** $(3, 1), (3, -5)$

**6.** You burn 108 calories playing basketball for 12 minutes and 135 calories playing basketball for 15 minutes. Draw a graph of calories burned for various amounts of time. Find and interpret the slope of the graph.

# Practice

Extra Practice
p. 507

**Tell whether the slope of the line is *positive, negative, zero,* or *undefined*. Then find the slope.**

**1.**

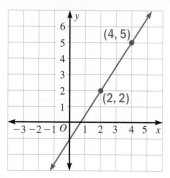

**2.**

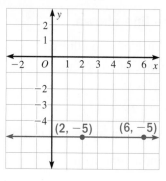

**3.**

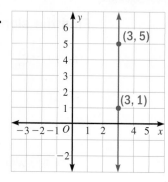

**4.** **FIND THE ERROR** *Describe* and correct the error in finding the slope of the line through the points $(-3, -4)$ and $(15, 16)$.

$$m = \frac{15 - (-3)}{16 - (-4)} = \frac{18}{20}$$
$$= \frac{9}{10}$$ ✗

**Find the slope of the line through the given points.**

**5.** $(9, 6), (21, 14)$

**6.** $(8, 0), (10, 10)$

**7.** $(3, 9), (16, 9)$

**8.** $(6, 1), (7, -2)$

**9.** $(-9, -2), (-7, -3)$

**10.** $(-5, -4), (-5, -7)$

**11.** $(-4, -8), (-6, -11)$

**12.** $(-2, -3), (10, 15)$

**13.** $(7, 6), (12, -14)$

**14.** $(-13, 6), (8, -17)$

**15.** $(20, -18), (1, -2)$

**16.** $(7, -13), (-33, 19)$

**17.** **REASONING** Two lines both have positive slope. The slope of one line is greater than the slope of the second line. Does this mean that the first line is *steeper* than the second line? *Explain* your reasoning.

**18.** A ladder is leaning against a house. The bottom of the ladder is 8 feet from the house. The top of the ladder is leaning against the house 15 feet above the ground. Find the slope of the ladder.

**19.** The graph shows the distance traveled by a car for various amounts of time.

**a.** Find the slope of the line.

**b.** What information about the car can you obtain from the slope?

**c.** A second car is traveling at 50 miles per hour. Suppose you make a graph showing the distance traveled by the second car for various amounts of time. How would the graph for the second car compare with the graph for the first car? *Explain* your reasoning.

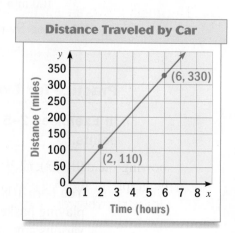

Distance Traveled by Car

**Tell whether the slope of the line is *positive, negative, zero*, or *undefined*. Then find the slope.**

**1.**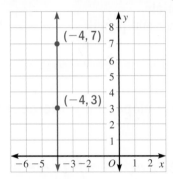

**2.**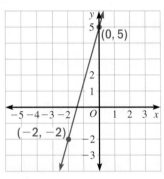

**3.**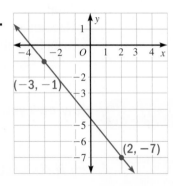

**4. FIND THE ERROR** *Describe* and correct the error in finding the slope of the line through the points $(-4, 15)$ and $(-9, 11)$.

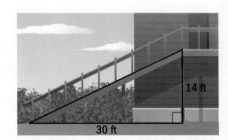

$$m = \frac{11 - (-4)}{-9 - 15} = \frac{15}{-24}$$

$$= -\frac{5}{8}$$

**Find the slope of the line through the given points.**

**5.** $(6, 3), (14, 19)$

**6.** $(10, 11), (15, 11)$

**7.** $(8, 48), (16, 24)$

**8.** $(1, 5), (36, 19)$

**9.** $(4, 4), (32, 18)$

**10.** $(9, 4), (32, 17)$

**11.** $(-6, -17), (-22, -12)$

**12.** $(-9, -7), (-11, -13)$

**13.** $(7, -20), (-13, 10)$

**14.** $(2, -11), (-13, 14)$

**15.** $(-6, -5), (-6, 7)$

**16.** $(4, 4), (14, 10)$

**17.** Find the slope of the ramp in the figure.

**18. REASONING** You find the slope of the line passing through the points $(-2, 4)$ and $(-3, 10)$ as follows:

$m = \dfrac{10 - 4}{-3 - (-2)}$. Your friend finds the slope as follows:

$m = \dfrac{4 - 10}{-2 - (-3)}$. Who is correct? *Explain.*

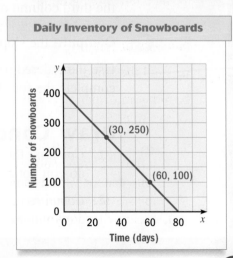

14 ft

30 ft

**19.** The graph shows the number of days a sporting goods store took to sell its inventory of snowboards.

**a.** Find the slope of the line.

**b.** What information about the sales can you obtain from the slope?

**c.** The store sold the same number of pairs of skis at a rate of 4 per day. Suppose you make a graph showing the daily inventory of skis. How would the graph for the skis compare with the graph for the snowboards? *Explain* your reasoning.

**Daily Inventory of Snowboards**

## Let's Explore
### Investigating Slope and y-Intercept

**Goal**
Recognize slopes and *y*-intercepts of lines from their equations.

**Materials**
• paper and pencil

**QUESTION** How can you use the equation of a line to find its slope and *y*-intercept?

**EXPLORE 1** *Find the slopes and the y-intercepts of lines*

Copy the table below.

| Line | $(0, y_1)$ | $(2, y_2)$ | Slope | y-intercept |
|------|------------|------------|-------|-------------|
| $y = 4x + 3$ | (0, 3) | (2, 11) | $\dfrac{11 - 3}{2 - 0} = 4$ | 3 |
| $y = -2x + 3$ | (0, ?) | (2, ?) | ? | ? |
| $y = \frac{1}{2}x + 4$ | (0, ?) | (2, ?) | ? | ? |
| $y = -4x - 3$ | (0, ?) | (2, ?) | ? | ? |
| $y = -\frac{1}{4}x - 3$ | (0, ?) | (2, ?) | ? | ? |

**1** **Find** *y* when *x* = 0.

Let $x_1 = 0$ and find $y_1$ for each equation in the table. Use your answers to complete the second and fifth columns of the table.

**2** **Find** *y* when *x* = 2.

Let $x_2 = 2$ and find $y_2$ for each equation. Use your answers to complete the third column of the table.

**3** **Compute** the slope.

Use the ordered pairs you found in the second and third columns to complete the fourth column of the table.

## Draw Conclusions

1. *Compare* the slope of each line with the equation of the line. What do you notice?

2. *Compare* the *y*-intercept of each line with the equation of the line. What do you notice?

**Predict the slope and the *y*-intercept of the line with the given equation. Then check your predictions by finding the slope and *y*-intercept as you did in Explore 1.**

**3.** $y = -5x + 1$      **4.** $y = \frac{3}{4}x + 2$      **5.** $y = -\frac{3}{2}x - 1$

**6.** Use the procedure you followed in Explore 1 to show that the *y*-intercept of the graph of $y = mx + b$ is $b$ and the slope of the graph is $m$.

**EXPLORE 2** *Graph a line using the slope and y-intercept*

**Graph the equation $y = 4x + 3$ from Explore 1.**

**①** **Plot** a point on the *y*-axis.

Since the *y*-intercept is 3, plot (0, 3).

**②** **Use** slope to plot a second point.

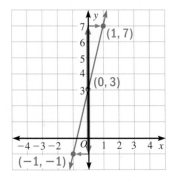

Since the slope is 4 or $\frac{4}{1}$, move up 4 units and right 1 unit to plot a second point. The point is (1, 7).

Alternatively, move down 4 units and left 1 unit to plot a second point. The point is (−1, −1).

**③** **Draw** a line through the points.

## Draw Conclusions

**7.** Consider Step 2 of Explore 2.

     **a.** *Explain* why the alternative method for plotting a second point works.

     **b.** Suppose you move up 8 units and right 2 units to plot a second point. Is that point on the line? *Explain.*

     **c.** *Generalize* the results of parts (a) and (b)

**8.** *Describe* the steps you would take to graph the equation $y = -\frac{1}{2}x + 1$.

**9.** Graph the remaining four equations from your completed table in Explore 1.

# Lesson 10.6 — Graph Equations in Slope-Intercept Form

## VOCABULARY and CONCEPTS

The **slope-intercept form** of a linear equation is $y = mx + b$ where $m$ is the slope and $b$ is the $y$-intercept of the equation's graph.

**EXAMPLE 1** *Identifying Slopes and y-Intercepts*

**Identify the slope and $y$-intercept of the line.**

**a.** $y = x - 4$

**b.** $3x + 2y = 4$

**Solution**

**a.** The equation $y = x - 4$ can be written as $y = 1x + (-4)$.

slope $m$ — y-intercept $b$

▸**Answer** The line has a slope of 1 and a $y$-intercept of $-4$.

**b.** Write the equation $3x + 2y = 4$ in slope-intercept form.

$$3x + 2y = 4 \qquad \text{Write original equation.}$$
$$2y = -3x + 4 \qquad \text{Subtract 3x from each side.}$$
$$y = -\frac{3}{2}x + 2 \qquad \text{Divide each side by 2.}$$

slope $m$ — y-intercept $b$

▸**Answer** The line has a slope of $-\frac{3}{2}$ and a $y$-intercept of 2.

### Practice for Example 1

**Find the slope and $y$-intercept of the line.**

**1.** $y = 4x + 9$

**2.** $y = -3x + 1$

**3.** $-5x + 2y = 8$

**EXAMPLE 2** *Graphing Using Slope-Intercept Form*

**Graph the equation $y = \frac{1}{3}x + 2$.**

**Step 1** The $y$-intercept is 2, so plot the point $(0, 2)$.

**Step 2** The slope is $\frac{1}{3}$, so plot two more points by twice moving up 1 unit and right 3 units. The points are $(3, 3)$ and $(6, 4)$.

**Step 3** Draw a line through the points.

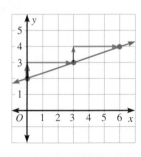

## Practice for Example 2

**Graph the equation.**

**4.** $y = 3x + 1$

**5.** $y = \frac{1}{3}x - 2$

**6.** $y = -x + 4$

### EXAMPLE 3 *Using Slope-Intercept Form*

Miguel bought a guitar for $125 and took lessons for $25 per lesson. Miguel's total cost $y$ is given by the equation $y = 25x + 125$ where $x$ is the number of lessons he takes.

**a.** Graph the equation.

**b.** Miguel spent a total of $250 on the guitar and lessons. How many lessons did he take?

**Solution**

**a.** Use the $y$-intercept and the slope to plot the points (0, 125) and (1, 150). Draw a line through the points.

**b.** Use the graph to find the number of lessons.

Find 250 on the $y$-axis. Move horizontally to the line, then vertically to the $x$-axis.

▶ **Answer** The $x$-coordinate of the point with $y$-coordinate 250 is 5. So, Miguel took 5 lessons.

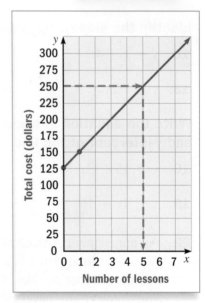

## Practice for Example 3

**7.** You are selling potted houseplants at a school sale. It costs you $12 for supplies, and you are selling the plants for $4 each. Your profit $y$ is given by the equation $y = 4x - 12$ where $x$ is the number of plants sold.

**a.** Graph the equation.

**b.** How many plants would you have to sell in order to make a profit of $16?

**Practice**

**Extra Practice**
p. 507

**Write the equation in slope-intercept form.**

**1.** $2x - y = 3$

**2.** $4x + y = 7$

**3.** $5x + 3y = 6$

**4.** $-x + 6y = 12$

**5.** $7x + 5y = 25$

**6.** $-2x - 3y = 9$

**Match the equation with its graph.**

**7.** $y = 2x + 5$

**8.** $y = -2x + 5$

**9.** $y = \frac{1}{2}x + 5$

**A.**
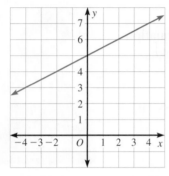

**B.**
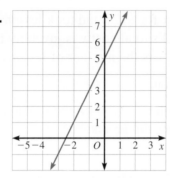

**C.**
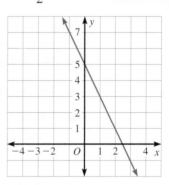

**Identify the slope and $y$-intercept of the line. Then graph the equation.**

**10.** $y = x + 4$

**11.** $y = \frac{1}{2}x - 7$

**12.** $y = -3x + 10$

**13.** $y = -2x + 3$

**14.** $y = 4$

**15.** $x = \frac{1}{2}$

**Write the equation in slope-intercept form. Then identify the slope and $y$-intercept of the line.**

**16.** $y = 15 - 3x$

**17.** $y + 4 = 5x$

**18.** $y - \frac{2}{5}x = 0$

**19.** $x - 4y = 16$

**20.** $\frac{1}{9}x - y = 6$

**21.** $2x - 3y = 21$

**22.** An amusement park charges \$12 for admission and \$3 for each ride. Your total cost $y$ is given by the equation $y = 3x + 12$ where $x$ is the number of rides. Graph the equation. How many rides can you go on if you have \$30 to spend?

**23.** You have \$120. You buy some CDs that cost \$15 each. The amount of money $y$ left over is given by $y = 120 - 15x$ where $x$ is the number of CDs you buy. Graph the equation. How many CDs can you buy and still have \$60 left over?

**24.** **REASONING** A line passes through the origin and the point $(5, 3)$.

    **a.** What is the $y$-intercept of the line? *Explain.*

    **b.** What is the slope of the line? *Explain.*

    **c.** What is an equation of the line? *Explain.*

# Practice

@HomeTutor
classzone.com

**Write the equation in slope-intercept form.**

**1.** $5x - y = 8$

**2.** $-11x + y = 13$

**3.** $7x + 2y = 12$

**4.** $-x + 9y = 45$

**5.** $3x + 7y = 21$

**6.** $-4x - 3y = -27$

**Match the equation with its graph.**

**7.** $y = 3x + 4$

**8.** $y = -3x + 4$

**9.** $y = \frac{1}{3}x + 4$

**A.**

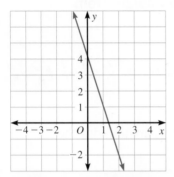

**B.**

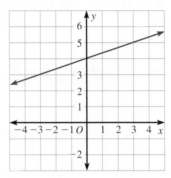

**C.**

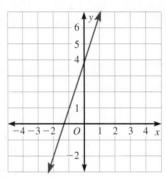

**Identify the slope and *y*-intercept of the line. Then graph the equation.**

**10.** $y = x + 9$

**11.** $y = \frac{1}{5}x - 2$

**12.** $y = -5x + 1$

**13.** $y = -x + 6$

**14.** $y = 7$

**15.** $y = \frac{3}{4}$

**Write the equation in slope-intercept form. Then identify the slope and *y*-intercept of the line.**

**16.** $y = 14 - 2x$

**17.** $y + 8 = 4x$

**18.** $y - \frac{3}{5}x = 0$

**19.** $6x - 3y = 15$

**20.** $\frac{1}{8}x - y = 7$

**21.** $15x - 10y = 32$

**22.** The Woodard family went camping at a park. The park entrance fee was $10 and the campsite fee was $6 per night. The family's total cost *y* is given by the equation $y = 6x + 10$ where *x* is the number of nights at the campsite. Graph the equation. The family's total cost was $46. For how many nights did the family camp?

**23.** The Bates family planted a young Leyland cypress tree when it was 2 feet tall. Leyland cypress trees grow at a rate of 3 feet per year. The height *y* of the tree is given by the equation $y = 3x + 2$ where *x* is the number of years since the tree was planted. Graph the equation. The tree is now 20 feet tall. How many years ago was the tree planted?

**24. REASONING** A line has a *y*-intercept of 3 and an *x*-intercept of 2. How can you use this information to write an equation of the line?

# Activity 10.7

## Let's Explore
### Investigating Direct Variation

**Goal**
Perform an experiment to find the relationship between two quantities.

**Materials**
- meter stick
- ball
- graph paper

**QUESTION**  **How is the bounce height of a ball related to the height from which it is dropped?**

**EXPLORE 1**  *Compare drop heights and bounce heights* .....

**1**  **Set up** the experiment.
Copy the table shown below. Hold a meter stick next to a wall with the zero mark touching the floor.

| Drop height (D) | Bounce height | | | | Mean bounce height (B) | $\frac{B}{D}$ |
|---|---|---|---|---|---|---|
| 1 m | 0.4 m | 0.5 m | 0.4 m | 0.4 m | 0.425 m | 0.425 |
| ? | ? | ? | ? | ? | ? | ? |

**2**  **Measure** the bounce height.
Choose a height from which to drop your ball. Record the drop height *D* in the table.

Drop the ball from the height you chose four different times. Each time, measure and record the height of the first bounce.

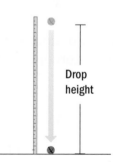

Drop height

**3**  **Find** the mean of the bounce heights.
Find the mean of the bounce heights you measured in Step 2. Record the mean bounce height *B* in the table.

**4**  **Find** the ratio of *B* to *D*.
Find the ratio of the mean bounce height *B* to the drop height *D*. Record this ratio in the table.

**5**  **Collect** additional data.
Repeat Steps 2–4 four times, using four different drop heights. Record the data in your table.

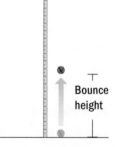

Bounce height

## Draw Conclusions

1. Compare the values of $\frac{B}{D}$ for the five rows in your table. As the ball's drop heights decrease, do the values of $\frac{B}{D}$ *increase*, *decrease*, or *remain approximately the same*?

2. Make a graph of your data. Label the horizontal axis "Drop height" and the vertical axis "Mean bounce height." Graph the ordered pairs $\left(D, \frac{B}{D}\right)$ from your table. *Describe* any patterns you see in your graph. Are you able to draw a line through the plotted points or a line that passes *close* to the plotted points? If so, what is the slope of the line?

**EXPLORE 2** *Measure heights of second bounce* ..............

1. **Set** up the experiment.
   You will be repeating the experiment of Explore 1, except this time you will let the ball bounce a *second* time. Make a table like the one in Explore 1, but this time "bounce height" refers to the height of the *second* bounce.

2. **Measure** the second bounce heights and complete the table.
   Drop the ball from the same heights used in Explore 1. Record the heights of the *second* bounces. Complete each row in the table by finding the mean of the second bounce heights $B$ and the ratio of mean second bounce height to drop height $D$.

## Draw Conclusions

3. Repeat Exercise 2 using the drop heights and mean second bounce heights from Explore 2.

4. Locate the mean bounce heights in your tables from Explore 1 and Explore 2. Compute the ratio of the mean *second* bounce height to the mean *first* bounce height for each drop height. What do you notice?

5. *Compare* the ratios from Exercise 4 with the ratios from Exercise 1.

6. *Compare* the ratio of mean second bounce height to drop height in your table from Explore 2 to the ratio of mean first bounce height to drop height in your table from Explore 1.

# Solve Direct Variation Problems By Graphing

### VOCABULARY and CONCEPTS

A set of paired data $(x, y)$ represents **direct variation** if the ratio $\frac{y}{x}$ for $x \neq 0$ is constant. The graph of the data pairs lies on a straight line that passes through the origin and has a slope equal to the constant ratio.

**EXAMPLE 1** *Using Ratios to Identify Direct Variation*......

**Three sizes of a photo appear below. Tell whether width and length show direct variation.**

15 in.

10 in.

5 in.

| 3 in. | 6 in. | 9 in. |
|-------|-------|-------|
| Photo 1 | Photo 2 | Photo 3 |

### Solution

Find the ratio of the width to the length for each photo.

**Photo 1**

$$\frac{\text{width}}{\text{length}} = \frac{3}{5}$$

**Photo 2**

$$\frac{\text{width}}{\text{length}} = \frac{6}{10} = \frac{3}{5}$$

**Photo 3**

$$\frac{\text{width}}{\text{length}} = \frac{9}{15} = \frac{3}{5}$$

Because the ratios are equal, the data show direct variation.

### Practice for Example 1

**Tell whether the data in the table show direct variation.** *Explain.*

**1.**

| x | 2 | 4 | 6 | 8 |
|---|---|---|---|---|
| y | 1 | 2 | 3 | 4 |

**2.**

| x | 1 | 2 | 3 | 4 |
|---|---|---|---|---|
| y | 1 | 4 | 9 | 16 |

Gr. 7 AF 3.4 Plot the values of quantities whose ratios are always the same (e.g., cost to the number of an item, feet to inches, circumference to diameter of a circle). Fit a line to the plot and understand that the slope of the line equals the ratio of the quantities.

Gr. 7 AF 4.2 Solve multistep problems involving rate, average speed, distance, and time or a direct variation.

**EXAMPLE 2** *Solve a Direct Variation Problem* . . . . . . . . . . . . . . .

You are arranging for a group of people to see a movie. The total ticket costs for various numbers of people are shown in the table. How much would 20 tickets cost?

| Number of people, *P* | 3 | 5 | 9 | 14 | 18 |
|---|---|---|---|---|---|
| Cost of tickets, *C* | 18 | 30 | 54 | 84 | 108 |

**Solution**

Check to see if the data show direct variation by finding the ratio of *C* to *P* for each data pair.

$$\frac{18}{3} = 6 \qquad \frac{30}{5} = 6 \qquad \frac{54}{9} = 6 \qquad \frac{84}{14} = 6 \qquad \frac{108}{18} = 6$$

Since the ratios are equal, the data show direct variation.

Graph the data pairs. Draw a line through the origin and the plotted points.

To find the slope of the line, choose any two points on the line, such as (3, 18) and (5, 30).

$$m = \frac{30 - 18}{5 - 3} = \frac{12}{2} = 6$$

Note that the slope of the line and the ratio of *C* to *P* are the same.

To find the total cost for a group of 20 people, start at 20 on the *P*-axis and move vertically to the line and then horizontally to the *C*-axis. You find that *C* = 120 when *P* = 20.

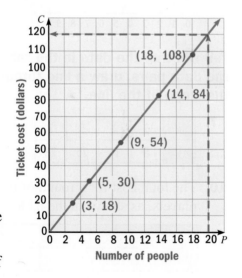

▸ **Answer** You will pay $120 for a group of 20 people.

**Practice for Example 2**

3. On a driving trip, Mr. Chung recorded the number of hours and number of miles he traveled as shown in the table.

| Time, *t* | 2 | 3 | 4 | 5 |
|---|---|---|---|---|
| Distance, *d* | 120 | 180 | 240 | 300 |

  a. Do the data in the table show direct variation? *Explain.*

  b. Graph the data pairs and draw a line through the origin and the plotted points. What is the slope of the line? How does it compare with the ratio of *d* to *t*?

  c. How many miles would you predict Mr. Chung could travel in 8 hours?

# Practice

**Extra Practice**
p. 507

**Tell whether the data in the table show direct variation. *Explain*.**

**1.**

| x | 3 | 4 | 5 | 6 |
|---|---|---|---|---|
| y | 12 | 16 | 20 | 24 |

**2.**

| x | 4 | 5 | 6 | 7 |
|---|---|---|---|---|
| y | 6 | 8 | 10 | 12 |

**3.**

| x | 4 | 8 | 12 | 16 |
|---|---|---|---|---|
| y | 2 | 4 | 6 | 8 |

**Tell whether the data in the graph show direct variation.**
***Explain*.**

**4.**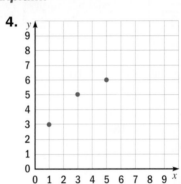

**5.**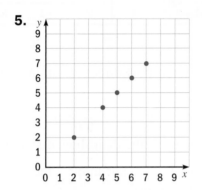

**6.**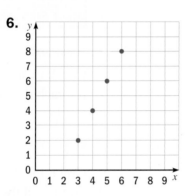

**Tell whether the data in the table show direct variation. If so, graph the data pairs, draw a line through the plotted points, and compute the slope of the line.**

**7.**

| x | 2 | 4 | 5 | 7 |
|---|---|---|---|---|
| y | 8 | 16 | 25 | 28 |

**8.**

| x | 3 | 5 | 6 | 8 |
|---|---|---|---|---|
| y | 9 | 15 | 18 | 24 |

**9.**

| x | 2 | 3 | 4 | 5 |
|---|---|---|---|---|
| y | 4 | 6 | 8 | 10 |

**10.** The total cost for a round of miniature golf depends on the number of players, as shown in the table.

| Number of players, P | 2 | 3 | 4 | 5 |
|---|---|---|---|---|
| Total cost (dollars), C | 8 | 12 | 16 | 20 |

**a.** Do the data show direct variation? If so, what is the constant ratio?

**b.** Make a graph of the data pairs and draw a line through the plotted points. What is the slope of the line?

**c.** What would the total cost be for a group of 8 players?

**REASONING Tell whether you would expect the given variables to show direct variation. *Explain*.**

**11.** Your heights at various ages

**12.** The lengths of boards in inches compared with the lengths in feet

**13.** The circumferences of circles having various diameters

Tell whether the data in the table show direct variation. *Explain*.

**1.**

| x | 6 | 7 | 8 | 9 |
|---|---|---|---|---|
| y | 78 | 91 | 104 | 117 |

**2.**

| x | 5 | 6 | 7 | 8 |
|---|---|---|---|---|
| y | 9 | 11 | 13 | 17 |

**3.**

| x | 30 | 45 | 60 | 75 |
|---|---|---|---|---|
| y | 2 | 3 | 4 | 5 |

Tell whether the data in the graph show direct variation. *Explain*.

**4.**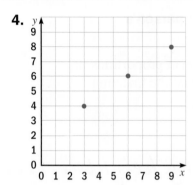

**5.**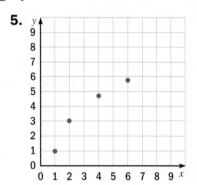

**6.**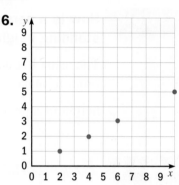

Tell whether the data in the table show direct variation. If so, graph the data pairs, draw a line through the plotted points, and compute the slope of the line.

**7.**

| x | 2 | 4 | 5 | 8 |
|---|---|---|---|---|
| y | 12 | 24 | 25 | 48 |

**8.**

| x | 0.5 | 1 | 1.5 | 2 |
|---|---|---|---|---|
| y | 1.5 | 3 | 4.5 | 6 |

**9.**

| x | 4 | 6 | 8 | 10 |
|---|---|---|---|---|
| y | 2 | 3 | 4 | 5 |

**10.** You are painting some walls in your home. The table shows the amount of paint needed to cover various areas of wall.

| Paint (gallons), *P* | 0.5 | 1 | 1.5 | 2 |
|---|---|---|---|---|
| Area (square feet), *A* | 125 | 250 | 375 | 500 |

**a.** Do the data show direct variation? If so, what is the constant ratio?

**b.** Make a graph of the data pairs and draw a line through the plotted points. What is the slope of the line?

**c.** If you want to paint 625 square feet of wall, how many gallons of paint will you need?

**d.** If you have 3 gallons of paint, how much wall can you paint?

**11.** **REASONING** If you triple an *x*-value in a direct variation, does the corresponding *y*-value also triple? *Explain*.

**12.** **REASONING** Three points are on the same line provided the slopes of any two line segments connecting the points are equal. Suppose the data pairs ($a$, $b$) and ($c$, $d$) show direct variation. *Explain* why the line drawn through the points ($a$, $b$) and ($c$, $d$) also passes through the origin.

## Let's Explore
### Writing Direct Variation Equations

**Goal**
Write a direct variation equation for real-world data.

**Materials**
- 2 meter sticks
- graph paper

**QUESTION** **How is a person's kneeling height related to the person's standing height?**

The artist Leonardo da Vinci (1452–1519) studied human proportions in order to make more accurate drawings. He observed that the kneeling height of a person is $\frac{3}{4}$ of the person's standing height.

**EXPLORE 1** *Examine kneeling and standing heights* ......

1 **Measure** and record heights.
Your teacher will have you work in groups. Copy and complete the table below. Add rows for each student in your group. Measure and record the kneeling and standing heights of each student.

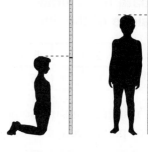

| Name | Standing height (cm) | Kneeling height (cm) | Kneeling height / Standing height |
|------|------|------|------|
| John | 158 | 117 | $\frac{117}{158} \approx 0.74$ |

2 **Find** ratios.
For each student, find the ratio of kneeling height to standing height and record the ratio in the last column of your table. Then calculate the mean of the ratios you have found. Compare your group's results with results from other groups.

3 **Graph** your data.
Plot the point (*standing height, kneeling height*) for each student. Do not connect the points.

4 **Graph** the equation $y = kx$.
Using the mean ratio you calculated in Step 2 as the value $k$, graph the equation $y = kx$.

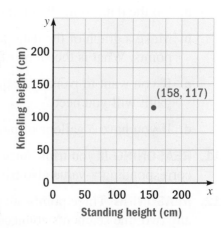

## Draw Conclusions

1. Do you agree with da Vinci's observation that the kneeling height of a person is $\frac{3}{4}$ of the person's standing height? Why?

2. What relationship do you observe between your plotted points and the line you drew?

3. Use the equation $y = kx$ to predict the kneeling height of a person who has a standing height of 190 centimeters. Check your answer by using the graph of $y = kx$ from Step 4.

4. Use the equation $y = kx$ to predict the standing height of a person who has a kneeling height of 125 centimeters. Check your answer by using the graph of $y = kx$ from Step 4.

**EXPLORE 2** *Examine standing height and a body length*

**Design your own study to see if there is a relationship between a person's standing height and some other body length.**

**1** **Set up** the study.

Decide what to compare with standing height. Some possibilities are length of a foot, distance from elbow to the end of the hand, and distance between tips of outstretched hands.

Make a table like the one from Explore 1.

**2** **Measure** and record heights and lengths.

**3** **Find** the ratio of height to length for each student. Then calculate the mean of the ratios.

**4** **Graph** your data and the equation $y = kx$ where $k$ is the mean ratio you calculated in Step 3.

## Draw Conclusions

5. Do the data in your study show direct variation? *Explain.*

6. Which study, the one in Explore 1 or the one in Explore 2, is better at accurately predicting a person's height? *Explain.*

# Solve Direct Variation Problems Using Algebra

## VOCABULARY and CONCEPTS

### Direct Variation Equations

If a set of paired data $(x, y)$ show direct variation, then $y$ is said to *vary directly* with $x$. Because each ratio $\frac{y}{x}$ $(x \neq 0)$ equals some nonzero constant $k$, called the **constant of variation**, the equation $y = kx$ relates $y$ to $x$ and is called a *direct variation equation.*

### Properties of Graphs of Direct Variation Equations

- The graph of a direct variation equation is a line through the origin.

- The slope of the graph of $y = kx$ is $k$.

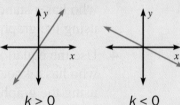

$k > 0$        $k < 0$

---

**EXAMPLE 1** *Writing a Direct Variation Equation* •••••••••••

**The graph of a direct variation equation is shown.**

  **a.** Write the direct variation equation.

  **b.** Find the value of $y$ when $x = 12$.

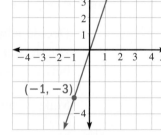

### Solution

  **a.** Because $y$ varies directly with $x$, the equation has the form $y = kx$. Use the fact that $y = -3$ when $x = -1$ to find $k$.

| | |
|---|---|
| $y = kx$ | **Write direct variation equation.** |
| $-3 = k(-1)$ | **Substitute.** |
| $3 = k$ | **Solve for k.** |

    The direct variation equation that relates $x$ and $y$ is $y = 3x$.

  **b.** When $x = 12$, $y = 3(12) = 36$. The value of $y$ when $x = 12$ is 36.

### Practice for Example 1

  **1.** The graph of a direct variation equation passes through the origin and the point $(3, -4)$.

    **a.** Write a direct variation equation that relates $x$ and $y$.

    **b.** Find the value of $y$ when $x = -12$.

**EXAMPLE 2** *Graphing a Direct Variation Equation* ·········

**Graph** $y = \frac{2}{3}x$.

The equation is in the form $y = kx$, so the slope of the graph is $\frac{2}{3}$.

Plot a point at the origin and plot another point using the slope $\frac{2}{3}$. Then draw a line through the two points.

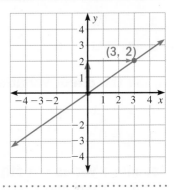

**Practice for Example 2**

**Graph the equation.**

  **2.** $y = \frac{2}{5}x$         **3.** $y = -\frac{2}{5}x$         **4.** $y = 6x$

**EXAMPLE 3** *Using a Direct Variation Model* ················

The total amount $A$ that the cheerleading squad pays for uniforms and pompoms depends on the number $n$ of cheerleaders on the squad. For 6 cheerleaders, the squad needs $420. Write an equation that relates $n$ and $A$. Find the amount of money the squad needs for 10 cheerleaders.

**Solution**

**Step 1** Find the constant of variation $k$.

     $A = kn$      **Write direct variation equation using $A$ and $n$.**

  $420 = k(6)$    **Substitute 420 for $A$ and 6 for $n$.**

   $70 = k$      **Solve for $k$.**

**Step 2** Find the amount of money needed for 10 cheerleaders.

     $A = 70n$    **Write direct variation equation using $A$ and $n$.**

    $= 70(10)$   **Substitute 10 for $n$.**

    $= 700$      **Multiply.**

  ▸**Answer** The squad needs $700 for 10 cheerleaders.

**Practice for Example 3**

  **5.** The cost $C$ of oranges depends on their weight $w$ (in pounds). Three pounds of oranges sell for $1.95. Write an equation that relates $C$ and $w$. Find the cost of 5 pounds of oranges.

**Tell whether the equation represents direct variation. If it does, give the constant of variation.**

**1.** $y = 7x$

**2.** $y + 1 = 2x$

**3.** $2y - 3 = 5x$

**4.** $3x + 4y = 0$

**5.** $-3x - 7y = 2$

**6.** $5y = \frac{5}{2}x$

**Graph the direct variation equation.**

**7.** $y = \frac{3}{4}x$

**8.** $y = -5x$

**9.** $y = -\frac{1}{6}x$

**10.** $y = 0.5x$

**11.** $y = 8x$

**12.** $y = -2x$

**Assume $y$ varies directly with $x$. Write an equation that relates $x$ and $y$. Then find $y$ when $x = 3$.**

**13.** $x = 2, y = 6$

**14.** $x = -3, y = 4$

**15.** $x = 8, y = 4$

**16.** $x = -4, y = 5$

**17.** $x = 8, y = 2$

**18.** $x = -6, y = 4$

**19.** $x = -3, y = -9$

**20.** $x = -10, y = -2$

**21.** $x = -5, y = 2$

**22. FIND THE ERROR** *Describe* and correct the error in graphing $y = -2x$.

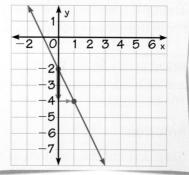

The slope is −2.
Plot a point at −2 on the y-axis.
Then go down 2 units and right
1 unit to plot the second point.
Draw a line connecting the
two points.

**23.** The total amount $A$ that a football team pays for uniforms depends on the number $n$ of players on the team. For 5 players, the team needs $240. Write an equation that relates $n$ and $A$. Find the amount the team needs for 11 players.

**24.** The distance $d$ that a hiker travels varies directly with the time $t$ spent hiking at a constant speed. A hiker travels 9 miles in 3 hours. Write an equation that relates $t$ and $d$. Predict the distance the hiker can travel in 1.5 hours.

**25.** The number $p$ of pages a student can read varies directly with the time $t$ spent reading. The student can read 60 pages in 30 minutes. Write an equation that relates $t$ and $p$. Predict the number of pages the student can read in 45 minutes.

**26. REASONING** Suppose $y$ varies directly with $x$, and the constant of variation is $k$. Does $x$ vary directly with $y$? If so, what is the constant of variation?

**Tell whether the equation represents direct variation. If it does, give the constant of variation.**

**1.** $y = -3x$

**2.** $y + 2 = 8x$

**3.** $3y - 5 = 0$

**4.** $6x + y = 2$

**5.** $-6x + 4y = 0$

**6.** $3y = \frac{9}{2}x$

**Graph the direct variation equation.**

**7.** $y = \frac{1}{2}x$

**8.** $y = 2x$

**9.** $y = -\frac{1}{3}x$

**10.** $y = 1.5x$

**11.** $y = -3x$

**12.** $y = -0.25x$

**Assume *y* varies directly with *x*. Write an equation that relates *x* and *y*. Then find *y* when *x* = 3.**

**13.** $x = 6, y = -8$

**14.** $x = -4, y = -16$

**15.** $x = 2, y = 14$

**16.** $x = -4, y = -20$

**17.** $x = 12, y = -4$

**18.** $x = 7, y = 4$

**19.** $x = -6, y = -1$

**20.** $x = -10, y = -15$

**21.** $x = 10, y = 4$

**22. FIND THE ERROR** *Describe* and correct the error in writing the direct variation equation for the graph shown.

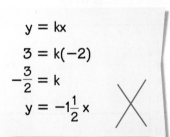

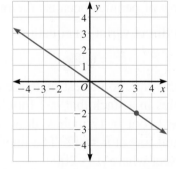

**23.** A library has a copier that you can use to make copies of book pages. The cost *C* varies directly with the number *n* of copies made. It costs $.08 to make 1 copy. Write an equation that relates *n* and *C*. Find the number of pages you can copy if you spend $.96.

**24.** The cost *C* of going to the movies varies directly with the number *n* of people attending. A group of 4 people paid $14 to go to the movies on Friday. Write an equation that relates *n* and *C*. Find how much it would cost for 7 people to go to the movies.

**25.** The distance *d* Christine walks varies directly with the time *t* she spends walking. She walked 2.5 miles in 50 minutes. Write an equation that relates *t* and *d*. Find how much time it takes her to walk 4 miles.

**26. REASONING** Suppose *y* varies directly with *x*, and the constant of variation is *k*. Also, suppose *z* varies directly with *y*, and the constant of variation is $\ell$. What is the relationship between *x* and *z*?

# Problem Solving and Reasoning

## Problem

Information about the height of a stack of pennies and the length of a line of pennies is given in the table below. About how many pennies would it take to make a stack that would reach from Earth to the moon? The distance from Earth to the moon when the moon is closest to Earth is about 225,700 miles.

| Number of pennies, p | Height, h (inches) | Length, ℓ (inches) |
|---|---|---|
| 25 | 1.5 | 18.75 |
| 50 | 3 | 37.5 |
| 75 | 4.5 | 56.25 |

## Solution

*Distinguish relevant from irrelevant information as part of MR 1.1, and break the problem into simpler parts as part of MR 1.3.*

**1** **Solve** a simpler problem. Since you want to know the height of a stack of pennies, use the second column in the table. It is easier to start with a shorter stack, so first find the number of pennies in a stack that is 1 foot high. The height $h$ varies directly with the number $p$ of pennies because the ratio $\frac{h}{p}$ in the table equals 0.06.

Write a direct variation equation.

$$h = 0.06p$$

*Use a graph to estimate, then use algebra to check as part of MR 2.3.*

Graph the equation to estimate the number of pennies in a stack that is 1 foot high. Because 1 foot = 12 inches, draw a horizontal line at $h = 12$. The lines appear to intersect where $p = 200$.

Use the equation to check:
$$h = 0.06(200) = 12$$
There are 200 pennies in a stack of pennies that is 1 foot high.

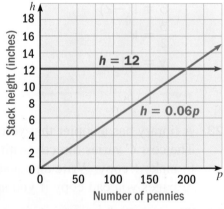

*Make precise calculations as part of MR 2.8.*

**2** **Solve** the problem. There are 200 pennies in a stack that is 1 foot high and there are 5280 feet in 1 mile. Find the number of pennies in a stack of pennies that is 225,700 miles high.

$$\frac{200 \text{ pennies}}{1 \text{ ft}} \cdot \frac{5280 \text{ ft}}{1 \text{ mi}} \cdot 225{,}700 \text{ mi} = 238{,}339{,}200{,}000 \text{ pennies}$$

It would take about 238,339,200,000 pennies to make a stack that would reach the moon.

*Use estimation to verify that results are reasonable as part of MR 2.1.*

**3** **Estimate** to check reasonableness.
Because $200 \cdot 5000 \cdot 230{,}000 = 230{,}000{,}000{,}000$, an answer of 238,339,200,000 is reasonable.

# Practice

1. The distance around Earth at the equator is about 24,900 miles. Use the information in the table on the previous page to find how many pennies it would take to make a line that would go around Earth at the equator. Use estimation to check that your answer is reasonable. **MR 2.1, MR 3.2**

2. Two different lines are *parallel* if they both have the same slope or both have an undefined slope. Use the graph to locate a point $D$ on the line $x = -3$ such that the line through points $C$ and $D$ is parallel to the line through points $A$ and $B$. Then describe how you could solve this problem without a graph. **MR 3.3**

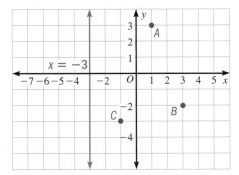

3. A car in need of repair requires $300 for parts and 3 hours of labor to install the parts. A car dealership charges $70 per hour for labor, and a repair shop charges $65 per hour for labor. Equations giving the total cost $C$ for a repair requiring $t$ hours of labor are shown below. **MR 2.3, MR 2.5**

   **Car dealership** $C = 300 + 70t$
   **Repair shop** $C = 300 + 65t$

   a. Graph the equations.

   b. Describe how you can use the graph from part (a) to find the savings when the car is taken to the repair shop.

   c. Give an alternative method for solving this problem.

4. Consider the equation $8x + 12y = k$. Give two possible values of $k$ so that the $x$-intercept and $y$-intercept of the graph of the equation are both integers. Make and justify a conjecture about all values of $k$ for which the $x$-intercept and $y$-intercept are both integers. **MR 1.1, MR 1.2**

5. The following table shows the sales tax on an item with a given price. **MR 2.3, MR 3.2**

   | Price (dollars) | Sales tax (dollars) |
   |---|---|
   | 20 | 1.20 |
   | 40 | 2.40 |
   | 60 | 3.60 |

   a. Write and graph a direct variation equation that describes the relationship between the price and the sales tax. Predict the sales tax on an item that costs $130.

   b. How is the process you used to solve this problem similar to that used in the problem on the previous page?

6. An equation of a line with given $x$-intercept $a$ and $y$-intercept $b$ is shown in each row of the table.

   | $a$ | $b$ | Equation |
   |---|---|---|
   | 4 | 5 | $5x + 4y = 20$ |
   | 7 | 2 | $2x + 7y = 14$ |
   | 3 | −3 | $-3x + 3y = -9$ |

   Use the pattern in the table to find an equation of a line with $x$-intercept $a$ and $y$-intercept $b$. *Explain* how you wrote the equation. Are there any values of $a$ and $b$ for which you could not write an equation in this way? **MR 1.1, MR 1.2**

# Chapter 10 Review Game

## Materials
• graph paper

## Guess That Object

Work with a partner. Copy the grid and line segments below onto a piece of graph paper. The segments on the grid have the following descriptions:

• The graph of a vertical line whose $x$-intercept is 8 for values of $y$ that satisfy $0 \leq y \leq 5$
• The graph of a horizontal line that passes through $(4, 2)$ for values of $x$ that satisfy $4 \leq x \leq 6$

You and your partner will take turns completing the exercises. The resulting figure will be a familiar object. After completing an exercise you may try to guess what the object is, then check the guess with your teacher. If you are correct, you win and the game ends. If you are incorrect, your partner takes his or her turn by completing the next exercise and making a guess. Play continues in this way until a guess is correct or all of the exercises have been completed.

### Exercises

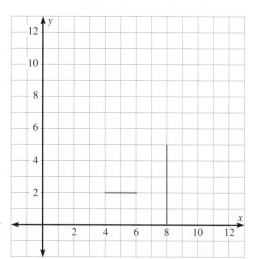

1. Graph the vertical line whose $x$-intercept is 12 for values of $y$ that satisfy $3 \leq y \leq 8$.

2. Graph the vertical line whose $x$-intercept is 4 for values of $y$ that satisfy $0 \leq y \leq 2$.

3. Graph the equation $3x - 4y = 4$ for values of $x$ that satisfy $8 \leq x \leq 12$.

4. Graph the equation $x - y = -3$ for values of $x$ that satisfy $2 \leq x \leq 5$.

5. Graph the equation $x + y = 20$ for values of $x$ that satisfy $9 \leq x \leq 12$.

6. Graph the equation $y = \frac{3}{4}x - 6$ for values of $x$ that satisfy $8 \leq x \leq 12$.

7. Graph the equation $3x - 4y = -17$ for values of $x$ that satisfy $5 \leq x \leq 9$.

8. Graph the horizontal line that passes through $(8, 0)$ for values of $x$ that satisfy $2 \leq x \leq 8$.

9. Graph the vertical line whose $x$-intercept is 2 for values of $y$ that satisfy $0 \leq y \leq 5$.

10. Graph the equation $x + y = 13$ for values of $x$ that satisfy $5 \leq x \leq 8$.

11. Graph the vertical line whose $x$-intercept is 6 for values of $y$ that satisfy $0 \leq y \leq 2$.

## VOCABULARY

- coordinate plane, p. 408
- *x*-axis, p. 408
- *y*-axis, p. 408
- origin, p. 408
- quadrants, p. 408
- ordered pair, p. 408
- *x*-coordinate, p. 408

- *y*-coordinate, p. 408
- solution of an equation in two variables, p. 414
- graph of an equation in two variables, p. 414
- linear equation, p. 414
- standard form of a linear equation, p. 414

- *x*-intercept, p. 428
- *y*-intercept, p. 428
- slope, p. 434
- slope-intercept form, p. 440
- direct variation, p. 446
- constant of variation, p. 452

### Vocabulary Exercises

**1.** Copy and complete: The axes divide the coordinate plane into four $\underline{\ ?\ }$.

**2.** Copy and complete: A set of paired data $(x, y)$ represents $\underline{\ ?\ }$ if the ratio $\dfrac{y}{x}$ for $x \neq 0$ is constant.

### 10.1 Graph in the Coordinate Plane • • • • • • • • • • • • • • • • • • • • pp. 408–411

Each point in a coordinate plane is represented by a pair of numbers $(x, y)$ called an ordered pair.

**EXAMPLE**   Plot the point $P(-3, 2)$ and describe its location.

Start at $(0, 0)$. Move 3 units to the left and 2 units up. The point is in Quadrant II.

**Plot the point and describe its location.**

**3.** $A(2, 1)$     **4.** $B(-3, -4)$     **5.** $C(-1, 0)$     **6.** $D(0, 3)$

### 10.2 Graph Linear Equations in Standard Form • • • • • • • • pp. 414–417

An equation whose graph is a line is called a linear equation.

**EXAMPLE**   Graph the equation $x - y = 1$.

Solve for $y$. Make a table. Plot the points and draw a line through them.

$$x - y = 1$$
$$-y = -x + 1$$
$$y = x - 1$$

| $x$ | $-1$ | $0$ | $1$ | $2$ |
|-----|------|-----|-----|-----|
| $y$ | $-2$ | $-1$ | $0$ | $1$ |

**Graph the equation.**

**7.** $3x + y = 2$     **8.** $x - 2y = 4$     **9.** $4x + 3y = 12$     **10.** $5x - 2y = 10$

**10.3**  *Graph Horizontal and Vertical Lines* . . . . . . . . . . . . . . **pp. 420–423**

The graph of the equation $x = a$ is a vertical line.
The graph of the equation $y = b$ is a horizontal line.

**EXAMPLE**   **Graph $y = -2$.**

All points on the graph of $y = -2$ must have a $y$-coordinate of
$-2$, such as $(0, -2)$, $(2, -2)$, $(3, -2)$. Plot the points, then draw a
horizontal line through them.

**Graph the equation on a coordinate plane.**

**11.** $y = -1$     **12.** $y = 3$     **13.** $x = -2$     **14.** $x = 4$

**10.4**  *Graph Linear Equations Using Intercepts* . . . . . . . . . **pp. 428–431**

The $x$-coordinate of a point where a graph crosses the $x$-axis is an $x$-intercept.
The $y$-coordinate of a point where a graph crosses the $y$-axis is a $y$-intercept.

**EXAMPLE**   **Find the $x$-intercept of the graph of $3x + 2y = 6$.**

| | |
|---|---|
| $3x + 2y = 6$ | **Write original equation.** |
| $3x + 2(0) = 6$ | **Substitute 0 for $y$.** |
| $x = \dfrac{6}{3} = 2$ | **Solve for $x$.** |

The $x$-intercept is 2.

**Find the $x$-intercept and $y$-intercept of the graph of the equation.**

**15.** $x + y = 5$     **16.** $x - 2y = 8$     **17.** $15 = 3x + 5y$     **18.** $7x - 2y = 14$

**10.5**  *Find Slopes of Lines* . . . . . . . . . . . . . . . . . . . . . . . . . . **pp. 434–437**

The slope of a nonvertical line is the ratio of the vertical change, called the rise,
to the horizontal change, called the run, between any two points on the line.

**EXAMPLE**   **Find the slope of the line through the points
(0, 1) and (3, 3).**

$$m = \frac{\text{rise}}{\text{run}} = \frac{\text{difference of } y\text{-coordinates}}{\text{difference of } x\text{-coordinates}}$$

$$= \frac{3 - 1}{3 - 0} = \frac{2}{3}$$

The slope is $\dfrac{2}{3}$.

**Find the slope of the line through the given points.**

**19.** $(2, 3), (3, 5)$     **20.** $(1, 4), (7, 10)$     **21.** $(-4, 3), (-5, 6)$     **22.** $(1, 3), (5, 3)$

## 10.6 *Graph Equations in Slope-Intercept Form* •••••• pp. 440–443

The slope-intercept form of a linear equation is $y = mx + b$, where $m$ is the slope and $b$ is the $y$-intercept of the equation's graph.

**EXAMPLE**

| $2x + 3y = 12$ | **Original equation** |
| $3y = -2x + 12$ | **Subtract 2x from each side.** |
| $y = -\dfrac{2}{3}x + 4$ | **Divide each side by 3.** |

The line has a slope of $-\dfrac{2}{3}$ and a $y$-intercept of 4.

**Find the slope and *y*-intercept of the graph of the equation.**

**23.** $y = 3x - 1$    **24.** $1 - 5x = y$    **25.** $2x - y = 4$    **26.** $20 = 4x + 5y$

## 10.7 *Solve Direct Variation Problems by Graphing* ••••• pp. 446–449

A set of paired data $(x, y)$ represents direct variation if the ratio $\dfrac{y}{x}$ for $x \neq 0$ is constant.

**EXAMPLE**

**Tell whether the data in the table show direct variation. *Explain.***

| $x$ | 2 | 4 | 6 | 8 |
|---|---|---|---|---|
| $y$ | 6 | 12 | 18 | 24 |

Find the ratios of the $y$-values to $x$-values.

$$\frac{6}{2} = 3 \qquad \frac{12}{4} = 3 \qquad \frac{18}{6} = 3 \qquad \frac{24}{8} = 3$$

Because the ratios are equal, the data show direct variation.

**Tell whether the data in the table show direct variation. *Explain.***

**27.**

| $x$ | 1 | 2 | 3 |
|---|---|---|---|
| $y$ | 3 | 6 | 9 |

**28.**

| $x$ | 6 | 7 | 8 |
|---|---|---|---|
| $y$ | 16 | 17 | 18 |

**29.**

| $x$ | 2 | 4 | 6 |
|---|---|---|---|
| $y$ | 20 | 40 | 60 |

## 10.8 *Solve Direct Variation Problems Using Algebra* •••• pp. 452–455

**EXAMPLE**

**Assume *y* varies directly with *x*, and *y* = 10 when *x* = 5. Write an equation that relates *x* and *y*.**

| $y = kx$ | **Write direct variation equation using *y* and *x*.** |
| $10 = k(5)$ | **Substitute 10 for *y* and 5 for *x*.** |
| $k = 2$ | **Solve for *k*.** |

The direct variation equation is $y = 2x$.

**30.** Assume $y$ varies directly with $x$, and $y = 8$ when $x = 2$. Write an equation that relates $x$ and $y$.

**Plot the point and describe its location.**

**1.** $A(-2, -2)$        **2.** $B(-4, 1)$        **3.** $C(-3, 0)$

**Tell whether the ordered pair is a solution of the equation.**

**4.** $-3x + 2y = -4; (2, 1)$    **5.** $5x - y = -3; (-1, 2)$    **6.** $5x = 6; (-2, 2)$

**Find the x-intercept and y-intercept of the graph of the equation.**

**7.** $x - 5y = 10$        **8.** $3x - 4y = -24$        **9.** $4x - 5y = -10$

**Draw the line with the given intercepts.**

**10.** $x$-intercept: 4        **11.** $x$-intercept: 3        **12.** $x$-intercept: $-4$
      $y$-intercept: $-3$            $y$-intercept: $-2$            $y$-intercept: $-1$

**Find the slope of the line through the given points.**

**13.** $(4, 5), (10, 3)$        **14.** $(-2, 5), (6, -3)$        **15.** $(-12, 3), (-9, -7)$

**Write the equation in slope-intercept form. Identify the slope and
y-intercept of the line. Then graph the equation.**

**16.** $3x - 2y = 6$        **17.** $3x - 5y = -15$        **18.** $5x + 2y = 8$

**Tell whether the data in the table show direct variation.** *Explain.*

**19.**

| x | 3 | 5 | 7 | 9 |
|---|---|---|---|---|
| y | 9 | 15 | 21 | 27 |

**20.**

| x | 2 | 4 | 6 | 8 |
|---|---|---|---|---|
| y | 8 | 10 | 12 | 14 |

**21.**

| x | 2 | 4 | 6 | 8 |
|---|---|---|---|---|
| y | 3 | 6 | 9 | 12 |

**Tell whether the equation represents direct variation. If it does, give
the constant of variation.**

**22.** $3x - 2y = 0$        **23.** $x - y = -2$        **24.** $6x = -5y$

**Assume y varies directly with x. Write an equation that relates
x and y. Then find y when x = 4.**

**25.** $x = 3, y = 4$        **26.** $x = 2, y = -5$        **27.** $x = -5, y = -3$

**28.** Student tickets for a school play cost $6 each. General public tickets
cost $10 each. Charlene spent $120 on tickets. An equation that models
this situation is $6x + 10y = 120$. Draw a graph and find three possible
combinations of tickets she bought.

**29.** The cost $C$ of going to an amusement park varies directly with the
number $p$ of people going. A group of 6 paid $168. Write an equation
that relates $C$ and $p$. How much would it cost for a group of 8 to go to
the amusement park?

1. Allison is building a sandbox for her backyard. She makes a scale drawing on a coordinate plane with each unit representing 1 foot. Points $A(-1, 2)$, $B(-1, -1)$, $C(3, -1)$, and $D(3, 2)$ represent the corners of the sandbox. What will the perimeter of her sandbox be?

   Ⓐ 7 ft      Ⓑ 12 ft

   Ⓒ 14 ft      Ⓓ 24 ft

2. Which ordered pair is *not* a solution of the equation $3x - 2y = 12$?

   Ⓐ $(0, -6)$      Ⓑ $(2, -3)$

   Ⓒ $(6, 3)$      Ⓓ $(-2, 9)$

3. The graph of which equation is shown?

   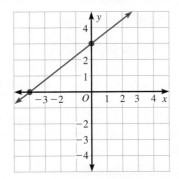

   Ⓐ $4x - 3y = 12$    Ⓑ $-3x + 4y = 12$

   Ⓒ $3x - 4y = 12$    Ⓓ $4x - 3y = -12$

4. Greg is buying tile for his kitchen floor. The boundaries of the floor can be modeled by the graphs of $x = 4$, $y = 8$, $x = 16$, and $y = -8$, where all the distances are in feet. How many square feet of tile are needed?

   Ⓐ $32 \text{ ft}^2$      Ⓑ $96 \text{ ft}^2$

   Ⓒ $192 \text{ ft}^2$      Ⓓ $56 \text{ ft}^2$

5. What is the $y$-intercept of the graph of $9x - 4y = 36$?

   Ⓐ 4      Ⓑ $-9$

   Ⓒ 9      Ⓓ $-4$

6. What is the slope of the line through the points $(-4, 3)$ and $(2, 3)$?

   Ⓐ 0      Ⓑ $-\dfrac{3}{2}$

   Ⓒ $-\dfrac{1}{2}$      Ⓓ Undefined

7. What is the slope-intercept form of $3x - 5y = 10$?

   Ⓐ $y = -\dfrac{3}{5}x - 2$    Ⓑ $y = \dfrac{3}{5}x + 2$

   Ⓒ $y = -\dfrac{3}{5}x + 2$    Ⓓ $y = \dfrac{3}{5}x - 2$

8. Which table has data showing direct variation?

   Ⓐ

   | $x$ | 1 | 2 | 3 | 4 |
   |---|---|---|---|---|
   | $y$ | 1 | 3 | 5 | 7 |

   Ⓑ

   | $x$ | 1 | 2 | 3 | 4 |
   |---|---|---|---|---|
   | $y$ | 2 | 3 | 4 | 5 |

   Ⓒ

   | $x$ | 1 | 2 | 3 | 4 |
   |---|---|---|---|---|
   | $y$ | 2 | 4 | 6 | 8 |

   Ⓓ

   | $x$ | 1 | 2 | 3 | 4 |
   |---|---|---|---|---|
   | $y$ | 2 | 4 | 8 | 10 |

9. Which equation represents direct variation with a constant of variation of 5?

   Ⓐ $5x - y = 0$      Ⓑ $x - 5y = 5$

   Ⓒ $5x + y = 0$      Ⓓ $5x - y = 5$

10. The distance $d$ that Marcus walks varies directly with the time $t$ spent walking at a constant speed. Marcus walks 10 miles in 4 hours. What distance did he walk in 2.5 hours?

    Ⓐ 2.5 mi      Ⓑ 5 mi

    Ⓒ 5.25 mi      Ⓓ 6.25 mi

# Contents of Student Resources

## Looking Ahead
pages 465–475

## Skills Review Handbook
pages 476–497

### Number Sense

| | |
|---|---|
| Place Value | 476 |
| Comparing and Ordering Whole Numbers | 477 |
| Comparing and Ordering Decimals | 478 |
| Rounding | 479 |
| Adding and Subtracting Whole Numbers | 480 |
| Multiplying Whole Numbers | 481 |
| Dividing Whole Numbers | 482 |
| Ratios | 483 |
| Factors and Multiples | 484 |

### Algebra and Functions

| | |
|---|---|
| Converting Units of Measurement | 486 |
| Converting Between Metric Units and Customary Units | 487 |

### Measurement and Geometry

| | |
|---|---|
| Perimeter and Area | 488 |
| Circumference and Area of a Circle | 490 |
| Surface Area and Volume | 492 |

### Statistics, Data Analysis, and Probability

| | |
|---|---|
| Reading Bar Graphs | 494 |
| Reading Circle Graphs | 495 |

### Mathematical Reasoning

| | |
|---|---|
| Problem Solving Strategies | 496 |

## Extra Practice for Chapters 1–10
pages 498–507

## Tables
pages 508–513

| | | | |
|---|---|---|---|
| Symbols and Formulas | 508 | Measures | 512 |
| Geometric Formulas | 509 | Squares and Square Roots | 513 |
| Properties | 510 | | |

## English-Spanish Glossary
pages 514–532

## Index
pages 533–543

## Credits
page 544

## Selected Answers
pages SA1–SA17

# Looking Ahead

## Introduction

The following Looking Ahead topics expand upon what you learned in Algebra Readiness, especially in Chapter 10. These topics will be covered in much greater depth in Algebra 1.

**California Standards**

Gr. 7 AF 1.1    **Topic 1**

Write and Graph Equations in Two Variables    **466**

Gr. 7 AF 1.1    **Topic 2**

Write and Graph Inequalities in Two Variables    **468**

Gr. 7 AF 1.1    **Topic 3**

Write and Graph Systems of Equations    **472**

Gr. 7 AF 1.1    **Topic 4**

Write and Graph Systems of Inequalities    **474**

**Writing and graphing an equation for the total cost of joining a BMX track, page 467**

> **VOCABULARY and CONCEPTS**
> • *x*-intercept, p. 428  • *y*-intercept, p. 428  • slope, p. 434
> Recall that for a linear equation in the form $y = mx + b$, the graph of the equation is a line with slope $m$ and *y*-intercept $b$.

**EXAMPLE 1** *Writing an Equation in Two Variables* ⋯⋯⋯⋯⋯⋯

|     | Verbal Sentence | Equation |
|-----|-----------------|----------|
| **a.** | The sum of three times a number *x* and two times a number *y* is eight. | $3x + 2y = 8$ |
| **b.** | The difference of five times a number *x* and half of a number *y* is six. | $5x - \frac{1}{2}y = 6$ |
| **c.** | A number *y* is equal to the sum of four times a number *x* and two. | $y = 4x + 2$ |

**EXAMPLE 2** *Writing and Graphing an Equation in Two Variables*

A landscape supply business charges $32 to deliver mulch. The mulch costs $24 per cubic yard. Write an equation that gives the total cost *y* (in dollars) of having mulch delivered to a site in terms of the number *x* of cubic yards ordered. Then graph the equation.

**Solution**

**Step 1** Write a verbal model. Then write an equation.

| Total cost (dollars) | = | Cost per cubic yard (dollars per cubic yard) | · | Number of cubic yards ordered | + | Delivery cost (dollars) |
|---|---|---|---|---|---|---|
| $y$ | = | 24 | · | $x$ | + | 32 |

**Step 2** Identify the slope and *y*-intercept: $m = 24$ and $b = 32$.

**Step 3** Plot the point that corresponds to the *y*-intercept, (0, 32).

**Step 4** Use the slope to locate a second point on the line. For this problem, only nonnegative values of *x* and *y* make sense, so draw a ray in Quadrant I as shown.

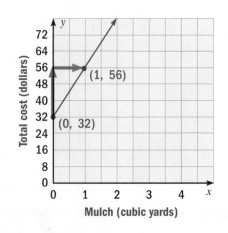

**EXAMPLE 3** *Writing and Graphing an Equation in Two Variables*

Advance tickets to the school play cost $6. Tickets sold at the door cost $8. Total ticket sales for $x$ advance tickets and $y$ tickets sold at the door were $480. Write an equation to represent this situation. Graph the equation.

**Solution**

**Step 1** Write a verbal model. Then write an equation.

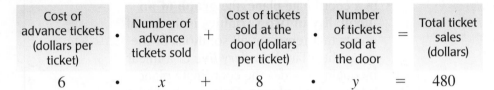

| Cost of advance tickets (dollars per ticket) | · | Number of advance tickets sold | + | Cost of tickets sold at the door (dollars per ticket) | · | Number of tickets sold at the door | = | Total ticket sales (dollars) |
|---|---|---|---|---|---|---|---|---|
| 6 | · | $x$ | + | 8 | · | $y$ | = | 480 |

**Step 2** Identify the intercepts.

| *x*-intercept | *y*-intercept |
|---|---|
| $6x + 8y = 480$ | $6x + 8y = 480$ |
| $6x + 8(0) = 480$ | $6(0) + 8y = 480$ |
| $x = 80$ | $y = 60$ |

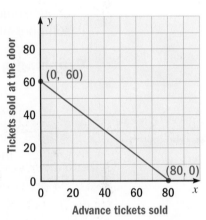

**Step 3** Plot points that correspond to the intercepts. Plot the points $(80, 0)$ and $(0, 60)$. For this problem, only nonnegative values of $x$ and $y$ make sense, so draw a segment in Quadrant I as shown.

## Practice

**In Exercises 1–3, write the verbal sentence as an equation in two variables.**

**1.** A number $y$ is the sum of half of a number $x$ and five.

**2.** The difference of a number $x$ and four times a number $y$ is thirty-two.

**3.** A number $x$ is equal to the sum of two thirds of a number $y$ and six.

**4.** You pay a one-year membership fee of $50 to a Bicycle Moto Cross (BMX) track plus $15 per race. Write an equation that gives the total cost (in dollars) in terms of the number of races in which you participate during the year. Graph the equation.

**5.** One pound of chicken costs $3.50, and one pound of ground beef costs $2.50. Write an equation that models the possible combinations of pounds of chicken and pounds of ground beef that you can buy for $35. Graph the equation.

# Write and Graph Inequalities in Two Variables

## VOCABULARY and CONCEPTS

- A **linear inequality in two variables,** such as $x - 3y < 6$, is the result of replacing the $=$ sign in a linear equation with $<$, $\leq$, $>$, or $\geq$.
- A **solution of an inequality in two variables**, $x$ and $y$, is an ordered pair $(x, y)$ that produces a true statement when the values of $x$ and $y$ are substituted into the inequality.
- In a coordinate plane, the **graph of an inequality in two variables** is the set of points that represent all solutions of the inequality. The *boundary line* of a linear inequality divides the coordinate plane into two **half-planes.** Only one half-plane contains the points that represent the solutions of the inequality.

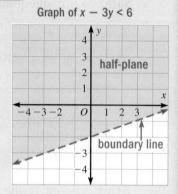

Graph of $x - 3y < 6$

half-plane

boundary line

## Graphing a Linear Inequality in Two Variables

**Step 1** Graph the boundary line. Use a *dashed line* for $<$ or $>$, and use a *solid line* for $\leq$ or $\geq$.

**Step 2** Test a point not on the boundary line by checking whether the ordered pair is a solution of the inequality.

**Step 3** Shade the half-plane containing the point if the ordered pair is a solution of the inequality. Shade the other half-plane if the ordered pair is *not* a solution.

**EXAMPLE 1** *Checking Solutions* ••••••••••••••••••••••••••••••••

**Tell whether the ordered pair is a solution of the inequality.**

**a.** $3x - y > 7$; $(4, 3)$ **b.** $4x - 3y \leq 8$; $(10, -3)$

**Solution**

**a.**

$$3x - y > 7 \qquad \text{Write original inequality.}$$
$$3(4) - 3 \overset{?}{>} 7 \qquad \text{Substitute 4 for } x \text{ and 3 for } y.$$
$$9 > 7 \checkmark \qquad \text{Simplify.}$$

So, $(4, 3)$ is a solution of $3x - y > 7$.

**b.**

$$4x - 3y \leq 8 \qquad \text{Write original inequality.}$$
$$4(10) - 3(-3) \overset{?}{\leq} 8 \qquad \text{Substitute 10 for } x \text{ and } -3 \text{ for } y.$$
$$49 \leq 8 \ \text{✗} \qquad \text{Simplify.}$$

Because $49 \leq 8$ is not true, $(10, -3)$ is not a solution of $4x - 3y \leq 8$.

## EXAMPLE 2 — Graphing a Linear Inequality in Two Variables

### a. Graph $x + 2y > 6$.

**Step 1** Graph the equation $x + 2y = 6$.

The inequality is $>$, so use a dashed line.

**Step 2** Test $(0, 4)$ in $x + 2y > 6$.

$$0 + 2(4) \stackrel{?}{>} 6 \quad \textbf{Substitute.}$$

$$8 > 6 \checkmark \quad \textbf{Simplify.}$$

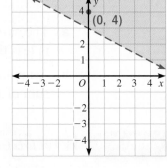

**Step 3** Shade the half-plane that contains $(0, 4)$, because $(0, 4)$ is a solution of the inequality.

### b. Graph $x + 2y \le 6$.

The boundary line is the same as in part (a), but the inequality is $\le$, so use a solid line.

You tested the point $(0, 4)$ in part (a) and found $8 > 6$. Because 8 is *not* less than or equal to 6, shade the other half-plane.

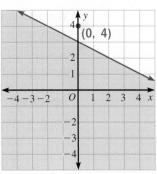

## EXAMPLE 3 — Graphing a Linear Inequality in Two Variables

### a. Graph $y < -1$.

**Step 1** Graph the equation $y = -1$. The inequality is $<$, so use a dashed line.

**Step 2** Test $(0, -2)$ in $y < -1$. You substitute only the $y$-coordinate because the inequality does not have the variable $x$. $-2 < -1 \checkmark$

**Step 3** Shade the half-plane that contains $(0, -2)$, because $(0, -2)$ is a solution of the inequality.

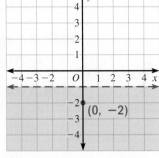

### b. Graph $x \ge 3$.

**Step 1** Graph the equation $x = 3$. The inequality is $\ge$, so use a solid line.

**Step 2** Test $(1, 0)$ in $x \ge 3$. You substitute only the $x$-coordinate because the inequality does not have the variable $y$. $1 \ge 3$ ✗

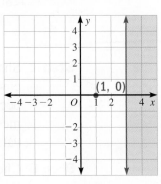

**Step 3** Shade the half-plane that does not contain $(1, 0)$, because $(1, 0)$ is *not* a solution of the inequality.

**EXAMPLE 4** *Writing an Inequality in Two Variables* ...............

| Verbal Sentence | Equation |
|---|---|
| **a.** The sum of a number $x$ and a number $y$ is less than three. | $x + y < 3$ |
| **b.** A number $y$ is greater than or equal to the sum of four times a number $x$ and five. | $y \geq 4x + 5$ |

**EXAMPLE 5** *Writing and Graphing an Inequality in Two Variables*

You are going shopping for clothes and can spend at most $140. A pair of pants costs $28, and a shirt costs $20. Write and graph an inequality that describes the numbers of pairs of pants and shirts that you can buy. Give three possible combinations of pants and shirts that you can buy.

**Solution**

**Step 1** Write a verbal model. Let $x$ represent the number of pairs of pants you can buy. Let $y$ represent the number of shirts you can buy. Then write an inequality.

| Cost of a pair of pants (dollars per pair) | · | Number of pairs of pants bought | + | Cost of a shirt (dollars per shirt) | · | Number of shirts bought | ≤ | Maximum amount you can spend (dollars) |
|---|---|---|---|---|---|---|---|---|
| 28 | · | $x$ | + | 20 | · | $y$ | ≤ | 140 |

**Step 2** Graph the inequality $28x + 20y \leq 140$.

The inequality is ≤, so use a solid line.

**Step 3** Test $(1, 2)$ in $28x + 20y \leq 140$.

$28x + 20y \leq 140$ **Write original inequality.**

$28(1) + 20(2) \overset{?}{\leq} 140$ **Substitute 1 for $x$ and 2 for $y$.**

$68 \leq 140$ ✓ **Simplify.**

**Step 4** Shade the part of the half-plane that contains $(1, 2)$ and lies in Quadrant I, because $(1, 2)$ is a solution of the inequality and only nonnegative values of $x$ and $y$ make sense.

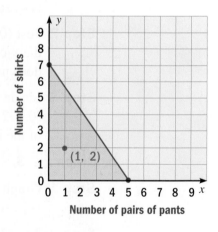

**Step 5** Choose three points on the graph, such as $(2, 2)$, $(4, 1)$, and $(1, 5)$. So, you can buy 2 pairs of pants and 2 shirts, or 4 pairs of pants and 1 shirt, or 1 pair of pants and 5 shirts.

## Practice

**Tell whether the ordered pair is a solution of the inequality.**

**1.** $x + y < 3$;
(0, 0)

**2.** $x - y < 12$;
(18, 6)

**3.** $x + 3y \le -15$;
(8, −8)

**4.** $x - 6y \ge 10$;
(−7, −3)

**5.** $4x + 3y \ge 11$;
(−3, 3)

**6.** $6x - 2y < 7$;
(3, −5)

**7.** $y \ge 2x - 1$;
(−3, −4)

**8.** $y < -3x + 2$;
(−1, 5)

**9.** $y > -6x + 5$;
(2, −8)

**Match the inequality with its graph.**

**10.** $y - x \ge 3$

**11.** $x - y \ge 3$

**12.** $y - x \le 3$

**A.**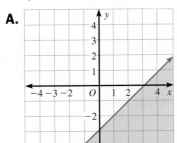

**B.**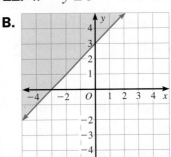

**C.**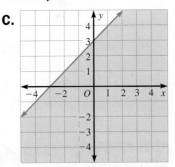

**Graph the inequality.**

**13.** $y > x - 2$

**14.** $y \le x + 4$

**15.** $y \ge -x$

**16.** $y - x \ge 6$

**17.** $y \ge 4$

**18.** $x \le 10$

**19.** $y - 2x < 4$

**20.** $x + y > 3$

**21.** $3x + y < 1$

**22.** To keep in shape, you try to swim and run at least 6 hours each week. Let $x$ represent the number of hours you swim each week, and let $y$ represent the number of hours you run each week.

    **a.** Write an inequality describing the number of hours you exercise each week in terms of $x$ and $y$.

    **b.** Graph the inequality. Then give three possible combinations of hours of swimming and running that allow you to meet your goal.

**23.** The debate club at your school has 20 members. Only sophomores, juniors, and seniors may participate. Let $x$ represent the number of sophomores, and let $y$ represent the number of juniors. Write and graph an inequality that describes the different numbers of sophomores and juniors in the debate club. Then give three possible combinations of numbers of sophomores and juniors in the club.

# Write and Graph Systems of Equations

## VOCABULARY and CONCEPTS

- A **system of linear equations**, or simply a *linear system*, consists of two or more linear equations in the same variables.
- A **solution of a system of linear equations** in two variables is an ordered pair that satisfies each equation in the system.

### EXAMPLE 1 · Checking a Solution

Tell whether (2, 0) is a solution of the linear system $2x + y = 4$, $x - 2y = 2$.

**Equation 1**

$$2x + y = 4$$
$$2(2) + 0 \stackrel{?}{=} 4$$
$$4 = 4 \checkmark$$

**Equation 2**

$$x - 2y = 2$$
$$2 - 2(0) \stackrel{?}{=} 2$$
$$2 = 2 \checkmark$$

> Substitute 2 for $x$ and 0 for $y$ in each equation.

The ordered pair (2, 0) is a solution of the system.

### EXAMPLE 2 · Writing and Solving a System of Equations

The sum of a number $x$ and a number $y$ is negative two. The sum of negative five times a number $x$ and a number $y$ is four. Write a system of linear equations, solve the system by graphing, and check your answer.

**Solution**

**Step 1** Write the system of linear equations.

$$x + y = -2$$
$$-5x + y = 4$$

**Step 2** Graph both equations.

**Step 3** Estimate the point of intersection.
The two lines appear to intersect at $(-1, -1)$.

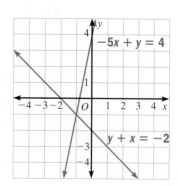

**Step 4** Check whether $(-1, -1)$ is a solution.

**Equation 1**

$$x + y = -2$$
$$-1 + (-1) \stackrel{?}{=} -2$$
$$-2 = -2 \checkmark$$

**Equation 2**

$$-5x + y = 4$$
$$-5(-1) + (-1) \stackrel{?}{=} 4$$
$$4 = 4 \checkmark$$

The ordered pair $(-1, -1)$ is a solution of the system.

**EXAMPLE 3** *Solving a Multi-Step Problem*

The Rosebud Shop charges $6 plus a rate of $.25 per mile to deliver a bouquet of flowers. Beautiful Bouquets charges $8 plus a rate of $.20 per mile to deliver. Determine the distance for which the total delivery charges for both shops would be the same.

**Solution**

**Step 1** Write a linear system. Let $x$ be the number of miles driven and $y$ be the total cost of delivery.

$$y = 6 + 0.25x \quad \textbf{Equation 1 for Rosebud Shop}$$

$$y = 8 + 0.20x \quad \textbf{Equation 2 for Beautiful Bouquets Shop}$$

**Step 2** Graph both equations.

**Step 3** Estimate the point of intersection. The two lines appear to intersect at $(40, 16)$.

**Step 4** Check whether $(40, 16)$ is a solution.

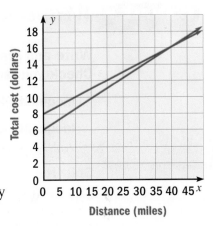

Distance (miles)

| Equation 1 | Equation 2 |
|---|---|
| $y = 6 + 0.25x$ | $y = 8 + 0.20x$ |
| $16 \stackrel{?}{=} 6 + 0.25(40)$ | $16 \stackrel{?}{=} 8 + 0.20(40)$ |
| $16 = 16 ✓$ | $16 = 16 ✓$ |

For a distance of 40 miles, the total delivery charges for both shops are the same.

## Practice

**Tell whether the ordered pair is a solution of the linear system.**

**1.** $(0, -4)$;
$x + y = -4$
$x - 5y = 20$

**2.** $(3, 3)$;
$x + 2y = 9$
$4x - y = 15$

**3.** $(1, -2)$;
$2x - 3y = 8$
$3x - 2y = -1$

**Solve the linear system by graphing. Check your solution.**

**4.** $5x - y = -4$
$-2x + y = 1$

**5.** $y = x$
$y = 4x - 9$

**6.** $y = -2x + 2$
$y = x + 5$

**7.** $3x + y = 7$
$-2x + y = -8$

**8.** $4x + 3y = 5$
$2x - y = 5$

**9.** $-x + 3y = 9$
$4x - y = 8$

**10.** Lee bought 14 one-gallon bottles of apple juice and orange juice for a school dance. The apple juice was on sale for $1.50 per bottle. The orange juice was $2 per bottle. He spent $24. Write a system of equations for this situation. Then graph the system. How many bottles of each type of juice did Lee buy?

# Write and Graph Systems of Inequalities

## VOCABULARY and CONCEPTS

- A **system of linear inequalities in two variables**, or simply a *system of inequalities*, consists of two or more linear inequalities in the same variables.
- A **solution of a system of linear inequalities** is an ordered pair that is a solution of each inequality in the system.
- The **graph of a system of linear inequalities** is the graph of all solutions of the system.

### Graphing a System of Linear Inequalities

**Step 1** Graph each inequality.

**Step 2** Find the intersection of the half-planes. The graph of the system is this intersection.

---

**EXAMPLE 1** *Writing and Graphing a System of Linear Inequalities*

Write and graph the system of linear inequalities described below. Check your solution.

**Inequality 1** A number $y$ is less than the sum of a number $x$ and 2.

**Inequality 2** A number $y$ is greater than or equal to the sum of 5 and $-2$ times a number $x$.

**Solution**

**Step 1** Write the system of inequalities.

> **Inequality 1** $y < x + 2$
>
> **Inequality 2** $y \geq -2x + 5$

**Step 2** Graph both inequalities in the same coordinate plane. The graph of the system is the intersection of the two half-planes, which is shown as the shaded region.

**Step 3** Check your solution. Choose a point in the shaded region, such as (3, 2). To check this solution, substitute 3 for $x$ and 2 for $y$ into each inequality.

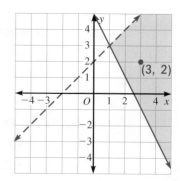

| **Inequality 1** | **Inequality 2** |
|---|---|
| $y < x + 2$ | $y \geq -2x + 5$ |
| $2 \overset{?}{<} 3 + 2$ | $2 \overset{?}{\geq} -2(3) + 5$ |
| $2 < 5\ \checkmark$ | $2 \geq -1\ \checkmark$ |

(3, 2) is a solution of each inequality, so the solution checks.

Gr. 7 AF 1.1 Use variables and appropriate operations to write an expression, an equation, an inequality, or a system of equations or inequalities that represents a verbal description (e.g., three less than a number, half as large as area A).

**EXAMPLE 2** *Writing and Solving a System of Linear Inequalities*

The tickets for a school play cost $8 for adults and $5 for students. The auditorium in which the play is being held can hold at most 525 people. The organizers of the school play must make at least $3000 to cover the costs of the set construction, costumes, and programs.

Write and graph a system of linear inequalities based on selling $x$ adult tickets and $y$ student tickets. Identify two possible combinations of adult and student tickets that could be sold.

**Solution**

**Step 1** Write a system of linear inequalities.

$8x + 5y \geq 3000$   **Ticket revenue**

$x + y \leq 525$   **Auditorium capacity**

**Step 2** Graph the inequalities.

**Step 3** Choose two points on the graph, such as (300, 150) and (400, 50). These ordered pairs represent selling 300 adult tickets and 150 student tickets, or 400 adult tickets and 50 student tickets.

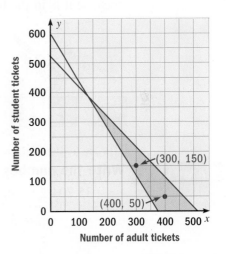

## Practice

**Graph the system of linear inequalities.**

**1.** $x + y > 1$
$x \leq y$

**2.** $x \geq y + 2$
$2x + y < 4$

**3.** $x \leq -y$
$2x - y < 4$

**4.** A number $y$ is less than the sum of half a number $x$ and $-1$. A number $y$ is greater than or equal to the sum of $-3$ times a number $x$ and 2. Write and graph the system of linear inequalities.

**5.** You are planning a cookout. You figure that you will need at least 8 pounds of ground beef and ground turkey to make burgers. Ground beef costs $2.40 per pound, and ground turkey costs $1.20 per pound. You want to spend at most $12 on the meat.

   **a.** Let $x$ represent the number of pounds of ground beef you buy, and let $y$ represent the number of pounds of ground turkey you buy. Write a system of linear inequalities for the meat that you can buy.

   **b.** Graph the system of inequalities.

   **c.** Identify two combinations of ground beef and ground turkey that you can buy.

# Skills Review Handbook

## Place Value

Gr. 3 NS 1.3, Gr. 3 NS 1.5

The **whole numbers** are the numbers 0, 1, 2, 3, . . . (the dots indicate that the numbers continue without end). A **digit** is any of the numbers 0, 1, 2, 3, 4, 5, 6, 7, 8, or 9. Decimals are numbers such as 121.32, 25.6, and 3.456. The decimal 4.5 has the digits 4 and 5. The place value of each digit in a whole number or a decimal depends on its position within the number. For example, in the number 491,037.892, the 8 has a value of $8 \times 0.1$, or 0.8, because it is in the tenths' place.

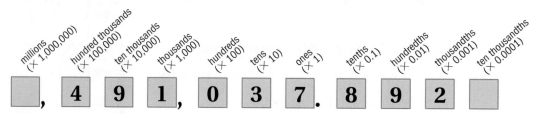

**EXAMPLE 1**

Write the number 35,704.2 in expanded form.

$35,704.2 = 30,000 + 5,000 + 700 + 4 + 0.2$

> The zero in the tens' place is a placeholder.

$= 3 \times 10,000 + 5 \times 1000 + 7 \times 100 + 4 \times 1 + 2 \times 0.1$

**EXAMPLE 2**

Write $2 \times 100 + 3 \times 1 + 5 \times 0.1 + 7 \times 0.01 + 9 \times 0.0001$ in standard form.

$2 \times 100 + 3 \times 1 + 5 \times 0.1 + 7 \times 0.01 + 9 \times 0.0001$

$= 200 + 3 + 0.5 + 0.07 + 0.0009$

$= 203.5709$

## Practice

**Write the number in expanded form.**

**1.** 2,462,027.6     **2.** 79.3672     **3.** 3905.83     **4.** 937.385

**5.** 1,008,635.369     **6.** 2378.186     **7.** 10,893.2     **8.** 0.9027

**Write the number in standard form.**

**9.** $8 \times 1,000,000 + 5 \times 10,000 + 7 \times 1 + 6 \times 0.1 + 4 \times 0.01$

**10.** $4 \times 10,000 + 2 \times 1000 + 3 \times 10 + 8 \times 0.01 + 7 \times 0.0001$

**11.** $2 \times 1,000,000 + 6 \times 100,000 + 5 \times 100 + 3 \times 0.01 + 8 \times 0.001$

**12.** $5 \times 100,000 + 8 \times 10,000 + 9 \times 0.1 + 2 \times 0.01 + 1 \times 0.001$

# Comparing and Ordering Whole Numbers

Gr. 2 NS 1.3, Gr. 3 NS 1.2

A **number line** is a line whose points are associated with numbers. You can use a number line to compare two whole numbers using the symbols at the right. You can also use a number line to order a list of whole numbers from least to greatest.

| Symbol | Meaning | Example |
|--------|---------|---------|
| < | is less than | 4 < 5 |
| ≤ | is less than or equal to | 4 ≤ 5 |
| = | is equal to | 4 = 4 |
| ≥ | is greater than or equal to | 6 ≥ 5 |
| > | is greater than | 6 > 5 |
| ≠ | is not equal to | 6 ≠ 5 |

**EXAMPLE 1** Copy and complete the statement 13 _?_ 4 using <, >, or =.

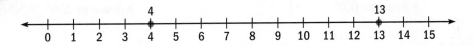

13 is to the right of 4, so 13 is greater than 4.

▸ **Answer** 13 > 4

**EXAMPLE 2** Order the numbers 15, 8, 1, 10, 7, and 3 from least to greatest.

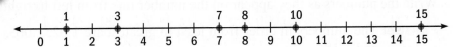

Write the numbers as they appear on the number line from left to right.

▸ **Answer** The numbers in order from least to greatest are 1, 3, 7, 8, 10, and 15.

## Practice

**Copy and complete the statement using <, >, or =.**

**1.** 8 _?_ 12  **2.** 656 _?_ 658  **3.** 1863 _?_ 1027  **4.** 67 _?_ 25

**5.** 75 _?_ 36  **6.** 118 _?_ 231  **7.** 1125 _?_ 1152  **8.** 85 _?_ 48

**9.** 152 _?_ 252  **10.** 2363 _?_ 2633  **11.** 321 _?_ 1230  **12.** 10,462 _?_ 1635

**Order the numbers from the least to greatest.**

**13.** 8, 12, 16, 32, 7, 5, 24

**14.** 9, 3, 11, 8, 0, 1, 13

**15.** 32, 64, 72, 26, 36, 62, 106, 98

**16.** 43, 88, 78, 28, 86, 108

**17.** 1123, 1157, 1104, 1018, 1016

**18.** 529, 267, 8627, 12,843, 1293

**19.** 246, 64, 358, 275, 2032

**20.** 3052, 3205, 605, 2062, 3004

# Comparing and Ordering Decimals

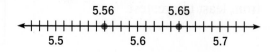Gr. 6 NS 1.1

You can use a number line to compare and order decimals. From left to right, the numbers on a number line appear in order from least to greatest.

**EXAMPLE 1** **Copy and complete the statement using <, >, or =.**

a. 0.06 _?_ 0.11

b. 5.65 _?_ 5.56

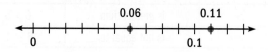 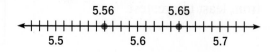

0.06 is to the left of 0.11, so 0.06 is less than 0.11.

5.65 is to the right of 5.56, so 5.65 is greater than 5.56.

▶ **Answer** 0.06 < 0.11

▶ **Answer** 5.65 > 5.56

**EXAMPLE 2** **Order the numbers 1.18, 1.02, 1.12, and 1.065 from least to greatest.**

Graph all the numbers on a number line.

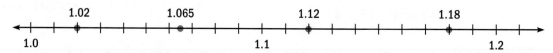

Write the numbers as they appear on the number line from left to right.

▶ **Answer** The numbers in order from least to greatest are 1.02, 1.065, 1.12, and 1.18.

## Practice

**Copy and complete the statement using <, >, or =.**

**1.** 8.31 _?_ 8.04      **2.** 0.98 _?_ 1.09      **3.** 0.664 _?_ 0.67      **4.** 32.391 _?_ 32.39

**5.** 7.201 _?_ 7.201      **6.** 12.21 _?_ 1.221      **7.** 18.4 _?_ 18.04      **8.** 0.007 _?_ 0.02

**9.** 1.25 _?_ 1.3      **10.** 6.821 _?_ 5.821      **11.** 0.356 _?_ 3.56      **12.** 0.0048 _?_ 0.004

**Order the numbers from least to greatest.**

**13.** 0.07, 0.06, 0.1, 0.12

**14.** 28.4, 28, 28.04, 28.24

**15.** 3.35, 3.4, 3.49, 3.53

**16.** 17.9, 18.3, 17.09, 18.1

**17.** 40.1, 40.11, 40.01, 41

**18.** 9.93, 10.09, 9.89, 9.099

**19.** 1.13, 1.02, 1.15, 1.2

**20.** 12.367, 12.382, 21.361, 21.238

**21.** 5.036, 5.006, 5.253, 5.025

**22.** 0.0175, 1.0248, 0.0053, 1.0058

**23.** 123.5, 123.05, 135.6, 123.036

**24.** 32.036, 23.681, 201.365, 3.2036

# Rounding

Gr. 5 NS 1.1

To **round** a number means to approximate the number to a given place value. When rounding, look at the digit to the right of that place value. If the digit to the right is less than 5 (0, 1, 2, 3, or 4), round down. If the digit to the right is 5 or greater (5, 6, 7, 8, or 9), round up.

**EXAMPLE 1**   **Round the number to the place value of the red digit.**

    **a.** 8357                          **b.** 2.5129

**Solution**

  **a.** Because the 5 is in the tens' place, round 8357 to the nearest ten. Since 8357 is between 8350 and 8360, it will round to one of these two numbers.

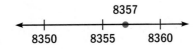

                                               **Notice that 8357 is closer to 8360 than to 8350.**

    The digit to the right of the 5 in the tens' place is the 7 in the ones' place. Because 7 is greater than 5, round up.

    ▸ **Answer** 8357 rounded to the nearest ten is 8360.

  **b.** Because the 1 is in the hundredths' place, round 2.5129 to the nearest hundredth. Notice that 2.5129 is between 2.51 and 2.52, so it will round to one of these two numbers.

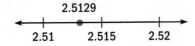

                                               **Notice that 2.5129 is closer to 2.51 than to 2.52.**

    The digit to the right of the 1 in the hundredths' place is the 2 in the thousandths' place. Because 2 is less than 5, round down.

    ▸ **Answer** 2.5129 rounded to the nearest hundredth is 2.51.

## Practice

**Round the number to the place value of the red digit.**

| | | | |
|---|---|---|---|
| **1.** 8755 | **2.** 16,241 | **3.** 4.226 | **4.** 158.36 |
| **5.** 29,003 | **6.** 7.5897 | **7.** 12,766,023 | **8.** 3397.2 |
| **9.** 54,564 | **10.** 9671 | **11.** 65.235 | **12.** 0.32246 |
| **13.** 32.8825 | **14.** 5,820,677 | **15.** 9471.5 | **16.** 7.93448 |
| **17.** 23,001.3 | **18.** 36.0578 | **19.** 1670.3485 | **20.** 32,264.246 |
| **21.** 0.3671258 | **22.** 3,021,364.84 | **23.** 321,655.216 | **24.** 1.0364872 |

# Adding and Subtracting Whole Numbers
**Gr. 4 NS 3.1**

To add and subtract whole numbers, start with the digits in the ones' place. Moving to the left, add or subtract the digits one place value at a time, regrouping as needed. The result of adding numbers is called the **sum**. The result of subtracting numbers is called the **difference**.

**EXAMPLE 1**  Find the sum 577 + 63.

**Step 1**
Add the ones.
Regroup 10 ones as
1 ten and 0 ones.

$$
\begin{array}{r}
\overset{1}{\phantom{0}} \\
577 \\
+\ 63 \\
\hline
0
\end{array}
$$

**Step 2**
Add the tens.
Regroup 14 tens as
1 hundred and 4 tens.

$$
\begin{array}{r}
\overset{1\,1}{\phantom{0}} \\
577 \\
+\ 63 \\
\hline
40
\end{array}
$$

**Step 3**
Add the hundreds.

$$
\begin{array}{r}
\overset{1\,1}{\phantom{0}} \\
577 \\
+\ 63 \\
\hline
640
\end{array}
$$

**EXAMPLE 2**  Find the difference 206 − 178.

**Step 1**
Start with the ones.
There are not
enough ones in 206
to subtract 8.

$$
\begin{array}{r}
206 \\
-\ 178 \\
\hline
\end{array}
$$

**Step 2**
Move to the tens.
There are no tens in 206,
so regroup 1 hundred as
9 tens and 10 ones.

$$
\begin{array}{r}
\overset{9}{1\ \cancel{10}\ 16} \\
\cancel{206} \\
-\ 178 \\
\hline
\end{array}
$$

**Step 3**
Subtract.

$$
\begin{array}{r}
\overset{9}{1\ \cancel{10}\ 16} \\
\cancel{206} \\
-\ 178 \\
\hline
28
\end{array}
$$

▶ **Check** Because addition and subtraction are inverse operations, you can check your answer by adding: 28 + 178 = 206.

## Practice

**Find the sum or difference.**

| | | | |
|---|---|---|---|
| **1.** 83 + 57 | **2.** 69 + 75 | **3.** 132 + 77 | **4.** 236 + 449 |
| **5.** 62 − 43 | **6.** 88 − 29 | **7.** 625 − 38 | **8.** 554 − 137 |
| **9.** 3478 + 37 | **10.** 1621 − 96 | **11.** 2406 − 187 | **12.** 7880 + 982 |
| **13.** 28,004 − 205 | **14.** 90,425 − 7116 | **15.** 75,944 + 5472 | **16.** 68,909 + 7681 |
| **17.** 653 + 15,482 | **18.** 8631 + 862 | **19.** 365 − 218 | **20.** 35,367 + 12,357 |
| **21.** 6321 − 6024 | **22.** 364,582 + 268 | **23.** 2658 − 378 | **24.** 23,548 − 21,035 |
| **25.** 2635 + 58,741 | **26.** 6812 − 5738 | **27.** 48,962 + 43,385 | **28.** 75,863 − 52,486 |

# Multiplying Whole Numbers

 Gr. 4 NS 3.2

When you multiply two numbers, the result you get is called the **product**. When numbers are multiplied together, each number is a **factor** of the product. You can indicate multiplication using a times sign (×), a multiplication dot (•), or parentheses: $3 \times 2 = 3 \cdot 2 = 3(2)$.

**EXAMPLE 1**  **Find the product 374 × 205.**

**Step 1**
Multiply 374 by the ones' digit in 205.

**Step 2**
Skip the 0 in the tens' place, and multiply by the hundreds' digit. Start the partial product in the hundreds' place.

**Step 3**
Add the partial products.

$$\begin{array}{r} {}^{3\,2} \\ 374 \\ \times\ 205 \\ \hline 1870 \end{array}$$

$$\begin{array}{r} {}^{1} \\ 374 \\ \times\ 205 \\ \hline 1870 \\ 748 \end{array}$$

$$\begin{array}{r} 374 \\ \times\ 205 \\ \hline 1870 \\ 748 \\ \hline 76{,}670 \end{array}$$

To multiply a whole number by a power of 10, such as 10, 100, or 1000, write the number followed by the number of zeros in the power. Because multiplying by such powers of 10 shifts each digit of the number to a higher place value, the zeros are needed as placeholders.

**EXAMPLE 2**  **Find the product.**

   **a.** 672 • 100

   **b.** 8450(1000)

**Solution**

   **a.** 100 is a power of 10 with 2 zeros, so write 2 zeros after 672.

   $672 \cdot 100 = 67{,}200$

   **b.** 1000 is a power of 10 with 3 zeros, so write 3 zeros after 8450.

   $8450(1000) = 8{,}450{,}000$

## Practice

**Find the product.**

1. $83 \times 64$
2. $491(227)$
3. $1420 \cdot 602$
4. $7245 \times 3050$
5. $491(100)$
6. $52 \times 10{,}000$
7. $59{,}000 \times 100$
8. $9300 \cdot 1000$
9. $268 \cdot 534$
10. $1268(257)$
11. $8653 \cdot 10{,}000$
12. $73{,}254 \times 15$
13. $723 \times 2783$
14. $2187 \cdot 7862$
15. $1260(100)$
16. $38{,}538 \times 329$
17. $74(12{,}539)$
18. $26{,}762 \cdot 1000$
19. $65 \times 7531$
20. $425(6754)$

# Dividing Whole Numbers

In a division problem, the number being divided is called the **dividend** and the number it is being divided by is called the **divisor**. The result of the division is called the **quotient**. If the divisor does not divide the dividend evenly, then there is a **remainder**.

**EXAMPLE 1** **Find the quotient 192 ÷ 8.**

**Step 1**
Because 8 is between 1 and 19, place the first digit above the 9. Because $8 \times 2 = 16$, estimate that 8 divides 19 about 2 times.

$$\text{divisor} \rightarrow 8\overline{)192} \leftarrow \text{dividend}$$
(with 2 above)

**Step 2**
Multiply 2 and 8. Then subtract 16 from 19. Be sure the difference is less than the divisor: $3 < 8$.

$$\begin{array}{r} 2 \\ 8\overline{)192} \\ \underline{16} \\ 3 \end{array}$$

**Step 3**
Bring down the next digit, 2. Divide 32 by 8 to get 4. Multiply 4 and 8. Subtract 32 from 32. There are no more digits to bring down.

$$\begin{array}{r} 24 \leftarrow \textbf{Quotient} \\ 8\overline{)192} \quad \textbf{is 24.} \\ \underline{16} \\ 32 \\ \underline{32} \\ 0 \end{array}$$

**EXAMPLE 2** **Find the quotient 5731 ÷ 95.**

**Step 1**
Because 95 is between 57 and 573, place the first digit above the 3. Because $90 \times 6 = 540$, estimate that 95 divides 573 about 6 times.

$$\begin{array}{r} 6 \\ 95\overline{)5731} \end{array}$$

**Step 2**
Multiply 6 and 95. Then subtract 570 from 573. Be sure the difference is less than the divisor: $3 < 95$.

$$\begin{array}{r} 6 \\ 95\overline{)5731} \\ \underline{570} \\ 3 \end{array}$$

**Step 3**
Bring down the last digit, 1. Because $31 < 95$, write a 0 in the quotient. Then write the remainder next to the quotient.

$$\begin{array}{r} 60 \text{ R31} \\ 95\overline{)5731} \\ \underline{570} \\ 31 \leftarrow \textbf{Remainder} \\ \textbf{is 31.} \end{array}$$

## Practice

**Find the quotient.**

1. $512 \div 8$
2. $848 \div 6$
3. $529 \div 17$
4. $966 \div 21$
5. $6640 \div 53$
6. $2016 \div 224$
7. $3426 \div 571$
8. $23,824 \div 425$
9. $468 \div 12$
10. $25,050 \div 25$
11. $6348 \div 122$
12. $9527 \div 500$
13. $6354 \div 3142$
14. $3160 \div 632$
15. $15,782 \div 5261$
16. $4518 \div 753$

# Ratios

A **fraction** is a number of the form $\frac{a}{b}$ where $a$ is a whole number called the **numerator** and $b$ is a nonzero whole number called the **denominator**. A fraction is one way of writing a *ratio*. A **ratio** uses division to compare two numbers. You can write the ratio of $a$ to $b$ as $\frac{a}{b}$, as $a : b$, or as "$a$ to $b$."

**EXAMPLE 1**  **There are 15 adults and 62 students on a field trip. Write the ratio of adults to students in three ways.**

$$\frac{\text{Number of adults}}{\text{Number of students}} = \frac{15}{62} = 15 : 62 = 15 \text{ to } 62$$

You can write a ratio as a decimal by carrying out the division. Two ratios are **equivalent ratios** when they have the same decimal form.

**EXAMPLE 2**  **In baseball, batting average is the ratio of a player's hits to times at bat. So far this season, Bill has had 32 hits in 128 times at bat. Don has had 24 hits in 96 times at bat. Do Bill and Don have the same batting average?** *Explain*.

Write the ratio of hits to times at bat as a decimal for each player.

**Bill:** $\dfrac{\text{Hits}}{\text{Times at bat}} = \dfrac{32}{128} = 0.25$        **Don:** $\dfrac{\text{Hits}}{\text{Times at bat}} = \dfrac{24}{96} = 0.25$

▶ **Answer**  Bill and Don have the same batting average because the ratio of hits to times at bat for both players is equal to 0.25.

## Practice

**There are 124 male campers, 165 female campers, and 43 staff members at a summer camp. Write the specified ratio.**

**1.** Staff members to female campers

**2.** Male campers to female campers

**3.** Male campers to all campers

**4.** Staff members to all campers

**5.** Staff members to male campers

**6.** Female campers to all campers

**Tell whether the ratios are equivalent.**

**7.** 16 to 40 and 46 to 115

**8.** $6 : 48$ and $3 : 25$

**9.** $\dfrac{27}{75}$ and $\dfrac{6}{20}$

**10.** $\dfrac{65}{104}$ and $\dfrac{45}{72}$

**11.** $42 : 125$ and $20 : 103$

**12.** 24 to 624 and 56 to 656

**13.** Evan has had 36 hits in 120 times at bat. Jack has had 28 hits in 112 times at bat. Do Evan and Jack have the same batting average? *Explain*.

# Factors and Multiples

Gr. 4 NS 4.2, Gr. 5 NS 1.4, Gr. 6 NS 2.4

A **prime number** is a whole number that is greater than 1 and has exactly two whole number factors, 1 and itself. A **composite number** is a whole number that is greater than 1 and has more than two whole number factors. The table below shows that the first five prime numbers are 2, 3, 5, 7, and 11.

| Number | Product(s) | Factor(s) | Prime or composite? |
|--------|------------|-----------|---------------------|
| 1 | 1 • 1 | 1 | Neither |
| 2 | 1 • 2 | 1, 2 | Prime |
| 3 | 1 • 3 | 1, 3 | Prime |
| 4 | 1 • 4, 2 • 2 | 1, 2, 4 | Composite |
| 5 | 1 • 5 | 1, 5 | Prime |
| 6 | 1 • 6, 2 • 3 | 1, 2, 3, 6 | Composite |
| 7 | 1 • 7 | 1, 7 | Prime |
| 8 | 1 • 8, 2 • 4 | 1, 2, 4, 8 | Composite |
| 9 | 1 • 9, 3 • 3 | 1, 3, 9 | Composite |
| 10 | 1 • 10, 2 • 5 | 1, 2, 5, 10 | Composite |
| 11 | 1 • 11 | 1, 11 | Prime |
| 12 | 1 • 12, 2 • 6, 3 • 4 | 1, 2, 3, 4, 6, 12 | Composite |

When you write a composite number as a product of prime numbers, you are writing its **prime factorization**. You can use a **factor tree** to write the prime factorization of a number.

**EXAMPLE 1** **Write the prime factorization of 150.**

Write 150 at the top of the factor tree. Draw two branches and write 150 as the product of two factors. Continue to draw branches until all factors are prime numbers (shown in red). Here are two possible factor trees for 150.

Start with 150 = 3 • 50.

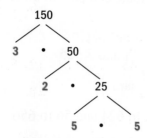

Start with 150 = 10 • 15.

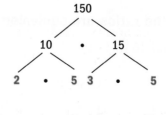

Both factor trees show that $150 = 2 \cdot 3 \cdot 5 \cdot 5$ or $150 = 2 \cdot 3 \cdot 5^2$.

▶ **Answer** The prime factorization of 150 is $2 \cdot 3 \cdot 5^2$.

For two or more nonzero whole numbers, a **common factor** is a whole number that is a factor of each number. The **greatest common factor (GCF)**, or *greatest common divisor*, of two or more nonzero whole numbers is the greatest of their common factors.

**EXAMPLE 2** **Find the greatest common factor of 45 and 60.**

Write the prime factorization of each number. The GCF is the product of the common prime factors.

$$45 = \mathbf{3} \cdot \mathbf{3} \cdot \mathbf{5} \qquad \text{and} \qquad 60 = 2 \cdot 2 \cdot \mathbf{3} \cdot \mathbf{5}$$

The common prime factors are 3 and 5. The GCF is the product $3 \cdot 5 = 15$.

▶ **Answer** The greatest common factor of 45 and 60 is 15.

A **multiple** of a nonzero whole number is the product of the number and any nonzero whole number. A **common multiple** of two or more nonzero whole numbers is a multiple of each number. The **least common multiple (LCM)** of two or more nonzero whole numbers is the least of their common multiples.

**EXAMPLE 3** **Find the least common multiple of 40 and 90.**

Write the prime factorization of each number using exponents. Circle the greatest power of each prime factor that appears in either factorization. The LCM is the product of these powers.

$$40 = \boxed{2^3} \cdot 5 \qquad \text{and} \qquad 90 = 2 \cdot \boxed{3^2} \cdot \boxed{5}$$

The LCM is the product $2^3 \cdot 3^2 \cdot 5 = 360$.

▶ **Answer** The least common multiple of 40 and 90 is 360.

## Practice

**Write the prime factorization of the number if it is not a prime number. If the number is prime, write *prime*.**

| | | | |
|---|---|---|---|
| **1.** 40 | **2.** 18 | **3.** 13 | **4.** 70 |
| **5.** 99 | **6.** 41 | **7.** 80 | **8.** 120 |

**Find the greatest common factor of the pair of numbers.**

| | | | |
|---|---|---|---|
| **9.** 12, 30 | **10.** 7, 15 | **11.** 75, 45 | **12.** 6, 42 |
| **13.** 48, 72 | **14.** 30, 84 | **15.** 51, 17 | **16.** 18, 63 |

**Find the least common multiple of the pair of numbers.**

| | | | |
|---|---|---|---|
| **17.** 12, 18 | **18.** 5, 14 | **19.** 8, 32 | **20.** 24, 30 |
| **21.** 38, 42 | **22.** 6, 8 | **23.** 28, 36 | **24.** 11, 121 |

# Converting Units of Measurement

The Table of Measures on page 512 gives many statements of equivalent measures. You can write two different conversion factors for each statement, as shown below. Each conversion factor is equal to 1.

| Statement of Equivalent Measures | Conversion Factors |
|---|---|
| 100 cm = 1 m | $\dfrac{100 \text{ cm}}{1 \text{ m}} = 1 \qquad \dfrac{1 \text{ m}}{100 \text{ cm}} = 1$ |

To convert from one unit of measurement to another, multiply by a conversion factor that will eliminate the starting unit and result in the desired unit.

**Convert meters to centimeters:**

$$3 \text{ m} \times \frac{100 \text{ cm}}{1 \text{ m}} = 300 \text{ cm}$$

**Convert centimeters to meters:**

$$400 \text{ cm} \times \frac{1 \text{ m}}{100 \text{ cm}} = 4 \text{ m}$$

Sometimes you will need to use more than one conversion factor.

**EXAMPLE 1**  **Copy and complete: 345,600 sec = _?_ days**

**Step 1** Find the appropriate statements of equivalent measures.

1 min = 60 sec, 1 h = 60 min, and 1 day = 24 h

**Step 2** Write conversion factors.

$$\frac{1 \text{ min}}{60 \text{ sec}}, \frac{1 \text{ h}}{60 \text{ min}}, \text{ and } \frac{1 \text{ day}}{24 \text{ h}}$$

**Step 3** Multiply by the conversion factors to convert seconds to days.

$$345{,}600 \text{ sec} \times \frac{1 \text{ min}}{60 \text{ sec}} \times \frac{1 \text{ h}}{60 \text{ min}} \times \frac{1 \text{ day}}{24 \text{ h}} = 4 \text{ days}$$

▶ **Answer** 345,600 sec = 4 days

## Practice

**Copy and complete.**

**1.** 1 day = _?_ sec

**2.** 15,840 ft = _?_ mi

**3.** 3 gal = _?_ c

**4.** 2 km = _?_ cm

**5.** 65,000 mL = _?_ L

**6.** 16 lb = _?_ oz

**7.** 8 yd = _?_ in.

**8.** 3600 sec = _?_ h

**9.** 2000 mg = _?_ g

**10.** 3 wk = _?_ h

**11.** 64 fl oz = _?_ qt

**12.** 10 qt = _?_ c

**13.** 1 kg = _?_ mg

**14.** 5 L = _?_ mL

**15.** 192 in. = _?_ ft

**16.** 11 days = _?_ h

**17.** 5 tons = _?_ lb

**18.** 25 m = _?_ mm

**19.** 24 qt = _?_ gal

**20.** 4 L = _?_ mL

**21.** 120 years = _?_ decades

**22.** 3 kg = _?_ g

**23.** 12 pt = _?_ c

**24.** 2 mi = _?_ yd

# Converting Between Metric and Customary Units

Gr. 6 AF 2.1

To convert between metric and customary units, use the approximate relationships shown below. The symbol ≈ means *is approximately equal to*.

| Length | Capacity | Weight |
|---|---|---|
| 1 mm ≈ 0.0394 in. | 1 mL ≈ 0.0338 fl oz | 1 g ≈ 0.0353 oz |
| 1 m ≈ 3.28 ft | 1 L ≈ 1.06 qt | 1 kg ≈ 2.2 lb |
| 1 km ≈ 0.621 mi | 1 kL ≈ 264 gal | |

**EXAMPLE 1**   **Copy and complete the statement. Round to the nearest whole number.**

    **a.** 131 km ≈ _?_ mi      **b.** 124 lb ≈ _?_ kg      **c.** 75 mL ≈ _?_ fl oz

**Solution**

    **a.** $131 \text{ km} \approx 131 \text{ km} \times \dfrac{0.621 \text{ mi}}{1 \text{ km}} = 81.351 \text{ mi} \approx 81 \text{ mi}$

    **b.** $124 \text{ lb} \approx 124 \text{ lb} \times \dfrac{1 \text{ kg}}{2.2 \text{ lb}} \approx 56.36 \text{ kg} \approx 56 \text{ kg}$

    **c.** $75 \text{ mL} \approx 75 \text{ mL} \times \dfrac{0.0338 \text{ fl oz}}{1 \text{ mL}} = 2.535 \text{ fl oz} \approx 3 \text{ fl oz}$

**EXAMPLE 2**   **Copy and complete using < or >: 225 m _?_ 685 ft**

| | |
|---|---|
| 225 m _?_ 685 ft | **Write the problem.** |
| 738 ft _?_ 685 ft | **Convert meters to feet:** $225 \text{ m} \approx 225 \text{ m} \times \dfrac{3.28 \text{ ft}}{1 \text{ m}} = 738 \text{ ft}$ |
| 738 ft > 685 ft | **Compare.** |

▶ **Answer**   225 m > 685 ft

## Practice

**Copy and complete the statement. Round to the nearest whole number.**

**1.** 6 kL ≈ _?_ gal      **2.** 5 in. ≈ _?_ mm      **3.** 22 g ≈ _?_ oz

**4.** 3 in. ≈ _?_ cm      **5.** 12 qt ≈ _?_ L      **6.** 36 kg ≈ _?_ lb

**7.** 60 fl oz ≈ _?_ mL      **8.** 15 L ≈ _?_ gal      **9.** 4 km ≈ _?_ mi

**Copy and complete the statement using < or >.**

**10.** 7 qt _?_ 6 L      **11.** 5 km _?_ 3.5 mi      **12.** 110 lb _?_ 55 kg

**13.** 5 in. _?_ 120 mm      **14.** 90 g _?_ 3 oz      **15.** 18 ft _?_ 6 m

**16.** 1.5 kL _?_ 400 gal      **17.** 50 mm _?_ 2 in.      **18.** 4 kg _?_ 8 lb

# Perimeter and Area

The **perimeter** $P$ of a figure is the distance around it. The **area** $A$ of a figure is the number of square units enclosed by the figure.

| Figure | **Triangle**: a three-sided figure | **Rectangle**: a four-sided figure with four right angles and opposite sides equal in length | **Square**: a rectangle with all sides equal in length |
|---|---|---|---|
| Drawing | $a$ $c$ $b$ | $w$ $\ell$ | $s$ |
| Perimeter | $P = a + b + c$ | $P = \ell + w + \ell + w$ $= 2\ell + 2w$ | $P = s + s + s + s$ $= 4s$ |
| Area | See below. | $A = \ell w$ | $A = s^2$ |

| Figure | **Triangle**: a three-sided figure | **Parallelogram**: a four-sided figure with both pairs of opposite sides parallel | **Trapezoid**: a four-sided figure with exactly one pair of opposite sides parallel |
|---|---|---|---|
| Drawing | $h$ $b$ | $h$ $b$ | $b_1$ $h$ $b_2$ |
| Area | $A = \frac{1}{2}bh$ | $A = bh$ | $A = \frac{1}{2}(b_1 + b_2)h$ |

**EXAMPLE 1** **Find the perimeter of the figure.**

**a.** Square

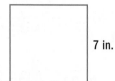

7 in.

**b.** Rectangle

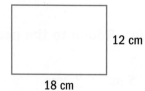

12 cm

18 cm

**c.** Triangle

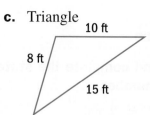

10 ft

8 ft

15 ft

**Solution**

**a.** $P = 4s$

$\quad = 4(7)$

$\quad = 28$ in.

**b.** $P = 2\ell + 2w$

$\quad = 2(18) + 2(12)$

$\quad = 60$ cm

**c.** $P = a + b + c$

$\quad = 8 + 10 + 15$

$\quad = 33$ ft

**EXAMPLE 2** **Find the area of the figure.**

**a.** Rectangle

8 m

6 m

$A = \ell w$
$\quad = 8(6)$
$\quad = 48 \text{ m}^2$

**b.** Triangle

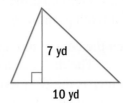

7 yd

10 yd

$A = \frac{1}{2}bh$
$\quad = \frac{1}{2}(10)(7)$
$\quad = 35 \text{ yd}^2$

**c.** Parallelogram

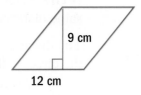

9 cm

12 cm

$A = bh$
$\quad = 12(9)$
$\quad = 108 \text{ cm}^2$

## Practice

**Find the perimeter of the figure.**

**1.** Square

5 cm

**2.** Rectangle

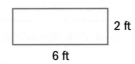

2 ft

6 ft

**3.** Triangle

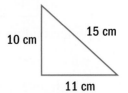

10 cm    15 cm

11 cm

**Find the area of the figure.**

**4.** Square

16 in.

**5.** Rectangle

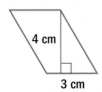

12 yd

8 yd

**6.** Triangle

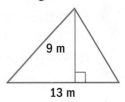

9 m

13 m

**7.** Parallelogram

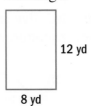

4 cm

3 cm

**8.** Trapezoid

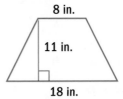

8 in.

11 in.

18 in.

**9.** Parallelogram

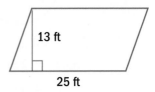

13 ft

25 ft

**10.** Rectangle

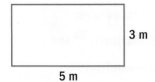

3 m

5 m

**11.** Triangle

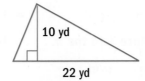

10 yd

22 yd

**12.** Trapezoid

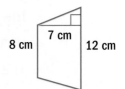

8 cm    7 cm    12 cm

# Circumference and Area of a Circle

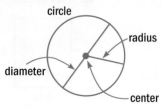 Gr. 7 MG 2.1

A **circle** consists of all points in a plane that are the same distance from a fixed point called the **center**.

The distance between the center and any point on the circle is the **radius**. The distance across the circle through the center is the **diameter**. The diameter of a circle is twice its radius.

The **circumference** of a circle is the distance around the circle. For any circle, the ratio of its circumference to its diameter is $\pi$ (pi), a number that is approximately equal to 3.14 or $\frac{22}{7}$.

| Circumference of a Circle |
|---|
| To find the circumference of a circle with radius $r$, use the formula $C = 2\pi r$. <br><br> To find the circumference of a circle with diameter $d$, use the formula $C = \pi d$. 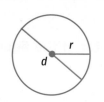 |

When finding the circumference of a circle, you can leave $\pi$ in the answer, which gives an exact result. You can also substitute either 3.14 or $\frac{22}{7}$ for $\pi$, which gives an approximate result. As a general rule, use $\frac{22}{7}$ for $\pi$ when the given value of $r$ or $d$ is a multiple of 7. Otherwise use 3.14 for $\pi$.

**EXAMPLE 1**   Find the circumference of the circle. Give an exact answer in terms of $\pi$ as well as an approximation rounded to the nearest tenth if necessary.

a.

5 cm

b.

14 in.

**Solution**

a. $C = 2\pi r$    **Write formula.**

     $= 2\pi(5)$    **Substitute 5 for *r*.**

     $= 10\pi$    **Simplify.**

     $= 10\pi$ cm    **Exact answer**

     $\approx 10(3.14)$    **Substitute 3.14 for $\pi$.**

     $= 31.4$ cm    **Approximation**

b. $C = \pi d$    **Write formula.**

     $= \pi(14)$    **Substitute 14 for *d*.**

     $= 14\pi$    **Simplify.**

     $= 14\pi$ in.    **Exact answer**

     $\approx 14\left(\frac{22}{7}\right)$    **Substitute $\frac{22}{7}$ for $\pi$.**

     $= 44$ in.    **Approximation**

| Area of a Circle |
|---|

To find the area of a circle with radius $r$,
use the formula $A = \pi r^2$.

To find the area of a circle with diameter $d$,
first find the radius $r = \dfrac{d}{2}$ and then use
the formula $A = \pi r^2$.

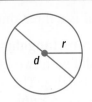

**EXAMPLE 2** Find the area of the circle. Give an exact answer in terms of $\pi$ as well as an approximation rounded to the nearest tenth if necessary.

a.

7 ft

b.

4 m

**Solution**

a. $A = \pi r^2$    **Write formula.**

$\quad = \pi(7)^2$    **Substitute 7 for $r$.**

$\quad = 49\pi$    **Simplify.**

$\quad = 49\pi \text{ ft}^2$    **Exact answer**

$\quad \approx 49\left(\dfrac{22}{7}\right)$    **Substitute $\dfrac{22}{7}$ for $\pi$.**

$\quad = 154 \text{ ft}^2$    **Approximation**

b. The radius is $r = \dfrac{d}{2} = \dfrac{4}{2} = 2$ m.

$\quad A = \pi r^2$    **Write formula.**

$\quad = \pi(2)^2$    **Substitute 2 for $r$.**

$\quad = 4\pi$    **Simplify.**

$\quad = 4\pi \text{ m}^2$    **Exact answer**

$\quad \approx 4(3.14)$    **Substitute 3.14 for $\pi$.**

$\quad = 12.6 \text{ m}^2$    **Approximation**

## Practice

Find the circumference and area of the circle. Give exact answers in terms of $\pi$ as well as approximations rounded to the nearest tenth if necessary.

1.

10 in.

2.

3 ft

3.

7 m

4.

28 cm

5.

21 ft

6.

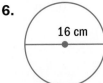

16 cm

# Surface Area and Volume

A **solid** is a three-dimensional figure that encloses part of space.

A **right rectangular prism**, or *rectangular prism*, is a solid with two identical parallel bases that are rectangles. The remaining surfaces are also rectangles. A **cube** is a rectangular prism for which all of the edges have the same length.

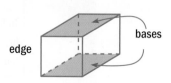

A **right circular cylinder**, or *cylinder*, is a solid with two identical parallel circular bases. The remaining surface of the cylinder consists of parallel circles of the same radius as the bases whose centers lie on the segment that joins the centers of the bases and is perpendicular to the bases.

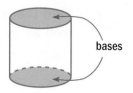

The **surface area** $S$ of a solid is the sum of the areas of all its surfaces. The **volume** $V$ of a solid is the amount of space that the solid occupies. In the formulas below, $B$ is the area of the base, $P$ is the perimeter of a rectangular prism's base, $C$ is the circumference of a cylinder's base, and $h$ is the height of the solid.

| Right Rectangular Prism | Cube | Right Circular Cylinder |
|---|---|---|
| $S = 2B + Ph$<br>$= 2\ell w + 2hw + 2\ell h$ | $S = 2B + Ph$<br>$= 6s^2$ | $S = 2B + Ch$<br>$= 2\pi r^2 + 2\pi rh$ |
| $V = Bh$<br>$= \ell wh$ | $V = Bh$<br>$= s^3$ | $V = Bh$<br>$= \pi r^2 h$ |

**EXAMPLE 1**

**Find the surface area of the solid.**

**a.** Rectangular prism

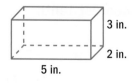

$S = 2\ell w + 2hw + 2\ell h$

$= 2(5)(2) + 2(3)(2) + 2(5)(3)$

$= 62 \text{ in.}^2$

**b.** Cube

$S = 6s^2$

$= 6(8)^2$

$= 384 \text{ m}^2$

**c.** Cylinder

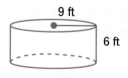

$S = 2\pi r^2 + 2\pi rh$

$= 2\pi(9)^2 + 2\pi(9)(6)$

$= 162\pi + 108\pi$

$= 270\pi \text{ ft}^2$

$\approx 270(3.14)$

$= 847.8 \text{ ft}^2$

**EXAMPLE 2** Find the volume of the solid.

**a.** Rectangular prism

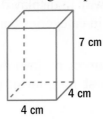

7 cm

4 cm

4 cm

$V = \ell wh$

$\quad = 4(4)(7)$

$\quad = 112 \text{ cm}^3$

**b.** Cube

10 ft

$V = s^3$

$\quad = (10)^3$

$\quad = 1000 \text{ ft}^3$

**c.** Cylinder

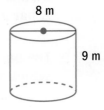

8 m

9 m

$r = \dfrac{d}{2} = \dfrac{8}{2} = 4 \text{ m}$

$V = \pi r^2 h$

$\quad = \pi(4)^2(9)$

$\quad = 144\pi \text{ m}^3$

$\quad \approx 144(3.14)$

$\quad = 452.2 \text{ m}^3$

## Practice

Find the surface area and volume of the solid. For cylinders, give exact answers in terms of $\pi$ as well as rounded to the nearest tenth if necessary.

**1.** Cube

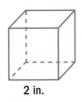

2 in.

**2.** Rectangular prism

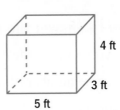

4 ft

3 ft

5 ft

**3.** Cylinder

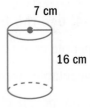

7 cm

16 cm

**4.** Rectangular prism

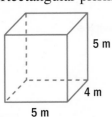

5 m

4 m

5 m

**5.** Cylinder

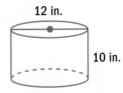

12 in.

10 in.

**6.** Cube

14 ft

**7.** Rectangular prism

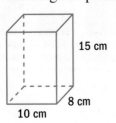

15 cm

8 cm

10 cm

**8.** Cube

9 m

**9.** Cylinder

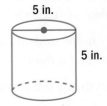

5 in.

5 in.

# Reading Bar Graphs

*Data* are numbers or facts. A *bar graph* is one way to display data.
A **bar graph** uses bars to show how quantities in categories compare.

**EXAMPLE 1** The bar graph below shows the results of a survey on favorite vegetables. Which vegetable was chosen by the greatest number of people?

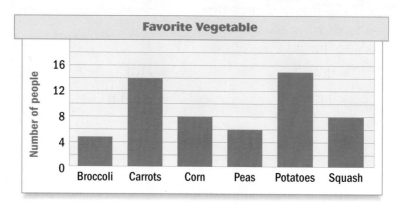

**Solution**

The longest bar on the graph represents the 15 people who chose potatoes. So, potatoes were chosen by the greatest number of people.

## Practice

In Exercises 1–4, use the bar graph above to answer the question.

1. How many people chose carrots as their favorite vegetable?

2. Which two vegetables were chosen by the same number of people?

3. How many more people chose potatoes than chose corn?

4. Which vegetables were chosen by fewer than 7 people?

In Exercises 5–8, use the bar graph, which shows the results of a survey on how students are most likely to spend their time after school.

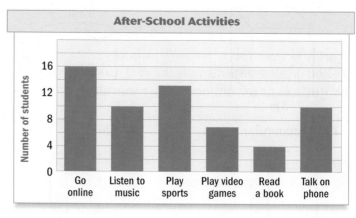

5. Which activity was chosen by the least number of students?

6. Which two activities were chosen by the same number of students?

7. How many more students chose *listen to music* than *read a book*?

8. Which activities were chosen by more than 10 students?

# Reading Circle Graphs

A **circle graph** displays data as sections of a circle. The entire circle represents all of the data. The sections of the graph may be labeled using the actual data or the data expressed as fractions, decimals, or percents. When expressed as fractions, decimals, or percents, the data have a sum of 1.

**EXAMPLE 1** The circle graph shows the results of a survey that asked 100 people the type of book they most recently read. How many more people read a suspense book than read a nonfiction book?

**Type of Books Last Read**

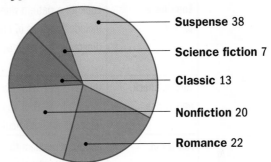

Suspense 38

Science fiction 7

Classic 13

Nonfiction 20

Romance 22

### Solution

The graph shows that 38 people read a suspense book and 20 people read a nonfiction book. Because $38 - 20 = 18$, there are 18 more people who read a suspense book than read a nonfiction book.

## Practice

**In Exercises 1–5, use the circle graph above to answer the question.**

1. Which type of book was read by the greatest number of people?

2. How many people read a romance book?

3. How many more people read a nonfiction book than read a classic book?

4. How many people read either a science fiction book or a classic book?

5. For how many people was their last book *not* a suspense book?

**In Exercises 6–8, use the circle graph, which shows the results of a survey that asked 100 students how long it takes them to get ready for school in the morning.**

**Time to Get Ready for School**

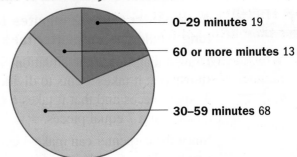

0–29 minutes 19

60 or more minutes 13

30–59 minutes 68

6. How many students take less than 30 minutes to get ready for school?

7. How many students take less than 1 hour to get ready for school?

8. How many students take 30 or more minutes to get ready for school?

# Problem Solving Strategies

 Gr. 6 MR 1.0, Gr. 6 MR 2.0

The following are strategies that you can use to solve problems.

| Strategy | When to use | How to use |
|---|---|---|
| **Draw a diagram** | Draw a diagram when a problem involves any relationships that you can represent visually. | Draw a diagram that shows the given information. Label any unknowns in your diagram and look for relationships between givens and unknowns. |
| **Look for a pattern** | Look for a pattern when a problem includes a series of numbers or diagrams that you need to analyze. | Look for a pattern in any given information. Apply, extend, or generalize the pattern to help you solve the problem. |
| **Guess, check, and revise** | Guess, check, and revise when you need a place to start or you want to see what happens for a particular number. | Make a reasonable guess. Check to see if your guess solves the problem. If it does not, revise your guess and check again. |
| **Act it out** | Act out a problem that involves any relationships that you can represent with physical objects and movement. | Act out the problem, using objects described in the problem or other items that represent those objects. |
| **Make a list or table** | Make a list or table when you need to record, generate, or organize information. | Generate a list systematically, accounting for all possibilities. Look for relationships across rows or down columns within a table. |
| **Solve a simpler or related problem** | Solve a simpler or related problem when a problem seems difficult and can be made easier by using simpler numbers or conditions. | Think of a way to make the problem easier. Solve the simpler or related problem. Use what you learned to help you solve the original problem. |
| **Work backward** | Work backward when a problem gives you an end result and you need to find beginning conditions. | Work backward from the given information until you solve the problem. Work forward through the problem to check your answer. |
| **Break into parts** | Break into parts when a problem cannot be solved all at once, but can be solved in parts or stages. | Break the problem into parts and solve each part. Put the answers together to help you solve the original problem. |

**EXAMPLE 1**

**A carpenter takes 2 minutes to cut a beam into 4 equal pieces. How long would the carpenter take to cut a beam into 7 equal pieces?**

Draw a diagram of the situation. The diagram shows that it takes 3 cuts to divide a beam into 4 equal pieces and that it takes 6 cuts to divide a beam into 7 equal pieces.

4 equal pieces

7 equal pieces

Since the carpenter can make 3 cuts in 2 minutes, you would expect the carpenter to make 6 cuts in 4 minutes.

▶ **Answer** The carpenter would take 4 minutes to cut a beam into 7 equal pieces.

## Practice

1. Max is ordering balloons for a party. He specifies that there are to be 2 mylar balloons for every 5 latex balloons. If Max orders a total of 35 balloons, how many are latex?

2. The lengths of three dowels are 3 inches, 4 inches, and 15 inches. How can the dowels be used to measure a length of 14 inches?

3. An arcade game involves rolling a ball up a ramp and into one of three holes. Each hole has the point value shown. If three balls are rolled, how many different point totals are possible?

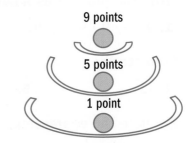

9 points

5 points

1 point

4. In a robotics competition, the first robot to push the other robot out of the ring is the winner of the match. In the first round of the competition, each robot must compete against every other robot. If there are 8 robots entered in the competition, how many matches are there in the first round?

5. Bob gives half of his money to Lisa. Lisa gives Carl double the amount he has. Bob then gives Carl $2. Bob, Lisa, and Carl now each have $8. With how much money did they each start?

6. Nina is setting up a display of hockey pucks at a sporting goods store. She wants 1 puck in the first stack, 2 pucks in the second stack, 3 pucks in the third stack, and so on, as shown. Each puck is 1 inch thick, and the display will be $1\frac{1}{4}$ feet tall. How many hockey pucks will be in the display?

7. Five students line up for a fire drill. Deb is last in line, Brad is between Suni and Kate, and Aaron is next to Suni and Deb. Which student is first in line?

8. In how many different ways can you make $.75 in change using only quarters, dimes, and nickels?

9. Four friends go camping. The table shows the amount of money each friend spends. The friends want to share the expenses equally, and Jen will pay the entire amount she owes to one person. To whom does Jen owe money, and how much?

| Person | Camping expenses |
|--------|------------------|
| Marci  | $29 for gas      |
| Sara   | $43 for food     |
| Grace  | $29 for camping site |
| Jen    | $15 for souvenirs |

10. Dan is 14 years old. In 4 years, Dan will be 3 times the age of his brother. How old is Dan's brother?

11. Seamus is fencing a rectangular area for his dog. He has 14 fence posts that must be placed every 2 feet along the perimeter of the rectangular area. One fence post must be placed at each corner. What is the perimeter of the fenced area?

# Extra Practice

## Chapter 1

**1.1**  **Write the product as a power.**

**1.** $9 \cdot 9 \cdot 9 \cdot 9 \cdot 9 \cdot 9$     **2.** $20 \cdot 20 \cdot 20 \cdot 20$     **3.** $12 \cdot 12 \cdot 12 \cdot 12 \cdot 12$

**Evaluate the power.**

**4.** $12^2$     **5.** $3^4$     **6.** $2^6$     **7.** $10^2$

**1.2**  **Evaluate the expression.**

**8.** $5 + 7 \cdot 2$     **9.** $12 \times 5 - 2$     **10.** $18 \div 3 + 3$     **11.** $10 - 7 + 3$

**12.** $30 - 4^2$     **13.** $82 \div (37 + 4)$     **14.** $\dfrac{15 + 6}{10 - 7}$     **15.** $6 \times (8 + 4) \div 2$

**1.3**  **Find the perimeter and area of the rectangle.**

**16.** 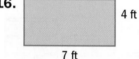 4 ft
7 ft

**17.** 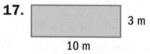 3 m
10 m

**18.**  9 yd
9 yd

**19.** Find the distance traveled when the rate is 45 miles per hour and the time is 3 hours.

**1.4**  **Write the unit rate as a fraction.**

**20.** $15 per square foot     **21.** 36 centimeters per second

**Copy and complete the statement by finding the missing number or unit.**

**22.** $50 \underline{\ ?\ } \times 4 \text{ h} = 200 \text{ mi}$     **23.** $5 \text{ persons} \times \underline{\ ?\ } \text{ days} = 40 \text{ person-days}$

**1.5**  **Evaluate the expression when $x = 4$ and $y = 12$.**

**24.** $x - 2$     **25.** $x + y$     **26.** $y - 2x$     **27.** $5x - 3y$

**Write the phrase as an algebraic expression using $n$.**

**28.** A number increased by 12     **29.** Twice the sum of a number and 7

**1.6**  **30.** A driver leaves Corona at noon and drives at an average rate of 50 miles per hour. At what time does the driver reach the town of Willowbrook 300 miles away?

**31.** A builder plans to install a hardwood floor in a room that is 12 feet wide and 16 feet long. The wood costs $6 per square foot. Find the total cost of the wood for the floor.

# Chapter 2

**2.1** Write two fractions, including one in simplest form, that are equivalent to the given fraction.

**1.** $\frac{9}{15}$      **2.** $\frac{4}{14}$      **3.** $\frac{8}{10}$      **4.** $\frac{21}{28}$

Copy and complete the statement using <, >, or =.

**5.** $\frac{2}{3} \underline{\ ?\ } \frac{5}{9}$      **6.** $\frac{7}{8} \underline{\ ?\ } \frac{9}{12}$      **7.** $\frac{3}{4} \underline{\ ?\ } \frac{9}{16}$      **8.** $\frac{7}{15} \underline{\ ?\ } \frac{1}{2}$

**2.2** Write the mixed number as an improper fraction or the improper fraction as a mixed number.

**9.** $4\frac{2}{3}$      **10.** $2\frac{5}{9}$      **11.** $\frac{43}{6}$      **12.** $\frac{35}{11}$

Order the numbers from least to greatest.

**13.** $7\frac{5}{16}, \frac{15}{2}, 7\frac{1}{4}, \frac{32}{5}$      **14.** $\frac{47}{8}, 5\frac{3}{5}, \frac{23}{4}, 5\frac{5}{6}$      **15.** $\frac{19}{4}, \frac{73}{16}, 4\frac{5}{9}, 4\frac{3}{10}$

Find the sum or difference.

**2.3** **16.** $\frac{7}{12} + \frac{3}{12}$      **17.** $\frac{3}{8} + \frac{7}{8}$      **18.** $\frac{9}{10} - \frac{1}{10}$      **19.** $\frac{23}{25} - \frac{8}{25}$

**20.** $5\frac{3}{8} + 2\frac{5}{8}$      **21.** $16\frac{3}{4} + 9\frac{3}{4}$      **22.** $7\frac{11}{13} - 2\frac{9}{13}$      **23.** $8\frac{2}{5} - 4\frac{3}{5}$

**2.4** **24.** $\frac{2}{5} + \frac{7}{20}$      **25.** $\frac{7}{15} + \frac{2}{3}$      **26.** $\frac{7}{8} - \frac{5}{6}$      **27.** $\frac{8}{9} - \frac{5}{6}$

**28.** $10\frac{1}{3} + 8\frac{1}{4}$      **29.** $4\frac{3}{4} + 3\frac{3}{5}$      **30.** $5\frac{7}{12} - 1\frac{1}{6}$      **31.** $7\frac{1}{2} - 3\frac{5}{6}$

**2.5** Find the product.

**32.** $\frac{4}{7} \cdot \frac{2}{3}$      **33.** $\frac{3}{8} \cdot \frac{1}{3}$      **34.** $\frac{3}{8} \cdot \frac{4}{9}$      **35.** $\frac{14}{21} \cdot \frac{3}{12}$

**36.** $4 \cdot \frac{11}{12}$      **37.** $5 \cdot 1\frac{7}{8}$      **38.** $2\frac{1}{2} \cdot 7\frac{2}{3}$      **39.** $1\frac{3}{7} \cdot 1\frac{1}{4}$

**2.6** Write the reciprocal of the number.

**40.** $\frac{15}{23}$      **41.** $\frac{13}{7}$      **42.** $6$      **43.** $18$

**44.** $4\frac{1}{3}$      **45.** $12\frac{1}{2}$      **46.** $\frac{25}{4}$      **47.** $5\frac{2}{5}$

**2.7** Find the quotient.

**48.** $\frac{7}{10} \div \frac{4}{5}$      **49.** $\frac{4}{3} \div \frac{4}{3}$      **50.** $\frac{12}{25} \div 4$      **51.** $7 \div \frac{7}{4}$

**52.** $9\frac{1}{3} \div 7$      **53.** $3\frac{2}{3} \div 2\frac{3}{4}$      **54.** $1\frac{5}{7} \div \frac{2}{3}$      **55.** $2\frac{3}{5} \div 13$

# Chapter 3

**3.1** **Find the sum or difference.**

**1.** $3.87 + 7.4$     **2.** $9.28 + 5.63$     **3.** $14.1 - 9.25$     **4.** $10.62 - 7.83$

**5.** $8.703 + 3.092$     **6.** $5.14 + 0.893$     **7.** $12 - 6.38$     **8.** $20 - 8.431$

**Evaluate the expression when $x = 8.7$ and $y = 3.74$.**

**9.** $x + 2.085$     **10.** $6 - y$     **11.** $x + y$     **12.** $x - y$

**3.2** **Find the product.**

**13.** $8 \times 2.3$     **14.** $15 \times 9.12$     **15.** $0.3 \times 0.7$     **16.** $4.6 \times 0.9$

**17.** $5.78 \times 3.91$     **18.** $2.51 \times 6.8$     **19.** $0.04 \times 7.553$     **20.** $6.104 \times 2.945$

**3.3** **Find the quotient. Then check your answer.**

**21.** $7.52 \div 8$     **22.** $55.8 \div 9$     **23.** $38 \div 4$     **24.** $12.6 \div 3$

**25.** $10.26 \div 3.8$     **26.** $15.12 \div 0.7$     **27.** $2.1125 \div 3.25$     **28.** $4.764 \div 0.6$

**3.4** **Write the fraction or mixed number as a decimal, or write the decimal as a fraction or mixed number.**

**29.** $\frac{7}{10}$     **30.** $\frac{5}{9}$     **31.** $4\frac{3}{8}$     **32.** $3\frac{5}{6}$

**33.** $0.8$     **34.** $0.45$     **35.** $4.625$     **36.** $2.3125$

**Order the numbers from least to greatest.**

**37.** $\frac{1}{4}, 0.3, \frac{1}{5}, 0.23$     **38.** $0.9, \frac{17}{20}, 0.83, \frac{4}{5}$     **39.** $0.11, \frac{1}{10}, \frac{1}{8}, 0.08$

**3.5** **Write the percent as a fraction or mixed number.**

**40.** $60\%$     **41.** $35\%$     **42.** $175\%$     **43.** $0.22\%$

**Write the percent as a decimal.**

**44.** $37\%$     **45.** $8\%$     **46.** $546\%$     **47.** $0.09\%$

**3.6** **Write the fraction or decimal as a percent.**

**48.** $\frac{13}{20}$     **49.** $\frac{19}{50}$     **50.** $\frac{7}{8}$     **51.** $\frac{21}{25}$

**52.** $0.7$     **53.** $0.48$     **54.** $0.094$     **55.** $0.3715$

**3.7** **Find the percent of the number.**

**56.** $75\%$ of $60$     **57.** $90\%$ of $200$     **58.** $33\frac{1}{3}\%$ of $45$     **59.** $66\frac{2}{3}\%$ of $120$

**60.** $10\%$ of $80$     **61.** $15\%$ of $92$     **62.** $48\%$ of $20$     **63.** $30\%$ of $76$

# Chapter 4

**4.1** **Use a number line to order the integers from least to greatest.**

**1.** $6, 8, -4, 10, -1, -3, 0$        **2.** $-21, 18, -17, 19, 15, -15$

**Write the opposite and the absolute value of the integer.**

**3.** $13$      **4.** $-7$      **5.** $-16$      **6.** $0$

**4.2** **Find the sum.**

**7.** $-18 + 16$      **8.** $-25 + 39$      **9.** $-31 + (-48)$

**10.** $-47 + (-93)$      **11.** $54 + (-60)$      **12.** $102 + (-77)$

**13.** $42 + (-73) + 18$      **14.** $-56 + 28 + (-14)$      **15.** $-30 + (-45) + (-27)$

**4.3** **Find the difference.**

**16.** $-17 - 8$      **17.** $-14 - 15$      **18.** $26 - 29$      **19.** $18 - 38$

**20.** $19 - (-35)$      **21.** $53 - (-24)$      **22.** $-71 - (-80)$      **23.** $-64 - (-33)$

**Evaluate the expression when $x = 5$ and $y = -18$.**

**24.** $x - 8$      **25.** $12 - y + 10$      **26.** $x - y - 3$      **27.** $17 + y - x$

**4.4** **Find the product.**

**28.** $-7(-9)$      **29.** $-12(-3)$      **30.** $-8(4)$      **31.** $16(-5)$

**32.** $-18(0)$      **33.** $3(-5)(-6)$      **34.** $-4(-7)(-2)$      **35.** $7(-9)(10)$

**Copy and complete the statement using < or >.**

**36.** $-6(-5) \underline{\ ?\ } 6(-5)$      **37.** $-3(8) \underline{\ ?\ } -3(-8)$

**38.** $|-4| \cdot (-9) \underline{\ ?\ } 4 \cdot |-9|$      **39.** $|-7| \cdot |-5| \underline{\ ?\ } 7(-5)$

**Evaluate the expression when $a = -3$ and $b = -8$.**

**40.** $ab - 4$      **41.** $b^2 + 2a$      **42.** $a^2 - b^2$      **43.** $5a + 3b$

**4.5** **Find the quotient.**

**44.** $\dfrac{15}{-5}$      **45.** $\dfrac{-63}{-9}$      **46.** $\dfrac{-72}{-8}$      **47.** $\dfrac{-132}{12}$

**48.** $\dfrac{0}{-16}$      **49.** $\dfrac{-82}{1}$      **50.** $\dfrac{-140}{-7}$      **51.** $\dfrac{182}{-13}$

**Find the mean of the numbers.**

**52.** $-4, -18, 13, 17, -8$      **53.** $-26, 16, -11, -18, 14$

**54.** $3, -4, -9, -9, 8, -1$      **55.** $-16, 0, 14, 22, -18, 15, 46$

# Chapter 5

**5.1** Show that the number is a rational number by writing it as a quotient of two integers.

    **1.** $8.5$              **2.** $2.3$              **3.** $-0.9$              **4.** $-7.6$

Order the rational numbers from least to greatest.

    **5.** $-5, 3.6, -4.5, 3\frac{1}{2}$              **6.** $-\frac{3}{4}, -\frac{9}{10}, 0, -0.8$

**5.2** Find the sum or difference.

    **7.** $7.6 + (-2.5)$     **8.** $-5.4 + (-9.1)$     **9.** $-0.8 - 1.7$     **10.** $11 - 14.3$

    **11.** $-4.2 + 6.1$     **12.** $88 - (-15.7)$     **13.** $\frac{11}{15} - \frac{8}{9}$     **14.** $-3\frac{7}{20} - 6\frac{7}{50}$

    **15.** $-5\frac{1}{2} + 6\frac{1}{4}$     **16.** $7\frac{5}{6} + \left(-8\frac{1}{3}\right)$     **17.** $3 - 5\frac{3}{8}$     **18.** $\frac{3}{5} - \left(-\frac{9}{10}\right)$

**5.3** Identify the property illustrated.

    **19.** $5.8 + (-1.7) = -1.7 + 5.8$              **20.** $\frac{3}{5} + \left(-\frac{3}{5}\right) = 0$

Simplify the expression. Justify your steps.

    **21.** $-3.5 - 1.6y + 4.9$     **22.** $0.7 + 0.4x - 0.7$     **23.** $-z + \frac{1}{4} + z$

**5.4** Find the product or quotient.

    **24.** $-8(2.5)$     **25.** $-0.6(-1.7)$     **26.** $4.8 \div (-0.5)$     **27.** $-6 \div (-3.2)$

    **28.** $-0.25 \div (-100)$     **29.** $9.9(-12.1)$     **30.** $-36\left(\frac{5}{8}\right)$     **31.** $4\frac{2}{7} \div \left(-\frac{3}{14}\right)$

    **32.** $\frac{5}{9}\left(-\frac{3}{5}\right)$     **33.** $-\frac{8}{9}\left(-\frac{1}{4}\right)$     **34.** $-24 \div \frac{3}{10}$     **35.** $-\frac{1}{8} \div \left(-\frac{5}{12}\right)$

**5.5** Identify the property illustrated.

    **36.** $-\frac{6}{7}\left(-\frac{7}{6}\right) = 1$     **37.** $1.4(-3.7) = -3.7(1.4)$     **38.** $-1(-8.2) = 8.2$

Simplify the expression. Justify your steps.

    **39.** $(-5 + 5)y$     **40.** $-4v\left(-\frac{1}{4}\right)$     **41.** $-\frac{1}{5}(5x)$

**5.6** Use the distributive property to write an equivalent expression.

    **42.** $5(6.3 + w)$     **43.** $-3.2(x - 7)$     **44.** $\frac{4}{5}\left(\frac{1}{2} - y\right)$

Simplify the expression by combining like terms.

    **45.** $r - 5.2r - 1.6r$     **46.** $4(s + 1.8) - 5.9s$     **47.** $7.3t - (3.4t - 2.5)$

# Chapter 6

**6.1** **Simplify the expression. Write your answer using exponents.**

**1.** $4^2 \cdot 4^5$

**2.** $7^8 \cdot 7^{11}$

**3.** $9^8 \cdot 9^2 \cdot 9^7$

**4.** $(-8)^{14} \cdot (-8)^{10}$

**5.** $(-3)^6 \cdot (-3)^5 \cdot (-3)^2$

**6.** $(-10)^{12} \cdot (-10)^{15}$

**Simplify the expression.**

**7.** $x^2 \cdot x^5$

**8.** $2y^5 \cdot 3y^9$

**9.** $9r^8 \cdot r^2$

**10.** $3m^3 \cdot 12m^4 \cdot m^{10}$

**11.** $5v^4 \cdot 4v^8 \cdot 2v^7$

**12.** $6p^4q^3 \cdot 7p^6q^2$

**6.2** **Simplify the expression. Write your answer using exponents.**

**13.** $\dfrac{7^8}{7^3}$

**14.** $\dfrac{9^{16}}{9^{10}}$

**15.** $\dfrac{(-11)^{14}}{(-11)^7}$

**16.** $\dfrac{(-5)^{15}}{(-5)^9}$

**Simplify the expression.**

**17.** $\dfrac{n^6}{n^2}$

**18.** $\dfrac{x^{22}}{x^{11}}$

**19.** $\dfrac{1}{h^5} \cdot h^9$

**20.** $m^{20} \cdot \dfrac{1}{m^6}$

**21.** $\dfrac{64z^8}{4z^5}$

**22.** $\dfrac{25w^{14}}{5w^9}$

**23.** $\dfrac{40s^{13} \cdot t^7}{12s^{10}}$

**24.** $\dfrac{42c^3 \cdot d^7}{4d^2}$

**6.3** **Evaluate the expression.**

**25.** $9^{-2}$

**26.** $(-2)^{-4}$

**27.** $15^0$

**28.** $(-5)^{-3}$

**Write the number in standard form.**

**29.** $8 \times 10^1 + 7 \times 10^0 + 4 \times 10^{-1}$

**30.** $3 \times 10^0 + 6 \times 10^{-1} + 5 \times 10^{-2}$

**31.** $7.62 \times 10^3$

**32.** $9.241 \times 10^{-4}$

**Write the number in scientific notation.**

**33.** $86,000$

**34.** $14,000,000$

**35.** $0.000365$

**36.** $0.000007$

**6.4** **Evaluate the expression.**

**37.** $12^{-8} \cdot 12^{10}$

**38.** $3^2 \cdot 3^{-5} \cdot 3^1$

**39.** $(-4)^2 \cdot (-4)^{-3} \cdot (-4)^4$

**40.** $\dfrac{5^{-3}}{5^{-6}}$

**41.** $\dfrac{(-2)^7}{(-2)^9}$

**42.** $\dfrac{10^{-4}}{10^{-1}}$

**Simplify the expression. Write your answer using positive exponents.**

**43.** $d^{-5} \cdot d^{14}$

**44.** $a^{-1} \cdot a^{-5} \cdot a^{-6}$

**45.** $c^{13} \cdot c^7 \cdot c^{-11}$

**46.** $\dfrac{m^{-2}}{m^8}$

**47.** $\dfrac{8n^{-7}}{32n^{-3}}$

**48.** $\dfrac{v^{-8}w^{-4}}{v^{-2}w^{-7}}$

# Chapter 7

**7.1** **Find the two square roots of the number.**

   **1.** 9           **2.** 64          **3.** 100        **4.** 4

   **5.** 49         **6.** 169        **7.** 81         **8.** 121

   **Evaluate the expression.**

   **9.** $\sqrt{36}$      **10.** $\sqrt{25}$      **11.** $\sqrt{16}$      **12.** $-\sqrt{900}$

  **13.** $-\sqrt{625}$    **14.** $-\sqrt{196}$    **15.** $\pm\sqrt{1600}$    **16.** $\pm\sqrt{256}$

**7.2** **Approximate the square root to the nearest integer.**

  **17.** $\sqrt{6}$      **18.** $\sqrt{15}$      **19.** $-\sqrt{43}$      **20.** $-\sqrt{75}$

   **Approximate the square root to the nearest tenth.**

  **21.** $\sqrt{21}$      **22.** $\sqrt{68}$      **23.** $-\sqrt{97}$      **24.** $-\sqrt{152}$

   **Order the numbers from least to greatest.**

  **25.** $\sqrt{25}, -3, 5.8, -\sqrt{16}$        **26.** $-7, -\sqrt{50}, 2.5, \dfrac{12}{5}$

**7.3** **Write the statement in if-then form and identify the hypothesis and the conclusion.**

  **27.** The square of an even number is an even number.

  **28.** All integers are rational numbers.

   **Let $a$ and $b$ represent the lengths of the legs of a right triangle, and let $c$ represent the length of the hypotenuse. Find the unknown length. Round to the nearest tenth if necessary.**

  **29.** $a = 6, b = 8$      **30.** $a = 5, b = 12$      **31.** $a = 7, b = 24$

  **32.** $a = 4, b = 9$      **33.** $a = 3, b = 8$      **34.** $a = 10, b = 13$

**7.4** **Write the converse of the if-then statement. Tell whether the converse is *true* or *false*. If it is false, explain why.**

  **35.** If a figure is a square, then the figure is a rectangle.

  **36.** If a number is negative, then its square is positive.

  **37.** If the product of two numbers is 0, then one of the numbers is 0.

   **Determine whether the triangle with the given side lengths is a right triangle.**

  **38.** $a = 8, b = 15, c = 17$      **39.** $a = 5, b = 6, c = 11$

  **40.** $a = 9, b = 18, c = 27$      **41.** $a = 9, b = 40, c = 41$

# Chapter 8

## 8.1 Write the verbal sentence as an equation. Let $n$ represent the number.

**1.** 18 less than a number equals 4.   **2.** The difference of 11 and a number is 5.

### Solve the equation. Check your solution.

**3.** $x + 14 = -18$   **4.** $y - 6 = 23$   **5.** $z + 2.1 = 1.7$   **6.** $m + 9 = 32$

**7.** $c - 1.3 = -0.6$   **8.** $n - 0.5 = -4.7$   **9.** $a - \frac{5}{8} = -\frac{1}{4}$   **10.** $p + \frac{2}{3} = \frac{1}{9}$

## 8.2 Solve the equation. Check your solution.

**11.** $4v = 48$   **12.** $-11f = -88$   **13.** $-3.2x = 24$

**14.** $\frac{z}{10} = 6$   **15.** $\frac{s}{-4} = -8$   **16.** $\frac{t}{2.1} = -7$

**17.** $\frac{2}{5}r = -12$   **18.** $-\frac{3}{4}w = 30$   **19.** $-\frac{1}{6}g = -14$

## 8.3 Solve the equation. Check your solution.

**20.** $-3x + 2 = 8$   **21.** $5y - 8 = 37$   **22.** $7m + 4 = -10$

**23.** $-4z - 2.3 = -5.5$   **24.** $\frac{n}{2} - 3 = 12$   **25.** $\frac{p}{6} + 8 = -3$

### Write the verbal sentence as an equation. Then solve the equation.

**26.** Ten less than 4 times $n$ is $-38$.   **27.** Seven more than 3 times $y$ is $-20$.

## 8.4 Solve the equation by first clearing the fractions or decimals.

**28.** $\frac{1}{3}x - \frac{3}{4} = \frac{5}{6}$   **29.** $\frac{3}{10}y + \frac{1}{3} = -\frac{4}{15}$   **30.** $-\frac{3}{20}x + \frac{3}{8} = -\frac{3}{5}$

**31.** $7.8 - 2.4x = 18$   **32.** $0.25d + 4.1 = -0.645$   **33.** $-3.2t - 0.8t = 1.88$

## 8.5 Solve the equation. Check your solution.

**34.** $18x - 3x + 4 = -11$   **35.** $-4m - 2m + 7 = 31$   **36.** $-9(3 - 2c) = -81$

**37.** $6(5q + 10) = -48$   **38.** $-8s + 2(9s - 3) = 37$   **39.** $-12r - (4r + 1) = 95$

## 8.6
**40.** Two cars travel in opposite directions from Los Angeles. The average speed of one car is 5 miles per hour greater than the average speed of the other car. After 2 hours the cars are 250 miles apart. Find the speed of each car.

**41.** Jeff and Tom are at the starting point of a race. Jeff gets a 2 minute head start and runs at a rate of 0.13 mile per minute. Tom then follows Jeff at a rate of 0.17 mile per minute. After how many minutes from the time Jeff starts running does Tom overtake Jeff?

# Chapter 9

**9.1** Graph the inequality.

**1.** $x < 9$      **2.** $m \geq -6$      **3.** $p \leq -1\frac{1}{2}$      **4.** $r > 4.2$

Write an inequality represented by the graph.

**5.**

**6.**

**7.**

**8.**

Write the common phrase as an inequality.

**9.** Less than 8             **10.** More than 5.6

**11.** 2 or more           **12.** No more than 0.7

**9.2** Tell whether the number is a solution of the inequality.

**13.** $x - 5 < 9;\ -3$           **14.** $y + 3 > -12;\ -15$

**15.** $v + 4.7 \geq -3.6;\ -9.1$      **16.** $w - 2\frac{1}{3} \leq -4;\ -1\frac{2}{3}$

Solve the inequality. Graph your solution.

**17.** $a - 11 \geq -6$    **18.** $c - 3 < 19$    **19.** $23 \leq n + 15$    **20.** $-44 > g + 30$

**21.** $m + 5.2 \leq 4.7$    **22.** $-2.8 \geq s + 9.4$    **23.** $-3\frac{2}{3} \geq t - 2\frac{1}{6}$    **24.** $p - 1\frac{3}{4} > -2\frac{1}{4}$

**9.3** Solve the inequality. Graph your solution.

**25.** $\frac{d}{5} > 3$    **26.** $7 \leq \frac{n}{-8}$    **27.** $-9k < 54$    **28.** $-102 \geq 6x$

**29.** $-14f \leq -84$    **30.** $-4.2 \geq 2z$    **31.** $-7 > \frac{p}{1.3}$    **32.** $\frac{w}{-12} < 3.5$

**9.4** Solve the inequality. Graph your solution.

**33.** $-2c - 15 \geq -8$    **34.** $7n + 12 < -2$    **35.** $\frac{d}{-5} + 9 \leq 7$    **36.** $\frac{m}{4} - 13 > -10$

**37.** $\frac{q}{3} + 4 \geq -16$    **38.** $\frac{z}{-7} - 5 \geq 3$    **39.** $0.8x - 10 \geq 4$    **40.** $-5s + 7.5 \geq -1$

Write the verbal sentence as an inequality. Then solve the inequality.

**41.** Three more than twice a number $x$ is less than or equal to $-19$.

**42.** Four less than three times a number $y$ is greater than 29.

# Chapter 10

**10.1 Plot the point and describe its location.**

**1.** $A(-4, -4)$    **2.** $B(-4, 1)$    **3.** $C(0, -1)$

**4.** $D(4, 4)$    **5.** $E(-2, 4)$    **6.** $F(4, -3)$

**10.2 Tell whether the ordered pair is a solution of the equation.**

**7.** $3x + 4y = 27; (1, 6)$    **8.** $-2x + 8y = -40; (-2, -6)$

**Graph the equation.**

**9.** $x - 2y = 8$    **10.** $-2x + 3y = 10$    **11.** $5x + 4y = -30$

**10.3 Tell whether the ordered pair is a solution of the equation.**

**12.** $y = 3; (-2, 3)$    **13.** $x = -16; (8, -16)$    **14.** $x = 0.5; (-0.5, 0.6)$

**Graph the equation on a coordinate plane.**

**15.** $x = -4$    **16.** $y = 7$    **17.** $y = -8$

**10.4 Find the *x*-intercept and the *y*-intercept of the graph of the equation. Then graph the equation.**

**18.** $x + y = 5$    **19.** $2x - 5y = 20$    **20.** $-3x + 4y = -36$

**21.** $x - y = -8$    **22.** $3x + 4y = 24$    **23.** $3x + 5y = 15$

**10.5 Find the slope of the line through the given points.**

**24.** $(2, 6), (-1, -4)$    **25.** $(2, -3), (8, -5)$    **26.** $(12, 4), (-6, 4)$

**27.** $(-10, -6), (-15, -9)$    **28.** $(7, -5), (-6, 3)$    **29.** $(-8, 0), (-8, 9)$

**10.6 Identify the slope and *y*-intercept of the line. Then graph the equation.**

**30.** $y = 5x - 2$    **31.** $y = -3x + 9$    **32.** $y = -\frac{1}{2}x - 4$

**33.** $x + 4y = 32$    **34.** $-4x + y = -10$    **35.** $3x - 2y = -8$

**10.7 Tell whether the data in the table show direct variation. Explain.**

**36.**

| x | 1 | 3 | 5 | 7 |
|---|---|---|---|---|
| y | -2 | -6 | -10 | -14 |

**37.**

| x | 1 | 2 | 3 | 4 |
|---|---|---|---|---|
| y | 1 | 4 | 9 | 16 |

**10.8 Graph the direct variation equation.**

**38.** $y = x$    **39.** $y = -x$    **40.** $y = 4x$    **41.** $y = -\frac{1}{2}x$

# Tables

## Symbols

| Symbol | Meaning | Page |
|---|---|---|
| $7^3$ | 7 to the third power, or $7 \cdot 7 \cdot 7$ | 6 |
| ( ) | parentheses—a grouping symbol | 12 |
| [ ] | brackets—a grouping symbol | 12 |
| $3x$ | 3 times $x$ | 32 |
| $\frac{a}{b}$ | $a$ divided by $b$, $b \neq 0$ | 54 |
| % | percent | 134 |
| $-a$ | the opposite of $a$ | 162 |
| $|a|$ | the absolute value of $a$ | 162 |
| $\frac{1}{a}$ | the reciprocal of $a$, $a \neq 0$ | 230 |
| $a^{-n}$ | $\frac{1}{a^n}$, $a \neq 0$ | 266 |
| $\sqrt{a}$ | the nonnegative square root of $a$, $a \geq 0$ | 288 |
| $\pm$ | plus or minus | 288 |

| Symbol | Meaning | Page |
|---|---|---|
| $\stackrel{?}{=}$ | is equal to? | 302 |
| $m$ | slope | 440 |
| $b$ | $y$-intercept | 440 |
| $k$ | constant of variation | 452 |
| . . . | continues on | 476 |
| $=$ | is equal to | 477 |
| $<$ | is less than | 477 |
| $>$ | is greater than | 477 |
| $\leq$ | is less than or equal to | 477 |
| $\geq$ | is greater than or equal to | 477 |
| $\neq$ | is not equal to | 477 |
| $3 \times 2$ $3 \cdot 2$ $3(2)$ | 3 times 2 | 481 |
| $a:b$ | the ratio of $a$ to $b$ | 483 |
| $\approx$ | is approximately equal to | 487 |

## Formulas

| | | | |
|---|---|---|---|
| Distance, rate, and time (p. 18) | $d = rt$ | Distance traveled $d$ is equal to the speed (rate of travel) $r$ times the travel time $t$. | |
| Total cost (p. 18) | $T = cn$ | The total cost $T$ of $n$ items is the cost $c$ of one item (the unit cost) times the number of items. | |
| Mass of an object (p. 27) | $m = DV$ | The mass $m$ of an object is the density $D$ of the object times the volume $V$ of the object. | |
| Simple interest (p. 146) | $I = Prt$ | The simple interest $I$ for the amount of money you save or borrow (the principal) is the product of the principal $P$, the annual interest rate $r$ (as a decimal), and the time $t$ (in years). | |

# Geometric Formulas

| | | |
|---|---|---|
| **Pythagorean Theorem (p. 302)**<br><br>In a right triangle, $a^2 + b^2 = c^2$ where $a$ and $b$ are the lengths of the legs and $c$ is the length of the hypotenuse. | **Rectangle (p. 488)**<br>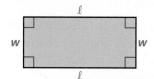<br>**Area**    **Perimeter**<br>$A = \ell w$    $P = 2\ell + 2w$ | **Square (p. 488)**<br><br>**Area**    **Perimeter**<br>$A = s^2$    $P = 4s$ |
| **Triangle (p. 488)**<br>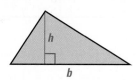<br>**Area**<br>$A = \frac{1}{2}bh$ | **Parallelogram (p. 488)**<br>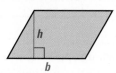<br>**Area**<br>$A = bh$ | **Trapezoid (p. 488)**<br>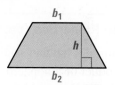<br>**Area**<br>$A = \frac{1}{2}(b_1 + b_2)h$ |
| **Circle (p. 490)**<br><br>**Circumference**    **Area**<br>$C = \pi d$ or    $A = \pi r^2$<br>$C = 2\pi r$ | **Rectangular Prism (p. 492)**<br><br>**Surface Area**<br>$S = 2B + Ph$<br>$\quad = 2\ell w + 2hw + 2\ell h$<br><br>**Volume**<br>$V = Bh$<br>$\quad = \ell wh$ | **Cylinder (p. 492)**<br><br>**Surface Area**<br>$S = 2B + Ch$<br>$\quad = 2\pi r^2 + 2\pi rh$<br><br>**Volume**<br>$V = Bh$<br>$\quad = \pi r^2 h$ |

# Properties

## Properties of Addition and Multiplication

**Commutative Properties** (pp. 216, 230)

The order in which you add two numbers does not change the sum.      $a + b = b + a$

The order in which you multiply two numbers does not change the product.      $a \cdot b = b \cdot a$

**Associative Properties** (pp. 216, 230)

The way you group three numbers in a sum does not change the sum.      $(a + b) + c = a + (b + c)$

The way you group three numbers in a product does not change the product.      $(a \cdot b) \cdot c = a \cdot (b \cdot c)$

**Identity Properties** (pp. 216, 230)

The sum of a number and the additive identity, 0, is the number.      $a + 0 = 0 + a = a$

The product of a number and the multiplicative identity, 1, is the number.      $a \cdot 1 = 1 \cdot a = a$

**Inverse Properties** (pp. 216, 230)

The sum of a number and its additive inverse, or opposite, is 0.      $a + (-a) = -a + a = 0$

The product of a nonzero number and its multiplicative inverse, or reciprocal, is 1.      $a \cdot \frac{1}{a} = \frac{1}{a} \cdot a = 1 \; (a \neq 0)$

**Distributive Property** (p. 236)

$$a(b + c) = ab + ac$$
$$(b + c)a = ba + ca$$
$$a(b - c) = ab - ac$$
$$(b - c)a = ba - ca$$

You can multiply a number and a sum by multiplying each term of the sum by the number and then adding these products. The same property applies to the product of a number and a difference.

## Properties of Equality

**Addition Property of Equality** (p. 324)

Adding the same number to each side of an equation produces an equivalent equation.      If $x - a = b$, then $x - a + a = b + a$, or $x = b + a$.

**Subtraction Property of Equality** (p. 324)

Subtracting the same number from each side of an equation produces an equivalent equation.      If $x + a = b$, then $x + a - a = b - a$, or $x = b - a$.

**Multiplication Property of Equality** (p. 330)

Multiplying each side of an equation by the same nonzero number produces an equivalent equation.      If $\frac{x}{a} = b$ and $a \neq 0$, then $a \cdot \frac{x}{a} = a \cdot b$, or $x = ab$.

**Division Property of Equality** (p. 330)

Dividing each side of an equation by the same nonzero number produces an equivalent equation.      If $ax = b$ and $a \neq 0$, then $\frac{ax}{a} = \frac{b}{a}$, or $x = \frac{b}{a}$.

# Properties of Inequality

**Addition Property of Inequality (p. 378)**

Adding the same number to each side of an inequality produces an equivalent inequality.

If $a < b$, then $a + c < b + c$.
If $a > b$, then $a + c > b + c$.

**Subtraction Property of Inequality (p. 378)**

Subtracting the same number from each side of an inequality produces an equivalent inequality.

If $a < b$, then $a - c < b - c$.
If $a > b$, then $a - c > b - c$.

**Multiplication Property of Inequality (p. 386)**

Multiplying each side of an inequality by a *positive* number produces an equivalent inequality.

If $a < b$ and $c > 0$, then $ac < bc$.
If $a > b$ and $c > 0$, then $ac > bc$.

Multiplying each side of an inequality by a *negative* number and *reversing the direction of the inequality symbol* produces an equivalent inequality.

If $a < b$ and $c < 0$, then $ac > bc$.
If $a > b$ and $c < 0$, then $ac < bc$.

**Division Property of Inequality (p. 386)**

Dividing each side of an inequality by a *positive* number produces an equivalent inequality.

If $a < b$ and $c > 0$, then $\frac{a}{c} < \frac{b}{c}$.
If $a > b$ and $c > 0$, then $\frac{a}{c} > \frac{b}{c}$.

Dividing each side of an inequality by a *negative* number and *reversing the direction of the inequality symbol* produces an equivalent inequality.

If $a < b$ and $c < 0$, then $\frac{a}{c} > \frac{b}{c}$.
If $a > b$ and $c < 0$, then $\frac{a}{c} < \frac{b}{c}$.

# Properties of Exponents

**Product of Powers Property (pp. 252, 272)**

To multiply powers having the same base, add the exponents.

$a^m \cdot a^n = a^{m+n}$

**Quotient of Powers Property (pp. 258, 272)**

To divide powers having the same nonzero base, subtract exponents.

$\frac{a^m}{a^n} = a^{m-n}, a \neq 0$

**Definition of zero exponent (p. 266)**

A nonzero number raised to the zero power is 1.

$a^0 = 1, a \neq 0$

**Definition of negative exponent (p. 266)**

A nonzero number raised to a negative power is the reciprocal of the number raised to the corresponding positive power.

$a^{-n} = \frac{1}{a^n}, a \neq 0$

# Measures

## Time

60 seconds (sec) = 1 minute (min)
60 minutes = 1 hour (h)
24 hours = 1 day
7 days = 1 week (wk)
4 weeks ≈ 1 month

$\left.\begin{array}{l}\text{365 days} \\ \text{52 weeks (approx.)} \\ \text{12 months}\end{array}\right\}$ = 1 year

10 years = 1 decade
100 years = 1 century

## Metric

### Length

10 millimeters (mm) = 1 centimeter (cm)

$\left.\begin{array}{l}\text{100 cm} \\ \text{1000 mm}\end{array}\right\}$ = 1 meter (m)

1000 m = 1 kilometer (km)

### Area

100 square millimeters = 1 square centimeter
(mm$^2$)                          (cm$^2$)
10,000 cm$^2$ = 1 square meter (m$^2$)
10,000 m$^2$ = 1 hectare (ha)

### Volume

1000 cubic millimeters = 1 cubic centimeter
(mm$^3$)                          (cm$^3$)
1,000,000 cm$^3$ = 1 cubic meter (m$^3$)

### Capacity

$\left.\begin{array}{l}\text{1000 milliliters (mL)} \\ \text{1000 cubic centimeters (cm}^3\text{)}\end{array}\right\}$ = 1 liter (L)

1000 L = 1 kiloliter (kL)

### Mass

1000 milligrams (mg) = 1 gram (g)
1000 g = 1 kilogram (kg)
1000 kg = 1 metric ton (t)

## United States Customary

### Length

12 inches (in.) = 1 foot (ft)

$\left.\begin{array}{l}\text{36 in.} \\ \text{3 ft}\end{array}\right\}$ = 1 yard (yd)

$\left.\begin{array}{l}\text{5280 ft} \\ \text{1760 yd}\end{array}\right\}$ = 1 mile (mi)

### Area

144 square inches (in.$^2$) = 1 square foot (ft$^2$)
9 ft$^2$ = 1 square yard (yd$^2$)

$\left.\begin{array}{l}\text{43,560 ft}^2 \\ \text{4840 yd}^2\end{array}\right\}$ = 1 acre (A)

### Volume

1728 cubic inches (in.$^3$) = 1 cubic foot (ft$^3$)
27 ft$^3$ = 1 cubic yard (yd$^3$)

### Capacity

8 fluid ounces (fl oz) = 1 cup (c)
2 c = 1 pint (pt)
2 pt = 1 quart (qt)
4 qt = 1 gallon (gal)

### Weight

16 ounces (oz) = 1 pound (lb)
2000 lb = 1 ton

## Conversions Between Systems

| | | | |
|---|---|---|---|
| **Length** | 1 in. = 2.54 cm | 1 ft = 0.3048 m | 1 mi ≈ 1.609 km |
| **Capacity** | 1 fl oz ≈ 29.573 mL | 1 qt ≈ 0.946 L | 1 gal ≈ 3.785 L |
| **Weight/Mass** | 1 oz ≈ 28.35 g | 1 lb ≈ 0.454 kg | |

# Squares and Square Roots

| No. | Square | Sq. Root | No. | Square | Sq. Root | No. | Square | Sq. Root |
|---|---|---|---|---|---|---|---|---|
| 1 | 1 | 1.000 | 51 | 2601 | 7.141 | 101 | 10,201 | 10.050 |
| 2 | 4 | 1.414 | 52 | 2704 | 7.211 | 102 | 10,404 | 10.100 |
| 3 | 9 | 1.732 | 53 | 2809 | 7.280 | 103 | 10,609 | 10.149 |
| 4 | 16 | 2.000 | 54 | 2916 | 7.348 | 104 | 10,816 | 10.198 |
| 5 | 25 | 2.236 | 55 | 3025 | 7.416 | 105 | 11,025 | 10.247 |
| 6 | 36 | 2.449 | 56 | 3136 | 7.483 | 106 | 11,236 | 10.296 |
| 7 | 49 | 2.646 | 57 | 3249 | 7.550 | 107 | 11,449 | 10.344 |
| 8 | 64 | 2.828 | 58 | 3364 | 7.616 | 108 | 11,664 | 10.392 |
| 9 | 81 | 3.000 | 59 | 3481 | 7.681 | 109 | 11,881 | 10.440 |
| 10 | 100 | 3.162 | 60 | 3600 | 7.746 | 110 | 12,100 | 10.488 |
| 11 | 121 | 3.317 | 61 | 3721 | 7.810 | 111 | 12,321 | 10.536 |
| 12 | 144 | 3.464 | 62 | 3844 | 7.874 | 112 | 12,544 | 10.583 |
| 13 | 169 | 3.606 | 63 | 3969 | 7.937 | 113 | 12,769 | 10.630 |
| 14 | 196 | 3.742 | 64 | 4096 | 8.000 | 114 | 12,996 | 10.677 |
| 15 | 225 | 3.873 | 65 | 4225 | 8.062 | 115 | 13,225 | 10.724 |
| 16 | 256 | 4.000 | 66 | 4356 | 8.124 | 116 | 13,456 | 10.770 |
| 17 | 289 | 4.123 | 67 | 4489 | 8.185 | 117 | 13,689 | 10.817 |
| 18 | 324 | 4.243 | 68 | 4624 | 8.246 | 118 | 13,924 | 10.863 |
| 19 | 361 | 4.359 | 69 | 4761 | 8.307 | 119 | 14,161 | 10.909 |
| 20 | 400 | 4.472 | 70 | 4900 | 8.367 | 120 | 14,400 | 10.954 |
| 21 | 441 | 4.583 | 71 | 5041 | 8.426 | 121 | 14,641 | 11.000 |
| 22 | 484 | 4.690 | 72 | 5184 | 8.485 | 122 | 14,884 | 11.045 |
| 23 | 529 | 4.796 | 73 | 5329 | 8.544 | 123 | 15,129 | 11.091 |
| 24 | 576 | 4.899 | 74 | 5476 | 8.602 | 124 | 15,376 | 11.136 |
| 25 | 625 | 5.000 | 75 | 5625 | 8.660 | 125 | 15,625 | 11.180 |
| 26 | 676 | 5.099 | 76 | 5776 | 8.718 | 126 | 15,876 | 11.225 |
| 27 | 729 | 5.196 | 77 | 5929 | 8.775 | 127 | 16,129 | 11.269 |
| 28 | 784 | 5.292 | 78 | 6084 | 8.832 | 128 | 16,384 | 11.314 |
| 29 | 841 | 5.385 | 79 | 6241 | 8.888 | 129 | 16,641 | 11.358 |
| 30 | 900 | 5.477 | 80 | 6400 | 8.944 | 130 | 16,900 | 11.402 |
| 31 | 961 | 5.568 | 81 | 6561 | 9.000 | 131 | 17,161 | 11.446 |
| 32 | 1024 | 5.657 | 82 | 6724 | 9.055 | 132 | 17,424 | 11.489 |
| 33 | 1089 | 5.745 | 83 | 6889 | 9.110 | 133 | 17,689 | 11.533 |
| 34 | 1156 | 5.831 | 84 | 7056 | 9.165 | 134 | 17,956 | 11.576 |
| 35 | 1225 | 5.916 | 85 | 7225 | 9.220 | 135 | 18,225 | 11.619 |
| 36 | 1296 | 6.000 | 86 | 7396 | 9.274 | 136 | 18,496 | 11.662 |
| 37 | 1369 | 6.083 | 87 | 7569 | 9.327 | 137 | 18,769 | 11.705 |
| 38 | 1444 | 6.164 | 88 | 7744 | 9.381 | 138 | 19,044 | 11.747 |
| 39 | 1521 | 6.245 | 89 | 7921 | 9.434 | 139 | 19,321 | 11.790 |
| 40 | 1600 | 6.325 | 90 | 8100 | 9.487 | 140 | 19,600 | 11.832 |
| 41 | 1681 | 6.403 | 91 | 8281 | 9.539 | 141 | 19,881 | 11.874 |
| 42 | 1764 | 6.481 | 92 | 8464 | 9.592 | 142 | 20,164 | 11.916 |
| 43 | 1849 | 6.557 | 93 | 8649 | 9.644 | 143 | 20,449 | 11.958 |
| 44 | 1936 | 6.633 | 94 | 8836 | 9.695 | 144 | 20,736 | 12.000 |
| 45 | 2025 | 6.708 | 95 | 9025 | 9.747 | 145 | 21,025 | 12.042 |
| 46 | 2116 | 6.782 | 96 | 9216 | 9.798 | 146 | 21,316 | 12.083 |
| 47 | 2209 | 6.856 | 97 | 9409 | 9.849 | 147 | 21,609 | 12.124 |
| 48 | 2304 | 6.928 | 98 | 9604 | 9.899 | 148 | 21,904 | 12.166 |
| 49 | 2401 | 7.000 | 99 | 9801 | 9.950 | 149 | 22,201 | 12.207 |
| 50 | 2500 | 7.071 | 100 | 10,000 | 10.000 | 150 | 22,500 | 12.247 |

TABLES

# English-Spanish Glossary

| | |
|---|---|
| **absolute value** (p. 162) The absolute value of a number $a$ is the distance between $a$ and 0 on a number line. The symbol $\lvert a \rvert$ represents the absolute value of $a$. | $\lvert 2 \rvert = 2,\ \lvert -5 \rvert = 5,$ and $\lvert 0 \rvert = 0$ |
| **valor absoluto** (pág. 162) El valor absoluto de un número $a$ es la distancia entre $a$ y 0 en una recta numérica. El símbolo $\lvert a \rvert$ representa el valor absoluto de $a$. | $\lvert 2 \rvert = 2,\ \lvert -5 \rvert = 5$ y $\lvert 0 \rvert = 0$ |
| **additive identity** (p. 216) The number 0 is the additive identity, because the sum of any number and 0 is the number: $a + 0 = 0 + a = a$. | |
| **identidad de la suma** (pág. 216) El número 0 es la identidad de la suma ya que la suma de cualquier número y 0 es ese número: $a + 0 = 0 + a = a$. | $-2 + 0 = -2,\ 0 + \frac{3}{4} = \frac{3}{4}$ |
| **additive inverse** (p. 216) The additive inverse of a number $a$ is its opposite, $-a$. The sum of a number and its additive inverse is 0: $a + (-a) = -a + a = 0$. | The *additive inverse* of $-5$ is 5, and $-5 + 5 = 0$. |
| **inverso aditivo** (pág. 216) El inverso aditivo de un número $a$ es su opuesto, $-a$. La suma de un número y su inverso aditivo es 0: $a + (-a) = -a + a = 0$. | El *inverso aditivo* de $-5$ es 5, y $-5 + 5 = 0$. |
| **algebraic expression** (p. 32) An expression that consists of numbers, operations, at least one variable, and sometimes grouping symbols. Also called *variable expression*. | $5n,\ \frac{14}{y},\ 6 + c,$ and $8 - x$ are *algebraic expressions*. |
| **expresión algebraica** (pág. 32) Expresión que consiste en números, operaciones, al menos una variable y a veces signos de agrupación. Llamado también *expresión variable*. | $5n,\ \frac{14}{y},\ 6 + c$ y $8 - x$ son *expresiones algebraicas*. |

| | |
|---|---|
| **average rate of change (p. 188)** A change in one quantity divided by a change in a second quantity. | The altitude of a hot air balloon changes $-884$ feet in 34 minutes. The *average rate of change* in the balloon's altitude is $\dfrac{-884\text{ ft}}{34\text{ min}}$, or $-26$ feet per minute. |
| **tasa promedio de cambio (pág. 188)** Un cambio en una cantidad dividido por un cambio en otra cantidad. | La altitud de un globo aerostático cambia $-884$ pies en 34 minutos. La *tasa promedio de cambio* de la altitud del globo es $\dfrac{-884\text{ pies}}{34\text{ min}}$, o $-26$ pies por minuto. |

### B

| | |
|---|---|
| **base of a power (p. 6)** The number that is used as a factor in a repeated multiplication. | In the power $3^4$, the *base* is 3. |
| **base de una potencia (pág. 6)** El número que se usa como factor en una multiplicación repetida. | En la potencia $3^4$, la *base* es 3. |

### C

| | |
|---|---|
| **coefficient (p. 236)** The number part of a term with a variable part. | The *coefficient* of $-6x$ is $-6$. |
| **coeficiente (pág. 236)** La parte numérica de un término que tiene una variable. | El *coeficiente* de $-6x$ es $-6$. |
| **constant term (p. 236)** A term that has no variable part. | In the expression $$3x + (-4) + (-6x) + 2,$$ the *constant terms* are $-4$ and 2. |
| **término constante (pág. 236)** Término que no tiene una parte variable. | En la expresión $$3x + (-4) + (-6x) + 2,$$ los *términos constantes* son $-4$ y 2. |
| **constant of variation (p. 452)** The nonzero constant $k$ in a direct variation equation $y = kx$. | The *constant of variation* in the direct variation equation $y = 7x$ is 7. |
| **constante de variación (pág. 452)** La constante $k$ no igual a cero, en una ecuación de variación directa $y = kx$. | La *constante de variación* en la ecuación de variación directa $y = 7x$ es 7. |

**converse of a statement (p. 308)** A statement formed by interchanging the hypothesis and the conclusion of a statement in if-then form. The converse of a true statement is not necessarily true.

**recíproco de un enunciado (pág. 308)** Enunciado formado al intercambiar la hipótesis y la conclusión de un enunciado en la forma "si..., entonces...". El recíproco de un enunciado verdadero no es necesariamente verdadero.

The *converse of the statement* "If $x = 5$, then $|x| = 5$" is "If $|x| = 5$, then $x = 5$." The original statement is true, but the converse is false.

El *recíproco del enunciado* "Si $x = 5$, entonces $|x| = 5$" es "Si $|x| = 5$, entonces $x = 5$". El enunciado original es verdadero, pero el recíproco es falso.

**coordinate plane (p. 408)** A coordinate system formed by the intersection of a horizontal number line, called the $x$-axis, and a vertical number line, called the $y$-axis.

**plano de coordenadas (pág. 408)** Un sistema de coordenadas formado por la intersección de una recta numérica horizontal, llamada eje $x$, y una recta numérica vertical, llamada eje $y$.

vertical axis/eje vertical
$y$-axis/eje $y$

| | |
|---|---|
| Quadrant II<br>Cuadrante II | Quadrant I<br>Cuadrante I |
| Quadrant III<br>Cuadrante III | Quadrant IV<br>Cuadrante IV |

horizontal axis
eje horizontal
$x$-axis/eje $x$

origin/origen
$(0, 0)$

## D

**direct variation (p. 446)** The relationship of two variables $x$ and $y$ if there is a nonzero number $k$ such that $y = kx$ or $k = \frac{y}{x}$.

**variación directa (pág. 446)** La relación entre dos variables $x$ e $y$ cuando hay un número $k$ distinto de cero, de manera tal que $y = kx$ o $k = \frac{y}{x}$.

$$y = 5x$$
$$y = kx$$

## E

**equation (p. 324)** A mathematical sentence formed by placing an equal sign between two expressions.

**ecuación (pág. 324)** Un enunciado matemático que se forma al colocar un signo igual entre dos expresiones.

$3 \cdot 6 = 18$ and $x + 7 = 12$ are *equations*.

$3 \cdot 6 = 18$ y $x + 7 = 12$ son *ecuaciones*.

| | |
|---|---|
| **equivalent equations** (p. 324)  Equations that have the same solution. | $2x - 6 = 0$ and $2x = 6$ are *equivalent equations* because the solution of both equations is 3. |
| **ecuaciones equivalentes** (pág. 324)  Ecuaciones que tienen la misma solución. | $2x - 6 = 0$ y $2x = 6$ son *ecuaciones equivalentes* porque la solución de ambas ecuaciones es 3. |
| **equivalent fractions** (p. 54)  Fractions that represent the same number. Equivalent fractions have the same simplest form. | $\frac{6}{8}$ and $\frac{9}{12}$ are *equivalent fractions* that both represent $\frac{3}{4}$. |
| **fracciones equivalentes** (pág. 54)  Fracciones que representan el mismo número. Las fracciones equivalentes tienen la misma mínima expresión. | $\frac{6}{8}$ y $\frac{9}{12}$ son *fracciones equivalentes* porque ambas representan $\frac{3}{4}$. |
| **equivalent inequalities** (p. 378)  Inequalities that have the same solutions. | $2t < 4$ and $t < 2$ are *equivalent inequalities*, because the solutions of both inequalities are all real numbers less than 2. |
| **desigualdades equivalentes** (pág. 378)  Desigualdades con las mismas soluciones. | $2t < 4$ y $t < 2$ son *desigualdades equivalentes* ya que las soluciones de ambas son todos los números reales menores que 2. |
| **evaluate an expression** (p. 12)  To find the value of an expression.  **hallar el valor de una expresión** (pág. 12)  Encontrar el valor de una expresión. | $$4(3) + 6 \div 2 = 15$$ |
| **exponent** (p. 6)  A number that represents how many times a base is used as a factor in a repeated multiplication. | In the power $5^3$, the *exponent* is 3. |
| **exponente** (pág. 6)  Un número que representa cuántas veces una base se usa como factor en una multiplicación repetida. | El *exponente* de la potencia $5^3$ es 3. |

## F

formula (p. 18) A relationship between two or more variables.

fórmula (pág. 18) Una relación entre dos o más variables.

The *formula d = rt* relates the distance traveled to the speed and travel time.

La *fórmula d = rt* relaciona la distancia recorrida con la velocidad y el tiempo transcurrido.

## G

graph of an equation in two variables (p. 414) The set of points in a coordinate plane that represent all solutions of the equation.

gráfica de una ecuación con dos variables (pág. 414) El conjunto de puntos de un plano de coordenadas que representa todas las soluciones de la ecuación.

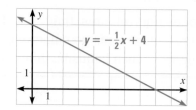

The line is the *graph of the equation* $y = -\frac{1}{2}x + 4$.

La recta es la *gráfica de la ecuación* $y = -\frac{1}{2}x + 4$.

graph of an inequality in one variable (p. 372) On a number line, the set of points that represent all solutions of an inequality.

gráfica de una desigualdad con una variable (pág. 372) En una recta numérica, el conjunto de puntos que representan todas las soluciones de una desigualdad.

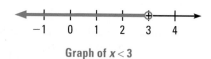

Graph of $x < 3$

Gráfica de $x < 3$

graph of an inequality in two variables (p. 468) In a coordinate plane, the set of points that represent all solutions of the inequality.

gráfica de una desigualdad con dos variables (pág. 468) En un plano de coordenadas, el conjunto de puntos que representan todas las soluciones de la desigualdad.

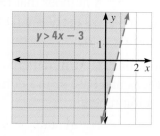

The graph of $y > 4x - 3$ is the shaded half-plane.

La gráfica de $y > 4x - 3$ es el semiplano sombreado.

**graph of a system of linear inequalities in two variables** (p. 474) The graph of all solutions of the system.

**gráfica de un sistema de desigualdades lineales con dos variables** (pág. 474) La gráfica de todas las soluciones del sistema.

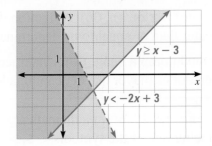

The *graph of the system* $y < -2x + 3$ and $y \geq x - 3$ is the intersection of the half-planes.

La *gráfica del sistema* $y < -2x + 3$ e $y \geq x - 3$ es la intersección de los semiplanos.

---

**grouping symbols** (p. 12) Symbols such as parentheses, brackets, or fraction bars that group parts of an expression.

**signos de agrupación** (pág. 12) Signos tales como paréntesis, corchetes o barras de fracción que agrupan partes de una expresión.

The parentheses in $12 \div (4 - 1)$ are *grouping symbols* that indicate that the subtraction is done first.

Los paréntesis en $12 \div (4 - 1)$ son *signos de agrupación* que indican que la resta se hace primero.

---

# H

**half-plane** (p. 468) In a coordinate plane, the region on either side of a boundary line.

**semiplano** (pág. 468) En un plano de coordenadas, la región situada a cada lado de una recta límite.

*See* graph of an inequality in two variables.

*Véase* gráfica de una desigualdad con dos variables.

---

**hypotenuse** (p. 302) The side of a right triangle that is opposite the right angle.

**hipotenusa** (pág. 302) El lado de un triángulo rectángulo que está opuesto al ángulo recto.

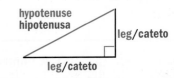

---

# I

**if-then form** (p. 302) A statement with an *if* part and a *then* part. The *if* part contains the hypothesis, and the *then* part contains the conclusion.

**forma "si..., entonces..."** (pág. 302) Enunciado con una parte de *si* y otra de *entonces*. La parte de *si* contiene la hipótesis, y la parte de *entonces* contiene la conclusión.

If $a = -1$, then $|a| = 1$.
The hypothesis is $a = -1$.
The conclusion is $|a| = 1$.

Si $a = -1$, entonces $|a| = 1$.
La hipótesis es $a = -1$.
La conclusión es $|a| = 1$.

| | |
|---|---|
| **improper fraction** (p. 60) A fraction whose numerator is greater than or equal to its denominator. | $\frac{8}{7}$ is an *improper fraction*. |
| **fracción impropia** (pág. 60) Una fracción en la cual el numerador es mayor que el denominador o igual a él. | $\frac{8}{7}$ es una *fracción impropia*. |
| **inequality** (p. 372) A mathematical sentence formed by placing one of the symbols $<$, $\leq$, $>$, or $\geq$ between two expressions. | $6n \geq 24$ and $x - 2 < 7$ are *inequalities*. |
| **desigualdad** (pág. 372) Enunciado matemático formado al colocar uno de los siguientes símbolos entre dos expresiones: $<$, $\leq$, $>$ o $\geq$. | $6n \geq 24$ y $x - 2 < 7$ son *desigualdades*. |
| **integers** (p. 162) The numbers . . . , $-4$, $-3$, $-2$, $-1$, 0, 1, 2, 3, 4, . . . consisting of the negative integers, zero, and the positive integers. | $-8$ and 14 are *integers*.<br>$-8\frac{1}{3}$ and 14.5 are not *integers*. |
| **números enteros** (pág. 162) Los números ..., $-4$, $-3$, $-2$, $-1$, 0, 1, 2, 3, 4, ... que constan de los números enteros negativos, cero y los números enteros positivos. | $-8$ y 14 son *números enteros*.<br>$-8\frac{1}{3}$ y 14.5 no son *números enteros*. |
| **inverse operations** (p. 324) Operations that "undo" each other. | Addition and subtraction are *inverse operations*.<br>Multiplication and division are also *inverse operations*. |
| **operaciones inversas** (pág. 324) Operaciones que se "deshacen" mutuamente. | La suma y la resta son *operaciones inversas*.<br>La multiplicación y la división también son *operaciones inversas*. |
| **irrational number** (p. 294) A number that cannot be written as the quotient of two integers. The decimal form of an irrational number neither terminates nor repeats. | $\sqrt{945} = 30.74085\ldots$ is an *irrational number*.<br>$1.666\ldots$ is *not* an irrational number. |
| **número irracional** (pág. 294) Número que no puede escribirse como cociente de dos números enteros. La forma decimal de un número irracional no termina ni se repite. | $\sqrt{945} = 30.74085\ldots$ es un *número irracional*.<br>$1.666\ldots$ *no* es un *número irracional*. |

**least common denominator (LCD) (p. 54)** The least common multiple of the denominators of two or more fractions.

**mínimo común denominador (m.c.d.) (pág. 54)** El mínimo común múltiplo de los denominadores de dos o más fracciones.

The *LCD* of $\frac{7}{10}$ and $\frac{3}{4}$ is 20, the least common multiple of 10 and 4.

El *m.c.d.* de $\frac{7}{10}$ y $\frac{3}{4}$ es 20, que es el mínimo común múltiplo de 10 y 4.

---

**legs of a right triangle (p. 302)** The two sides of a right triangle that form the right angle.

**catetos de un triángulo rectángulo (pág. 302)** Los dos lados de un triángulo rectángulo que forman el ángulo recto.

*See* hypotenuse.

*Véase* hipotenusa.

---

**like terms (p. 236)** Terms that have identical variable parts with corresponding variables raised to the same power. Constant terms are also like terms.

**términos semejantes (pág. 236)** Términos que tienen partes variables idénticas con variables correspondientes elevadas a la misma potencia. Los términos constantes también son términos semejantes.

In the expression
$$3x + (-4) + (-6x) + 2,$$
$3x$ and $-6x$ are *like terms*, and $-4$ and 2 are *like terms*.

En la expresión
$$3x + (-4) + (-6x) + 2,$$
$3x$ y $-6x$ son *términos semejantes*, y $-4$ y 2 también son *términos semejantes*.

---

**linear equation (p. 414)** An equation whose graph is a line or a part of a line.

**ecuación lineal (pág. 414)** Una ecuación cuya gráfica es una recta o una parte de una recta.

*See* standard form of a linear equation.

*Véase* forma general de una ecuación lineal.

---

**linear inequality in two variables (p. 468)** An inequality that is the result of replacing the equal sign in a linear equation with $<$, $\leq$, $>$, or $\geq$.

**desigualdad lineal con dos variables (pág. 468)** Desigualdad que se obtiene al reemplazar el signo de igualdad de la ecuación lineal por $<$, $\leq$, $>$ o $\geq$.

$x - 3y < 6$ is a *linear inequality in two variables*, $x$ and $y$.

$x - 3y < 6$ es una *desigualdad lineal con dos variables*, $x$ e $y$.

**mean (p. 188)** The sum of the numbers in a set of data divided by the number of items in the set. Also called the *average*.

**media (pág. 188)** La suma de los números en un conjunto de datos dividida por el número de elementos en el conjunto. Llamado también *promedio*.

The *mean* of the data set

$$85, 59, 97, 71$$

is $\frac{85 + 59 + 97 + 71}{4} = \frac{312}{4} = 78$.

**La *media* del conjunto de datos**

$$85, 59, 97, 71$$

es $\frac{85 + 59 + 97 + 71}{4} = \frac{312}{4} = 78$.

---

**mixed number (p. 60)** The sum of a whole number and a proper fraction.

**número mixto (pág. 60)** La suma de un número natural y una fracción propia.

$2\frac{5}{8}$ is a *mixed number*.

$2\frac{5}{8}$ es un *número mixto*.

---

**multiplicative identity (p. 220)** The number 1 is the multiplicative identity, because the product of any number and 1 is the number: $a \cdot 1 = 1 \cdot a = a$.

**identidad de la multiplicación (pág. 220)** El número 1 es la identidad de la multiplicación ya que el producto de cualquier número y 1 es ese número: $a \cdot 1 = 1 \cdot a = a$.

$$3.6(1) = 3.6, \ 1(-7) = -7$$

---

**multiplicative inverse (p. 220)** The multiplicative inverse of a number $\frac{a}{b}$ ($a, b \neq 0$) is the reciprocal of the number, or $\frac{b}{a}$. The product of a number and its multiplicative inverse is 1.

**inverso multiplicativo (pág. 220)** El inverso multiplicativo de un número $\frac{a}{b}$ ($a, b \neq 0$) es el recíproco de dicho número, es decir $\frac{b}{a}$. El producto de un número y su inverso multiplicativo es 1.

The *multiplicative inverse* of $\frac{3}{2}$ is $\frac{2}{3}$, so $\frac{3}{2} \cdot \frac{2}{3} = 1$.

El *inverso multiplicativo* de $\frac{3}{2}$ es $\frac{2}{3}$, por lo tanto $\frac{3}{2} \cdot \frac{2}{3} = 1$.

---

**negative exponent (p. 266)** If $a \neq 0$, then $a^{-n}$ is the reciprocal of $a^n$; $a^{-n} = \frac{1}{a^n}$.

**exponente negativo (pág. 266)** Si $a \neq 0$, entonces $a^{-n}$ es el recíproco de $a^n$; $a^{-n} = \frac{1}{a^n}$.

$$3^{-2} = \frac{1}{3^2} = \frac{1}{9}$$

| | |
|---|---|
| **negative integers** (p. 162) The integers that are less than zero. | The *negative integers* are $-1, -2, -3, -4, \ldots$ . |
| **números enteros negativos** (pág. 162) Números enteros menores que cero. | Los *números enteros negativos* son $-1, -2, -3, -4, \ldots$ . |
| **numerical expression** (p. 12) An expression consisting of numbers, operations, and sometimes grouping symbols. | $4(3) + 24 \div 2$ |
| **expresión numérica** (pág. 12) Una expresión compuesta por números, operaciones y a veces signos de agrupación. | |

## O

| | |
|---|---|
| **opposites** (p. 162) Two numbers that are the same distance from 0 on a number line but are on opposite sides of 0. | 4 units   4 units<br>4 unidades   4 unidades<br><br>$-6 \quad -4 \quad -2 \quad 0 \quad 2 \quad 4 \quad 6$<br><br>4 and $-4$ are *opposites*.<br>4 y $-4$ son *opuestos*. |
| **opuestos** (pág. 162) En una recta numérica, dos números que están a la misma distancia de 0 pero en lados opuestos de 0. | |
| **ordered pair** (p. 408) A pair of numbers $(x, y)$ that can be used to represent a point in a coordinate plane. The first number is the *x*-coordinate, and the second number is the *y*-coordinate. | $(-2, 1)$<br>$-5\ -4\ -3 \quad -2 \quad 1\ 2\ x$ |
| **par ordenado** (pág. 408) Par de números $(x, y)$ que se puede usar para representar un punto en un plano de coordenadas. El primer número es la coordenada *x* y el segundo número es la coordenada *y*. | |
| **order of operations** (p. 12) A set of rules for evaluating an expression involving more than one operation. | To evaluate $3 + 2 \cdot 4$, you perform the multiplication before the addition:<br><br>$3 + 2 \cdot 4 = 3 + 8 = 11$ |
| **orden de las operaciones** (pág. 12) Conjunto de reglas para hallar el valor de una expresión que tiene más de una operación. | Para hallar el valor de $3 + 2 \cdot 4$, haz la multiplicación antes que la suma:<br><br>$3 + 2 \cdot 4 = 3 + 8 = 11$ |

**origin** (p. 408) The point (0, 0) where the *x*-axis and the *y*-axis meet in a coordinate plane.

*See* coordinate plane.

**origen** (pág. 408) El punto (0, 0) donde se encuentran el eje *x* y el eje *y* en un plano de coordenadas.

*Véase* plano de coordenadas.

**P**

**percent** (p. 134) A ratio that compares a number to 100. The symbol for percent is %.

**porcentaje** (pág. 134) Razón que compara un número con 100. El símbolo de porcentaje es %.

$$43\% = \frac{43}{100} = 0.43$$

**perfect square** (p. 288) A number that is the square of an integer.

49 is a *perfect square*, because $49 = 7^2$.

**cuadrado perfecto** (pág. 288) Número que es el cuadrado de un número entero.

49 es un *cuadrado perfecto* ya que $49 = 7^2$.

**positive integers** (p. 162) The integers that are greater than zero.

The *positive integers* are 1, 2, 3, 4, . . . .

**números enteros positivos** (pág. 162) Números enteros mayores que cero.

Los *números enteros positivos* son 1, 2, 3, 4, ....

**power** (p. 6) A product formed from repeated multiplication by the same number. A power consists of a base and an exponent.

$2^4$ is a *power* with base 2 and exponent 4.

**potencia** (pág. 6) Producto que se obtiene de la multiplicación repetida por el mismo número. Una potencia está compuesta de una base y un exponente.

$2^4$ es una *potencia* con base 2 y exponente 4.

**proper fraction** (p. 60) A fraction whose numerator is less than its denominator.

$\frac{7}{8}$ is a *proper fraction*.

**fracción propia** (pág. 60) Una fracción cuyo numerador es menor que su denominador.

$\frac{7}{8}$ es una *fracción propia*.

## Q

**quadrant (p. 408)** One of the four regions that a coordinate plane is divided into by the $x$-axis and the $y$-axis.

**cuadrante (pág. 408)** Una de las cuatro regiones en las que el eje $x$ y el eje $y$ dividen un plano de coordenadas.

*See* coordinate plane.

*Véase* plano de coordenadas.

## R

**rate (p. 26)** A ratio of two quantities measured in different units.

**tasa (pág. 26)** Razón entre dos cantidades medidas en unidades diferentes.

An airplane climbs 18,000 feet in 12 minutes. The airplane's *rate* of climb is $\frac{18,000 \text{ ft}}{12 \text{ min}} = 1500$ ft/min.

Un avión asciende 18,000 pies en 12 minutos. La *tasa* de ascenso del avión es $\frac{18,000 \text{ pies}}{12 \text{ min}} = 1500$ pies/min.

**rational number (p. 204)** A number that can be written as $\frac{a}{b}$ where $a$ and $b$ are integers and $b \neq 0$.

**número racional (pág. 204)** Un número que se puede escribir como $\frac{a}{b}$ donde $a$ y $b$ son números enteros y $b \neq 0$.

$6 = \frac{6}{1}, -\frac{3}{5} = \frac{-3}{5}, 0.75 = \frac{3}{4}$, and $2\frac{1}{3} = \frac{7}{3}$ are all *rational numbers*.

$6 = \frac{6}{1}, -\frac{3}{5} = \frac{-3}{5}, 0.75 = \frac{3}{4}$ y $2\frac{1}{3} = \frac{7}{3}$ son todos *números racionales*.

**real numbers (p. 294)** The set of all rational and irrational numbers.

**números reales (pág. 294)** El conjunto de todos los números racionales e irracionales.

$8, -6.2, \frac{6}{7}, \pi$, and $\sqrt{2}$ are *real numbers*.

$8, -6.2, \frac{6}{7}, \pi$ y $\sqrt{2}$ son *números reales*.

**reciprocals (p. 86)** Two nonzero numbers whose product is 1.

**recíprocos (pág. 86)** Dos números distintos de cero cuyo producto es 1.

$\frac{2}{3}$ and $\frac{3}{2}$ are *reciprocals*.

$\frac{2}{3}$ y $\frac{3}{2}$ son *recíprocos*.

**repeating decimal (p. 128)** A decimal that has one or more digits that repeat without end.

**decimal periódico (pág. 128)** Decimal que tiene uno o más dígitos que se repiten infinitamente.

$0.7777\ldots$ and $1.\overline{29}$ are *repeating decimals*.

$0.7777\ldots$ y $1.\overline{29}$ son *decimales periódicos*.

**right triangle** (p. 302)  A triangle with one right angle.

**triángulo rectángulo** (pág. 302)  Un triángulo que tiene un ángulo recto.

---

## S

**scientific notation** (p. 266)  A number is written in scientific notation if it has the form $c \times 10^n$, where $c$ is greater than or equal to 1 and less than 10, and $n$ is an integer.

**notación científica** (pág. 266)  Un número está escrito en notación científica si tiene la forma $c \times 10^n$ donde $c$ es mayor que o igual a 1 y menor que 10, y $n$ es un número entero.

In *scientific notation*, **328,000** is written as **$3.28 \times 10^5$**, and **0.00061** is written as **$6.1 \times 10^{-4}$**.

En *notación científica*, **328,000** se escribe como **$3.28 \times 10^5$** y **0.00061** se escribe como **$6.1 \times 10^{-4}$**.

---

**simplest form of a fraction** (p. 54)  A fraction is in simplest form if its numerator and denominator have a greatest common factor of 1.

**mínima expresión de una fracción** (pág. 54)  Una fracción está en su mínima expresión si el máximo común divisor del numerador y del denominador es 1.

The *simplest form of the fraction* $\frac{6}{8}$ is $\frac{3}{4}$.

La *mínima expresión de la fracción* $\frac{6}{8}$ es $\frac{3}{4}$.

---

**slope** (p. 434)  The slope of a nonvertical line is the ratio of the rise (vertical change) to the run (horizontal change) between any two points on the line.

**pendiente** (pág. 434)  La pendiente de una recta no vertical es la razón entre la distancia vertical (cambio vertical) y la distancia horizontal (cambio horizontal) entre dos puntos cualesquiera de la recta.

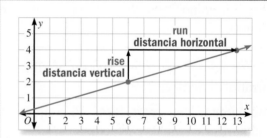

The *slope* of the line above is:

$$\text{slope} = \frac{\text{rise}}{\text{run}} = \frac{2}{7}$$

La *pendiente* de la recta anterior es:

$$\text{pendiente} = \frac{\text{distancia vertical}}{\text{distancia horizontal}} = \frac{2}{7}$$

| | |
|---|---|
| **slope-intercept form of a linear equation** (p. 440) A linear equation written in the form $y = mx + b$ where $m$ is the slope and $b$ is the $y$-intercept of the equation's graph. | $y = 3x + 4$ is in *slope-intercept form*. The slope of the line is 3, and the $y$-intercept is 4. |
| **forma de pendiente e intersección de una ecuación lineal** (pág. 440) Ecuación lineal escrita en la forma $y = mx + b$, donde $m$ es la pendiente y $b$ es la intersección en $y$ de la gráfica de la ecuación. | $y = 3x + 4$ está en la *forma de pendiente e intersección*. La pendiente de la recta es 3, y la intersección en $y$ es 4. |
| **solution of an equation in one variable** (p. 324) A number that produces a true statement when substituted for the variable in an equation. | The number 3 is a *solution of the equation* $8 - 2x = 2$, because $8 - 2(3) = 2$. |
| **solución de una ecuación con una variable** (pág. 324) Número que, al sustituirse por la variable de la ecuación, produce un enunciado verdadero. | El número 3 es una *solución de la ecuación* $8 - 2x = 2$ ya que $8 - 2(3) = 2$. |
| **solution of an equation in two variables** (p. 414) An ordered pair $(x, y)$ that produces a true statement when the values of $x$ and $y$ are substituted into the equation. | $(3, 8)$ is a *solution of the equation* $y = 3x - 1$. |
| **solución de una ecuación con dos variables** (pág. 414) Par ordenado $(x, y)$ que produce un enunciado verdadero cuando se sustituyen los valores de $x$ e $y$ en la ecuación. | $(3, 8)$ es una *solución de la ecuación* $y = 3x - 1$. |
| **solution of an inequality in one variable** (p. 372) A number that produces a true statement when substituted for the variable in an inequality. | The number 3 is a *solution of the inequality* $5 + 3n \le 20$, because $5 + 3(3) = 14$ and $14 \le 20$. |
| **solución de una desigualdad con una variable** (pág. 372) Número que, al sustituirse por la variable de la desigualdad, produce un enunciado verdadero. | El número 3 es una *solución de la desigualdad* $5 + 3n \le 20$ ya que $5 + 3(3) = 14$ y $14 \le 20$. |
| **solution of an inequality in two variables** (p. 468) An ordered pair $(x, y)$ that produces a true statement when the values of $x$ and $y$ are substituted into the inequality. | $(-1, 2)$ is a *solution of the inequality* $x - 3y < 6$ because $-1 - 3(2) = -7$ and $-7 < 6$. |
| **solución de una desigualdad con dos variables** (pág. 468) Par ordenado $(x, y)$ que, al sustituirse los valores de $x$ e $y$ en la desigualdad, produce un enunciado verdadero. | $(-1, 2)$ es una *solución de la desigualdad* $x - 3y < 6$ ya que $-1 - 3(2) = -7$ y $-7 < 6$. |

| | |
|---|---|
| **solution of a system of linear equations in two variables** (p. 472) An ordered pair that is a solution of each equation in the system. | (3, 2) is a *solution of the system of linear equations* $$x + 2y = 7$$ $$3x - 2y = 5$$ because each equation is a true statement when 3 is substituted for $x$ and 2 is substituted for $y$. |
| **solución de un sistema de ecuaciones lineales con dos variables** (pág. 472) Par ordenado que es una solución de cada ecuación del sistema. | (3, 2) es una *solución del sistema de ecuaciones lineales* $$x + 2y = 7$$ $$3x - 2y = 5$$ ya que cada ecuación es un enunciado verdadero cuando $x$ se sustituye por 3 e $y$ se sustituye por 2. |
| **solution of a system of linear inequalities in two variables** (p. 474) An ordered pair that is a solution of each inequality in the system. | (6, −5) is a *solution of the system of linear inequalities* $$x - y > 7$$ $$2x + y < 8$$ because each inequality is a true statement when 6 is substituted for $x$ and −5 is substituted for $y$. |
| **solución de un sistema de desigualdades lineales con dos variables** (pág. 474) Par ordenado que es una solución de cada desigualdad del sistema. | (6, −5) es una *solución del sistema de desigualdades lineales* $$x - y > 7$$ $$2x + y < 8$$ ya que cada desigualdad es un enunciado verdadero cuando $x$ se sustituye por 6 e $y$ se sustituye por −5. |
| **square root** (p. 288) A square root of a real number $a$ is a real number $b$ such that $b^2 = a$. | The *square roots* of 9 are 3 and −3, because $3^2 = 9$ and $(-3)^2 = 9$. So, $\sqrt{9} = 3$ and $-\sqrt{9} = -3$. |
| **raíz cuadrada** (pág. 288) La raíz cuadrada de un número real $a$ es un número real $b$, tal que $b^2 = a$. | Las *raíces cuadradas* de 9 son 3 y −3 ya que $3^2 = 9$ y $(-3)^2 = 9$. Así pues, $\sqrt{9} = 3$ y $-\sqrt{9} = -3$. |

| | |
|---|---|
| **standard form of a linear equation** (p. 414) $Ax + By = C$ where $A$, $B$, and $C$ are real numbers and $A$ and $B$ are not both zero. | The linear equation $y = 2x - 3$ can be written in *standard form* as $2x - y = 3$. |
| **forma general de una ecuación lineal** (pág. 414) $Ax + By = C$ donde $A$, $B$ y $C$ son números reales, y donde $A$ y $B$ no son ambos cero. | La ecuación lineal $y = 2x - 3$ puede escribirse en la *forma general* como $2x - y = 3$. |
| **system of linear equations in two variables** (p. 472) Two or more linear equations in the same variables; also called a *linear system*. | The equations below form a *system of linear equations in two variables*: $$x + 2y = 7$$ $$3x - 2y = 5$$ |
| **sistema de ecuaciones lineales con dos variables** (pág. 472) Dos o más ecuaciones lineales con las mismas variables; llamado también *sistema lineal*. | Las siguientes ecuaciones forman un *sistema de ecuaciones lineales con dos variables*: $$x + 2y = 7$$ $$3x - 2y = 5$$ |
| **system of linear inequalities in two variables** (p. 474) Two or more linear inequalities in the same variables; also called a *system of inequalities*. | The inequalities below form a *system of linear inequalities in two variables*: $$x - y > 7$$ $$2x + y < 8$$ |
| **sistema de desigualdades lineales con dos variables** (pág. 474) Dos o más desigualdades lineales con las mismas variables; llamado también *sistema de desigualdades*. | Las siguientes desigualdades forman un *sistema de desigualdades lineales con dos variables*: $$x - y > 7$$ $$2x + y < 8$$ |

# T

| | |
|---|---|
| **terminating decimal** (p. 128) A decimal that has a final digit. | 0.4 and 3.6125 are *terminating decimals*. |
| **decimal exacto** (pág. 128) Decimal que tiene un dígito final. | 0.4 y 3.6125 son *decimales exactos*. |
| **terms of an expression** (p. 236) The parts of an expression that are added together. | The *terms* of $2x + 3$ are $2x$ and 3. |
| **términos de una expresión** (pág. 236) Las partes de una expresión que se suman entre sí. | Los *términos* de $2x + 3$ son $2x$ y 3. |

**unit analysis (p. 26)** Evaluating expressions with units of measure and checking that your answer uses correct units; also called *dimensional analysis*.

$$\frac{\text{miles}}{\cancel{\text{hour}}} \cdot \cancel{\text{hours}} = \text{miles}$$

**análisis de unidades (pág. 26)** Hallar el valor de expresiones con unidades de medida y comprobar que la respuesta usa unidades correctas; también llamado *análisis de dimensiones*.

$$\frac{\text{millas}}{\cancel{\text{hora}}} \cdot \cancel{\text{horas}} = \text{millas}$$

**unit rate (p. 26)** A rate written as a fraction with a denominator of 1 unit.

$\dfrac{55 \text{ miles}}{1 \text{ hour}}$, or 55 mi/h, is a *unit rate*.

**tasa unitaria (pág. 26)** Tasa escrita en forma de fracción cuyo denominador es 1 unidad.

$\dfrac{55 \text{ millas}}{1 \text{ hora}}$, o 55 mi/h, es una *tasa unitaria*.

**variable (p. 18)** A letter that is used to represent one or more numbers.

In the expressions $5n$, $n + 1$, and $8 - n$, the letter $n$ is the *variable*.

**variable (pág. 18)** Letra que sirve para representar uno o más números.

En las expresiones $5n$, $n + 1$ y $8 - n$, la letra $n$ es la *variable*.

**verbal model (p. 38)** A verbal model describes a real-world situation using words as labels and using math symbols to relate the words.

A *verbal model* and algebraic expression for dividing *a* dollars in a tip jar among 6 people:

**modelo verbal (pág. 38)** Un modelo verbal describe una situación de la vida real mediante palabras que la exponen y símbolos matemáticos que relacionan esas palabras.

Un *modelo verbal* y una expresión algebraica utilizados para dividir entre 6 personas *a* dólares del recipiente de las propinas:

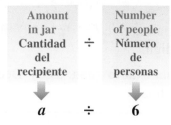

| Amount in jar Cantidad del recipiente | $\div$ | Number of people Número de personas |
|:---:|:---:|:---:|
| $\downarrow$ | | $\downarrow$ |
| $a$ | $\div$ | $6$ |

**x-axis (p. 408)** The horizontal axis in a coordinate plane.

**eje x (pág. 408)** Eje horizontal de un plano de coordenadas.

*See* coordinate plane.

*Véase* plano de coordenadas.

**x-coordinate (p. 408)** The first number in an ordered pair representing a point in a coordinate plane.

**coordenada x (pág. 408)** El primer número en un par ordenado que representa un punto en un plano de coordenadas.

The *x-coordinate* of the ordered pair $(-2, 1)$ is $-2$.

La *coordenada x* del par ordenado $(-2, 1)$ es $-2$.

**x-intercept (p. 428)** The x-coordinate of a point where a graph crosses the x-axis.

**intersección en x (pág. 428)** La coordenada x de un punto donde la gráfica interseca con el eje x.

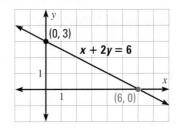

The *x-intercept* is 6.

La *intersección en x* es 6.

**y-axis (p. 408)** The vertical axis in a coordinate plane.

**eje y (pág. 408)** Eje vertical en un plano de coordenadas.

*See* coordinate plane.

*Véase* plano de coordenadas.

**y-coordinate (p. 408)** The second number in an ordered pair representing a point in a coordinate plane.

**coordenada y (pág. 408)** El segundo número de un par ordenado que representa un punto en un plano de coordenadas.

The *y-coordinate* of the ordered pair $(-2, 1)$ is 1.

La *coordenada y* del par ordenado $(-2, 1)$ es 1.

***y*-intercept** (p. 428) The *y*-coordinate of a point where a graph crosses the *y*-axis.

**intersección en *y*** (pág. 428) La coordenada *y* de un punto donde la gráfica interseca con el eje *y*.

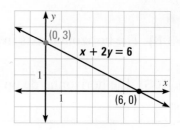

The *y-intercept* is 3.

La *intersección en y* es 3.

## Z

**zero exponent** (p. 266) If $a \neq 0$, then $a^0 = 1$.

**exponente cero** (pág. 266) Si $a \neq 0$, entonces $a^0 = 1$.

$$(-7)^0 = 1$$

# Index

## A

**Absolute value,** 160, 162-165, 178, 195
  integer addition and, 169-171, 196
  integer division and, 187
  rational number addition and, 210-213, 244
**Act it out,** problem solving strategy, 496-497
**Activities,** *See also* Games
  algebra
    direct variation, 444-445
    equations with fractions and decimals, 342-343
    equations involving addition and subtraction, 322-323
    equations involving multiplication, 328-329
    evaluating expressions, 30
    expressions involving exponents, 270-271
    inequalities involving addition and subtraction, 376-377
    inequalities involving multiplication and division, 384-385
    multi-step equations, 348-349
    rate problems, 354-355
    simple inequalities, 370-371
    two-step equations, 334-335
    two-step inequalities, 390-391
    writing direct variation equations, 450-451
    writing expressions, 31
  graphing
    equations using intercepts, 426-427
    equations in two variables, 412-413
    horizontal and vertical lines, 418-419
    modeling slope, 432-433
    points in a coordinate plane, 406-407
    using slope and *y*-intercept, 438-439
  measurement
    area, 17
    converse of the Pythagorean theorem, 306-307
    perimeter, 16
    Pythagorean triples, 307
    relationship of sides and hypotenuse of a right triangle, 300-301
    unit conversion, 24-25

  number sense
    comparing integers, 160-161
    distributive property, 234-235
    equivalent fractions, 52-53
    evaluating powers, 4-5
    fractions and decimals, 126-127
    mixed numbers and improper fractions, 58-59
    ordering numbers on a number line, 202-203
    percent of a number, 144-145
    percents, decimals, and fractions, 132-133, 138-139
    products of powers, 250-251
    quotients of powers, 256-257
    reciprocals, 84-85
    square root, 286-287
    zero and negative exponents, 264-265
  operations
    decimal addition, 106-107
    decimal division, 118-119
    decimal multiplication, 112-113
    decimal subtraction, 107
    fraction addition, 64, 72
    fraction division, 90-91
    fraction multiplication, 78-79
    fraction subtraction, 65, 73
    integer addition, 166-167
    integer division, 186-187
    integer multiplication, 180-181
    integer subtraction, 172-173
    order of, 10-11
    rational number addition, 208-209
    rational number multiplication and division, 222-223
  problem solving, using strategies, 36-37
  properties
    of addition, 214-215
    of multiplication, 228-229
**Addition**
  decimal, 106-111, 124, 153
    estimating sums, 109-111
  equations, 322-327, 340, 363
  fraction
    different denominators, 72, 74, 76-77, 100
    same denominator, 64, 66-69, 70, 100
  integer, 166-171, 178, 196
    using absolute value, 169-171, 196

  as inverse of subtraction, 173
  mixed number, 64, 67-69, 70, 74, 76-77, 100
  order of operations and, 10-15, 45
  properties, 214-219, 220, 324-327, 378-381
  rational number, 208-213, 220, 244
    rule of signs for, 210
  repeated, 180
  for solving inequalities, 376-381, 400
  sum, 480
  whole number, 480
  words indicating, 32
**Addition property of equality,** 324
**Addition property of inequality,** 378
**Additive identity,** 216
**Additive inverse,** 216
**Algebraic expression(s),** *See also* Numerical expression(s), 32
  coefficients and, 236
  decimal, 108, 110-111, 123
  evaluating, 30, 32-35, 47
    using addition properties, 217, 218, 219
    using the distributive property, 237-239
    using multiplication properties, 231-233
  exponential, 250-261, 262, 264-276, 279-281
  formulas and, 18-21, 46
  integer, 174, 176-177, 183-185, 190-191
  for properties
    addition, 214-216
    multiplication, 228-230
  rational number, 80, 82, 92, 95, 206, 207, 211, 212, 213, 225, 226, 227, 231, 232, 233, 244, 245
  simplest form, 348-353
  square root, 289-291, 316, 317
  variables and, 18
  writing, 31, 33-35, 47, 96, 97, 234, 235, 240
**Algebra tiles**
  for modeling integer addition, 166
  for modeling integer subtraction, 172
  for solving addition and subtraction equations, 322-323
  for solving multiplication equations, 328-329

for solving multi-step equations, 348-349

for solving two-step equations, 334-335

***Always, sometimes, never* questions,** 83, 171, 177, 190

**Angle(s)**

Pythagorean theorem and, 300-305, 316

right triangles and, 300, 302

**Annual interest rate,** 146

**Applications**

art, 77

astronomy, 259, 277, 283

baseball, 55, 142, 233, 290, 291, 483

basketball, 15, 33, 435

bicycling, 49, 367

botany, 277

bowling, 102, 238

business, 56, 183, 206, 219, 227, 345, 347, 394, 396, 397, 416, 425, 437, 441, 457, 466, 473

camping, 225, 311, 345, 443, 497

chemistry, 27, 28, 46, 226, 267, 268, 269, 275

competitions, 34, 387, 497

computers and internet, 8, 9, 20, 217, 260, 261, 283, 296

construction, 46, 241, 305, 310, 311, 313, 338, 422, 423, 463, 496

consumer economics, 13, 14, 19, 20, 21, 23, 40, 212, 213, 395, 397, 402, 467

crafts, 15, 310

design, 93

diving, 165, 177

domestic animals, 68, 69, 497

earth science, 175, 176, 183, 212, 226, 253, 254, 255, 273, 457

education, 380

employment, 15, 27, 28, 29, 40, 57, 69, 88, 89, 116, 122, 137, 219, 331, 333, 338, 388, 389

entertainment, 13, 14, 41, 148, 374, 375, 442, 447, 455, 462, 475

exercise, 326, 403, 431

farming, 77, 397, 422

finance, 137, 147, 151, 179, 190, 199, 206, 207, 226, 247

fishing, 67, 170

food preparation, 61, 62, 63, 68, 69, 80

football, 41, 169, 185, 218, 232, 429, 454

fundraising, 29, 40, 41, 395, 416

games, 7, 193

gardening, 21, 76, 94, 123, 289, 296, 299, 331, 410, 411, 421, 425, 443

golf, 137, 191, 448

hiking, 68, 184, 351, 365, 454

history, 254, 255, 278, 374

hockey, 63, 497

home decor, 8, 232, 240, 290, 291, 296, 299, 303, 421

maps, 131, 406, 409, 410, 411

measurement, 8, 9, 40, 41, 49, 56, 67, 82, 93, 94, 95, 102, 110, 111, 115, 116, 117, 129, 157, 163, 177, 185, 241, 255, 263, 268, 273, 274, 295, 296, 297, 305, 313, 325, 327, 331, 352, 353, 425, 449, 497

money management, 35, 122, 123, 125, 151, 157, 170, 184, 206, 207, 239, 326, 327, 341, 345, 346, 347, 361, 381, 383, 387, 388, 389, 393, 403, 415, 416, 417, 427, 429, 430, 442, 475

monuments, 21

music, 57, 75, 397, 441

physics, 275

physiology, 77, 352, 380, 402, 435, 450

population, 95, 254

recreation, 211, 212, 227

running, 19, 28, 41, 109, 171, 360, 381

school activities, 7, 22, 55, 175, 394, 453, 471, 483, 494

shopping, 110, 111, 116, 117, 147, 148, 149, 151, 156, 157, 325, 332, 338, 339, 467, 470

soccer, 18

structures, 130, 131, 241, 290, 433, 434

surveys, 81, 83, 135, 136, 141, 142, 143, 157, 332, 494, 495

swimming, 354, 355, 397, 435, 471

telephone, 76, 261

temperature, 189, 190, 193, 198, 199, 205, 211, 212, 213, 225, 246, 247, 375, 403

track and field, 63, 68, 130

travel, 20, 23, 26, 28, 38, 41, 47, 57, 87, 88, 89, 97, 103, 109, 117, 121, 327, 332, 352, 353, 356, 357, 358, 359, 365, 366, 367, 373, 379, 380, 381, 383, 402, 447

vehicles, 189, 190, 199, 310

volleyball, 33, 121

volunteer work, 217

weather, 383

wild animals, 19, 20, 76, 82, 231

winter sports, 13, 170, 191

**Approximation,** *See also* Estimation

area of a circle, 491

circumference of a circle, 490-491

length of a hypotenuse, 303-305

measurement conversions, 487

of pi, 490

rounding and, 479

of square root, 292-297, 315, 316

for writing a fraction as a percent, 139

**Area,** *See also* Surface area, 488

of a circle, 297

of a compound figure, 41, 43

of a parallelogram, 488-489

of a rectangle, 17, 18-21, 488-489

effect of changing dimensions, 240

of a square, 18-21, 488-489

effect of changing dimensions, 277, 286

of a trapezoid, 488-489

of a triangle, 488-489

**Area model**

for showing adding fractions, 64, 72

for showing adding mixed numbers, 64

for showing decimals, 138

for showing the distributive property, 235-236, 238-239

for showing equivalent fractions, 52-53

for showing fractions, 139

for showing mixed numbers and improper fractions, 58-59

for showing multiplying fractions, 78

for showing multiplying mixed numbers, 79

for showing percent, 132, 138-139

for showing reciprocals, 84-85

for showing relationship between legs and hypotenuse of a right triangle, 300-301

for showing square root, 286, 292

for showing subtracting fractions, 64, 73

for showing subtracting mixed numbers, 65

**Assessment,** *See also* Readiness; Reviews

Chapter Test, 48, 102, 156, 198, 246, 282, 318, 366, 402, 462

Mid-Chapter Test, 23, 71, 125, 179, 221, 263, 299, 341, 383, 425

Multiple Choice Chapter Test, 49, 103, 157, 199, 247, 283, 319, 367, 403, 463

Pre-Course Test, xxi-xxiii

prerequisite skills check, 3, 51, 105, 159, 201, 249, 285, 321, 369, 405

**Associative property**

of addition, 216-219

of multiplication, 230-233

**@Home Tutor,** *Throughout. See for example* 9, 15, 21, 29, 35, 41, 45, 47, 57, 63, 69, 77, 83

**Average,** *See also* Mean, 188, 197

**Average rate of change,** 188-191

**Bar graph,** 494
  reading, 494
**Bar notation,** for repeating decimals, 128
**Base(s)**
  of a power, 4, 6
  of a right circular cylinder, 492
  of a right rectangular prism, 492
**Base-ten pieces**
  for modeling decimal addition, 106-107
  for modeling decimal division, 118-119
  for modeling decimal multiplication, 112-113
  for modeling decimal subtraction, 107
**Boundary line,** of a linear inequality, 468
**Break into parts,** problem solving strategy, 150, 240, 496-497

**Change,** 175-177, 211-213
  average rate of, 188-191, 225-227
**Changing dimensions**
  effect of changing dimensions
    area and perimeter, 240
    circumference and area of a circle, 241
    radius and area of a circle, 277
    side length and area of a square, 277, 286
  side lengths of inscribed squares, 312
**Chapter problem,** *See* Problem Solving and Reasoning
**Chapter review,** 45-47, 99-101, 153-155, 195-197, 243-245, 279-281, 315-317, 363-365, 399-401, 459-461
  game, 44, 98, 152, 194, 242, 278, 314, 362, 398, 458
**Chapter Test,** *See* Assessment
**Checking reasonableness,** 150
  using estimation, 42, 80-81, 82, 83, 114, 116, 117, 125, 193, 231, 456
  using mental math, 231, 360
**Checking solutions**
  using inverse operations, 47, 120-123, 187, 480
  using operations, 86, 91, 192
  using substitution, 322, 323, 325-330, 334-335, 340, 342, 350, 363, 378, 386-387, 392, 396, 412, 418, 419, 420, 468, 472-474
**Chord,** of a circle, 43
**Circle,** 490
  area of, 297, 491
  chord of, 43

circumference of, 490-491
  diameter of, 490
  effect of changing dimensions, 241
  radius of, 490
**Circle graph,** 495
  exercises, 142, 143, 151, 157
  percent and, 135-137
  reading, 495
**Circumference,** of a circle, 490-491
**Classifying**
  real numbers, 296
  terminating and repeating decimals, 128, 130, 131
**Coefficient,** 236
**Common factor,** 485
**Common multiple,** 485
**Communication,** *See also* Writing
  describing in words, *Throughout. See for example* 15, 20, 21, 34, 41, 43, 57, 63, 76, 77, 82
**Commutative property**
  of addition, 216-219
  of multiplication, 230-233
**Comparing**
  decimals, 478
  exponents, 250, 256, 264
  fractions, 54, 56-57, 61-63
  integer products, 183-185
  integers, 160-162, 164, 165, 178, 195
  numbers in scientific notation, 267-269
  using ratio, 483
  rational numbers, 204-207, 220, 243
  ratios, 445
  whole numbers, 477
**Composite number,** 484-485
**Conclusion,** *See also* Draw conclusions, 302
  if-then statements and, 302, 304, 305, 316
**Conjecture**
  justifying, 96, 97, 240, 457
  making, 96, 97, 193, 240, 300, 457
**Constant term,** 236
**Constant of variation,** 452
  direct variation equations and, 452-455
**Converse**
  of the Pythagorean theorem, 306-311, 317
  of a statement, 308, 310, 311, 317
**Conversion,** *See also* Unit analysis
  between fractions and decimals, 126-131
  between improper fractions and mixed numbers, 58-63, 70, 99
  between percents and decimals, 133, 135-137
  between percents and fractions, 133-137

factors
  for customary and metric units, 231, 233, 487
  for customary units, 24-25, 232, 233, 486
  for metric units, 232, 233, 486
**Coordinate plane,** 408
  describing paths in, 406-407
  distance in, 406-407, 409-411, 421-423
  graphing inequalities in, 468-471, 474-475
  graphs of horizontal lines in, 419-423, 424
  graphs of linear equations in, 412-423, 424, 426-451, 459-461
  graphs of vertical lines in, 418, 420-423, 424
  half-plane, 468
  ordered pair, 408
  origin, 408
  plotting points in, 406-411, 459
  quadrants, 408
  $x$-axis, 408
  $x$-coordinate, 408
  $y$-axis, 408
  $y$-coordinate, 408
**Critical thinking,** *See* Reasoning
**Cube,** 492
  surface area of, 276, 492-493
  volume of, 276, 492-493
**Customary units,** *See also* Area; Perimeter; Surface area; Volume
  converting among, 24-25, 486
  converting to metric units, 487
  length, 24-25
**Cylinder,** *See* Right circular cylinder

**Data,** 494
  analyzing
    mean, 188-191, 197
    relevant and irrelevant information, 36-37
    sequencing and prioritizing information, 36-37
    using unit analysis, 26-29, 46, 87
  displaying
    in a bar graph, 494
    in a circle graph, 495
  organizing
    in a diagram, 38, 97, 169, 286, 312, 354-355, 496-497
    in a table, 214, 215, 222, 228, 229, 240, 286, 287, 376, 377, 390, 438, 484
    in a tree diagram, 484
    in a Venn diagram, 296

paired, 446

**Decimal(s),** *See also* Rational number(s), 476

   adding, 106-111, 124, 153

   clearing to solve equations, 343-347

   comparing, 478

   dividing, 118-123, 124, 154

   equations with, 343-347, 364

   estimating sums and differences, 109-111

   expanded form, 476

   fractions and, 126-131, 154

   multiplying, 112-117, 124, 153

   ordering, 478

   percents and, 133, 135-137, 138, 140-143, 154-155

   place value, 476

   repeating, 128

   rounding, 479

   standard form, 476

   subtracting, 107-111, 124, 153

   terminating, 128

   written as powers of ten, 266-269

**Denominator,** 483

**Density,** unit analysis and, 27-29, 46

**Diagrams,** *See also* Area model; Number line

   drawing to solve a problem, 97, 286, 312, 354-355, 496-497

   for modeling integer addition, 169

   organizing data in, 38

   tree, 484

   Venn, 296

**Diameter,** of a circle, 490

**Difference,** 480

**Digit,** 476

**Dimensional analysis,** *See* Unit analysis

**Direct variation,** 452, 461

   equations, 450-455, 461

     writing, 452-455

   experiment, 444-445

   graphing, 445-449, 461

**Discount,** percent and, 147-149

**Discrete mathematics**

   composite numbers, 484-485

   greatest common divisor, 485

   greatest common factor (GCF), 485

   least common denominator (LCD), 54

   least common multiple (LCM), 485

   prime factorization, 484-485

   prime numbers, 484-485

   tree diagram, 484

**Distance,** *See also* Rate

   in a coordinate plane, 406-407, 409-411, 421-423

   formula, 18-21, 351, 356-359, 365

   rate and, 18-21, 38-39, 46

**Distributive property,** 236, 245

   modeling, 234-235

   for solving equations, 350-353, 365

**Dividend,** 482

**Division**

   decimal, 118-123, 124, 154

   dividend, 482

   divisor, 482

   equations, 330-333, 340, 363

   for finding equivalent fractions, 53-57

   with fractions, 90-95, 101

   integer, 186-191, 197

   as inverse of multiplication, 186

   mixed number, 93-95, 101

   order of operations and, 10-15, 45

   of powers with the same base, 256-261, 262, 279

   properties, 330-333, 386-389

   quotient, 482

   quotient of powers, 256-261, 262, 271-275, 279

   rational number, 222-227, 245

   ratios and, 483

   with remainders, 482

   for solving inequalities, 384-389, 401

   whole number, 482

   words indicating, 32

**Division property of equality,** 330-333

**Division property of inequality,** 386-389

**Division rule**

   for dividing by a fraction, 90, 91, 92

   for dividing rational numbers, 224-227

   proving, 91

**Divisor,** 482

**Draw conclusions,** exercises, *Throughout. See for example* 4, 5, 11, 16, 17, 24, 25, 30, 31, 37, 53, 58, 59

**Draw a diagram,** problem solving strategy, 312, 496-497

**E**

**Equality**

   addition property of, 324-327

   division property of, 330-333

   multiplication property of, 330-333

   subtraction property of, 324-327

**Equation(s),** *See also* Formula(s); Linear equation(s), 322, 324

   addition, 322-327, 340, 363

   with decimals, 343-347, 364

   division, 330-333, 340, 363

   equivalent, 324, 330

   with fractions, 342-347, 364

   multiplication, 328-333, 340, 363

   multi-step, 348-353

   in one variable, 322-339, 342-353

   rate, 354-359, 365

   solution of, 322, 324

   solving

     using the distributive property, 350-353

     using properties of equality, 324-327, 330-333

   subtraction, 323, 325-327, 340, 363

   systems of, 472-473

   two-step, 334-339, 340, 364

   in two variables, 412-423, 426-457, 466-467

     solution of, 412, 414

   verbal sentences for, 324-327, 331-333, 337-339, 365, 466-467, 473

   writing, 325-327, 331-333, 337-339, 345-347, 351-353, 466-467, 472-473

**Equivalent equations,** 324

**Equivalent fractions,** 52-57

**Equivalent inequalities,** 376-381

**Equivalent ratios,** 483

**Error analysis,** *Throughout. See for example* 15, 29, 34, 41, 63, 82, 88, 94, 110, 116, 136, 170, 171

**Estimation,** *See also* Approximation

   for checking reasonableness, 42, 80-81, 82, 83, 114, 116, 117, 125, 193, 231

   decimal products, 114, 116, 117, 153

   decimal sums and differences, 109-111

   from a graph, 360, 361, 451, 456

   percent of a number, 145-149

   point of intersection in a linear system, 472-473

   techniques

     using a model, 145

     rounding, 109-111, 114, 116, 117

**Expanded form,** 476

   powers and, 4-9

   using powers of ten, 266-269

**Experiment,** direct variation, 444-445

**Exponent(s),** *See also* Powers, 4, 6

   adding to multiply powers, 250-255, 262, 270-275, 279

   evaluating expressions involving, 6-9, 22, 45, 81-83, 250-261, 264-276

   negative, 264-269, 280

   order of operations and, 10-15, 22, 45

   properties of, 250-261, 270-275, 279-281

   scientific notation and, 266-269, 280

   subtracting to divide powers, 256-261, 262, 271-275, 279

   zero as, 264-269, 280

**Expression(s),** *See* Algebraic expression(s); Numerical expression(s)

**F**

**Factor(s), 481**
  common, 485
  conversion, 24-25, 231-233, 486, 487
  greatest common, 485
  prime, 484-485
**Factor tree, 484**
**Formula(s), 18, 46**
  area
    of a circle, 277, 297, 490
    of a parallelogram, 488
    of a rectangle, 18, 115, 488
    of a square, 18, 289, 488
    of a trapezoid, 488
    of a triangle, 488
  circumference, of a circle, 490
  distance, 18, 46, 356
  interest, simple, 146, 147
  mass, 27
  perimeter
    of a rectangle, 18, 488
    of a square, 18, 488
    of a triangle, 18, 488
  rate, 354, 356
  slope, 432, 434
  surface area
    of a cube, 276, 492
    of a right circular cylinder, 492
    of a right rectangular prism, 492
  table of, 508
    geometric, 509
  temperature, Celsius/Fahrenheit, 193
  total cost, 18
  volume
    of a cube, 276, 492
    of a right circular cylinder, 492
    of a right rectangular prism, 232, 492
**Fraction(s),** *See also* Rational number(s), 483
  adding
    with different denominators, 72, 74, 76-77, 100
    with same denominator, 64, 66-69, 70, 100
  comparing, 54, 56-57
  decimals and, 126-131, 154
  denominator, 483
  dividing, 90-95, 101
  equations with, 342-347, 364
  equivalent, 52-57
  improper, 58-63, 70, 99
  mixed numbers and, 58-63, 70, 99
  multiplying, 78-83, 101
  numerator, 483
  percent and, 133-137, 139-143, 154-155

  proper, 60
  raised to a power, 81-83
  ratios and, 483
  reciprocals and, 84-89, 101
  simplest form, 54-57, 70, 99
  subtracting
    with different denominators, 73, 75-77, 100
    with same denominator, 65-69, 70, 100
  unit rate and, 26-29

**G**

**Games,** *See also* Activities
  algebra
    equations, 362
    inequalities, 398
  fractions, 98
    decimals, and percents, 152
  graphing
    linear equations, 458
    locating points in a coordinate plane, 407
  measurement
    area and perimeter, 44
    unit conversion, 25
  number sense
    comparing integers, 161
    exponential expressions, 278
    properties of rational numbers, 242
    squares and square roots, 314
  operations
    with exponents, 251, 257
    integer, 194
    with rational numbers, 222-223, 242
**Generalize results, 180, 312**
**Geometric formulas,** table of, 509
**Geometry,** *See* Geometric formulas; Measurement
**Graphs**
  bar, 494
  circle, 495
    exercises, 142, 143, 151, 157
    percent and, 135-137
  of direct variation, 445-449, 461
  double bar, 34
  of an equation in two variables, 415
  of horizontal lines, 419, 421-423, 460
  of inequalities
    in one variable, 372-375, 378-381, 382, 386-389, 392-396
    systems of, 474-475
    in two variables, 468-471
  of linear equations
    direct variation, 445-449, 461
    using intercepts, 426-431, 460

  using ordered pairs, 360-361, 412-413, 415-417, 420-423, 424, 459
  using slope-intercept form, 439-443, 461
  systems of, 472-473
  in two variables, 412-417, 420-423, 459-461, 466-467
  predicting from, 360, 361
  scatter plot, 448, 449
  of vertical lines, 418, 420-423, 460
**Greatest common divisor, 485**
**Greatest common factor (GCF), 485**
  for simplifying fractions, 55-57
**Grouping property,** *See* Associative property
**Grouping symbol(s), 12**
  order of operations and, 10-15, 22, 45
**Guess, check, and revise,** problem solving strategy, 496-497

**H**

**Half-plane, 468**
  boundary line of, 468
**Horizontal line(s), 420**
  equations for, 420-423, 460
  graph of, 421-423, 460
    modeling, 419
**Hypotenuse, 300, 302**
  approximating length of, 303-305
  Pythagorean theorem and, 302-303
  relationship to legs in a right triangle, 300-301
**Hypothesis, 302**
  if-then statements and, 302, 304, 305, 316

**I**

**Identity property**
  of addition, 216
  of multiplication, 230
**If-then statement, 302, 304, 305, 316**
  converse of, 308
**Improper fraction(s), 58, 60**
  mixed numbers and, 58-63, 70, 99
**Indirect measurement, 304, 305**
**Inequality (Inequalities), 370, 372**
  addition and subtraction, 376-381, 382, 400
  equivalent, 376-381, 382
  graphing
    in a coordinate plane, 468-471, 474-475
    on a number line, 372-375, 378-381, 382, 386-389, 392-397, 399-401
  multiplication and division, 384-389, 401

in one variable, 370-375, 378-381, 382, 384-395, 399-401
properties of, 378-381, 382, 386-389
solution of, 372
systems of, 474-475
two-step, 390-395, 401
in two variables, 468-471, 474-475
verbal sentences for, 386-389, 393-395, 470-471, 474-475
writing, 371-375, 379-381, 387-389, 393-395, 399-401

**Inference,** *See* Draw conclusions

**Integer(s),** *See also* Rational number(s), 162
adding, 166-171, 178, 196
using absolute value, 169-171, 196
comparing, 160-161, 164, 165, 178, 195
dividing, 186-191, 197
multiplying, 180-185, 197
negative, 162
ordering, 162, 164, 165, 178, 195
positive, 162
rational numbers and, 202-207
subtracting, 172-177, 178, 196
by adding the opposite, 173-177, 196

**Intercept(s),** 426, 428, 460
finding, 428-431, 460
for graphing linear equations, 428-431, 460

**Interest,** simple, 146-149

**Inverse operations,** 324
addition and subtraction, 173
multiplication and division, 186
for solving equations, 324-327, 330-333 336-339

**Inverse property**
of addition, 216
of multiplication, 230

**Irrational number,** 294

**Irrelevant information,** identifying, 36-37

**Justify,** *See also* Reasoning
a conjecture, 96, 97, 457
steps, 217, 218, 219, 231, 232, 233, 240, 241, 244, 245

**Lattice,** using to solve a problem, 426

**Least common denominator (LCD),** 54
for adding fractions, 74, 76-77, 100
for comparing fractions, 54, 56-57
for solving equations, 344-347
for subtracting fractions, 75-77, 100

**Least common multiple (LCM),** 485

**Legs,** of a right triangle, 300, 302
Pythagorean theorem and, 302-303
relationship to hypotenuse, 300-301

**Length,** *See also* Measurement
converting customary units of, 24-25
in a coordinate plane, 409-411

**Like terms,** 236
combining
using the distributive property, 237-239
to solve equations, 348-353

**Linear equation(s),** *See also* Equation(s), 414
direct variation, 450-455, 461
of the form $x = a$, 420-423, 424, 460
of the form $y = b$, 421-423, 424, 460
graphing
using intercepts, 426-431, 460
using ordered pairs, 360-361, 412-413, 415-417, 420-423, 424, 459
using slope-intercept form, 439-443, 461
horizontal lines and, 420-423, 424, 460
slope and, 432-443, 460, 461
solutions of, 412, 414
standard form, 412-417, 424, 459
systems of, 472-473
vertical lines and, 420-423, 424, 460
writing, 450-455, 466-467
$y$-intercept and, 438-443

**Linear function(s),** *See* Linear equation(s)

**Linear graph(s)**
drawing to solve problems, 360-361
predicting from, 360, 361

**Linear inequality,** in two variables, *See also* Linear system, 468-471

**Linear system,** 472-473
graphing, 472-473
solution of, 472

**Line slope,** *See* Slope

**Logical reasoning,** *See* Error analysis; Games; Number sense; Reasoning

**Look for a pattern,** problem solving strategy, 96, 240, 286, 496-497

**Magic squares,** 192, 193

**Make a list,** problem solving strategy, 496-497

**Make a table,** problem solving strategy, 150, 240, 250, 256, 376, 377, 390, 391, 496-497

**Manipulatives**
algebra tiles, 166, 172, 322-323, 328-329, 334-335, 348-349

base-ten pieces, 106-107, 112-113, 118-119
index cards, 10-11, 161, 194, 202-203, 222, 257, 370, 384, 398
number cube, 25, 30, 44, 251
real-world objects, 202-203, 412-413, 418-419, 432-433, 444-445
ruler, 90, 208-209, 432-433, 444-445, 450-451
straightedge, 426-427

**Mass,** density and, 27-29, 46

**Mathematical reasoning,** *See* Reasoning

**Mean,** 188-191, 197, 450

**Measurement**
area, 17-21, 41, 43, 240, 297, 488-489
of a circle, 297
of a compound figure, 41, 43
of a parallelogram, 488-489
of a rectangle, 17-21, 488-489
of a trapezoid, 488-489
of a triangle, 488-489
circumference, 490-491
converting units, 24-29
between metric and customary systems, 487
within systems, 486
indirect, using the Pythagorean theorem, 304, 305
length, customary units, 24-25
mass and density, 27-29, 46
perimeter
of a rectangle, 16, 18-21, 488-489
of a square, 18-21, 488-489
of a triangle, 488-489
surface area, 276, 492-493
volume, 276, 492-493

**Measures,** table of, 512

**Mental math,** addition properties and, 217, 218, 219

**Metric units,** *See also* Area; Perimeter; Surface area; Volume
converting among, 486
converting to customary units, 487

**Mid-Chapter Test,** *See* Assessment

**Missing information,** identifying, 36-37, 42

**Mixed number(s),** *See also* Rational number(s), 58, 60
adding, 64, 67-69, 70, 74, 76-77, 100
comparing, 61-63
division with, 93-95, 101
improper fractions and, 58-63, 70, 99
multiplying, 79, 81-83, 101
ordering, 61-63
reciprocals of, 87-89
subtracting, 65, 67-69, 70, 75-77, 100

**Modeling,** *See also* Algebra tiles; Graphs; Number line

addition
    decimal, 106-107
    fraction, 64, 72
    integer, 166-171
    mixed number, 64
    rational number, 208-209
decimals, 138
direct variation, 444-445, 450-451, 453
the distributive property, 234-235
division
    decimal, 118-119
    by a fraction, 90-91
equations
    addition, 322-323
    multiplication, 328-329
    multi-step, 348-349
    rate, 354-355
    subtraction, 323
    two-step, 334-335
fractions, 139
    equivalent, 52-53
    mixed numbers and, 58-59
graphs
    of equations in two variables, 412-413
    of horizontal and vertical lines, 418-419
multiplication
    decimal, 112-113
    fraction, 78
    mixed number, 79
percent, 132, 138
    of a number, 144-145
powers of two, 5
rational numbers, 202-203
reciprocals, 84-85
relationship between legs and hypotenuse of a right triangle, 300-301
slope, 432-433
square root, 286, 292
subtraction
    decimal, 107
    fraction, 65, 72
    integer, 172-173
    mixed number, 65
**Models,** *See* Area model; Base-ten pieces; Number line; Verbal model
**Money**
    discount, 147-149
    simple interest, 146-149
**Multiple(s),** 485
    common, 485
    least common, 485
**Multiple choice chapter test,** *see* Assessment
**Multiple representations,** *See also* Manipulatives; Modeling

*Throughout. See for example* 52-53, 58-59, 64-65, 78-79, 80, 92, 126-127, 135, 138-139, 144-145, 166-168, 172-173
**Multiplication**
    checking, 114, 116, 117
    decimal, 112-117, 124, 153
    equations, 328-333, 340, 363
    factors, 481
    to find equivalent fractions, 53-54, 56-57
    with fractions, 78-83, 101
    integer, 180-185, 197
    as inverse of division, 186
    with mixed numbers, 79, 81-83, 101
    order of operations and, 10-15, 45
    of powers with the same base, 250-255, 262, 279
    by powers of ten, 481
    product, 481
    product of powers, 250-255, 262, 270-275, 279
    properties, 228-233, 245, 330-333, 386-389
    rational number, 222-227, 245
    repeated, powers and, 4-9, 45
    repeated addition and, 180
    for solving inequalities, 384-389, 401
    whole number, 481
    words indicating, 32
**Multiplication property of equality,** 330
**Multiplication property of inequality,** 386
**Multiplicative identity,** 230
**Multiplicative inverse,** *see also* Reciprocals, 230
**Multi-step equation(s),** 348-353
**Multi-step problems**
    examples, *Throughout. See for example* 26-27, 38-39, 61, 96, 109, 150
    exercises, *Throughout. See for example* 28, 39, 40, 41, 42, 43, 62, 63

N

**Negative exponent,** 264-269, 280
**Negative integer,** *See also* Integer(s), 162
**Negative number,** *See also* Integer(s); Rational number(s), 160
**Negative slope,** 434-437
**Negative square root,** 287-288, 298
**Number(s),** *See also* Decimal(s); Fraction(s); Integer(s); Mixed number(s); Percent; Properties
    absolute value of, 160, 162-165, 178, 195
    classifying, 296
    composite, 484-485

expanded form, 476
factors of, 481
greatest common factor of, 485
irrational, 294
least common multiple of, 485
negative, 160, 162
opposites, 162-165, 178, 195
perfect square, 288
pi, 490
positive, 160
prime, 484-485
prime factorization of, 484-485
rational, 204, 243
real, 294-297
reciprocals, 84-89, 101
relationships among, 296
repeating decimals, 128-131
in scientific notation, 266-269, 280
terminating decimals, 128-131
**Number line,** 477
    for adding integers, 167-171
    for comparing integers, 160, 162, 164, 195
    for comparing and ordering decimals, 478
    for comparing and ordering whole numbers, 477
    for graphing inequalities, 372-375, 378-381, 382, 386-389, 392-397, 399-401
    for identifying and ordering rational numbers, 202-203, 204, 205, 243
    for ordering real numbers, 295
    for rounding decimals, 479
    for rounding whole numbers, 479
    for subtracting integers, 173
**Number sense,** *See also* Approximation; Comparing; Estimation; Ordering; Property; Reasoning
    absolute value, 160, 162-165, 178
    additive identity, 216
    additive inverse, 216
    common factor, 485
    common multiple, 485
    composite number, 484-485
    expanded form, 476
    greatest common factor, 485
    irrational number, 294
    least common multiple, 485
    multiple, 485
    multiplicative identity, 230
    multiplicative inverse, 230
    opposites, 162-165, 178
    perfect square, 288
    place value, 476
    prime factorization, 484-485
    prime number, 484-485
    real number, 294

rounding, 121-123, 141-143, 479
scientific notation, 266-269, 280
square root, 286-291, 292-297
standard form of a number, 476
**Numerator,** 483
**Numerical expression(s),** *See also*
        Algebraic expression(s), 12
    absolute value, 163, 164, 165
    exponential, 6-9, 22, 45, 81-83, 250,
        252-261, 262, 264-275, 279-281
    order of operations and, 10-15, 22, 45
    rational number, 210-213, 224-227
    simplifying
        using addition properties, 217-219
        using the distributive property, 236,
            238-239
        using multiplication properties, 231-
            233
    square root, 288-291, 314, 316, 318

**Opposites,** 162-165, 178, 195
    integer subtraction and, 173-177, 196
**Ordered pair(s),** 408
    for graphing linear equations, 360-361,
        412-413, 415-417, 420-423, 424,
        459
    as solution of an equation in two
        variables, 414
    as solution of an inequality in two
        variables, 468
    as solution of a system of linear
        equations, 472-473
    *x*-coordinate, 408
    *y*-coordinate, 408
**Ordering**
    decimals, 478
    fractions and decimals, 129-131
    fractions, decimals, and percents, 143
    integers, 162, 164, 165, 178, 195
    mixed numbers and fractions, 61-63
    rational numbers, 205-207, 220, 243
    real numbers, 295-297
    whole numbers, 477
**Order of operations,** 10-15, 22, 45
**Order property,** *See* Commutative
        property
**Origin,** in a coordinate plane, 408

**Paired data,** *See also* Coordinate plane;
        Ordered pair(s), 446
**Parallel lines,** 457
**Parallelogram,** 488
    area of, 488-489
**Pattern(s),** *See also* Direct variation;
        Linear equation(s)

examples, 5, 96, 264, 286
exercises, 39, 40, 41, 43, 76, 77, 95, 97,
    130, 131, 457
**Percent(s),** 132, 134
    circle graphs and, 135-137
    decimals and, 133, 135-138, 140-143,
        154-155
    discount, 147-149
    fractions and, 133-143, 154-155
    interest, 146-149
    modeling, 132
    of a number, 144-149, 155
    rounding, 141-143
    symbol for, 132, 134
**Percent bar,** to model percent of a
        number, 144-145
**Perfect square,** 288
**Perimeter,** 488
    of a rectangle, 16, 18-21, 488-489
        effect of changing dimensions, 240
    of a square, 18-21, 488-489
    of a triangle, 488-489
**Person-days,** unit analysis and, 27-29
**Pi,** 490
    area of a circle and, 297, 491
    circumference of a circle and, 490-491
    surface area of a cylinder and, 492-493
    volume of a cylinder and, 492-493
**Pie chart,** *See* Circle graph
**Place value,** 476
    rounding and, 479
**Point(s)**
    distance between on a coordinate plane,
        406-407, 409-411
    graphing in a coordinate plane, 406-
        411, 459
**Positive integer,** *See also* Integer(s), 162
**Positive number,** 160
**Positive slope,** 434-437
**Positive square root,** 287-288, 298
**Powers,** *See also* Exponent(s), 4, 6
    dividing, 256-261, 271-275, 279
    evaluating, 4-9, 22, 45
    multiplying, 250-255, 270-275, 279
    negative, 264-269, 280
    order of operations and, 10-15, 22, 45
    raising fractions to, 81-83
    of ten, 266-269, 280
        multiplying by, 481
    verbal phrases for, 7-9
    writing, 6-9, 45
    zero as, 264-269, 280
**Pre-Course Test,** xxi-xxiii
**Prediction,** exercises, 264, 277, 312, 360,
    439, 447, 451, 457
**Prerequisite skills,** *See also* Skills
        Review Handbook, 3, 51, 105,
        159, 201, 249, 285, 321, 369, 405

**Prime factorization,** 484-485
    greatest common factor and, 485
    least common multiple and, 485
**Prime factors,** 484-485
**Prime number,** 484-485
**Principal,** interest and, 146
**Prioritizing information,** *See also* Multi-
        step problems, 36-37, 192
**Prism,** *See also* Right rectangular prism,
        492
**Problem solving,** *See also* Problem
        solving plan; Problem Solving
        and Reasoning; Problem solving
        strategies
    examples, *Throughout. See for example*
        7, 19, 26, 27, 55, 61, 67, 75, 87, 93
    identifying missing information, 36-
        37, 42
    making a generalization, 312
    relevant and irrelevant information,
        36-37, 42, 456
    sequencing and prioritizing
        information, 36-37, 192
    using strategies, 36-37
**Problem solving plan,** 38, 47
**Problem Solving and Reasoning,** 42-43,
        96-97, 150-151, 192-193, 240-
        241, 276-277, 312-313, 360-361,
        396-397, 456-457
**Problem solving strategies,** 36-37, 496-
        497
    act it out, 496-497
    break into parts, 150, 240, 496-497
    draw a diagram, 312, 496-497
    guess, check, and revise, 496-497
    look for a pattern, 96, 240, 286, 496-497
    make a list, 496-497
    make a table, 150, 240, 250, 256, 376,
        377, 390, 391, 496-497
    solve a simpler problem, 192, 240,
        496-497
    work backward, 496-497
**Product,** 481
**Product of powers property,** 252, 270,
        272
**Proof,** of division rule, 91
**Proper fraction,** 60
**Property (Properties)**
    of addition, 214-219, 220, 244, 324-
        327, 378-381
    associative, 215-219, 229-233
    commutative, 214, 216-219, 228, 230-
        233
    distributive, 234-239, 245, 350-353
    of division, 330-333, 386-389
    of equality, 324-327, 330-333

**Term(s)**
coefficient of, 236
constant, 236
of an expression, 236
like, 236
**Terminating decimal(s),** 128
fractions and, 128-131
rational numbers and, 204
**Tests,** *See* Assessment
**Theorem,** Pythagorean, 302-305, 312, 316
**Three-dimensional figure,** *See* Solid(s); Surface area; Volume
**Total cost,** formula, 18
**Trapezoid,** 488
area of, 488-489
**Tree diagram,** factor tree, 484
**Triangle,** *See also* Right triangle, 488
area of, 488-489
perimeter of, 488-489
*True or false questions, Throughout. See for example* 14, 89, 161, 190, 214, 215, 310, 311, 317, 318
**Two-step equation(s),** 334-339, 340, 364
with fractions and decimals, 342-347, 364
writing, 337-339
**Two-step inequalities,** 390-395, 401
writing, 393-395, 401

**Undefined slope,** 435
**Unit analysis,** *See also* Conversion; Rate, 26
converting measurements, 24-25
density and, 27-29, 46
examples, 87
person-days and, 27-29, 46
speed and, 26, 28-29
**Unit rate,** 26

**V**

**Variable,** 18
**Variable expression,** *See* Algebraic expression(s)
**Venn diagram,** to show number relationships, 296
**Verbal model,** 38-41
examples, *Throughout. See for example* 44, 109, 175, 211, 253, 325, 331, 337, 345, 351, 353, 379, 387, 393, 466, 467, 470
**Verbal phrases,**
for absolute value, 163, 164, 165
for inequalities, 372-375
for integer subtraction, 176, 177
for powers, 7-9, 22

for unit rate, 26
writing expressions for 31, 33-35
**Verbal sentence(s),** 324
translating, 324-327
writing as equations, 325-327, 331, 333, 337-339, 365, 466-467,
writing as inequalities, 386-389, 3 395, 470-471, 474-475
**Vertical line(s),** 420
equations for, 420-423, 460
graph of, 420-423, 460
modeling, 418
**Visual thinking,** *See* Graphs; Manipulatives; Modeling; Number line; Spatial reasoni
**Vocabulary**
chapter, 2, 50, 104, 158, 200, 248, 320, 368, 404
lesson introduction to, *Throughout for example* 6, 12, 18, 26, 32, 54, 60, 66, 74, 80, 86
prerequisite, 3, 51, 105, 159, 201, 285, 321, 369, 405
review
chapter, 45, 99, 153, 195, 243, 2 315, 363, 399, 459
mid-chapter, 22, 70, 124, 178, 2 262, 298, 340, 382, 424
**Volume,** 492
of a cube, 276, 492-493
of a right circular cylinder, 492-493
of a right rectangular prism, 492-49

**Whole number(s),** 476
adding, 480
comparing, 477
composite, 484
dividing, 482
expanded form, 476
multiplying, 481
ordering, 477
place value, 476
prime, 484-485
reciprocals of, 86, 88, 89
rounding, 479
standard form, 476
subtracting, 480
**Work backward,** problem solving strategy, 496-497
**Writing,** *See also* Communication; Ve model
algebraic expressions, 31, 33-35, 47 96, 97, 234, 235, 240
decimals
as fractions, 126, 129, 130, 131, as percents, 138, 140-143, 155

of exponents, 250-261, 270-275, 279-281
of graphs of direct variation equations, 452
identity, 216-219, 230-233
of inequality, 378-381, 386-389
inverse, 216-219, 230-233
of multiplication, 228-233, 245, 330-333, 386-389
of −1, 230
of subtraction, 324-327, 378-381
table of, 510-511
of zero, 230
**Proportional reasoning,** *See also* Dimensional analysis; Spatial reasoning
circle graphs and, 135-137, 142, 143, 151, 157, 495
interest and, 146-149
percent and, 135-137, 144-149
rate and, 188-191, 354-359
**Puzzles,** 98
magic squares, 192, 193
**Pythagorean theorem,** 302, 316
converse of, 306-311, 317
indirect measurement and, 304, 305
modeling, 300-301
**Pythagorean triples,** 307

**Q**

**Quadrants,** in a coordinate plane, 408
**Quotient,** 482
**Quotient of powers property,** 258, 271, 272

**R**

**Radius,** 490
area of a circle and, 491
circumference and, 490-491
surface area of a cylinder and, 492-493
volume of a cylinder and, 492-493
**Rate,** 26
of change
average, 188-191, 225, 226, 227
slope and, 435-437
distance and, 18-21, 38-39, 46
equations, 354-359, 365
interest, 146
modeling, 354-355
of speed, 26, 28-29
unit, 26
**Ratio(s),** 483
circumference and area of a circle, 490-491
direct variation, 444-455
equivalent, 483
percent as, 132, 134

pi, 490
slope, 432-437
**Rational number(s),** *See also* Decimal(s); Fraction(s); Integer(s), 204, 243
adding, 208-213, 220, 244
comparing and ordering, 204-207, 220, 243
dividing, 222-227, 245
modeling on a number line, 202-203, 204, 205
multiplying, 222-227, 245
properties
of addition, 216-219, 244
distributive, 236-239
of multiplication, 228-233
subtracting, 210-213, 220, 244
**Readiness**
prerequisite skills, 3, 51, 105, 159, 201, 249, 285, 321, 369, 405
Skills Review Handbook, 476-497
**Real number(s),** 294
approximating square root of, 294-297
graphing on a number line, 295
ordering, 295-297
Venn diagram showing relationships, 296
**Reasonableness,** *See also* Checking solutions
checking, 42, 80-81, 82, 83, 114, 116, 117, 125, 150, 193, 231, 360, 456
**Reasoning,** *See also* Error analysis; Estimation; Problem solving; Problem solving strategies; Proportional reasoning
conclusion, 302
conjecture
justifying, 96, 97, 240
making, 96, 97, 193, 240, 300
converse of a statement, 308, 310, 311
dimensional analysis, 286, 312, 313
draw conclusions, *Throughout. See for example* 4, 5, 11, 16, 17, 24, 25, 30, 31, 37, 53, 58, 59
exercises, *Throughout. See for example* 8, 9, 14, 15, 20, 21, 28, 29, 34, 35, 56, 57
generalize results, 180, 312
hypothesis, 302
identifying missing information, 36-37, 42
if-then statement, 302, 304, 305, 316
converse of, 308, 310, 311
justifying
a conjecture, 96, 97, 457
steps, 217, 218, 219, 231, 232, 233, 240, 241, 244, 245
problem solving plan, 38, 47

proof, 91
relevant and irrelevant information, 36-37
sequencing and prioritizing information, 36-37
tree diagram, 484
Venn diagram, 296
**Reciprocals,** 84-89, 101
division with fractions and, 90-95, 101
using to solve an equation, 331-333
**Rectangle(s),** 488
area of, 17, 240, 488-489
effect of changing dimensions, 240
perimeter of, 16, 18-21, 240, 488-489
effect of changing dimensions, 240
**Relevant information,** identifying, 36-37
**Remainder,** 482
**Repeating decimal(s),** 128
bar notation for, 128
fractions and, 128-131
rational numbers and, 204
**Reviews,** *See also* Assessment; Prerequisite skills
Chapter, 45-47, 99-101, 153-155, 195-197, 243-245, 279-281, 315-317, 363-365, 399-401, 459-461
games, 44, 98, 152, 194, 242, 278, 314, 362, 398, 458
Mid-Chapter, 22, 70, 124, 178, 220, 262, 298, 340, 382, 424
Skills Review Handbook, 476-497
**Right circular cylinder,** 492
surface area of, 492-493
volume of, 492-493
**Right rectangular prism,** 492
surface area of, 492-493
volume of, 492-493
**Right triangle,** 300, 302
converse of the Pythagorean theorem and, 306-311, 317
hypotenuse of, 300, 302
legs of, 300, 302
Pythagorean theorem and, 300-305, 316
relationship between legs and hypotenuse, 300-301
**Rise,** slope and, 432, 434, 460
**Rounding,** *See also* Approximation; Estimation, 479
decimals, 479
percents, 141-143
whole numbers, 479
**Run,** slope and, 432, 434, 460

**S**

**Sale price,** *See* Discount
**Scientific notation,** 266-269, 280
comparing numbers in, 267-269

**Sequencing information,** 36-37, 192
**Simple interest,** 146-149
  formula, 146, 147
**Simplest form**
  expression, 348-353
  fraction, 54-57, 70, 99
    in addition and subtraction, 64-69,
      100
**Skills Review Handbook,** 476-497
  graphs
    reading bar graphs, 494
    reading circle graphs, 495
  measurement
    area of a circle, 490-491
    area of a polygon, 488-489
    circumference, 490-491
    converting between metric and
      customary units, 487
    converting units, 486
    perimeter, 488-489
    surface area, 492-493
    volume, 492-493
  number sense
    comparing decimals, 478
    comparing whole numbers, 477
    factors, 484-485
    multiples, 484-485
    ordering decimals, 478
    ordering whole numbers, 477
    place value, 476
    ratios, 483
    rounding, 479
  operations
    adding whole numbers, 480
    dividing whole numbers, 482
    multiplying whole numbers, 481
    subtracting whole numbers, 480
  problem solving strategies, 496-497
**Slope,** 432, 434, 460
  direct variation and, 446-449, 452
  formula, 432, 434
  modeling, 432-433
  as rate of change, 435-437
  rise and, 432, 434, 460
  run and, 432, 434, 460
  undefined, 435
  *y*-intercept and, 438-443, 461
  zero, 435
**Slope-intercept form,** 440, 461
  for graphing linear equations, 439-443,
    461
**Solid(s),** 492
  surface area of, 492-493
  volume of, 492-493
**Solution**
  of an equation
    in one variable, 322, 324
    in two variables, 412, 414

  of an inequality
    in one variable, 372
    in two variables, 468
  of a system of linear equations, 47
  of a system of linear inequalities, 4
**Solve a simpler problem,** problem
    solving strategy, 192, 240, 49
    497
**Spatial reasoning,** *See also* Area mod
    Diagram(s); Graphs; Modelin
    Number line
  area, 17-21, 41, 43, 240, 297, 488-
  perimeter, 16, 18-21, 240, 488-489
  surface area, 276, 492-493
  tree diagram, 484
  Venn diagram, 296
  volume, 276, 492-493
**Speed,** unit analysis and, 26, 28-29
**Square,** 488
  area of, 18-21, 488-489
  perimeter of, 18-21, 488-489
  side length and area relationship, 2
    289-291
**Square numbers**
  using to approximate square root, 2
    297, 298
  perfect squares and, 288
  table of, 513
**Square root(s),** 287, 288, 315
  approximating, 292-297, 298, 315
  of perfect squares, 286-291, 298, 31
  positive and negative, 287, 288, 298
  Pythagorean theorem and, 300-311,
    312, 316
  symbol for, 288
  table of, 513
  of zero, 288
**Standard form of a linear equation,**
    *also* Linear equation(s), 414
**Standard form of a number,** 476
  written as powers of ten, 266-269, 2
**Stem-and-leaf plot,** 241
**Substitution,** to check answers, 322, 3
    325, 326, 327, 328, 329, 330,
    334, 335, 340, 342, 350, 363,
    378, 386, 387, 392, 396, 412,
    418, 419, 420, 468, 472, 473, 4
**Subtraction**
  decimal, 107-111, 124, 153
    estimating differences, 109-111
  difference, 480
  equations, 323, 325-327, 340, 363
  fraction
    different denominators, 73, 75-77
    100
    same denominator, 65-69, 70, 100
  integer, 172-177, 178, 196
  as inverse of addition, 173

# Credits

## Photography

**Cover** *center* Timothy Large/Shutterstock; *bottom left* IT Stock Free/PictureQuest; *bottom right* Image 100 LTD; *center left* PhotoDisc/Getty Images; *center right* Brand X/SuperStock; **iii** *Austin* Jostens Photography/Lifetouch; *Cliffe* Timothy Cliffe; *Kohn* Sharon Kohn; *Miyata* Courtesy of Greg Miyata; *Sass* Courtesy of Rudy Sass; **iv** Comstock; **v** RubberBall; **vi** RubberBall/Getty Images; **vii** Eric J. Enger/Shutterstock; **viii** PhotoDisc/Getty Images; **ix** PhotoDisc/Getty Images; **x** Digital Vision Ltd./SuperStock; **xi** RubberBall Productions/Getty Images; **xii** PhotoDisc/Getty Images; **xiii** Royalty-Free/Corbis; **xv, 2** *all* Comstock; **9** PhotoDisc/Getty Images; **13** IT Stock Free/PictureQuest; **15** Jorge Alban/McDougal Littell/Houghton Mifflin Co.; **19** PhotoDisc/Getty Images; **21** Comstock; **26** Nick Rowe/PhotoDisc/Getty Images; **28** RubberBall; **33** Brand X Pictures; **34** Andrew Paterson/Alamy; **38** ThinkStock/age fotostock; **50** RubberBall; **55** PhotoDisc/Getty Images; **57** Stockbyte/Royalty-Free; **61** Big Cheese Photo/FotoSearch; **63** Comstock; **68** PhotoDisc/Getty Images; **75** Comstock Images/Alamy; **76** Jorge Albán/McDougal Littell/Houghton Mifflin Co.; **82** Gert Johannes Jacobus Vrey/Shutterstock; **87** Brandon Laufenberg/iStockPhoto; **88, 104** RubberBall Productions/Getty Images; **109** Michael Stevens/Fog Stock; **115** Corel Corporation; **121** BananaStock/PictureQuest; **122** PhotoDisc/Getty Images; **129** Ken O'Donoghue/McDougal Littell/Hougton Mifflin Co.; **141** FoodCollection/SuperStock; **142** Jorge Albán/McDougal Littell/Houghton Mifflin Co.; **147** Royalty-Free/Corbis; **148** Comstock; **158** Eric J. Enger/Shutterstock; **163** Royalty-Free/Corbis; **165** Steve Allen/Brand X Pictures/PictureQuest; **170** Think-Stock LLC/Index Stock Imagery; **177** Ken Usami/Getty Images; **183** PhotoObjects/Jupiterimages Corp.; **185** Simone van de Berg/Shutterstock; **189** PhotoDisc/Getty Images; **191** Brand X Pictures; **200** PhotoDisc/Getty Images; **205** WizData, Inc./Shutterstock; **211** PhotoDisc/Getty Images; **212** Artville; **217** BananaStock/Alamy; **225, 226** Royalty-Free/Corbis; **231** Digital Vision Ltd./SuperStock; **238** Digital Vision/Getty Images; **248** PhotoDisc/Getty Images; **253** Royalty-Free/Corbis; **259** NASA Jet Propulsion Laboratory (NASA-JPL); **261** Stockbyte/Royalty-Free; **268** Artville; **273** Yaroslav/Shutterstock; **274** image100/Alamy; **284** Digital Vision Ltd./SuperStock; **297** Salvador Garcia Gil/Shutterstock; **309** PhotoObjects/Jupiterimages Corp.; **320** RubberBall Productions/Getty Images; **325** Comstock; **326** Royalty-Free/Corbis; **331** Brand X Pictures; **337** Shane Lighter/Shutterstock; **338** Ken O'Donoghue/McDougal Littell/Houghton Mifflin Co.; **345** Brand X Pictures; **346** Digital Vision/Getty Images; **351** Digtial Vision/Corbis; **352** Duncan Smith/Getty Images; **357** Shutterstock; **358** iStockPhoto; **359** Seb Rogers/Alamy; **368** PhotoDisc/Getty Images; **373** Royalty-Free/Corbis; **374** Andrew F. Kazmierski/Shutterstock; **379** James Lauritz/Digital Vision/Getty Images; **381** RubberBall Productions/Getty Images; **387** Chris Mole/Shutterstock; **389** Ann Summa/McDougal Littell/Houghton Mifflin Co.; **393** Brand X Pictures; **394** Robert Deal/iStockPhoto; **404** Royalty-Free/Corbis; **415** Lisa Vivona/Shutterstock; **416** Greg Nicholas/iStockPhoto; **422** Digital Stock; **430** Allan Penn/McDougal Littell/Houghton Mifflin Co.; **441** Take A Pix Media/Shutterstock; **442** Brand X Pictures; **446** Comstock; **447** Scott Rothstein/Shutterstock; **448** PhotoDisc/Getty Images; **453** Brand X Pictures; **454** Shawn Pecor/Shutterstock; **465** RubberBall.

## Illustration

**236** Dan Stuckenschneider/McDougal Littell/Houghton Mifflin Co.; **254** Karen Minot/McDougal Littell/Houghton Mifflin Co.; **290** Patrick Gnan/McDougal Littell/Houghton Mifflin Co.; **432** Argosy/McDougal Littell/Houghton Mifflin Co.

All other illustrations by McDougal Littell/Houghton Mifflin Co.

# Selected Answers

## Chapter 1

**1.1 Practice A (p. 8)** **1.** base **3.** $8^3$ **5.** $6^5$ **7.** $2^6$
**9.** C **11.** F **13.** A **15.** 8 **17.** 125 **19.** 64 **21.** $6^2$; 36
**23.** $3^4$; 81 **25.** $8^3$; 512 **27.** 6561; Since the exponent
8 is one more than the exponent 7, multiply the value
of $3^7$ one time by the base, 3; $2187 \cdot 3 = 6561$.
**29.** 100 cm

**1.1 Practice B (p. 9)** **1.** 3 to the eighth power
**3.** 4 to the fifth power **5.** 4 to the ninth power **7.** $2^6$
**9.** $6^4$ **11.** $5^7$ **13.** 32 **15.** 1000 **17.** 216 **19.** $7^2$; 49
**21.** $6^4$; 1296 **23.** $12^3$; 1728 **25.** $5^2$ **27.** $8^2$ or $4^3$ or $2^6$
**29.** $10^3$ **31.** $1^2, 2^2, 3^2, 4^2, 5^2, \ldots$ **33.** 1024 bytes
**35.** $200^2$

**1.2 Practice A (p. 14)** **1.** multiplication
**3.** addition **5.** multiplication **7.** multiplication
**9.** division **11.** division **13.** 22 **15.** 42 **17.** 28 **19.** 9
**21.** 2 **23.** 9 **25.** false; 4 **27.** true **29.** false; 37
**31.** false; 85 **33.** true **35.** $590 **37.** 640 ft$^2$

**1.2 Practice B (p. 15)** **1.** 40 **3.** 36 **5.** 19
**7.** 16 **9.** 1088 **11.** 3 **13.** 2 **15.** 8 **17.** C **19.** A
**21.** The numbers 5 and 2 were multiplied first and
then the result was squared. The value of the power
$5^2$ should have been computed first and the result, 25,
multiplied by 2. Then 15 should have been subtracted
from 50. The correct answer is 35. **23.** $89 **25.** 21

**1.3 Practice A (p. 20)** **1.** $P = 40$ in.; $A = 96$ in.$^2$
**3.** $P = 16$ cm; $A = 15$ cm$^2$ **5.** $P = 12$ m; $A = 9$ m$^2$
**7.** 80 ft **9.** 75 in. **11.** $48 **13.** $45 **15.** Divide the
perimeter by 4. **17.** $P = 46$ in.; $A = 130$ in.$^2$
**19.** 15 mi **21.** $24 **23.** $99

**1.3 Practice B (p. 21)** **1.** $P = 18$ in.; $A = 20$ in.$^2$
**3.** $P = 18$ yd; $A = 18$ yd$^2$ **5.** $P = 32$ in.; $A = 64$ in.$^2$
**7.** 312 mi **9.** 168 ft **11.** $18 **13.** $138 **15.** Divide
the area by the width. **17.** $P = 24$ ft; $A = 36$ ft$^2$
**19.** 24 km **21.** $30

**1.4 Practice A (p. 28)** **1.** $\dfrac{25 \text{ ft}}{1 \text{ sec}}$ **3.** $\dfrac{\$3}{1 \text{ gal}}$ **5.** $\dfrac{19 \text{ oz}}{1 \text{ ft}^3}$

**7.** h **9.** 4 **11.** 5 **13.** Not reasonable;
$r = \dfrac{600 \text{ mi}}{3 \text{ h}} = 200$ mi/h, which is too fast for

someone to drive. **15.** 60 g **17.** 20 more miles

**19a.** $\dfrac{6 \text{ miles}}{1 \text{ hour}}$ **19b.** $\dfrac{60}{20} = 3$, so there are 3 20-minute

periods in 1 hour. The man runs $\dfrac{6}{3} = 2$ miles in each

period, so he runs a total of $6 + 2 = 8$ miles.

**1.4 Practice B (p. 29)** **1.** 13 **3.** cm$^3$ **5.** 1 h
**7.** Units are not compatible. Convert 3 minutes
to 180 seconds; $11 \times 180 = 1980$. **9.** Not
reasonable; to walk 18 miles in 120 minutes, you
would have to walk at a rate of 9 miles per hour.
$r = \dfrac{18 \text{ mi}}{120 \text{ min}} = \dfrac{18 \text{ mi}}{2 \text{ h}} = 9$ mi/h **11.** The mercury and
zinc samples have the same mass of 154 grams.
The nickel sample has a mass of 144 grams, which
is 10 grams less than the mass of the other two
samples. **13.** 6 days

**1.5 Practice A (p. 34)** **1.** 11 **3.** 45 **5.** 17 **7.** 50
**9.** 22 **11.** 8 **13.** 1 **15.** 7 **17.** 27 **19.** 28 **21.** 42
**23.** 4 **25.** $n + 7$ **27.** $\dfrac{n}{6}$ **29.** $4n - 6$ **31.** $9(4 - n)$
**33.** Substituted wrong numbers for variables.
$3(4) - 6 = 6$ **35.** 3 **37.** $v + m$ **39.** 176 points

**1.5 Practice B (p. 35)** **1.** 4 **3.** 48 **5.** 31 **7.** 28
**9.** 39 **11.** 68 **13.** 30 **15.** 7 **17.** $\dfrac{s^2}{4}$ **19.** $56 \div n$
**21.** $3n \div 2$ **23.** $\dfrac{100}{19 - n}$ **25.** $2g + a$; 49 points **27.** $7b$
**29.** 50 books

**1.6 Practice A (p. 40)** **1.** B **3.** D **5.** weight of
bag $\div$ weight of one serving **7.** number of
T-shirts $\cdot$ cost of one T-shirt **9.** total number of
muffins $\div$ number of muffins in one batch
**11.** Round 576 to 600 and round 36 to 40. Then
$600 \div 40 = 15$, so 16 batches is reasonable.
**13.** 34 km

**1.6 Practice B (p. 41)** **1.** You should order
5 pizzas, because a pizza is needed for the remainder.
**3.** 8:05 P.M. **5.** 31, 40 **7.** 49, 38 **9.** Not enough
information; Need to know number of miles he walks
and how much each pledge will be per mile.
**11.** 1 P.M.

# Chapter 2

**2.1 Practice A (p. 56)** **1–7.** *Sample answers are given.* **1.** $\frac{2}{14}, \frac{3}{21}$ **3.** $\frac{2}{3}, \frac{4}{6}$ **5.** $\frac{6}{16}, \frac{9}{24}$ **7.** $\frac{1}{3}, \frac{14}{42}$ **9.** > **11.** < **13.** > **15.** = **17.** $\frac{1}{2}$ **19.** $\frac{7}{8}$ **21.** $\frac{4}{5}$ **23.** $\frac{4}{5}$ **25.** $\frac{5}{8}$ **27.** $\frac{2}{5}$ **29.** Kayla **31.** $\frac{3}{4}, \frac{3}{4}$, yes **33.** The greatest common factor of the numerator and denominator is not 1. Both are divisible by 3, 5, and 15.

**2.1 Practice B (p. 57)** **1–7.** *Sample answers are given.* **1.** $\frac{7}{11}, \frac{14}{22}$ **3.** $\frac{1}{2}, \frac{3}{6}$ **5.** $\frac{14}{32}, \frac{21}{48}$ **7.** $\frac{11}{17}, \frac{44}{68}$ **9.** < **11.** > **13.** > **15.** < **17.** $\frac{1}{2}$ **19.** $\frac{3}{4}$ **21.** $\frac{3}{4}$ **23.** $\frac{5}{6}$ **25.** Monday **27.** $\frac{2}{9}, \frac{3}{8}$; no **29.** The fractions are equivalent fractions obtained by multiplying both the numerator and the denominator of $\frac{3}{8}$ by consecutive whole numbers starting with 1; $\frac{15}{40}, \frac{18}{48}, \frac{21}{56}$. **31.** No; 108 is not divisible by 24.

**2.2 Practice A (p. 62)** **1.** fraction **3.** improper **5.** proper fraction **7.** improper fraction **9.** improper fraction **11.** $\frac{3}{1}$ **13.** $\frac{27}{1}$ **15.** $\frac{22}{3}$ **17.** $3\frac{1}{4}$ **19.** $1\frac{1}{10}$ **21.** $2\frac{1}{2}$ **23.** > **25.** < **27.** < **29.** The apples from the first store. **31.** An improper fraction is greater than 1, and a proper fraction is less than 1. So, an improper fraction is greater.

**2.2 Practice B (p. 63)** **1.** $\frac{17}{4}$ **3.** $\frac{20}{7}$ **5.** $\frac{23}{4}$ **7.** $\frac{122}{15}$ **9.** $5\frac{1}{2}$ **11.** $5\frac{3}{10}$ **13.** $7\frac{2}{3}$ **15.** $3\frac{5}{16}$ **17.** The numerator should be $5 \cdot 9 + 4$. The improper fraction should be $\frac{49}{9}$. **19.** B **21.** $4\frac{3}{16}, 4\frac{1}{2}, \frac{37}{8}, \frac{19}{4}$ **23.** $4\frac{11}{24}, \frac{57}{12}, \frac{31}{6}, 5\frac{1}{4}$ **25.** $9\frac{1}{6}, \frac{83}{9}, \frac{61}{6}, 10\frac{1}{4}$ **27.** $97\frac{1}{8}$ ft, $97\frac{2}{9}$ ft, $97\frac{1}{4}$ ft, $97\frac{3}{5}$ ft **29.** The whole-number parts are all 3, so compare only the fractions by writing equivalent fractions. Use this information to order the numbers from least to greatest.

**2.3 Practice A (p. 68)** **1.** $\frac{1}{8}$ **3.** $\frac{2}{3}$ **5.** $1\frac{1}{5}$ **7.** $1\frac{11}{21}$ **9.** $1\frac{1}{2}$ **11.** $5\frac{2}{3}$ **13.** $\frac{1}{2}$ mi **15.** $\frac{1}{2}$ mi **17.** $1\frac{1}{2}$ lb

**2.3 Practice B (p. 69)** **1.** $\frac{5}{6} - \frac{2}{6} = \frac{3}{6}$, or $\frac{1}{2}$ **3.** $\frac{1}{3}$ **5.** $3\frac{1}{2}$ **7.** $3\frac{2}{3}$ **9.** $10\frac{1}{5}$ **11.** $\frac{1}{2}$ **13.** $15\frac{1}{9}$ **15.** a, b **17.** $\frac{4}{20}$ or $\frac{1}{5}$ **19.** $\frac{3}{4}$ lb **21.** $12\frac{1}{8}$ lb

**2.4 Practice A (p. 76)** **1.** 20 **3.** 12 **5.** 24 **7.** 36 **9.** $\frac{17}{24}$ **11.** $\frac{13}{28}$ **13.** $\frac{29}{40}$ **15.** $\frac{23}{30}$ **17.** $\frac{9}{10}$ **19.** $\frac{1}{2}$ **21.** $6\frac{11}{15}$ **23.** $5\frac{7}{8}$ **25.** $2\frac{13}{14}$ **27.** $5\frac{5}{24}$ **29.** $1\frac{3}{10}$ h **31.** $16\frac{1}{4}$ min **33.** $4\frac{1}{4}$ ft **35.** $6\frac{5}{6}$ ft

**2.4 Practice B (p. 77)** **1.** $1\frac{17}{60}$ **3.** $\frac{71}{85}$ **5.** $\frac{19}{33}$ **7.** $\frac{21}{80}$ **9.** $\frac{25}{33}$ **11.** $\frac{29}{45}$ **13.** $12\frac{19}{42}$ **15.** $5\frac{13}{18}$ **17.** $5\frac{27}{28}$ **19.** $1\frac{21}{80}$ **21.** $2\frac{29}{48}$ **23.** $\frac{37}{40}$ **25.** $1\frac{1}{2}$ in. **27.** $2\frac{5}{8}$ mi **29.** $8\frac{13}{24}$ lb **31.** $66\frac{5}{16}$ in. **33.** Add $\frac{1}{16}$ to each fraction; $\frac{5}{16}, \frac{3}{8}, \frac{7}{16}$.

**2.5 Practice A (p. 82)** **1.** $\frac{43}{5}$ **3.** $\frac{113}{11}$ **5.** $\frac{4}{15}$ **7.** $1\frac{3}{4}$ **9.** $4\frac{9}{10}$ **11.** $3 = \frac{3}{1}$, not $\frac{3}{3}$. The answer is $\frac{5}{4}$, or $1\frac{1}{4}$. **13.** $\frac{8}{729}$ **15.** $\frac{27}{512}$ **17.** $3\frac{2}{3}; \frac{11}{15} \approx \frac{12}{15} = \frac{4}{5}; \frac{4}{5}$ of 5 = 4. **19.** $1\frac{1}{2}; \frac{3}{20} \approx \frac{2}{20} = \frac{1}{10}; \frac{1}{10}$ of 10 is 1. **21.** $\frac{55}{72}$ ft² **23.** $\frac{7}{12}$ mi **25.** $3\frac{3}{4}$ gal

**2.5 Practice B (p. 83)** **1.** $\frac{3}{56}$ **3.** $\frac{45}{56}$ **5.** 9 **7.** $4\frac{4}{5}$ **9.** $61\frac{1}{3}$ **11.** 3 **13.** $\frac{27}{50}$ **15.** $\frac{729}{1331}$ **17.** $\frac{64}{15,625}$ **19.** $1\frac{4}{5}; \frac{9}{20} \approx \frac{10}{20} = \frac{1}{2}; \frac{1}{2}$ of 4 is 2. **21.** $10\frac{1}{2}; \frac{21}{60} \approx \frac{20}{60} = \frac{1}{3}; \frac{1}{3}$ of 30 is 10. **23.** $16\frac{7}{15}$ ft² **25.** 150 families **27.** 420 calories **29.** sometimes

**2.6 Practice A (p. 88)** **1.** $\frac{7}{6}$ **3.** $\frac{1}{3}$ **5.** $\frac{9}{4}$ **7.** $\frac{1}{21}$ **9.** $\frac{6}{13}$ **11.** $\frac{3}{14}$ **13.** $\frac{8}{99}$ **15.** $\frac{5}{57}$ **17.** yes; $\frac{9}{10} \cdot \frac{10}{9} = 1$ **19.** no; $\frac{3}{8} \cdot \frac{3}{8} \neq 1$ **21.** no; $\frac{1}{9} \cdot \frac{19}{1} \neq 1$ **23.** yes; $\frac{3}{2} \cdot \frac{2}{3} = 1$ **25.** The student should not have found the reciprocal of the fraction in the first step. $4\frac{2}{3} = \frac{14}{3}$; The reciprocal of $\frac{14}{3}$ is $\frac{3}{14}$. **27.** 5 h **29.** 6 h

**2.6 Practice B (p. 89)** 1. $\frac{9}{7}$ 3. $\frac{1}{96}$ 5. $\frac{80}{1}$ or 80
7. $\frac{1}{1}$ or 1 9. $\frac{15}{62}$ 11. $\frac{4}{15}$ 13. $\frac{11}{197}$ 15. $\frac{12}{265}$
17. no; $\frac{13}{19} \cdot \frac{13}{19} \neq 1$ 19. no; $\frac{9}{15} \cdot \frac{15}{19} \neq 1$
21. yes; $\frac{5}{29} \cdot \frac{29}{5} = 1$ 23. no; $\frac{34}{5} \cdot \frac{34}{5} \neq 1$
25. 1000, 100, 10, 2, $\frac{10}{9}$, $\frac{100}{99}$ Their reciprocals are
also close to 1. 27. $9\frac{1}{2}$ h 29. 5 h 31. 13 h 33. true

**2.7 Practice A (p. 94)** 1. $\frac{2}{3}$ 3. $\frac{80}{81}$ 5. $\frac{9}{98}$
7. $1\frac{5}{22}$ 9. $1\frac{23}{102}$ 11. $2\frac{2}{3}$ 13. $\frac{1}{4}$ 15. 24
17. The reciprocal of the dividend, $\frac{4}{5}$, was used
instead of the reciprocal of the divisor,
$\frac{11}{3}$; $\frac{4}{5} \times \frac{3}{11} = \frac{12}{55}$. 19. $\frac{3}{40}$ 21. $2\frac{2}{9}$ 23. $\frac{3}{7}$
25. $2\frac{7}{9}$ 27. 8 placemats 29. $4\frac{3}{5}$ m 31. Greater;
dividing by $\frac{1}{2}$ is the same as multiplying by 2.

**2.7 Practice B (p. 95)** 1. $1\frac{1}{3}$ 3. $1\frac{44}{81}$ 5. $\frac{8}{75}$
7. $1\frac{37}{56}$ 9. $3\frac{5}{108}$ 11. $2\frac{1}{7}$ 13. 1 15. 35 17. $\frac{2}{15}$
19. $2\frac{13}{16}$ 21. 9 23. $2\frac{2}{3}$ 25. 3 27. $2\frac{13}{15}$ 29. $\frac{28}{39}$
31. 54 times longer 33. Dividing a number by $\frac{2}{3}$
results in a greater quotient because the reciprocal
of $\frac{2}{3}$ is greater than the reciprocal of $\frac{3}{2}$.
35. The quotients are reciprocals of consecutive
multiples of 4, starting with 8.

# Chapter 3

**3.1 Practice A (p. 110)** 1. 10.84 3. 2.33
5. 0.177 7. 6.35 9. 9.057 11. 1.56 13. 4.11
15. 15.19 17. 5.82 19. 11.66 21. The student forgot
to add 1 in the ones' place after regrouping; 10.3.
23. 5 25. 3 27. 3 29. 34 31. 18 33. 23.56 cm
35. $24.86 37. $2.3 + 4.5 = \frac{23}{10} + \frac{45}{10} = \frac{68}{10} = 6.8$

**3.1 Practice B (p. 111)** 1. 6.3 3. 2.67 5. 3.06
7. 5.63 9. 22.243 11. 36.79 13. 5.77 15. 21.731
17. 9.09 19. 15.74 21. 12.04 23. 2.235 25. 16
27. 7 29. 2 31. 17 33. 29 35. 155 37. 44.23 mm

39. $57.85 41. $4.84 43. $3.75 - 0.25 =$
$\frac{375}{100} - \frac{25}{100} = \frac{350}{100} = 3.50$, or 3.5

**3.2 Practice A (p. 116)** 1. 7.2 3. 8.32 5. 90.24
7. 45.91 9. 125.616 11. 5 13. 4 15. 7 17. There
should be a placeholder after the 64. The product is
6.72. 19. 1.17 21. 20.25 23. 57.144377 25. 0.1369
27. 0.027 29. 37.989 mm$^2$ 31. $25.76 33. $19.25

**3.2 Practice B (p. 117)** 1. 296.9424
3. 4.3696433 5. 162 miles 7. 0.36 9. 3.66
11. 67.54944 13. 32.44501 15. 17.7289
17. 4.2025 19. 0.4096 21. 86.49 mm$^2$ 23. <
25. $3.60 27. Belt; the cost of the belt is greater than
the cost of the poster. 29. 450; 0.001; The product
of $18 \times 25$ and $0.1 \times 0.01$ is equal to $1.8 \times 0.25$, or
$450 \times 0.001 = 0.45$.

**3.3 Practice A (p. 122)** 1. B 3. A 5. 5.5 7. 6.3
9. 7.9 11. 9.8 13. 5.4 15. 1.2 17. 18.1 19. 5.8
21. 21.0 23. 2.5 25. 90 27. 1.15 29. 0.45
31. $4.99 33. $4.97 35. $.90

**3.3 Practice B (p. 123)** 1. B 3. C 5. 49 7. 21.9
9. 14.9 11. 2.3 13. 7.15 15. 0.13 17. 1.6 19. 0.55
21. 0.36 23. 6.76 25. 2.10 27. 10.93 29. 7.57
31. $5.24 33. $.24; $2.88 35. The dividend
and divisor in $23.4 \div 60$ are the dividend and
divisor in $2.34 \div 6$ each multiplied by 10, so that
$2.34 \div 6 = \frac{2.34}{6} = \frac{2.34 \times 10}{6 \times 10} = \frac{23.4}{60} = 23.4 \div 60$.

**3.4 Practice A (p. 130)** 1. terminating
3. repeating 5. terminating 7. $0.\overline{4}$ 9. $2.\overline{3}$ 11. $3.\overline{7}$
13. 2.8 15. $\frac{7}{10}$ 17. $2\frac{3}{8}$ 19. $\frac{3}{16}$ 21. $\frac{17}{25}$ 23. $\frac{3}{25}$
25. < 27. < 29. > 31. 0.6, $\frac{13}{20}$, 0.7, $\frac{3}{4}$
33. $\frac{1}{4}$, 0.30, $\frac{1}{3}$, 0.35 35. 0.75, $\frac{4}{5}$, $\frac{21}{25}$, 0.9
37. $\frac{167}{5}$, $33\frac{2}{5}$ 39. $3\frac{3}{4}$, 3.75

**3.4 Practice B (p. 131)** 1. C 3. A 5. 0.4;
terminating 7. 5.75; terminating 9. $3.\overline{2}$; terminating
11. $0.\overline{4}$ 13. $3.6\overline{7}$ 15. $\frac{3}{5}$ 17. $3\frac{1}{4}$ 19. $\frac{1}{8}$
21. 0.3, $0.\overline{3}$, 0.34, $\frac{2}{5}$, $\frac{7}{3}$ 23. 1.01, $\frac{23}{20}$, $1.\overline{15}$, $1\frac{1}{5}$
25. 0.58, $\frac{7}{12}$, $\frac{2}{3}$, 0.67 27. $0.325 \approx \frac{1}{3}$; $\frac{1}{3} = \frac{5}{15} < \frac{7}{15}$, so
$0.325 < \frac{7}{15}$ 29. $\frac{11}{40}$; 0.28

**3.5 Practice A (p. 136)** **1.** hundred; 100 **3.** left **5.** C **7.** $\frac{23}{100}$ **9.** $\frac{13}{25}$ **11.** $4\frac{2}{5}$ **13.** $12\frac{1}{2}$ **15.** 0.65 **17.** 0.37 **19.** The decimal point was not included in the numerator; $5.5\% = \frac{5.5}{100} = \frac{55}{1000} = \frac{11}{200}$. **21.** $\frac{7}{20}$; 0.35 **23.** $\frac{2}{5}$; 0.4 **25.** $\frac{1}{50}$; 0.02

**3.5 Practice B (p. 137)** **1.** C **3.** D **5.** $\frac{9}{25}$, 0.36 **7.** $\frac{1}{8}$, 0.125 **9.** $\frac{24}{25}$ **11.** $\frac{31}{200}$ **13.** $1\frac{51}{500}$ **15.** $\frac{13}{250}$ **17.** 3.54 **19.** 0.0098 **21.** $\frac{3}{5}$; 0.6 **23.** $\frac{2}{25}$; 0.08 **25.** $\frac{7}{100}$; 0.07

**3.6 Practice A (p. 142)** **1.** C **3.** D **5.** 54% **7.** 4% **9.** 90% **11.** 8.2% **13.** 45.7% **15.** 37.5% **17.** 55.6% **19.** 27.3% **21.** 60% **23.** Your score was better. **25.** Blue **27.** Blue **29.** Since $\frac{1}{8}$ is half of $\frac{1}{4}$, $\frac{1}{8}$ written as a percent is half of 25%, or 12.5%.

**3.6 Practice B (p. 143)** **1.** 50% **3.** 37% **5.** 85% **7.** 14.6% **9.** 56.3% **11.** 400% **13.** 61.1% **15.** 9.0% **17.** $\frac{1}{2}$, 0.53, 55% **19.** 0.61, $\frac{13}{20}$, 69% **21.** 37.5% **23.** 25% **25.** The group favoring dogs represents a greater percent of those surveyed; $\frac{204}{503} \approx 40\%$, 40% > 30%, so $\frac{204}{503} > 30\%$. **27.** Technology **29.** 77.5%

**3.7 Practice A (p. 148)** **1.** 8 **3.** 21 **5.** 11 **7.** 105.3 **9.** 24 **11.** 19 **13.** $14.40 **15.** $5.10 **17.** 4 **19.** 16 **21.** 675 **23.** 12.2 **25.** 44.8 **27.** 138 **29.** $534 **31.** Yes; the tax is $1.40, so the total is $29.40. **33.** Dee's estimate is closer because $\frac{1}{3} = 33\frac{1}{3}\%$ is closer to 32% than 0.30 = 30% is.

**3.7 Practice B (p. 149)** **1.** 8.4 **3.** 11 **5.** 64.8 **7.** 79.3 **9.** 36 **11.** 19.8 **13.** $.55 **15.** $16.20 **17.** $30 **19.** $75 **21.** 1500 **23.** 10 **25.** 57 **27.** 90 **29.** 24 **31.** 75 **33.** $11.16 **35.** The estimate using $\frac{2}{9}$ is closer because $\frac{2}{9}$ is closer in value to 22% than 0.2 is.

# Chapter 4

**4.1 Practice A (p. 164)** **1.** integers **3.** greater than **5.** the number; 0 **7.** $-36, -21, -4, 0, 3, 7, 14$

**9.** $-24, -15, -4, -1, 0, 5, 17, 24$ **11.** 4; 4 **13.** 15; 15 **15.** $-10$; 10 **17.** 5; 5 **19.** > **21.** < **23.** D **25.** A **27.** 8 **29.** $-14$ **31.** $-3$ **33.** Bird is at 6 ft; you are at $-5$ ft; your depth is 5 ft; you are closer to the surface.

**4.1 Practice B (p. 165)** **1.** negative **3.** $-24, -16,$ $-8, 2, 7, 17, 23$ **5.** $-10, -7, -5, -1, 0, 2, 4, 6$ **7.** $-7$; 7 **9.** $-106$; 106 **11.** < **13.** < **15.** > **17.** > **19.** E **21.** C **23.** B **25.** 9 **27.** $-6$ **29.** $-34$ **31.** $-15$ ft; 15 ft; yes; 15 ft above the surface of the water

**4.2 Practice A (p. 170)** **1.** $-6 + 11 = 5$ **3.** $-1$ **5.** absolute values of the integers **7.** 2 was added to $-5$ instead of $-2$. Correct sum is $-7$. **9.** 8 **11.** $-92$ **13.** $-23$ **15.** 6°F; yes, 6°F is above 5°F. **17.** $-34$ **19.** $-51$ **21.** No; she needs $7 more.

**4.2 Practice B (p. 171)** **1.** $-4 + 11 = 7$ **3.** $-5$ **5.** The sum should have the same sign as the integers.
$$-9 + (-6) = -(\left|-9\right| + \left|-6\right|)$$
$$= -(9 + 6)$$
$$= -15$$
**7.** 9 **9.** $-97$ **11.** 9 **13.** $-43$ **15.** $-121$ **17.** never **19.** sometimes **21.** $-9$ **23.** $-140$ **25.** $-32$ **27.** 2 seconds

**4.3 Practice A (p. 176)** **1.** $a, (-b)$ **3.** Error is using a negative sign in the answer. Answer is 12. **5.** $-7$ **7.** $-30$ **9.** 2 **11.** $-15$ **13.** $-17$ **15.** 7 **17.** $13 - (-4) = 17$ **19.** 10 **21.** 4 **23.** $-126$ cm **25.** 4 **27.** 4 **29.** $-5$ **31.** $-47$ **33.** Because distance is positive, you must subtract the lesser number, $-174$, from the greater number, 146. $146 - (-174) = 146 + 174 = 320.$

**4.3 Practice B (p. 177)** **1.** $-4$ **3.** 7 **5.** $-5$ **7.** 40 **9.** $-16$ **11.** $-12$ **13.** $-6 - 19 = -25$ **15.** $-15 - (-28) = 13$ **17.** The order of the integers was changed; $-7$. **19.** $-29$ **21.** 3 **23.** $-24$ **25.** $-8$ **27.** $-31$ **29.** 9 **31.** $-12$ **33.** 16 ft **35.** sometimes

**4.4 Practice A (p. 184)** **1.** C **3.** D **5.** $-24$ **7.** 0 **9.** 33 **11.** $-98$ **13.** $-240$ **15.** 432 **17.** 21 **19.** 135 **21.** Error is that absolute value is always positive, so $5 \cdot 5 = 25$ and $25 \cdot (-2) = -50$. **23.** > **25.** < **27.** > **29.** $-504$ **31.** 79 **33.** $-72$ **35.** 66 ft **37.** $-24$ lb or a loss of 24 lb

**4.4 Practice B (p. 185)** **1.** $-36$ **3.** 0 **5.** $-96$ **7.** $-306$ **9.** $-210$ **11.** 0 **13.** 48 **15.** 160

**17.** Error is that absolute value is always positive, so $-3 \cdot 6 = -18$ and $-18 \cdot 1 = -18$. **19.** < **21.** < **23.** < **25.** $-462$ **27.** $-474$ **29.** $-378$ **31.** The team's own 17 yard line **33.** $-1014$ **35.** $-23$ steps **37.** $n$ must be an odd number in order for the value of the power to be negative because $n$ determines the number of times that $-1$ is used as a factor.

**4.5 Practice A (p. 190)** **1.** false **3.** true **5.** $-5$ **7.** $-7$ **9.** 0 **11.** $-4$ **13.** $-9$ **15.** $-3$ **17.** $-5$ **19.** $-5$ **21.** $-2$ **23.** $-4$ **25.** $-16$ **27.** 2 **29.** 0 **31.** $-4$ **33.** $-8°F$ **35.** $-587$ ft/min, or descent of 587 ft/min

**4.5 Practice B (p. 191)** **1.** 8 **3.** $-5$ **5.** 0 **7.** $-2$ **9.** $-9$ **11.** $-21$ **13.** 4 **15.** $-2$ **17.** $-6$ **19.** $-4$ **21.** 4 **23.** $-6$ **25.** $-4$ **27.** 284 strokes **29.** Pat: $-7$ ft/sec, Julia: $-3$ ft/sec

# Chapter 5

**5.1 Practice A (p. 206)** **1.** $\frac{4}{5}$ **3.** $\frac{28}{5}$ **5.** $\frac{-12}{5}$ **7.** $\frac{-5}{2}$ **9.** 0 **11.** $-2.3$ **13.** $-7.4$ **15.** 0.5; Terminates **17.** $-0.75$; Terminates **19.** $-0.6$; Terminates **21.** $0.\overline{1}$; Repeats **23.** $-1$, $0$, $\frac{1}{4}$ **25.** $-7$, $\frac{1}{8}$, 3.5 **27.** $-3.5$; 3.5 **29.** $2\frac{1}{7}$; $2\frac{1}{7}$ **31.** $\frac{4}{5}$ **33.** $\frac{14}{5}$ **35a.** August **35b.** December **37.** $-\frac{1}{a+1}$; You know that $a + 1 > a$. The greater number has the lesser reciprocal, so $\frac{1}{a+1} < \frac{1}{a}$. With $\frac{1}{a+1}$ to the *left* of $\frac{1}{a}$ on a number line, their opposites have the reverse orientation. That is, $-\frac{1}{a+1}$ is to the *right* of $-\frac{1}{a}$, so $-\frac{1}{a+1}$ is greater.

**5.1 Practice B (p. 207)** **1.** $\frac{28}{25}$ **3.** $\frac{43}{5}$ **5.** $\frac{-11}{2}$ **7.** $\frac{-3}{100}$ **9.** 1.4; Terminates **11.** $-2.\overline{1}$; Repeats **13.** $-0.8\overline{3}$; Repeats **15.** $-0.875$; Terminates **17.** $-2.4$ **19.** $-3\frac{1}{3}$ **21.** $-3\frac{1}{8}$ **23.** $-3$, $-1.9$, $\frac{3}{4}$, 0.8 **25.** $-2$, $\frac{1}{5}$, $\frac{3}{4}$, 4.7 **27.** 2.5 **29.** $-1.5$ **31.** Monday; Wednesday **33.** $-\frac{1}{2a}$; You know that $a > 0$, so $2a > a$. The greater number has the lesser reciprocal, so $\frac{1}{2a} < \frac{1}{a}$. With $\frac{1}{2a}$ to the *left* of $\frac{1}{a}$ on a number line, their opposites have the reverse orientation. That is, $-\frac{1}{2a}$ is to the *right* of $-\frac{1}{a}$, so $-\frac{1}{2a}$ is greater.

**5.2 Practice A (p. 212)** **1.** $\frac{2}{3}$ **3.** $\frac{1}{2}$ **5.** $\frac{1}{8}$ **7.** $-\frac{1}{9}$ **9.** $\frac{2}{5}$ **11.** $-\frac{13}{22}$ **13.** 0 **15.** $\frac{43}{6}$ or $7\frac{1}{6}$ **17.** 37.2 **19.** $-45.2$ **21.** 42.7 **23.** 36.7 **25.** $-5\frac{1}{2}°F$ **27.** $-134.3$ meters **29.** 111.8 meters **31.** $2\frac{7}{10}$ ft; up **33.** Change the fraction to a decimal or the decimal to a fraction and add; $-\frac{1}{5}$ or $-0.2$.

**5.2 Practice B (p. 213)** **1.** 2 **3.** $-907.3$ **5.** 20.8 **7.** 468.7 **9.** $-16.9$ **11.** $-179.9$ **13.** $17\frac{1}{5}$ **15.** $-17\frac{1}{5}$ **17.** $-19\frac{4}{5}$ **19.** $9\frac{9}{10}$ **21.** $6\frac{2}{5}$ **23.** $24\frac{2}{5}$ **25.** $10.5°C$ **27.** $-3\frac{3}{4}$ yards **29.** $-28\frac{1}{12}$ feet **31.** Alaska: $100°C$, North Dakota: $100.5°C$, Wyoming: $100.5°C$, Virginia: $77.7°C$, Nevada: $97.3°C$. Wyoming showed the greatest temperature difference.

**5.3 Practice A (p. 218)** **1.** Inverse **3.** Comm. **5.** Inverse **7.** Comm. **9.** Identity **11.** 29 **13.** 49.2 **15.** $-0.9$ **17.** $y + 10.7$ **19.** $\frac{9}{4} + m$ **21.** $-\frac{1}{7}z - 8\frac{5}{6}$ **23.** 1.8 miles from his house; east **25.** Changing the order when subtracting two numbers changes the sign: $a - b = -(b - a)$.

**5.3 Practice B (p. 219)** **1.** Inverse **3.** Assoc. **5.** Inverse **7.** Assoc. **9.** Identity **11.** $-6$ **13.** $-40.25$ **15.** $-0.99$ **17.** $y + 17.1$ **19.** $m$ **21.** $-\frac{1}{7}z - 8$ **23.** 5.75 mi west **25.** Counterexample: $(6 - 5) - 4 = (1) - 4 = -3$, but $6 - (5 - 4) = 6 - (1) = 5$. For $a$, $b$, and $c$, $(a - b) - c = a + (-b) + (-c)$ and $a - (b - c) = a + [-(b - c)] = a + (-b + c) = a + (-b) + c$. Any example with $c \neq 0$ shows that there is no associative property of subtraction.

**5.4 Practice A (p. 226)** **1.** $-\frac{1}{22}$ **3.** $-\frac{1}{4}$ **5.** 3 **7.** $-\frac{1}{2}$ **9.** $-10$ **11.** 24 **13.** $-36$ **15.** $-32.5$ **17.** 0.04 **19.** $-\frac{1}{3}$ **21.** $-2\frac{1}{3}$ **23.** $-1\frac{1}{5}$ **25.** $-\frac{3}{14}$ **27.** $-2\frac{5}{8}$ **29.** $-1\frac{1}{2}$ **31.** $1\frac{5}{8}$ **33.** $\frac{7}{25}$ **35.** $\frac{4}{7}$ **37.** $-9.6$ **39.** 0.48 **41.** First write 0.8 as a fraction: $\frac{4}{5}$. Then multiply $\frac{4}{5}$ by the reciprocal of $-\frac{2}{5}$, or $-\frac{5}{2}$: $\frac{4}{5} \cdot \left(-\frac{5}{2}\right) = -\frac{20}{10}$, or $-2$. **43.** 67.7 **45.** $-1.45$ mi$^2$/yr

**5.4 Practice B (p. 227) 1.** $\frac{3}{2}$ **3.** $-\frac{1}{4}$ **5.** $\frac{3}{4}$ **7.** $\frac{2}{3}$
**9.** $-64.5$ **11.** $35.34$ **13.** $-56.875$ **15.** $-64.8$ **17.** $-\frac{1}{7}$
**19.** $-\frac{3}{4}$ **21.** $-7\frac{1}{2}$ **23.** $1\frac{1}{2}$ **25.** $\frac{9}{49}$ **27.** $-\frac{1}{21}$ **29.** $-\frac{3}{10}$
**31.** $5$ **33.** $\frac{4}{7}$ **35.** $\frac{2}{7}$ **37.** $96$ **39.** $0.4$ **41.** Negative,
because the product of a nonzero number and its
reciprocal is 1, and if the number is negative, its
reciprocal must be negative for the product to be
positive. **43.** $0.28°C$ per minute **45.** $\$.36$

**5.5 Practice A (p. 232) 1.** Multiplicative property
of 0 **3.** Commutative property of multiplication
**5.** Identity property of multiplication
**7.** Commutative property of multiplication
**9.** Multiplicative property of $-1$ **11.** $-7x$ **13.** $-15y$
**15.** $12.6x$ **17.** $5$ **19.** $-24x$ **21.** $0$ **23.** $13,200$ ft
**25.** $1.57$ cm **27.** $215.6$ lb **29.** $1.91$ m, $1.40$ m;
$2.67$ m²; The area in square feet is $(3.28)^2$ times the
area in square meters. **31.** Since division is
multiplication by the reciprocal, $\frac{1}{\frac{a}{b}} = 1 \cdot \frac{b}{a}$, which
is $\frac{b}{a}$.

**5.5 Practice B (p. 233) 1.** Multiplicative property
of 0 **3.** Commutative property of multiplication
**5.** Identity property of multiplication
**7.** Commutative property of multiplication
**9.** Multiplicative property of $-1$ **11.** $-49x^2$
**13.** $-60x$ **15.** $168x$ **17.** $-6x$ **19.** $9.9a$ **21.** $-\frac{5}{7}$
**23.** $1600$ m **25.** $7.05$ lb **27.** $86$ quarts **29.** $1.62$ cubic
meters **31.** $441$ square feet

**5.6 Practice A (p. 238) 1.** B **3.** A **5.** $-24x - 21$
**7.** $3x + 3.5y$ **9.** $5x + 3\frac{1}{3}$ **11.** $5m$ **13.** $15m + 10p$
**15.** $\frac{3}{2}x - \frac{4}{3}y$ **17.** $126.5$ square feet **19.** $\frac{3}{2}x - \frac{1}{2}y$
**21.** $-2x - 3$ **23.** $\frac{17}{5}p$ **25a.** $(2.75 + 1.50)(4)$; $\$17$
**25b.** $4(2.75) + 4(1.50) = 11 + 6 = \$17$
**25c.** They are the same, which shows that finding
the cost per player and multiplying by the number
of players is equal to the sum of the cost of games
for four players and the cost of shoes for four
players.

**5.6 Practice B (p. 239) 1.** $-\frac{1}{3}y - 1$ **3.** $-\frac{1}{8}m - \frac{3}{10}$
**5.** $\frac{1}{3}z - 2$ **7.** $\frac{3}{4}w - 6$ **9.** $6x - \frac{1}{3}$ **11.** $\frac{3}{4}m + \frac{4}{9}k$ **13.** $\frac{5}{8}d$
**15.** $19.5x + 2.9y$ **17.** $3.6$ cm² **19.** The $0.2$ was not
distributed to both terms in the parentheses.

$0.2(5 + x) = 0.2(5) + 0.2(x) = 1 + 0.2x$
**21.** $4.5y + 15$ **23.** $-14.4d$ **25.** $\frac{5}{3}g - \frac{5}{6}$ **27.** $\$11.94$
**29.** $a(b - c) = a[b + (-c)] = ab + a(-c) = ab - ac$.

# Chapter 6

**6.1 Practice A (p. 254) 1.** add, exponents
**3.** no **5.** yes **7.** $2^6$ **9.** $4^{16}$ **11.** $8^{11}$ **13.** $(-13)^{15}$
**15.** $a^5$ **17.** $x^{12}$ **19.** $3g^9$ **21.** The student should have
multiplied $2 \cdot 2$; $4x^9$. **23.** $11$ **25.** $4$ **27.** $10^6, 10^5$
**29.** $10^{41}$ water molecules

**6.1 Practice B (p. 255) 1.** yes **3.** no **5.** $5^{21}$
**7.** $6^{17}$ **9.** $9^{25}$ **11.** $(-6)^{18}$ **13.** $(-15)^{24}$ **15.** $12h^{11}$
**17.** $56e^{19}$ **19.** $20v^{13}$ **21.** $121f^{11}$ **23.** $18$ **25.** $25$
**27.** $2x^2$ **29.** $4.8x^3$ **31.** $10^6$ metric tons

**6.2 Practice A (p. 260) 1.** denominator,
numerator **3.** yes **5.** no **7.** $5^1$ **9.** $12^1$ **11.** $8^2$
**13.** $(-13)^3$ **15.** $k^2$ **17.** $y^6$ **19.** $n^4$ **21.** $4d^2$ **23.** $\frac{4w^6t^2}{3}$
**25.** $11$ **27.** *Sample answer*: $c = 2, d = 1$; Yes; Any
pair of integers where the difference between $c$ and $d$
is 1 will make the statement true.

**6.2 Practice B (p. 261) 1.** $3^8$ **3.** $11^4$ **5.** $16^3$
**7.** $(-10)^1$ **9.** $(-25)^6$ **11.** $v^8$ **13.** $y^6$ **15.** $m^4$
**17.** $15x^5z^5$ **19.** $9m^4$ **21.** $\frac{18d^3}{7}$ **23.** $\frac{17t^3v^2}{36}$
**25.** The student divided the exponent in the
numerator by the exponent in the denominator; $4r^4$.
**27.** I could write seven 4's in the numerator and
three 4's in the denominator. I could then divide,
leaving four 4's in the numerator. **29a.** $10^3$ times
as great **29b.** $10^4$ times as great

**6.3 Practice A (p. 268) 1.** $a^n$ **3.** $\frac{1}{36}$ **5.** $\frac{1}{343}$ **7.** $\frac{1}{27}$
**9.** $1$ **11.** $1 \times 10^1 + 8 \times 10^0 + 4 \times 10^{-1}$
**13.** $2 \times 10^1 + 7 \times 10^0 + 3 \times 10^{-1}$ **15.** $6.53$
**17.** $19.89$ **19.** yes **21.** no **23.** $0.00000000439$
**25.** $76,500,000$ **27.** $887,000,000,000$ **29.** $9.3 \times 10^3$
**31.** $4.219 \times 10^{-2}$ **33.** $8.3 \times 10^{-9}$ **35.** Carpenter
**37.** Bulldog

**6.3 Practice B (p. 269) 1.** $\frac{1}{625}$ **3.** $\frac{1}{1024}$ **5.** $\frac{1}{81}$
**7.** $1$ **9.** $1 \times 10^1 + 1 \times 10^0 + 4 \times 10^{-1}$
**11.** $6 \times 10^{-1} + 3 \times 10^{-2}$ **13.** $527$ **15.** $237.5$
**17.** $0.0000804$ **19.** $0.0139$ **21.** $7,610,000$
**23.** $7.3 \times 10^5$ **25.** $8.915 \times 10^9$ **27.** $9.3 \times 10^{-4}$

**29.** The decimal point moves 3 places to the right, so the exponent should be negative; $4.8 \times 10^{-3}$.
**31.** The exponent is positive. **33.** 0.3, 0.165, 15; $9.75 \times 10^1$, $2.4 \times 10^{-4}$

**6.4 Practice A (p. 274)** **1.** C **3.** B **5.** $\frac{1}{121}$
**7.** 1 **9.** 64 **11.** $\frac{1}{16}$ **13.** yes **15.** yes **17.** 1 **19.** $\frac{1}{f^{10}}$
**21.** 1 **23.** $\frac{1}{m^8}$ **25.** $h^8$ **27.** $\frac{k^{20}}{m^{21}}$ **29.** $-5$ **31.** $-7$ **33.** 7
**35.** $10^4$, or 10,000 times as great **37.** $10^2$ kg, or 100 kg

**6.4 Practice B (p. 275)** **1.** 81 **3.** 2197 **5.** 8
**7.** $\frac{1}{256}$ **9.** yes **11.** yes **13.** $g^3$ **15.** $\frac{1}{c^{14}}$ **17.** $\frac{1}{b^7}$ **19.** $\frac{3}{d^{11}}$
**21.** $\frac{1}{x^6 z^9}$ **23.** 35 **25.** The student divided the
exponents $-9$ and 3 instead of subtracting them; $\frac{5}{b^{12}}$.
**27.** $-8$ **29.** 8 **31.** $10^4$, or 10,000 times as great
**33.** $10^6$, or 1,000,000 times as long

# Chapter 7

**7.1 Practice A (p. 290)** **1.** 2, $-2$ **3.** 9, $-9$
**5.** 6, $-6$ **7.** 4, $-4$ **9.** 7 **11.** $-5$ **13.** 9 **15.** $\pm 4$
**17.** $-3$ **19.** 13 **21.** $\pm 8$ **23.** $-6$ **25.** 5 ft **27.** 200 ft
**29.** 24 in. **31.** 44 ft **33.** 60.5 ft$^3$

**7.1 Practice B (p. 291)** **1.** 3, $-3$ **3.** 11, $-11$
**5.** 60, $-60$ **7.** 17, $-17$ **9.** 30 **11.** $-14$ **13.** $-4$
**15.** $\pm 9$ **17.** $-20$ **19.** 70 **21.** $-29$ **23.** 31 **25.** $\pm 0.6$
**27.** $\pm 2.1$ **29.** $\pm 0.5$ **31.** $\pm 1.1$ **33.** 18 **35.** $-45$
**37.** 60 ft **39.** 2.5 ft **41.** 2.5 in. **43.** $a$; by the
definition of square root, $\sqrt{a}$ is a number whose
square is $a$, so $(\sqrt{a})^2 = a$.

**7.2 Practice A (p. 296)** **1.** 3, 4 **3.** $-6$, $-7$ **5.** 2
**7.** $-5$ **9.** $-7$ **11.** 8 **13.** 5 **15.** $-12$ **17.** 1.7 **19.** $-3.3$
**21.** 8.7 **23.** 11.9 **25.** $-5$, 2, $\sqrt{9}$, $\sqrt{64}$ **27.** $-3.6$,
$-\sqrt{1}$, $\frac{2}{3}$, $\sqrt{4}$ **29.** 11 ft **31.** 48.6 cm **33.** integer,
rational, real **35.** whole, integer, rational, real

**7.2 Practice B (p. 297)** **1.** 4 **3.** 9 **5.** $-5$ **7.** $-7$
**9.** 12 **11.** 25 **13.** $\sqrt{39} \approx \sqrt{36}$, not 36; 6. **15.** 5.2
**17.** 9.6 **19.** 11.4 **21.** $-15.2$ **23.** $-8.15$, $-8$, $\sqrt{53}$, 7.4
**25.** $-4.7$, $-\sqrt{21}$, $-\sqrt{\frac{2}{5}}$, $-\frac{5}{9}$ **27.** Using $\sqrt{2} \approx 1.4$,
832 mm **29.** 3.2 cm **31.** Rational because $\frac{2}{11}$ has the
form $\frac{a}{b}$. **33.** Irrational because 15 is not a perfect
square. **35.** 3.4 **37.** 0.101001000100001. . .

**7.3 Practice A (p. 304)** **1.** If a glass is $\frac{3}{5}$ full, then
the glass is 60% full; Hypothesis: a glass is $\frac{3}{5}$ full;
Conclusion: the glass is 60% full **3.** If $a = -4$, then
$a^2 = 16$; Hypothesis: $a = -4$; Conclusion: $a^2 = 16$
**5.** 4.5 **7.** 5.8 **9.** 7.6 **11.** 15 **13.** 8.9 **15.** 6.7 mm
**17.** 30.5 ft **19.** The length of the hypotenuse
doubles. For example, if the legs are 4 inches and
5 inches long, the length of the hypotenuse is
$\sqrt{4^2 + 5^2} \approx 6.4$ inches. If the legs are 8 inches and
10 inches long, the length of the hypotenuse is
$\sqrt{8^2 + 10^2} \approx 12.8$ inches long.

**7.3 Practice B (p. 305)** **1.** If a fish tank is 80%
full, then the fish tank is $\frac{4}{5}$ full; Hypothesis: the
fish tank is 80% full; Conclusion: the fish tank is
$\frac{4}{5}$ full **3.** If $a = 0$, then $a^2 = 0$; Hypothesis: $a = 0$;
Conclusion: $a^2 = 0$ **5.** 5.1 **7.** 8.5 **9.** 7.3 **11.** 50
**13.** 24.6 **15.** Yes; The diagonal of the window
is 5 feet long. **17.** The length of the hypotenuse
becomes half of its original length. For example,
$8^2 + 10^2 = c^2$, $c \approx 12.8$ and $4^2 + 5^2 = c^2$, $c \approx 6.4$.

**7.4 Practice A (p. 310)** **1.** If you are an athlete,
then you are a soccer player; false; athletes play
many different sports. **3.** If an animal is a mammal,
then the animal is a whale; false; many mammals
are not whales. **5.** no **7.** yes **9.** no **11.** no **13.** yes
**15.** no **17.** no **19.** no **21.** no **23.** No; the diagonal
should measure about 15.6 inches. **25.** Measure
the sides and a diagonal of the rectangle and if
$a^2 + b^2 = c^2$, then the triangle is a right triangle and
the frame is a rectangle.

**7.4 Practice B (p. 311)** **1.** If an animal is a
reptile, the animal is a lizard; false; many reptiles are
not lizards. **3.** If the temperature is below freezing,
then it is snowing; false; the temperature can be
below freezing without snow falling. **5.** yes **7.** no
**9.** yes **11.** no **13.** yes **15.** no **17.** no **19.** yes **21.** no
**23.** No; $15^2 + 18^2 \stackrel{?}{=} 23^2$, $549 \neq 529$. **25.** To use
the Pythagorean theorem, you must know that you
have a right triangle and you can use the formula
$a^2 + b^2 = c^2$ to find the length of a missing side if
you know the lengths of two sides. For the converse,
the formula can be used to determine if a given
triangle is a right triangle if you know the lengths of
all three sides.

# Chapter 8

**8.1 Practice A (p. 326) 1.** $n + 3 = 7$
**3.** $-8 = n - 5$ **5.** yes **7.** no **9.** yes **11.** 16, 16;
Subtract 16; 1 **13.** $y = -19$ **15.** $x = -9$
**17.** $b = -1$ **19.** $a = 29$ **21.** $r = 35$ **23.** $c = 20$
**25.** $h - 5.45 = 7.95$; $13.40 **27.** $w + 5 = 21$;
16 games

**8.1 Practice B (p. 327) 1.** yes **3.** no
**5.** $n = -37$ **7.** $a = 40$ **9.** $s = 55$ **11.** $c = 8.8$
**13.** $t = \frac{1}{2}$ **15.** $x = -\frac{1}{3}$ **17.** 16 was added only
to the right side; $y = 35$. **19.** $n + 9 = 24$; $n = 15$
**21.** $n - 15 = 7$; $n = 22$ **23.** $11.3 = 1.8 + 5 +$
$1.3 + x$; $x = 3.2$ mm **25.** $p + 37 = 54$; 17 people
**27.** Add $-3$ to each side of the equation.

**8.2 Practice A (p. 332) 1.** yes **3.** yes **5.** no **7.** C
**9.** B **11.** Error is getting 7 when dividing 42 by
$-6$, $\frac{42}{-6} = -7$; $a = -7$. **13.** $w = 4$ **15.** $r = 21$
**17.** $n = -52$ **19.** $b = -8$ **21.** $g = -9$ **23.** $y = 7.5$
**25.** Yes, multiply each side by $\frac{1}{3}$, the reciprocal of 3.
**27.** $11x = 363$, $x = 33$; Her car gets 33 miles per
gallon.

**8.2 Practice B (p. 333) 1.** no **3.** no **5.** yes
**7.** $p = 12$ **9.** $c = -35$ **11.** $m = -301$
**13.** $a = -28.8$ **15.** $r = -16$ **17.** $q = 0.27$
**19.** $d = -12$ **21.** $f = 8.4$ **23.** The equation was not
multiplied by 4; $x = 32$. **25.** $3x = 14.4$; $x = 4.8$
**27.** In two steps, first multiply each side of the
equation by 3. Then divide each side of the equation
by 2 and simplify. In one step, multiply each side by
the reciprocal, $\frac{3}{2}$, and simplify. **29.** $3.2p = 4.8$,
$p = 1.5$; The cost of 1 lb of peanuts is $1.50.

**8.3 Practice A (p. 338) 1.** $x = 2$ **3.** $m = 5$
**5.** $p = 30$ **7.** $m = -24$ **9.** $g = 9$ **11.** $x = 49$
**13.** $g = 18$ **15.** $c = -2\frac{2}{3}$ **17.** $q = 4\frac{1}{4}$
**19.** In step 4, each side is divided by 6 instead of
$-6$. $\frac{15}{-6} = \frac{-6n}{-6}$; $-2\frac{1}{2} = n$ **21.** Yes, but you must
use the distributive property when multiplying the
left side by 2. **23.** $3 + 7n = 45$; $n = 6$
**25.** $2.90b + 3.18 = 20$; $b = 5.8$; 5 bracelets
**27.** $60t + 45 = 225$; $t = 3$; It took the plumber
3 hours to do the job.

**8.3 Practice B (p. 339) 1.** $x = 4$ **3.** $r = 200$
**5.** $p = -2$ **7.** $m = -3$ **9.** $g = 11$ **11.** $x = 64$
**13.** $c = -1\frac{3}{4}$ **15.** $q = 6\frac{1}{7}$ **17.** $a = -833$
**19.** In step 2, 12 is subtracted instead of added.
$\frac{n}{5} - 12 + 12 = 32 + 12$; $\frac{n}{5} = 44$; $\frac{n}{5} \cdot 5 = 44 \cdot 5$;
$n = 220$. **21.** For the first equation, multiply each
side by 2, then subtract 1 from each side. For the
second equation, subtract 1 from each side, then
multiply each side by 2. **23.** $9.8 + \frac{n}{5} = 10.4$; $n = 3$
**25.** $4c + 2.89 = 12.25$; $c = 2.34$; $2.34
**27.** $5(25) + 25p = 260$; $p = 5.4$; Jessica needs
6 more packages of 25 sheets.

**8.4 Practice A (p. 346) 1.** 10 **3.** 100 **5.** 12
**7.** $x = \frac{1}{4}$ **9.** $n = -\frac{1}{17}$ **11.** $t = -\frac{1}{14}$ **13.** $c = \frac{7}{8}$
**15.** $m = \frac{5}{12}$ **17.** $w = 2\frac{13}{25}$ **19.** Only the right
side of the equation was multiplied by 10; $y = 25.5$
**21.** $g = 2.4$ **23.** $z = 2$ **25.** $x = 4.5$ **27.** $y = 0.5$
**29.** $r = -3.9$ **31.** $m = 13$ **33.** $25.5 + 1.2d + 1.3d = 30$, $d = 1.8$; 1 of each **35.** Write 0.5 as $\frac{1}{2}$ and
multiply both sides of the equation by 2 or write
each $\frac{1}{2}$ as 0.5 and multiply both sides of the equation
by 10. The solution is $x = 2$.

**8.4 Practice B (p. 347) 1.** $t = -\frac{8}{17}$ **3.** $x = \frac{7}{16}$
**5.** $h = -1\frac{1}{2}$ **7.** $p = \frac{19}{28}$ **9.** $b = -\frac{1}{4}$ **11.** $a = \frac{8}{13}$
**13.** Each side of the equation should be multiplied
by the same number, in this case, 12; $x = 1\frac{7}{8}$.
**15.** $x = 6$ **17.** $d = -2.1$ **19.** $v = 2.4$ **21.** $z = -0.7$
**23.** $p = 2$ **25.** $w = 8$ **27.** $6.95x + 7.45x + 86.1 = 250$, $x = 11$; 11 bags of each **29.** $32.45 + 1.308d = 50$; $d \approx 13.4$; 14 U.S. dollar bills.

**8.5 Practice A (p. 352) 1.** no **3.** yes
**5.** Use the distributive property to get $5a - 20$.
**7.** Use the distributive property to get $6w - 18$.
**9.** Use the distributive property to get $-3p - 18$.
**11.** $x = -15$ **13.** $x = -11$ **15.** $x = 4$ **17.** $p = 6$
**19.** $w = -7.5$ **21.** $b = 5\frac{1}{5}$ **23.** $x = 3$ **25.** $x = 1.75$
**27.** The Donati family was not driving for 66 hours
of the trip.

**8.5 Practice B (p. 353) 1.** $x = 3$ **3.** $a = 2$
**5.** $c = -3$ **7.** $n = 3$ **9.** $z = 3$ **11.** $x = 5$ **13.** $x = 6$

**15.** Yes; The solution of the first equation is $x = 2$ and the solution of the second equation is $x = 2$, so the two equations are equivalent. **17.** 12 h

**8.6 Practice A (p. 358) 1.** 50 km/h; 60 km/h
**3.** 65 km/h; 75 km/h **5.** $6\frac{2}{3}$ h **7.** They will meet two-thirds of the fixed distance measured from where the faster object began moving (or one-third of the fixed distance from where the slower object began moving) because the faster object travels twice the distance traveled by the slower object.

**8.6 Practice B (p. 359) 1.** 58 km/h; 65 km/h

**3a.** 1.3, 1.3$r$; $r$ + 5, 2.4, 2.4($r$ + 5)

**3b.**
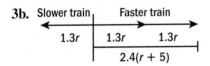

**3c.** 2.4($r$ + 5) = 2(1.3$r$) **3d.** Slower train: 60 km/h; Faster train: 65 km/h **3e.** Slower train: 78 km; Faster train: 156 km **5.** 1.2 h **7.** 3 h

# Chapter 9

**9.1 Practice A (p. 374)**

**1.** [number line graph: open circle at −2, −3 −2 −1 0 1]

**3.** [number line graph: closed circle at 0, −1 0 1]

**5.** $x \le 4$ **7.** $x \ge 9$ **9.** C **11.** A **13.** $x \ge 10$ **15.** $x < 5$
**17.** D **19.** A

**21.** $h \ge 48$; [number line: closed circle at 48, 47 48 49]

**23.** $a \ge 35$; [number line: closed circle at 35, 34 35 36]

**25.** $d > 2.2$; [number line: open circle at 2.2, 2 3]

**9.1 Practice B (p. 375)**

**1.** [number line: open circle at −9.1, −10 −9 −8]

**3.** [number line: closed circle at −0.3, −1 0]

**5.** $x \ge 5$ **7.** $x < 10$ **9.** B **11.** A **13.** $x \le 6$ **15.** $x \ge 2$

**17.** C **19.** A
**21.** $h \ge 52$; [number line: closed circle at 52, 51 52 53]

**23.** $a \ge 16$; [number line: closed circle at 16, 15 16 17]

**25.** $t < 65$; [number line: open circle at 65, 64 65 66]

**9.2 Practice A (p. 380) 1.** Not a solution
**3.** Solution
**5.** $m \le 11$; [number line: closed circle at 11, 10 11 12]

**7.** $f > 9$; [number line: open circle at 9, 8 9 10]

**9.** $y > -5$; [number line: open circle at −5, −6 −5 −4]

**11.** $v \le -12$; [number line: closed circle at −12, −13 −12 −11]

**13.** $x < -7$; [number line: open circle at −7, −8 −7 −6]

**15.** $y > 0$; [number line: open circle at 0, −1 0 1]

**17.** $v > -1$; [number line: open circle at −1, −2 −1 0]

**19.** 7 should be subtracted from both sides. The solution should be $x > -11$.
**21.** $x + 80 \ge 170$; $x \ge 90$; at least 90 points on the English section **23.** $x + 100 \ge 348.50$; $x \ge 248.50$; at least $248.50 **25.** Yes; $x - 2 \le 4$ can be transformed to obtain $x \le 6$ by adding 2 to each side, and reading $6 \ge x$ from right to left gives $x \le 6$.

**9.2 Practice B (p. 381) 1.** Solution **3.** Solution
**5.** $m \le 13$; [number line: closed circle at 13, 12 13 14]

**7.** $f < 8$; [number line: open circle at 8, 7 8 9]

**9.** $y > -2$; [number line: open circle at −2, −3 −2 −1]

**11.** $v \le -22$; [number line: closed circle at −22, −23 −22 −21]

**13.** $x > \frac{3}{5}$; [number line: open circle at $\frac{3}{5}$, −1 0 1]

**15.** $m \le 4.25$; [number line: closed circle at 4.25, 3 4 5]

**17.** c $\ge -24.9$; [number line: closed circle at −24.9, −26 −25 −24 −23]

**19.** $-3.6 - 2.8 = -6.4$; The solution should be $y > -6.4$. **21.** $5 + 7 + 8 + 6 + x < 30$; $x < 4$; less than 4 minutes **23.** $x + 8.5 + 8.5 + 25.5 \le 50$; $x \le 7.5$; 7.5 pounds or less **25.** No; the solution is $x \ge 2$, so the number line should include all numbers greater than or equal to 2.

**9.3 Practice A (p. 388)** **1.** E **3.** A **5.** B

**7.** $h \le -10$;

**9.** $p < -48$;

**11.** $n \ge -4$;

**13.** $q \ge -15$;

**15.** $c \le -9$;

**17.** $j \le 3$;

**19.** $9.5x \le 38$; $x \le 4$; four CDs or fewer. **21.** $15w \ge 180$, $w \ge 12$; at least 12 weeks **23.** Divide by $-1$ because $-x = -1 \cdot x$.

**9.3 Practice B (p. 389)**

**1.** $m \ge 12$;

**3.** $y \ge -145$;

**5.** $g < 6$;

**7.** $k < -11$;

**9.** $u > -108$;

**11.** $b > -427$;

**13.** You must multiply, rather than divide, by $-2$ on each side of the inequality; $w < 20$. **15.** $4x \ge 350$; $x \ge 87.5$; at least \$87.50 each month **17.** $1.6b \le 40$; $b \le 25$; 25 or fewer balloons **19.** $4c \le 300$; $c \le 75$; \$75 or less per person **21.** Divide each side by $-\frac{1}{2}$, or multiply each side by $-2$.

**9.4 Practice A (p. 394)** **1.** Subtract 6. **3.** Add 4. **5.** Subtract $\frac{1}{2}$.

**7.** $x > -3$;

**9.** $x \le 1.2$;

**11.** $y \ge -14$;

**13.** $x \le -46$;

**15.** $b > -0.14$;

**17.** $c > -36$;

**19.** A **21.** B

**23.** $3x + 5 < 8$; $x < 1$;

**25.** $-3.2x - 1 \le 5.4$; $x \ge -2$;

**27.** Yes. $4\left(\frac{3}{4}\right) - 5 \overset{?}{<} 10$; $-2 < 10$ **29.** $120p + 220 \ge 400$; $p \ge 1.5$; You need to make at least 1.5 pins per minute.

**9.4 Practice B (p. 395)** **1.** Subtract 4. **3.** Subtract 1.09. **5.** Add 15.

**7.** $x < 2$;

**9.** $w > 16$;

**11.** $c < 15$;

**13.** $w < -60$;

**15.** $x \ge -12$;

**17.** $x < -9$;

**19.** C **21.** A

**23.** $5x + 6 \ge 31$;

$x \ge 5$

**25.** $-2x + 10 < 8$;

$x > 1$

**27.** Yes. $-5 \le \frac{-20}{4} + 2$; $-5 \le -3$ **29.** $7.5p - 34 \ge 50$; $p \ge 11.2$; You must sell at least 12 paintings.

# Chapter 10

**10.1 Practice A (p. 410)** **1.** $(1, -2)$ **3.** $(-2, 3)$
**5.** $(-1, 0)$

**7, 9, and 11.**

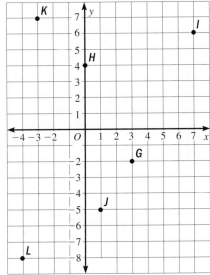

**7.** In Quadrant IV **9.** In Quadrant I
**11.** In Quadrant II **13.** rectangle; 10 units; 6 square
units **15.** square; 16 units; 16 square units **17.** The
$x$-coordinate is $-3$, so move 3 units to the left.
**19.** $(-2, 2)$ **21a.** $A(-6, 3)$, $B(3, -1)$ **21b.** 9 mi; 4 mi
**21c.** 13 mi

**10.1 Practice B (p. 411)** **1.** $(3, -2)$ **3.** $(4, 0)$
**5.** $(1, 5)$

**7, 9, and 11.**

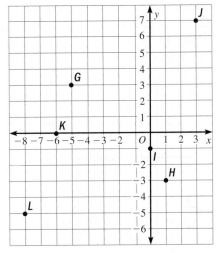

**7.** In Quadrant II **9.** On the $y$-axis **11.** On the $x$-axis

**13.** rectangle; 14 units; 12 square units **15.** square;
20 units; 25 square units **17.** Error is subtracting
the $y$-coordinate of $H$ from the $x$-coordinate of $G$.
Should subtract the $x$-coordinate of $H$.
$|-2 - 4| = |-6| = 6$ units **19.** 60 ft; 221 ft$^2$
**21.** The new rectangle has a perimeter that is 2 times
the perimeter of the original rectangle.

**10.2 Practice A (p. 416)** **1.** Yes **3.** No **5.** Yes
**7.** Error is switching $x$ and $y$ when substituting.
It should be $4(1) + 2(2) = 8$, so $(1, 2)$ is a solution.
**9.** $y = 12$ **11.** $y = 6$

**13.**

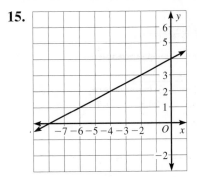

**15.**

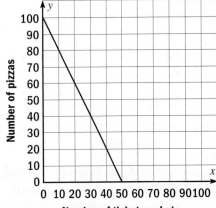

**19.** $a = 3$

**21a.**

**21b.** *Sample answer*: 0 ticket packets and 100 pizzas, 10 ticket packets and 80 pizzas, 20 ticket packets and 60 pizzas, 50 ticket packets and 0 pizzas.

**10.2 Practice B (p. 417) 1.** No **3.** Yes **5.** No **7.** $y = 306$ **9.** $y = 4$ **11.** $y = \frac{3}{2}$ **13.** Error is in $(6, -1)$. The values of $x$ and $y$ are reversed in the ordered pair. One solution should be $(-1, 6)$.

**15.**

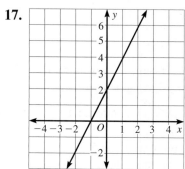

**17.**

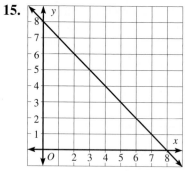

**23.** $a = 6$

**25a.**

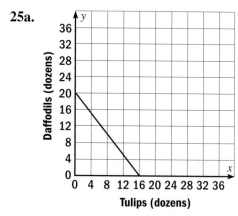

**25b.** *Sample answer*: 0 dozen tulips and 20 dozen daffodils, 4 dozen tulips and 15 dozen daffodils, 8 dozen tulips and 10 dozen daffodils, 16 dozen tulips and 0 dozen daffodils.

**10.3 Practice A (p. 422) 1.** B **3.** C **5.** No **7–13.** *Sample answers are given.* **7.** $(-25, 3)$, $(-25, -9)$, $(-25, 5)$ **9.** $(4, 12)$, $(-8, 12)$, $(-2, 12)$ **11.** $(40, 59)$, $(41, 59)$, $(42, 59)$ **13.** $(-10, -17)$, $(-2, -17)$, $(8, -17)$

**15.**

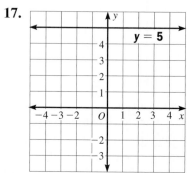

**17.**

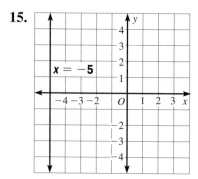

**23.** $y = 3$ **25.** $375$ ft$^2$ **27a.** *B* must equal 0. **27b.** *A* must equal 0.

**10.3 Practice B (p. 423) 1.** A **3.** C **5.** Yes **7–13.** *Sample answers are given.* **7.** $(-32, 4)$, $(-32, -7)$, $(-32, 0)$ **9.** $(11, -56)$, $(-9, -56)$, $(8, -56)$ **11.** $(-0.2, -5)$, $(-0.2, -1)$, $(-0.2, 3)$ **13.** $(-5, 0)$, $(1, 0)$, $(8, 0)$

**15.**

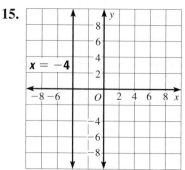

**17.**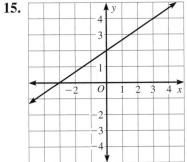

**23.** $y = -2$ **25.** $(5, -2)$; use the value of $x$ from the equation $x = 5$ as the $x$-coordinate and the value of $y$ from the equation $y = -2$ as the $y$-coordinate; $(-7, -6)$ **27.** 500 in.²

**10.4 Practice A (p. 430) 1.** $x$-intercept $= -4$, $y$-intercept $= -1$ **3.** $x$-intercept $= -3$, $y$-intercept $= -2$ **5.** $x$-intercept $= 6$, $y$-intercept $= 4$ **7.** $x$-intercept $= 2$, $y$-intercept $= -6$ **9.** $x$-intercept $= 5$, $y$-intercept $= -3$ **11.** 12 should not be multiplied by 0; $y$-intercept $= 6$.

**13.**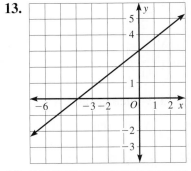

**15.**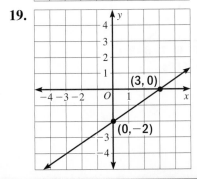

**19.**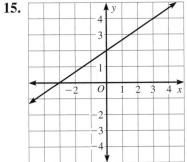

**21.**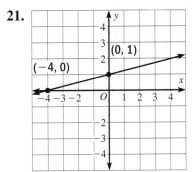

**25.**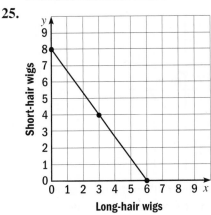

6 long-hair and 0 short-hair, 3 long-hair and 4 short-hair, or 0 long-hair and 8 short-hair

**10.4 Practice B (p. 431) 1.** $x$-intercept $= 1$, $y$-intercept $= -4$ **3.** $x$-intercept $= -5$, $y$-intercept $= 5$ **5.** $x$-intercept $= -0.5$, $y$-intercept $= 1$ **7.** Error is substituting 0 for $x$-intercept and solving for $y$; $x$-intercept $= 5$.

**9.**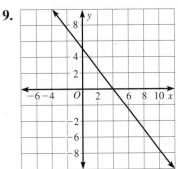

**11.**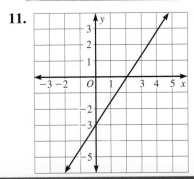

**13.**

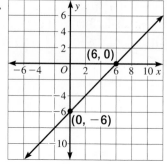

**15.**

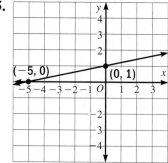

**19.** If the *x*-intercept is 0, then the line passes through the origin, so you know the *y*-intercept is also 0.

**10.5 Practice A (p. 436)** **1.** positive; $\frac{3}{2}$
**3.** undefined **5.** $\frac{2}{3}$ **7.** 0 **9.** $-\frac{1}{2}$ **11.** $\frac{3}{2}$ **13.** $-4$
**15.** $-\frac{16}{19}$ **17.** Yes, a greater slope means the line is steeper because the rise will be greater for a given run. **19a.** 55 **19b.** Its speed, 55 miles per hour **19c.** It would be less steep because the car is traveling more slowly.

**10.5 Practice B (p. 437)** **1.** undefined
**3.** negative; $-\frac{6}{5}$ **5.** 2 **7.** $-3$ **9.** $\frac{1}{2}$ **11.** $-\frac{5}{16}$ **13.** $-\frac{3}{2}$
**15.** undefined **17.** $\frac{7}{15}$ **19a.** $-5$ **19b.** The store sold the snowboards at a rate of 5 snowboards per day. **19c.** The line would be less steep because skis are being sold at a slower rate.

**10.6 Practice A (p. 442)** **1.** $y = 2x - 3$
**3.** $y = -\frac{5}{3}x + 2$ **5.** $y = -\frac{7}{5}x + 5$ **7.** B **9.** A
**11.** slope $= \frac{1}{2}$; *y*-intercept $= -7$

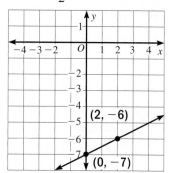

**13.** slope $= -2$; *y*-intercept $= 3$

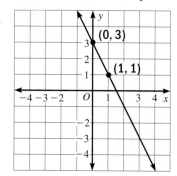

**17.** $y = 5x - 4$; slope $= 5$, *y*-intercept $= -4$
**19.** $y = \frac{1}{4}x - 4$; slope $= \frac{1}{4}$, *y*-intercept $= -4$
**21.** $y = \frac{2}{3}x - 7$; slope $= \frac{2}{3}$; *y*-intercept $= -7$
**23.** 4 CDs

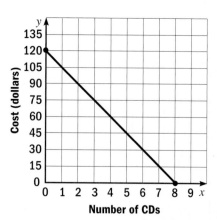

**10.6 Practice B (p. 443)** **1.** $y = 5x - 8$
**3.** $y = -\frac{7}{2}x + 6$ **5.** $y = -\frac{3}{7}x + 3$ **7.** C **9.** B

**11.** slope $= \frac{1}{5}$; $y$-intercept $= -2$

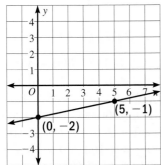

**13.** slope $= -1$; $y$-intercept $= 6$

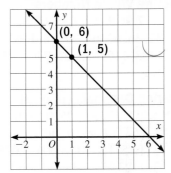

**17.** $y = 4x - 8$; slope $= 4$, $y$-intercept $= -8$
**19.** $y = 2x - 5$; slope $= 2$, $y$-intercept $= -5$
**21.** $y = \frac{3}{2}x - \frac{16}{5}$; slope $= \frac{3}{2}$, $y$-intercept $= -\frac{16}{5}$
**23.** 6 years

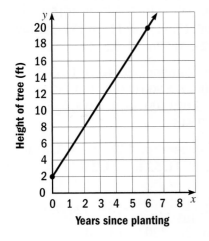

**10.7 Practice A (p. 448)** **1.** Yes; the ratios of
$y$-values to $x$-values all equal 4. **3.** Yes; the ratio of
$y$-values to $x$-values all equal $\frac{1}{2}$. **5.** Yes; the ratios of
$y$-coordinates to $x$-coordinates all equal 1. **7.** No
**9.** Yes, the slope is 2.

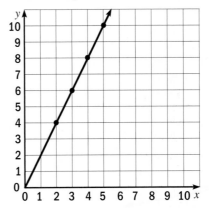

**11.** No, because a young person grows at various
rates. **13.** Yes, because the diameter is always
multiplied by $\pi$ to get the circumference.

**10.7 Practice B (p. 449)** **1.** Yes; the ratios of
$y$-values to $x$-values all equal 13. **3.** Yes; the ratios
of $y$-values to $x$-values all equal $\frac{1}{15}$. **5.** No; the ratios
of $y$-coordinates to $x$-coordinates are not equal.
**7.** No **9.** Yes; the slope is $\frac{1}{2}$.

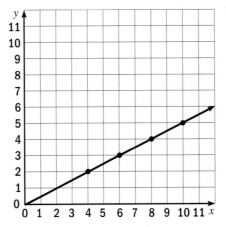

**11.** Yes, for the ratio $\frac{y}{x}$ to be constant, multiplying
$x$ by 3 requires multiplying $y$ by 3.

**10.8 Practice A (p. 454)** **1.** Yes; 7 **3.** No **5.** No

**7.**

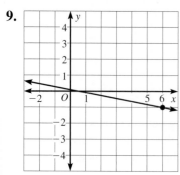

**9.**

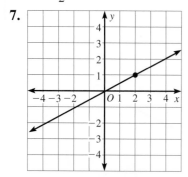

**13.** $y = 3x$; 9 **15.** $y = \frac{1}{2}x$; $1\frac{1}{2}$ **17.** $y = \frac{1}{4}x$; $\frac{3}{4}$

**19.** $y = 3x$; 9 **21.** $y = -\frac{2}{5}x$; $-1\frac{1}{5}$ **23.** $A = 48n$; $528

**25.** $p = 2t$; 90 pages

**10.8 Practice B (p. 455)** **1.** Yes; $-3$ **3.** No
**5.** Yes; $1\frac{1}{2}$

**7.**

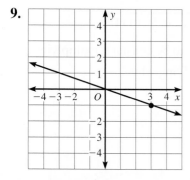

**9.**

**13.** $y = -\frac{4}{3}x$; $-4$ **15.** $y = 7x$; 21 **17.** $y = -\frac{1}{3}x$; $-1$

**19.** $y = \frac{1}{6}x$; $\frac{1}{2}$ **21.** $y = \frac{2}{5}x$; $1\frac{1}{5}$ **23.** $C = 0.08n$;

12 pages **25.** $d = 0.05t$; 80 minutes

# Skills Review Handbook

**Place Value (p. 476)** **1.** $2 \times 1,000,000 + 4 \times$
$100,000 + 6 \times 10,000 + 2 \times 1000 + 2 \times 10 + 7 \times$
$1 + 6 \times 0.1$ **3.** $3 \times 1000 + 9 \times 100 + 5 \times 1 +$
$8 \times 0.1 + 3 \times 0.01$ **5.** $1 \times 1,000,000 + 8 \times 1000 +$
$6 \times 100 + 3 \times 10 + 5 \times 1 + 3 \times 0.1 + 6 + 0.01 +$
$9 \times 0.001$ **7.** $1 \times 10,000 + 8 \times 100 + 9 \times 10 + 3 \times$
$1 + 2 \times 0.1$ **9.** 8,050,007.64 **11.** 2,600,500.038

**Comparing and Ordering Whole Numbers
(p. 477)** **1.** < **3.** > **5.** > **7.** < **9.** < **11.** < **13.** 5, 7, 8,
12, 16, 24, 32 **15.** 26, 32, 36, 62, 64, 72, 98, 106
**17.** 1016, 1018, 1104, 1123, 1157 **19.** 64, 246, 275,
358, 2032

**Comparing and Ordering Decimals (p. 478)**
**1.** > **3.** < **5.** = **7.** > **9.** < **11.** < **13.** 0.06, 0.07, 0.1,
0.12 **15.** 3.35, 3.4, 3.49, 3.53 **17.** 40.01, 40.1,
40.11, 41 **19.** 1.02, 1.13, 1.15, 1.2 **21.** 5.006, 5.025,
5.036, 5.253 **23.** 123.036, 123.05, 123.5, 135.6

**Rounding (p. 479)** **1.** 8800 **3.** 4.2 **5.** 29,000
**7.** 12,770,000 **9.** 54,560 **11.** 65.24 **13.** 32.883
**15.** 9470 **17.** 23,001 **19.** 1670.3 **21.** 0.36713
**23.** 321,655.22

**Adding and Subtracting Whole Numbers
(p. 480)** **1.** 140 **3.** 209 **5.** 19 **7.** 587 **9.** 3515
**11.** 2219 **13.** 27,799 **15.** 81,416 **17.** 16,135 **19.** 147
**21.** 297 **23.** 2280 **25.** 61,376 **27.** 92,347

**Multiplying Whole Numbers (p. 481)** **1.** 5312
**3.** 854,840 **5.** 49,100 **7.** 5,900,000 **9.** 143,112
**11.** 86,530,000 **13.** 2,012,109 **15.** 126,000
**17.** 927,886 **19.** 489,515

**Dividing Whole Numbers (p. 482)** **1.** 64 **3.** 31 R2
**5.** 125 R15 **7.** 6 **9.** 39 **11.** 52 R4 **13.** 2 R70
**15.** 2 R5260

**Ratios (p. 483)** **1.** $\frac{43}{165}$ **3.** $\frac{124}{289}$ **5.** 43 : 124 **7.** yes
**9.** no **11.** no **13.** No; $36 : 120 = 0.3$ and
$28:112 = 0.25$.

**Factors and Multiples (p. 485)** **1.** $2^3 \cdot 5$
**3.** prime **5.** $3^2 \cdot 11$ **7.** $2^4 \cdot 5$ **9.** 6 **11.** 15 **13.** 24
**15.** 17 **17.** 36 **19.** 32 **21.** 798 **23.** 252

**Converting Units of Measurement (p. 486)**
**1.** 86,400 **3.** 48 **5.** 65 **7.** 288 **9.** 2 **11.** 2
**13.** 1,000,000 **15.** 16 **17.** 10,000 **19.** 6 **21.** 12
**23.** 24

**Converting Between Metric and Customary**
**Units (p. 487) 1.** 1584 **3.** 1 **5.** 11 **7.** 1775 **9.** 2
**11.** < **13.** > **15.** < **17.** <

**Perimeter and Area (p. 489) 1.** 20 cm
**3.** 36 cm **5.** 96 yd$^2$ **7.** 12 cm$^2$ **9.** 325 ft$^2$
**11.** 110 yd$^2$

**Circumference and Area of a Circle (p. 491)**
**1.** $C = 20\pi \approx 62.8$ in.; $A = 100\pi \approx 314$ in.$^2$
**3.** $C = 7\pi \approx 22$ m; $A = 12.25\pi \approx 38.5$ m$^2$
**5.** $C = 42\pi \approx 132$ ft; $A = 441\pi \approx 1386$ ft$^2$

**Surface Area and Volume (p. 493)**
**1.** $S = 24$ in.$^2$; $V = 8$ in.$^3$
**3.** $S = 136.5\pi \approx 428.6$ cm$^2$; $V = 196\pi \approx 615.4$ cm$^3$
**5.** $S = 192\pi \approx 602.9$ in.$^2$; $V = 360\pi \approx 1130.4$ in.$^3$
**7.** $S = 700$ cm$^2$; $V = 1200$ cm$^3$
**9.** $S = 37.5\pi \approx 117.8$ in.$^2$; $V = 31.25\pi \approx 98.1$ in.$^3$

**Reading Bar Graphs (p. 494) 1.** 14 **3.** 7
**5.** Read a book **7.** 6

**Reading Circle Graphs (p. 495) 1.** Suspense
**3.** 7 **5.** 62 **7.** 87

**Problem Solving Strategies (p. 497) 1.** 25 **3.** 7
**5.** Bob had $20; Lisa and Carl each had $2. **7.** Kate
**9.** Sara; $14 **11.** 28 ft